C Programmer's Guide to
Serial Communications

HOWARD W. SAMS & COMPANY
HAYDEN BOOKS

Related Titles

C with Excellence:
Programming Proverbs
Henry Ledgard with John Tauer

QuickC™ Programming for
the IBM®
Carl Townsend

C Programmer's Guide to
Microsoft® Windows 2.0
Carl Townsend

The Waite Group's Advanced
C Primer++
Stephen Prata

The Waite Group's C++
Programming (Version 2.0)
Edited by The Waite Group

The Waite Group's C Primer
Plus, Revised Edition
Mitchell Waite, Stephen Prata, and
Donald Martin

The Waite Group's Microsoft®
C Programming for the IBM®
Robert Lafore

The Waite Group's Turbo C®
Programming for the IBM®
Robert Lafore

Programming in C, Revised
Edition
Stephen G. Kochan

Topics in C Programming
Stephen G. Kochan, Patrick H. Wood

Data Communications,
Networks, and Systems
Thomas C. Bartee, Editor-in-Chief

Digital Communications
Thomas C. Bartee, Editor-in-Chief

Modem Connections Bible
Carolyn Curtis and Daniel Majhor, The
Waite Group

Handbook of
Computer-Communications
Standards:
The OSI Model and
OSI-Related Standards,
Volume 1
William Stallings

Handbook of
Computer-Communications
Standards:
Local Network Standards,
Volume 2
William Stallings

Handbook of
Computer-Communications
Standards:
Department of Defense
Protocol Standards, Volume 3
William Stallings

For the retailer nearest you, or to order directly from the publisher,
call 800-428-SAMS. In Indiana, Alaska, and Hawaii call 317-298-5699.

C Programmer's
Guide to
Serial Communications

Joe Campbell

HOWARD W. SAMS & COMPANY

A Division of Macmillan, Inc.

11711 North College, Carmel, Indiana 46032 USA

International Standard Book Number: 0-672-22584-0
Library of Congress Catalog Card Number: 87-60387

Acquisitions Editor: *James S. Hill*
Editor: *Marie Butler-Knight*
Interior Designer: *T. R. Emrick*
Illustrators: *Wm. D. Basham* and *Ralph E. Lund*
Cover Designer: *Keith J. Hampton, Visual Graphic Services*
Cover Illustrators: *Jerry Bates* and *Patrick Sarles, Visual Graphic Services*
Compositor: *Photo Comp Corporation*

Printed in the United States of America

Trademark Acknowledgments

Contents

II ASYNCHRONOUS PROGRAMMING IN C

Preface

Considering that every programmer—from the professional working on a Cray to the hobbyist hacking a Radio Shack Color Computer—must inevitably do battle with the serial port, it is odd that this book has not already been written. An obvious reason for this void is the breadth of the subject. An author writing about most topics can actually expect to cover it thoroughly; however, because of its almost limitless scope, undertaking a book on data communications is as daunting as one entitled, say, *Life*. In humble recognition of the demands of such an epic subject, this book is about one tiny subtopic—*asynchronous serial communications* as it is found on microcomputers. Other important topics—synchronous communications, networks, and so forth—will have to wait for another book.

Our chosen subject is the simplest form of digital electronic communication. Tersely put, in asynchronous serial communications, data is disassembled into bits, transmitted bit-by-bit as binary electronic pulses, then reassembled by the receiver. Little technical knowledge is required to comprehend the idea behind this form of communication because it is analogous to many things in everyday life. Take riding a ski lift, for example. While waiting for a lift chair, groups of skiers (bits) stand in parallel (bytes). Once on the lift, they are transported (transmitted) one after the other (serially). At the top of the hill, they hop off the lift (are received) and again form into groups (bytes).

Although homey, simple-minded analogies like this are usually unnecessary in books designed for a technically sophisticated audience, it is offered here to counterbalance the decidedly non-technical and widely held opinion that serial communications is somehow inherently arcane or mysterious. Even in programmer's publications, we often read how an otherwise intelligent writer is confounded by this "black art." Evidence of this notion is everywhere, even in the names of the suppliers of hardware for serial communications: Syzygy, which evokes images of astrology and necromancy, and The Black Box Catalog, whose implication is clear. Even I succumbed to this attitude in *The RS-232 Solution*, which contains a chapter entitled "Elves in the Basement."

Much of what is perceived as "weird science" is a result of the technology's having evolved in the essentially mechanical world of the middle and late nineteenth century. Design decisions that seem absurd by modern standards were the products of an age when AC current was essentially unknown, the DC motor was still a toy, and communications devices were powered by clockwork mechanisms. The miracle is not that this technology worked well, but that it worked at all. That this hundred-year-old technology persists, no, even thrives in a world of high-powered computers is testimony to its vigor and reliability. One of our first undertakings, then, will be to understand today's technology in terms of how it came to be.

Although the subject of this book sounds relatively narrow, each area of study seems to touch another, which in turn embraces others, and so on. In order to understand the ins and outs of asynchronous I/O, therefore, several related topics must first be studied. To this end, the book comprises three sections: *Basics*, *Asynchronous Programming in C*, and *Appendixes*.

Section One: Basics

The first eight chapters present the theoretical and practical background information required to understand the objectives of the programming section. Topics in this section are of general interest to all programmers, independent of language.

- ASCII
- The mechanics of asynchronous communications viewed from an historical perspective
- Error detection, including an intelligible explanation of CRCs (Cyclic Redundancy Checks)
- Flow-control procedures such as XON/XOFF and ETX/ACK
- The XMODEM and Kermit file-transfer protocols
- Modems—why they are necessary, how they work, and their limitations
- RS-232—a practical, realistic look at this feared topic
- The UART—an IC controller for asynchronous communications
- Detailed coverage of all Hayes Smartmodem products

Section Two: Asynchronous Programming in C

Using the first eight chapters as a backdrop, the next eleven chapters develop the programming tools to accomplish everyday serial programming chores. The programming examples are in C. This section develops a library of *portable* functions modeled upon the standard C library's concept of "stream" I/O. By careful design, machine dependencies are wrung from high-level functions and placed in one or two hardware-specific configuration files. This design, dubbed the "virtual UART," provides a level of generality and portability not previously known in libraries for asynchronous I/O.

With only one or two small configuration files to write, moving programs from one environment to another requires only hours of work instead of days or weeks. To illustrate this flexibility, sample configuration files are developed simultaneously for the IBM PC family and the popular Kaypro CP/M computers. No one will question the choice of the IBM PC, but some will wonder why an "obsolete" machine such as the Kaypro was selected. The answer is simple. More recent computers such as the Macintosh and the Amiga are flashier, but their serial hardware is much more sophisticated and therefore less challenging than the Kaypro's. The Kaypro sports such wonderful "features" as an operating system located in ROM, bank-switched RAM, no real-time clock, no heartbeat interrupt, and a serial I/O controller with read-only registers. Simply put, the Kaypro was chosen for purely pedagogical reasons—its oddities best demonstrate the powers of the virtual UART.

In particular, this section contains:

- Functions to perform the precise timing necessary for serial I/O
- Portable functions to set baud rate, data format, and other parameters
- Portable functions to control and monitor the RS-232 interface
- Portable functions to "open" and "close" a serial port
- Portable functions to perform formatting of serial input and output
- A complete library of functions to control the entire family of Hayes Smartmodems
- A high-performance XMODEM file-transfer module
- CRC functions that use *fast* table-lookup algorithms
- A mechanism for transparently integrating asynchronous interrupts into the system

Appendixes

Seven appendixes supply important information that does not fit logically into any chapter.

- Listings for several non-serial functions used but not explained in the body of the text
- The 8086 and 8080 assembly-language routines to create the efficient console functions needed in the programming section
- Instructions for adapting the book's assembly-language functions to the format required by popular PC DOS compilers
- Listings of all header files developed in the programming sections
- Listings of the configuration files for the IBM PC and Kaypro

What You Need To Know To Read This Book

This is an intermediate-to-advanced book. As such, it assumes that you have a grasp of fundamental computer concepts and terminology. If you are unfamiliar with terms such as "FIFO," "polling," "RAM," "vector," and so forth, you will need a good computer dictionary and a supple mind.

The first section of this book contains no code, so it should be of interest to all programmers. Chapters 1 and 2 might even appeal to advanced users. Chapter 3 has a certain egghead appeal, if for no other reason than that much of it is devoted to the esoteric topic of CRCs (Cyclic Redundancy Checks). But at Chapter 4, the pedal goes hard to the metal and every purely theoretical notion is juxtaposed with a practical example. Chapter 5, for example, is a theoretical look at modems, but Chapter 8 spends 46 pages discussing the Hayes Smartmodem in molecular detail. Chapter 6 looks at what serial I/O hardware *ideally ought* to do, then Chapter 7 counters immediately by judging how well two real ICs (the INS8250 and the Z80SIO) measure up.

The second section is devoted entirely to programming, with examples written in C. Although the design and goal of these programming examples apply to *all* languages, if you do not have at least a *reading* knowledge of C, you will soon find yourself foundering. To be completely candid, beginners in C will probably sink rather quickly. If this happens to you, do not abandon hope, but mount a new attack from time to time as your fluency increases. After all, there is no better way to learn C than to see real code doing real work in the real world.

Acknowledgment

Many people deserve thanks for their contributions to this book. At the top of this list belongs my wife Cynthia whose harassment motivated me to finish the book, followed by my two children, Ben and Aaron, who no longer think that their father doesn't work.

My friend Roger Purves gets credit for the penny-and-dime CRC simulator in Chapter 3, and for other common-sense suggestions on the subject. Thanks also to Dave Schwaderer for long telephone conversations about CRC. Steve Strand, as always, generously donated his expertise in C. Fred Cisin gets one general-purpose kudos.

Several companies helped, too. Manx Software graciously donated their excellent Aztec C compilers. Thanks also to the Technical Support department at Hayes Microcomputer Products in general for providing the Smartmodem manuals; in particular, a tip of the hat to Joe Browning for digging out the answers to dozens of obscure and niggling questions.

As this book grew longer (and later), Howard W. Sams showed incredible patience, generosity, and faith in me. In particular, Jim Hill and Jim Rounds fought to keep it alive. I hope they feel the final product was worth the battle. Thanks also to Marie Butler-Knight for her sensitive, non-intrusive editing and for her good humor.

Among the material contributors, no one worked harder than my technical assistant Fred Spindler. He read every word of the manuscript, checked the code for errors, offered suggestions, and drafted most of the book's artwork.

Finally, thanks to two men I never knew, Cole Porter and Johnny Mercer, who provided joy and inspiration.

Joe Campbell
Berkeley, California
February, 1987

I

Basics

Although the stated purpose of this first section is to provide background information for the second (programming) section, Chapters 1 through 6 are stand-alone treatments of their respective topics. As you read through this first section, you may be puzzled by occasional references to topics not yet completely covered. For example, Chapter 4 is about flow controls and protocols; these subjects by nature overlap with the subject of modems and line usage conventions, which are not covered until Chapter 5. Similarly, the discussion of parity—an error detection scheme—belongs in Chapter 3, but the discussion of ASCII in Chapter 1 would be feloniously incomplete without pointing out the relationship between the 7-bit code and the parity bit.

This problem is brought on by the connected-ness of the subtopics within the main subject of serial communications. The foundation of communications technology is so broad, encompassing so many other ideas, that it is impossible—if not intellectually dishonest—to try to treat it as a group of disassociated, solitary topics. The organization of the first section of this book may, therefore, vex you from time to time, depending upon your prior knowledge of the information covered in each chapter. While it is probably true that this problem could have been alleviated by introductory chapters on each topic, it is also true that a forklift would be required to get such a book off the shelf.

This brings up the matter of how to read this section. Paradoxically, the close interrelationship of the topics creates a book that is best read in the spirit of a novel instead of as a technical dissertation. Each chapter should be read not only for the information it contains about its declared topic, but also with an eye toward filling in a larger plot. Characters that seem sketchily drawn in one chapter inevitably appear full-blown in another. Your ultimate understanding of these characters is enriched by the earlier brief encounters. In other words, in return for your tolerance of an occasional forward reference, you are rewarded with a book of succinct, tightly structured chapters that *collectively* illuminate a subject that somehow is larger than the sum of its parts.

1

ASCII

Since the topic of this book is communications, we first need to discuss the medium in which we intend to communicate. Despite all the hi-tech glitter surrounding computers in general, the most straightforward way to analyze computer communications is with the rather old-fashioned tools of traditional morphology; that is, if we don't go overboard in doing so, we can apply the same analysis to communication between computers as we do to communication between humans. The study of human communication is, in the last couple of thousand years or so anyway, largely the study of written language.

At its most basic level, a written language can ultimately be viewed as an encoding scheme. Spelling teaches us the rules for encoding, and reading is just rapid decoding. Languages are partially identified by their coding elements (characters) and by their coding array (alphabets). For example, any valid English word can be coded into written form with only 26 unique elements, or "letters." Since there is no limitation on word length in English, it is theoretically possible to create an infinite number of words from these 26 letters, provided we are willing to tolerate words that take forever to pronounce. According to the rules of English, certain sequences of letters are prescribed (e.g., 'u' must always follow 'q'), while others are eschewed because they are phonetically unpleasant. All in all, human languages can be extremely complex.

How can we describe a computer's language? Remember, it must be a language understandable to an utter simpleton (which the computer is). By comparison to human languages, the computer's vocabulary is trivial: it possesses only two "letters" and *all* words are exactly 8 letters long. From this description, you can easily conclude that a dictionary of the computer language comprises only 2^8, or 256 words. None of these words is idiomatic or colloquial, and there are no spelling rules.

Before we examine the details of this little language, be careful not to draw a parallel between language as we are discussing it now and computer *programming* languages such as BASIC, Pascal, or C. While it is amusing to debate whether *programming* languages are really languages at all, this is not the sense in which the term "language" is used here.

As you doubtless already know, the two "letters" of the computer "alphabet" are 0 and 1. A computer "word"[1] is known as a byte and a computer character is a "bit."

---

[1]Because "word" to microcomputer users has the special meaning of "16 bits" or "2 bytes," this analogical ice is admittedly pretty thin. Here we use "word" to refer to a logical grouping of bits, whereas "word" in the other sense applies to a physical grouping of bits generally dictated by the physical architecture of the computer itself. Hence on large computers, a "word" may comprise 32, 64, or any number of bits.

Contextual Meaning

With such a small vocabulary, computers are hopelessly inarticulate. (Imagine the banality of your own conversations if you knew only 256 words.) The problem, then, is how to use the same 256 words to represent a much greater number of entities. The solution is *contextual meaning*.

In human languages, words generally have absolute meanings; that is, each word represents only one thing. The degree to which a word is bound to a single meaning is sometimes called its *truth value*. However, because of oddities in etymology, the meaning of many words cannot be unambiguously deduced from their spellings—for example, "bow," "row," and "sanction." These words must be interpreted according to the meaning of the sentence in which they are used. In other words, their meanings become clear only in context.

Contextual meaning is the only way to extend the expressiveness of the computer's 256 word vocabulary. This means that we can assign different meanings to the 256 words, depending upon how we intend them to be interpreted. Each contextual assignment is called a *set*.

Machine Contexts: Instruction Sets

When the byte 0100_0001 is used as an instruction to an 8080 microprocessor, it represents the machine-language instruction that causes the microprocessor to move the contents of the C register into the B register. Each microprocessor interprets the 256 possible words differently: the 8086 microprocessor, for example, interprets the same 0100_0001 byte as an instruction to increment the CX register. Where compatibility between processors' *instruction sets* is desired, the instruction set of one processor includes that of another. For example, the Z80's instruction set is identical to the 8080's except that the Z80 additionally employs the unused instructions—bytes 10H, 20H, and 30H for example. When this relationship exists, the expanded character set is said to be a *superset* of the original.

Human Contexts: Character Sets

These two examples illustrate how the computer's vocabulary can be employed in non-human contexts. It is obviously possible to define contexts in which the same 256 words stand for ordinary English language letters, punctuation, digits, etc. These contexts are called *character sets*.

Sets of characters are invented as the need arises; indeed there are hundreds of character sets in use today, including those for optical code readers, paper tape, robots, and one for almost every science or academic discipline. As long as there is agreement within a field of discipline, standards evolve ipso facto. A slightly different situation exists among computer equipment manufacturers who wish to make their equipment broadly compatible with other equipment. Clearly, if each manufacturer invented its own set of codes, the interchange of data among different brands of equipment would be prohibitively difficult. For this reason, industry standards have been created through various standards organizations in cooperation with the computer industry itself.

By far the most important character set to the English-speaking world is the American Standard Code for Information Interchange, or ASCII for short. The ASCII code (pronounced ASS-key) is a product of the American National Standards Institute (ANSI), where it is referred to simply as *ANSI Standard X3.4-1977 (Revised 1983), Code for Information Interchange*, or just AS-CII. (It is unclear why the code is called ASCII instead of ANSCII.) There are two other, virtually identical standards from other world standards organizations: the 7-Bit Coded Character Set for Information Processing (standard number 646) of the ISO (International Standards Organization), and Alphabet No. 5 of CCITT (the International Consultative Committee for Telephone and Telegraph).[2]

Virtually every computer worldwide employs some form of these human-readable character sets. The notable exception is International Business Machines, which invented its own character set, the Extended Binary Coded Decimal Interchange Code (EBCDIC, pronounced EBB-si-dik) which, unfortunately, is incompatible with all the standards listed above. Following the clearly defined trend of the microcomputer industry, however, IBM graciously chose to employ ASCII in its microcomputer product.

A Bit About ASCII

Before we look at the details of the ASCII character set, let's first summarize some of the considerations that went into its development.

ASCII was from the start intended to be primarily a "human-readable" code. Before you get carried away with that notion, however, it should be pointed out that the distinction between human- and computer-readable codes is artificial, because humans cannot—in a physical sense, anyway—read computer codes. Computer codes are merely electronic potentials existing across the barrier layers of semiconductors. In short, *all* computer codes are designed to interact at some primary level with other, non-human, electronic devices. The important thing to remember, though, is that the ASCII character set was designed *for use with* ordinary devices that ultimately are looked at or listened to by humans. Since a device is required for "translating" the computer code into a form that humans can read, that same code must also contain a few characters for controlling the display device itself. Hence some of the ASCII codes are explicitly designed to control other devices.

Somewhat at odds with the "human" aims of the writers of the code, was the acknowledged fact that a large fraction of the world's computers are dedicated to that vague-sounding activity, "data processing." The needs of the data processing "community" were naturally high in the minds of the creators of ASCII. As we shall see, some of the characters in the ASCII code as well as the sequence (ordering) of the characters have a distinctly data-processing flavor. Similarly, any proposed code must serve the field of data communications, which by nature relies heavily upon codes. Along these same lines, everyone realized that if ASCII were to become the standard vocabulary of computers, it had to accommodate computer programmers. ASCII therefore incorporates the character requirements of common programming languages such as FORTRAN, BASIC, and COBOL.

Also in the minds of the ASCII "fathers" was the desire to accommodate the unique alphabets of different nations, reserving certain codes for "national" usage, such as unique characters, special punctuation, and diacritical markings.

"ASCII" as an Adjective

ASCII is a 7-bit code, so the 128 positions from 128 to 255 are not defined. Character sets that employ the 8th bit (bit 7) exist, but are not, by definition, ASCII. Although the size and scope of

---

[2]ANSI and ISO standards and proposals can be ordered from: American National Standards Institute, 1430 Broadway, New York, NY 10018, (212) 354-3300. CCITT standards are available from: Global Engineering Documents, 2625 Hickory Street, Santa Anna, CA 92707, (800) 854-7179.

the ASCII code are unambiguously defined in the X3.4 document, there has always been some confusion about the meaning of the term "ASCII." Commodore, for example, calls its character set "PET ASCII" (after their PET model computer), although it bears little resemblance to ASCII. IBM refers to the encoding scheme for the "special" keys (such as "function" keys) on IBM PCs as "Extended ASCII," even though such keys as F1, Alt, and PgDn on the IBM keyboard clearly have nothing to do with ASCII. Many word processing programs employ the undefined "upper" (i.e., those from 80H to FF) 128 characters as end-of-line, margin, and justification markers. In the WordStar program, for example, an A0 byte (**SP** with bit 7 TRUE) represents spaces added for line justification. WordStar also sets bit 7 in the final character of every word (including Carriage Return) to simplify line reformation.

The ASCII Table

The ASCII table is shown in Figure 1-1 and, for handy reference, is also included as a removable wall chart. When reproduced in chart form, it is all too often banished to a remote appendix where its sole purpose is to list the characters and their numerical equivalents. This is a regrettable practice—there is much to be learned about the nature of computer communications just by studying the configuration and layout of this chart.

The official chart in the ASCII document (ANSI X3.4) is in octal; that is, it is 8 units wide by 16 long. More befitting the practice among microcomputer programmers, however, our chart is laid out in hexadecimal format; that is, it is 16 units wide by 8 long. Above the graphic representation of each character are its decimal and binary values. The horizontal rows of characters are called *sticks* (a quaint sounding term) by the designers of ASCII. The *position* of any character can be expressed by its stick and its rank within the stick: 'A' is 4/1, '$' is 2/4, and so forth. The ASCII document gives row/column coordinates in decimal, but we will use hexadecimal throughout this book. Unlike ANSI's version of the chart, the consistent use of hexadecimal means that a character's coordinates on the chart are also its rank in the code. For example, official ASCII lingo refers to the letter 'k' as 6/11, whereas we would refer to it as 6B; 4/1 in ANSI notation is just plain 41 here, and 4/15 becomes 4F.

The most obvious characteristic of the ASCII code is that it defines only 128 of the 256 possible bit patterns. Specifically, the ASCII character set is a 7-bit code; this means that in systems that employ 8-bit bytes, including all microcomputers, the ASCII character set is represented in the lower 7 bits, occupying the bit positions from 0 to 127. Sometimes when we look at a byte in the range 80H to FF, we wonder what its ASCII equivalent is—that is, what its value is with a high-order bit of 1. If you are not adept at hexadecimal subtraction, the right side of the chart has indexes in hexadecimal for characters whose high-order nibble is 8 through F. Suppose, for example, that you wish to find the character that results when the high-order bit is stripped from the byte E4; quickly subtracting 8 from E yields row 6, and moving down column 4 then leads to the letter 'd'. Alternatively, you can go directly to the correct column simply by using the 'E' index on the right side of the chart.

ASCII has an organizing principle, or rather, several organizing principles, so it is easier to analyze if we regard it as several smaller groups of characters (or character *subsets*, if you will) instead of a single large one. The most general division is between the *graphics* characters and the *controls*. Control characters are those from position 0 to 1F and the DEL at 7F; the graphics characters comprise everything else.

Figure 1-1 The ASCII chart.

	0	1	2	3	4	5	6	7	8	9	A	B	C	D	E	F
0	NUL	SOH	STX	ETX	EOT	ENQ	ACK	BEL	BS	HT	LF	VT	FF	CR	SO	SI
1	DLE	DC1	DC2	DC3	DC4	NAK	SYN	ETB	CAN	EM	SUB	ESC	FS	GS	RS	US
2	SP	!	"	#	$	%	&	`	(	)	*	+	,	-	.	/
3	0	1	2	3	4	5	6	7	8	9	:	;	<	=	>	?
4	@	A	B	C	D	E	F	G	H	I	J	K	L	M	N	O
5	P	Q	R	S	T	U	V	W	X	Y	Z	[	\	]	^	_
6	`	a	b	c	d	e	f	g	h	i	j	k	l	m	n	o
7	p	q	r	s	t	u	v	w	x	y	z	{	|	}	~	DEL

The Graphics

Within the *graphics* are several subcategories; two of these—the *digits* and the *Latin alphabet*—are familiar to all and contain no great surprises. We shall discuss them first. The remaining category of graphics characters is known somewhat boringly as the *Specials*. These contain the more interesting characters, which we need to look at more carefully.

The Digits

Figure 1-2 The Digits.

	0	1	2	3	4	5	6	7	8	9	A	B	C	D	E	F	
0	00 NUL	01 SOH	02 STX	03 ETX	04 EOT	05 ENQ	06 ACK	07 BEL	08 BS	09 HT	10 LF	11 VT	12 FF	13 CR	14 SO	15 SI	**8**
1	16 DLE	17 DC1	18 DC2	19 DC3	20 DC4	21 NAK	22 SYN	23 ETB	24 CAN	25 EM	26 SUB	27 ESC	28 FS	29 GS	30 RS	31 US	**9**
2	32 SP	33 !	34 "	35 #	36 $	37 %	38 &	39 '	40 (	41)	42 *	43 +	44 ,	45 -	46 .	47 /	**A**
3	48 0	49 1	50 2	51 3	52 4	53 5	54 6	55 7	56 8	57 9	58 :	59 ;	60 <	61 =	62 >	63 ?	**B**
4	64 @	65 A	66 B	67 C	68 D	69 E	70 F	71 G	72 H	73 I	74 J	75 K	76 L	77 M	78 N	79 O	**C**
5	80 P	81 Q	82 R	83 S	84 T	85 U	86 V	87 W	88 X	89 Y	90 Z	91 [	92 \	93]	94 ^	95 _	**D**
6	96 `	97 a	98 b	99 c	100 d	101 e	102 f	103 g	104 h	105 i	106 j	107 k	108 l	109 m	110 n	111 o	**E**
7	112 p	113 q	114 r	115 s	116 t	117 u	118 v	119 w	120 x	121 y	122 z	123 {	124 |	125 }	126 ~	127 DEL	**F**

The group highlighted in Figure 1-2 is the digits—that is, graphic representations of the ordinary cardinal decimal numbers. Note that they are specifically referred to as *digits*, not numbers, not numerals; the ASCII *number* 1 (i.e., bit pattern 0000_0001) is at position 01 in the chart, whereas the *digit* 1 is at 31. The distinction between numbers and digits is a fine one for many people and the source of much confusion. When values are used in arithmetic operations such as adding or subtracting, they are most efficiently and conveniently stored in binary form according to *value*—that is, the number 1 is stored as 0000_0001, 2 is 0000_0010, 3 is 0000_0011, and so on. On the other hand, the digits are *arbitrarily* assigned to specific graphic characters. In other words, the number 9 is stored as a "raw" binary value, 0000_1001; but the ASCII character (digit) used to display the graphic '9' is at position 39 (0011_1001) in the ASCII table.

As long as quantities in the range 0 to 9 are involved, there is no penalty for storing them as ASCII digits—a single byte suffices in either case. The ASCII storage of numbers as digits becomes increasingly expensive as the quantities become larger, because one byte of storage is required for every decade. As an example, consider the number 26,581 (67D5). It can be stored as a binary value with 2 bytes: 0110_0111 1101_0101. Its ASCII representation, however, requires 5 bytes:

> 0011_0010 (32H) for the "2"
> 0011_0110 (36H) for the "6"
> 0011_0101 (35H) for the "5"
> 0011_1000 (38H) for the "8"
> 0011_0001 (31H) for the "1"

There is a partial solution to this problem. You may have noticed that the lower nibble of the digits contains the binary value of the number they represent. This enables the use of *packed ASCII* or *binary coded decimal* (BCD) representation wherein two ASCII digits are encoded into a single byte. Using packed ASCII, 26,581 (right-justified) becomes:

> 0000_0010 for the "2"
> 0110_0101 for the "65"
> 1000_0001 for the "81"

Storing numbers as ASCII digits, even in BCD format results in substantial overhead—both programming and storage. Yet schemes to perform arithmetic (even floating-point arithmetic) on packed ASCII numerical data are quite common. The 8086 microprocessor, for example, provides a group of instructions to adjust the results of arithmetic instructions when the operands are in packed BCD format. Despite such conveniences, calculations performed in ASCII are woefully slow in comparison to the same operation performed on binary numbers.

In view of these serious disadvantages—speed, storage, and coding overhead—one might wonder why this form of representation exists at all. The answer is simple—storing data in ASCII format is, if not convenient, portable. In other words, because ASCII coding is universally recognized, virtually every computer system is equipped to handle it.

The Arabic Zero

The Arabic zero is notoriously imitated by the Latin capital 'O.' Oddly, this lack of differentiation is perpetuated in ASCII. Although many display devices already display the "slashed zero," (0) this form is easily confused with an alphabetical character in the Scandinavian alphabet. To avoid confusion altogether, our chart uses a special upper-case 'O': Ꝺ , or the capital 'Q' rotated 180 degrees. Lest some consider this to be too eccentric, it is the "official" method prescribed in ANSI X3.45-1982, "The Character Set for Handprinting," a facsimile of which is given in Figure 1-3.

The Latin Alphabet

Rows four through seven, highlighted in Figure 1-4, contain the ordinary characters of our alphabet. Notice that the first character in both cases is offset in its row by one; that is, **A** and **a** appear in column 1 instead of column 0. Users are often perplexed that the capital letters rank lower in the chart than the small letters. The most obvious reason for this order is historical. The lower position of the capitals creates a 5-bit ASCII subset, thus making it possible to adapt the code to the most common display device at the time, the teleprinter. (Many teleprinters, as well as early video terminals, displayed only upper case.) For speculation about why upper case was selected for 5-bit

Figure 1-3   The character set for handprinting from ANSI X3.45.

Figure 1-4 The Latin alphabet.

	0	1	2	3	4	5	6	7	8	9	A	B	C	D	E	F	
0	00 NUL	01 SOH	02 STX	03 ETX	04 EOT	05 ENQ	06 ACK	07 BEL	08 BS	09 HT	10 LF	11 VT	12 FF	13 CR	14 SO	15 SI	8
1	16 DLE	17 DC1	18 DC2	19 DC3	20 DC4	21 NAK	22 SYN	23 ETB	24 CAN	25 EM	26 SUB	27 ESC	28 FS	29 GS	30 RS	31 US	9
2	32 SP	33 !	34 "	35 #	36 $	37 %	38 &	39 '	40 (	41)	42 *	43 +	44 ,	45 –	46 .	47 /	A
3	48 0	49 1	50 2	51 3	52 4	53 5	54 6	55 7	56 8	57 9	58 :	59 ;	60 <	61 =	62 >	63 ?	B
4	64 @	65 A	66 B	67 C	68 D	69 E	70 F	71 G	72 H	73 I	74 J	75 K	76 L	77 M	78 N	79 O	C
5	80 P	81 Q	82 R	83 S	84 T	85 U	86 V	87 W	88 X	89 Y	90 Z	91 [	92 \	93]	94 ^	95 _	D
6	96 `	97 a	98 b	99 c	100 d	101 e	102 f	103 g	104 h	105 i	106 j	107 k	108 l	109 m	110 n	111 o	E
7	112 p	113 q	114 r	115 s	116 t	117 u	118 v	119 w	120 x	121 y	122 z	123 {	124 |	125 }	126 ~	127 DEL	F

codes instead of the more readable lower case, see "Why a Five-Unit Code?" in Chapter 2.

Since the cases differ only in bit 5, upper case can be forced by ANDing with 5F and lower case can be forced by ORing with 20H.

The Specials

The "Specials" that follow the digits in row 3 are familiar punctuation, **: ; ?** and the arithmetic symbols **< = >**. The troublesome characters all reside in row 2. Let's discuss them one at a time.

- The space (20H) is considered to be a Special, one suspects, because people tend not to think of it as a character at all; to most, a space is the same thing as a blank. In fact, some of the designers of ASCII argued for calling this character a "blank," but this name was probably rejected on the grounds it suggests a character with no graphic value—that is, a "non-printing" character. This is indeed true on "hard copy" devices such as printers and teletypes where a space is actually just a specified quantity of skipped space. This is decidedly not true, however, on video devices where an **SP** obliterates any pre-existing character that occupies the same position on the screen. The important thing to remember is that, as far as ASCII is concerned, this "blank" character is as important as any other.

  Important problems arise from the use of **SP**. Writers of user's manuals often assume that the operator is totally unfamiliar with computers. Even though writers may know that an **SP** is an important part of a command's syntax, there is no "nothing" character with which to represent it. For example, in the UNIX operating system, the careless use of **SP** in conjunction with wildcards can have cataclysmic consequences: the UNIX command *rm −r *.bak* would purge your file system of all backup files, but *rm −r *b̸.bak* (the same command with an errant and seemingly harmless **SP**) would erase the entire file system!

From the preceding example, you can see the occasional extreme need for a visible character with which to represent the **SP** in this position. Following the suggestions given in the ANSI standard for handprinting (see Figure 1-3), many books use a "b" with a slant overstrike: b̸. In this book, however, an explicit **SP** is represented with a small block of highlighting. (See page 1-16 for a discussion of the backspace character **BS** and how to create overstrike characters.)

" The Quotation Mark (22H). In ASCII, this single character must stand for both opening and closing quotation marks, whereas a typesetter has a different symbol for each. This is not really an oversight, but a simple way for a single character to serve two functions. Despite popular usage, the name of this character is "quotation mark" (a noun), not "quote" (a verb).

Figure 1-5   The Specials.

	0	1	2	3	4	5	6	7	8	9	A	B	C	D	E	F	
0	NUL	SOH	STX	ETX	EOT	ENQ	ACK	BEL	BS	HT	LF	VT	FF	CR	SO	SI	8
1	DLE	DC1	DC2	DC3	DC4	NAK	SYN	ETB	CAN	EM	SUB	ESC	FS	GS	RS	US	9
2	SP	!	"	#	$	%	&	'	(	)	*	+	,	−	.	/	A
3	0	1	2	3	4	5	6	7	8	9	:	;	<	=	>	?	B
4	@	A	B	C	D	E	F	G	H	I	J	K	L	M	N	O	C
5	P	Q	R	S	T	U	V	W	X	Y	Z	[	\	]	^	_	D
6	`	a	b	c	d	e	f	g	h	i	j	k	l	m	n	o	E
7	p	q	r	s	t	u	v	w	x	y	z	{	|	}	~	DEL	F

Specials: International Usage Positions

The positions shown highlighted in Figure 1-6 are designated International Usage positions. These positions are intended to promote compatibility with other alphabets and character sets around the world. Presumably, countries with alphabets of more than 26 characters—the Scandinavian alphabet, for example, has 29—must squeeze in the additional characters in these positions. Some positions, such as the "commercial at" sign (@, 40H), are part of most foreign character sets and alternative characters are seldom seen. As a general rule, though, avoid this group of characters in the textual portions of software if there is even a remote chance of international distribution.

Of the International Usage group, positions 5E, 60H, and 7E are *secondary* positions that "have been designated as supplementary use positions, which are replaceable by national characters in only those countries having an extraordinary requirement in this regard." Just what might constitute an *extraordinary* requirement is not discussed, but some countries substitute a straight overbar for the tilde at 7E and an up arrow for the circumflex at 5E. (An early version of ASCII placed an up arrow at 5E, too.)

Figure 1-6 International Usage positions.

	0	1	2	3	4	5	6	7	8	9	A	B	C	D	E	F	
0	NUL	SOH	STX	ETX	EOT	ENQ	ACK	BEL	BS	HT	LF	VT	FF	CR	SO	SI	8
1	DLE	DC1	DC2	DC3	DC4	NAK	SYN	ETB	CAN	EM	SUB	ESC	FS	GS	RS	US	9
2	SP	!	"	#	$	%	&	'	(	)	*	+	,	—	.	/	A
3	0	1	2	3	4	5	6	7	8	9	:	;	<	=	>	?	B
4	@	A	B	C	D	E	F	G	H	I	J	K	L	M	N	O	C
5	P	Q	R	S	T	U	V	W	X	Y	Z	[	\	]	^	_	D
6	`	a	b	c	d	e	f	g	h	i	j	k	l	m	n	o	E
7	p	q	r	s	t	u	v	w	x	y	z	{	|	}	~	DEL	F

The Currency Positions

The characters at 23H and 24H are reserved for international currency symbols.

\# When used internationally, the character at 23H may be replaced by the national currency symbol, such as the pound sterling symbol, £.

The \# is interesting because it doesn't have a name of its own, but is variously called:

1. *Sharp sign*. It is, in fact, not exactly like the "sharp" symbol in music, which is more slanty.

2. *Number sign*. True, it is occasionally used to identify ordinal measurement, as in "a #3 wash tub" or "#6/32 screw," but this quaint usage is diminishing as more precise

measuring standards evolve. The current practice is to use "Nr." or "No." to stand for ordinal measurement.

3. *Pound sign.* This usage greatly confounds the British, for whom the pound sign is £ and which, in the UK, occupies this position.

4. Ticktacktoe sign. This name, especially when enhanced by the gesture of overlaying the index and middle fingers of both hands, has the virtue of clarity, though its use invariably draws stares in professional circles.

$ In other countries, the dollar sign (24H) is replaced by a second national currency symbol. The ISO standard places the international currency symbol, ¤ , at this position.

The nanogram

Considering the pretense of precision in computer science, it is amazing that 1/128th of the code, **#**, has no name. I propose the name "nanogram" which means, roughly, "nine squares," and is easy to pronounce and remember. Other names that have been proposed include Hatch, Chiffer, Corral, Quadrux, Dunphy, Sidfrigand, Jang, and Bradgard—all submitted in a contest recently held by the Washington newsletter *Privacy*. The winning names in that contest were Octothorpe, judged "most authentic," and Gridlet, judged "most intriguing."

Specials: Punctuation and Diacritical Marks

To represent languages other than English, several punctuation marks may, in conjunction with backspacing (see page 18), be used to form commonly used diacritical marks. These correspondences are shown in Table 1-1.

Table 1-1 Punctuation used as diacritical markings.

Position	Symbol	As punctuation	As diacritical mark
22	"	Quotation mark	Diaeresis (umlaut)
27	´	Apostrophe	Acute accent
2C	,	Comma	Cedilla
5E	^	(None)	Circumflex
60H	`	Opening single quotation mark	Grave accent
7E	~	(None)	Tilde

The ASCII Collating Sequence

The sequence achieved when items are sorted strictly and solely according to their order in the ASCII table is called the ASCII *collating sequence*. Lists "sorted" in this way are not very useful and, in fact, are usually downright counter-intuitive. That numbers (digits) collate before the alphabet is not particularly disturbing, but consider what happens when raw numerals are sorted:

Unsorted	ASCII Order
−500	+1
−10	−1
−1	−10
+1	−500
2	10
3	100
4	2
10	3
100	4

The position of **SP** at the head of graphic characters in the ASCII table is important: groups of characters containing **SP** appear at the top of any list that is sorted into ASCII order. If it seems abstractly correct that nothing (the **SP**) should come before something, consider how the following list (taken from the Oakland, CA phone book) is arranged by a purely ASCII "sort."

Phone Book Order		ASCII Order	
Delabette	(1)	De La Cruz	(3)
Delacour	(2)	de la Cruz	(5)
De La Cruz	(3)	De la Cruz	(11)
delacruz	(4)	De laCruz	(8)
de la Cruz	(5)	Dela Cruz	(12)
Delacruz	(6)	DeLa Cruz	(13)
DeLaCruz	(7)	Delabette	(1)
De laCruz	(8)	Delacour	(2)
DelaCruz	(9)	delacruz	(4)
DeLaCruz	(10)	Delacruz	(6)
De la Cruz	(11)	DeLaCruz	(7)
Dela Cruz	(12)	DelaCruz	(9)
DeLa Cruz	(13)	DeLaCruz	(10)

Rather than belabor the point with further examples, let us just conclude that ASCII order does not a sort make.

The Controls

All characters discussed so far have one thing in common—they have graphic value. That is, they cause a specified graphic character to appear on a display device such as a printer or a video display terminal. By contrast, the characters in rows 0 and 1, together with **DEL** at 7F do not generate graphics characters. These are the *control characters*, thirty-three in all, shown in Figure 1-7.

As defined in X3.4, a control character, "initiates, modifies, or stops an action that affects the recording, processing, transmission, and interpretation of data." This definition hardly stirs the imagination, so it is helpful to divide the controls into several general categories for discussion:[3]

- Physical device controls
- Logical communications controls
- Physical communications controls
- Information separators
- Code extension controls

Before we consider the individual members in these categories, however, let's first clear up a few misunderstandings and establish a vocabulary for discussing control characters.

Figure 1-7 The control characters.

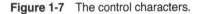

	0	1	2	3	4	5	6	7	8	9	A	B	C	D	E	F	
0	NUL	SOH	STX	ETX	EOT	ENQ	ACK	BEL	BS	HT	LF	VT	FF	CR	SO	SI	8
1	DLE	DC1	DC2	DC3	DC4	NAK	SYN	ETB	CAN	EM	SUB	ESC	FS	GS	RS	US	9
2	SP	!	"	#	$	%	&	'	(	)	*	+	,	-	.	/	A
3	0	1	2	3	4	5	6	7	8	9	:	;	<	=	>	?	B
4	@	A	B	C	D	E	F	G	H	I	J	K	L	M	N	O	C
5	P	Q	R	S	T	U	V	W	X	Y	Z	[	\	]	^	_	D
6	`	a	b	c	d	e	f	g	h	i	j	k	l	m	n	o	E
7	p	q	r	s	t	u	v	w	x	y	z	{	|	}	~	DEL	F

The Control Key

On virtually every keyboard, control characters are generated by a shift key, the *Control key*. The Control key makes it possible to generate the thirty-two contiguous control characters by subtracting 40H from the keys in rows 4 and 5. (There is no way to generate a **DEL** with the Control key.) **SOH**, for example, is generated by pressing the control key and the 'A' key. When it is necessary to describe these keystrokes, the notation is **Ctrl-A**. In practice, keyboards ignore the state of bit 5

---

[3]These categories are not part of the ASCII standard.

while the Control key is depressed, thus making **Ctrl-a** and **Ctrl-A** equivalent. As shown in Table 1-2, separate ("dedicated") keys usually duplicate frequently used key combinations.

Table 1-2 How control characters are generated from the keyboard.

Control Character	Key Strokes	Dedicated Key
BEL	Ctrl-G	Bell
BS	Ctrl-H	Backspace
HT	Ctrl-I	Tab
LF	Ctrl-J	Line Feed
CR	Ctrl-M	Carriage Return
DEL	None	DEL

Because of the use of a shift key, an understandable but still regrettable confusion has arisen about control characters and the keys required to produce them. The problem is this: control characters are not popularly known by their formal names—SOH, CAN, NAK, for example—but by the keys required to create them: Control-A, Control-X, and Control-U or, worse, Ctrl-A, Ctrl-X, and Ctrl-U. We can avoid this minor form of illiteracy simply by agreeing upon a few simple rules. We will use the constuction **Ctrl-** to refer to a combination of *keystrokes*. In general, we will call the characters by their formal names, often adding (reluctantly) the popular *Control-* designation for reference.

Physical Device Controls

The eleven control characters shown in Figure 1-8 are dedicated to controlling physical computer equipment such as printers, plotters, terminals, and so forth. Within the Physical Control group, six are *Format Effectors*. These alter the layout or positioning of graphics characters on display devices and are often represented on keyboards with discrete keys.

Format Effectors

Today our interaction with computers is mostly through a video terminal that may possess more computing power than some computers of just a few years ago. This power makes it easy to forget that the names of the ASCII "Format Effectors" describe the mechanical motions of the teletypewriter (TTY). Early video terminals in turn were designed to emulate the teletypewriter and were even called "glass TTYs." In short, the fancy capabilities taken for granted in modern display devices—cursor positioning, attribute (e.g, inverse video), graphics, selective screen erasure—not only are missing in ASCII, they are irrelevant to it. ASCII is a modest, very general standard not intended to embrace all needs. As we shall soon see, however, ASCII contains several trapdoors through which we can easily escape into other standards and character sets.

Instead of a cursor, ASCII refers to an "active position," where the next character will be displayed. The sole dimension recognized by ASCII is that used by a continuous spool of paper.

BS   (Backspace, 8, Control-G, ∩) This character is "a one-active-position Format Effector that moves the position backwards on the same line." The final phrase "on the same line," is important—BS cannot be used to move from the beginning of one line to the end of the previous one.

Figure 1-8 Physical Device Controls—the Format Effectors.

	0	1	2	3	4	5	6	7	8	9	A	B	C	D	E	F	
0	00 NUL	01 SOH	02 STX	03 ETX	04 EOT	05 ENQ	06 ACK	07 BEL	08 BS	09 HT	10 LF	11 VT	12 FF	13 CR	14 SO	15 SI	**8**
1	16 DLE	17 DC1	18 DC2	19 DC3	20 DC4	21 NAK	22 SYN	23 ETB	24 CAN	25 EM	26 SUB	27 ESC	28 FS	29 GS	30 RS	31 US	**9**
2	32 SP	33 !	34 "	35 #	36 $	37 %	38 &	39 '	40 (	41)	42 *	43 +	44 ,	45 -	46 .	47 /	**A**
3	48 0	49 1	50 2	51 3	52 4	53 5	54 6	55 7	56 8	57 9	58 :	59 ;	60 <	61 =	62 >	63 ?	**B**
4	64 @	65 A	66 B	67 C	68 D	69 E	70 F	71 G	72 H	73 I	74 J	75 K	76 L	77 M	78 N	79 O	**C**
5	80 P	81 Q	82 R	83 S	84 T	85 U	86 V	87 W	88 X	89 Y	90 Z	91 [	92 \	93]	94 ^	95 _	**D**
6	96 `	97 a	98 b	99 c	100 d	101 e	102 f	103 g	104 h	105 i	106 j	107 k	108 l	109 m	110 n	111 o	**E**
7	112 p	113 q	114 r	115 s	116 t	117 u	118 v	119 w	120 x	121 y	122 z	123 {	124 |	125 }	126 ~	127 DEL	**F**

BS can be used to create a number of special effects: underscoring, overstriking, bold print, and inflected characters. There are three ways to create these effects in text; for example, underscoring:

1. The most "natural" way is to type your text, followed by an equal number of BS's, followed by an equal number of underscores.

2. Type a single character, followed by a single BS, followed by an underscore, followed by another single character, another BS, and so forth.

3. The same as number 2, but the underscore and BS precede the character.

If video terminals behaved as printers, all of these methods would produce the same results on both devices. Unfortunately, the next character following a BS on a video terminal obliterates the character at that position. If method 1 or 2 is used, only the underscores remain. If method 3 is used, the special effec.s are lost on video terminals, but at least the text remains.

HT (Horizontal Tab, 9, Control-I, ≻) The behavior of this character is analogous to the Tab key on a typewriter—it "advances the active position to the next predetermined character position on that line." Predetermination of the next position is performed locally; that is, there is no corresponding ASCII code for setting the tabulation intervals.

LF (Line Feed, 0A, Control-J, ≡) This character "advances the active position to the same character on the next line." In other words, an LF moves the active position down one line, but does not affect its column. See "A Modest Proposal," later in this chapter for a discussion of an alternative definition of this character.

VT (Vertical Tab, 0B, Control-K, ∨) This character "advances the active position to the same character position on the next predetermined line." It is intended as a sort of super line feed—a rapid method to jump more than one line at a time. Significantly, it may also, when agreed upon in advance by all concerned, change the active position to the first character of the same line (i.e., perform a Carriage Return).

FF (Form Feed, 0C, Control-L, ↡) This advances the active position to a predetermined line on the next page. The exact number of lines advanced must be predetermined locally; that is, the device receiving the FF is responsible for the actual line counting. Unbelievably, some printers do not support FF. For these devices, pagination is performed by issuing the suitable number of Line Feeds followed by Carriage Returns. On some video terminals, FF clears the screen—a logical usage.

CR (Carriage Return, 0D, Control-M, ◄) The purpose of this character is to advance the active position to the first column of the same line. This horizontal motion is generally used together with the vertical motion of LF to create a new line. On printers, it can be used to embolden, underscore, or overstrike entire lines. On video terminals, however, the second line obliterates the first—a serious limitation to the technique.

Other Device Controls

The remaining control characters in the Physical Control group have more general usage.

BEL (Bell, 7, Control-G, ⌐) As its name implies, this control triggers some sort of attention-getting signal. Although most terminals respond to this character with an audio tone, the signal need not be an audible one. Some terminals, for example, can be configured to issue "visual bells," which might cause a portion of the screen to flash. Although it may seem a bit far-fetched, in some environments a tactile signal (a vibrator perhaps) might be required.

DC1,DC2
DC3,DC4 (Device Control, 11-14H, Control Q - T, ☉ ☉ ☉ ☉) These device controls have no assigned meaning in ASCII. They can be used for any purpose at hand, but two of them used in concert, DC1 and DC3, have become a de facto standard of flow control, a subject discussed at length in Chapter 4.

Logical Communications Control

These ten control characters, highlighted in Figure 1-9, are employed to control the flow of data between two communicating devices. Although we will examine the topic of *file-transfer protocols* in detail in Chapter 4, a brief summary of the subject will help in understanding how this group of control characters is used.

A common method of transferring data is to break it into arbitrarily sized smaller blocks of data referred to as *messages*. At transmission, the message itself is "framed," or delimited with control characters. The message is preceded by a *header*, which may contain information about the length and sequence of the following message. Next comes the message block itself, followed by some sort of error-checking information.

Based on the information contained in the header, the receiver parses the data stream back into header, message, and error-checking information. Using the error-checking information, the

Figure 1-9 Logical communications controls.

	0	1	2	3	4	5	6	7	8	9	A	B	C	D	E	F	
0	00 NUL	01 SOH	02 STX	03 ETX	04 EOT	05 ENQ	06 ACK	07 BEL	08 BS	09 HT	10 LF	11 VT	12 FF	13 CR	14 SO	15 SI	**8**
1	16 DLE	17 DC1	18 DC2	19 DC3	20 DC4	21 NAK	22 SYN	23 ETB	24 CAN	25 EM	26 SUB	27 ESC	28 FS	29 GS	30 RS	31 US	**9**
2	32 SP	33 !	34 "	35 #	36 $	37 %	38 &	39 '	40 (	41)	42 *	43 +	44 ,	45 −	46 .	47 /	**A**
3	48 0	49 1	50 2	51 3	52 4	53 5	54 6	55 7	56 8	57 9	58 :	59 ;	60 <	61 =	62 >	63 ?	**B**
4	64 @	65 A	66 B	67 C	68 D	69 E	70 F	71 G	72 H	73 I	74 J	75 K	76 L	77 M	78 N	79 O	**C**
5	80 P	81 Q	82 R	83 S	84 T	85 U	86 V	87 W	88 X	89 Y	90 Z	91 [	92 \	93]	94 ^	95 _	**D**
6	96 `	97 a	98 b	99 c	100 d	101 e	102 f	103 g	104 h	105 i	106 j	107 k	108 l	109 m	110 n	111 o	**E**
7	112 p	113 q	114 r	115 s	116 t	117 u	118 v	119 w	120 x	121 y	122 z	123 {	124 |	125 }	126 ~	127 DEL	**F**

receiver then signals that the data block is good or bad. Bad data blocks are normally retransmitted until correctly received. This process continues for each block in the message, at the end of which time the transfer is terminated.

In this kind of data transfer, the *logical* communications control characters actually mark the boundaries between header, message, and error checking. Others are used as signaling codes in the transmission itself, indicating, for example, that a data block has been correctly or incorrectly received.

SOH (Start of Header, 1, Control-A, ⌐) This character marks the beginning of the header information. The header itself may be of any length.

STX (Start of Text, 2, Control-B, ⊥) This character marks the beginning of the data block (referred to in ASCII as the "text") and, ipso facto, the end of the header.

ETX (End of Text, 3, Control-C, ⌐) This character marks the end of the data (text) block.

EOT (End of Transmission, 4, Control-D, ↘) EOT is usually transmitted where SOH would normally occur, telling the receiver that the transmission is over.

ENQ (Enquiry, 5, Control-E, ⊠) When two computers begin to establish communications, one of them transmits ENQ to mean "Are you there?" In many cases it is a request for actual identification or status, a sort of "Who are you?"

ACK (Acknowledge, 6, Control-F, ✓) This character is transmitted by the receiver in response to the error-free reception of a message.

HOWARD W. SAMS & COMPANY

Bookmark

DEAR VALUED CUSTOMER:

Howard W. Sams & Company is dedicated to bringing you timely and authoritative books for your personal and professional library. Our goal is to provide you with excellent technical books written by the most qualified authors. You can assist us in this endeavor by checking the box next to your particular areas of interest.

We appreciate your comments and will use the information to provide you with a more comprehensive selection of titles.

Thank you,

Vice President, Book Publishing
Howard W. Sams & Company

COMPUTER TITLES:

Hardware
- ☐ Apple 140
- ☐ Macintosh 101
- ☐ Commodore 110
- ☐ IBM & Compatibles 114

Business Applications
- ☐ Word Processing J01
- ☐ Data Base J04
- ☐ Spreadsheets J02

Operating Systems
- ☐ MS-DOS K05
- ☐ OS/2 K10
- ☐ CP/M K01
- ☐ UNIX K03

Programming Languages
- ☐ C L03
- ☐ Pascal L05
- ☐ Prolog L12
- ☐ Assembly L01
- ☐ BASIC L02
- ☐ HyperTalk L14

Troubleshooting & Repair
- ☐ Computers S05
- ☐ Peripherals S10

Other
- ☐ Communications/Networking M03
- ☐ AI/Expert Systems T18

ELECTRONICS TITLES:
- ☐ Amateur Radio T01
- ☐ Audio T03
- ☐ Basic Electronics T20
- ☐ Basic Electricity T21
- ☐ Electronics Design T12
- ☐ Electronics Projects T04
- ☐ Satellites T09

- ☐ Instrumentation T05
- ☐ Digital Electronics T11

Troubleshooting & Repair
- ☐ Audio S11
- ☐ Television S04
- ☐ VCR S01
- ☐ Compact Disc S02
- ☐ Automotive S06
- ☐ Microwave Oven S03

Other interests or comments: _____

_____

Name _____
Title _____
Company _____
Address _____
City _____
State/Zip _____
Daytime Telephone No. _____

A Division of Macmillan, Inc.

4300 West 62nd Street Indianapolis, Indiana 46268   22584

Bookmark

HOWARD W. SAMS
& COMPANY

BUSINESS REPLY CARD

FIRST CLASS   PERMIT NO. 1076   INDIANAPOLIS, IN

POSTAGE WILL BE PAID BY ADDRESSEE

HOWARD W. SAMS & COMPANY
ATTN: Public Relations Department
P.O. Box 7092
Indianapolis, IN 46209-9921

DLE (Data Link Escape, 10H, Control-P, ⊟) This character signals that a limited number of contiguous characters that follow have a special meaning. In effect, DLE is used to create *control code sequences* to supplement existing control characters.

NAK (Negative Acknowledge, 15H, Control-U,) This character is transmitted by the receiver when an error is detected in a message.

SYN (Synchronous Idle, 16H, Control-V, ⎍) This character is used in *synchronous* systems to establish and maintain synchronization on a communications line on which no data is flowing.

ETB (End of Transmission Block, 17H, Control-W, ⊣) This character may be used in place of ETX, although its use suggests that the length of the preceding message may have been artificially forced by the communications apparatus (such as the end of a data volume) and is not necessarily of the size expected. For example, block size is often chosen to correspond to some logical record size in the data. If the physical volume containing the data to be transmitted is exhausted in the middle of a record, ETB might be sent instead of ETX.

Physical Communications Control

This group of controls is used for communications with physical devices such as printers, terminals, and computers.

Figure 1-10 Physical communications controls.

	0	1	2	3	4	5	6	7	8	9	A	B	C	D	E	F	
0	00 0000 0000 NUL	01 0000 0001 SOH	02 0000 0010 STX	03 0000 0011 ETX	04 0000 0100 EOT	05 0000 0101 ENQ	06 0000 0110 ACK	07 0000 0111 BEL	08 0000 1000 BS	09 0000 1001 HT	10 0000 1010 LF	11 0000 1011 VT	12 0000 1100 FF	13 0000 1101 CR	14 0000 1110 SO	15 0000 1111 SI	8
1	16 0001 0000 DLE	17 0001 0001 DC1	18 0001 0010 DC2	19 0001 0011 DC3	20 0001 0100 DC4	21 0001 0101 NAK	22 0001 0110 SYN	23 0001 0111 ETB	24 0001 1000 CAN	25 0001 1001 EM	26 0001 1010 SUB	27 0001 1011 ESC	28 0001 1100 FS	29 0001 1101 GS	30 0001 1110 RS	31 0001 1111 US	9
2	32 0010 0000 SP	33 0010 0001 !	34 0010 0010 "	35 0010 0011 #	36 0010 0100 $	37 0010 0101 %	38 0010 0110 &	39 0010 0111 '	40 0010 1000 (	41 0010 1001)	42 0010 1010 *	43 0010 1011 +	44 0010 1100 ,	45 0010 1101 -	46 0010 1110 .	47 0010 1111 /	A
3	48 0011 0000 0	49 0011 0001 1	50 0011 0010 2	51 0011 0011 3	52 0011 0100 4	53 0011 0101 5	54 0011 0110 6	55 0011 0111 7	56 0011 1000 8	57 0011 1001 9	58 0011 1010 :	59 0011 1011 ;	60 0011 1100 <	61 0011 1101 =	62 0011 1110 >	63 0011 1111 ?	B
4	64 0100 0000 @	65 0100 0001 A	66 0100 0010 B	67 0100 0011 C	68 0100 0100 D	69 0100 0101 E	70 0100 0110 F	71 0100 0111 G	72 0100 1000 H	73 0100 1001 I	74 0100 1010 J	75 0100 1011 K	76 0100 1100 L	77 0100 1101 M	78 0100 1110 N	79 0100 1111 O	C
5	80 0101 0000 P	81 0101 0001 Q	82 0101 0010 R	83 0101 0011 S	84 0101 0100 T	85 0101 0101 U	86 0101 0110 V	87 0101 0111 W	88 0101 1000 X	89 0101 1001 Y	90 0101 1010 Z	91 0101 1011 [	92 0101 1100 \	93 0101 1101]	94 0101 1110 ^	95 0101 1111 _	D
6	96 0110 0000 `	97 0110 0001 a	98 0110 0010 b	99 0110 0011 c	100 0110 0100 d	101 0110 0101 e	102 0110 0110 f	103 0110 0111 g	104 0110 1000 h	105 0110 1001 i	106 0110 1010 j	107 0110 1011 k	108 0110 1100 l	109 0110 1101 m	110 0110 1110 n	111 0110 1111 o	E
7	112 0111 0000 p	113 0111 0001 q	114 0111 0010 r	115 0111 0011 s	116 0111 0100 t	117 0111 0101 u	118 0111 0110 v	119 0111 0111 w	120 0111 1000 x	121 0111 1001 y	122 0111 1010 z	123 0111 1011 {	124 0111 1100 |	125 0111 1101 }	126 0111 1110 ~	127 0111 1111 DEL	F

NUL (Nul, 0, Control-@, □) This character is a time-waster inserted in the data stream, usually to give a hardware device time to perform some function. When devices (such as teletypewriters and video terminals) process the incoming data stream one character at a time, the time required for mechanical operations—such as returning the print head or scrolling the screen—exceeds the time between characters. To avoid the loss of data during this time, the sending equipment inserts an agreed-upon number of NULs after each Format Effector to allow the device to complete its slow operation.

In ASCII jargon, this practice of inserting do-nothing characters into the data stream is referred to as *media fill time,* but less formally as *padding*. The standard states that NUL should not change the information content of the data stream, but "addition or removal of these characters may affect the information layout or the control of equipment." In simple terms, it means that NUL has no information value, but it *may* have special meaning to external equipment or, for that matter, may be part of a logical record structure. In other words, use it at your own risk!

Since NUL is a valid character, the amount of time it actually wastes varies with the speed of the transmission. That is, twice as many NULs are required to control the same device at 120 characters per second as at 60 characters per second.

Only in the most imprecise sense is the character NUL interchangeable with the word "null." The former is a character in the ASCII character set, the latter a synonym for zero or a "nothing." The NUL was assigned the position at 00 because that value does not punch holes in paper tape. Aside from this convenience, the function of the NUL character might have been assigned to any of the control characters.

DEL (Delete, FF, DEL) Everything the standard ascribes to NUL it also ascribes to DEL with two exceptions: (1) DEL is "used primarily to erase or obliterate an unwanted or erroneous character in punched tape" and, (2) it punches *all* the holes on paper tape. The choice between NUL or DEL as a padding character is usually dictated by system conventions or by hardware requirements.

CAN (Cancel, 18H, Control-X, X) This character means that an agreed-upon number of preceding characters should be ignored. Some operating systems use CAN to allow a user to clear a partially typed command.

EM (End of Medium, 19H, Control-Y, ⊦) This character indicates that the preceding character was the last usable character currently on the medium; it does not necessarily mean that the medium is exhausted.

SUB (Substitute, 1A, Control-Z, ⸮) If, at any point in the communications link, a character is determined to be in error, a SUB should be installed in its place. A truly "ASCII" device displays this character as a mirror-image question mark.

Information Separators

These four control characters, highlighted in Figure 1-11, are used to impart hierarchical order to data.

FS (File Separator, 1C, Control-\, ⊟)
GS (Group Separator, 1D, Control-], ⊟)
RS (Record Separator, 1E, Control-^, ⊞)

US (Unit Separator, 1F, Control-__, 🖵) The ASCII standard states, somewhat obliquely, "These information separators may be used with data in optional fashion, except that their hierarchical relationship shall be: FS as the most inclusive, then GS, then RS, and US as least inclusive. The content and length of a file, group, record, or unit are not specified." In other words, these characters may have arbitrary meanings provided only that when they appear together, a hierarchical order is presumed. As an example of how they may be used, some computerized typesetting systems use these codes to delimit indentation levels and type face changes associated with different headings.

Figure 1-11 Information separators.

	0	1	2	3	4	5	6	7	8	9	A	B	C	D	E	F	
0	00 NUL	01 SOH	02 STX	03 ETX	04 EOT	05 ENQ	06 ACK	07 BEL	08 BS	09 HT	10 VT	11 FF	12 CR	13 SO	14 SI	15	**8**
1	16 DLE	17 DC1	18 DC2	19 DC3	20 DC4	21 NAK	22 SYN	23 ETB	24 CAN	25 EM	26 SUB	27 ESC	28 FS	29 GS	30 RS	31 US	**9**
2	32 SP	33 !	34 "	35 #	36 $	37 %	38 &	39 '	40 (	41)	42 *	43 +	44 ,	45 —	46 .	47 /	**A**
3	48 0	49 1	50 2	51 3	52 4	53 5	54 6	55 7	56 8	57 9	58 :	59 ;	60 <	61 =	62 >	63 ?	**B**
4	64 @	65 A	66 B	67 C	68 D	69 E	70 F	71 G	72 H	73 I	74 J	75 K	76 L	77 M	78 N	79 O	**C**
5	80 P	81 Q	82 R	83 S	84 T	85 U	86 V	87 W	88 X	89 Y	90 Z	91 [	92 \	93]	94 ^	95 _	**D**
6	96 `	97 a	98 b	99 c	100 d	101 e	102 f	103 g	104 h	105 i	106 j	107 k	108 l	109 m	110 n	111 o	**E**
7	112 p	113 q	114 r	115 s	116 t	117 u	118 v	119 w	120 x	121 y	122 z	123 {	124 |	125 }	126 ~	127 DEL	**F**

Controls for Code Extension

Clearly, there are not enough characters in the ASCII alphabet to satisfy every need. Indeed, almost every computer user at one time or another has wished for a special character or even an entirely different character set: writers bemoan the absence of a copyright mark, business needs the penny symbol, doctors need an "Rx," mathematicians need a host of special symbols, and so on indefinitely. The writers of ASCII were aware of this problem:

> . . .a fundamental decision had to be made as to the size of the code. In making such a decision there is usually a conscious effort to avoid the most obvious problems with a code that is either too large or too small. Should the number of characters included be too small, many users will find their needs not accommodated and will be forced to adopt "parochial" codes for their ap-

plications. Should the number of characters be too large, many users will find the code disproportionately costly to implement, or untenably inefficient in transmission or storage, and will again be driven to the use of some other code.

—ANSI Standard X3.4-1977 (Revised 1983)

ISO Standard 2375 describes the procedures for registering *alternative* character sets for international use. The actual registry is carried out by the French standards group, the Association Francaise de Normalization (AFNOR), but the listing of codes is available through ANSI.

Figure 1-12 Code extension controls.

	0	1	2	3	4	5	6	7	8	9	A	B	C	D	E	F
0	NUL	SOH	STX	ETX	EOT	ENQ	ACK	BEL	BS	HT	LF	VT	FF	CR	SO	SI
1	DLE	DC1	DC2	DC3	DC4	NAK	SYN	ETB	CAN	EM	SUB	ESC	FS	GS	RS	US
2	SP	!	"	#	$	%	&	'	(	)	*	+	,	-	.	/
3	0	1	2	3	4	5	6	7	8	9	:	;	<	=	>	?
4	@	A	B	C	D	E	F	G	H	I	J	K	L	M	N	O
5	P	Q	R	S	T	U	V	W	X	Y	Z	[	\	]	^	_
6	`	a	b	c	d	e	f	g	h	i	j	k	l	m	n	o
7	p	q	r	s	t	u	v	w	x	y	z	{			}	~	DEL

Invocation of Alternative Character Sets

SI, **SO**, and **ESC** are used to activate extended character sets. In ASCII documents, an *Escape Sequence* is a string of characters beginning with the ESC character and is used to convey compound identifying or control information (much more on this later). An Escape sequence in conjunction with the SI and SO characters invokes alternative sets of control or graphics (i.e., noncontrol) characters, but not both simultaneously. First, the desired set of alternative characters is identified in an Escape sequence. The next SO in the data stream invokes the new character set, which remains in effect until an SI causes a return to the original character set. In systems that require multiple alternative character sets, the invocations may be nested; that is, other alternative sets may be invoked while in the "Shift Out" mode.

The complicated procedures for manipulating and managing character sets are beyond the scope of this book, but are exhaustively detailed in American National Standards Institute, "Code Extension Techniques with the 7-Bit Coded Character Set" (ANSI X3.41-1974).

Control Character Woes

Earlier in this chapter we discussed how users often confuse control characters with the keys required to generate them. In fact control characters cause a good deal of grief. Connecting a computer to a terminal or printer for which it is not configured is an almost sure-fire way to ruin a day. Even trying to transmit an "ASCII" file to a friend via modem can produce confounding and, at times, startling effects. Computer users have come to regard control characters as a kind of "X-factor" in their lives—control characters are summarily blamed for anything that goes awry in the system.[4]

Why should this be? The answer is simple: control characters are incredibly powerful, but (and here's the rub), they are *invisible*. Control characters, by definition, have no graphic value, and because they cannot be seen, their effects are mysterious. The problems began with the earliest design of ASCII keyboards when a "control" key was installed purely as a mechanical convenience. That is, the key marked "Control" simply forced upper case and subtracted 40H from any key in rows 4 or 5. Users were then (and still are) instructed to "hit a Control-A," without receiving an explanation of what a Control-A is or what it does. What, exactly, is the conceptual relationship between the control character **SOH** and the letter 'A'? Precisely the same intellectual relationship as, say, the asterisk has to the digit 8; namely, none at all. Calling control characters by the names of alphabetical characters is inherently misleading and uninformative. Relegated to an undefined, inferior subcategory of other keys, having no names or symbols of their own, it is no wonder that control characters have become, in the minds of the ordinary user at least, dark denizens of the keyboard.

If this sort of rhetoric seems bombastic, consider that perfectly competent touch-typists must remove their fingers from "home" to fumble for the Backspace, Tab, Line Feed, and Escape "function" keys. Once informed, however, touch-typists unanimously prefer to generate control characters with **Ctrl-H**, **Ctrl-I**, **Ctrl-J**, and **Ctrl-[**. Touch-typists are not alone here—a surprising number of computer "professionals" never make the association between the dedicated keys and their Control key equivalents.

Graphic Representation of Control Characters

Perhaps the most unusual feature of the ASCII chart in Figure 1-1 is its use of graphic figures to represent control characters. These figures are seldom seen or used, although they are a bona fide ANSI standard: ANSI X3.32-1973, "Graphic Representation of the Control Characters of ASCII." Promulgation of these graphic representations is a first step toward erasing the difficulties that users and programmers have with control characters. First, the graphic representations of the control characters shown in Figure 1-1 should be painted on the stick 4 and 5 keytops or, at the very least, on the H, I, J, and M keys. This will impart to control characters an importance at least equal to the shifted characters that now occupy other keytops. Suddenly, control characters are no longer "functions," but legitimate characters that can be generated from the keyboard. Second, every character display device should have an optional mode that will display these symbols (or miniatures of the abbreviations for the control characters' names). Imagine how many hours of useless "debugging" would be saved by this feature. How easy it would be to solve many "communications" problems if your terminal were capable of reproducing *every* received or typed

---

[4]Overheard: A computer salesman cautioning a new user against typing too many control characters because "they can burn out your screen."

character. A fair number of terminals with this feature were once manufactured, but are now hard to find due to lack of consumer interest.

ANSI X3.64: Control Code Extension

Of rather more general interest is the subject of control codes for character-imaging devices. The meager array of control characters in sticks 0 and 1 of the ASCII code are obviously grossly inadequate to control such modern devices as video terminals, laser printers, microfiche readers, and the myriad of devices as yet uninvented. In the absence of standards for device control codes, manufacturers have been forced to employ home-made codes (the "parochial" codes mentioned in ANSI X3.41). Consequently, the computer world is awash with incompatible equipment whose very uniqueness causes endless grief for professional and amateur alike.

The computer industry has responded to this disconcerting variety with ANSI X3.64-1979, "Additional Controls for Use with American National Standard Code for Information Interchange." (The equivalent ISO standard is DP6429.) This document sets forth a set of standard Escape sequences to control almost every imaginable aspect of a character display device. Table 1-3 shows some of the ANSI X3.64 video terminal control codes.

Table 1-3   Video terminal control codes in ANSI X3.64.*

Mnemonic	Action	Escape Sequence	Parameter Defaults	Function Type**
CBT	Cursor Backward Tabulation	Esc [Pn Z	1	Edit
CHA	Cursor Horizontal Absolute	Esc [Pn G	1	Edit
CHT	Cursor Horizontal Tabulation	Esc [Pn I	1	Edit
CNL	Cursor Next Line	Esc [Pn E	1	Edit
CPL	Cursor Preceding Line	Esc [Pn F	1	Edit
CPR	Cursor Position Report	Esc [Pn ; Pn R	1,1	
CSI	Control Sequence Introducer	Esc [		
CTC	Cursor Tabulation Control	Esc [Ps W	0	Edit
	0 Set HT stop at active position			
	1 Set VT stop at active line			
	2 Clear HT at active position			
	3 Clear VT at active line			
	4 Clear all HT stops in active line			
	5 Clear all HT stops in device			
	6 Clear all VT stops in device			
CUB	Cursor Backward	Esc [Pn D	1	Edit
CUD	Cursor Down	Esc [Pn B	1	Edit
CUF	Cursor Forward	Esc [Pn C	1	Edit
CUP	Cursor Position	Esc [Pn ; Pn H	1,1	Edit
CUU	Cursor Up	Esc [Pn A	1	Edit
CVT	Cursor Vertical Tab	Esc [Pn Y		Edit

*Note: Spacing is added for readability. Actual SPs are indicated by ▪.
**Format—Format Effector   Edit—editing function

Table 1-3 cont.   Video terminal control codes in ANSI X3.64.*

Mnemonic	Action	Escape Sequence	Parameter Defaults	Function Type**
DA	Device Attributes	Esc [Pn c	0	
DAQ	Define Area Qualification	Esc [Ps o	0	
	0 Accept all input			
	1 Accept no input (protected); do not transmit (guarded)			
	2 Accept graphics			
	3 Accept numerics			
	4 Accept alphabetics			
	5 Right justify in area			
	6 Zero-fill in area			
	7 HT at start of area (field)			
	8 Accept no input (protected); permit transmit (unguarded)			
	9 Space-fill in area			
DCH	Delete Character	Esc [Pn P	1	Edit
DL	Delete Line	Esc [Pn M	1	Edit
DSR	Device Status Report	Esc [Ps n	0	
	0 Ready, no malfunctions detected			
	1 Busy—retry later			
	2 Busy—DSR will notify when ready			
	3 Malfunction—retry later			
	4 Malfunction—DSR will notify when ready			
	5 Please report status via DSR or DSC			
	6 Please report status active position via CPR			
EA	Erase in Area	Esc [Ps O	0	Edit
	0 From active position through end			
	1 From start through active position			
	2 All of qualified area			
ECH	Erase Character	Esc [Pn X	1	Edit
ED	Erase in Display	Esc [Ps J	0	Edit
	0 From active position through end			
	1 From start through active position			
	2 All of display			
EF	Erase in Field	Esc [Ps N	0	Edit
	0 From active position through end			
	1 From start through active position			
	2 All of field			
EL	Erase in Line	Esc [Ps K	0	Edit
	0 From active position through end			
	1 From start through active position			
	2 All of line			
EPA	End of Protected Area	Esc W		
ESA	End of Selected Area	Esc G		

*Note: Spacing is added for readability. Actual SPs are indicated by ▮.
**Format—Format Effector   Edit—editing function

Table 1-3 cont. Video terminal control codes in ANSI X3.64.*

Mnemonic	Action	Escape Sequence	Parameter Defaults	Function Type**
FNT	Font Selection	Esc [Pn ; Pn■D	0,0	Format
	0;0 Primary font			
	1;0 First alternative font			
	⋮			
	9;0 Ninth alternative font			
GSM	Graphic Size Modify	Esc [Pn ; Pn■B	100,100	Format
GSS	Graphic Size Selection	Esc [Pn■C	none	Format
HPA	Horizontal Position Absolute	Esc [Pn '	1	Format
HPR	Horizontal Position Relative	Esc [Pn a	1	Format
HTJ	Horiz. Tab with Justification	Esc |		Format
HTS	Horizontal Tab Set	Esc H		Format
HVP	Horiz. and Vertical Position	Esc [Pn ; Pn f	1,1	Format
ICH	Insert Character	Esc [Pn @	1	Edit
IL	Insert Line	Esc [Pn L	1	Edit
IND	Index	Esc D		Format
JFY	Justify	Esc [Ps; … ;PS■F	0	Format
	0 Terminate all justify actions			
	1 Fill action			
	2 Interword spacing			
	3 Letter spacing			
	4 Hyphenation			
	5 Flush left margin			
	6 Center text between margins			
	7 Flush right margin			
	8 Italian form (underscore last)			
MW	Message Waiting	Esc U		
NEL	Next Line	Esc E		Format
NP	Next Page	Esc [Pn U	1	Edit
PLD	Partial Line Down	Esc K		Format
PLU	Partial Line Up	Esc L		Format
PP	Preceding Page	Esc [Pn V	1	Edit
REP	Repeat Character or Control	Esc [Pn b	1	
RI	Reverse Index	Esc M		Format
RM	Reset Mode	Esc [Ps |	none	
SD	Scroll Down	Esc [Pn T	1	Edit
SEM	Select Extent Mode	Esc [Ps Q	O	
	0 Edit in display			
	1 Edit in active line			
	2 Edit in field			
	3 Edit in qualified area			
SGR	Select Graphics Rendition	Esc [Ps m	0	Format
	0 Primary rendition			
	1 Bold or increased intensity			
	2 Faint or decreased intensity or			
	secondary color			
	3 Italic			

*Note: Spacing is added for readability. Actual SPs are indicated by ■.
**Format—Format Effector   Edit—editing function

Table 1-3 cont.   Video terminal control codes in ANSI X3.64.*

Mnemonic	Action	Escape Sequence	Parameter Defaults	Function Type**
	4 Underscore			
	5 Slow blink (< 150 per minute)			
	6 Rapid blink rate (> = 150 per minute)			
	7 Inverse negative image			
	8 Reserved			
	9 Reserved			
	10 Primary font as designated by FNT			
	11 First alternative font as designated by FNT			
	⋮			
	19 Ninth alternative font as designated by FNT			
	20 Fraktur (Archaic German manuscript font)			
SL	Scroll Left	Esc [Pn■@	1	Edit
SM	Select Mode	Esc [Ps h	none	
SPA	Start of Protected Area	Esc V		
SPI	Spacing Increment	Esc [Pn; Pn■G	none	Format
SR	Scroll Right	Esc [Pn■A	1	Edit
SSA	Start of Selected Area	Esc F		
SU	Scroll Up	Esc [Pn S	1	Edit
TBC	Tab Clear	Esc [Ps g	0	Format
	0 Clear HT stop at active position			
	2 Clear VT stop at active line			
	3 Clear all HT stops in active line			
	4 Clear all HT stops			
	5 Clear all VT stops			
TSS	Thin Space Specification	Esc [Pn■E	none	Format
VPA	Vertical Position Absolute	Esc [Pn d	1	Format
VPR	Vertical Position Relative	Esc [Pn e	1	Format

*Note: Spacing is added for readability. Actual SPs are indicated by ■.
**Format—Format Effector   Edit—editing function

The ANSI X3.64 Control Code Format

The general format for ANSI X3.64 control codes is:

    CSI   P...P   I...I   F

where CSI is the *Control Sequence Introducer*, P is a series of zero or more *parameter strings*, I is zero or more *Intermediate* characters, and F is a *Final* character. Let's examine these parts one at a time.

The Control Sequence Introducer

The control codes for character devices consist of Escape sequences that unambiguously identify the desired action. The first portion of the sequence is a *control sequence introducer*, or CSI. For 7-bit systems (i.e., those based upon the ASCII character set), the CSI is "**ESC [**" or 1B 5B. A few of the codes—IND, for example—are introduced by a single **ESC**.

After the CSI come the optional parameters, for which there are several formats:

- *Single numeric* parameters, indicated with Pn in Table 1-3, are expressed using the digits 30H through 39H in stick 3. For example, three digits—31H, 30H, and 30H—are required to express a numeric parameter of 100.

- *Multiple numeric parameters*, if required, are separated by semicolons indicated with "Pn;Pn. . ." in Table 1-3.

- *Selective parameters*, indicated by Ps in Table 1-3, are also expressed with digits (30H through 39H) separated by colons, but their meaning is not numeric. In this context the digits select options or modes. See "Programming for ANSI X3.64," below, for an illustration of selective parameters.

- Default parameters are assumed when parameters are omitted from functions that require them (cursor positioning, for instance).

Intermediate Characters

The Intermediate's sole purpose is to extend the number of functions beyond the seventy-nine Final characters. Intermediates come only from the sixteen characters in stick 2, yielding $16 \times 79 = 1264$ possible functions. If more than 1264 functions are ever required, additional Intermediates will be introduced. Any number of Intermediates can appear in a sequence as long as they appear between the parameters and the Final.

To understand how Intermediates work, notice that the only difference between the ICH and SL commands in Table 1-3 is the Intermediate ▧ **(SP)** before the Final @ (40).

The Final Character

The Final actually defines the function, and must come from sticks 3 through 7, excluding **DEL**. The Final character in the Select Graphics Rendition code, for example, is **m** (6D). Finals from stick 7 are reserved for private use; that is, for home-made controls.

Programming for ANSI X3.64

Let's look at a couple of examples of the ASCII extended control codes. Assume that we need to clear the screen, position the cursor to the center of the screen, and change the video mode to inverse video. First, we will decide which functions are required, then examine the formal definition of those functions, and finally put together the correct control sequences.

Clearing the Screen: ED, Erase in Display

This function erases some or all of the display according to the parameter supplied. The coding is

ESC [Ps F

where "Ps" is a selective parameter and 'F' stands for the Final. The possible *selective* parameters are

0 (30H)—Erase from active position to end of display.

1 (31H)—Erase from beginning of display to active position.

2 (32H)—Erase entire display.

From Table 1-3, we find that the final for ED is **J** (4A). The control sequence to clear the screen is therefore

ESC [2 J   (1B,5B,32,4A)

Cursor Motion: CUP, Cursor Position

This function moves the active position to the position specified by the parameters, which default to 1. The first parameter specifies the vertical position (row), the second parameter specifies the horizontal (column). A parameter value of 0 is converted to 1. A CUP with default parameters is therefore equivalent to a "Cursor Home" function. The format is

ESC [Pn;Pn F

The two "Pn"s are the numeric parameters for row and column screen coordinates and the Final for this function is **H** (48). The control code to position the cursor at row 12, column 40 is

ESC [12;40H   (1B,5B,31,32,3B,34,30,48)

Changing to Inverse Video: SGR, Select Graphics Rendition

This function changes the next character and all subsequent characters in the data screen according to the graphics "rendition" (i.e., characteristics) described by the parameter(s). Parameters 10 through 19 invoke a font that may have been previously designated by FNT (Font Selection). The format is

ESC [Ps F

where F is the Final character, **m** (6D). The possible parameters are shown in Table 1-3.
The code to invoke inverse video is therefore

ESC [7m   (1B,5B,37,6D)

Since the default for SGR is 0, if the parameter field is omitted, the display returns to normal:

ESC [m   (1B,5B,6D)

Although manufacturers haven't exactly rushed headlong to abandon their own "parochial" codes in favor of those in ANSI X3.64, an increasing number, led by Digital Equipment Corporation, Zenith, and others, have begun to implement ANSI X3.64 in parallel with in-house codes. Thus terminals are appearing that support an "ANSI mode." The IBM PC family, which employs memory-mapped video, implements a tiny[5] subset of ANSI X3.64 via the device driver *ANSI.SYS* that is optionally loaded during power-up.

---

[5]The following functions are supported by IBM PC with *ANSI.SYS* installed: CPR, CUB, CUD, CUF, CUP, CUU, DSR, ED, EL, HVP, RM, SGR, and SM. In addition, three "local use" functions are defined: SCP (save cursor position), RCP (restore cursor position), and keyboard reasssignment.

There are good reasons why ANSI X3.64 has met with a lukewarm reception. First, certain manufacturers, especially those with an established customer base, have little or no interest in compatibility—customers are more apt to become locked into a particular brand of equipment if it is incompatible with other brands. Second, there is a decided performance disadvantage to expressing numeric parameters in ASCII instead of binary because several bytes may be required in ASCII where one would do in binary. This large coding overhead is not apparent at high data rates, but in certain applications the inefficiency is painfully apparent. Word processing over a 1200 bps modem is maddeningly slow on any terminal, but on an ANSI one it is positively an unnatural act.

From the programmer's point of view, writing a driver for ANSI *output* is slightly more difficult than for other kinds of terminals because ANSI expresses all numeric parameters as ASCII digits instead of binary numbers. But if ANSI output is not particularly difficult, writing code for an ANSI *input* driver is a Herculean[6] labor. Because the identifying code (the "Final") occurs last or next to last (if an Intermediate is present), there is no way to ascertain at the beginning of a control sequence how long it will be. Remember, there may be a variable number of ASCII numeric parameters *and/or* selective parameters. If necessary parameters are missing from the control string, defaults must be supplied. All input from the CSI through the Final (or Final-Intermediate combination) must therefore be buffered, then parsed into functions and parameters.

The Newline

Before we leave the subject of control characters and ASCII, we must touch upon an eternal problem—ASCII's omission of a definitive end-of-line character. The problem is this: two distinct motions are required to begin a new line on a display device—one to change the current line position and one to change the current column position. These two motions are represented by the control characters CR and LF. In another way of thinking, these two physical actions constitute a single concept—the beginning of a new line—so a single character should suffice. ASCII actually authorizes the use of a single character, calling it the "New Line option," but warns, with just a hint of disapproval, that its use "requires agreement between sender and recipient of data." ASCII assigns the LF to this role, adding that when used in this context LF should be called a New Line (NL).

Almost everyone agrees that a single end-of-line character is a good idea because it is possible to create a new line efficiently while preserving CR and LF for fancier formatting applications. But the obvious problem with ASCII's definition of the New Line is its ambiguity—its bit

---

[6]The labors of Hercules were:
1. Kill Nemean Lion.
2. Slay nine-headed hydra of Lerna.
3. Capture elusive Stag of Arcadia.
4. Capture wild boar on Mt Erymanthus.
5. Clean stables of King Augeas of Elis.
6. Shoot monstrous man-eating birds of the Stymphalian marshes.
7. Capture mad bull of Crete.
8. Kill man-eating mares of King Diomedes.
9. Steal Girdle of Hippolyta.
10. Seize cattle of Geryon of Erytheia.
11. Fetch golden apples of Hesperidies.
12. Retrieve three-headed dog Cerberus from Hell.
13. Emulate Terminal of ANSI.

pattern is the same as the Line Feed. Moreover, the name "New Line" is unfortunate because it imparts the name of a logical concept, a *new line*, to a physical entity, the ASCII character LF. When we say "output a new line," we mean "output whatever character sequence is required to return to column 1 and advance to the next line." By contrast, the phrase "output a New Line," means "output a 0A byte." In other words, the newline is a concept, only one embodiment of which is ASCII 0A. A much more general name would have been, say, EOL.

The point of a standardized character set is that each element is clearly defined independent of the environment in which it appears. At present, the single character LF simply has no standard, unambiguous meaning. In some contexts, it means LF, in others it means end-of-line. UNIX employs the New Line convention, while PC DOS and CP/M use CRLF. Apple, Tandy (Radio Shack), and Commodore use CR. The result is that text files are not portable across operating systems with different end-of-line conventions.

Conclusion: A Modest Proposal

The lack of a single end-of-line character clearly is a glaring weakness in ASCII. Although X3.4's muted approval of the "New Line Option" is an open admission of the need, the selection of an existing character may have further compounded the problem. But where would we put a new character? All positions in ASCII are in use. In fact, the problem could be solved not by adding a new *position*, but by changing the name and definition of the existing Format Effector **VT**, which has gone virtually unused in the industry. Few terminals and even few printers support it in its defined context. One of the authors of X3.4, R. W. Bemer, has stated,

> This is a very dangerous character to use. It cannot be used directly on any terminal I know of. Even if it could, the implementation rules are not supplied unambiguously in the ASCII standard.
> —*The Best of Interface Age,* Forest Grove, Oregon: dilithium Press, 1978.

One alters standards as porcupines make love—very carefully. As their name implies, standards are intended to be bulwarks against whim and frivolity. An industry creates and adopts standards to buffer itself against the caprice of fashion; if changes are effected too easily, the standard will have failed and conformity to it will quickly decrease. In a tightly packed standard like ASCII, even the most trivial change invites a visit from Chaos. Proposed alteration must therefore be scrutinized from every perspective and subjected to exhaustive public review. But if any change in ASCII can be called harmless, surely it is the changing of **VT** to **EOL**.

End-of-line Vocabulary

Because much of this book deals with programming, the discussion of end-of-line nomenclature is not a mere philosophical exercise. Even though it would be presumptuous to think we can solve all the problems raised in the issue, we must agree upon a vocabulary just to discuss it. Here is the end-of-line dictionary for this book:

CR   The ASCII Carriage Return, 0D

LF   The ASCII Line Feed, 0A

CRLF   The ASCII couplet, 0D,0A

New Line   The ASCII Line Feed, 0A

Newline   EOL, the character or sequence of characters that advances the active position to column 1 of the next row. This is the term used in the C programming language.

2

Fundamentals of Asynchronous Technology

In this chapter we will examine the manner in which data is transmitted and received serially. Most computer users at some time in their careers have had to deal with serial technology when installing a peripheral such as a video terminal, mouse, modem, printer, or plotter. Unfortunately, not everyone's encounter with this technology is altogether pleasant. Its vocabulary— terms such as baud rate, MARK, SPACE, STOP bits, START bits—is so foreign-sounding that to the casual user the term "serial" has become synonymous with "incomprehensible." But precisely because unpleasant experiences tend to be memorable, most of the topics in this chapter are probably familiar to you. In fact, it is likely that you are approaching this chapter with a working knowledge of the subject, seeking only to refine your ideas.

Since computer users are clearly not averse to learning technical gobbledygook, we should point out that the strangeness in the terminology comes from its being archaic, not "foreign." There is a good reason for this—it is a very old technology. Messages sent across the Transatlantic Cable in about 1886 employed essentially the same technology as the mouse in your microcomputer. Yet the outdated language associated with the subject tends to obscure an important quality— the technology's almost childlike *simplicity*. Students of serial technology are often taken aback to discover that the principles underlying asynchronous I/O, like most computer topics, are disarmingly easy to comprehend and can be completely mastered in only a few minutes. This is not surprising—the crude hardware in those early years demanded nothing more of a communications medium than that it be robust and uncomplicated. Frills, subtleties, and refinements made no sense in a world when the biggest problem was making the machinery work at all.

You may be a bit surprised to discover that this book contains no academic definition of the serial and parallel methods of communications (which you probably understand anyway); we will explore them in terms of the historical milieu in which they occurred.

History of Electronic Communications

On the philosophical assumption that an incomprehensible present is always clarified by an astute examination of the past, the first part of this chapter will briefly (and selectively) discuss the evolution of electronic communications. Although the development of the telegraph—we can hardly say it was *invented*—proved to be a milestone in electronic communications, the technology associated with the telegraph itself—the key, the sounder, the operator with arm bands and visor—are actually incidental to our story. The telegraph, that Romantic instrument fixed in our minds by countless Western movies and our how-the-West-was-won mythos, has pretty much disappeared now. More important to our story is the parallel evolution of the specialized branches of *printing telegraphy* or *teleprinting*, from which the modem and the RS-232 interface are directly descended. Indeed, modern computer communications are as deeply rooted in teleprinting as the automobile design is rooted in carriage building.

Early Parallel Systems

Attempts to communicate electronically over long distances began in Europe as early as 1790. By 1810 the German von Soemmering devised a signaling device that consisted of twenty-six wires (one for each letter of the alphabet) attached to the bottom of an aquarium. When electrical current was passed through these wires, the electrolytic action produced bubbles. By selectively energizing the wires, Soemmering was able to send encoded messages with bubbles. Although Soemmering's fantastical system sounds as if it came from *Gulliver's Travels*, it is nevertheless extraordinarily important because it drew the attention of the military, who saw the tactical advantage of long-distance communications during battle.

Before long, much of the world became fascinated with the commercial and civil potential of communications. The race was on. By 1839 the two Englishmen W.F. Cooke and Charles Wheatstone had a thirteen-mile telegraph installation in commercial use by a British railroad. Their instrument consisted of five wires that powered small electromagnets, which were used to deflect low-mass needles. By selectively applying current to only two wires at a time, the corresponding needles were deflected so that they pointed at letters of the alphabet arranged in a matrix. This arrangement is shown in Figure 2-1. In this *two-of-five code* only twenty valid combinations were possible, so the letters C, J, Q, U, V and Z were omitted.

Figure 2-1   The Wheatstone-Cooke five-needle telegraph.

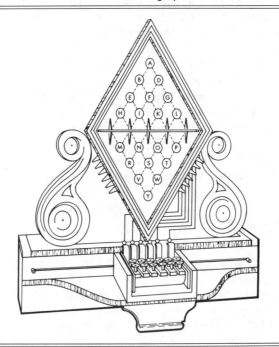

Although the Wheatstone-Cooke five-needle telegraph was a giant advance over von Soemmering's twenty-six-wire telebubble, the code was trinary, not binary; that is, a needle could be deflected left, right, or not at all. Code structure aside, the most crippling aspect of these designs lay in their reliance on multiple *parallel* wires carrying simultaneous signals. Indeed, one of Wheatstone and Cooke's most difficult problems was overcoming the sheer weight and bulk of the conductors (which they constructed themselves). The use of a parallel medium, at least for long-distance communication, was quickly abandoned in favor of a serial method in which the individual elements of the code were transmitted sequentially along a two-wire communications line. It should be noted that the impetus to convert from parallel to serial came not from the early inventors' belief that the serial medium was somehow theoretically superior, but because they were physically overwhelmed by the engineering problems associated with building an infrastructure for the parallel system.

A Serial Binary System

Although Wheatstone and Cooke eventually produced a two-wire serial device—the single-needle telegraph—they were intellectually stuck on the idea of *graphic* coding, insisting that the system yield *readable* characters (their indicator needle, for example). Indeed, this way of thinking was from the beginning embodied by the very name of the instrument: *tele-graph* (Greek for "making marks from afar").

The first practical, fully serial binary system—code and hardware—is generally credited (with protest from the British) to S.F.B. Morse. In the Morse code, shown in Figure 2-2, characters are represented by a series of dots and dashes (1s and 0s, if you will). Morse's first telegraph, however, was not the simple click-clacking instrument we remember from countless movies. Instead, Morse's instrument (on display at the Smithsonian Museum), was a rather complicated system in which a stylus contacted a rotating drum of paper, creating a continuous mark. Code impulses in the form of electrical current energized an electromagnet, momentarily deflecting the stylus from the paper, producing an undulating line on the paper. Here, still, the concept is one of a tele-*graph*.

Soon, telegraph operators discovered that they did not have to look at the paper created by the Morse recorder, but could interpret the code by the sound of the stylus scratching on the paper. The recorder was quickly replaced by a much simpler instrument known as a *sounder* that produced loud clicks instead of marks. It is interesting to note that at this point the "unschooled" Americans should have changed the name of the instrument from the telegraph to the *telephone* ("making sound from afar"). Would Bell have chosen the name "telepheme" ("speech from afar") for his invention?

Although the transcription of telegraphic code soon turned into the separate technology of teleprinting, for a brief period the sounder coexisted with a simplified recording device. On this device, which seems to have been known only as the "Automatic Recorder," an electronic impulse merely lifted the stylus from the rotating drum of paper. This device's practical value was an accurate graphic reproduction of the dots and dashes of the Morse code, but its greatest significance lay in its legacy of terminology. The state during idle periods when the stylus was in contact with the paper was given the no-nonsense name *MARKING*; the lifting of the stylus by a pulse was simply named the *SPACING* state. These terms, which are still in use today, are customarily written entirely in capital letters because codes of this period lacked a lower-case alphabet. This book observes this tradition.

Figure 2-2 The International Morse code.

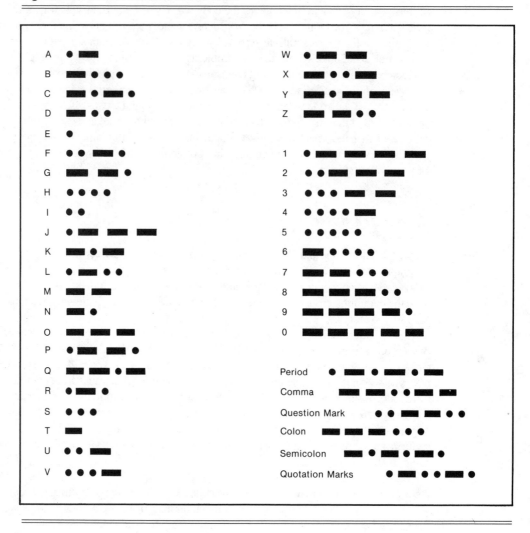

Early Printing Telegraphs

Here we leave the manual telegraph because its limitations (so obvious that we need not even discuss them) led inevitably to its extinction. From the outset, the commercial value of a machine that somehow produced *printed* characters was so obvious that early inventors and entrepreneurs expended much energy and money on research to develop it. Early versions of this machine consisted of a wheel with inked type uniformly spaced around its circumference. The code—a train of electrical impulses— sequentially ratcheted the type wheel to the desired character. Once the wheel was correctly positioned, a paper tape was brought into contact with it to produce the image of the character. Later methods employed a rotating type wheel at both the sender and the receiver. When the desired character rotated into position at the sender's wheel, a single "printing" pulse was sent that caused the receiver's type wheel to engage the paper tape. This machine and its complicated rotating mechanism were the progenitors of what we now refer to as asynchronous serial communications. The rotating-head system and countless others like it relied heavily on an almost unattainable factor—*synchronism* between sender and receiver. In the head-ratchet system, synchronism was required between the position of the sender's and receiver's heads. If even a single ratchet-positioning pulse in the sequence was lost during transmission, the receiver's message would be hopelessly and endlessly garbled. For this reason, frequent long "rest" periods were observed to return the heads to a null position every few characters. In the rotating-head system, strict synchronism was required between the *rate* of rotation of the sender's and receiver's type wheel.

Its oversensitivity to minor discrepancies in receiver-transmitter synchronization would probably have smothered the rotating mechanism technology, but one timely historical event breathed new life into the idea: the almost universal adoption by about 1900 of AC over DC current. Spurred, among other factors, by the inherent simplicity and superiority of Nikola Tesla's AC motor, AC power systems began to supplant DC systems. In 1896 the sheer volume of AC current produced by the new mammoth AC Niagara Falls Hydroelectric Project assured the swift adoption of AC current.

The universality of AC electrical current quickly led to the development of the *synchronous* AC motor, whose rate of rotation was dependent *only* on the frequency of the AC current. The new synchronous AC motor assured the future of teleprinting because it meant that once synchronized, the rotating mechanisms of distant machines would—in theory, at least—remain in synchronization indefinitely. The AC motor worked so well that speeds up to 60 words per minute were claimed (perhaps apocryphally) for even the delicate rotating-head systems.

Amazingly, rotating-head teleprinter systems, pioneered in the early 1870's, were used extensively in the United States until the 1920's and for about ten years longer in Europe. They were ultimately brought down by the lack of *precise* stability between AC power sources. There was no guarantee, for example, that a power company in, say, Chicago was *precisely* synchronized with one several hundred miles away. As we will discuss in a moment, the maximum *rate* of communication depends to a large degree upon the ability of the sender and receiver to remain in synchronization. The frequency of many early power companies was given as "nominally" 60 Hz. Today, federal laws require the short-term (one minute) accuracy of the AC line frequency to be within a few tenths of a percent of 60 HZ and its long-term accuracy to be within a few *thousandths* of a percent. Such a high degree of stability was not only unavailable, it was not technologically practical until perhaps the late thirties. In the absence of speed stability in the AC supply, it was inevitable that a system highly tolerant to line-frequency variations would eventually dominate telecommunications technology.

The Five-Unit Code

Neither of the teleprinting systems described above employed a *bona fide* code. In the head-ratchet system, as many pulses as necessary were sent in order to rotate the type-head to the desired position. In the rotating head system, the "code" consisted of a single pulse. Free-form codes such as the Morse Code contain a variable number of elements: one element for an E, two for an A, six for a comma, and so on. (The length of the codes is roughly in inverse order of their frequency of use in English.) Although this sort of code is easily mastered by humans, who bring an intuitive sense of language to any code, it is very difficult to devise a machine to receive a variable-length code.

Jean Maurice Emile Baudot, an officer in the French Telegraph Service, is generally credited with the invention of the first uniform-length code in about 1874. The International Telegraph

(CCITT) Alphabet #2, which is sometimes referred to as the BAUDOT[1] code, is shown in Table 2-1. Since you are probably accustomed to a binary representation of codes, the code is shown in that format as well as hexadecimal.

Table 2-1 The CCITT International Alphabet #2. The LTRS/FIGS character serves as a shift key between two sets, for a total of sixty-two characters.

Hex	Binary	LETTERS Shift	FIGURES Shift	Hex	Binary	LETTERS Shift	FIGURES Shift
0	00000	Blank	Blank	10	10000	T	5
1	00001	E	3	11	10001	Z	+
2	00010	LF	LF	12	10010	L	)
3	00011	A	-	13	10011	W	2
4	00100	Space	Space	14	10100	H	reserved
5	00101	S	'	15	10101	Y	6
6	00110	I	8	16	10110	P	0
7	00111	U	7	17	10111	Q	1
8	01000	CR	CR	18	11000	O	9
9	01001	D	WRU	19	11001	B	?
0A	01010	R	4	1A	11010	G	reserved
0B	01011	J	BELL	1B	11011	FIGS	FIGS
0C	01100	N	,	1C	11100	M	.
0D	01101	F	reserved	1D	11101	X	/
0E	01110	C	:	1E	11110	V	=
0F	01111	K	(	1F	11111	LTRS	LTRS

Character 5 is an apostrophe; 0C is a comma. Shifted F, G, and H positions are reserved for national usage.

Although this is a five-unit code and therefore has only thirty-two primary characters, characters at positions 27 and 32 are used to shift in and out a supplementary or alternative set of characters in much the same manner as a shift key on a typewriter. The "primary" character set, shown in Table 2-1 under the column "LETTERS Shift" comprises the upper-case alphabet, CR and LF. Under the column "FIGURES Shift" is the "secondary character set which includes the digits 0–9, common punctuation, and a few symbols such as BELL and the control character WRU (who are you?).

The characters in the LETTERS or FIGURES column are selected by the control characters LTRS and FIGS, respectively. (See "Invocation of Alternative Character Sets" in Chapter 1 for a description of this technique.) Notice that some characters are present in both columns and that three positions are reserved for national usage.

Automatic Coding and Decoding by Machine

The uniform length of characters in the 5-bit[2] code greatly simplifies encoding and decoding by machine: the transmitter merely copies the character, one bit at a time, *low-order* bit first, onto the

---

[1]The attribution is incorrect. Baudot's code is The International Telegraph Alphabet #1. The International Telegraph Alphabet #2 was the invention of Donald Murray.

[2]Although it is obviously anachronistic to refer to teleprinter characters as "data" and the code units as "bits," these terms are irresistible.

transmission line. By "copy," we mean that the transmitter translates the binary value of the bits—0 or 1—to a physical voltage connected to a physical piece of wire. In Chapter 5 we will examine these voltage level conventions, but for now their magnitude and polarity are unimportant. The voltage representing each bit is "impressed" on the *transmission line* for a fixed, uniform time period. Synchronous AC motors are used for accurate timing. The number of these intervals in 1 second is called the *baud rate* (after Emile Baudot). Transmitting a raw 5-bit code at the rate of forty characters per second, for example, could be expressed as 200 baud. The *bit time* is how long the bit remains on the line, in this case, 1/200th of a second, or .005 second.

Figure 2-3 The receiver mechanism of a hypothetical teleprinter.

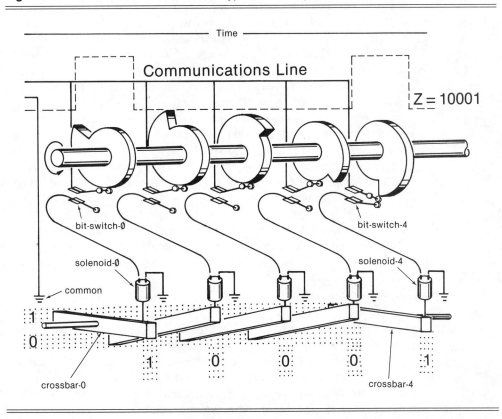

To understand how this train of electrical impulses is decoded, refer to the drawing in Figure 2-3, which shows a hypothetical[3] teleprinter's receiving mechanism. The heart of this machine's operation is its cam shaft, which rotates in tight synchronism with the transmitter. As the receiver's shaft rotates, its cam lobes sequentially operate a bank of *bit-switches*. When closed, a bit-switch connects the transmission line to one of five electromagnetic latches, or solenoids. If the rotation of the cam is properly synchronized with the transmitter, the bit-switches close at precisely the instant that electrical impulses (i.e., data bits) are present on the communications line. The closure of a bit-switch connects the electrical energy represented by each bit to the corresponding solenoid. When the solenoid "fires," its plunger operates a pivoting see-saw lever called

---

[3]The mechanism depicted in Figure 2-3 is a composite of technologies used at various times in the evolution of the teleprinter. Eventually the cam system was replaced entirely by a distributor.

a *crossbar*. The crossbar is initially in the up position, but the plunger from an energized solenoid pushes it downward if the bit on the communications line happens to be a 1. If the bit is a 0, no energy flows through the switch to the solenoid, the plunger does not move, and the position of the crossbar is unchanged.

The important point here is that the crossbar's indirect connection to the communications line makes it, in effect, a mechanical memory. The cam maintains the switch in a closed position for exactly one bit time, capturing into the corresponding crossbar any voltage that appeared on the communications line during this period. As the cam continues around, it sequentially opens and closes all five switches, only one of which can be closed at any instant. After one complete rotation of the cam, the binary value of the communications line during switch closures is remembered in the up-down pattern of the array of crossbars.

Figure 2-3 shows how this mechanism would decode the bit pattern 10001, the letter 'Z' in 5-bit code. If the receiver is correctly synchronized with the transmitter, the receiver's bit-0 switch closes while the transmitted bit 0 is present on the communications line; the bit-1 switch closes during bit 1, and so on. In order to see the effect of the mechanism on all bits of the character, the action in the drawing is "frozen" at the instant when the cam closes the bit-4 switch, capturing the final '1' pulse that is present on the communications line. Although the drawing depicts the capturing of a '1' pulse, it is important to realize that the absence of a pulse—i.e., a 0—is just as significant, even though the position of the corresponding crossbar is not changed. For example, notice that the position of the crossbars 1, 2, and 3 are still in their '0' position because no bits (voltages) were present on the communications line while their switches were closed.

The closure of the last switch on the cam coincides with the final 1 bit on the communications line. At the end of the pulse sequence, then, the up-down pattern in the crossbars duplicates the pattern of the received pulse exactly. Now, with all the bits captured, the crossbars are jammed against a moving type-head. The up-down pattern of the crossbars causes the type-head to stop at a unique position for each encoded character (a similar mechanism is used in slot machines). A striker then drives the printing mechanism against the type-head.

Synchronization

As you can see, the decoding of a fixed-length code, though mechanically intense, is conceptually simple. Even from the oversimplified depiction in Figure 2-3 it should be apparent that such a system is completely at the mercy of precise synchronism between the cams of the sending and the receiving stations. For example, a bit-switch at the receiving station must close at almost the same instant that its corresponding pulse is transmitted. If this synchronism slips, the bits are captured into the incorrect crossbar and the wrong character is decoded. Before electrical motors, and later synchronous motors, were available, the mechanisms were powered by a large deadbeat escapement such as is found in clocks. Because of its reliance on synchronism, this form of communications is even today known as *synchronous serial communications*.

Despite the use of a fixed-length code and high-quality synchronous motors, early teleprinters were prone to drifting out of synchronism due to slight manufacturing differences between mechanical parts or, inevitably, a difference between the frequency of the power sources at the transmitter and receiver. To minimize the need to maintain synchronism over the entire length of a message, characters on early teleprinters were not generated by human typists, but by pre-encoded perforated paper tape. Even using machine-generated codes, it was still inevitable that the mechanism would drift out of synchronism. Accordingly, early teleprinters required constant monitoring by skilled operators whose job was to make mid-message adjustments at the first sign of loss of synchronism. As you might imagine, even under the best of conditions these machines were temperamental, and at worst, maddeningly unreliable. Clearly, if the technology was to go forward, a new system had to be found.

The problem of synchronism is not as awful as it sounds. As a matter of fact, even before electrical motors were used, the combination of a deadbeat and a mechanical governor was able to maintain synchronism over the short term. The real problem with such a system is that once communication begins, the sender and receiver must remain in synchronism for the *entire* message. In other words, although the basic unit of encoding is the character, the unit of transmission is the message. The flaw of the system, then, is not in its *use* of synchronism, which is common to all forms of electronic communications, but in the period of time over which synchronism must be maintained. If the system could somehow be resynchronized for each character, a fair amount of drift in frequency between sender and receiver would be tolerable. The solution to the problem of receiver/transmitter synchronization changed the history of communications.

The START Bit

The solution, credited to E. E. Kleinschmidt during W.W. I, was to transmit a *synchronizing bit* just before the first bit of each character. This additional pulse, which is identical in every way to an ordinary data bit, signals the teleprinter mechanism that the very next pulse is the first bit of a character.

Adding the sync pulse to the character, of course, required modification of the teleprinter mechanism as well. During periods of idle—that is, between characters—the cam continues to rotate,[4] but the bit-switches are completely retracted from the cam lobes. Obviously, in this arrangement no switch action and no bit capture occur. Upon the arrival of a sync pulse, the whole bit-switch assembly is repositioned by means of a clutch so that the switches contact the cam lobes. After each character—i.e., one complete revolution of the cam—the clutch once again disengages the cam and the bit-switches, and the system returns to rest.

Before we discuss Figure 2-4, which shows how the synchronization pulse is prepended to the code bits, notice that it employs traditional notation, which defines the *idle state* (i.e., MARK) of the communications line as logical 1, and a negative-going pulse (i.e., SPACE) as logical 0. The reasons for this are partly historical (Morse's telegraph), but mostly because electromechanical devices that possess contacts (relays, for example) operate much more reliably with current perpetually passing through them. For whatever reasons, though, electrical current normally flows in the communications line during idle periods.

Figure 2-4a shows a timing diagram of a communications line bearing the letter 'F' (01101) preceded by its sync pulse. Because transmission of a character proceeds from least- to most-significant bit, the bit patterns given in Table 2-1 and those shown graphically in Figure 2-4 are reversed.

The addition of a sync pulse alone would have advanced the art of the teleprinter enormously. By providing automatic per-character instead of per-message synchronization, it unconditionally cures the problems caused by discrepancies such as differences in the frequency of the AC power line. But the sync pulse alone cannot defend against the eternal nemesis—data deformation or corruption by an imperfect communications line. To illustrate the havoc wreaked by this phenomenon, consider Figure 2-4b, which shows several iterations of the letter 'F' and their sync pulses. The sync pulse on the first 'F' properly engages the cam of our hypothetical teleprinter, causing 5 bits to be correctly sampled from the communications line. On the second 'F', however, the sync pulse has somehow been transformed from a SPACE into a MARK and the teleprinter

---

[4]Actually, early systems simply started and stopped the cam shaft completely. This worked satisfactorily at low speeds but inertia caused overshoot at high speeds.

Figure 2-4 Synchronization pulse for code bits.

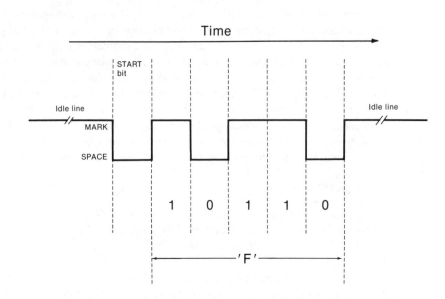

a. The Letter 'F' (01101) and Its Sync Pulse

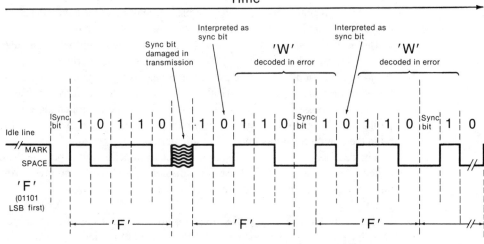

b. Several Iterations of the Letter 'F' (01101) and Its Sync Pulse

mechanism does not engage. The mechanism now thinks that the next 0 bit—the first data bit of the character—is the sync bit, and subsequently copies data bit 0 into crossbar 0, data bit 1 into crossbar 1, and so forth. As shown in Figure 2-4b, when the first data bit in the 'F' is interpreted as the sync bit, the next 5 bits are interpreted as 01001—the letter 'D' (received as 10010). During continuous transmission, where one character follows the next with no intervening idle period, a single damaged sync bit can theoretically cause subsequent characters to be garbled indefinitely.

Re-establishment of synchronization can be guaranteed only by allowing the communications line to idle for one entire character interval.

The STOP Bit

The loss of synchronization when the sync bit is damaged is inherent in a binary system where all pulses are identical. To complement the sync bit, which identifies the first bit of the character, an additional bit is required to identify the *last* bit of the character. This new bit, a MARK, is simply appended to the data bits at the transmitter. The letter 'F' in this new format is shown in Figure 2-5.

The teleprinter modifications necessary to implement this new end-of-character bit are simple. During reception, the end-of-character bit is "read" and latched into a crossbar just like the other 5 bits. After all 6 bits are received, however, a 0 in the final crossbar prevents the activation of the printing assembly. In this way an out-of-sync character can still be received, but is discarded if its final bit is not a 1. As far as the teleprinter is concerned, a valid character must begin with a SPACE and end with a MARK.

Figure 2-5 Two iterations of the letter 'F' with sync bit and an additional bit to mark the end of the character.

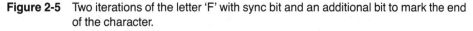
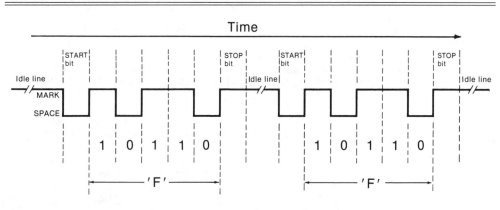

Before we proceed, it is time we decide on some official terminology. As you probably know, the sync and end bits are traditionally referred to as *START* and *STOP* bits, respectively. Because these bits set the character off from surrounding bits, they are collectively referred to as *framing* bits and the entire "package" of START, data, and STOP bits is given the name of *character frame* or simply *frame*. The form of serial communications we call "asynchronous," then, is properly "START/STOP asynchronous."

It is impossible to appreciate the robustness of this START/STOP communications method without seeing it in action. Figure 2-6 illustrates how the START and STOP bits *automatically* restore proper character framing following a loss of synchronization. Using the 5-bit code given in Table 2-1, the transmitted message, a ten-character portion of the familiar "HOW NOW BROWN COW" is shown in Figure 2-6a. Figure 2-6b shows the same message, but with the bit-order reversed as during transmission. Figure 2-6c marks the START and STOP bits symbolically with the letters 'x' and 'y', respectively. In Figure 2-6d the framing bits are actual 0s and 1s, which, to make them more easily discerned, are bold. Thus, Figure 2-6d shows the bit stream without errors, as it might look as it leaves the transmitter. Figure 2-6e, however, shows the message as it might look as it arrives at the receiver with an error in the START bit of the second character, O.

Figure 2-6 Automatic resynchronization after a framing error with START and STOP bits.

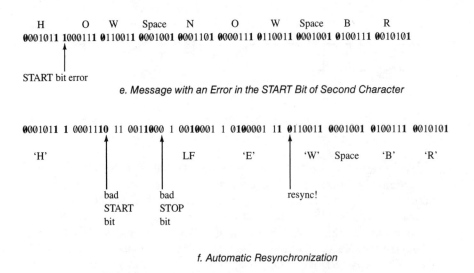

H O W Space N O W Space B R
10100 11000 10011 00100 01100 11000 10011 00100 11001 01010

a. Ten Characters of the Message "HOW NOW BROWN" in Five-Unit Code

H O W Space N O W Space B R
00101 00011 11001 00100 00110 00011 11001 00100 10011 01010

b. Ten-Character Message with Bit Order Reversed as in Transmission

H O W Space N O W Space B   R
x00101y x00011y x11001y x00100y x00110y x00011y x11001y x00100y x10011y x01010y

c. Message with Symbolic 'x' for START Bits and 'y' for STOP Bits

H O W Space N O W Space B   R
0001011 0000111 0110011 0001001 0001101 0000111 0110011 0001001 0100111 0010101

d. Message with Binary START and STOP Bits Installed

H O W Space N O W Space B   R
0001011 1000111 0110011 0001001 0001101 0000111 0110011 0001001 0100111 0010101

START bit error

e. Message with an Error in the START Bit of Second Character

0001011 1 0001110 11 0011000 1 0010001 1 0100001 11 0110011 0001001 0100111 0010101

'H'   LF   'E'   'W' Space 'B'   'R'

       bad   bad   resync!
       START STOP
       bit   bit

f. Automatic Resynchronization

Finally, Figure 2-6f shows how the teleprinter almost immediately recovers from the bad START bit. The first character 'H' is received correctly. Loss of synchronization occurs, however, when the receiver interprets the damaged START bit as a period of MARK time (line idle). The next 0 bit—data bit 0 in the letter 'O'—is interpreted as a START bit and the next six bits are decoded; since the sixth of these is not a 1 (i.e., a START bit), the character is discarded and nothing is displayed. This peg-legged stumbling continues, with the receiver occasionally printing a garbage character after assembling a valid, but erroneous, frame. The error resulting from a defective START or STOP bit is given the general name *framing error*. Framing errors occur

twice, resulting in an erroneous Line Feed and the letter 'E'. Eventually, though, the receiver synchronizes on one of the *original* START bits and the message is back in synchronization. The teleprinter would probably display the message like this:

H
    EW BROWN COW

We have discussed the addition of a STOP bit as if it were an intellectual or theoretical invention. The truth is, however, that long before the START bit was hit upon as a foolproof method of character framing, an equivalent resting period after each character was part of teleprinter operating procedure. The reason for its existence, however, derives not from the abstract concept of character framing, but from the intensely mechanical nature of teleprinters. A period of line idle (MARK) was inserted between characters to allow time for the teleprinter mechanism to clear the previous character and reset itself for the next.[5] The duration of these "inertial" STOP bits is quite long in early models, but came to be standardized at about 1½ to 1 bit times for "modern" teleprinters. This amount of time, though small, is absolutely critical to correct operation of the machine.

Why a Five-Unit Code?

The absence of a lower-case alphabet and the paucity of punctuation and graphics characters often lead modern users to wonder why a 5-bit code was used instead of, say, a 7-bit one. No one seems to know for certain (or cares!) why upper case was chosen over lower, especially since it was known at the time that lower case is easier to read than upper. There are several plausible reasons. First, because the Latin alphabet was entirely upper case, there was a centuries-old sentiment that upper case was somehow more "classical," somehow more dignified and formal. In fact, until well into this century, diplomatic documents such as treaties, proclamations, and accords were printed almost exclusively in upper case. Because of these ideas, lower case was thought to be, well, vulgar. The second and more likely reason for the choice of upper case has to do with the graphic ambiguity of the lower-case alphabet. A poorly printed 'a' or 'f', for example, can easily be mistaken for a half-dozen other lower-case letters—depending upon which portion of the character is ill-formed or omitted. Lower case is easier to read than upper case only when comparing accurate and perfectly formed characters. A poorly printed 'A', on the other hand, can hardly be confused with other members of the alphabet. If the print quality of "sophisticated" modern teleprinters is any indication, early mechanisms must have produced crude output indeed. The upper-case alphabet was therefore probably selected in self defense against the early error-prone teleprinter mechanism.

The second question—why the code is limited to five units—is easier to guess. The most obvious reasons are economic—the fewer bits per character, the quicker any given message can be sent; expressed in modern computerese, the use of a five-unit code "maximized system throughput." It is impossible to say whether such crassly commercial reasons entered into the choice of a five-unit code, but it is certain that these early engineers understood how a frame length affects reliable synchronization. To understand this, visualize a receiver detecting a START

---

[5]If you look closely at the drawing in Figure 2-3 you can discern a definite dead spot in the cam—a period in its rotation when no switch is closed. This is the resting period during which, among a myriad of other things, the crossbars are reset to all 0s.

bit at *precisely* the middle of its bit time. If the transmitter's and receiver's bit times differ by more than one-half a bit time over the next 6 bits the STOP bit is missed. Since this cumulative timing error is greater over a larger number of bits, codes with longer character lengths are inherently more susceptible to the effects of speed mismatches than shorter codes. Considering the variety of electrical environments around the world in which the teleprinter has been successful over the last hundred years, the five-unit code has proven to be a good choice. As a matter of fact, a considerable amount of international teleprinter communications is still encoded in the five-unit CCITT Alphabet #2.

The BREAK Signal

One special framing error is treated not as an error, but as a form of communication. We mentioned earlier that teleprinters are designed so that electrical current flows in the communications line during idle periods. As we have seen, bits are electrically encoded by interrupting this quiescent line current at regular intervals. One consequence of this design, and one of the major factors in its persistence, is its ability to detect a failure in the communications line itself. When the line is interrupted, the cessation of current is detected as a START bit. After sampling the agreed-upon number of data bits (which are all 0s), the receiver finds a SPACE where the STOP bit should be. Since this condition—an all-0 frame—cannot occur as a result of any legitimate character, it signals a "break" in the transmission line. Consistent with the no-nonsense upper-case naming conventions of the period, this condition was dubbed a *BREAK*—any SPACE condition on the communications line that lasts longer than a character and its framing bits. The term is still used today.

When generated intentionally for short, agreed-upon periods, the BREAK becomes a primary communications signal instead of just a fault indicator. In general, the BREAK is employed as a brute-force override of coded communication. A BREAK can be used to reset a mechanism, to ring a bell, to interrupt a process that would otherwise ignore coded data arriving on the communications line. Because it is often employed in this "In case of fire, break glass" fashion, BREAK detection is usually electrically separate from and parallel to the serial decoding process. The BREAK is often incorrectly called a "character," though it is manifestly just the opposite. As a matter of fact, its distinct "uncharacter"-ness gives it significance.

Character Framing in Electronic Communications

Even though we must concede that the STOP bit historically antedates the START bit, it is important to recognize that a *framing* STOP bit is required even in the frictionless and inertia-less world of modern electronic communications. In fact, some purely electronic devices still require an inertial STOP bit *in addition* to the framing STOP bit. Some older terminals, for example, are notorious for losing character synchronization when scrolling a full screen at high data rates. The problem can usually be cured by using a frame with 2 STOP bits instead of 1, thus giving an extra instant for the electronics to perform the scroll.

Transmission of ASCII Code

Since most computer equipment is byte-oriented, it is "natural" to handle data in an eight-unit form. Although ASCII and the closely related CCITT V.3 alphabet are officially *seven-unit* codes, they are seldom transmitted in that format. Instead, the eighth bit is often used as a *parity bit* for error-checking (see Chapter 3), thus making ASCII in practice an eight-unit code. In addition to the format of 7 data bits and 1 parity bit, a considerable amount of computer data is *binary* (as opposed to textual) in nature. By binary, we mean that the meaning of the bits lies in their *pattern* (as in processor instructions) rather than in their representation (as in an ASCII code). In binary data, all bits are of equal value and must be included in the frame.

Serial Nomenclature

Considering that asynchronous serial technology is a century old, it is incredible that no standardized vocabulary has developed to express its concepts. In the absence of standardized terminology, the popular microcomputer press has happily responded with terms and definitions that are inaccurate, fatuous, or just plain ignorant. To avoid association with pop terminology, we will now establish a vocabulary and apply it consistently throughout the remainder of the book.

The Serial Data Unit

First, we require a name for the entire physical "package" that is impressed upon the communications line—the START bits, data bits, parity bits (if any), and the STOP bit(s). So far we have used the word "frame" to refer to a unit of transmitted data, but this is an ambiguous term because it incorrectly evokes the image of a "perimeter" or "framework." To avoid this connotation, we will simply use the phrase *serial data unit,* or *SDU* for short.

Data Format

With the imputation of meaning to the eighth bit of an ASCII character, we sorely need a notation that can describe the layout and contents of any SDU. Accordingly, we will refer to these variable transmission parameters—baud rate, number of data bits, parity bit, and number of STOP bits—as the *data format*. We will employ the following notation for the rest of this book:

[baudrate]-[data bits][parity][STOP bits]

For example, we would describe the data format of 1200 baud, 7 data bits, NO parity and 2 STOP bits in the form *1200-7N2* or, for variety, *1200-7-N-2*.

More on Baud[6] Rate

Since "baud" is often incorrectly used to mean "bits per second," it is worth spending a few moments to differentiate between these two terms. Baud rate is the measure of the fundamental *electrical signaling* rate of a communications line. Stated another way, *baud rate* is the frequency at which electrical impulses are transferred to the communications line. Because it is an electrical unit of measure and not a unit of information, baud rate implies no relationship between the voltages that appear on the communications line and the data represented by those voltages.

Although it sounds simple-minded to say out loud, the rate of transfer of information is the *bit transfer rate*, and is expressed in *bits per second* (bps). The baud rate and the bit transfer rate are therefore equal *only* when one data bit is encoded during one signaling period. If this distinction strikes you as a trifle precious, consider that 1200 and 2400 bps modems operate at a signaling rate of only 600 baud. In other words, these modems manage to encode 2 and 4 bits, respectively, in one electrical impulse. We'll return to this point in Chapter 5.

---

[6]Please remember that "baud" should be abbreviated with a capital letter in honor of Emile Baudot.

"Serialization"

We must discuss one final term before proceeding. We have seen that asynchronous transmission is essentially the translating of the individual bits of compound ("parallel") data into instants of voltage. Asynchronous reception is the opposite, building compound data from periodical voltage samples taken from a wire. There is, incredibly, no perfectly apt single word to describe the idea embodied in both processes. For want of a more concise term, and in full recognition that it is only half correct, we will use the word *serialization*. As used in this book, serialization is a concept that applies *both* to reception and transmission. In this way of thinking, therefore, the *framing* error demonstrated in Figure 2-6 is a *serialization error*, even though it is literally an error of deserialization or, better perhaps, "parallelization."

Communications Line Usage

The amount of information that could be transferred over very early telegraph and teleprinter systems was amazingly small. At first, the only solution to this limitation on "throughput" was to erect more wires to handle the additional traffic. Because of the enormous expense and difficulty in erecting telegraph and telephone lines, researchers constantly searched for a way to send more than one message *simultaneously* (or apparently so) over the same line. They used the following terminology to describe the traffic on communications lines:

Simplex: Communication is single-direction with a receiving or a transmitting device (but not both) at either end. The classic "ticker-tape" is a simplex receiver.

Half-duplex: Communication is possible in both directions, but not simultaneously. Early telegraphs worked in this manner as do many modern forms of communication (CB radio, for example).

Full-duplex: Communication can occur *simultaneously* in both directions. The telegraph quickly became a full-duplex, and, thanks to Thomas Edison, a *quadruplex* instrument. Today, most two-way communication is full-duplex.

Multiplex: This form of communication, which eventually supplanted quadruplex, is used if more than a single channel of information is required. Pioneered by Baudot, multiplexing is a technique for creating several communications channels by sequentially allocating frequencies or time slices from a single channel. Modern communications increasingly relies on multiplexing.

Most of these terms are in use today, as is other jargon from this period. For example, many early telegraphs used lines that had to be oppositely *polarized* during transmission and reception. When changing over from transmission to reception, or vice versa, operators had to reverse the positive and negative connections on their half-duplex instruments. Their term for this, "turning the line around," is still very much alive today in half-duplex modem operations, although, as we shall see, its use is now figurative.

Synchronous vs Asynchronous Serial Communications

As we have seen, asynchronous communications relies heavily upon synchronism: characters *arrive* asynchronously, but the reception of the individual bits of each character is synchronized by the START bit. For this reason, "asynchronous" was (and still is) a poor choice to describe this technology. In fact, the fundamental differences between asynchronous and synchronous communications are ones of degree— the former requires a sync bit with every character, while the latter requires a sync *byte* much less often.

The "sync/async" nomenclature also tends to obscure the practical differences between the two methods of serial communications. When efficiency is of paramount importance and when data can be supplied in a carefully time-controlled, continuous bit stream, synchronous transmission is vastly superior to asynchronous START/STOP transmission. After all, adding a START and STOP bit to an 8-bit character results in a transmission overhead of one-fifth: fully 20 percent of the bits carry *no* data. Yet, as we saw in our discussion of early teleprinters, even if *perfect* synchronism had been possible, the system would still have failed in many areas simply because it required data in an *unbroken* stream. In other words, it was transmitting "characterized" data with a technology that had no way to differentiate one character from another. Even in a perfect universe, therefore, purely *synchronous* systems are impractical for applications where characters do not arrive according to a schedule. Without the START/STOP "asynchronous" serial format, all interaction between human and computer over serial lines would be impossible—we simply do not type, speak, or think synchronously. In other words, without the old-fashioned START/STOP form of communication, computer programmers would probably still be punching cards and paper tape.

Conclusion

The descriptions of teleprinters just presented are understandably oversimplified and several major questions remain unanswered. If you have a burning curiosity about teleprinter technology, consult the bibliography for sources of further information.

Do not be concerned at this point about unresolved inconsistencies in your understanding of asynchronous serial communications. Most of these topics are taken up again in later chapters where they are treated in greater detail and examined in the context of microcomputers instead of teleprinters. There you will learn that the grimy details of asynchronous serial I/O— START bits, STOP bits, data format, and the like—are completely taken over by microcomputer hardware. Once the hardware is configured for a particular data format, sending and receiving data is almost as simple as reading and writing memory variables. In other words, the conversion from parallel to serial during transmission and back again during reception is hidden from the programmer.

Before we return to the subject of asynchronous communications technology, we will spend several chapters studying some of the larger issues in communications in general. During these discussions, you should take asynchronous I/O more or less on faith—as something that just magically happens—without undue concern for *how* it happens. After we have looked at some of the larger issues that face the programmer, we will undertake a microscopic examination of the technology available to solve them.

3

Errors and Error Detection

A t the end of the previous chapter we mentioned the "larger" issues in communications. One such issue is certainly that of errors. In that chapter, for example, we saw that the consequences of just a single error in a single bit can result in a train of errors that persist for many characters beyond the original error. Although in this chapter we will briefly discuss the origin of such errors, our main goal will be to examine the tools available to the programmer for detecting and correcting them.

Origin of Errors

Errors are produced by two fundamentally different kinds of failures: *static* events whose behavior and existence are well known, and *transient* events that occur randomly. Signal distortion and attenuation loss are examples of static failures; atmospheric electromagnetic disturbances such as lightning or sun spots are examples of transient errors.

Errors arising from static events are much easier to handle because their effects are predictable. Since the behavior of AC signals is well known, engineers can compensate for the problems caused by almost any environment. Equalization amplifiers can compensate for high-frequency attenuation; low-capacity or low-inductance cable can prevent bias distortion; shielding can exclude radio frequency interference—in short, given foreknowledge of an event or a phenomenon, most can be engineered into harmlessness. Thus by careful analysis, planning, and design, it is possible to communicate with a minuscule number of static errors.

Alas, transient causes of error are not so easily dealt with, if for no other reason than that they often involve imperfectly understood forces that occur at unpredictable times. Most transient errors, however, are caused by electrical interference (or "noise") on the communications line. Interference may result from atmospheric events (lightning), local "static" (commutator noise), or dirty relay contacts in a communications device. Where the communications line is the telephone system, a whole new category of noises are possible—dropouts, crosstalk, echoes, and so forth.

The most common kind of noise, especially on telephone lines, is *impulse noise* or *burst noise*; that is, periods of disrupting noise bounded on either side by periods of no noise. Although all forms of communication are susceptible to errors, serial is more vulnerable than parallel because the bit-by-bit nature of transmission exposes the data to the vagaries of the communications line for a longer time. Even seemingly tiny noise bursts inevitably manifest errors in several bits.

For example, a noise burst of .01 second during 1200 baud communication will contaminate fully 12 bits; more bits are affected at higher data rates—96 bits at 9600 baud. Recalling from Figure 2-6 how a single framing error can cause a ripple of errors across many characters, START/STOP asynchronous communications is particularly vulnerable to burst noise.

Error Detection

The acceptability of errors in communications depends upon the content of the data, the ultimate use to which the data is put, and the difficulty of correcting the error. Extremely high error rates are sometimes acceptable in pure text, which is still intelligible to the human eye even with 20 percent of the characters *missing*. At the other extreme are sensitive applications, such as the launch and guidance systems for thermonuclear weapons, where *no* errors can be tolerated.

Correcting errors is an entirely separate issue from detecting them. Again, the response to an error depends upon the content, importance, and uniqueness of the data. In general, if the information is still available, retransmission is the most straightforward means of correcting errors. For example, the receiver of a message containing "casual" text (such as newspaper copy) can simply request retransmission of the message or, more likely, that portion of the message containing errors. In some situations, however, retransmission is impossible or impractical. Raw "real-time" data transmitted between a remote recording instrument and its decoder cannot be repeated because the instant of time cannot be repeated. Retransmission between earth and interplanetary space vehicles, though clearly possible, is impractical because the turn-around time would be far too long. In situations that preclude retransmission, there must be not only a means to detect errors, but also a way to *correct* them. Since the asynchronous style of communication is not likely to become the communications medium for NASA, we will largely ignore the subject of error correction.

Redundancy

Most error detection schemes involve some degree of *redundancy*; that is, additional bits that somehow represent the content of the message are transmitted along with the message itself. These various methods for deriving *redundancy codes* differ in the amount of the message represented and the complexity of the coding algorithm.

Character Redundancy: Parity

In Chapter 2 we noted that a *parity* bit is often appended to ASCII characters for error checking. This form of error detection is named from the mathematical idea of parity, which is the odd-even property of integers. A parity bit is formed to enforce an *arbitrary* rule that all characters shall have either an odd (or even) number of 1 bits. When ODD parity is in effect during transmission of ASCII, for example, 0100001 becomes 01000011 because the highlighted **1** is required to *create* an ODD number of 1s in the byte; in an EVEN parity scheme, the byte must be 01000010 to *maintain* an even number of 1s. Similarly, 0100010 under EVEN parity would become 01000100, but 1000101 under ODD parity.

During transmission, the sender calculates the parity bit, then appends it to the outgoing character. (EVEN parity is the Exclusive-OR of all data bits.) At the receiver, parity for the 7-bit data bytes is calculated and compared to the parity bit received. If the two do not agree, an error occurred.

Although in the strictest meaning of the term "parity," only EVEN and ODD make sense, dispensation of the eighth bit is often expressed in other ways:

NONE   The parity bit is unused and its value is unspecified.

MARK   The parity bit is always 1.

SPACE   The parity bit is always 0.

Parity is the lowest level of redundancy possible because it aims at discovering errors at the level of the individual character. Since it is a binary value reporting a binary (ODD-EVEN) relationship, it is capable of providing only minimal error detection. Specifically, parity can detect only errors that affect an *odd* number of bits. This is illustrated by Table 3-1, where the parity bit is the left-most bit.

Table 3-1   Parity detects errors only in an odd number of bits
(damaged bits are highlighted).

Transmitted	Received	Results for EVEN parity
01000001	01000001	Even number of 1s—parity OK.
01000001	01000011	Single-bit error: odd number of 1s, error detected.
01000001	00000011	Double-bit error: even number of 1s, error not detected.
01000001	01011101	Triple-bit error: odd number of 1s, error detected.

This insensitivity to such a wide range of bit patterns makes parity generally ineffective in asynchronous serial communications, where most errors come in bursts. Considering this fallibility, it is a wonder that parity is used at all, especially in the hostile environment of telecommunications with its relatively high probability of errors. In fact, one suspects that the use of parity in today's asynchronous applications (such as dial-up lines to mainframes) is due mainly to habit or intellectual inertia.

"Overhead"

A few hardware devices such as video terminals indicate parity errors by somehow highlighting the offending character, but this feature is becoming rare today. Nevertheless, parity is often designed into all-ASCII text systems, then seldom used. Because modern ICs (i.e., UARTs) have so simplified manipulation of data format, many programmers feel that the parity bit is somehow a "freebie," or that "it's there, so why not use it?" Why not indeed? Consider that in a 10-bit SDU (1 START, 7 data, 1 parity, 1 STOP), 10 percent of the system's time is spent transmitting an error-checking bit that fails to detect errors 40 percent of the time.[1]

Block Redundancy: Parity

Its poor return upon bit investment makes character parity's *overhead* usuriously high. Its accuracy can be somewhat improved, however, by supplementing the parity check on individual characters with a parity check on a *block* of characters. With this concept, the basic unit of trans-

---

[1]In *Telecommunications and the Computer* (Prentice-Hall, 1976), author Martin shows that based upon the statistical character of burst errors at 1200 baud on the public (switched) telephone network, the simple parity check fails to detect nearly 40 percent of the errors.

mission changes from the character to the *message*. In the *block-check* strategy, message characters are treated as a two-dimensional array. A parity bit is appended to each character (row) of bits as usual. After an agreed-upon number of characters, a *block-check character* (BCC), which represents a parity check on the columns, is transmitted. At the receiver, the incoming characters are checked for parity as usual; after the agreed-upon number of characters has arrived, the receiver calculates the parity character and compares it against the one just received. The assumption here is that an error that is missed in one dimension may be visible in another.

Table 3-2 illustrates this method by calculating a parity EVEN block check for the four ASCII characters *CfyU*: a bit is appended to each 7-bit character so that the resulting 8-bit byte contains an even number of 1 bits. An EVEN parity bit is also figured for each column.

Table 3-2 Vertical and longitudinal redundancy checks using EVEN parity (errors are highlighted).

TRANSMITTED		RECEIVED	
	Message	Double-bit error in 1 row	Double-bit error in 2 rows
C	11000011	11000011	11000011
f	01100110	01100110	01100110
y	11111001	11100001	11100001
U	01010101	01010101	01001101
BCC	00001001	00001001	00001001
BCC calculated by receiver	⟶	00010001 (error detected)	00001001 (error not detected)

On the "TRANSMITTED" side of Table 3-2 are the individual transmitted characters and BCC as they are transmitted. The parity bit is left-most. On the "RECEIVED" side are the same characters as they would be received, with one and then two occurrences of 2-bit errors.

The first receive error has a single 2-bit error in the third row. The character parity bit does not reveal an error because an even number of bits are damaged. But notice how in the next heading those same double-bit row errors become single-bit errors when parity is calculated on the columns. The error is detected because the BCC (parity byte) calculated (00010001) for the column does not agree with the one received (00001001).

The second example in Table 3-2 shows the same message, but with a pair of 2-bit errors—one in the third row and one in the fourth. Again, the double-bit errors are not detected by row parity. Because these double-bit errors extend across an even number of rows, no error is detected by the row-parity calculation.

Though column parity (also referred to as the *Vertical Redundancy Check*) improves the chances of detecting an error substantially, it is blind to an even number of errors in a column in the same way character parity (also referred to as the *Longitudinal Redundancy Check*) is susceptible to an even number of errors in the rows.

About the only virtue of parity checking in serial I/O is its simplicity—it can be implemented in hardware with just a few Exclusive-OR gates. In microcomputers, however, the asynchronous serial functions are handled completely by dedicated ICs which support single-character parity, but not a Vertical/Longitudinal Redundancy check.

The Checkvalue

Before proceeding, we must once again tackle the vocabulary surrounding the topic of error-checking and error codes, which is hopelessly inconsistent and vague. These inconsistencies are easily explained. Much of the literature on the subject has sprung from the commercial sector, where the engineer-authors (notoriously oblivious to charges of parochialism) simply adopt the jargon extant in their companies. For example, the redundant bits that bear the error-checking code in one book are referred to as the "block-check character," another uses the simpler "check character," while still another calls them a "frame check sequence." For one reason or another, none of these is precise enough. Is it not misleading to refer to a single "character" when there may be more than one? For the same reason, isn't "sequence" misleading when applied to a single entity? The word "frame" is already overused in computer jargon. To avoid these ambiguities, we will henceforth use the numerical term *checkvalue* to denote the redundant bits added for error checking.

Block Redundancy: Checksum

The Vertical/Longitudinal Redundancy Check introduced an important technique—checking for errors on blocks of data instead of on individual characters. An extension of that technique is the arithmetic checksum, a simple sum of the numerical value of characters in the block.

Table 3-3   The arithmetic checksum (damaged bits are highlighted).

TRANSMITTED		RECEIVED		
Message	Double-bit error in 1 row	Double-bit error in 2 rows	Single-bit error in 2 columns	
C	1000011	1000011	1000011	1000010
f	1100110	1100110	1100110	1100111
y	1111001	1100001	1100001	1111001
U	1010101	1010101	1001101	1010101
BCC	101110111	101101111	101110111	101110111
BCC calculated by receiver ———▶	101011111 (detected)	101010111 (detected)	101110111 (not detected)	

In Table 3-3, our familiar four-character ASCII message is shown in 7-bit format *without* parity. The checksum detects double-bit errors in one or two rows, but fails to detect even-numbered bit errors in columns.

Significantly, the checksum cannot detect errors of sequence; that is, an identical checksum is produced even if the message is sent in random order. The example in Table 3-3 also reveals that the size of the arithmetic checksum varies according to the numerical value of the individual members of the message, and is at least n where n is the number of bits in each member. In Table 3-3, for example, the four-character message of 7-bit ASCII characters results in a 9-bit checksum. Transmitting this whole value would require two 7-bit characters or truncation of the 9-bit value to a single 7-bit one (i.e., modulo-128). The former greatly increases the accuracy, but, depending upon the length of the message, also increases the overhead. In general, however, if the size of the block to be checked is sufficiently large, the extra byte is insignificant in comparison to the additional margin of safety from the longer checkvalue.

Cyclic Redundancy Checks

An extremely powerful kind of error checking is available with the same overhead as the checksum. Consider these promises[2] for a checkvalue of only 16 bits:

Single-bit errors:	100 percent
Double-bit errors:	100 percent
Odd-numbered errors:	100 percent
Burst errors shorter than 16 bits:	100 percent
Burst errors of exactly 17 bits:	99.9969 percent
All other burst errors:	99.9984 percent

In comparison to the relatively anemic parity and checksum methods, this method, the *Cyclical Redundancy Check* or *CRC*, seems magically powerful. The CRC is good at detecting all kinds of errors, but especially those that occur in bursts over a relatively long time.

Modulo-2 Arithmetic

You should understand from the outset that the *starting point* for designing any CRC system is the number of bits desired in the checkvalue. Because computer hardware usually manipulates in 8-bit bytes, the most common checkvalue size is 16 bits although 12 bits is sometimes used and, for extremely critical applications, 32 bits. Although the examples, formulas, and discussions in this chapter center about 16-bit CRC checkvalues, keep in mind that the principles are true for CRCs of other lengths.

Despite the efforts of various "expositors," the theory and implementation of CRCs are surprisingly simple. As a matter of fact, CRCs are best understood as a variation of the simple arithmetic checksum explained earlier. Whereas the arithmetic checksum is derived by addition, CRC-style checkvalues are derived by division. To illustrate, let's return to our earlier 4-byte message **CfyU**, but this time with the characters expressed in 8 bits and EVEN parity:

C 11000011

f 01100110

y 11111001

U 01010101

For simplicity's sake, let's assume that we wish to transmit a 16-bit checkvalue for these 4 bytes of data. Instead of considering the 4 bytes individually as before, or as a two-dimensional matrix, we will treat them as if they were one single large binary number:

11000011011001101111100101010101

or in decimal: 3,278,305,621.

The checkvalue is derived by dividing this number by another number (the divisor) chosen for its magical properties; since we are being hypothetical, let's say the divisor is decimal 525.

---

[2]Tanenbaum, Andrew S., *Computer Networks*, Prentice-Hall, 1981.

$$\frac{3278305621}{525} = 624439 \text{ with } 346 \text{ remainder}$$

A problem now arises: although the 23-bit quotient is a perfectly good checkvalue, it would have to be truncated to 16 bits, compromising its accuracy. Unfortunately, there is no way to guarantee the number of bits in a quotient. There is no reason why we have to use the quotient of the division. Why not use the *remainder*, taking advantage of the fact that a remainder is by definition at least one less than the divisor? In other words, we can control the size of the remainder by our choice of divisors. In the example above, a divisor of 17 bits *guarantees* a remainder no larger than 16 bits. A divisor of, say, 65540 will produce

$$\frac{3278305621}{65540} = 50019 \text{ with } 60361 \text{ remainder}$$

where the remainder is clearly significant to 16 bits:

$$60361 = EBC9 = 1110101111001001$$

Longhand Modulo-2 Division

CRC procedures, which existed long before microprocessors, were first implemented in hardware where simplicity of design and operating efficiency are important economic considerations. For reasons we will discuss later, the checkvalue remainder is not obtained by ordinary binary arithmetic, but in *modulo-2*. This technique simplifies the hardware design enormously because modulo-2 arithmetic has no carries or borrows. For example, the binary addition of

$$\begin{array}{r} 01010101 \\ 01010101 \\ \hline 10101010 \end{array}$$

is laborious because of the carries into every place. In modulo-2 addition, however, there are no carries:

$$\begin{array}{r} 01010101 \\ 01010101 \\ \hline 00000000 \end{array}$$

If the result of the modulo-2 addition operation looks familiar, it is because modulo-2 addition is identical to the Exclusive-OR. To refresh your memory, the truth table for XOR is shown below. Note that addition and subtraction are identical under these rules.

The only mechanical difference between modulo-2 division and ordinary binary division is that the intermediate results are obtained by Exclusive-OR instead of subtraction. The engine that drives binary division is the forcing of the left-most bit in the previous remainder to 0. One by one the message bits are brought down from the dividend and appended to the right-hand end of the intermediate result. The brought-down bits are shown in bold. If the high-order bit of the intermediate remainder is 1, a 1 goes into the quotient and the divisor is subtracted (i.e, XORed) from the remainder; if the first bit of the intermediate answer is 0, a 0 goes into the quotient and sixteen 0 bits are subtracted. To ease the strain on the eyes, an 'x' marks the "dead" 0s produced by each step.

Truth table for XOR (modulo-2)

$$0 \oplus 0 = 0$$
$$0 \oplus 1 = 1$$
$$1 \oplus 0 = 1$$
$$1 \oplus 1 = 0$$

$\oplus$ is the symbol for Exclusive-OR.

Figure 3-1 shows the modulo-2 division of our 4-byte message by the divisor 69665 (10001000000100001).

Figure 3-1   Modulo-2 division of the 4-byte message "CfyU" by 10001000000100001.

```
                               0000000000000000110011111110000111
           10001000000100001 │ 11000011011001101111100101010101
                               10001000000100001
                               x10010110111011001
                               10001000000100001
                               x00111101111110001
                               00000000000000000
                               x01110111111100011
                               00000000000000000
                               x11110111111000111
                               10001000000100001
                               x11111111111001100
                               10001000000100001
                               x11101111110011010
                               10001000000100001
                               x11001111111110111
                               10001000000100001
                               x10001111110101100
                               10001000000100001
                               x00001111100011011
                               00000000000000000
                               x00011111000110110
                               00000000000000000
                               x00111110001101101
                               00000000000000000
                               x01111100011011010
                               00000000000000000
                               x11111000110110101
                               10001000000100001
                               x11100001100101000
                               10001000000100001
                               x11010011000010011
                               10001000000100001
                               x1011011000110010
```

Intermediate remainders are obtained by XORing, not by ordinary subtraction

← Final remainder

Modulo-2 Division and Hardware

Students of the subject of CRCs usually assume that there is a dark, mystical mathematical reason why the division is performed in modulo-2 instead of ordinary binary arithmetic. In fact, the reason is disappointingly mundane. CRC procedures were intended from the outset for implementation in hardware communications devices, and later in disk controllers. Modulo-2 division was selected because its arithmetic can be implemented with just a few shift registers and gates; ordinary binary arithmetic, by contrast, requires additional logic to handle borrows and carries. Naturally, the simplicity of the modulo-2 design also means an increase in operating speed.

The example of longhand division makes a good point of reference, but does not illuminate the internal process that makes CRC such a good error-checking code. To remedy this omission, we will now study the pseudo-schematic diagram in Figure 3-2 of a hardware circuit that performs modulo-division, graphically illustrating the turbulent bit action that characterizes CRC check-values. In this figure, the boxes stand for the individual elements of a shift register while the encircled plus symbols stand for Exclusive-OR gates.

Figure 3-2   Hardware simulation of longhand modulo-2 division using shift registers and Exclusive-OR gates.

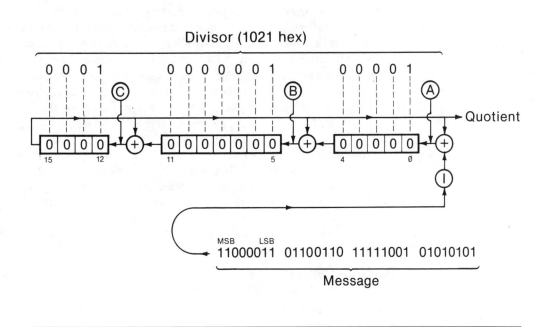

In Figure 3-1 we saw that the procedure in longhand modulo-2 division is to bring down a bit from the dividend into the LSB of the remainder. The divisor is then XORed with the remainder to produce a new remainder; XORing forces the left-most bit of the previous remainder to 0. This is exactly the hardware approach as well, where the remainder register is represented by the sixteen elements of the shift register. Message (dividend) bits are shifted into (brought down) the LSB of the remainder register, which is then shifted left. During the shift, XOR gates between the elements perform the modulo-2 subtraction. The value in the remainder register after the shift is the new remainder.

The application of the divisor (1021H) to the remainder register is denoted by shaded lines. We will discuss the significance of the divisor later, but for now simply notice that (1) it is 16, not 17 bits in length, and (2) for every 1 bit in the divisor, there is a corresponding Exclusive-OR gate immediately to the right in the remainder register. The bit shifted out of bit 15 of the remainder register is the quotient.

A Trial Run of 2 Bits

At the beginning, the remainder register consists of all 0s. The first bit of the message, 1, is presented to the input at point I. Point I is actually one input of a two-input XOR gate whose other input comes from the high-order bit of the remainder register via the line marked QUOTIENT. Since bit 15 is 0, the output of the XOR gate at point A is also a 1. At output point B, the 0 in bit 4 is XORed with 0 in bit 15 to produce a 0; at output point C the 0 in bit 11 is XORed with the 0 in bit 15 to yield 0. When the shifting pulse occurs, the 1 at point A is shifted into the remainder register's bit 0. All other 0s shift left one place. The remainder now contains 0000_0000000_00001.

The 1 in the first message bit produces less than startling results, but is a good warmup for things to come. As the movement of the bits within the remainder soon becomes complex, it is a good idea to construct a visual aid. It is recommended that you draw an enlarged version of Figure 3-2 and simulate the movement of the 1s and 0s with tokens of some sort—pennies and dimes work well. Physically moving these coins about and noting the contents of the remainder register after each step is an excellent way to get a feel for the process. Write the bits of the message in a column and, beside each message bit, write down the state of the remainder register *before* the shift. This record will help you find your place if you make mistakes or become confused.

Using the truth table in the box on page 60, apply the next message bit, also a 1, to the point marked I. Decode the two inputs of the right-most XOR gate. Since the message bit is 1 and bit 15 of the remainder is still 0, temporarily place the result—a dime for a 1—in the circle labeled A. Repeat the procedure for points B and C. This will result in a dime in the circle at A, and a penny at B, and C.

Before proceeding, try to get the *static* situation just described in your mind. Now snap your fingers (to simulate the shift pulse) and discard the "dead" message bit coin and the coins from bits 4, 11, and 15. Next move all bits to the left one place, moving the penny at point C into bit 12, the penny at point B into bit 5, and the dime at point A into bit 0. This completes two steps in the division. The state of the remainder register is given in Figure 3-3a.

Now stop and reflect. Write down the contents of the remainder after the second bit—0000 _0000000_00011. Repeat the entire procedure for each message bit:

1. Use the truth table in the box on page 60 to decode the inputs to the XOR gates, placing a dime or penny at the circles marked A, B, and C.
2. Snap your fingers to signify the shift.[3]
3. Discard the message bit coin and the coins from bits 4, 11, and 15.
4. Shift the remaining bits left one place.
5. Move the coins at A, B, and C into bits 0, 5, and 12 respectively.
6. Pause and record the remainder.
7. Repeat until there are no more message bits.
8. The value remaining in the register is the checkvalue.

---

[3]Failure to snap your fingers (which produces the *Purves Effect*) may result in incorrect answers.

Figure 3-3   The remainder register.

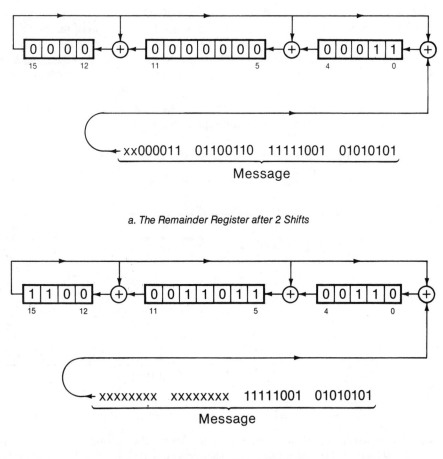

a. The Remainder Register after 2 Shifts

b. The Remainder Register after 16 Shifts

As you process the first few bits, you will probably notice that as long as bit 15 contains 0, the XOR gates do not affect the message bits as they pass through. Because the first bit in the message is 0, bit 15 remains a 0 for the first seventeen shifts, causing the circuit simply to produce *transparent shifts*. (This parallels the beginning of longhand division, where, according to convention, we do not include in the quotient the leading 0s produced by applying the divisor to the first few places of the dividend.) Regardless of the value of the first message, then, the first sixteen shifts always simply copy the first 16 bits of the message into the remainder register. As soon as the first bit of the message is shifted out of the remainder, subsequent remainders correspond perfectly with the intermediate remainders in Figure 3-1.

Figure 3-3b shows the situation after 16 shifts. As predicted, the register is just a copy of bits 0 through 15 of the message. With this knowledge you can now save yourself some work if you are using tokens to simulate the register action. Starting with the first 1 bit in the message, duplicate the next 16 message bits in the remainder register.

The Bit Hits the Fan

The 17th shift, however, produces a profound effect because the initial 1 bit from the message, now in bit 15 of the remainder, is applied to the QUOTIENT line. The presence of a 1 at one input of the XOR gate means that 0 bits immediately to the right of the gate are transformed to 1 bits during the shift. Figure 3-4 shows the remainder register after the 17th step.

The 1 of the incoming message bit and the 1 in bit 15 of the remainder are XORed to produce a 0 (penny) for circle A; the 0s at both bit 4 and 11 are XORed with bit 15 to produce 1s (dimes) in circles C and D. The very next shift, therefore, will produce the result shown in Figure 3-4. It is also the first intermediate remainder from our longhand division in Figure 3-1. This process is repeated for every bit in the message.

Figure 3-4   The remainder register after 17 shifts: the first 1 message bit reaches the XOR gates.

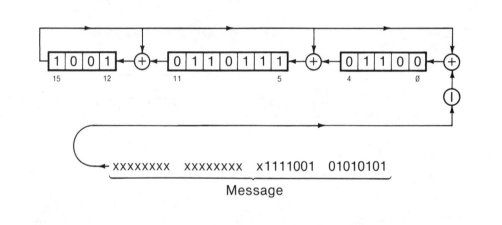

Message

The important action in this simulator is that as long as a 0 appears on the gate feedback (Quotient) line, the bits shift transparently; when a 1 appears, however, the bits are XORed with 1 as they pass. Bits and ghosts of bits incestuously recirculate in the remainder long after the bit itself has died. This, together with the dramatic effect often wrought by a single bit, means that the value in the remainder register any instant depends upon a great deal of history. The remainder from modulo-2 division not only detects the bit errors missed by the arithmetic checksum discussed earlier, it detects errors in the *order* in which the message bits are sent.

Students of this method are often troubled by the location of the XOR gates to the *right* of their corresponding 1 bits in the divisor. Try to keep in mind that the XOR gates decode the QUOTIENT-line feedback *before* the shift occurs. The earlier admonition to snap your fingers to simulate the shift was not intended as a facetious suggestion, but was to emphasize the correspondence between the behavior of the hardware circuit and longhand division. In short, it is important to understand fully that the action of the XOR gates on the remainder is the same as XORing the entire register with the divisor 1021 Hex; this, in turn, is equivalent to the modulo-2 subtraction in longhand division.

This brings up another frequently misunderstood point—how the hardware can get by with a 16-bit divisor (1021 Hex) when a 17-bit divisor (11021 Hex) is required in longhand division. First, recall the obvious: *all* divisors must contain a 1 in their high bits. Second, in longhand division, the high-order bit of the 17-bit divisor serves only to force the high-order bit of the remainder to 0, and thereafter serves no further purpose in the calculation. Because this "dead" bit is super-fluous (it is the 'x' in Figure 3-1), it can be altogether ignored in the design of hardware, and, as we will discover in Chapter 19, software.

Purging the Remainder Register

We now encounter another vocabulary problem: there is no single, unambiguous definition of a CRC. One is tempted to dub the remainder of modulo-2 division a CRC, but one additional step is required. To understand why the remainder of modulo-2 division is not yet a CRC, recall that after 16 shifts, the remainder register contains a copy of the first 16 bits of the message. Kindly put, an error-checking method that simply duplicates the message wins no awards for cleverness.

As we noted earlier, the register does not even begin to percolate until the first 1 bit in the message reaches the QUOTIENT line and is fed back to the XOR gates. In a real sense, then, we can complain that the very effect we seek from any given bit does not occur until that bit is actu-ally *shifted out* of the remainder! This means that when the last bit of the message has been shifted into the remainder register, it is still fully 16 bits away from exerting an *active* influence on the remainder. This minor problem is easy to solve: the residual message bits are forced into the XOR feedback path by "flushing" the CRC remainder register with sixteen 0s. Seen another way, six-teen extraneous 0 bits are appended to the message itself. (For yet another way to view the 0 bits, see "Achieving a Zero Remainder," below.)

So important is the technique of using 0s to flush the remainder, that we can, ipso facto, make the following definition: a CRC is the remainder obtained from modulo-2 division in which a number of 0 bits equal to the number of bits in the remainder register is appended to the message.

The "Classical" CRC Circuit

The need to purge the remainder register with 0 bits actually presents a design problem: who or what actually does the purging? Must the bits be manually appended to the message? Is software somehow supposed to signal the hardware when the 0s are to be added? This dilemma can be resolved by making a subtle change in the design of the circuit itself. This new circuit, shown in Figure 3-5, actually eliminates the need to purge the remainder with 0s.

If you construct a penny-and-dime simulator for this circuit, you will discover that after the very first shift its remainder corresponds to the intermediate remainders of longhand division. As before, the incoming message bit is XORed with the high-order bit of the accumulator, then shifted into the accumulator. The important difference is the manner in which the divisor is sub-tracted from the remainder. In the earlier circuit, the feedback for the XOR gates was provided by bit 15 directly; in this new circuit, however, the bit produced by XORing the data with bit 15 is actually the QUOTIENT line. Note that by placing the message bits immediately into the XOR feedback stream, their effect upon the remainder is felt immediately, without the 16-bit propaga-tion delay incurred by the simple division circuit. Processing a message through this circuit, then, produces the same remainder as the polynomial division circuit with 16 bits of 0s appended to the message.

Since the circuit in Figure 3-5 produces a CRC directly, and in order to differentiate it from the earlier circuit which performs "pure" modulo-2 division, we will henceforth refer to it as the *classical* CRC prototype. (See "The Classical CRC," on page 71.)

Figure 3-5 Modification of division circuit eliminates flushing the remainder with 0s.

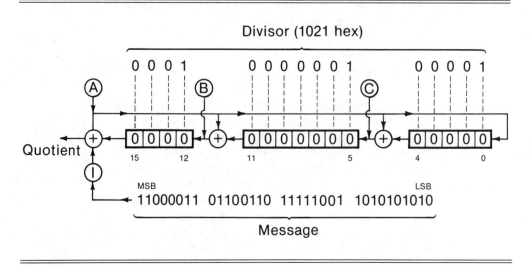

CRC and Polynomials

So far we have used the language of modulo-2 division to describe the various aspects of CRC calculations. In practice, though, CRCs are usually described in the language of *polynomials*. In this language, the message is expressed as a long polynomial whose bits form the coefficients of the polynomial term. The exponent for each term in the polynomial is derived from that bit's ordinal rank in the message. For example, our 4-byte message (11000011011001101111100101010101) is expressed as a polynomial like this:

$$1 \quad 1 \quad 0 \quad 0 \quad 0 \quad 0 \quad 1 \quad 1 \quad 0 \quad 1 \quad 1 \quad 0 \quad 0 \quad 1 \quad 1 \quad 0$$
$$1X^{31}+1X^{30}+0X^{29}+0X^{28}+0X^{27}+0X^{26}+1X^{25}+1X^{24}+0X^{23}+1X^{22}+1X^{21}+0X^{20}+0X^{19}+1X^{18}+1X^{17}+0X^{16}+$$
$$1 \quad 1 \quad 1 \quad 1 \quad 1 \quad 0 \quad 0 \quad 1 \quad 0 \quad 1 \quad 0 \quad 1 \quad 0 \quad 1$$
$$1X^{15}+1X^{14}+1X^{13}+1X^{12}+1X^{11}+0X^{10}+0X^9+1X^8+0X^7+1X^6+0X^5+1X^4+0X^3+1X^2+0X^1+1X^0$$

and our divisor (10001000000100001) is

$$1 \quad 0 \quad 0 \quad 0 \quad 1 \quad 0 \quad 0 \quad 0 \quad 0 \quad 0 \quad 0 \quad 1 \quad 0 \quad 0 \quad 0 \quad 0 \quad 1$$
$$1X^{16}+0X^{15}+0X^{14}+0X^{13}+1X^{12}+0X^{11}+0X^{10}+0X^9+0X^8+0X^7+0X^6+1X^5+0X^4+0X^3+0X^2+0X^1+1X^0$$

By convention, however, non-leading terms with a 0 coefficient are not shown. In this shorthand, our message polynomial is

$$X^{31}+X^{30}+X^{25}+X^{24}+X^{22}+X^{21}+X^{18}+X^{17}+X^{15}+X^{14}+X^{13}+X^{12}+X^{11}+X^8+X^6+X^4+X^2+X^0$$

and the divisor polynomial is

$$X^{16}+X^{12}+X^5+1$$

The convenience of this notation is clearly one of the reasons why the polynomial language is adopted. There are new names for the other parts of the process:

Message polynomial — the message itself (i.e., the dividend), expressed as a polynomial

Generator polynomial — the divisor, expressed as a polynomial

CRC generator — a circuit or, by extension, software algorithm for calculating CRCs

CRC accumulator — the CRC remainder or remainder register

Although these terms are not entirely satisfactory, for the sake of consistency with the existing literature on the subject, we will adopt them for the remainder of this chapter.

Selecting a Generator Polynomial (Divisor)

Aside from noting that all divisor polynomials must begin and end with a 1 term, a discussion of the criteria for selecting polynomials is far beyond the scope of this book. A thorough discussion of this subject requires knowledge of advanced mathematics. Further references are provided in the bibliography for those who wish to pursue the subject further.

There are two popular 16-bit CRC polynomials. The first is specified by the CCITT in the following deadly prose:

> The. . .information bits, taken in conjunction, correspond to the coefficients of a message polynomial having terms from x^{n-1} (n = total number of bits in a block or sequence) down to X^{16}. This polynomial is divided, modulo 2, by the generating polynomial $x^{16} + x^{12} + x^5 + 1$. The check bits correspond to the coefficients of the terms from x^{15} to x^0 in the remainder polynomial found at the completion of this division.
> —*The CCITT Red Book*, Volume VIII, International Telecommunications Union, Geneva, 1986. Recommendation V.41, "Code-Independent Error Control System."

You may recognize this polynomial as the "hypothetical" in the examples of this chapter. Known simply as *CRC-CCITT*, it was used by IBM for the first floppy disk controller (Model 3770) and quickly became a standard for microcomputer disk controllers. This polynomial is also employed in IBM's popular synchronous protocols HDLC/SDLC (High-level Data Link Control/Synchronous Data Link Control), and we will encounter it in the XMODEM file transfer protocols in Chapters 4 and 19.

Another widely used CRC polynomial is CRC-16:

$$X^{16} + X^{15} + X^2 + 1$$

This polynomial, though not quite as efficient at catching errors as CRC-CCITT, is nevertheless still popular due to its long history in IBM's BYSYNC (Binary Synchronous Communications Protocol) method of data transfer.

Achieving a Zero Remainder

After all bytes of a message have been transmitted, the 16-bit CRC checkvalue must then be transmitted. What is the easiest way to check that this received CRC value matches the CRC locally calculated by the receiver? The method that comes immediately to mind is for the receiver to fetch the two transmitted CRC bytes and perform a simple integer comparison of the two values: "if the received CRC equals the calculated CRC." Although this method gives the right answer, a simpler and faster way exists, thanks to the peculiarities of modulo-2 arithmetic.

Let's assume that both receiver and transmitter are using the CRC circuit in Figure 3-5 and have successfully transferred a message without errors. It is now time for the receiver to fetch the CRC checkvalue. Instead of fetching the transmitted CRC bytes separately and comparing them to the value in its own accumulator, the receiver simply treats them as part of the message, processing them through its own CRC generator. When the message and the CRC are both error-free, the receiver's CRC accumulator is 0!

If this phenomenon seems to be magic, you can watch it happen with a penny-and-dime simulator for Figure 3-5. When the receiver's CRC calculation is complete and before the CRC bytes are sent, the CRC in the accumulator is identical to the sender's CRC. Thus, as each message bit is applied to the accumulator, it is XORed with a copy of itself in bit 15 of the accumulator. The result, always 0, is shifted into the low-order bit of the accumulator. After 16 bits, the accumulator contains all 0s.

Another View of Accumulator Purging

Our explanation of the need to purge the modulo-2 division circuit with 0s was based upon the common-sense perception that the message bits do not participate actively in the remainder until they are shifted out onto the XOR gate feedback (QUOTIENT) line. While this observation remains valid, we now turn to a more mathematical explanation to illuminate several aspects of the subject.

Whenever programmers discuss CRCs, there is always one point of confusion. Someone complains that although their algorithm generates the correct CRC value, it does not produce a 0 remainder when the CRC is appended to the message as described above. Using the pennies-and-dimes CRC simulator we can easily resolve this mystery and, along the way, arrive at a fundamental point about the relationship between CRC circuits and circuits that perform "pure" polynomial division. A simulator shows that although modulo-2 division produces the correct CRC remainder after purging with 0 bits, it cannot be used to produce the 0 remainder just discussed. Clearly, then, the production of a remainder of 0 is somehow related to the purging of the CRC accumulator with 0s. To understand why, let's recall some basic arithmetic. We know that

$$\text{Message} = (\text{Quotient} \times \text{Divisor}) + \text{Remainder}$$

By adding *Remainder* to both sides, we achieve

$$\text{Message} + \text{Remainder} = (\text{Quotient} \times \text{Divisor}) + \text{Remainder} + \text{Remainder}$$

This equation is seemingly useless until we remember that in modulo-2 arithmetic, addition is equivalent to Exclusive-ORing. The expression

$$\text{Remainder} + \text{Remainder}$$

is equivalent to

$$\text{Remainder} \oplus \text{Remainder}$$

From the Exclusive-OR truth table on page 60, we see that any value XORed with itself is 0. This leaves us with the more interesting equation

$$\text{Message} \oplus \text{Remainder} = \text{Quotient} \times \text{Divisor}$$

then

$$\frac{\text{Message} \oplus \text{Remainder}}{\text{Divisor}} = \text{Quotient}$$

which plainly states that in modulo-2 arithmetic, XORing the remainder of division to the orginal message creates a new message that is *evenly* divisible by the original divisor (produces a remainder of 0).

Stating it somewhat differently: when the remainder of message A is XORed with message A to form message B, division of message B by the original divisor produces a remainder of 0. Applying this principle to the longhand division in Figure 3-1 yields:

```
1100001101100110111110010101010101 ◄─────────── Original message A
          1011011000110010 ◄─────────── Remainder
─────────────────────────────────
1100001101100110010011110110111 ◄─────────── New message B evenly divisible
                                              by original divisor
```

Although this procedure indeed achieves a remainder of 0, the accomplishment is, you must concede, a bit of a Pyrrhic victory—we have altered the message! Luckily, there is a simple way to preserve the original content of the message. Before performing the first division, we concatenate sixteen extra 0s to the original message.

This means that we need to rephrase our principle. Message A is right-padded with 0s to form message B. The remainder of message B is appended to message B to form message C. After division the remainder of message C is 0. Let's see this in action.

```
1100001101100110111110010101010101 ◄─────────────────── Message A
110000110110011011111001010101010100000000000000000 ◄───────── Message B
```

We now calculate the remainder for message B.

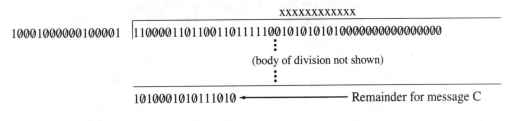

```
                              XXXXXXXXXXXX
                          ────────────────────────────────────────────
1000100000100001 |110000110110011011111001010101010100000000000000000
                          ⋮
                          (body of division not shown)
                          ⋮
                  ──────────────────────────────
                   1010001010111010 ◄─────────── Remainder for message C
```

Now we create the *final message* by XORing the remainder with the 0-paddded message to produce the final message that is evenly divisible.

```
110000110110011011111001010101010100000000000000000 ◄───── Message C added to
                               1010001010111010 ◄───────── Remainder of Message C
────────────────────────────────────────────────────
110000110110011011111001010101011010001010111010 ◄───── New message is evenly
                                                         divisible by divisor
```

This procedure works only with the classical CRC model, which "pre-appends" the sixteen 0s, and not with simple modulo-2 division. It is therefore likely that programmers who are frustrated by the failure of their "correct" algorithms to achieve the expected 0 remainder are probably using modulo-2 division algorithms, not CRC algorithms.

In view of this discussion, it is worthwhile to examine the remainder of the CCITT specification quoted earlier:

The complete block [of] message bits followed by the check bits, corresponds to the coefficients of a polynomial which (*sic*) is integrally divisible in modulo 2 fashion by the generating polynomial.

At the transmitter the . . . information bits are subjected to an encoding process equivalent to a division by the generator polynomial. The resulting remainder is transmitted to the line immediately after the information bits, commencing with the highest order bits.

At the receiver, the incoming block is subjected to a decoding process equivalent to a division by the generator polynomial, which in the absence of errors will result in a zero remainder. If the division results in other than a zero remainder, errors are indicated.

The important phrase here is "integrally divisible," because it means that the classic CRC (as opposed to the polynomial division) model is intended. It is interesting to note that the term CRC appears neither in this excerpt nor in the body of the specification from which it was taken.

More CRC Variations

It should come as no shock to learn that CRC procedures are not performed on one long, continuous message. Since hardware must interface to a processor, the message is usually fed into the hardware in 8-bit bytes. In serial devices that contain CRC hardware, however, the bits are sent to the CRC generator 1 bit at a time as they are transmitted or received. Since a byte is transmitted with the low-order bit first, the resulting CRC is calculated in reverse order. As long as there is a complementary CRC hardware circuit in the receiver, this process is transparent because the bits go into the receiver's generator in the same sequence as they went into the sender's.

Microcomputers seldom contain hardware for processing CRC during asynchronous I/O. In the event you are called upon to write software in support of CRC checkvalues created by hard-

Figure 3-6   A "reverse" circuit using the CRC-16 polynomial.

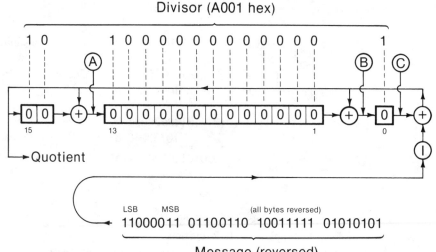

ware, you will need to perform the necessary bit reversals. Figure 3-6 shows a common reverse CRC, depicted here using the CRC-16 generator polynomial. This circuit assumes that message bits are applied low-order bit first. To compensate for bit reversal, the circuit is designed with bit flow in the opposite direction from previous models. Here, incoming message bits enter the high-order end and shift right. Notice also that even the polynomial represented by the position of the XOR gates is in inverse order as well—A001 Hex instead of 8005 Hex as expected. This circuit, which is of the "auto-purge" variety, produces a CRC remainder correctly reversed.

The Classical CRC

Because CRCs are so closely linked with communications hardware, which processes bits in "reverse" order, some would argue that the circuit in Figure 3-5 should not be called the "classical" CRC model. These authors point out, with some validity, that since CRC error checking virtually was born in serial communications hardware, which reverses the bit order of bytes during transfer, the reverse CRC deserves the honorific "classical." In other words, the only "real" CRC is, a priori, the one performed by hardware.

While it is probably true that the circuit in Figure 3-5 probably never existed in real-world hardware, it is a good bet that it was built as an evolutionary step in the development of the bit-reversed CRCs that eventually were used. Besides, this book is about software, not hardware, applications of CRCs. Due to modern ICs that automate every aspect of asynchronous communications, software does not have to deal with incoming bytes bit-by-bit, but as entire bytes. Since bytes are received whole, software CRC calculations need not be concerned with the peculiarities of the processes of serialization inside the ICs. Software, therefore, can more obviously and directly parallel the CRC's theoretical roots in polynomial division. For our purposes, then, the *classical* CRC model continues to be that of Figure 3-5.

Leading Zeroes

Like the CCITT document quoted above, a surprising number of error-checking procedures specify that the CRC accumulator be initialized to 0. This is an odd requirement, since this makes the algorithm vulnerable to leading spurious 0s. There are two popular alternatives to initialization with 0s.

The most obvious way around susceptibility to leading extraneous 0s is to initialize the accumulator to any other value but 0. A more imaginative method is that used in IBM's popular synchronous protocol SDLC, in which the accumulator is initialized to all 1s. Upon completion of the CRC calculation, the *1s complement* of the CRC accumulator is transmitted. Through some unexplored miracle of modulo-2 arithmetic, if the receiver processes these inverted bytes as appendages to the message, the resulting remainder is 1D0F Hex instead of 0.

CRCs on Byte-Size Data

As we just noted, software implementations of CRCs feed the message into the generator 1 byte at a time. It is interesting to examine exactly how the 8 bits of a byte combine with the existing 16-bit accumulator to produce a new accumulator. Our goal in this section is to analyze the new accumulator in terms of the *ancestry* of its bits—that is, *exactly* which of the original data bits combined with which of the original accumulator bits. For our example we will use the reverse CRC-16 model shown in Figure 3-6.

Although you can duplicate this experiment with the purely manual penny-and-dime CRC simulator, be forewarned that it is an extremely tedious procedure. If you choose to do this, begin by labeling each bit in the data and the accumulator with its bit number—D0 through D7 and A0 through A15, respectively. On a separate piece of paper, maintain a cumulative chart showing each bit in the accumulator and the original bits—both data and accumulator—that were XORed to produce it. Figure 3-7 shows this chart before shifting begins. Bit numbers are represented with capital letters, while the contents of the registers use lower-case letters.

Figure 3-7 Reverse CRC-16 bit-combining chart before shifting.

DATA BITS

	MSB							LSB
Bit number	D7	D6	D5	D4	D3	D2	D1	D0
Contents	d7	d6	d5	d4	d3	d2	d1	d0

CRC ACCUMULATOR

	MSB															LSB
Bit number	A15	A14	A13	A12	A11	A10	A9	A8	A7	A6	A5	A4	A3	A2	A1	A0
Contents	a15	a14	a13	a12	a11	a10	a9	a8	a7	a6	a5	a4	a3	a2	a1	a0

Figure 3-8 Reverse CRC-16 bit-combining chart after one shift.

DATA BITS

	MSB							LSB
Bit number	D7	D6	D5	D4	D3	D2	D1	D0
Contents	—	d7	d6	d5	d4	d3	d2	d1

CRC ACCUMULATOR

	MSB															LSB
Bit number	A15	A14	A13	A12	A11	A10	A9	A8	A7	A6	A5	A4	A3	A2	A1	A0
Contents	—	a15	a14	a13	a12	a11	a10	a9	a8	a7	a6	a5	a4	a3	a2	a1
	a0		a0													a0
	d0		d0													d0

Figure 3-8 shows the chart after only one shift. This chart now shows the ancestry of each bit: bits 15, 13, and 0 of the accumulator (C15, C13, C0) now contain the XOR of c0 and d0 (the *original* contents of C0 and D0).

Figure 3-9 shows the registers after the fourth shift. Notice that after only four shifts, the columns already contain many duplicate bits, making the whole chart appear hopelessly confusing. This clutter of duplicates can be greatly simplified, however, when we realize that the XOR of identical bits produces 0; these bits can therefore be eliminated from the chart. Figure 3-10 shows

Figure 3-9 Reverse CRC-16 bit-combining chart after four shifts.

DATA BITS

	MSB							LSB
Bit number	D7	D6	D5	D4	D3	D2	D1	D0
Contents	—	—	—	—	d7	d6	s5	d4

CRC ACCUMULATOR

	MSB															LSB
Bit number	A15	A14	A13	A12	A11	A10	A9	A8	A7	A6	A5	A4	A3	A2	A1	A0
Contents	—	—	—	—	a15	a14	a13	a12	a11	a10	a9	a8	a7	a6	a5	a4
	a3	a2	a1	a0	a1	a0										a3
	a2	a1	a0	d0	a0	d0										a2
	a2	a0	d0	a2	d0											a1
	a0	d0	d1	a1	d1											a0
	d0	d1	a3	a0												d0
	d1	d2	a2	d0												d1
	d2		a1	d1												d2
	d3		a0	d3												d3
			d0													
			d1													
			d2													
			d3													

the chart after eight shifts with the duplicates cancelled and removed. The bits have also been rearranged to juxtapose like-numbered data and accumulator bits.

Figure 3-10 CRC-16 bit-combining chart after eight shifts (duplicates cancelled).

DATA BITS

	MSB							LSB
Bit number	D7	D6	D5	D4	D3	D2	D1	D0
Contents	—	—	—	—	—	—	—	—

CRC ACCUMULATOR

	MSB															LSB
Bit number	A15	A14	A13	A12	A11	A10	A9	A8	A7	A6	A5	A4	A3	A2	A1	A0
Contents	—	—	—	—	—	—	—	—	a15	a14	a13	a12	a11	a10	a09	a08
	a0	a0	a6	a5	a4r	a3	a2	a1	a0	a0						a0
	d0	d0	d6	d5	d4	d3	d2	d1	d0	d0						d0
	a1	a1	a7	a6	a5	a4	a3	a2	a1							a1
	d1	d1	d7	d6	d5	d4	d3	d2	d1							d1
	a2	a2														a2
	d1	d2														d2
	a3	a3														a3
	d3	d3														d3
	a4	a4														a4
	d4	d4														d4
	a5	a5														a5
	d5	d5														d5
	a6	a6														a6
	d6	d6														d6
	a7															a7
	d7															d7

After eight shifts, the low-order byte of the new accumulator contains only bits created by XORing the data bytes with bits D7 through A15 of the original accumulator. In other words, a data byte is XORed only with the *low-order byte* of the existing accumulator, producing an 8-bit value we refer to as the *combining value*. Sparing you the tiresome mathematical proof, it is fairly apparent that the new CRC accumulator is simply the *CRC of the combining value* plus (XOR in modulo-2) the original high-order byte of the accumulator.

For non-reversed CRC algorithms, the message byte combines only with the *high*-order bits of the existing accumulator. The new CRC accumulator is simply the *CRC of the combining value* XORed with the original low-order byte of the accumulator.

So What?

Although the historical relationships among the bits are interesting in themselves, it is unlikely that you can perceive their absolute worth, for they are here presented completely out of practical context. In fact, they are offered here solely as background reference to assist in writing table-driven CRC software generators in Chapter 19. Further discussion of the subject is deferred until then.

4

Information Transfer

The previous chapter dealt with what asynchronous communication is, how it evolved, how to do it, and errors that can occur during it. This chapter will look at how the medium can be used to transfer information from one place to another intact. The first portion of this chapter deals with *flow control*—procedures to prevent overwhelming the receiver with unexpected or improperly formatted data. Here we discuss flow-control *procedures* in which regulation of the flow of data is the responsibility of the sender, and flow-control *protocols* where sender and receiver cooperatively control the flow of data. In the second portion, we turn our attention to the more complicated topic of *file-transfer protocols* where sender and receiver together not only regulate the flow of traffic, but also assure the *accuracy* of the data.

Flow Control

Before communications can begin, a *physical communications link* must be established. This link may take the form of a simple cable connecting a computer to its CRT; it may consist of two computers exchanging data over the telephone network with modems, or it may be a radio-telemetry conversation between two space satellites. Regardless of how simple or how complicated the physical link, there is no guarantee that the receiver is *unconditionally* able to accept the sender's data. Consider a few examples:

- You are sending characters to a printer. To compensate for the computer's ability to send characters faster than they can be printed, the printer thoughtfully provides a few bytes of buffer storage where characters can wait their turn to be printed. When the buffer becomes full, the printer output becomes garbled.

- Your microcomputer is reading bytes from the communications line and storing them one-by-one onto a floppy disk file. Even though your operating system buffers the characters for you, sooner or later it must perform a physical write to the floppy. During the eternity required to write to the floppy, bytes are lost.

- You wish to transmit a file to a mainframe that treats all data as if it were created by human fingers; bytes arriving faster than humans can type are mysteriously lost.

These are all examples of a need for *flow control*—the modification of the amount or rate of transmitted data based upon the needs or responses of the receiver. The modifications may be as simple as performing the data transfer at a slower data rate, or as complicated as wholesale refor-matting of the outgoing data to match that of the receiver.

Software Flow-Control Procedures

As the examples above clearly illustrate, flow control is not necessarily an aberrant situation, but a fact of everyday life. Every time you press **Ctrl-S** (or **Ctrl-NumLock** on the IBM PC) to pause a screen listing, you have participated in flow control by signaling the computer that it is over-whelming a peripheral device (you!) with data. Hardware devices such as printers, plotters, and to a lesser degree, video terminals inevitably require flow control. This often takes the form of volt-age changes on the pins of the serial interface connector. This is *hardware flow control*, which we examine more closely in Chapter 5. Where a physical connection between the communicating devices is impossible (such as over a modem) or when hardware flow control is not supported, *software flow control* is necessary.

Flow control between identical computers and operating sytems is usually no problem, be-cause both obey the same set of rules. But very special kinds of flow-control problems confront the programmer trying to *upload* (transmit) or *download* (receive) data between operating sys-tems or hardware devices that possess fundamentally different concepts about I/O. We will now look at a few of the common kinds of serial I/O problems that you are likely to encounter.

The most important thing to keep in mind when dealing with "foreign" systems, especially large timesharing computers, is that responsibility for character I/O is usually relegated to auxili-ary input hardware equipment, simply called *a communication front-end* (the IBM Model 3705, for example). These devices, which actually qualify as small computers themselves, gather input from the communications lines and package it according to the rules of the system. Incoming characters are stored in a buffer until the buffer is full or until a designated *logical terminator* character (usually a CR) is detected in the input. When the front-end signals the computer that input is ready, the computer empties the buffer as soon as it can.

During the input procedure, incoming data may be altered. The alterations may be per-formed by the communications front-end during receipt of the characters, or by the computer it-self through its device-controlling subroutines, or *device drivers*. On virtually every system, one or more of the following functions is performed on the incoming data:

- Translation of control characters to printable equivalents
- Upper- or lower-case translation
- Truncation of lines that are too long
- New line translation: converting CR to LF (or vice versa), or inserting CR before an LF (or vice versa)
- Ignoring ("*swallowing*") control characters. Although any given system may consider any character to be "*hot,*" most discard NUL and DEL, which are characteristically used as *device padding*, or time-wasting characters sent to accommodate slow devices such as printers.
- Imparting special meaning to control characters, especially DC1, DC2, DC3, and DC4
- Acting upon primitive command line editing control characters, especially NAK (Control-U), CAN (Control-X), and ESC
- Transmitting a copy of the received character (possibly modified as just described) back to the sender. This function, known as *echoplexing*, is available only on full-duplex systems.

On some systems it may be possible to enter a *raw* mode to disable most of this preprocessing of the character stream, but on some systems it isn't. To complicate matters, systems often apply one set of rules to a console device, but another set of rules for I/O performed by applications programs.

The method of communications-line access also varies from one system to another: half- or full-duplex, or half-duplex over full-duplex channels. Mercifully, half-duplex systems are becoming increasingly rare. Since a system's "plex" is exclusively a hardware concern, it is addressed in Chapter 5.

Character-by-Character Flow-Control Procedures

The purpose of listing these characteristics is not to provide a compendium of computer idiosyncrasies—such a list would be endless—but to emphasize how hostile one environment can be to characters originating in another. As you enter these battlefields, bear two mottos on your shield: "Assume nothing!" and "Forewarned is forearmed."

Intercharacter Delay

Before the modern video terminal was developed, interactive keyboard input was generated on teleprinters. The operator could either send characters to the computer directly from the keyboard or could punch them into paper tape for automatic uploading. Input systems designed during this stage of technology have been amazingly slow to die. Other systems, such as the DEC-system 2060, were simply designed to receive characters at a rate slightly higher than humans can type. This is not a design flaw so much as shortsightedness, but it clearly poses problems when uploading data, even at the modest rate of 60 cps. Although these problems can usually be cured by lowering the raw communications (e.g., data) rate, it is not always possible to do so, especially on dial-up lines, where only one or two modem speeds may be available. Even where it is possible to use a slower speed, the choice is not necessarily a good one. A system that can accept data at a rate of only 60 cps, for example, will certainly be overwhelmed by 120 cps (assuming a 10-bit SDU), but may perform perfectly at 55 cps. Stepping down to the next lower standard modem data rate of 30 cps would unnecessarily reduce throughput by almost 50 percent.

A fixed delay introduced between characters, often referred to as *pacing*, is a much better solution than reducing the signaling rate, because it enables the sender to customize the data rate to the system in question. Using the example above, then, how much delay would be required? Assuming a 10-bit SDU, the time required to transmit characters at 120 and 55 cps is

$$55 \text{ char/sec} = 1 \div 55 = .01818 \text{ sec/char}$$
$$120 \text{ char/sec} = 1 \div 120 = .00833 \text{ sec/char}$$

The difference between the two rates,

$$
\begin{array}{r}
0.01818 \\
\underline{0.00833} \\
0.00985 \text{ sec/char}
\end{array}
$$

or approximately 10 milliseconds (.01 second), is the amount of intercharacter delay that must be added to slow 120 bps to 55 bps.

Intercharacter delay is a valuable tool, but it is a successful flow-control technique only if it is individually tailored for each system. Moreover, the same delay is not always effective. On time-sharing systems, periods of heavy usage can bog the input response of an ordinarily fast system down to a few tens of characters per second; during such cases of severe loading, the system may accept no input at all for several seconds. Clearly, intercharacter delay is useless if the system remains insensitive to input for periods longer than the delay interval.

Echo-Wait

The problem with intercharacter delay as a flow-control method is that the sender does not interact with the receiver. The transmission of the next character is in no way related to the successful reception of the previous one. A transfer performed without feedback between sender and receiver to confirm the receipt of data is called a *one-sided*, or *blind transfer* (or even "send and pray"). A two-sided transfer requires that the receiver respond in some way to the receipt of the data.

Most full-duplex systems echo input immediately back to the sender. Some systems provide echo to the user's console by default (but not always to the user's programs). When transferring data to an echoplex system, the system's echo can be used as a form of feedback between characters. After each character is transmitted, the sender enters a time-limited loop, awaiting the return echo from the receiver. If no echo arrives within a certain amount of time (the *timeout interval*), the sender retransmits the same character until an echo arrives. When the receiver fails to echo a character after several retransmissions, the software may react in several ways.

The first response is simply to send the next character anyway. Recall that many systems quietly swallow certain characters, especially control characters that are likely to be disruptive to system operations. For example, NUL and DEL traditionally are not echoed by systems that use them for device padding. Automatically transmitting the next character prevents a transmission from getting stuck if the data contains a "hot" character, or if an otherwise acceptable character is transformed into a hot character by an error. After several timeout errors in succession or a large total of timeout errors indicate that the transfer may be seriously flawed, the system should give you the opportunity to terminate the transfer or simply to abandon the echo-wait and proceed with a blind transfer.

Reverting to a blind transfer may sound like a foolish response, but under certain circumstances can be very useful. Although it is unlikely, you may learn *after* beginning the transfer that the receiving I/O channel is not full-duplex. Thus the option of switching to a blind transfer is essential for dealing with systems that provide echo only to the user's console, but not to other communications channels.

Comparing the original character to the echoed character is a crude test for errors during transfer. Because a character may be damaged during the return echo portion of its voyage (when it doesn't matter), however, the number of errors reported will be about 50 percent too high under ideal circumstances. In addition, some systems do not echo an exact copy of their input (CR may be echoed as CRLF, for example).

Line Flow Control

Although character-by-character flow control is effective in the right environment and under the right circumstances, there are several conditions under which it cannot be employed at all. On half-duplex systems, for instance, the time required to reverse the communications line (see Chapter 5) between each character is prohibitively long in comparison to the time required to transmit a single character.

The success of character-by-character flow control depends upon a single, dubious assumption: the receiver's echo proves that the character has been received. This assumption is decidedly false on systems that process input as lines, or, to use a more pretentious term, *logical records*. On such a system, characters are gathered into a buffer until a delimiter (a CR or LF, for example) is encountered, at which time the system accepts the entire buffer at one gulp. Such systems differ in the details of managing the input buffer. One point of difference is the system's response to a full buffer. Some respond by playing dead—ignoring the input and turning off echo; others ignore the input, but echo a BEL character to alert the sender that something is amiss. A few systems, however, have a most insidious response—they ignore the incoming character but continue to return the echo as if all were well.[1]

Transmitting data to line-oriented systems such as these can be treacherous. At the minimum, the sender must assume that the data contains end-of-line delimiting characters often enough to empty the receiver's input buffer before it becomes full. If the data does not contain delimiters at the correct intervals, the sender must insert them; if the sender's data contains delimiters of the wrong kind, the sender must translate its delimiters to those of the receiver. As you see, the list is endless.

Interline Delays

On many systems, even inserting the correct delimiters at the correct intervals does not guarantee a successful transfer. During periods of heavy usage, some systems take an inordinately long time to empty the buffer after receiving the correct delimiter. During this period, the system loses bytes that come on the heels of the previous line. Historically, the sender solves this problem by padding every line with a few NULs (usually), thus giving the receiving system time to empty its buffer. The same effect can be achieved more efficiently by adding a slight *delay* after transmitting each delimiter.

Flow-Control Protocols

The flow-control measures discussed so far are just *procedures*; that is, they assume that the sender has intimate, detailed knowledge of the receiver's ordinary response to arriving data. In each case, the sender adjusts one parameter—pace, end-of-line delimiter, and so forth—based upon prior knowledge about the receiver. Although such procedural techniques can be quite effective, they are haunted by the prospect of uncertainty—namely, is *enough* known about the way the receiver behaves? Flow-control procedures based upon timing are inherently unreliable because of the number of variables in the receiver's delay mechanism. For example, any of the following changes may cause a change in the receiver's timing: an increase in the number of users or jobs, installation of new device drivers, and changes in hardware (especially communications front-ends). In short, purely procedural flow-control techniques that worked perfectly yesterday may fail today.

The alternative to procedural flow control is *cooperative flow control* in which sender and receiver agree upon and observe a common set of rules to govern the exchange of data between

---

[1] It is interesting how the design of an input system reflects the designer's view of human nature.

them. The term ordinarily applied to these rules is *protocol*.[2] Echo-wait flow control is sometimes erroneously described as a protocol, presumably because the sender's behavior is dependent upon the receiver. This definition is incorrect: although the sender shows a good-natured willingness to cooperate, the receiver is oblivious. Remember, the two ingredients that transform a procedure into a protocol are *cooperation* and *agreement*, both of which are metaphorically implied in the informal name for a protocol, *handshaking*.

Flow-Control Protocols for Hardware Devices

So far the transferring of data has been discussed almost as if it were exclusively the province of computers. As noted earlier, many computer systems are designed to operate without any flow control whatever on their input. Hardware devices such as printers, plotters and to a lesser degree, video terminals, however, inevitably require flow control. Often this takes the form of voltage changes on the pins of the serial interface connector. We will examine this *hardware flow control* more closely in Chapter 5.

Where a physical connection between the communicating devices is impossible (such as over a modem) or when hardware flow control is not supported, *software flow* control is necessary. That is, instead of signaling by means of control wires, they make known their intentions by sending data over the communications line.

Character Protocols

The most popular (or at least the most famous) character flow-control protocol is known as *XON/XOFF*. Here, the sender and receiver assign special meaning to two characters, which are then inserted into the stream of data as flow control markers. These characters are given the functional names XON and XOFF, and their actual identity varies from system to system. By far the most common assignment is DC3 (Control-S) for XOFF and DC1 (Control-Q) for XON.

The receiver sends the XOFF character when it wishes the sender to pause in sending data, and an XON character when it wishes the sender to resume. (XOFF is often referred to as the *holdoff* character, and XON as the *release* character.)

XON/XOFF High Jinks

XON/XOFF is so uncomplicated that it seems foolproof so long as both sender and receiver respect the protocol. Nevertheless, many an unsuspecting computer user has been perplexed by a

---

[2]Through the childish behavior of diplomats, the word now connotes "superficial etiquette," but its Greek roots refer to the table of contents affixed to a treaty. Whatever its real meaning, "protocol" is so often misapplied that it is in danger of becoming too misleading for technical use. As usual, the culprit is the trade press, which appears willing to sacrifice accuracy in the name of its war on what it calls "computerese." It is quite common, for example, to read that START, STOP, and parity bits are protocols, when in fact they are encoding parameters. Even the ASCII character set is sometimes called the "ASCII protocol." This fuzzy usage extends fairly high up: a respected communications book repeatedly refers to the RS-232 *interface* as a "Physical-Layer Protocol." This kind of error is more subtle (and perhaps more dangerous): the EIA document number RS-232 defines a set of modem-control protocols *and* presents the electrical specifications for a hardware interface. Moral: be wary of things called protocols.

transfer that stopped midstream for no apparent reason. To illustrate this, let's look at a real-life example—one that occurred while sending the manuscript for Chapter 2 of this book through a UNIX electronic mail system. The sender was an IBM PC AT microcomputer using the XON/XOFF "UPLOAD" option in the *TERM* program developed in the programming chapters of this book. The data was in the form of an MS DOS text file created with the WordStar word processing program. The UNIX console driver was adjusted to XON = DC1, XOFF = DC3, and echo was enabled.

The UNIX command *cat > test.tmp* received the incoming text into a file named *test.tmp*. After only a few characters, the transfer stalled and could not be restarted. On successive attempts the transfer always stalled in the same spot, so that point in the file was examined using the MS DOS debugger *DEBUG*. The printed version of the text around the failure point and the debugger's display are shown in the box below.

Text around the file's failure point and how it appears in the debugger

"outdated language associated with the subject tends to obscure an important quality—the technology's almost childlike *simplicity*. Students of serial technology are often taken aback to discover that the underlying principle, like most computer topics, is . . . ."

```
0A 6F 75 74 64 61 74 65-E4 20 6C 61 6E 67 75 61     .outdate. langua
67 E5 20 61 73 73 6F 63-69 61 74 65 E4 20 77 69     g. associate. wi
74 E8 20 74 68 E5 20 73-75 62 6A 65 63 F4 20 74     t. th. subjec. t
65 6E 64 F3 20 74 EF 20-6F 62 73 63 75 72 E5 20     end. t. obscur.
61 EE 20 8D 0A 8D 0A 69-6D 70 6F 72 74 61 6E F4     a. ....importan.
20 71 75 61 6C 69 74 F9-AD 2D 74 68 E5 20 74 65     qualit.-th. te
63 68 6E 6F 6C 6F 67 79-27 F3 20 61 6C 6D 6F 73     chnology'. almos
F4 20 63 68 69 6C 64 6C-69 6B E5 20 13 73 69 6D     . childlik. .sim
70 6C 69 63 69 74 79 13-AE 20 20 8D 0A 8D 8A 53     plicity.. ....S
74 75 64 65 6E 74 F3 20-6F E6 20 73 65 72 69 61     tudent. o. seria
EC 20 74 65 63 68 6E 6F-6C 6F 67 F9 20 61 72 E5     . technolog. ar.
20 6F 66 74 65 EE 20 74-61 6B 65 EE 20 61 62 61     ofte. take. aba
63 EB 20 74 EF 20 64 69-73 63 6F 76 65 F2 20 74     c. t. discove. t
68 61 F4 20 8D 0A 8D 0A-74 68 E5 20 75 6E 64 65     ha. ....th. unde
72 6C 79 69 6E E7 20 70-72 69 6E 63 69 70 6C 65     rlyin. principle
AC 20 6C 69 6B E5 20 6D-6F 73 F4 20 63 6F 6D 70     . lik. mos. comp
75 74 65 F2 20 74 6F 70-69 63 73 AC 20 69 F3 20     ute. topics. i.
```

NOTE: To simplify automatic right-column justification, WordStar marks the last character in each word by setting its high-order bit. Since there is no ASCII equivalent for the resulting bytes, *DEBUG* displays them as a period. These high-order bits are stripped off by some mainframe front-ends.

The failure point in the file was always within the first three characters of the word "simplicity." Looking closely, we see that "simplicity" is bracketed by two 13H bytes. Experimentation revealed that WordStar uses DC3s (generated with the keystrokes **Ctrl-P Ctrl-S**) as internal markers for the beginning and end of underscoring.[3] But why do XOFFs in the outgoing data

---

[3]It is impossible to say whether this incredibly bad choice was the result of naivety or stupidity.

stream hang the transfer? After each byte the *TERM* program looks on the incoming communications line for an XOFF character. Meanwhile, UNIX busily echoes each byte it receives. When *TERM* sends the DC3 preceding "simplicity," UNIX innocently echoes it. *TERM*, not recognizing the stream of characters on its input as its own echo, detects the echoed XOFF and promptly goes into a loop awaiting an XON. The XON, of course, never comes.[4] Disabling the console echo (with the command *stty -echo*) before beginning the transfer solved the problem.

There is one important variation to the XON/XOFF protocol: instead of defining XON as a single character, the receiver accepts *any* character as a signal to resume transmission. Used in an echoing environment, this variant, which is generally found only on video terminal drivers, enables a *human* user to stop and start screen output with a single key. When a non-human receiver uses this style of XON/XOFF, however, the sender occasionally seems to ignore an XOFF. To understand why, visualize this: the sender transmits the letter 'A', and at exactly the same instant the receiver sends an XOFF. When the sender receives the XOFF, it ceases transmission and awaits an XON. Meanwhile, after sending the XOFF, the receiver immediately receives *and* echoes the letter 'A', which was already "in the pipe." The sender regards this echo of its own 'A' as its "any character XON" and immediately begins to transmit. Although this problem can be partially alleviated by building a delay into the code that senses the XON, the only certain remedy is turning off echo at the receiving end.

Whole-Line Protocols

Earlier we discussed how an end-of-line delay must be used when sending data to systems that accept input a line at a time. Like all flow controls that rely upon delays, this one is easily upset by minor variations in the receiving system's timing. A better solution is a protocol in which the sender appends a delimiting character to its data, then waits for the receiver to request another line by sending an acknowledgment character. Because computers are so individualized in their concept of I/O, there is an almost endless variety of these *prompted upload* protocols. We will therefore discuss only the most common one, the *ETX/ACK* protocol, which has its roots in IBM's VM/370 hybrid[5] upload protocol. Reflecting their ancestry in half-duplex communications, the two protocol characters are often referred to as the *outbound* and *inbound turn-around* characters. The sender transmits an ETX after each line of data and immediately begins a wait for the receiver's ACK (acknowledgment), which is also implicitly a request for the next line.

File-Transfer Protocols

We have examined flow control at the level of single characters and lines. A larger, far more complicated kind of protocol governs transfer of arbitrary *blocks* of data. Although used for a variety of applications in synchronous communications, block protocols in asynchronous communications are usually found only in programs that transfer entire files. In this context, they are referred to as *file-transfer protocols* (FTP).

---

[4]This problem is known as the *Godot Syndrome*.

[5]See Chapter 5 for a discussion of half-duplex protocols over a full-duplex communications line.

In virtually every asynchronous file-transfer protocol used on microcomputers, the basic unit of transfer is the *packet*, a grouping of various byte-elements or *fields*. Only one of these fields contains the file data, however; the remaining fields, known as *service fields,* contain the information required for the receiver to verify that the packet is error-free. The number and purpose of the control fields vary from protocol to protocol, but in general most contain a *packet-signature field* (usually beginning with an SOH byte), a packet-sequence number, a data field, and a checkvalue. Aside from differences in the number and kinds of fields, there are also many variations in the protocols that define how the packets are exchanged.

Automatic Repeat Request (ARQ) Protocols

The most common type of packet protocol is the *automatic repeat request* (ARQ) in which an error detected in a received packet or an unacknowledged packet automatically results in the re-transmission of that packet. There are several types of ARQ protocols.

Send-and-Wait ARQ

During transmission, data from the file is "*packetized*" by surrounding it with the service fields. An entire packet is then transmitted blindly (i.e., with no flow control), after which the sender waits for the receiver to acknowledge its receipt.

The receiver inputs the packets and, after verifying that the packet is in the correct sequence relative to the previous packet, computes a *local* checkvalue on the data portion of the packet. If the local checkvalue matches the one in the packet, the receiver acknowledges by sending an ACK; otherwise the receiver *negatively* acknowledges with a NAK (both ACK and NAK are considered acknowledgments). The ACK and NAK may actually be in the form of entire packets instead of single characters. Upon receipt of an ACK, the sender transmits the next packet; if a NAK is received, the same packet is transmitted again. Transmission proceeds in this manner until the entire file has been transferred.

The diagram in Figure 4-1 oversimplifies the process somewhat. We tend to forget that this is a two-way conversation and that the receiver's acknowledgments are just as susceptible to damage as the packets themselves. Consider the following scene: the receiver inputs and verifies a packet, sends an ACK, then proceeds to input what it expects to be the next packet in the sequence. Somehow, though, the receiver's ACK never reaches the transmitter who, after an appropriate timeout interval, obligingly retransmits the same packet. To prevent a duplicate block of data, the receiver must recognize that it has received the same block twice. How does the receiver get back on track? Simply by ignoring the packet and then sending another ACK.

Continuous ARQ

In a *continuous ARQ* protocol, the transmitter does *not* pause after each packet but transmits several packets in a row (the *packet group*). The receiver examines each packet and, as in send-and-wait ARQ, sends an acknowledgment (ACK or NAK) based upon the content. In this case, however, the packet's number is included along with the acknowledgment. During transmission, the sender continually examines the stream of acknowledgments returning from the receiver and keeps track of the packets that are received in error. After the entire group of packets has been transmitted, the sender then retransmits the ones that contain errors.

There are two methods for retransmitting the erroneous packets. In continuous ARQ *with fallback*, the first packet number received in error and every subsequent packet in the group are retransmitted. In continuous ARQ *with selective repeat*, only the actual packets containing errors are retransmitted.

Despite the send-and-wait protocol's obvious inefficiency (it was originally a half-duplex protocol) it is the most common file-transfer protocol found on microcomputers, including the two discussed later in this chapter. Continuous ARQ protocols, also known as *windowing* protocols, have never become popular on micros because they require substantially more computer resources and programming skill than the simpler send-and-wait protocols. For example, both continuous methods require that both sender and receiver buffer the entire packet *group* (window) in memory at one time.

Figure 4-1   Send-and-wait ARQ.

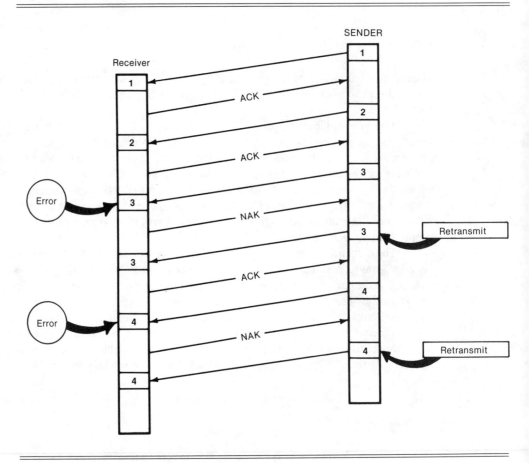

Packets

The number of packet designs is unlimited, but their most obvious differences lie in the manner in which the DATA field is delimited within the packet. There are three basic approaches: (1) marking the beginning and end of the DATA field with control characters, (2) including the length of the DATA field in the packet, and (3) fixed-length DATA field.

The Control Character Delimited Packet

The simplest form of packet is that used for transferring strictly *textual* data; that is, the file is expected to contain only ASCII plain-text: the alphanumeric characters plus the six control characters defined as Format Effectors (BS, HT, LF, VT, FF, and CR). The other control characters may not appear in the DATA field, but they may appear in other fields. A hypothetical version of such a packet is shown in Figure 4-2.

Figure 4-2 The layout of a hypothetical packet for transfer of text files.

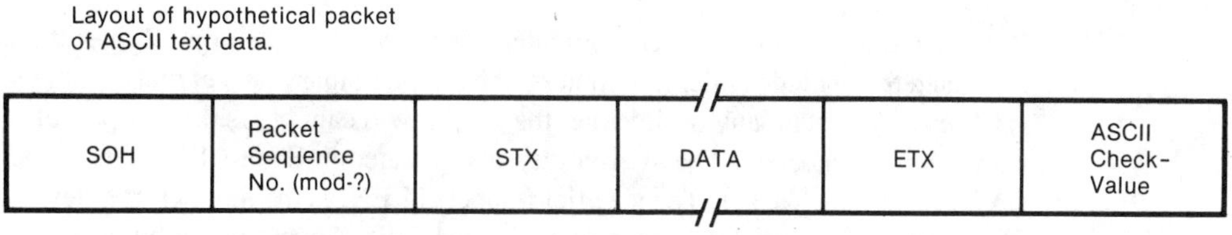

Layout of hypothetical packet of ASCII text data.

SOH	Packet Sequence No. (mod-?)	STX	DATA	ETX	ASCII Check-Value

SOH (Start of Header) This control character marks the beginning of a packet. This is the official purpose in ASCII.

Packet Sequence Number The next byte describes the packet's position in the current transfer. Its purpose is to enable the receiver to verify that the packet received is the one expected. To achieve this goal it is not necessary to know the packet's absolute position in the overall transfer (which may be a huge number), but merely its *relative* position in a limited sequence of packets. Accordingly, this field is usually limited to a single byte and, in some cases, the sequence number may be confined to a few significant bits of the field. This is expressed in the label "Packet number modulo-?." In simple send-and-wait ARQ protocols, the sequence field can even be modulo-2; i.e., "this" packet or "that" packet. If all 8 bits of this field are significant, the packet number is calculated modulo-256; 6 bits are modulo-64, and so on.

STX (Start of Text) This control character marks the beginning but is not part of the textual data.

DATA This contains the textual data.

ETX (End of Text) This control character marks the end but is not part of the textual data.

CHECKVALUE The redundant byte(s) used for error checking. To preserve the ASCII character of the protocol, the checkvalue may be represented with ASCII digits.

The data in an STX/ETX-delimited packet may be of variable length, although the penalty of having to retransmit a very long packet dictates that the maximum length of the packet should be short. Packet lengths for popular protocols range from 64 to 512 bytes. Regardless of its length, the receiver knows that the data begins at the byte after the STX byte in the packet and ends with the byte before the ETX byte.

Text-only protocols are necessary in some mainframe environments where the programmer cannot control the communications lines directly. These systems may use the high-order bit for parity (or even arbitrarily toss it altogether). Despite their rigorous ACSII format, text-only protocols are not portable across operating systems because each system processes input and output differently. The STX/ETX protocol, for example, does not work on a system that swallows or translates control these characters as described early in this chapter.

Size-Field Delimited Packet

When communicating between computers that have absolute control over the communications lines, and this includes microcomputers, the use of a binary packet makes more sense. Since binary files may contain any 8-bit value, the DATA field cannot, as the text packet can, be delimited with control characters. The alternative, as illustrated in Figure 4-3, is to include the *size* of the DATA field in the packet. The size field, labeled LEN, is the number of bytes in the DATA field. The number of bytes allotted to the length field limits the number of bytes that can be sent in one packet; a 1-byte length field, for example, limits the DATA field to 256 bytes.

Figure 4-3   The layout of a hypothetical packet for transfer of binary files.

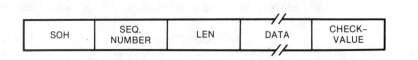

The Fixed-Length Data Field Packet

The third type of packet simply assumes a fixed length for the DATA field. If this seems like a reasonable approach, it has one major drawback—there is no way to send a *"short"* packet. A short packet is necessary whenever the original file's length is not evenly divisible by the fixed block size chosen. In other words, at the end of file transfer, there are probably not enough bytes in the file to fill an entire packet. The final packet therefore contains some non-file data: either garbage bytes or a padding byte specified in the protocol. In any case, because a file created by a fixed-length protocol likely contains one or more garbage bytes at the end, it is not an exact copy of the original. This brings up the subject of *invertibility*: if a file is transferred from one system to another, then back again, the recovered version on the first system should be identical to the original. The destination system can alter the file during its residence there, but must reverse (invert) the changes during retransmission.

Protocols with fixed-length DATA fields create inherently non-invertible files. The extra bytes at the end of the file often affect the file's utility or serviceability. Utilities that rely upon the number of bytes in a file as given in its directory entry ("TYPE" for example) find the garbage bytes as well. At first thought, one would think that executable files would be unaffected by superfluous bytes appended during transfer. Suppose, though, that you write a program that relies upon indexing from the end of a file. Calculations based upon these indexes will be incorrect if the file contains extra bytes. The popular XMODEM protocol, to which we now turn our attention, is a good example of a protocol that uses fixed-length DATA fields.

The XMODEM Protocol

The XMODEM file-transfer protocol was composed in 1977 by Ward Christensen, a programmer who has contributed many useful programs to the public domain. (In honor of his effort, the protocol is frequently referred to as the Christensen Protocol.) Christensen released into the public domain his file-transfer protocol surrounded by an extremely basic terminal emulator program simply called MODEM (and later MODEM2). Multi-file transfer capability and a multitude of smart terminal features were promptly added by public domain hackers. In this enlarged form, the program acquired the name MODEM7, which persists today in the form MODEM7xx, where xx is the current version number. The protocol is so widely known and so popular that scarcely a communications program now comes to market for microcomputers without support for XMODEM.

Technical Description of XMODEM

XMODEM is a simple send-and-wait ARQ protocol using a fixed-length data field. The checkvalue is a single-byte arithmetic checksum. Since CRC and multi-file transfer were added later and are not actually part of the Christensen protocol, we will deal with them separately. Figure 4-4 shows the layout of the XMODEM packet. All fields except DATA are 1 byte in length.

Figure 4-4 Layout of Christensen's XMODEM packet.

| SOH | Packet Sequence No. | 1's Complement of Packet Sequence No. | DATA (128 bytes) | Arithmetic Checksum |

All fields but DATA are 1 byte.

SOH The Start-of-Header byte announcing the first byte in the packet.

Packet Sequence The current packet number, modulo-256. The number of the first packet is 1.

1s Complement of Packet Sequence	The 1s complement of the current packet number in the previous field.
DATA	The length of the DATA field is fixed at 128 bytes. There are no restrictions upon the content—i.e., data may be binary or text.
Arithmetic Checksum	A 1-byte arithmetic sum of the content of the DATA field *only*, modulo-256.

Figure 4-5   XMODEM send. Timeouts and giveups are not shown.

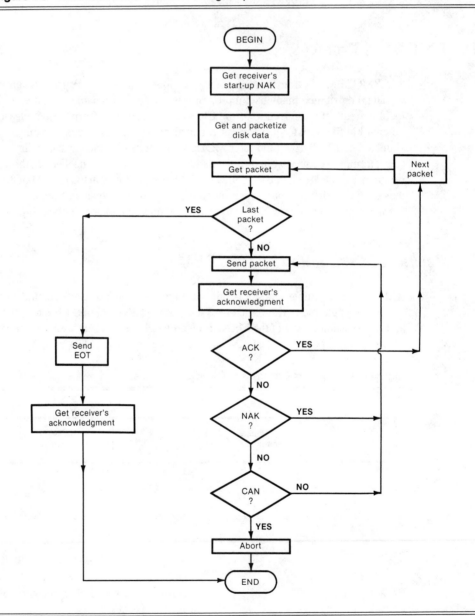

XMODEM Send

As in all protocols, the sender's job under XMODEM is considerably simpler than the receiver's. Figure 4-5 shows a flow chart of the transmission portion of the protocol.

Start-Up Phase

The first task in any protocol must be the establishment of contact between sender and receiver. One side always assumes the dominant role in this phase. The XMODEM protocol is said to be *receiver-driven*; that is, the receiver is responsible for stimulating and maintaining the flow of packets. Accordingly, the transmitter's role in the *start-up* or *synchronization* phase of the transfer consists of patiently waiting for a NAK from the receiver. When the first NAK arrives, the sender interprets it as "send the first packet." Arrival of the initial NAK ends the start-up phase.

Middle Phase

Once the sender receives the start-up NAK, it packetizes a 128-byte block of file data, transmits it, then waits for the receiver's acknowledgment of the just-transmitted packet. An ACK from the receiver means that the packet was received without error and is interpreted as an implicit request for the next packet; a NAK requests retransmission of the same packet; a CAN unconditionally terminates the transfer.[6] When there is no more file data to send, the middle phase of the transfer is completed.

Ending Phase

If the middle phase ends normally, the sender transmits a solitary EOT (End-of-Transmission) to inform the receiver that no more files are forthcoming. The receiver acknowledges the sender's EOT with an ACK. An orderly shutdown follows—files are closed, memory freed, and so forth. If the middle phase ends abnormally—with a CAN (abort) from the receiver, for example—no EOT is sent.

XMODEM Receive

It is the receiver's job not only to input the packet, but also, based upon the information contained in the service fields, to verify that the packet just received is the one expected and that it contains no errors. The XMODEM receiver therefore has much more to worry about than the transmitter. Figure 4-6 shows a flow chart of the receiver portion of the protocol.

Start-Up Phase

Aside from housekeeping chores—allocating buffers, opening files, and so on—the receiver's start-up phase consists entirely of sending a single NAK to announce its readiness to receive packets.

---

[6]Despite Christensen's protests, a CAN is used for this purpose in every known implementation.

Figure 4-6   XMODEM receive. Only packet timeout is shown.

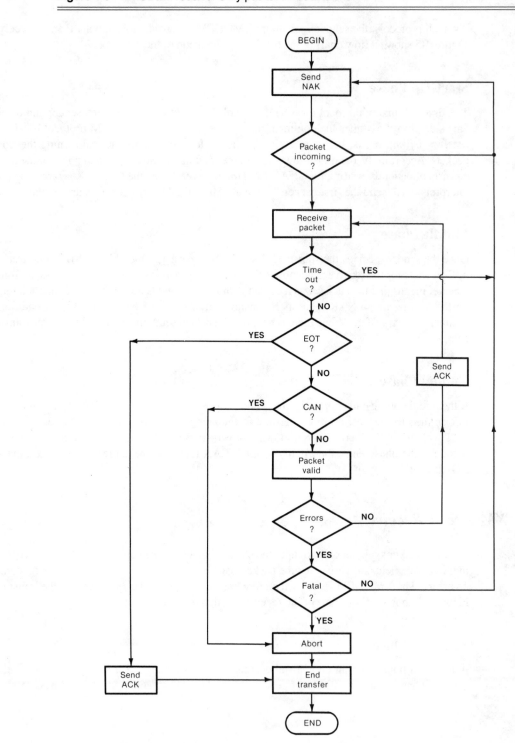

Middle Phase

The receiver now enters the receive loop—waiting for a packet and sending a NAK if none arrives in 10 seconds. The arrival of an SOH signals the arrival of a packet, which the receiver evaluates as follows:

1. Although a packet is formally identified as starting with an SOH, a solitary EOT byte in its place is interpreted as a sign that there are no more packets and the middle portion of the transfer ends.

2. The *integrity* of the packet sequence number is checked. In other words, the receiver makes certain that the second and third fields are not corrupt. Typically, this is accomplished by complementing one of the two packet-sequence fields and XORing it with the other. A result of 0 means that neither of the fields is damaged. If not identical, the receiver sends a NAK to request retransmission and loops back to await retransmission of the same packet.

3. Next, the receiver makes certain that the sequence number is the one expected. In general, if the packet sequence number is incorrect, something dreadful is wrong. Since there is no method for the receiver to recover from a sequence error, a CAN is sent to abort the transmission and the transfer ends. There is a single exception to this behavior. If the packet sequence number is the *same as that of the previous packet*, the receiver assumes that the sender never got the ACK for that packet. The receiver simply ignores the redundant packet, sends another ACK to get the transmitter back in sync, then loops back to await the next packet.

4. Finally, the receiver calculates an arithmetic sum (modulo-256) of the DATA field *only*, and compares it to the checksum field of the packet. If the two agree, the receiver sends an ACK; if they do not agree, the receiver sends a NAK.

End Phase

If the receiver's transfer ends normally, it performs an orderly shutdown—closing files, freeing memory, and so forth. If no errors occur during shutdown (a disk I/O error, for example), an ACK is transmitted to acknowledge the sender's EOT, and the transfer is concluded.

XMODEM-CRC

The XMODEM protocol had not been in the public domain long before a version appeared that employed a 2-byte CRC instead of Christensen's single-byte arithmetic checksum.[7] The layout of the XMODEM-CRC packet shown in Figure 4-7 is identical to that of the original XMODEM packet except for the additional byte for the enlarged value.

XMODEM uses a non-reversed CRC algorithm with the CCITT divisor polynomial $X^{16} + X^{12} + X^5 + 1$. The remainder (CRC) generated is the same as the remainder from performing polynomial division on a message with sixteen 0 bits appended. The bit-order of the bytes is *not* reversed before feeding them to the CRC-generating function. The high-order byte is transmitted before the low-order byte.

---

[7]It is unclear who is responsible for this enhancement. Although Christensen himself seems to credit John Mahr, most versions contain a note that the CRC was designed by Paul Hansknecht of Bloomfield Hills, Michigan.

Figure 4-7 Layout of the XMODEM-CRC packet.

SOH	Packet* Sequence No.	1's Complement of Packet Sequence No.	DATA (128 bytes)	CRC** high byte	low byte

*First packet is 1
**CCITT polynomial

Start-Up under XMODEM CRC

Although the CRC packet is only slightly changed, the start-up protocol is considerably altered to maintain compatibility with earlier versions that do not support CRC versions of XMODEM. A flow chart of the XMODEM-CRC receiver is given in Figure 4-8. Besides the obvious differences of a larger packet and the CRC checkvalue, the receiver's start-up protocol is also altered. A receiver desiring to use XMODEM-CRC sends the letter 'C' as an initial synchronization byte instead of the NAK used by the checksum version of XMODEM. Do not confuse the sync byte with the acknowledgment—both checksum and CRC variants *always* send NAK for a negative acknowledgment.

No flow chart is given for the sender under XMODEM-CRC. The receiver has only to look for the 'C' at start-up instead of a NAK, to be prepared for the longer packet, and, of course, to perform the local CRC calculations on the packet's data.

CRC/Checksum Hybrids

Most public domain derivatives of MODEM7 incorporate both CRC and checksum versions of the protocol. Under the assumption that during start-up a checksum-only sender will not respond to the CRC sync character, the receiver alternates between sync characters—a 'C' for CRC and, after 10 seconds of no response, a NAK for checksum. The transfer takes place in the mode whose sync character elicits a packet from the sender. For reasons we will explore in Chapter 18, under certain conditions these hybrid programs can establish incorrect synchronization. When this occurs, the two parties attempt transfer under different checkvalue protocols—a doomed effort.

Timeouts

Timeouts are a very important part of any protocol, where their function is to prevent the program from getting hung up if an expected event does not occur. In fact, timeouts must be built into any section of the program that waits for input from the communications line. For example, the flow chart in Figure 4-8 shows a receiver timeout after the box "RECEIVE PACKET." This timeout guaranatees that a NAK is sent if an expected packet does not arrrive (or if only a partial packet arrives). Software usually maintains a count of timeouts, giving the user the opportunity to cancel a transfer that moves along haltingly.

Figure 4-8 Flow chart of a receiver under XMODEM-CRC.

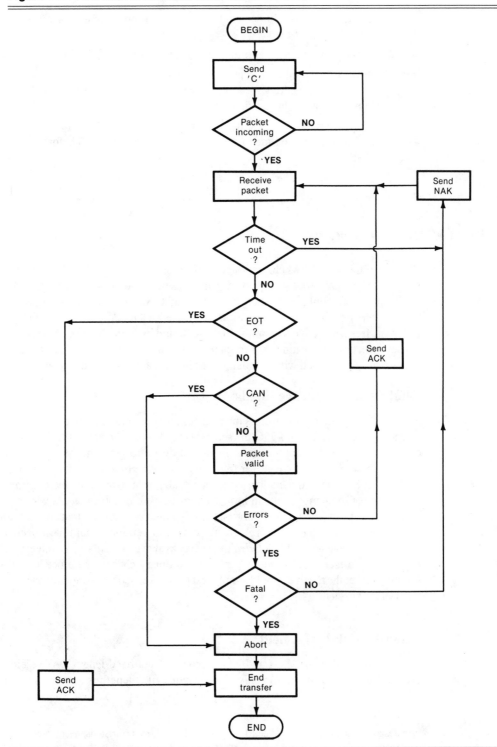

Here are the timeout rules for XMODEM as published by Christensen:[8]

1. The receiver has a 10-second timeout while waiting for a packet to arrive. A NAK is sent after each timeout.

2. While receiving a packet, the timeout interval for *each* character is 1 second.

3. In keeping with the concept of a receiver-driven protocol, the sender should not timeout when waiting for a synchronization (start-up) byte. (Most XMODEM implementations have a timeout here.)

4. Once the transfer begins, the sender should use a single 1-minute timeout. This gives the receiver ample time to perform any necessary disk I/O before sending its ACK, NAK, or CAN.

5. All timeouts (and errors) are retried at least ten times.

XMODEM Problems

Because of the XMODEM protocol's grass-roots origins in the public domain, there is a tendency to wax sentimental about it. In fact, as Christensen would doubtless agree, XMDODEM has all the earmarks of midnight basement hacking. Had Christensen been writing for public consumption, or if he were appointed to revise it today, the XMODEM protocol would doubtless be quite different. It is instructive to examine the shortcomings of the XMODEM protocol, not as an exercise in dead-horse-beating, but to gain insight into the problems that inevitably arise when a protocol is not designed with foresight or, as in this case, is pushed too far.

Dual Packet-Sequence Fields

The XMODEM protocol transmits the packet sequence number in two forms—the first is the actual packet number, modulo-256; the second is the 1s complement of the first. This redundancy is difficult to justify, but appears to stem from a desire to pinpoint the precise nature of packet-sequence errors. When the receiver finds an error in the first packet number, it must ascertain if the byte itself is bad or if a numbering error actually exists (for which there is no recovery). Comparing the packet number with an inverted copy of itself is not, in fact, a very robust method because, due to the bursty nature of errors, there is a high probability[9] that an error affecting the first byte will also affect the second. A greater degree of certainty could have been achieved with a single packet sequence field *included* in the checkvalue calculation. The integrity of the sequence number would then be checked as part of the ordinary checkvalue procedure; if no checkvalue error occurred, the receiver would simply test the packet-sequence field to make certain that it was the packet expected.

Fixed-Length DATA field

As discussed earlier, a file created by a protocol with a fixed-length DATA field will contain an exact image of the original file only if the original file's length is an even multiple of the DATA

---

[8]As described in an open letter dated 1/1/82, downloaded from Christensen's bulletin board in Chicago.

[9]At 1200 bps on the public telephone network, about one-fourth of all errors affect more than 8 bits.

field length. Otherwise, the new file will contain superfluous bytes. In general, the presence of useless bytes at the end of non-executable text files causes no problem—the system loads the file, extra bytes and all, into memory. However, on some systems, especially multi-tasking ones, executable files contain a block of additional data that contains detailed information used by the system to load the program into memory. In most cases, the system is able to calculate the size of an executable file based upon the information in this *load header*, which contains both the length of the executable portion of the file and the length of the header itself.

If the actual size of a file (as reported by its directory entry) differs from the size given in the header, the system can justifiably decline to load or execute it. One such case is the Commodore Amiga computer. The Amiga Public Forum on BIX (Byte Information Service), for example, shows many complaints from Amiga, who claim that programs transferred via the XMODEM users protocol will not run on their computers.[10] This problem, caused by applying XMODEM in an environment for which it was not designed, has produced a wealth of modified versions of XMODEM with names like "Extended XMODEM" and "Enhanced-XMODEM." In most cases, these modifications consist largely of somehow including the file's actual size in the protocol.

XMODEM Ambiguities

There are several ambiguities in the XMODEM protocol; that is, its behavior is not clear under some circumstances. Here are three:

1. Exactly how is a transfer terminated? In most programs, including those in Chapter 18, receiving a CAN where an ACK, NAK, SOH, or EOT is expected cancels the transfer. Yet Christensen himself (in the letter quoted earlier) declaims this practice, warning that "a single 'abort' character makes the transmission susceptible to false termination due to an <ack>, <nak>, or <soh> being corrupted into a <can> and canceling transmission."

2. Once all records have been sent and the last packet has been acknowledged, the sender transmits an EOT. The receiver acknowledges with an ACK. What is the receiver's negative response—a NAK or a CAN? Under what circumstances would the receiver not send an ACK? Is a disk I/O error on the final disk write grounds for not sending an ACK?

3. Is the sender expected to be ready to transmit *immediately* after receiving the start-up NAK? For example, should the transmitter perform preliminary disk I/O (file opening, reading, buffer filling, and so forth) before initiating start-up?

Multi-File XMODEM

The Christensen protocol is just that—a protocol. It knows nothing about other *layers*[11] of activity involved in the file-transfer process. In a simple modem linkage, for example, there are several layers that the file-transfer protocol knows nothing about:

1. The hardware layer, RS-232 interface

2. The method of tone-signaling or modulation employed by the modem

---

[10]For a sample, see "The Best of Bix," *BYTE Magazine*, April, 1986, p. 354.

[11]The concept of layers is embodied in the International Standards Organization's (ISO) reference model for *Open System Interconnect*, a topic for another book.

3. The sending and receiving systems' definition of a file

4. The storage media at either end of the transfer

The user, or more precisely, the system, is responsible for assigning a filename and making sure that the file is properly opened, read from or written to, and then closed at the end of the transfer. Although typing filenames does not require much effort, it quickly becomes boring when there are many files to transfer. It is not surprising, therefore, that most file-transfer protocols contain provisions for transferring more than one file at a session.

Designing a multi-file layer to a protocol requires no earth-shaking skill. Let's quickly concoct a multi-file version of XMODEM. For unknown reasons, Christensen chose to give the first packet the number 1 instead of 0. This is actually quite handy — we will commandeer packet 0 for use in multi-file transfers. How? When the receiver sees that the first packet is numbered 0, it knows not only that it is engaged in a multi-file transfer, but also that this *herald* (initialization) packet contains important information about the file — its name, its size, perhaps its contents, whether it is read/write, and so forth. Only the meaning of packet-sequence number and the DATA field of a herald packet differ from an ordinary packet; the functions of the other fields — SOH, 1s complement of the sequence number, and checkvalue — are unchanged. For flexibility and portability, the DATA field is pure ASCII — that is, all numerical data is expressed as ASCII numerals, not as binary values. One field in this contains the number of files in the transfer. Of course, we will leave several fields "reserved."[12]

Our imaginations could go on and on, but the point here is that if the XMODEM protocol itself is a bit myopic, there is a kind of primitive elegance to it. Each part seems to fit well with the overall design. With a little thought, a multi-file extension of the protocol can be designed that integrates well into the basic XMODEM way of doing things. Instead, the multi-file version of XMODEM is a cluttered, amateurish kludge with which Christensen is wise to disavow any connection. Because of its poor design and because it is completely incompatible with the orginal single-file version, it all but precludes further extension of the protocol.

Figure 4-9 shows the flow chart for the XMODEM multi-file protocol. The sender waits for the receiver to send a synchronizing NAK. Once the NAK is received, the sender transmits an ACK followed immediately by the first character of an 11-character filename. The filename must be in the MS-DOS (CP/M) format: 8 characters in the base name with an optional extension of 3 characters. Both name fields are right-padded with spaces (i.e., 20H) with no period delimiter. All filename characters must be in *upper case* and their high-order bits must be 0.

The receiver ACKs *each* character in the name. If an ACK does not arrive within the time-out period, the sender transmits a 75H (the letter 'K') and the process starts anew. After all 11 characters in the filename have been transmitted, the sender transmits a SUB (1AH) to signal the end of the filename. The receiver responds to this "eof" by sending a 1-byte arithmetic checksum that, oddly, includes the 1A byte itself. If the receiver's checksum does not agree with the sender's, the sender sends a 75H and the process recommences. If the checksums agree, the sender transmits an ACK and the ordinary XMODEM protocol takes over.

To signal that there are no more files in the multi-file transfer, the sender transmits an EOT in place of the first filename character.

---

[12]A popular extension of XMODEM, named YMODEM, employs a herald packet much like the one described here.

Figure 4-9 Flow chart for XMODEM multi-file protocol.

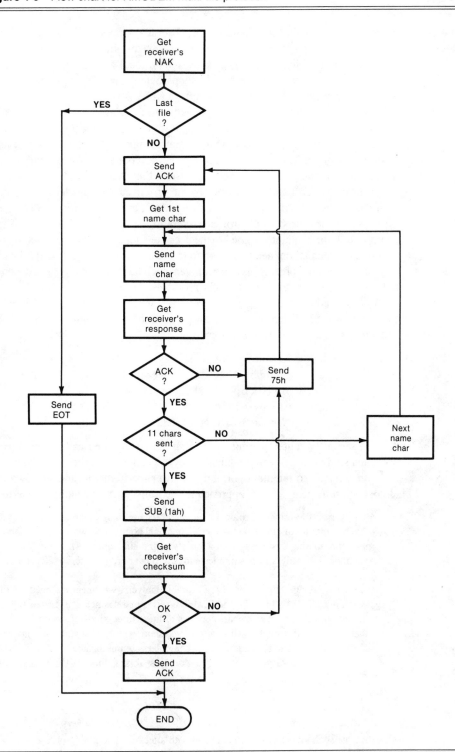

Kermit

Although this book focuses on the subject of serial communications as found on microcomputers, we will now take a brief look at a protocol that makes almost no assumptions about the nature of the computer on which it runs. This study of a protocol with a more generalized design is offered as an intellectual antidote to the hopelessly parochial XMODEM protocol, whose structure is inextricably wedded to the narrow system from which it sprang.

Even if XMODEM had been designed with the utmost generality it would still have been a distinctly *microcomputer* protocol. That is, it would have made the one assumption that characterizes software written for microcomputers: that a single program has absolute and undeniable control over all of the system's resources. On larger computers (or on multi-user or multi-tasking micros) this assumption does not hold true. For example, one cannot predict whether the "asynchronous I/O channel" provided by the system can be adjusted to the 8-bit, no parity format required for the transmission of binary files. And, as we have repeatedly noted, most operating systems somehow process control characters in the serial input stream. To make matters more complicated, the channel assigned to the user's terminal may have one set of characteristics while an auxiliary channel opened under program control may have quite different characteristics. The goal of the Kermit[13] protocol is to circumvent such hardware and system dependencies altogether, to become the Espranto of file-transfer protocols.

Kermit comes from Columbia University where it was written by Frank Da Cruz and Bill Catchings in 1981. The protocol is in the public domain for non-commercial use. Both a technical and a user's manual are available from:

> Kermit Distribution
> Columbia University Center for Computing Activities
> 7th Floor, Watson Laboratory
> 612 West 115th Street
> New York City, NY 10025

Anyone seriously contemplating composing the Great American Protocol would do well to acquire and study these Kermit manuals—they are textbook studies in software design.

In an effort to maintain portability between systems, no matter how dissimilar, Kermit is almost *painfully* general in its approach to file transfer. As the authors describe it,

> The Kermit file-transfer protocol is intended for use in an environment where there may be a diverse mixture of computers—micros, personal computers, workstations, laboratory computers, timesharing systems—from a variety of manufacturers. All these systems need have in common is the ability to communicate in ASCII over ordinary serial telecommunications lines.
>
> Kermit was originally designed at Columbia University to meet the need for file transfer between our DECSYSTEM-20 and IBM 370-series mainframes and various microcomputers. It turned out that the diverse characteristics of these three kinds of systems resulted in a design that was general enough to fit almost any system. The IBM mainframe, in particular, strains most common assumptions about how computers communicate.
>
> —*Kermit Protocol Manual*, New York: Columbia University, April, 1984, p. 3.

---

[13]Despite the sophomoric efforts to come up with a technical-sounding phrase from which to backform an acronym, Kermit remains just the name of the famous frog.

The Kermit Protocol

Although Kermit is much too complex (not to say complicated) to treat exhaustively here, we can at least look at its grand design and how it pursues its lofty goal of portability.

The "basic" Kermit is a send-and-wait ARQ packet protocol: the sender transmits a packet, then awaits the receiver's acknowledgment of the packet. The receiver can either request the next packet (ACK) or retransmission of the previous packet (NAK). At this level, Kermit is fundamentally quite similar to the XMODEM protocol. There are several important areas of difference, however:

1. Kermit oversees an entire file-transfer *session* that may include any number of files. As we discussed earlier, XMODEM is a single-file transfer onto which is kludged an ugly and poorly designed mechanism for transferring multiple files.

2. Kermit makes only minimal assumptions about the serial I/O channel over which the transfer occurs; namely that the channel is capable of sending and receiving all *printable* ASCII characters (i.e., characters in the range 20H − 7E). It also requires that the system be able to send and receive an SOH control character (see footnote on page 105).

3. Packets may be of variable length.

4. Several types of packets are defined.

5. The receiver's responses must consist of *entire packets*, although these packets may be "empty." (In XMODEM, responses are single characters.) The presence of SEQ fields in the ACK and NAK packets makes possible a continuous ARQ version of Kermit.

6. The sender and receiver negotiate important operating parameters such as device padding, metacharacters, and so forth. This negotiation takes place through an exchange of herald packets at the beginning of the session.

7. The name of the file is included in the protocol.

8. The herald packets make the protocol *extendible*. That is, new features and capabilities can be added without affecting the behavior of earlier versions.

Figure 4-10 shows a rough block diagram (not a complete flow chart) for transfer under the Kermit protocol. Although not depicted, the receiver's response (ACK and NAK packets) must be fetched after every transmission. Start-up takes place as in XMODEM—by the receiver sending repeated NAK (packets) until the transmitter responds by sending a herald packet, which in Kermit is called a *send-initiate* (or simply *send-init*) packet. The herald packet contains the sender's preferred settings for certain important communications parameters. As shown in the chart, the receiver makes its own preference (or agreement) known by including them in its ACK packet. Next, the name of the file is transmitted in a special File Header packet; when the receiver sends its ACK, it may optionally include in the packet the name under which it is storing the file.

The transfer proceeds under the ARQ rules until the entire file is transferred. The sender then transmits a special end-of-file packet. If there are more files to transmit, it sends the file header packet for the next file. When all files have been sent, the sender transmits an end-of-transmission packet to signal the end of the session.

As you can see, there is nothing earth-shaking about the design of Kermit's outer layer. The main differences lie in the *details* of implementation. Its most interesting characteristic stems from its minimalistic view of the transmission line. Because it expects control characters and possibly even non-ASCII characters to be somehow transformed by the transmission medium, Kermit converts such high-risk characters to a safer form.

Figure 4-10 A block diagram of a Kermit transmission.

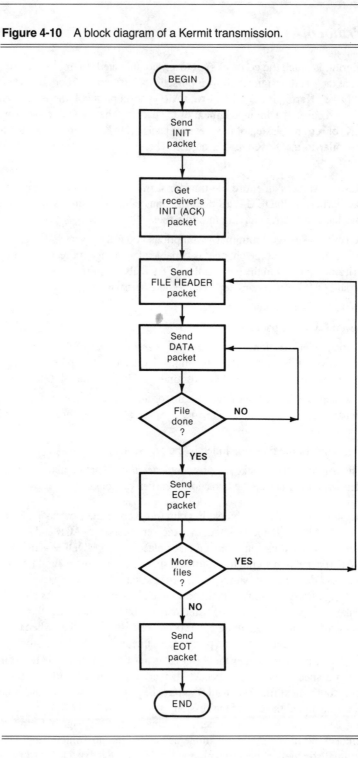

Control Character Encoding in the Kermit Packet

The Kermit packet, shown in Figure 4-11, comprises six fields. The contents of the DATA field, which may be of variable length, vary with the packet type; in a "data" packet, this field contains a portion of the contents of the file being transferred. The Kermit manual refers to the other, non-DATA fields as "control fields." This term is dangerous because of the erroneous semantical implication that these fields contain ASCII control characters. To avoid this confusion, which would prove deadly in the discussion that follows, we will continue to use the term "service field" to describe Kermit's non-DATA fields.

Figure 4-11   The Kermit packet.

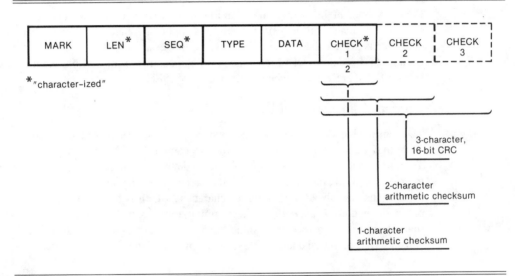

Each service field consists *entirely* of ASCII characters ($0-128$) and, with the exception of the MARK field, *printable* ASCII characters in the range 20H—7E (i.e., SP to ~). Although the DATA field may contain non-ASCII (i.e., 80H—FF) characters, all ASCII characters must be printable. Since the Kermit protocol so heavily relies upon printable ASCII, we must discuss the manner in which the information in the fields is encoded before we discuss the meaning of the fields themselves.

We have already noted how operating systems inevitably process, translate, or swallow control characters. Since the console is usually the most heavily processed and filtered I/O channel in any system, Kermit's stated worst-case design goal is to effect file transfers from an ordinary user's terminal. But there is a problem: if control characters in the I/O channel are liable to be abused by the system, how can we protect the packet? Suppose, for example, that Kermit packet were to arrive with an SEQ (packet-sequence number) of 0A; what would prevent the system from treating it as a Line Feed? (A UNIX console driver would probably expand it to a CRLF *pair*.) The solution is to convert high-risk characters to printable characters before transmission.

Control Characters in Service Fields

The system does not know that the service fields contain numerical information. From its point of view, a byte in the range ($0-20$H, and 7F) is a control character and therefore fair game for processing. The solution, for which we will use the tongue-in-cheek name *character-ization*, is quite simple: control characters are "promoted" to printable form before transmission with the *char* function:

$$\text{char}(x) = x + 20H$$

and transformed back again after reception with the `unchar` function (*decharacter-ization*):

$$\text{unchar}(x) = x - 20H$$

In this way, a byte of numerical data in the packet becomes printable by elevating it two sticks in the ASCII table. An ETX (3) byte becomes '#', an LF (0AH) becomes '*', and so on. Fields encoded in this way are noted in Figure 4-11 with an asterisk.

Unfortunately, if the `char` function is applied to characters greater than 5F, the resulting character is greater than FF and therefore no longer an ASCII character. The actual limit is 5E because 5F becomes a DEL, itself a control character. For this reason, the numerical data in the service fields in Kermit can be no larger than 94 (5EH).

Control Characters in DATA Fields

The control characters problem clearly exists in a more serious form in the DATA field. Because a file may legitimately contain *any* byte, we cannot limit the DATA field in the packet to 5E. Therefore control characters cannot be encoded merely by promoting them to printing status with the `char` and `unchar` functions. Instead, a printable character (nanogram, '#', by default) is actually inserted ahead of the control character, which is then XORed with 40H.[14] This technique, dubbed *prefix encoding* in the Kermit manual, is analogous to C's use of the reverse slant (backslash) to impart special meaning to certain characters within a string. As in C, a literal occurrence of a prefix character is "escaped" by a duplicate of itself. Thus, "#1" is encoded as "##1."

As an example of Kermit's prefix encoding of control characters, let's look at two lines created in WordStar's non-document format:

Mary had
a <u>little</u>
lamb.

literally contains

---

[14]Kermit defines the function `ctl( )` for use *only* where control characters are expected:

$$\text{ctl}(x) = x \text{ XOR } 40H$$

XORing with 40H is preferable to adding 40H because the former preserves the high bit. As an added bonus, no `unctl` function is required because the XOR makes the function self-inverting:

$$\text{ctl}(\text{ctl}(x)) = x$$

The manual refers to successive calls of `ctl( )` as *controlification*.

M a r y ■ h a d   a ■
4D 61 72 79 20 68 61 64 0A 0D 61 20 13

l i t t l e   l a m b .
6C 69 74 74 6C 65 13 0A 0D 6C 61 6D 62 2E 0D 0A

Note that WordStar uses DC3 (13H) bytes to begin and end the underlining of the word ''little'' and the CRLF pairs at the ends of both lines. Kermit would transmit the line like this:

M a r y ■ h a d # M # J a ■ # S
4D 61 72 79 20 68 61 64 23 4D 23 4A 61 20 23 53

l i t t l e # S # M # J l a m b . # M # J
6C 69 74 74 6C 65 23 53 23 4D 23 4A 6C 61 6D 62 2E 23 4D 23 4A

This elevates control characters to ASCII rows four and five and prefixes them with nanograms.

High-Order Bit Encoding in Kermit's DATA Field

In many systems, the data format of the serial communications line is a system-wide constant. In such installations, a program often has no way to control the data format. If the system happens to be a 7-bit parity system, the transfer of 8-bit binary files is obviously impossible without some form of encoding.

A byte with a TRUE high-order bit is subjected to a similar prefix encoding as control characters; namely, a printable character (a '&' is ''recommended'') is inserted and the byte is ANDed with 7F to make it printable. Let's look at the same file created in WordStar *document* mode where the high-order bits denote a word or character that is marked for line reformatting. A file containing the line

Mary had
a <u>little</u>
lamb.

literally contains

M a r   h a
4D 61 72 F9 A0 68 61 E4 8D 0A E1 A0 13

l i t t l e   l a m   .
6C 69 74 74 6C 65 13 8D 0A 6C 61 6D E2 2E 0D 0A

in which bytes with TRUE high-order bits are those greater than 7F. Kermit transmits this file like this:

M a r & y & ■ h a & d & # M # J & a & ■
4D 61 72 26 79 26 20 68 61 26 64 26 23 4D 23 4A 26 61 26 20

 # P l i t t l e & # M # J l a m & b . # M # J
 23 50 6C 69 74 74 6C 65 26 23 4D 23 4A 6C 61 6D 26 62 2E 23 4D 23 4A

Notice that the "soft" Carriage Return (as 8D is called in WordStar) must be subjected both to control character prefixing *and* high-order bit prefixing. A single 8D byte is thus transmitted as three ASCII characters: **&#M**.

Repeat-Count Encoding in Kermit's DATA Field

The expanding of control characters and bytes with high-order bits can result in a huge increase in overhead. This penalty is worst in a binary file, where the overhead is more than 75 percent.[15] To reduce this high overhead on binary files and, to some degree on text files as well, Kermit provides a simple compression scheme called *repeat-count prefixing*. A designated character (the '~' is "recommended") signals the beginning of a repeat-count sequence. Next comes a "character-ized" numerical count argument itself, followed immediately by the character to repeat.

For example, the sequence below repeats the letter 'X' eleven times.

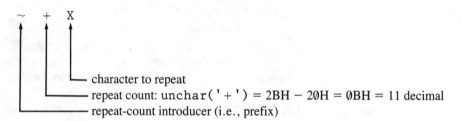

character to repeat
repeat count: `unchar('+')` = 2BH − 20H = 0BH = 11 decimal
repeat-count introducer (i.e., prefix)

Because of the limitations on the range of the `char` functions, repeat counts cannot exceed 94. When repeat-count, control-character, and high-order prefixing appear in a single expansion expression, the repeat count has the highest precedence followed by the 8-bit prefix, the control-character prefix, and the data character itself. We will not pursue the topic of precedence further since copious illustrations of this hierarchy are given in the Kermit Protocol Manual.[16]

Fields in the Kermit Packet

Now that we understand the various ways in which Kermit transforms the meanings of characters, let's quickly examine the meanings of the fields in the packet shown in Figure 4-11.

---

[15]Assuming that all 256 possible bit combinations are distributed evenly in a file,

33 × 2 =	66	(0−20H, and 7F) control characters expand to 2 bytes.
95 × 2 =	190	(A0−FE) high-bit bytes expand to 2 bytes.
33 × 3 =	99	(80H−9F, and FF) require both kinds and expand to 3 bytes.
95 × 1 =	95	(20H−7E) remain as 1 byte.
2 × 2 =	4	Escapes for prefix characters.
	454	

When 256 bytes expand to 454 the result is an overhead of 198 bytes, or 77 percent.

[16]The repeat count illustration on page 26 of the Fifth Edition (3 April, 1984) of this manual incorrectly shows `unchar('(')` to be 6. It is 8.

MARK　This is the start-of-packet signature byte, SOH. This is the only *canonical* control character permitted in the packet; that is, its value is a 1. Why is a control character permitted in this field? Since they do not appear anywhere else in the packet, a bona fide control character makes a good packet-signature byte. The authors of Kermit chose the SOH byte because of their observation that SOH, unlike other control characters, passes through most operating systems unchanged.[17]

LEN　This is the number of bytes in the packet following this field. In other words, the total packet length minus two. This field is character-ized, which limits total packet length to 96.

SEQ　This field contains the character-ized packet sequence number, modulo-64. Sequence numbering begins with the first packet transmitted, the 'S' packet. Its starting value is 0 and it resets to 0 after 63.

TYPE　This single, *literal* (i.e., unencoded) ASCII character identifies the type[18] of the packet as follows:

'D'　Data

'Y'　Acknowledge (ACK)

'N'　Negative acknowledge (NAK)

'S'　Send initiate (exchange parameters)

'B'　Break transmission (EOT)

'F'　File Header

'Z'　End of file (EOF)

'E'　Error

'T'　Reserved

'X'　Display text on screen

'A'　Attribute

We will discuss some of these in more detail shortly.

DATA　The content of this field varies with the packet type. In a 'D' (data) packet, it contains data from the file being transmitted, but in an 'F' (file header) packet it contains the name of the file. In some packet types, it contains nothing.

Whatever the type, all characters must be prefix encoded. Prefix encoding of high-order bits and repeat-count encoding are optional.

CHECK　This is the packet checkvalue and includes the LEN and SEQ fields, but not the MARK. The default checkvalue is a single-character arithmetic checksum, but a 2-byte arithmetic checksum or a 3-byte, 16-bit CRC are optional. To compensate for the lost accuracy incurred by encoding with char( ), bits 6 and 7 are extracted and added back to the low-order 6 bits before encoding. This odd-looking technique

---

[17]Should one encounter a system that does not pass SOHs, the authors state: ''It is possible to redefine the start-of-packet byte to be any other control character.'' Unfortunately, they do not explain the mechanism for redefinition.

[18]Kermit also defines a *server* mode in which it acts as an unattended host. This feature, which will not be discussed further, uses 'C' and 'G' packets to pass commands and responses between the local and remote systems.

assures that all 8 bits participate in checkvalue calculation. If x is the arithmetic sum of the packet, then

$$check = char((x + ((x \text{ AND } C0)/40H)) \text{ AND } 3F)$$

Types of Kermit Packets

Before we look at the interesting way various packets are used, let's straighten out yet another linguistic ambiguity. The Kermit Protocol Manual speaks of empty packets and blank packets. These are never satisfactorily defined. An *empty packet* is defined as a packet whose LEN indicates that there are no characters in the DATA field. An empty single-byte checksum packet, for example, contains a LEN argument of 3, or, in its character-ized format, '#'. When the Kermit manual uses the term "blank" it is referring to a *non-empty* packet whose DATA field contains one or more ASCII SP characters.[19]

Some types of packets always contain information in their DATA fields. A 'D' packet, for example, always contains data from the file being transmitted (otherwise, it would be a 'Z' (EOF) packet). Conversely, some packets *always* have an empty DATA field (the 'Z', for example). Still others may have an empty DATA field only some of the time. The ACK packet, for example, is normally empty, except when it is responding to an 'S' (Send-init) or 'F' (File Header) packet.

With these preliminary details out of the way we will now look at some of the packet types, their contents, and uses.

The 'S' (Send-init) Packet

This is the most interesting of all the packets. Its function is to inform the receiver of the sender's preferences with regard to several important communications parameters. The SEQ number of the 'S' packet is 0. Its DATA field is structured as shown in Figure 4-12. Since sender and receiver exchange this information, personal pronouns are used to help distinguish sides.

Figure 4-12 The DATA field of an 'S' (Send-initiate) packet.

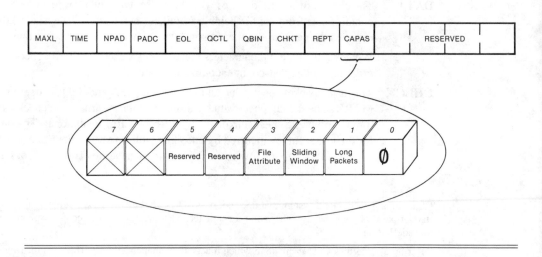

---

[19]"Blank" and space are often used interchangeably. See the warning in Chapter 1, "The Specials."

MAXL The maximum packet size I can receive (character-ized). This enables the two sides to allow for small buffers, poor-quality transmission lines, etc. Default: none.

TIME The maximum number of seconds you should wait for a packet before timing out (character-ized). This adjusts for habitually slow systems or networks. Default: none.

NPAD The number of padding characters you should send before each packet. This gives half-duplex systems time to switch from receive to transmit mode or vice versa (character-ized). Default: 0, no padding.

PADC The identity of the padding character, usually a NUL or a DEL (controlified). Default: NUL. (This field is ignored if NPAD is 0.)

EOL The character I need to terminate a packet. Line-oriented systems do not fetch the packet from their buffers unless the packet is followed by the system's line terminator. (Most systems that require a terminator accept a CR.) This character is *not* part of the packet (does not figure in the LEN or CHECK fields), but rather is appended to the packet at transmission. Unfortunately, there is no mechanism to state that no terminator is needed, as is the case on single-user microcomputers. This field is character-ized, not control-ified. Default: CR.

QCTL The prefix character I will use in control-character encoding (literal). Default: '#'.

The following fields are optional; that is, they do not have to be present on a "minimum" Kermit.

QBIN The prefix character I will use in high-bit encoding (literal). Only characters in the range 21H−3F or 60H−7F are permitted. Instead of specifying a character, a 'Y' or an 'N' can be used to indicate willingness to participate in high-bit prefixing. Default: SP—don't do high-bit prefixing.

CHKT The type of checkvalue to use: '1' for single-byte arithmetic, '2' for 2-byte arithmetic, and '3' for CRC.[20] Default: '1', single-character arithmetic.

REPT The prefix character I will use in repeat-count encoding (literal). Only characters in the range 21H−3F or 60H−7E are permitted. An SP here indicates that no repeat-count encoding is to be done.

CAPA This is the "Advanced Capability" field—a bit mask of unspecified length organized as a linked list of bytes (character-ized). Linkage between bytes is achieved by placing a 1 in bit 0 to indicate that another bit-mask byte follows; a 0 in bit 0 therefore indicates the end of the linkage chain.

Only the first 6 bits are significant in each byte, so only 5 Capabilites can be mapped to each byte. Bits are allocated from MSB to LSB, starting at bit 5. Support for a Capability is indicated by a 1 in its assigned bit.

As of mid-1986, bits 5 and 4 were reserved. Bit 3 marks support for Attribute packets. Bit 2 indicates the ability to use a continuous ARQ ("sliding window" in Kermitese) protocol instead of the usual send-and-wait ARQ. Bit 1 supports packets greater than 94 bytes in length.

---

[20]The only thing certain about the CRC checkvalue specification is the use of the CCITT polynomial. In fact, the checkvalue may not be a CRC at all, but polynomial division: "The 16-bit CRC is the remainder after dividing the data bit string by the CCITT polynomial." The authors then make the oblique observation that the Kermit CRC agrees with "common hardware implementations" such as the CRC instruction on the VAX minicomputer; this seems to imply that Kermit's is a reverse CRC model. Because of the lack of a coherent written specification, it is not possible to design a CRC algorithm for Kermit; instead, programmers are forced to rely upon inscrutable examples provided by the Kermit support group.

Because of the linkage among its bytes, the CAPAS field can expand to occupy the entire 94-character DATA field. The ability to add new Capabilities to the end of the CAPAS field enables each site to customize its own Kermit without fear of colliding with pre-existing Capabilities.

The 'Y' (ACK) Packet

When the receiver wishes to accept a packet, it sends a 'Y' (for "yes") packet. This must be a fully constructed packet, complete with SEQ, LEN, and CHECK fields. Although the DATA field of a 'Y' packet is usually empty, it can contain the receiver's response to the sender's packet. The 'Y' packet in response to an 'S' (Send-init) packet, for example, contains the receiver's initial configuration data in the same format as the DATA field of an 'S' packet.

The 'F' (File Header) Packet

This contains the name of the file being transmitted. To avoid clashes with metacharacters on the destination system, the name should be limited to digits and upper-case alphabetical characters (30−39H, 41H−5A). A single period (2E) is also permitted. Although there are no restrictions on length, the name should contain no device or system information such as drive identifier or path.

When the receiver ACKs with a 'Y' packet, its DATA field may optionally contain the file-name under which the file is stored on the destination system.

The 'N' (NAK) Packet

When the receiver wishes to reject a packet, it sends an 'N' (for "no") packet. This must be a fully constructed packet, complete with SEQ, LEN, and CHECK fields. Its DATA field packet is ordinarily empty.

The 'D' (Data) Packet

The DATA field of this packet contains data from the file being transmitted. Like all DATA fields, control characters must be prefix encoded. If both sides agree in their initial exchange of parameters, this field may also contain high-order bit and repeat-count prefixing.

The 'Z' (EOF) and 'B' (EOT) Packets

The transmitter sends a 'Z' packet when each file has been entirely transmitted. The transmitter sends a 'B' (for "break") packet when all files have been transmitted. In both cases, the receiver responds with a 'Y' (ACK) packet.

The 'E' (Error) Packet

Both sender and receiver send error packets when either encounters a *fatal* error. There is currently no way to send informational or warning messages.

The 'A' (Attribute) Packet

The ability to receive an 'A' packet is one of only three "advanced capabilities" currrently defined in the CAPAS field of the Send-init packet. This is the medium for passing auxiliary, usually system-dependent information about the file being transmitted. These "attributes" include file size (in Kbytes), contents (text, binary, image, etc.), date, time, path, security and access information (password, protection level, etc.), computer and operating system of origin, and type of encoding (ASCII, EBCDIC, hexadecimal, etc.).

A Sample Kermit Session

After what must seem an eternity of explanation, let's now snoop on the communications line during a Kermit transfer session, shown on page 110. The line numbers in the left column are for reference only and are *not* part of the conversation. To make the contents of the transfer totally unambiguous, the sample uses the ASCII symbol ⌐ for SOH and ▮ for SP. A brief description of the packet traffic is at the right, and a discussion of the interesting and important points follows.

1. Send-init   The first packet in the sample Kermit session above contains the sender's settings for the parameters given in Figure 4-12. Let's analyze this packet completely.

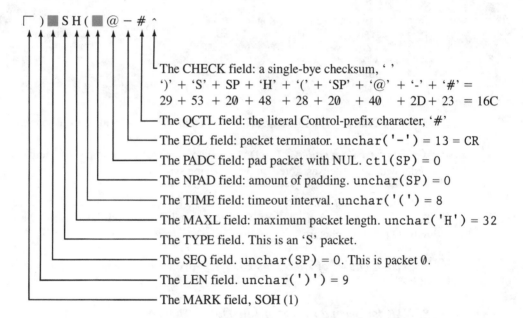

The CHECK field: a single-bye checksum, ' '
')' + 'S' + SP + 'H' + '(' + 'SP' + '@' + '-' + '#' =
29 + 53 + 20 + 48 + 28 + 20 + 40 + 2D + 23 = 16C

The QCTL field: the literal Control-prefix character, '#'

The EOL field: packet terminator. unchar('-') = 13 = CR

The PADC field: pad packet with NUL. ctl(SP) = 0

The NPAD field: amount of padding. unchar(SP) = 0

The TIME field: timeout interval. unchar('(') = 8

The MAXL field: maximum packet length. unchar('H') = 32

The TYPE field. This is an 'S' packet.

The SEQ field. unchar(SP) = 0. This is packet 0.

The LEN field. unchar(')') = 9

The MARK field, SOH (1)

The checksum is calculated according to the formula given on page 106:

$$16C + (16C/C0) = 16C + 2 = 16E$$
$$16E \text{ AND } 3F = 3E$$
$$char(3E) = 5E$$
$$5E = \text{'}\hat{}\text{'}a$$

2. ACK (with Receiver's Parameters)   The receiver responds with a 'Y' packet, whose parameters agree with the sender. Notice that neither high-bit prefixing nor repeat-count prefixing is in effect. The SEQ field contains the sequence number of the packet being ACKed— unchar(SP) = 0.

109

A Kermit file transfer[21]

1	⌐)▦SH(▦@−# ^	Send-init
2	⌐)▦YH(▦@−#%	ACK (with receiver's parameters)
3	⌐ + !FMOON.DOC2	File header
4	⌐ #!Y?	ACK for file header
5	⌐ E"D▦No▦celestial▦body▦has▦required▦J	First packet of file data
6	⌐ #"Y@	ACK of first packet
7	⌐ E#Das▦m%%%uch▦labor▦for▦the▦study▦of▦its#	Second packet has errors
8	⌐ ##N8	NAK for second packet
9	⌐ E#Das▦much▦labor▦for▦the▦study▦of▦its#	Retransmission of second packet
10	⌐ ##YA	ACK of second packet
11	⌐ E$D#M#Jmotion▦as▦the▦moon. ▦Since▦ClaA	Third packet of file data
12	⌐ #$YB	ACK of third packet
	⋮	
13	⌐ D"Dout▦300▦terms▦are▦sufficient.#M#JU	Last packet in file
14	⌐ #"Y@	ACK of third packet
15	⌐ ##ZB	EOF packet
16	⌐ ##YA	ACK of EOF packet
17	⌐ #$B +	EOT packet
18	⌐ #$YB	ACK of EOT packet

3. File Header   The filename is transmitted in the DATA field of an 'F' packet.

4. ACK for File Header   The DATA field of this packet is empty, but could contain the name under which the file was stored on the receiving system.

5. First Packet of File Data   Notice that the first packet of file data has the sequence number 2. In accordance with the MAXL field negotiated in the Send-init packets, the DATA contains only 32 (20H) characters.

7. Second Packet of Data Has Errors   An error occurred: the DATA field contains a burst of '%'.

8. NAK for Second Packet of File Data   The receiver discovers the error when the checksums don't match and sends an 'N' (NAK) packet to request retransmission.

9. Retransmission of Second Data Packet   Sender retransmits second of 'D' packets (SEQ '#').

10. ACK of Second Packet   The checksum of the retransmitted packet is valid, so receiver sends a 'Y' (ACK) packet.

15. EOF Packet   After the entire file is transmitted, sender transmits a 'Z' (EOF) packet.

17. EOT Packet   After receiver ACKs the 'Z' packet, the sender transmits a 'B' (EOT) packet to tell the receiver that the session is over.

---

[21]Source: Da Cruz and Catchings, "Kermit: A File-Transfer Protocol for Universities," *BYTE* (July, 1984), p. 400.

18. ACK of EOT Packet   Receiver's ACK of the 'B' packet ends the session.

Terminating a Transfer

As we have seen, the sender manages the session and is responsible for sending 'Z' (EOF) and 'B' (EOT) packets. To terminate the current file prematurely, the sender transmits a 'Z' packet as usual, but puts a 'D' (for "discard") in the data field. This instructs the receiver not to save the file. The receiver, too, may prematurely terminate the current file or the entire session by placing an 'X' or a 'Z', respectively, in the data field of a 'Y' (ACK) packet.

Recent Kermit Extensions

Kermit is a masterly combination of imaginative conception, generalized thinking, and realistic observation. Only on the most refractory system would a Kermit implementation fail to succeed. But this portability is not without its cost. With all its encoding vestments in action, Kermit is tortoise-like slow in comparison to the lapine XMODEM protocol. Because of its inefficiency, Kermit has always been a protocol of last resort, called upon when nothing else will do.

Two new extensions to the Kermit protocol, however, promise to increase Kermit's efficiency dramatically. By relaxing many of the pessimistic assumptions about the serial I/O channel, these Capabilities, shown in the inset in Figure 4-12, seem aimed directly at microcomputer users. Because these extensions appeared too late for thorough discussion in this book (these very paragraphs are 11th-hour additions to this book), we can only briefly examine them.

Continuous ARQ

As was mentioned earlier, the basic Kermit protocol is a send-and-wait ARQ protocol in which the sender pauses after every packet to await the receiver's acknowledgment. Such protocols have their roots in half-duplex communications, where sending and receiving are not simultaneously possible. Kermit's "sliding window" protocol extension, on the other hand, assumes a full-duplex communications line in which a packet acknowledgment may arrive at any time, even during the transmission of another packet.

In the sliding window extension, instead of transmitting a single packet, the sender transmits a *group* of packets, called, for some reason, a "window." The window is illustrated in Figure 4-13. As soon as the receiver acknowledges the first packet in the group (packet 'X'), the window advances (slides) and the next packet (packet X + 8) is sent. The number of packets in the window is declared the first byte following the CAPAS field of the 'S' (Send-init) packets. The default window size is 8.

Within the current window, packet numbers may be acknowledged in any order. Assuming a group of 2−9, if the sender transmits packets 2−9, the receiver may ACK packets 2−6, NAK packet 7, and ACK packets 8−9. As ACKs for the first five packets arrive, the sender immediately transmits five new packets, 10−14, then retransmits packet 7. The only rule is that the sender may not advance the window beyond an outstanding ACK. If, for example, the ACKs for packets 8−9 and 10−14 arrive before the ACK for the retransmitted packet 7, the sender cannot advance the window until the ACK for packet 7 arrives. As soon as the ACK for packet 7 arrives, however, eight new packets are sent.

The sliding window extension to the protocol is likely to prove most advantageous when communicating over networks such as Telenet or Tymnet. On such networks (which employ a packet protocol of their own), delays between transmission and reception can amount to tens of seconds. During these delays, Kermit's stop-and-wait ARQ protocol would have to sit idle awaiting the acknowledgment of each packet. Under Kermit's continuous ARQ, however, the sender can transmit up to thirty-one packets during idle periods before pausing for an ACK.

Figure 4-13 Kermit's sliding window before and after receiving the ACK on packet 'X'.

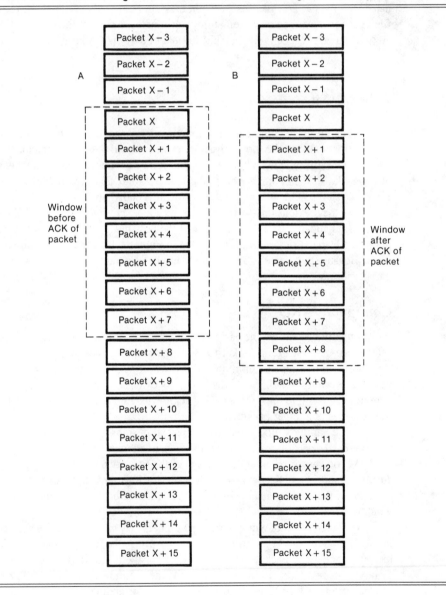

Long Packets

Since the number of bytes required for service fields in the Kermit protocol is independent of the length of its DATA field, the overall efficiency of the protocol is greatly improved by increasing the maximum number of bytes in a packet. As shown in Figure 4-14, 2 bytes instead of 1 are allocated to the LEN field. To make this extension easier to patch into an already-existing Kermit, the original LEN field is left blank. For the same reason, the 2-byte LEN field together with a new field, HCHECK, are squeezed between the TYPE and DATA fields. To insure integrity of the enlarged header, the HCHECK ("header check") field contains a Kermit-style, single-byte check-value of the LEN, SEQ, TYPE, LENX1, AND LENX2 fields.

The 2-byte maximum length of the extended data field is declared in the second and third byte following the CAPAS field of the 'S' (Send-init) packets. The 'S' packets themselves are still transferred with the basic Kermit 94-character maximum DATA fields; extended packets commence at the first 'D' packet. The maximum packet length is increased from 94 to 9024.[22]

Figure 4-14 Extension of Kermit's packet length.

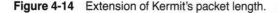
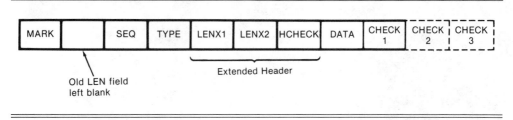

Which To Use

If not used carefully, these two extensions may turn out to be a plenitude of riches. Although both may be used simultaneously, they may work at cross-purposes. In general, the sliding window extension greatly increases Kermit's performance on full-duplex systems where many errors or network delays are expected. The long packet extension, on the other hand, works best on half-duplex lines or when the sender and receiver are directly connected through an essentially noise-less and wait-less cable. Because of the increased time to retransmit ACKed packets, the performance of Kermit under the long packet extension is seriously affected by errors.

Conclusion

Although we will not create a version of Kermit in the programming section of this book, the Kermit Protocol Manual gives the C source code listing for a "minimum" Kermit. The Kermit User's Guide (Sixth Edition, March, 1985) contains implementation and usage information for many systems, including CP/M, CP/M-86, AppleDOS, and PC DOS micros.

---

[22]A further extension is proposed to extend packet length to 857,374!

5

Modems and Modem Control

This chapter explores the fascinating topic of how computer data is transferred across ordinary telephone lines. We will examine the modem—the device that performs this technical wizardry. In the first section, we will look at some of the more technical aspects of exactly how the modem effects communications. Having arrived at a basic understanding of the principles involved, the second part of this chapter will discuss how computers and related peripherals interact with modems to control their behavior. Along the way, we'll look at some of the all-too-practical problems that are likely to crop up when writing programs to control modems.

The Modem

Since the first telegraph message was transmitted by Morse, telecommunications has been limited by the number of "communications lines" (wires) in existence. Due to the expense of creating and maintaining telegraph lines, even the ubiquitous telegraph found its way into only a fraction of the world's communities, and the teleprinter even fewer. Because these machines required special skills to operate, they could never be mass-marketed directly to the consumer. Consequently, the costs of these technologies were born largely by service businesses (such as Western Union), but government at all levels provided assistance in the form of land grants, trade monopolies, and generously fixed rates.

The telephone changed this picture drastically. Here was an instrument that required no special technical skill to operate, and, compared to a teleprinter, at least, was compact and physically unobtrusive. The telephone was a milestone because it was the first telecommunications product sold directly to a mass public. Driven by the consumer demand, it took only a few years for the number of telephones to exceed the combined number of telegraphs and teleprinters. In only a few more years, such a web of telephone wires was spun around the globe that today scarcely a community exists without telephone service.

While the importance of the telephone's proliferation as a cultural asset cannot be overstated, it has another, less obvious significance. As handy as the telephone is, it does not replace printed communications. Indeed, the telephone so stimulated economic growth that the need for a telecommunications print medium was more pressing than ever. Almost paradoxically, then, telephony resuscitated a moribund teleprinter industry, not only by increasing the demand for it, but also by providing the physical means to meet the demand. Put yourself in the place of a teleprinter mogul who, inundated with new demand for his product, contemplates the expense of erecting countless thousands of miles of new wires. Why invest in more wires and poles for teleprinters when the telephone company already has them?

Thus began the use of telephone lines for non-voice communications. Today, the telephone companies rent two kinds of lines for such communications. A *public* telephone line is the ordinary voice-grade line used in residences and businesses. Because this line is routed through countless relay systems and electromechanical circuits, it is also referred to as the *switched* telephone network. The other type of telephone line is the private line, or *leased* line. The term "private" means that the line is not subjected to the same amount of switching as the public lines and, at the lessee's option, may also accommodate a wider range of frequencies than contained in the human voice. In many, if not most cases, *leased* lines are actually four-wire lines consisting of two complete telephone circuits, one for traffic in each direction. Much commercial traffic is carried on leased lines, but our discussions will deal only with the public or switched telephone network.

Modem Fundamentals

Digital signals from devices such as teleprinters cannot be sent directly over telephone lines. Because a telephone line is intended to carry only human speech, which contains frequencies in the range of 200-8000 Hz, its frequency response (*bandwidth*) is rather limited. As a matter of fact, since the goal of the telephone network is not fidelity, but intelligibility, the telephone does not even reproduce voices particularly well. Figure 5-1 shows the bandwidth of the public telephone system.

Figure 5-1   The bandwidth of a public, switched telephone line.

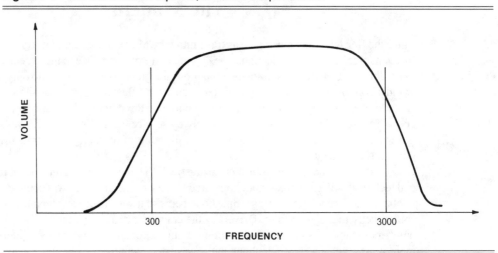

This bandwidth limitation enormously complicates the transmission of digital pulses over the ordinary public telephone network. As we have repeatedly depicted, telecommunications requires digital signals to be converted at some point into digital electrical pulses, or bits. From the standpoint of circuit design, an instantaneous transition between the 1 and 0 states is ideal. In other words, the perfect digital signal consists of clean, sharp, square (actually, rectangular) waves with perfectly vertical sides and perfectly flat tops.

Now, a square wave can be mathematically analyzed[1] as if it were a composite of sine waves at odd multiples of its frequency. A square wave of 200 Hz, for example, can be viewed electrically as progressively smaller amounts of 600 Hz, 1000 Hz, and 1400 Hz, and so on. Frequencies further from that of the fundamental square wave contribute less "squareness" to the composite. To transmit an acceptably square digital signal, the communications medium must have a significantly wider bandwidth than the frequency of the square wave itself. Otherwise, the high-frequency components are stripped out and along with them the sharpness of the square waves. If the bandwidth is too narrow, then, the resulting waves are not recognizably "square." At the receiver, the logic levels of the digital signal become ambiguous and communication fails. Figure 5-2 shows how a 2000 bps signal would be deformed by progressively narrower bandwidths. Notice that the pulse becomes recognizable as a square wave only at a bandwidth of 2500 Hz and reproduction of the wave is barely acceptable when the bandwidth is 4000 Hz.

Figure 5-2   The effects of bandwidth on square digital signals.

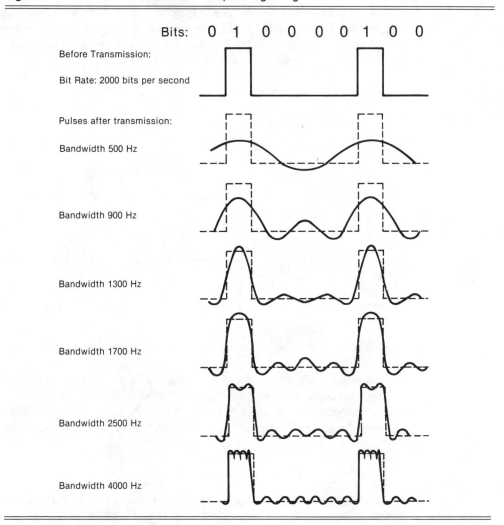

---

[1]Through Fourier analysis.

Modulation

The problem depicted in Figure 5-2 would occur if we attempted to transmit a computer's square waves over the voice-grade lines of the public telephone network. Clearly, a method is needed to convert data from square waves to a form that can pass unscathed over the telephone network. Sine waves are the best candidate because they can be easily created in a harmonically "pure" form that is less radically affected by the frequency roll-off inherent in the telephone line. The ultimate method of signaling should consist of sine waves whose frequencies are near the center of the bandwidth shown in Figure 5-1.

The process of encoding one signal with another is *modulation* and the recovery of the original signal is *demodulation*. The simplest form of modulation is *amplitude shift keying* or ASK modulation, depicted in Figure 5-3. During transmission, modulation occurs when a single sine wave tone is switched between two amplitudes (volume levels) to represent 1 and 0. In practice, one of the amplitudes is usually 0, so the modulation is attained merely by switching the tone on and off.[2] A MARK is therefore defined as the presence of a tone and a SPACE as its absence or vice versa. Since the transmission line idles at a MARK state, the continuous tone is transmitted even when no data is being encoded. The receiver demodulates the signal by outputting 1s and 0s as the tone on the communications line appears and disappears.

Figure 5-3   Amplitude modulation.

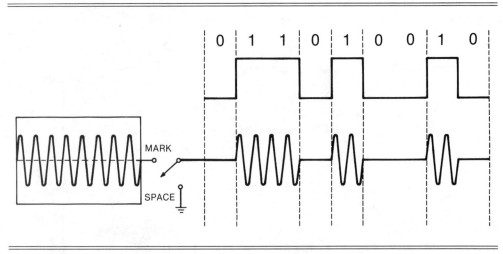

A device that performs modulation and demodulation on a communications line is known as a *modem*.[3] Although in computerdom the term "modem" is used almost exclusively to describe devices that operate over telephone lines, in fact modems are used on many different communications lines. A great deal of data, for example, is sent between computers at radio frequencies via

---

[2]Sometimes called ON/OFF keying.

[3]"Modem," as we have been told ad nauseam, is a portmanteau word formed from "modulate" and "demodulate." One can only marvel at the heights to which the human imagination soared for this name. Equally sublime is "codec" (from "code" and "decode"), a device that encodes analog signals in a digital format. The telephone company's name for a modem is the equally imaginative "data set."

RTTY (radio-teletype) modems. Another non-telephone modem is the *short-haul* modem, which sends modulated tones over ordinary wire. Short-haul modems are usually found where both pieces of equipment are located on the premises or where a noisy electrical environment precludes the use of ordinary cables.

"Plexes" or Bandwidth Usage

Before we examine more sophisticated modulation techniques, let's quickly review the "plex" terminology (presented briefly at the end of Chapter 2) describing the various ways of utilizing the available bandwidth of a communications line.

The Simplex Connection

A transmitter (such as the simple ASK modulator just described) at one end of the telephone line and a receiver at the other end form a *simplex* connection—that is, a connection in which data traffic moves in only one direction. This arrangement is illustrated in Figure 5-4a. Because they are inherently non-interactive, simplex installations have limited applications, but are found in one-sided applications such as stock tickers or printers at remote sites.

The Half-Duplex Connection

A limited kind of two-way system can be built from two simplex connections. As illustrated in Figure 5-4b, each modem contains a transmitter *and* a receiver, one of which is connected to the communications line through a "talk/listen" switch. For West-to-East traffic, modem W connects its transmitter to the line and modem E connects its receiver. This arrangement is reversed for East-to-West traffic. Changing the position of the "talk/listen" switch is called "turning the line around," a term from early telegraph days when operators had to reverse the physical connections on the equipment.

   The "talk/listen" switch is, of course, not a physical switch but an electronic one controlled by software. The two ends convey the need to turn the line around through *half-duplex protocols* such as the ETX/ACK protocol explained in Chapter 4. In general, half-duplex protocols are analogous to the familiar words "over" and "over and out" used in half-duplex radio conversions. In digital communications, the software controlling the two modems agree upon a *turnaround character* to signal the need to switch from sender to receiver. If the data to be transferred is of a binary (as opposed to textual) nature, block transfer protocols like those described in Chapter 4 must be used.

The Full-Duplex Connection

Although the half-duplex arrangement is considerably more flexible than the simplex, it is nevertheless inefficient. The time required to switch the circuitry from transmit to receive mode is commonly on the order of 200 milliseconds, but even longer delays are common in older equipment. A delay of such duration is intolerable in time-sensitive, interactive applications such as remote instrumentation monitoring and control systems. In addition, the cumulative delay incurred from repeated line reversals is responsible for the poor performance of half-duplex data transfer protocols such as the "stop-and-wait" protocol described in Chapter 4.

   The shortcomings of half-duplex communications can be avoided simply by taking the idea of channel-sharing one step further. Instead of alternately sharing receiver and transmitter, in the *full-duplex* connection shown in Figure 5-4c, each end of the connection contains both a transmitter *and* a receiver—one pair for communicating East-to-West and another for West-to-East. To prevent interference, a separate distinct tone is assigned to traffic in each direction. The general idea of dividing a communications channel into smaller frequency bands is called *frequency division multiplexing* or FDM.

Figure 5-4 "Plexes," or bandwidth usage.

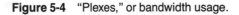

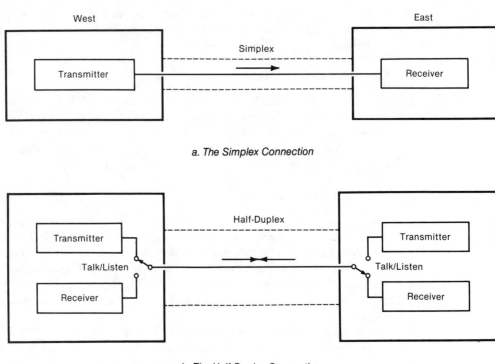

a. The Simplex Connection

b. The Half-Duplex Connection

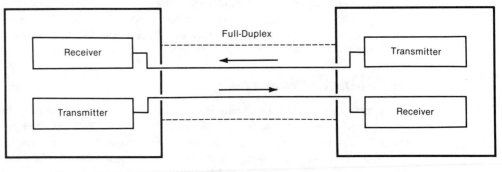

c. The Full-Duplex Connection

Half-Duplex Protocols on Full-Duplex Lines

It should be noted that even after full-duplex connections are installed, many computer systems (IBM, for example) continue to use the older half-duplex software protocols from the past. Such usage is entirely harmless, but usually represents a serious sacrifice in overall performance.

Channel Usage Conventions

Since a full-duplex connection consists of two complete channels in use simultaneously, two modems operating in full-duplex mode must agree upon how they will allocate the signals. For example, the modems might agree beforehand that the modem that uses the higher-frequency channel should be called a Girl modem, while those that use the lower are Boy modems. The problem with this approach is that, when the telephone rings, there is no way to know whether the caller is a Boy or Girl. Instead of using fixed definitions such as Boy and Girl, channel assignments are determined by the point of origin of the call. When new modems are designed, one channel is *arbitrarily* designated *originate* and the other *answer*. In use, the modem placing the call is expected to use the originate channel and the modem receiving the call is expected to use the answer channel.

Modems that both place and answer calls must contain circuitry to switch the channel assignments between originate and receive, depending upon the situation. In many applications, however, a modem either places or receives calls, but not both. Modems servicing the dial-up lines to timesharing computers, for example, never originate calls; modems connected to dedicated terminals (e.g., airline reservations) never need to answer calls. Modems for such situations, known as *originate-* and *answer-only* modems, have fixed channel assignments. Because complicated switching circuitry is unnecessary, dedicated modems are considerably less complicated and therefore less expensive than full-featured originate/answer modems.

Frequency Modulation

Noise causes spurious variations in an electrical signal's amplitude. Figure 5-5 shows how small noise "spikes" may transform one amplitude logic level into the other, producing a data error. Because it uses amplitude variations to encode digital logic levels, ASK modulation's greatest weakness is its susceptibility to noise. So profound is this limitation that ASK modulation is rapidly disappearing as low-noise environments become difficult to achieve in an increasingly electronic world.

Whereas electrical noise changes a signal's amplitude, no known natural phenomenon changes its frequency. Much more reliable encoding can therefore be attained by *frequency modulation*. Since modems need only transmit 1s and 0s, data can be represented by switching between two tones of different frequencies. This technique, known as *frequency shift keying*, would be superior to ASK even if judged solely on its immunity to noise, but FSK is also more robust because each logic level can be decoded not only as the presence of one tone but also as the absence of the other. In other words, a 1 is decoded as: *1 AND $\overline{0}$*. Figure 5-6a depicts FSK modulation, but the frequency difference between the two tones is exaggerated for clarity. Figure 5-6b, however, shows how the dual tones are actually assigned in the Bell model 202, a half-duplex 1200 bps modem using FSK modulation. This modem uses two tones 1000 Hz apart, centered about 1700 Hz. The 1200 Hz tone represents a MARK and the 2200 Hz tone a SPACE.

Figure 5-5   Effects of noise upon a digital signal.

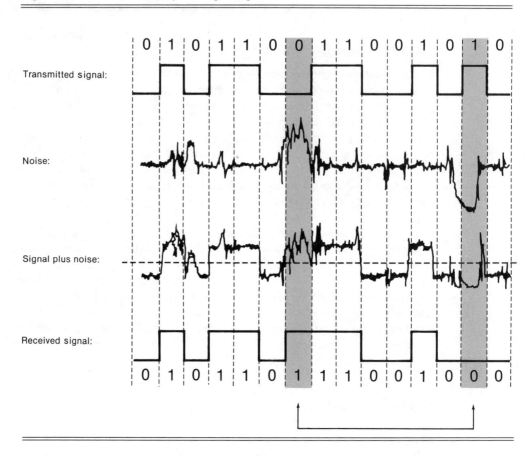

FSK modulation at 1200 bps produces a wide spectrum of frequencies, indicated by the shaded area in Figure 5-6. Note that this area occupies most of the available bandwidth of the telephone line. This modem also devotes a very small amount of bandwidth to a "backwards" (i.e., from receiver back to sender) channel. This channel consists of a continuous tone of 387 Hz and is used to inform the transmitting station that the receiver is still connected. If necessary, the tone can be modulated with *ON/OFF keying* at a maximum rate of 5 baud, thus providing very limited full-duplex capabilities. This capability is used in half-duplex protocols to indicate an error in transmission.

Figure 5-7 shows the FSK tone assignment for a Bell model 103, a full-duplex, 110-300 bps FSK modem. The originate modem on the left uses two tones, 100 Hz apart, centered about the frequency 1170; a SPACE is 1070 and a MARK is 1270. The answer modem tones are also 100 Hz apart, but centered about 2125 Hz; here, a SPACE is 2025 and a MARK is 2225. Notice that the frequencies are chosen so that there is very little overlap between their spectra and consequently little interference between the two.

Figure 5-6 FSK modulation.

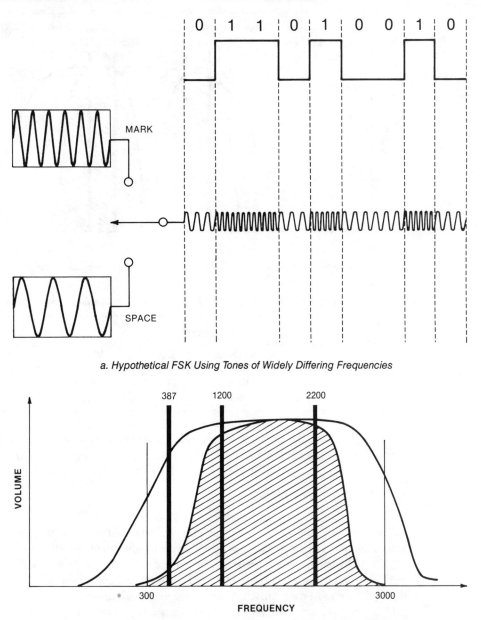

a. Hypothetical FSK Using Tones of Widely Differing Frequencies

b. Tone Assignments for a Bell 202 Half-Duplex, FSK 1200 bps Modem

So far, our discussion of tone frequencies and their originate/answer assignments are for Bell (AT&T) modems. Table 5-1 compares the 110-300 bps, full-duplex modem assignments with those of its European (CCITT V.21) counterparts.

Figure 5-7 Tone assignments for a Bell model 103, a full-duplex, 110-300 bps FSK modem.

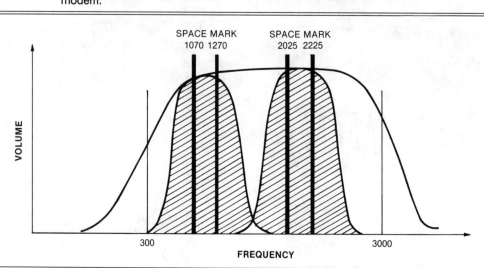

Table 5-1 Bell 103 vs CCITT V.21 300 bps, full-duplex tone assignments.

	Originate		**Answer**	
	MARK	**SPACE**	**MARK**	**SPACE**
Bell	1270	1070	2225	2025
CCITT	980	1180	1650	1850

In both cases, the answer mode is assigned to the higher tone-pair, but CCITT modems employ different frequency pairs and the lower of the two tones produces a MARK.

Bandwidth Limitations

At first thought, modulation sounds like the ultimate solution to the telephone bandwidth problems. After all, as long as the tones lie within the bandwidth of the telephone line, they should be unaffected by the transmission speed. The temptation, then, is to think that the telephone line can bear modulation at any baud rate. The cruel fact is that in any form of modulation the communications medium must have sufficient bandwidth to pass *all* primary components of modulation. In half-duplex FSK there are three primary components: the two FSK tones themselves and the baud rate of the data. In full-duplex communications, however, there are six primary components—the four FSK tones and two baud frequencies. In other words, to achieve a given data rate in full-duplex mode requires approximately the same channel bandwidth as a half-duplex connection at twice that rate.

We have seen examples of 1200 bps half-duplex and 300 bps full-duplex modems. We have also seen that the total frequency spectra produced by these modems fit comfortably within the bandwidth of the telephone line. Although there is room for a minor increase in baud rate, as the modem spectra begin to flirt with bandwidth limits, heroic (and expensive) electronic designs are necessary to compensate for the ugly phase and group delays that occur. Considering the expense, a *total* data rate of 1200 baud—either 1200 baud half-duplex or 600 baud full-duplex— is about the practical maximum modulation rate that can be reliably attained at reasonable cost on the switched telephone network.

Phase Modulation

So far we have legitimately been able to refer to modems as operating at 300, 600, or 1200 baud, because the *data* rate (in bps) of the modem is exactly equal to the *modulation rate* (in baud). That is, every bit is encoded into a single cycle of the modulated carrier. We have just noted that the practical limit of "modulation cycles" on a telephone line is about 1200 baud total. Clearly, in order to increase the amount of data that can be put through the telephone line, a way must be devised to encode more than one bit into each modulation cycle. Let's see how this is possible.

A waveform has three properties: amplitude, frequency, and phase. We have already examined modulation techniques that encode digital data into amplitude (ASK) and frequency (FSK). We will now briefly examine *phase modulation*, where information is encoded in the temporal *relationship* between two otherwise identical waveforms. In particular, we will examine the technique known as *phase shift keying* (PSK).

Two-Level Phase Shift Keying

Figure 5-8 shows three waveforms, all exactly the same amplitude and frequency, but differing in phase. One complete cycle of any period waveform is expressed as 360°. With respect to waveform A, waveform B is said to be *in phase* or, stated differently, its *phase angle* is 0°. Waveform C, however, lags behind waveform A by 180° and its phase angle is −180°.

Although these expressions may be foreign to you, it is fairly easy to see how this relationship can be used to encode data. Modulation consists of sending waveform C for a SPACE, and waveform B for a MARK. (We assume that both sender and receiver already have local copies of waveform A, so it need not be transmitted.) To demodulate the signal, the receiver adds the incoming waveform to its local copy of waveform A. If the result of this addition is 0 (C + A = 0) a SPACE is decoded. Conversely, if the result is non-0 (B + A ≠0) a MARK is decoded.

Although phase modulation is nifty, the example just discussed does not change the basic 1-to-1 ratio of the data and modulation rates. Let's see how to attain this goal.

Quadrature (Four-Phase) PSK

We all have the following phrase built in our mental ROMs: "in asynchronous I/O, a byte is broken up into bits. . ." To understand how a modem attains a bit rate of, say, 1200 bps from a modulation rate of 600 baud, we have to change this phrase to "in asynchronous I/O, a byte is broken up into dibits . . ." The new basic unit of data is no longer the bit, but the 2-bit pair, or *dibit*. Figure 5-9 shows how a dibit is encoded as one of four phase angles.

This encoding process, known as *quadrature*[4] phase shift keying (QPSK) is identical to the previous example except instead of encoding bits in two phase angles (0° and −180°), four phase angles are used—0°, 90°, 180°, and 270°.

---

[4]Quadrature just means "four-quadrant."

Demodulating the quadrature phase-encoded signal is conceptually identical to demodulating the binary phase-encoded signal. Again, the incoming waveform is added to the reference waveform, but this time both the polarity *and* magnitude of the sum are used to decode the dibits. Phase modulation has been around for many years—in fact, it is the technique used to modulate the RGB signal in an ordinary color television signal.

Figure 5-8 Two-level phase shift keying.

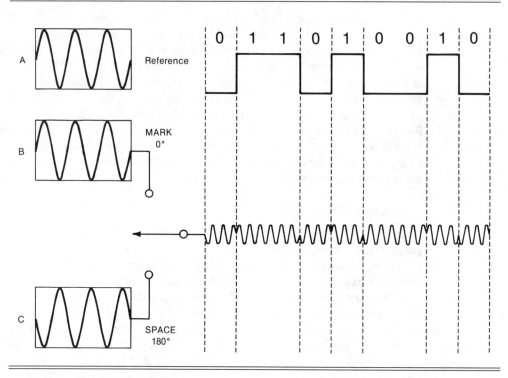

Differential Phase Shift Keying

Our earlier examples assume that both sender and receiver have local copies of the reference waveform. If this is so (you ask), what keeps the sender's and receiver's reference waveforms synchronized? (This sounds a lot like the teleprinter problem from Chapter Two, doesn't it.) In other technologies, a small *sync tone* is transmitted along with the carrier to enable the sender to reconstruct its copy of the reference waveform.[5] This is not practical on a telephone line because the energy required to transmit the sync pulse itself would consume some of the precious bandwidth.

The solution, called *differential* phase shift keying (DPSK), abandons altogether the idea of deriving phase differences from a quiescent reference signal (i.e., a sync pulse). Instead, the phase angle for each cycle is calculated relative to the *previous* cycle. Thus, for any given modulation cycle, the dibit is encoded in the phase relationship between the current cycle and its immediate predecessor.

---

[5]In a color television signal, this sync pulse is called the "burst." In a similar application in FM stereo, it is called the "pilot tone."

Figure 5-9   Quadrature phase shift keying.

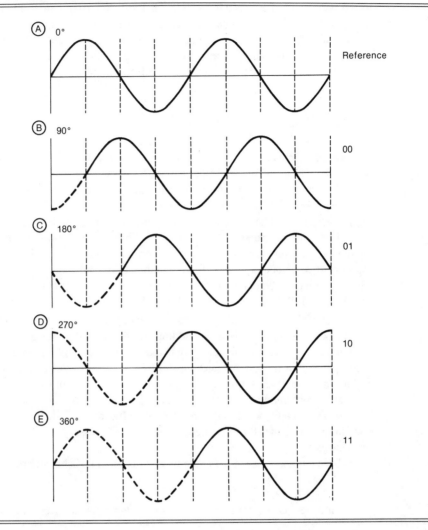

A modulation rate of 600 baud using four-level PSK provides a data rate of 2400 bps. This can be used in its entirety as a single 2400 bps half-duplex channel as in the Bell 201 modem, or divided into two full-duplex 1200 bps channels. The latter is the configuration of the popular Bell 212A modem whose frequency assignments are shown in Table 5-2.

Table 5-2   Tone assignments for the Bell 212A.

Originate		Answer	
Transmit	**Receive**	**Transmit**	**Receive**
1200	2400	2400	1200

The Bell 212A modem has become the 1200 bps standard for microcomputers, largely due to the popularity of Hayes Microcomputer Inc.'s Smartmodem 1200. It should be mentioned, however, that a similar competing system (which actually predates Bell's 212A) is used in the Racal-Vadic VA3400 1200 bps modem. The CCITT standard V.22 describes a 1200/600 bps modem that differs mainly in minor internal details and can communicate at 1200 bps with Bell 212A-type modems under all but the most adverse conditions.

Quadrature Amplitude Modulation

We have seen how data can be encoded into a signal's amplitude (ASK) and its phase (PSK). Aspects of both of these forms of modulation are combined to produce yet another modulation technique known as Quadrature Amplitude Modulation, or QAM. This technique results in a total data rate of 4800 bps with 600 baud modulation. QAM is specified by the CCITT V.22 *bis*[6] full-duplex standard and has been adopted by the Hayes Smartmodem 2400 and others.

Just as the basic data unit for PSK is the dibit, QAM uses the *quadbit*, or nibble. The CCITT version of QAM employs twelve phase angles in conjunction with three amplitudes. Of the resulting thirty-two unique phase/amplitude combinations, only sixteen are used to encode a quadbit. The remaining sixteen combinations will be used in the future to attain a data rate of 9600 bps (4800 bps in full-duplex). These are depicted in the phase "constellation" in Figure 5-10.

One of the chief benefits of frequency and phase modulation techniques such as FSK and PSK is their immunity to noise. By adding amplitude modulation to PSK, QAM sacrifices some noise immunity to achieve increased data rate. Indeed, in noisy environments where a 1200-baud full-duplex DPSK modem operates flawlessly, the 2400 bps full-duplex QAM modem may be unusable. In recognition of this problem, some manufacturers of CCITT-compatible 2400 bps modems are incorporating an "automatic fallback" feature that senses when an excessive amount of noise is present and switches the modem into 1200 bps, DPSK mode. The modem informs the transmitting computer that a change of data rate is necessary by changing a voltage on the hardware interface.

The characteristics of the modems mentioned in this chapter are summarized in Table 5-3.

Table 5-3   Characteristics of common modems designed for public telephone network.

Modem	Model	Data Rate	Baud Rate	Modulation	Duplex
Bell	103	110,300	300	FSK	Full
CCITT	V.21	200,300	200,300	FSK	Full
Bell	202	1200	300	FSK	Half*
Bell	212	1200,110	600,110	DPSK	Full
CCITT	V.22	1200,600	600,600	DPSK	Full
CCITT	V.22b	2400	600	QAM	Full
Racal-Vadic	VA3400	1200	600	DPSK	Full

*The "backward" ON/OFF channel at 387 Hz is limited to 5 bps.

---

[6]The suffix *bis* in CCITT document numbers refers to the second revision. This looks so odd in English that such references in this book simply append the letter 'b' (e.g., V.22b).

Figure 5-10   CCITT-style QAM modulation for 4800 bps at 600 baud (V.22b, p. 26).

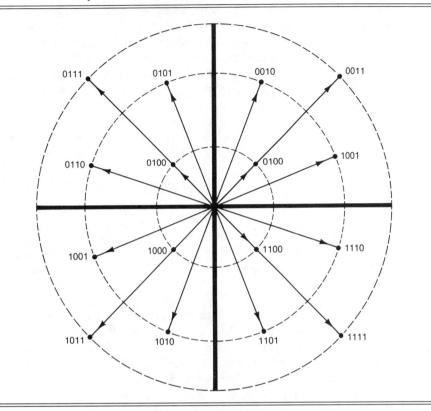

Establishing a Data Link

When an originate modem initiates a call, it listens patiently on the line for an answering modem to assert its carrier tone. When the answer modem comes online, it asserts its carrier tone. If the originate modem recoginzes the tone as belonging to one of its own species, it replies with its own carrier tone and the two are ready to communicate happily ever after. The remainder of this book will refer to two modems locked in this conjugate audio embrace as a *data link* or a *carrier link*. The link is broken when either carrier is turned off or interrupted for more than a few tenths of a second.

The precise tones used to negotiate the data link depend upon the types of modems in use. If the answer modem uses FSK modulation, its carrier is the answer transmitter's MARK; if a PSK modem, the carrier is just the answer modem's carrier (e.g., 2400 Hz for a Bell 212A). As soon as the FSK originate modem recognizes the MARK of the answer modem, it asserts its own transmitter's MARK; if a PSK modem, the originator asserts its carrier (e.g., 1200 Hz for a Bell 212A).

Modem Enhancements

Before 1968, the telephone companies forbade connecting "foreign" (i.e., non-Bell) equipment such as modems to the telephone line. Their argument, not without merit, was that the connection of untested circuitry to the telephone line made it impossible for them to guarantee the performance of the telephone system. After a long legal battle, the Federal Communications Commission in the "Carterphone" ruling declared that the telephone company's restrictions were unreasonable and ordered it to permit customers to use innerconnecting devices. In the same ruling the commission granted the telephone company the rights (1) to approve devices that will be connected to the telephone line and (2) to know when such a device is actually connected. The telephone company responded to the Carterphone decision by authorizing connection to the telephone line only through a *direct access adaptor* (DAA). These devices, which had to be rented from the telephone company, were essentially transformers to isolate the telephone line from the connected equipment and a few components to suppress potentially harmful voltages. Due to subsequent FCC rulings (or the threat of them), DAAs are no longer required as long as the connected equipment meets telephone company standards and the user reports to the telephone company whenever an approved modem is connected to or disconnected from the telephone lines.[7]

Acoustic Modems

Before direct connection to the telephone line was so easy, the *acoustic coupler* modem was common. This odd-looking device was often just a set of carbon-filled transmitter and receiver elements much like those found in the telephone handset itself. The user placed the telephone handset in a cradle consisting of rubber cups, which kept the telephone's mouthpiece and earpiece in close proximity to the coupler's transmitter and receiver elements, respectively. Tones were thus "coupled" between modem and telephone line using sound waves.

Acoustically coupled modems were hateful beasts and the source of perpetual headaches. Their most important failing was the necessity for total acoustic isolation between the two cups. Without this isolation, the originate and answer frequencies would intermix, creating *crosstalk* or, worse, oscillation, between the modem channels.

Describing these devices in the past tense is, perhaps, wishful thinking because a fair number of them still exist. If the direct connection rulings needed any assistance doing in the acoustic coupler, help came from the most unlikely of quarters—from the telephone company itself. If you examine the tone assignments for the Bell 212A modem in Table 5-2, you will notice that the upper carrier frequency is the first harmonic of the lower and that both are harmonically related to the data rate. This choice of tones—the worst possible for producing crosstalk—almost guaranteed that the world would see no 1200 bps acoustic couplers.

Auto-Dial, Auto-Answer Modems

The simplicity of direct connection (a blessing that the telephone company itself always enjoyed), brought a flood of new products to the telecommunications market, including modems that provide not only basic modulation functions but also a physical interface to the telephone line. Features such as automatic dial and automatic answer, heretofore found mainly on the telephone company's modems, now became standard.[8]

---

[7]At the same time you may report all the mattress and pillow tags you have removed in your lifetime.

[8]A few acoustic modems exist that "connect" to the telephone by using solenoids to physically operate the telephone's switch hook and dialer!

Using built-in dialing and ring detecting circuitry, auto-dial and auto-answer modems not only dial and answer the telephone, but manage the carrier handshaking required to establish a data link. When a call is originated by Bell 212A at 1200 bps, but answered by a 300 bps (Bell 103A) modem, the 212A makes no attempt to step down to 300, and a data link is not established. However, a 212A answers incoming calls in its 103A mode (i.e., with a 2225 Hz tone); if the calling modem is a 103A, the data link is established in that mode. Otherwise, the 212A steps up to its 1200 bps mode, asserts its 2400 Hz carrier, and attempts to establish a link at 1200 bps. The same answer/step-up relationship exists between 1200 and 2400 bps modems as between the 300 and 1200. CCITT V.22 modems perform in the same manner except that 1200 bps modems start at 600 bps, not 300.

Most originate/answer modems—even those that automatically answer and dial the telephone—provide some mechanism to override these tone assignment conventions. This enables them to use answer tones physically to place a call to an originate-only modem, or to use originate tones when answering a call from a receive-only modem.

Many people find the idea in the last paragraph to be confusing. The problem, as usual, is in the nomenclature. Remember, the "-only" names refer to the *convention* of tone usage, not to the call's *physical* point of origin. To illustrate this point, let's assume that you wish to transfer a file to a client who, for some reason, owns an originate-only modem. Your modem, however, is an originate/answer modem. If your modem places the call in the ordinary manner, it assumes the originate mode; that is, after dialing, it listens for an answer tone from the other modem. When the telephone rings, your client manually answers the telephone and manually switches on the modem (originate-only modems do not contain answering circuits). Do you see the problem yet? Since both modems are in originate mode, both are waiting to hear the carrier of an answer modem on the other end—a standoff.

What to do? Luckily, your modem has both answer *and* originate, so you hang up and call again. This time you instruct it to dial as always, but, and here's the important point, you also instruct it to behave *as if it were an answer modem*. Your modem dials again, but instead of waiting for an answer carrier as usual, it immediately asserts its own *answer* carrier. Your client's originate-only modem hears the answer tones and the data link is established.

Modem Control

Knowing how a watch works does not teach you to tell time. Understanding how modems work does not help you make them work. We have learned that modems, among other activities, establish data links, dial and answer the telephone, and go online and offline, and that half-duplex modems must perodically turn the line around. This portion of the chapter, therefore, is an explanation of how such modem functions are controlled and monitored by the programmer.

As we shall see, there are two fundamental ways to control or monitor the behavior of a modem—through hardware (wires between the computer and modem) and software (sending commands in the data stream). Formal standards for the first method are embodied in the Recommended Standard Number 232, Revision C from the Engineering Department of the Electronic Industries Association—better known as EIA RS-232C, or simply RS-232. The CCITT's V.24 is an almost identical standard. There are no formal standards for controlling modems via commands in the data stream, but the *Smartmodems* of Hayes Microcomputer Products, Inc. have become so popular that they (and imitations of them) have become microcomputer standards by acclamation if not by decree.

The RS-232 Standard

Making the leap from theoretical to practical understanding, our feet unavoidably land in the great intellectual pile known as RS-232. Of all the formal documents ever written, RS-232 is certainly one of the least understood. If it is also one of the least read standards, there is a good reason—it is one of the least read*able*. Why? The tip-off is on the front page: "*Engineering* Department of the *Electronics* Industries Association." Because documents of electrical engineering are seldom paragons of prose style, almost no one reads the RS-232 document first-hand. When a technical document is considered too difficult to understand, hack writers are summoned to craft a "user-friendly" explanation of the document. This has produced many well-written but quite inaccurate articles about RS-232.

The formal name of the RS-232C is *Interface between Data Terminal Equipment and Data Communication Equipment Employing Serial Binary Data Interchange*. Data Terminal Equipment (DTE) and Data Communications Equipment (DCE) are, for our purposes at least, the generic terms for "computer equipment" and "modem," respectively. Even though DTE and DCE are not particularly memorable terms, they are both popular and unambiguous. For these reasons, they are adopted in this chapter.

The most important words in the title of the EIA document are "serial interchange" and "interface," which tell us that this document describes how to perform serial I/O in the real world of modems. The definition of the term "interface" is uncharacteristically broad for an engineering concept. The document actually describes three separate aspects of the DTE/DCE connection:

1. Mechanical description of interface circuits
2. Functional description of interchange circuits
3. Electrical signal characteristics

Our study will follow the same organization.

Mechanical Description of Interface Circuits

The mechanical definitions are unexpectedly sparse in the RS-232 standard. One of the most common misconceptions about the standard is the matter of the physical connector. The standard says only that there should be two connectors—female for the DCE, male for the DTE.[9] It gives some guidelines about where the connectors should be placed. Conspicuously absent is any definition of the physical characteristics of the connector itself. The maximum capacitance of the cable (2500 picofarads) is also stated.

Twenty-five "interchange circuits" are defined and assigned pin numbers on the connector. These assignments are given in Table 5-4.

Culling the circuits in Table 5-4 that are unassigned or relate exclusively to synchronous transmission leaves us with the 11 pins given in Table 5-5. Each pin number is followed by the abbreviation of its function (instead of the circuit name), and a synopsis of how it is used.

---

[9]When the IBM PC was released, members of the trade press excoriated it because of its "non-standard" male connector. The fact is, earlier microcomputers universally used female connectors solely because they are less expensive than males.

Table 5-4   Pin assignments for the twenty-five RS-232 interchange circuits.

Pin	Circuit	Name
1	AA	Protective Ground
2	BA	Transmitted Data
3	BB	Received Data
4	CA	Request to Send
5	CB	Clear to Send
6	CC	Data Set Ready
7	AB	Signal Ground or Common
8	CF	Received Line Signal Detect*
9	—	Reserved for testing
10	—	Reserved for testing
11	—	Unassigned
12	SCF	Secondary Received Line Signal Detect
13	SCB	Secondary Clear to Send
14	SBA	Secondary Transmitted Data
15	DB	Transmission Signal Element Timing
16	SBB	Secondary Received Data
17	DD	Receiver Signal Element Timing
18	—	Unassigned
19	SCA	Secondary Request to Send
20	CD	Data Terminal Ready
21	CG	Signal Quality Detector
22	CE	Ring Indicator
23	CH/CI	Data Signal Rate Detector
24	DA	Transmit Signal Element Timing
25	—	Unassigned

*This chapter uses the more popular term Data Carrier Detect, DCD.

Table 5-5   The RS-232 circuits for asynchronous I/O on microcomputers.

Pin	Abbreviation	Name	Direction	Function
1	---	Protective Ground	------	Safety ground
2	TD	Transmitted Data	to DCE	Outbound DTE data
3	RD	Received Data	to DTE	Inbound DTE data
4	RTS	Request to Send	to DCE	DTE wants to switch to transmit mode
5	CTS	Clear to Send	to DTE	DCE is ready to transmit
6	DSR	Data Set Ready	to DTE	DCE ready to communicate with DTE
7	---	Signal Common	------	Common line for circuitry
8	DCD	Data Carrier Detect (RLSD)	to DTE	Data link in progress
20	DTR	Data Terminal Ready	to DCE	Enable modem for action
22	RI	Ring Indicator	to DTE	Announces incoming call
23	DSRD	Data Signal Rate Detector	either	Data rate indicator

Data vs Control Functions

RS-232 functions are sharply divided into *data functions* and *control functions*. The data functions are, quite simply, the transmitter and receiver on pins 2 and 3, respectively. These are the only two pins through which data flows. All remaining functions are control functions, so named because they carry the status or command for controlling the modem's behavior.

Input/Output Conventions

One of the less intuitive aspects of Tables 5-4 and 5-5 is that the two sides of an RS-232 interface are logically *complementary*—an output on one side of the interface becomes an input on the other. Remembering that the functional names of the circuits reflect the point of view of the DTE helps to clarify the counter-intuitive nomenclature. For example, the name "Transmitted Data" clearly denotes an output. Transmitted Data (2) is, however, an output *only* on a DTE ouput; on a DCE, it is an input. To alleviate this problem, Table 5-5 gives the direction of the intended signal.

RS-232 from a Programmer's Point of View

Control functions on the RS-232 interface are, of course, controlled through hardware. As we will see in the next chapter, commonly used asynchronous functions are built into a single controller IC known as a UART (Universal Asynchronous Receiver/Transmitter). This device provides both data (transmit and receive) as well as many control functions. When UARTs are employed, the inner timing details of START/STOP asynchronous I/O, data format, and RS-232 interfacing are largely hidden from the programmer. In fact, transmitting or receiving a byte with a UART is simply a matter of reading or writing to a RAM location or I/O port. In a similar fashion, RS-232 inputs and outputs can be monitored and manipulated almost effortlessly.

Formal Functional Descriptions of Interchange Circuits

We will now look at the formal EIA definitions of the circuit functions in Table 5-5. Later we will discuss many of these same functions in the light of *real-world* usage in "Real-World RS-232."

Protective Ground (Pin 1)

This pin should be connected internally to the chassis of the device, and thence to the earth ground provided at the AC outlet.

Signal Common (Pin 7)

This is the common return for all circuits and must be present on all interfaces. Connection of this pin to Protective Ground (pin 1) can prevent catastrophic destruction of equipment in the event of a transformer malfunction somewhere in the system.

Request to Send (RTS, Pin 4)
Clear to Send (CTS, Pin 5)

The RS-232 standard says that Request to Send (pin 4) "conditions" the modem for transmission. In fact, its only function is to switch a half-duplex modem between transmit and receive mode (i.e., turn the line around). While a half-duplex modem is receiving, the DTE keeps Request to Send inhibited; when it becomes the DTE's turn to transmit, it informs the modem of its desire to transmit by asserting Request to Send. The DTE must not start sending data to the modem immediately because the modem cannot perform the switchover instantaneously. After asserting Request to Send, therefore, the DTE begins monitoring Clear to Send (pin 5) which is held low by the modem in receive mode. When the modem completes the switchover, it asserts Clear to Send to inform the DTE that it is now safe to send data. This RTS/CTS *handshaking* is performed in reverse when switching from transmit back to receive.

Since full-duplex connections are two-way channels, there is clearly no need for RTS/CTS handshaking. Accordingly, in full-duplex modems, Clear to Send (pin 5) is permanently asserted or tied to Data Carrier Detect (pin 8).

Data Set Ready (DSR, Pin 6)

Data Set Ready is asserted only when the following conditions exist *simultaneously*:

1. The modem is "connected to a communications channel"; that is, off-hook, but not in test, voice, or dial mode.

2. The modem has performed "any timing functions required by the switching system to complete call establishment." In originate mode, this means dialing, monitoring call progress, and anything else required to usher the call through the telephone network.

3. The modem has begun "the transmission of a discrete answer tone. . ." In answer mode, the answer tone and Data Set Ready are asserted two seconds after the telephone goes off-hook. The originate modem does not transmit or assert its Data Set Ready until the answer tone is received from the remote modem.

The term "Data Set" is the telephone company's name for a modem. The EIA standard calls it a DCE. (Is "modem" a dirty word?)

Data Carrier Detect (DCD, Pin 8)

This pin, whose official name is Received Line Signal Detect, is asserted when the modem receives a remote carrier and remains asserted for the duration of the link. On half-duplex modems, of course, Data Carrier Detect is asserted only by the receiving modem.

Data Terminal Ready (DTR, Pin 20)

This signal "prepares" modems "to be connected" to the communications line and "maintains the connection established by external means." This means that Data Terminal Ready enables (but does not cause) the modem to switch onto the line. In originate mode, Data Terminal Ready must be asserted in order to auto-dial; in answer mode, Data Terminal Ready must be asserted to auto-answer.

Once the modem is connected to the line, Data Terminal Ready must remain asserted to maintain the connection; its inhibition causes disconnection from the communications line, disrupting a data link in progress. Since an asserted Data Terminal Ready is also required for transmitting data on the Transmitted Data (pin 2) line, Data Terminal Ready is, in effect, a "master control" for the modem.

Transmitted Data (TD, Pin 2)

The Transmitted Data line carries serial data from the DTE to the modem. In conformity with long-established technology, the transmitter is held at MARK during periods of line idle.

The DTE may not transmit data unless the following circuits are asserted:

1. Request to Send (pin 4)

2. Clear to Send (pin 5)

3. Data Set Ready (pin 6)

4. Data Terminal Ready (pin 20)

Requirements 1 and 2 make little sense in full-duplex modems where Request to Send and Clear to Send have no meaning.

Received Data (RD, Pin 3)

The performance of RD is not dependent upon any other RS-232 function. The standard requires that Received Data be held at MARK when no carrier is present or, in half-duplex modems, for a "brief" interval after switching from transmit to receive mode.

Ring Indicator (RI, Pin 22)

This pin is asserted during a ring on the line. Ring Indicator is supposed to be asserted "approximately coincident" with the ON segment of the ringing signal and inhibited between rings. This signal appears regardless of the state of Data Terminal Ready (pin 20).

Data Signal Rate Detector (DSRD, Pin 23)

If two data rates are possible (Bell 212A modems, for example) the higher of the two is represented by asserting DSRD. Note from Table 5-5 that this function can, by user agreement, be bidirectional. That is, the DTE may assert DSRD (pin 23) to force the modem to use the higher of the two rates, or the modem may assert DSRD to report the data rate of data link.

Electrical Signal Characteristics

Although most of the electrical characteristics of the RS-232 interface are irrelevent to the programmer, some knowledge of the subject is necessary for a well-rounded understanding of the topic.

Speed and Power

EIA allows speeds from "zero to a nominal upper limit of 20,000 bits per second." In most installations, the data rate is limited to 19,200 bps. The standard also cautions against cable lengths in excess of 50 feet unless the total cable capacitance is less than 2500 picofarads.

The interface must be able to sustain a short circuit of indefinite duration between any two of its pins without sustaining damage. In such cases, current must not exceed .5 ampere. These characteristics result in a safe, robust interface, which, importantly, is highly tolerant of cabling goofs.[10]

Logic Levels

The RS-232 standard specifies a *bipolar* logic level. That is, logic levels are represented not only by the magnitude of voltage levels, but by the polarities as well. The maximum voltage permitted on any circuit is ± 15 volts.

---

[10]While the interface cannot be harmed by connection among its own pins or those of another RS-232 device, it is easily damaged by connection to a device that does not observe the same current and voltage limitations.

The RS-232 standard actually defines *four* logic levels. Inputs have different definitions from outputs, and the data functions—Transmitted Data (pin 2) and Received Data (pin 3)—are different from control functions. Figure 5-11 shows the logic-level definitions of RS-232 for inputs and outputs. Binary logic levels for outputs are +5 to +15 and −5 to −15; voltages between +5 and −5 are undefined. Binary logic levels for inputs are +3 to +15 and −3 to −15; voltages between +3 and −3 are undefined. The different logic level from input to output is referred to as the *noise margin*. It also means that the interface can tolerate 2 volts of noise (peak) or a 2-volt Ohm's Law drop between DTE and DCE.

Figure 5-11 Logic levels for RS-232 *control* functions.

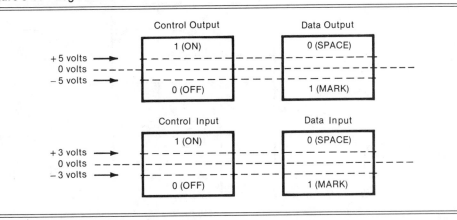

If this seems like an odd interface for computer equipment, remember that it was designed largely to accommodate teleprinter technology where, by a century of tradition, the bipolar communications line idles (MARKs) at a negative voltage.

RS-232 Level Conversion

Because RS-232 voltages and logic levels are not normally used in computer circuitry, level conversion is necessary. This is performed by special ICs known as EIA (RS-232) *line drivers* and *line receivers*. For electronic reasons, these devices are usually inverters, which means that the inputs and outputs of an asynchronous I/O controller IC (UART) must compensate for this inversion. Figure 5-12 shows how, for instance, the RTS and the CTS inputs of a UART must actually be $\overline{\text{RTS}}$ and $\overline{\text{CTS}}$ to compensate for the level inversion caused by the interface driver ICs. This subject, which affects the programmer's view of the interface, is addressed again in Chapter 7 where it is discussed in more concrete terms.

Real-World RS-232

The descriptions of the RS-232 interface presented so far are essentially recitations of the formal descriptions presented in the EIA document. We will now examine these same subjects under the harsh light of reality. In a later section, "Non-Standard Uses of RS-232," we will examine some of the unauthorized uses to which the RS-232 interface is put.

Figure 5-12 Typical RS-232 logic-level conversion hardware.

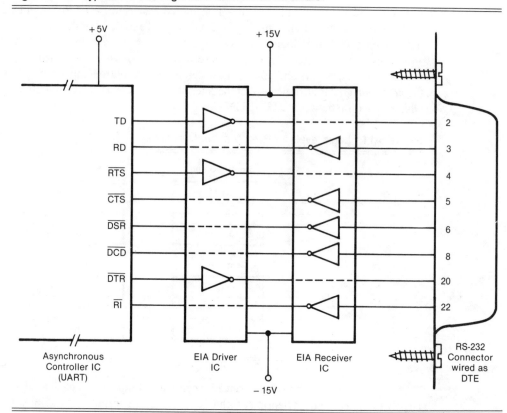

Modems and the RS-232 Interface

The control functions found on the typical microcomputer modem RS-232 interface scarcely resemble the descriptions presented earlier. Here is a brief and necessarily incomplete discussion of these control leads as you are likely to find them. Remember, this refers only to the modem interface; the microcomputer side of the interface will be discussed separately later.

Request to Send
Clear to Send

(RTS, Pin 4)
(CTS, Pin 5) Since half-duplex modems are not popular among microcomputer users, Request to Send/Clear to Send handshaking is seldom supported. On virtually every modem intended for use with microcomputers, the Request to Send input is not used and the Clear to Send output is permanently asserted.

Data Set Ready

(DSR, Pin 6) Usually, Data Set Ready is permanently asserted on microcomputer modems. Its sole value in this role is as an indicator that the modem is powered up and ready. Occasionally, however, it is permanently wired to the Data Carrier Detect (pin 8) output. It should be noted that the Hayes Smartmodem 2400 provides a command to force its Data Set Ready to behave in true RS-232 fashion.

Data Carrier Detect   (DCD, Pin 8) Data Carrier Detect is supported on virtually every microcomputer and modem.

Data Terminal Ready   (DTR, Pin 20) Luckily, most microcomputer modems support Data Terminal Ready in a fairly standard way—that is, as a "master control" for the modem. When Data Terminal Ready is inhibited, the modem does not transmit data to or receive data from the DTE, answer or dial the telephone—in short, without Data Terminal Ready, the modem goes functionally limp. Remember, though, that Ring Indicator (pin 22) operates independently of Data Terminal Ready.

Received Data   (RD, Pin 3) The EIA standard requires that Received Data be held at MARK when no carrier is present. The fact that this is *never* observed and that the same requirement for the transmitter is *always* observed provides an almost foolproof method to classify an unknown interface. The transmitter can be located simply by locating the negative voltage (MARK).

Ring Indicator   (RI, Pin 22) This signal is supported by most microcomputer modems. The voltage pulse produced does not occur at the ringer frequency, but remains asserted for the duration of the ring.

Data Signal Rate Detector   (DSRD, Pin 23) Not all microcomputer modems support this feature and where support exists, the pin designation varies. On the Bell 212A-compatible modems DSRD is on pin 12, while on CCITT V.22b-compatible modems it is supported on pin 23, as specified by the EIA and CCITT standards.

Figure 5-13   Typical connection beween microcomputer and modem.

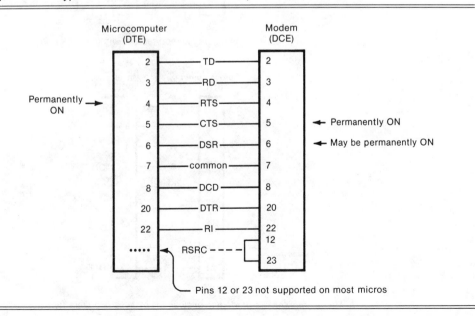

Of the signals on this list, it is safe to assume only that Transmitted Data (pin 2), Received Data (pin 3), Data Carrier Detect (pin 8), Data Terminal Ready (pin 20), Ring Indicator (pin 22), and *perhaps* Data Set Ready (pin 6) are always present and active. Request to Send (pin 4) and Clear to Send (pin 5) are usually present but not active (i.e., permanently asserted). An illustration of the resulting connection is shown in Figure 5-13. DSRD is also likely to be present in dual-speed modems, but should be discounted because neither of the pins on which it is commonly found (12 and 23) are supported on the typical microcomputer. Although other RS-232 inputs on the micro may be available for this purpose, a special cable would be required to cross-connect DSRD on the modem to the micro's input. (As we all know, there is no quicker way to deter customers than to require special cabling.)

Figure 5-14   RS-232 interchange for answering an incoming call.

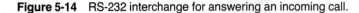

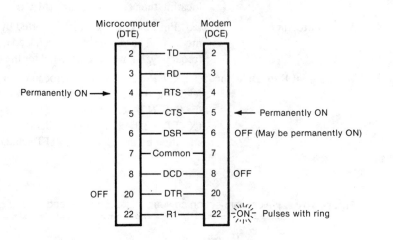

a. An incoming ring is reported on Ring Indicator (pin 22).

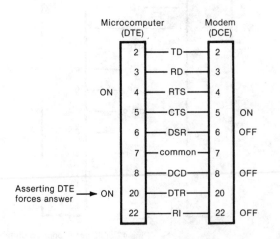

b. Microcomputer tells modem to answer call by asserting Data Terminal Ready (pin 20).

Figure 5-14 cont. RS-232 interchange for answering an incoming call.

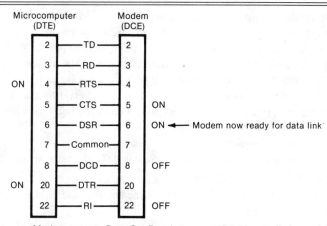

c. Modem asserts Data Set Ready to report finishing preliminary duties.

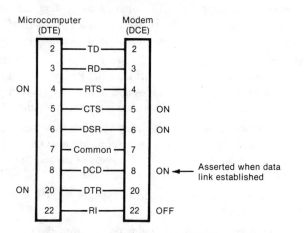

d. Modem's Data Carrier Detect reports that data link has been established.

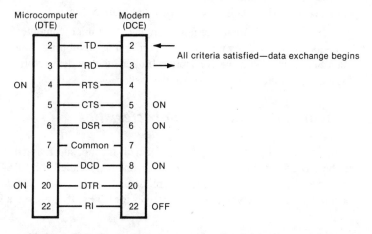

e. Modem's Data Carrier Detect reports that data link has been established.

A Sample RS-232 Interchange

The interrelationship of the RS-232 signals is best understood by a step-by-step analysis of the procedure for answering an incoming call. We are assuming that the modem is full-duplex and that, uncharacteristically, Data Set Ready (pin 6) is present both as an output on the modem and as an input on the microcomputer, and that it behaves in the manner prescribed by the RS-232 standard. The word ON is used to mean "asserted"—that is, logic 1.

The state of the two devices just as a ring occurs is shown in Figure 5-14a. Since our modem is full-duplex, there is no need for RTS/CTS handshaking. Therefore, the microcomputer always keeps RTS ON and the modem keeps CTS ON.

1. The software in the microcomputer (DTE) constantly monitors Ring Indicator (pin 22), waiting for it to be asserted (ON).

2. A ring occurs on the telephone line and the modem (DCE) asserts Ring Indicator for the duration of the ringing pulse.

3. The software notices that Ring Indicator is asserted and begins to count the number of rings by counting the number of ON/OFF transitions of Ring Indicator. When the programmed ring count is reached, the software asserts Data Terminal Ready (pin 20), which forces the modem to go off-hook (i.e., answer the telephone). This is shown in Figure 5-14b.

4. After waiting 2 seconds (an FCC rule), the modem automatically begins to transmit its answer carrier. The modem now asserts its Data Set Ready (pin 6) to inform the microcomputer that it has performed all preliminary duties and is awaiting a carrier. (Recall that many modems permanently assert Data Set Ready.) This state is shown in Figure 5-14c.

5. While keeping Data Terminal Ready (pin 20) asserted, the microcomputer's software monitors Data Set Ready (pin 6). When Data Set Ready goes ON, the microcomputer knows that the modem is ready for a data link; the microcomputer immediately begins to monitor Data Carrier Detect (pin 8) for evidence that the data link exists.

6. When the originate modem's carrier appears on the telephone line, the answer modem asserts Data Carrier Detect (pin 8).

7. Full-duplex communication begins on Transmit Data (pin 2) and Received Data (pin 3).[11] During data link, the microcomputer monitors Data Carrier Detect to make certain that a data link still exists. This state is shown in Figure 5-14e.

8. Communications are now complete. The microcomputer inhibits Data Terminal Ready. The modem responds by removing its carrier tone, inhibiting Data Carrier Detect, and inhibiting Data Set Ready. With the connection broken, the modem returns to the state shown in Figure 5-14a, ready to receive or make another call.

Mechanical and Electrical Characteristics

Considering that twenty-five pins are defined, it is not surprising that the most popular connector is the DB-25, or that it is sometimes erroneously called the "RS-232 connector." While the DB-25 is likely to remain standard on modems for the foreseeable future, the DB-9 and DB-15 are becoming increasingly popular alternatives for DTEs. If, however, a 9 or 15 pin connector is em-

---

[11]If this were a half-duplex connection, the modem and microcomputer would begin RTS/CTS line-turnaround handshaking on pins 4 and 5.

ployed, the standard pin assignments for Data Terminal Ready (pin 20), Ring Indicator (pin 22), and DSRD (pin 23) cannot be preserved. Therefore, when a connector other than a DB-25 is used, standard pin numbering goes out the window. Table 5-6, for example, shows the pin assignments for the IBM PC AT's DB-9 connector.

Table 5-6 RS-232 pin assignments for the IBM AT's 9-pin serial connector.

Pin	Function	Pin	Function
1	Received Line Signal Detect	6	Data Set Ready
2	Received Data	7	Request to Send
3	Transmit Data	8	Clear to Send
4	Data Terminal Ready	9	Ring Indicator
5	Signal Ground		

The EIA's limitation of speed to about 19.2KB is more of a warning than a prohibition. In fact, the RS-232 interface on most microcomputers is driven by UARTs capable of speeds up to 56KB. The upper limit on speed is often imposed by cable length instead of the frequency capabilities of the ICs.

In most RS-232 interfaces, the logic level for control signal inputs is effectively monopolar, so any voltage less than +3 volts inhibits the input. As a general rule, a disconnected, or "floating" input behaves as an inhibited one. Although these are precisely the kind of "facts" that eventually lead to trouble, they can save time when troubleshooting problems on the interface.

The Microcomputer Interface

Because of their enormous variety, it is difficult to make general observations about the RS-232 interfaces found on microcomputers. There is a very good reason why this is so—the micro lies completely outside of RS-232 considerations. As a matter of fact, microcomputers did not exist when the EIA formulated RS-232. This raises an interesting question—is a microcomputer DTE or DCE? Should computer manufacturers configure their serial ports as DTEs to interface with modems, or as DCEs to drive DTEs such as printers or terminals? Computers with two serial ports have a simple solution: configure one each way and label one "Printer" for driving a DTE and the other "Modem" for driving a DCE.

There are no ground rules in serial port configuration— manufacturers respond according to how they foresee the uses to which their equipment will be put. Two other factors shape the character of the microcomputer serial port. First, most microcomputer operating systems support modem I/O and printer I/O through the same physical port. As we shall see shortly, the needs of an operating system's printer driver are totally different from those of a modem driver. Second, the number of RS-232 control functions on current UARTs is limited. The typical UART, for example, provides two RS-232 outputs and two to four RS-232 inputs. With such a paucity of control signals, designers are understandably conservative and tend to allocate them to standard pin numbers and, where possible, standard functions.

A "System" View

As just mentioned, a single microcomputer serial port usually serves several logical system functions such as modem, printer, and "AUX" device. Therefore do not be surprised to discover that the *system* enforces arbitrary RS-232 rules on all serial I/O. The IBM PC family represents the height of folly in this regard, where the system—DOS and ROM BIOS—does not contain simple, unadorned functions to perform character-by-character serial I/O. For *every* byte, the serial output function perfunctorily asserts the Request to Send (pin 4) and Data Terminal Ready (pin 20) outputs, then tests that both Clear to Send (pin 5) and Data Set Ready (pin 6) inputs are enabled before transmitting the byte. Likewise, the serial input function refuses to read data from the serial port unless Data Set Ready is asserted. If these constraints are not bad enough, the system provides no mechanism to defeat them.

There is an important lesson to be learned here. Programmers like to regard the serial port as a portable medium through which to communicate with dissimilar (non-standard) devices that may or may not support RS-232 control signals. Indeed, in many cases, the lowly serial port is the only way to bring down a hardware Tower of Babel. Be forewarned: as far as microcomputer operating systems are concerned, all serial I/O is to some degree RS-232 I/O. There is no such thing as "general-purpose" serial I/O. If you wish to perform I/O through the *system's* resources (operating system calls, ROM routines, etc.), be prepared to obey an arbitrary subset of the RS-232 modem control rules even for simple tasks that manifestly have nothing to do with modems or RS-232.

Non-Standard Uses of RS-232

A pair of modems is functionally just a wire with awful transmission characteristics. The ends of this wire ultimately connect two DTEs. This leads to the obvious observation that two devices that function properly through modems should work identically if connected directly by a cable.

The Null Modem

Attempting to cable two DTE devices directly—that is, without going through modems—immediately gives rise to problems because the *RS-232 interface* in each DTE is designed for connection to a DCE (modem). The first is a hardware problem: two devices of the same sex[12] have the same connector. The second problem, illustrated in Figure 5-15, shows how an ordinary, "straight-through" cable produces an unworkable I/O arrangement by connecting inputs to inputs, outputs to outputs.

At the time the special cable is built to solve the connector mismatch, the two devices can also be custom-wired in such a manner that they cooperatively satisfy the handshaking requirements. This kind of connection, known as a *null modem* and shown in Figure 5-16, "tricks" the two interfaces by using the DTEs' own output voltages to satisfy the necessary RS-232 input logic.[13]

---

[12]The term "gender," which is a grammatical attribute of words, is often used to describe the physical conformation of plugs and jacks and even the concept of DTE and DCE. Null modems are even sometimes called "gender changers." "Male" and "female" are sexes; "masculine" and "feminine" are genders. To say a plug is of the "male gender," therefore, is not only incorrect, it is somehow insufferably prudish.

[13]It should be pointed out that although the null modem configuration can be used to interconnect two DCEs, such a connection is, in RS-232 terms anyway, an absurdity.

Figure 5-15 Same-sex connection produces unworkable I/O connection.

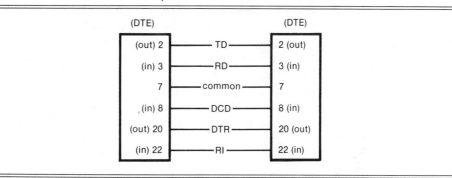

Figure 5-16 The null modem cable trick.

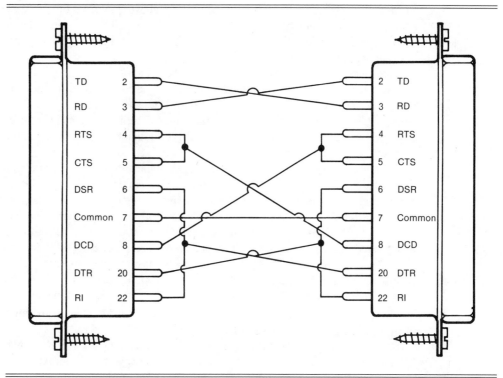

The most important connection on the null modem is the crossing of Transmitted Data (pin 2) and Received Data (pin 3) so that the data path is correct. The remaining connections satisfy control, or handshaking logic. For example, assertion of Request to Send (pin 4, an output) results in enabling Clear to Send (pin 5, an input) *and*, to simulate a data link, also enables Data Carrier Detect (pin 8) on the other interface. Similarly, assertion of Data Terminal Ready (pin 20) output simulates an incoming call by enabling its Data Set Ready (pin 6) and Ring Indicator (pin 22) inputs.

Connecting Non-Modem Devices: Hardware Handshaking

Although it is beyond the scope of this book to delve very deeply into the subject of non-RS-232 hardware interfacing,[14] we will take a look at the most common problem in this area—interfacing a computer to a serial printer.

A device that cannot use data as fast as the interface can send it requires some sort of flow control. Printers are the classic case of the need for *buffer-full handshaking*. If characters are sent to the printer at a faster rate than the printer can print them (as is usually the case), the printer places the incoming characters in a queue until they can be printed. The queue is in the form of an internal buffer whose size ranges from a few tens of bytes to several Kbytes in length. Because data is added to the buffer faster than it is removed, however, a buffer of any size eventually becomes full.

There are two basic methods by which a peripheral and a computer can perform flow control (handshaking): through software or through hardware. Software handshaking consists of a flow-control protocol such as the XON/XOFF or ETX/ACK protocols described in Chapter 4. The advantage of this method is that it can be performed over a modem link; its disadvantage is that many printers are send-only devices that cannot generate a TX data signal. The second and most common method is for the printer to use an RS-232 control signal to notify the computer of an impending full buffer.

But what is the correct RS-232 pin for the printer to use? The answer is that there is no "correct" way because the EIA standard does not address the need for interconnecting to non-modem devices. Indeed, flow control between a DTE and a modem is unnecessary because they must operate at the same baud rate. Since the standard itself is quiet on this subject, manufacturers are forced to choose handshaking pins arbitrarily. Although there is, predictably, little agreement on this topic, two broad views are discernible.

The first view, held mainly by peripheral manufacturers, uses one of the "undefined" pins in the EIA standard (see Figure 5-3) or, failing that, a pin that is unlikely to be in use. The advantage of this method is that buffer-full handshaking, being out of the way, does not interfere with standard RS-232 modem control signals. The second view, held mainly by computer manufacturers, explicitly uses *one or more* RS-232 modem control pins for buffer-full handshaking. As was pointed out a few pages ago, microcomputer controller ICs (UARTs) support only a few RS-232 inputs; consequently, computer manufacturers do not wish to waste an input by devoting it exclusively to an eccentric pin. Figure 5-17, for example, shows the cable required between an IBM PC family and an NEC Spinwriter printer—a very popular combination.

On the IBM PC side, the handshaking is performed on Data Set Ready (pin 6). Since system firmware enables the PC's transmitter only when Clear to Send (pin 5) *and* Data Set Ready are asserted, the positive voltage from the normally asserted Request to Send (pin 4) is jumpered to Clear to Send (pin 5) to form a *trick*. On the Spinwriter side, the printer refuses to print unless its Clear to Send, Data Set Ready, and Data Carrier Detect (pin 8) inputs are all enabled. These requirements are satisfied by tricks from Request to Send and Data Terminal Ready. Buffer-full handshaking is provided on pin 19[15] and connected to the IBM PC's Data Set Ready.

In a sense it is foolish even to talk about standards in this area—none exist. Considering the prodigious amount of pain and suffering that printer interfacing has inflicted upon computer users, it is surprising that no standard has been proposed.

---

[14]A complete discussion of this subject is contained in *The RS-232 Solution*, by Joe Campbell (Sybex, 1984).

[15]Warning—The Spinwriter contains an internal switch which determines whether the voltage produced on pin 19 is positive or negative.

Figure 5-17   Cable required between an IBM PC and an NEC Spinwriter model 3510.

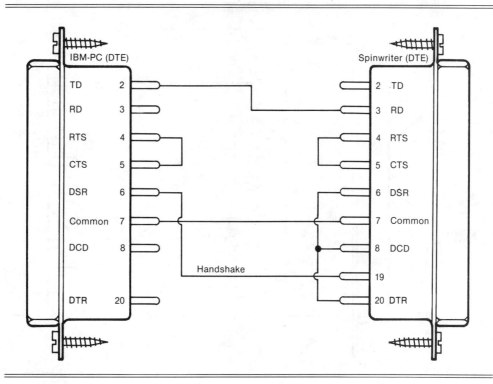

The Smart Modem

Formal RS-232 modem control, when viewed from the point of view of microcomputers, is suffocatingly medieval and certainly far more complicated than it needs to be. In this sense, the *"smart"* or *"intelligent"* modem is the microcomputer world's Enlightenment. Although Chapter 8 is devoted entirely to the study of the Hayes Smartmodem, the subject is worth a few paragraphs here, if for no other reason than to contrast its implicit philosophy with that of the "dumb" (RS-232-controlled) modem.

The conventional modems studied so far interact with their computer equipment at the hardware level; that is, by sending voltages across wires and interpreting them according to a complicated set of rules. Data and control information are always separate. By contrast, the smart modem interacts with computer equipment by exchanging ASCII messages on the Transmitted Data (pin 2) and Received Data (pin 3) data leads. No RS-232 control lines are needed because all modem control functions—dialing, answering, hanging up the telephone, and so forth—are accomplished by sending the smart modem strings of ordinary ASCII characters. The smart modem, in turn, replies to each command with its own ASCII messages. These range from simple messages acknowledging receipt of a command to more complicated ones that narrate the progress of a telephone call.

Today, virtually every modem sold for use with microcomputers is a smart modem. Why? Because its ASCII communication invites interaction with humans who can issue commands and monitor progress in their own language instead of via invisible electronic signals with obscure names and meanings. Figure 5-18 depicts the simplicity of the connection required to control a smart modem.

Figure 5-18   A theoretical three-wire cable for a smart modem.

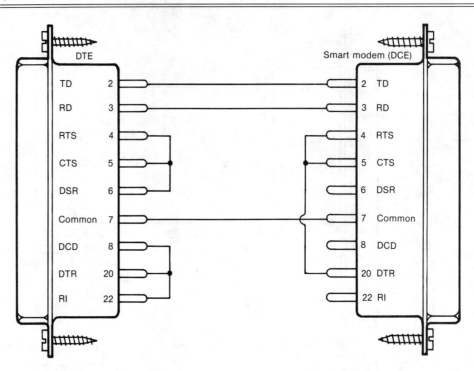

Notice that the only wires between the smart modem and the computer are Transmitted Data (pin 2), Received Data (pin 3), and Signal Common (pin 7). Although the smart modem itself may not require RS-232 controls, the computer's operating system may demand them. Accordingly, Figure 5-18 shows standard output-to-input handshaking tricks. The same cable could be used to connect a modem to a computer configured DCE simply by cross-connecting Transmitted Data and Received Data.

Conclusion

It would be nice to report that intelligent peripherals such as smart modems have relieved the vexation associated with asynchronous serial I/O. Unfortunately, modems and the RS-232 dominate the character of serial I/O on computers in general. This is particularly true on micros where there are usually not enough resources to justify a "vanilla" serial port (i.e., non-RS-232).

The lamentable conclusion to be drawn is that in order to circumvent the system's draconian enforcement of RS-232 rules, microcomputer programmers have to address the hardware directly. Yet we cannot always escape these rules by bypassing system software—RS-232 logic is actually built into some UARTs. Some, for example, refuse to transmit and receive unless the Clear to Send and Data Carrier Detect inputs are enabled. Although this *auto-handshake* mode is usually (and thankfully) under software control, its mere presence indicates how deeply intertwined serial I/O is with the RS-232 way of doing things. In summary, serial I/O and RS-232 seem, for better or worse, inextricably wed 'til death them do part.

In almost every chapter we have mentioned the asynchronous controller IC known as the UART. Since this device seems to dominate the conversation, it is finally time to explore it in depth. In the next chapter we will construct a "conceptual UART" based upon a survey of the tasks such a device must perform. In Chapter 7 we will examine two radically different real UARTs. Chapter 8 is devoted entirely to an exhaustive analysis of the Hayes Smartmodem family.

6

The UART—A Conceptual Model

In Chapter 2, we "reinvented" asynchronous I/O and in Chapter 5 we examined the workings of a modem and a typical microcomputer RS-232 interface. In this chapter, we'll see how these concepts are implemented in the real world. Luckily, today this world is more pleasant than just a few years ago when only indentured programmers could be persuaded to write asynchronous serial I/O. The rudiments of serial I/O in software, however, are deviously simple. A byte is output by writing its individual bits to a hardware latch which, in turn, drives an interface to the outside world (RS-232, for example). Conversely, input is performed by successively reading bits from a similar latch and assembling them into bytes. The difficulty in these processes arises when trying to implement the intricate timing relationships of the data and framing bits. Today, these problems are all handled almost transparently by an integrated circuit known as a UART.[1]

Asynchronous I/O in Software

There is no better way to gain an appreciation of the UART than to see what a programmer's life would be like without it. To this end, we'll briefly study what is required to perform asynchronous serial I/O in software. Figure 6-1 shows a flow chart for a hypothetical assembly-language routine to output a single byte using only the processor's clock cycle as a time reference. This chart assumes the existence of a processor instruction, SRC, that shifts all bits of the byte right and shifts the least significant bit into the carry flag. This instruction provides a rapid method for ascertaining the value of each bit. This flow chart also assumes the existence of a data port into which data is "latched," or written.

---

[1]The UART has many other names: ACE (Asynchronous Communications Element) and ACIA (Asynchronous Communications Interface Adaptor). All describe the same device. If the device also supports synchronous I/O, it is referred to as a USART.

Figure 6-1   A hypothetical flow chart for transmitting a single byte in software.

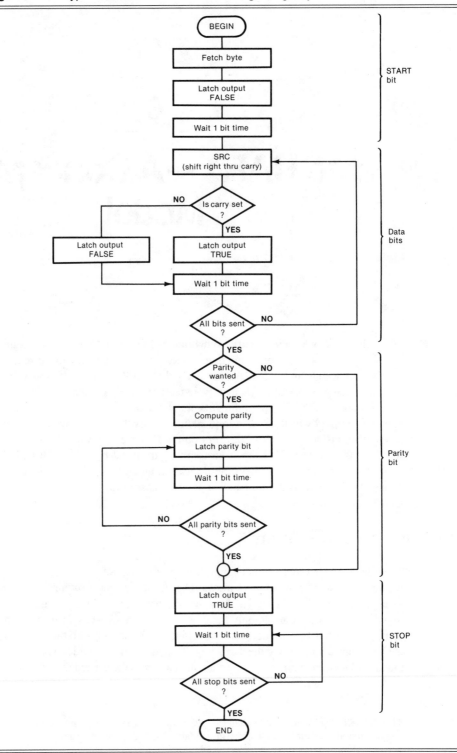

Software Asynchronous Output

After fetching the byte for transmission, the program immediately generates a START bit by latching the output FALSE for one bit-time. Next, the SRC instruction shifts the byte right once, placing the least significant bit into the carry flag. The value of the carry flag is then latched to the output for one bit-time. This process of shifting right and outputting the carry flag continues until all bits have been transmitted. If parity is enabled, the parity bit is calculated and latched to the output for one bit-time. The STOP bit is created by latching the output TRUE and the routine ends, leaving the output in this state (MARKING). The number of bits passed through the "All bits sent?" and "All STOP bits sent?" loops depends upon the data format currently in effect.

> Although most microprocessors have SRC-like instructions, the same effect can be achieved manually by successively applying AND masks to the output byte. After the AND operation, the Zero flag reflects the value of the bit to be output. This approach is slower and clumsier, however, because the value of the AND mask must correspond to the bit *number* being transmitted, 0000_0001 for the least significant bit, 1000_0000 for the most significant.

If writing the routine represented in the flow chart doesn't seem too difficult, consider the innocent-looking box labeled, "Wait one bit-time." Given the clock frequency and the number of clock cycles required for each instruction, writing a calibrated delay routine is not particularly difficult. Such a routine typically employs a register for counting the iterations of a loop of instructions of known duration. The routine depicted in Figure 6-1, however, requires a *variable* delay because the duration of a bit depends upon the current baud rate. At 300 baud, for example, a bit lasts 3.333 milliseconds (.00333 second), but at 19.2 Kbaud only 52 microseconds (.000052 second). A routine to provide an accurate variable delay over a *wide range* is rather more difficult to construct. Variable delay routines use the same principle as fixed delay routines, but add one or more outer loops that repeatedly call a fixed delay routine. Unfortunately, such multi-nested loop routines are not accurate over a wide range due to the time wasted in managing the loops.

An alternative to software timing loops is the use of a hardware timer, usually a crystal oscillator whose frequency is a multiple (harmonic) of the maximum baud rate desired. In this scheme, instead of counting iterations of processor instructions, software counts timer pulses, whose duration is known. We will return to the problem of timing again in Chapter 11 in another connection, so we will leave this topic for now. It is important to understand, though, that the code represented in the flow chart block "Wait one bit time" is deceptively simple and inherently dependent on such system factors as processor type, clock frequency, and system interrupt structure.

Software Asynchronous Input

The logic to assemble an inbound byte is, as you might expect, almost the inverse of that for transmitting a byte. The timing is similar, as is the need to deal with a variable number of data bits, the possibility of a parity bit, as well as a variable number of STOP bits. The flow chart for receiving

Figure 6-2 Flow chart for receiving a single byte in software.

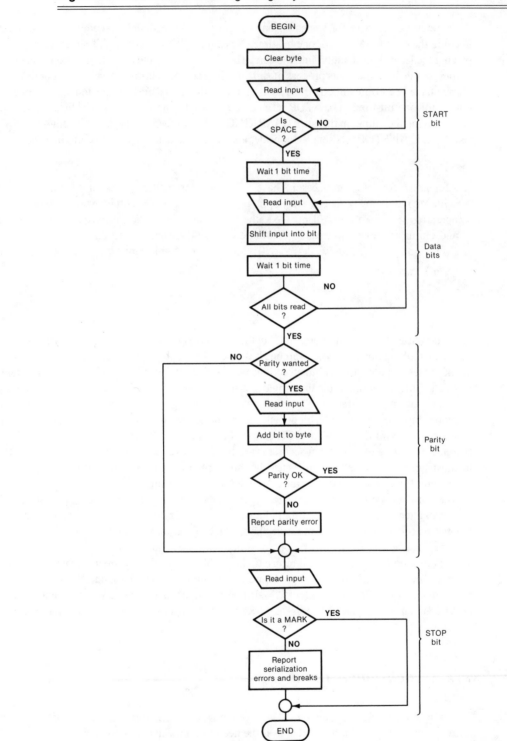

an inbound byte is shown in Figure 6-2. Despite these similarities, however, there are important differences. The receiver continually polls the input, waiting for a START bit (FALSE) to signal the beginning of an SDU. After the START bit is detected, the specified number of data bits is successively fetched and shifted into the byte under construction. The reception of the parity bit (if needed) followed by the STOP bit complicates the receive routine, for it is at this point that serialization errors and BREAKs must be detected. The first error test occurs after the reception of the parity bit: a parity bit that differs from the one expected must be reported. Once the parity bit has been processed, the input latch is read again to verify that a valid (i.e., TRUE) STOP bit is present. If not, a serialization error must be reported. The manner in which errors are reported depends on the system: a flag may be set in memory, a system interrupt may be generated, or, as in some implementations, errors are not reported at all.

Although you can probably conceive of writing these software functions to transmit and receive data, the flow charts in Figures 6-1 and 6-2 ignore an important aspect of asynchronous serial I/O: line sharing. As shown, these functions would be suitable only for simplex or half-duplex transmission. Why? Consider the program timing problems that result from *simultaneously* transmitting and receiving data. In between the transmitted bits, the program must also monitor the incoming line for activity. Now suppose, for example, that while transmitting a byte, a valid START bit is detected on the data input line. Your software is now responsible for maintaining two separate timing sequences—one to keep the outbound bits flowing at the prescribed baud rate and another to correctly fetch bits and assembly bytes from the input line. In other words, each function—receive and send—must adjust its timing loop based upon the activity of the other. Add to this picture the possibility that the incoming and outgoing baud rates may differ and you will quickly understand why full-duplex transmission has until recently been the bane of system programmers.

As complicated and distasteful as software-controlled, full-duplex, polled I/O may be, it is attainable on single-user microcomputers because the processor can be devoted entirely to maintaining the interrelated timing loops. Multi-user systems, on the other hand, share processor time among many tasks. In the days when asynchronous serial I/O was still performed in software on larger computers, full-duplex I/O could be attained only through complex interrupt schemes and then only if these interrupts were given the highest priority in the system. Because of this high priority, asynchronous serial I/O jobs tended to dominate a system, usurping time from other jobs.

Introduction to the UART

The basic asynchronous serial I/O functions just described, plus many others we will soon describe, are built into the Universal Asynchronous Receiver/Transmitter, or UART. The idea behind a UART is to relieve both programmer and processor of the toil associated with asynchronous serial I/O. To receive and send data, the program simply reads and writes bytes to the UART, which appears to the processor as one or more ordinary memory locations or I/O ports. The UART's circuitry handles the grimy details of assembling and reassembling bytes, handles the timing, and in general unburdens the processor.

Appliance-level UARTs first appeared about 1973 and quickly became ubiquitous. Because of the degree of simplicity UARTs brought to the previously arcane endeavor, software asynchronous I/O faded without much protest. Because many companies had huge investments in equipment and software to perform software asynchronous serial I/O, however, one can understand that even after UARTs became permanently entrenched in new computer designs, software asynchronous serial I/O did not instantly disappear from the scene. Because the popularity of the UART coincides roughly with the inception of the microcomputer, some early micro I/O boards did not contain UARTs. Instead, these boards provided support for what was essentially software I/O: an on-board clock, local RAM, address decoding, and, in some cases, a ROM containing the actual I/O routines.[2] Considering that high-quality, low-cost UARTs are now widely available (blister-packed UARTs are sold at Seven-Eleven stores in Silicon Valley), the absence of UARTs in a few otherwise "modern" designs, such as the Radio Shack Color Computer, is surprising.

Figure 6-3   A complete block diagram for our hypothetical UART.

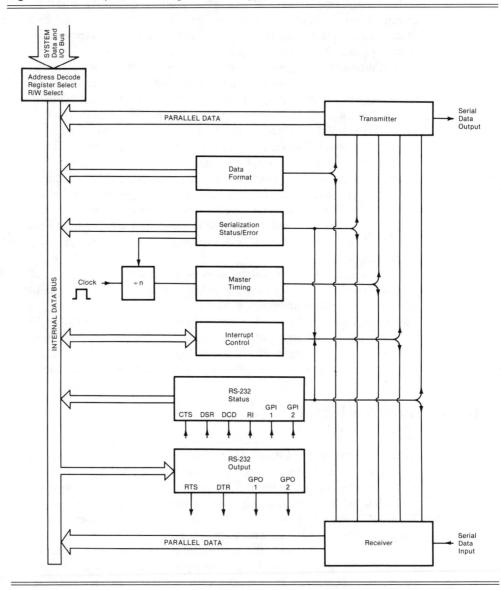

[2]Morrow's "Keyed-up 8080" and "Speak-Easy I/O Board" are good examples of this hardware. In what must be one of the great oxymorons of all times, boards such as these later became known as "software UARTs."

A block diagram for a hypothetical full-function UART is shown in Figure 6-3. For the remainder of this chapter we will study the details of each section of a hypothetical UART, pointing out how the various sections interact with the controlling program. Try to keep in mind that the UART presented here is conceptual— *exactly* no such device exists in nature. In the real world, for instance, you may find UARTs that use *inverted logic*—a 0 bit to represent a TRUE condition. Because such inner details of internal UART design are irrelevant to a conceptual understanding of how the devices work, we will ignore them in our discussions.

In the next chapter, we'll look at two representative samples of real UARTs. Now, before we begin an examination of how the UART transmits and receives serial data, let's take a brief and preliminary look at the *serial data clock*.

The Serial Data Clock

Before we begin our discussion of the serial data clock, it should be noted that in much of the literature on serial communications, the term *baud rate* and *data clock* are used interchangeably. While this causes no harm in casual discussion, we need the distinction here. As you will soon see, this is more than just an intellectual nicety—the correct functioning of a UART actually depends upon the existence of separate clocks for baud rate and internal timing. We postpone further illumination of this point until we have a better understanding of how the UART transmitter and receiver sections actually work.

Although our block diagram shows the serial data clock to be external to the UART, the actual circuitry for generating the clock may be part of the UART itself. If so, the frequency of the data clock is determined by the contents of a software programmable *baud rate register* (another misnomer). When the clock circuitry is external to the UART, however, the frequency of the data clock may be determined in several other ways:

- *Fixed frequency.* This, of course, occurs only in dedicated applications where the communication rate is not variable. The circuitry for these clock generators tends to be extremely simple, consisting of little more than a crystal and two or three logic gates. In some cases, the UART uses the processor's clock.

- *Variable frequency, software adjustable.* An external clock generator with adjustable frequency is programmable in much the same manner as when the generator is on the UART—by programming a specified register, memory address, or I/O port.

- *Variable frequency, hardware adjustable.* The clock generators of many early microcomputers derived their frequency from the binary value of microswitches (or jumpers) on the pc board. There are two variations to this scheme: first, the frequency of the generator can be dynamically (on the fly) altered by changing the position of the switches; second, the generator loads the value of the switches only at start-up and subsequent changes in the switch positions do not affect the frequency.

There is no reason why data must be received and transmitted at the same baud rate. Indeed, in certain full-duplex modem protocols, control and handshaking information is transmitted in a secondary reverse channel at a much lower rate than in the main data channel. In many UARTs, separate clock inputs are provided for transmitter and receiver. The system designer then decides whether to provide separate clocks or to use the same clock signal for both.

The UART Transmitter

A byte to be transmitted is written to the address of the UART's transmitter where it eventually is presented to the transmission section. This section consists largely of a shift register, the control logic to load the byte into the shift register, and one or more transmitter buffers. Figure 6-4 shows these functions.

Figure 6-4   Block diagram of hypothetical UART's transmitter.

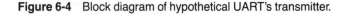

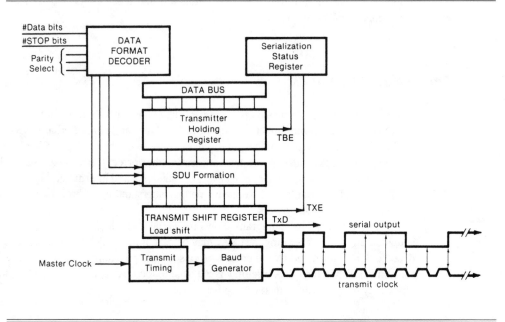

The transmitter itself consists of a parallel input, serial output shift register. The bits to be transmitted are loaded into the shift register, then shifted out on the negative transition of the *transmit data clock*. When all bits have been shifted out of the transmitter's shift register, the next SDU[3] is loaded and the process repeats. Not counting the START bit, the shift register must be large enough to accommodate from 7 bits (5N1) to 11 bits (8P2), although the latter is rare.

The data bits may be loaded directly from the system data bus, but most UARTs contain a transmitter buffer, or *Transmitter Holding register* which forms a small queue in which data can be temporarily stored while awaiting serialization. A byte for transmission can therefore be written into the UART's holding register while the previous byte is still being clocked out of the shift register. This buffering is not only a convenience, it makes the transmitter more efficient. Because there is an entire SDU within which the processor may replenish the buffer, it is easier to keep the shift register perpetually occupied. There may be several transmitter buffers, but most UARTs contain only one.

---

[3]To refresh your memory, SDU stands for "Serial Data Unit," the term developed in Chapter 2 for the collective START, data, parity, and STOP bits.

Framing

Since by definition an SDU begins with a SPACE (∅) bit, a ∅ can be automatically loaded into the first bit of the SDU. Three elements of the SDU, however, are variables: the number of STOP bits, parity, and the number of data bits. Interposed between the transmit buffer and the shift register, therefore, is a section labeled *SDU Formation*. Using signals decoded from user-programmable Data Format registers, this section fabricates the actual SDU that is eventually loaded into the shift register. For example, if the UART were programmed for 7E2, the data format logic section would build an SDU for the letter 'E' like this:

Figure 6-5   Building an SDU for the letter 'E' at 7E2.

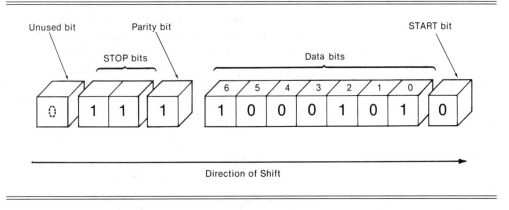

Notice that regardless of the format in effect, unused SDU bit positions are left-filled with ∅s. Zeroes are also shifted into the vacated left-hand positions. With unused positions guaranteed to be ∅, the transmitter contains a value of 1 only when all bits except the final STOP bit have been shifted out. This condition is used to announce that the transmitter buffer will be empty after the next shift/clock cycle. If the transmitter buffer contains a byte when the next clock cycle occurs (i.e., when the transmitter becomes empty), that byte is automatically loaded into the transmitter and transmission proceeds anew.[4] If, on the other hand, the transmitter buffer is also empty, the next clock cycle sets the *transmitter empty flag (TXE)*, but suppresses the final shift. The TD line therefore continues to assert the level of the final STOP bit and the line idles at a TRUE (MARK-ING) level until another byte arrives to begin the transmission process anew.

Transmitter Status

Writing programs to transmit data requires only two items of information about the transmitter: whether both the Transmitter Buffer and the transmitter's shift registers are empty. Each of these conditions is reported through a bit in a *Serialization Status register*. When the data from the buffer is loaded into the transmitter, a *transmitter buffer empty* (TBE) flag signals that the UART can accept another byte. If TBE is clear after the final bit of the SDU is clocked from the transmitter's shift register, the TXE flag signals that the shift register is also empty.

During full-duplex communication, software need only test the value of the TBE bit (in the Serialization Status register) to make certain that the buffer is empty before writing a byte to the UART. At various points in half-duplex communication, however, the modems must reverse their

---

[4]If 1½ STOP bits are selected, the format control logic arranges fractional bit timing on the last STOP bit.

roles—from transmitter to receiver and vice versa. (This action is called "turning the line around.") Before software can instruct a transmitting modem to become a receiver, it must know not only that the transmitter buffer is empty but also that the transmitter's shift register itself is empty. Otherwise the line may be reversed in mid-SDU, causing loss of data. (This is called "leaving one in the pipe.")

The UART's Receiver

A received byte is acquired by reading the address of the UART's receiver section, whose job is to construct an SDU from bits fetched from the serial input line. The UART must then extract the data byte from the surrounding formatting information in the SDU and make the byte available to the data bus. A block diagram of a UART receiver is shown in Figure 6-6. The receiver perpetually monitors the incoming serial line, waiting for a START bit. Once a START bit is detected, successive bits are shifted into the receiver's shift register according to the format described in the UART's user-programmable Data Format registers. After assembly, the byte is moved into a first-in, first-out buffer. Every modern UART has a FIFO, but the size varies from 1 to 5 bytes. (Chapter 20 shows how to obtain a FIFO of essentially unlimited size.)

Figure 6-6 A block diagram of a UART receiver.

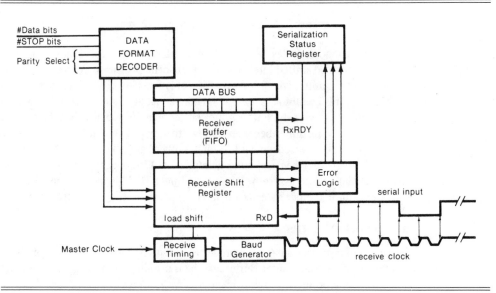

Receiver Status

When a byte has been moved into the receiver's FIFO, the RxRDY flag is set TRUE and remains TRUE until all elements of the FIFO are empty. For every element in the FIFO, there is a corresponding Serialization Status register.

Errors

The UART in no way forces a response to an error. Once a START bit is detected, the UART dutifully assembles a byte even in the face of cataclysmic errors. There is nothing to prevent your software from reading the resulting ersatz "byte" as it would a valid byte. Although software is under no obligation to test for errors, UARTs inevitably provide a mechanism for reporting them. The responsibility for testing for and handling errors, however, always lies entirely with the software. Throughout this discussion, please keep in mind that the term "serialization error" applies to errors in *reception* and transmission.

Transmitter Errors

As might be supposed, few errors are possible in the transmission process. Writing into a non-empty transmitter buffer results in a *transmitter overwrite* error (also sometimes referred to as *transmitter underrun* error). Under the assumption that this error is easily avoided, many UARTs do not even report a transmitter overwrite.

Receiver Errors

Unlike the transmission process, a number of problems may arise during reception.

- When bytes arrive faster than they can be read, they are placed in the receiver's FIFO buffer. When this buffer becomes full, it "wraps around" upon itself, with each new byte overwriting an older, and as yet unread, byte in the buffer. This is a *receiver overrun* error.
- If the value of the parity bit does not agree with that decoded from the user-programmable Data Format registers, a *parity error* is reported.
- If an invalid STOP bit is received, and if all data bits and the parity bit are 0, the serial line is assumed to have been FALSE for a time equal to one SDU, and a BREAK is reported.
- If an invalid STOP bit is received, the UART ascertains whether the assembled SDU contains *at least* one TRUE data bit. If so, either the START bit was invalid, or succeeding bits were damaged during transmission. Since it is not possible to ascertain the nature of the error more precisely, the catch-all *framing error* is reported.

The receiver errors just listed assume, of course, that transmitter and receiver are operating at identical baud rates and data format. A mismatch in either always generates an error.

Error Reporting

Serialization errors are reported in the UART's *Serialization Status* register, which is also often used to report the TXE (transmitter's shift register empty), TBE (transmitter buffer empty), and RxRDY flags. Each error or flag is mapped to a single bit in this register. Figure 6-7a shows an example of how these bits may be mapped.

Figure 6-7b depicts how some UARTs, especially those that also support synchronous transmission (i.e., USARTs), devote an entire register to error reporting. The occurrence of an error not only sets a designated bit in this register, it also sets a bit in a general-purpose status

Figure 6-7 Two versions of a UART's Serialization Status register.

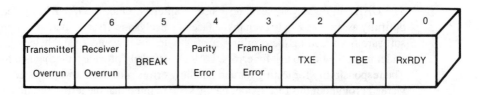

7	6	5	4	3	2	1	0
Transmitter Overrun	Receiver Overrun	BREAK	Parity Error	Framing Error	TXE	TBE	RxRDY

a. Single UART Serialization Status Register

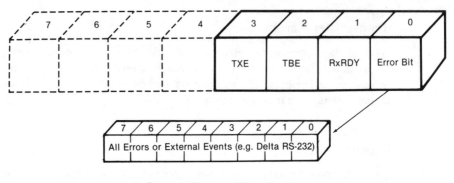

7	6	5	4	3	2	1	0
				TXE	TBE	RxRDY	Error Bit

7	6	5	4	3	2	1	0
All Errors or External Events (e.g. Delta RS-232)							

b. Separate Status and Error Registers

register. In this scheme, any transmitter/receiver status and serialization error can be detected by reading a single register. To identify the exact nature of the error, however, another register must be read. In addition to serialization errors, this register may also report the change in status of the RS-232 inputs or a BREAK.

Error Reading

Reading the Error register usually resets all error flags, although, rarely, an explicit *error reset* operation is required. The presence of the error status bits and the transmitter/receiver empty status bits in the same register potentially gives rise to a minor programming problem. When writing receiver routines, it is somehow natural to poll the receiver until its status bit becomes TRUE, then read the byte, then test for errors. Polling in this manner resets the error bits with each poll; the error status must be held in temporary storage until time to act upon it. Of course, the same caution holds for transmitter routines.

Receiver Timing

In describing how the UART transmitter works, we have glossed over the important subject of timing. Although designers of hardware devices strive to make the device's internal timing invisible to the programmer, the UART programmer is actually expected to participate in one important area. You will remember from our discussion in Chapter 2 that the purpose of the START bit is to synchronize the receiver with the transmitter at the beginning of each SDU. Until now, we have discussed this synchronization as it occurs under ideal conditions in which the receiver and transmitter operate at identical baud rates. When the periods of the two baud rates are identical, the point at which the receiver samples the incoming data is *theoretically* unimportant. But since this never happens in practice, we need to examine how different baud rates affect operation.

Figure 6-8 shows the same relationship, but with the receiver operating at a slightly higher baud rate. To dramatize the timing relationships involved, this figure shows the data bits on the incoming line as heavy square waves. The receiver's data clock is shown as an arrow that represents the point at which the receiver actually samples the line.

Figure 6-8 Incoming data sampled by two receivers of different phases.

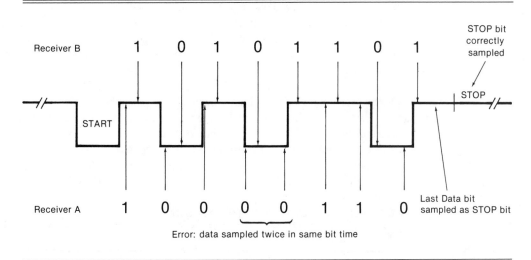

The byte transmitted is the binary value 1011_0101 at 8-NO-1 (remember, the low-order bit is transmitted first). As the diagram shows, receiver A detects the START bit relatively early in its period. Since receiver A's baud rate is slightly higher than the period of the incoming data, the receiver samples the first data bit yet nearer the trailing edge of the *preceding* incoming bit. So far so good. On each successive bit, however, the receiver samples the line earlier and earlier until its sampling pulse "falls over the edge" and actually occurs twice during bit 3. Sampling continues until the UART receives what it assumes is a correct STOP bit, which, due to the sampling "creep," is really just bit 7 of the data. It is important to see that receiver A assembles the wrong byte (0110_0001, the ASCII character 'e'), but *no framing error* is detected. Likewise, you should understand why this phenomenon is possible only with bytes whose low-order bit is TRUE.[5]

Now examine receiver B in Figure 6-8. Its period and bit-to-bit creep are precisely the same as receiver A. The only difference between the two receivers is the difference in the points at which they sample the incoming data (i.e., their *phase relationship*). Because receiver A begins so early in the data bit, its sampling point quickly creeps backwards into the previous data bit. Re-

---

[5]Although the use of parity would also have caught this particular error, there is a disturbing aspect about this type of error. Indeed, one can posit a situation where virtually *any* single byte might be received incorrectly, but without generating an error condition. Although it is unlikely that such a condition would go undetected for more than 1 or 2 bytes, the inability to associate an error with the byte that caused it is obviously a serious problem in any form of communication.

ceiver B, however, begins precisely in the center of the incoming data bit. Because it has farther to creep, receiver B samples the correct incoming data bit for the entire SDU.

Since sampling earlier in the input seems to immunize against sampling creep, there is a temptation to start sampling at the earliest possible moment, say, on the leading edge. That would certainly provide the maximum protection when the receiver's baud rate is higher than the transmitter's, but would have the opposite effect when the speed relationships are reversed. While there is no cure for errors caused by widely different baud rates, the UART is clearly much more tolerant when its receiver begins serialization near the center of the START bit.

Earlier in this chapter, we discussed the necessity of separate clock signals—one for the UART's internal operations and one to drive the shifting operations in the transmitter and receiver sections. The reason for these two clock signals can now be explained. The frequency of the master serial clock signal is designed to be several times higher than that of the baud rate. The ratio between the baud rate clock and the master data clock is called the *clocking factor*. A clocking factor of 16 is standard, but is programmable on some UARTs. The higher frequency of the master clock signal enables us to make a major improvement in the way START bits are detected.

Instead of sampling the input line at the baud rate frequency, the improved START bit detector samples the incoming line at the rate of the master clock. When the leading edge of a START bit is detected, the START bit detector waits for 8 data clock cycles (which together constitute one-half of a bit time), then begins reading bits from the line. Thereafter sampling of the input occurs once per bit-time (i.e., at the baud rate). By pausing to wait 8 clock cycles for the *center* of the STOP bit, the receiver is effectively "ideally" synchronized to the incoming data.

Figure 6-9 Best and worst case START bit detection with a clocking factor of 16.

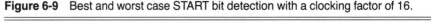

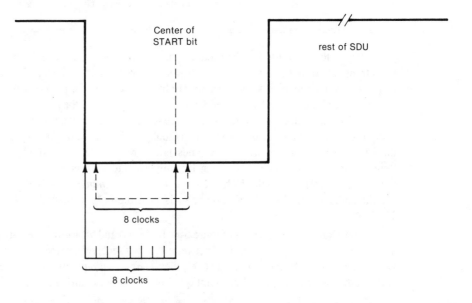

Figure 6-9 illustrates how well the improved START bit detector works. Under the best conditions—when the line is sampled at the instant the START bit begins—the UART locates the exact center. Under worst conditions—when the line is sampled one full clock cycle into the START bit—synchronization occurs $\frac{1}{16}$ of a bit-time past the center. This means that when the receiver's period is shorter than the transmitter's, the receiver's *cumulative* "backward" creep can be about $\%_{16}$ of a bit-time over the remainder of the SDU. When the receiver's period is longer than the transmitter's, the receiver's *cumulative* "forward" creep can be about $\frac{7}{16}$ of a bit-time. Remember, sampling is resynchronized (recentered) with each new START bit. For a 10-bit SDU, (7E1) for example, the cumulative error is spread over all 10 bits. For a fast receiver, this means that no error occurs if the baud rate error does not exceed $\%_{16} \times 10$, or about 5.6 percent; for a slow receiver, the baud rates may differ by $\frac{7}{16} \times 10$, or 4.3 percent.[6]

If a clocking factor of 16 provides good tolerance of baud rate errors, wouldn't a factor of 32 or even 64 improve performance even more? In fact, higher clocking factors force the UART and baud rate circuitry to work at higher frequencies. Considering that the performance improvement attained in this manner is insignificant (a few tenths of a percent) the trade-off hardly seems worth it. There is, however, one situation where the ability to switch clocking factors is important. As mentioned earlier, some computers do not support baud rate selection in software, but by switches or jumpers. If these switches are set to produce a reasonable baud rate with a clock factor of 32, the baud rate can be altered by reprogramming the UART's clocking factor. Suppose, for example, that the switches are adjusted to achieve 1200 baud with a clocking factor of 32. Switching to a factor of 16 produces a baud rate of 2400 while selecting a factor of 64 results in 300 baud. Although some UARTs offer a clocking factor of 1, this is not likely to prove satisfactory because, as shown by Figure 6-8, START bit synchronization cannot be achieved.

Before we leave the subject of synchronization, we should mention another refinement in the START bit detector that makes it even more reliable. After detecting the START bit and waiting for 8 clock cycles, synchronization does not automatically begin. Instead, the UART retests the communications line to make certain that the START bit is *still* present. If not, the UART assumes that the START bit was a noise spike on the line and does not begin reception.

Data Format

Predictably, the study of how a UART assembles an SDU closely follows the asynchronous theory in Chapter 2. It is especially interesting to see how modern UARTs replace the solenoids and cross bars depicted in Figure 2-3 with silicon wizardry.

Unlike mechanical devices, where the data format is frozen in hardware, a UART obtains its definition of the SDU by decoding the bits in its user-programmable *Data Format register*. Figure 6-10 shows the bit mapping for our hypothetical UART.

Figure 6-10 Bit map of a UART's Data Format register.

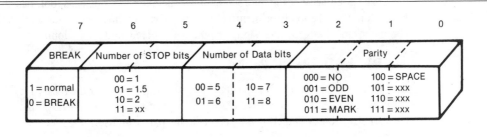

---

[6]This figure is theoretical because it ignores the sampling times and settling delays built into the UART. In actual practice, the range of immunity seems about $+4.5$ and -2.5 percent.

Parity

As described in Chapter 3, parity is a binary checkvalue. In the *ODD parity* scheme, the parity bit is added so there are an odd number of TRUE bits. Conversely, *EVEN parity* generates the parity bit necessary to make an even number of TRUE bits. ANSI X3.25-1967[7] designates bit 7 to be the parity bit for the ASCII code, but most UARTs support parity with any number of data bits including, although almost no one does it, 8.

If parity is enabled when a byte is received, the UART calculates the parity bit based upon the values of the data bits received. It then compares this calculated value according to the one described in the Data Format register. If the values differ, the "parity error" bit is set in the UART's Serialization Status register.

It is interesting to note that 100 percent parity errors occur when systems attempt to communicate with mismatched parity settings (ODD/EVEN), but only 50 percent when one of the systems is set to 8-NO. Using this fact, software can ascertain the SDU of the sending system and, if desired, adjust its own. The sensing software sets its own system to 7-EVEN and emits a query that is likely to elicit a response that contains both ODD and EVEN bytes. If it is an echoplex system, for instance, you might send several consecutive ASCII characters followed by the line terminator (CR). If the response generates parity errors in about half of the bytes, the software adjusts to 8-NO; if a parity error occurs on every byte, the software adjusts to 7-ODD. After adjustment of the data format, the test is performed again until no parity errors occur.

In general, parity is falling out of favor in modern communications. There are several good reasons for this.

1. Improvement of local computer communications hardware has removed many of the causes for error. The introduction of the UART is a good example.

2. A high proportion of errors in modem communications are caused by noise, especially burst noise. Parity is almost useless in the presence of burst noise (see the footnote on page 55).

3. Parity's usurpation of the high-order bit precludes the transmission of binary data such as executable files (see "8-bit Parity," below). As discussed in Chapter 4, the unavailability of a high-order bit causes enormous problems when binary data must be moved across serial data links. Such is the case in many mainframe systems which were not designed to exchange data through asynchronous serial ports. In such systems, asynchronous serial ports are designed for use with the user's terminals either connected directly or through modems; the "serious" matter of data transfer is intended to take place through synchronous data links or through interchangeable storage media.

The popularity of the microcomputer, especially as a business tool, has changed the industry's outlook on the lowly asynchronous serial port. As the need to transport data between micro and mainframe has grown, system designers are increasingly abandoning parity altogether.

MARK AND SPACE Parity

Besides NO, ODD, and EVEN parity settings, it is possible for the parity bit to be always TRUE or always FALSE. The former is called MARK parity, the latter SPACE parity. MARK and SPACE parity are capable of detecting only errors in the parity bit itself: the receiver reports an error only

---

[7]The name of this 2-page document is almost as long as its content: *Character Structure and Character Parity Sense for Parallel-by-bit Data Communication in the American National Standard Code for Information Exchange.*

if the parity bit is not TRUE or FALSE, respectively. Despite their ineffectiveness as error detection codes, MARK and SPACE parity can be found in a surprising number of applications. (Many IBM systems, for example, use MARK parity.)

Since MARK and SPACE settings are obviously not useful for error detection, when are they useful? To an 8-NO receiver, 7-SPACE parity looks exactly like an 8-NO transmission of ASCII data (i.e., bytes in the range $0-127$). Because of its effect of resetting the high-order bit, 7-SPACE is occasionally useful to prevent sending non-ASCII data to an ASCII device such as a printer. MARK parity can be used to sneak in an additional STOP bit to any receiver that is not expecting a parity bit. Despite these arcane uses, however, MARK and SPACE parity have little value in modern communications.

8-Bit Parity

It is worth noting here that virtually every UART supports 8 data bits *with parity*. For no apparent reason, most computer users find it conceptually difficult to deal with this format. In their minds, this format is somehow illegal—"it has too many bits," or it is "un-ASCII." Of course, neither of these statements is true. (Those who have qualms about its ASCII-ness do not seem to be bothered by the equally "illegal" 8-NO format.) In truth, the only valid objection to the 8-bit parity format is the additional 1-bit overhead incurred during transmission.

Number of Data Bits

Although seldom encountered by microcomputer programmers, there is still a fair number of 5- and 6-bit codes in use today. Five-bit codes can still be found in Western Union Telex (especially international) and in many teleprinters. The standard US military codes are all 6-bit codes. Six-bit codes persist in "ticker" output from the New York Stock Exchange and even in some more recent Teletype models. The ubiquitous Teletype US M35 is available in 5-, 6-, 7-, and 8-bit versions.

Although 5- and 6-bit codes provide a comparatively Spartan character set—usually just upper-case alphabet, numerals, and minimum graphics and punctuation—their smaller SDU allows for a higher data transmission rate than larger codes. So, despite the dwindling number of new applications for 5- and 6-bit codes, they are likely to continue where speed and efficiency is more important than subtlety of expression (in the military and in stock tickers, for example).

Bit Padding in Codes of Less Than 8 Bits

The use of codes smaller than 8 bits brings up an interesting problem. Even though the UART receiver may assemble an SDU of only, say, 5 data bits plus a parity bit, ultimately it must construct an 8-bit byte to output on the system bus. As we might suppose, the parity bit (if present) is inserted after the most significant data bit. But with what value does the UART fill the unused data bits 6, 7, and 8? Most UART data sheets ignore this question altogether. In practice, some UARTs pad unused bits with 0s, some with 1s, and others with *random* values. In the absence of a standard, therefore, the programmer must assume that unused bits are padded randomly. Accordingly, unused bits should be masked off whenever the combination of data and parity bits is less than 8.

Number of Stop Bits

Our conceptual model of the Data Format register includes bit mapping for 1, 1½, and 2 STOP bits. Most UARTs permit all three values, but there is a recent tendency to correlate the number of

STOP bits to the number of data bits. Two STOP bits are seldom necessary in the 5-bit format because START bit synchronization occurs so frequently that the receiver has no time to creep. At any rate, some UARTs permit 1½ STOP bits only with 5-bit data formats, but permit 1 or 2 STOP bits with any format. Some automatically switch to 1½ whenever 5 data bits are selected.

The "Send BREAK" Bit

The BREAK bit does not logically fit in the Data Format register, or, for that matter, anywhere else; it is shown here for lack of a better place. The BREAK bit is implemented in a fairly standard manner in all UARTs: when TRUE, the UART's transmitter output is held at SPACE. There is one interesting variation: *programmable BREAK timing*. In this mode, the UART's transmitter is held at SPACE for exactly 1½ SDUs, after which it returns to its normal MARK condition. This convenience feature, intended to free the programmer from manually timing the duration of the BREAK, is of limited usefulness because the duration of a BREAK is always defined locally.

The RS-232 Interface

Programmers new to asynchronous serial I/O are often puzzled by the presence of RS-232 input and output names on a UART. We have already discussed how asynchronous serial I/O and RS-232 are inseparably, and perhaps, unfortunately wedded. Generally speaking, a UART's so-called *modem control* inputs and outputs have nothing whatsoever to do with the basic processes of serial transmission and reception. That is, the RS-232 functions could just as well exist in a totally separate device. In fact, their presence in the same package with a transmitter, receiver, and serialization support circuitry ought to be viewed more as a programming convenience than a declaration of their participation in these processes.

On the other hand, it is naive to suppose that RS-232 devices are not a part of the serial I/O universe. Serial input and output almost presume that serial data will be transmitted to or received from a device external to the computer. After all, unless the data is bound for the outside world, why use serial (as opposed to parallel) I/O at all?[8] By convention, most serial I/O is performed through an RS-232 interface. Therefore, to program asynchronous serial I/O is, like it or not, to grapple with RS-232. Our UART model, therefore, acknowledges this close practical relationship by devoting two entire registers to RS-232 functions.

RS-232 Output Register

Only two RS-232 control outputs are commonly integrated into UARTs. These are shown in Table 6-1.

Before continuing our discussion, however, it is essential to understand two important points that many programmers find confusing. First, by convention, the UART names given the

---

[8]This is perhaps unduly harsh. There are actually many applications in which serial communications is preferable. The use of serial technology is increasingly popular in *distributed processing* (where several processors must communicate), where the failure of a single parallel device will disable the entire bus. Serial I/O also sees heavy use in robots, where signals must travel long distances through noisy environments.

Table 6-1 RS-232 outputs supported by most UARTs.

Output	Pin	"Official" Function (DTE)
RTS	4	(Request to Send) This line is meaningful only during full-duplex modem transmission, to instruct the modem to change from receiver to transmit or vice versa.
DTR	20	(Data Terminal Ready) This output is the modem's master enabling signal without which the modem will not go or remain "online."

RS-232 inputs and outputs assume that the UART is connected as a DTE device. This means that names such as DTR and RTS are *outputs* while CTS and DSR are inputs. Second, all inputs and outputs, whatever their names, are really just general-purpose outputs and are not necessarily intended to perform modem-like tasks.

To illustrate the second point, there is a tale—apocryphal, no doubt—about a journeyman programmer who had worked for years doing asynchronous programming in software. Upon purchasing his first microcomputer, he discovered that its UART was defective—its receiver worked fine, but its transmitter was inoperative. Undaunted, and anxious to establish communications with the outside world, the fellow soon discovered that by writing to a specific register, he could toggle the DTR output line between MARK and SPACE. He then proceeded to write the software asynchronous serial I/O routines to transmit using, yes, the DTR pin! The moral of this story is simple: what you choose to do with them, *if anything*, depends entirely upon your application and your imagination. Nevertheless, you should realize that most devices expect the computer to supply one or more control voltages through its RS-232 outputs.

RS-232 Inputs

Four RS-232 inputs are commonly integrated into UARTs. These are shown in Table 6-2.

Table 6-2 RS-232 inputs supported by most UARTs.

Input	Pin	"Official" Function (DTE)
CTS	5	(Clear to Send) A half-duplex modem asserts this line when it has successfully responded to the RTS (above) by turning the line around and is ready to act as a receiver.
DSR	6	(Data Set Ready) This input announces that a modem is online and ready for communications (actually, that the modem is not doing anything else).
DCD	8	(Data Carrier Detect) This is input on which a modem announces that a data link has been established with another modem.
RI	22	(Ring Indicator) This is the input where a modem announces an incoming call.

Despite their RS-232 names, these inputs, like the outputs, are actually just general-purpose inputs whose interpretation depends upon the application. The programmer in the tale of the defective UART, instead of using an RS-232 output as a transmitter, could just as plausibly have written software to operate one of these inputs as a serial data receiver.

Handshaking

After laboring to convince you that the RS-232 inputs and outputs are "user-definable" and do not necessarily interact with basic UART transmitter and receiver functions, we must now examine the significance of the word "necessarily."

As in most hardware appliance devices, there are two schools of thought in UART design. The "flexibility" school maintains that a UART should provide the basic functions required to perform asynchronous serial I/O, but should not include specialized features that favor one application at the expense of others. This is essentially the philosophy we have followed in developing our UART model.

By contrast, the "convenience" school holds that UARTs should take over as much drudgery as possible in their area of application. So what if the device becomes difficult to use for a few applications if it is significantly more convenient for most? This philosophy is revealed in the use of the two RS-232 inputs, CTS and DCD.

In some UARTs, the transmitter status flags (TXE and TBE) are ANDed with the CTS input. This means that unless the CTS line is asserted, the transmitter remains busy. Similarly, the receiver's RxRDY flag is ANDed with the DCD input. To understand why, in heavens name, a designer would ever hardwire these "features" into his product, let's look at some of the design criteria involved in two common UART applications: a modem and serial printer.

The Serial Printer   Since printers are not capable of printing characters as fast as computers can send them, the printer must somehow signal when its input buffer is full. How convenient to have a *hardware handshaking* (flow-control) pin built right in the UART so when the printer needs to stop the flow of data, it merely inhibits the RS-232 CTS line, which automatically turns off the UART's transmitter.

The Modem   The official use of DCD in the RS-232 standard is to inform the computer or terminal that a modem/data link is in progress. By tying RxRDY to DCD, we effectively shut off the reception of data in the absence of a modem to send it. Similarly, by tying the UART's transmitter to the CTS input, we prohibit the transmission of data until the modem is ready to receive.

The design criteria in both cases are correct, but hopelessly optimistic. Moreover, only a very few applications require full modem control, and those that do inevitably find a UART's built-in modem support to be inadequate. In the mind of a programmer, therefore, the minor convenience of automatic handshaking is usually outweighed by the inevitable loss of software design flexibility.

There is a more practical, almost political reason not to include automatic handshaking in UARTs: applications that specifically wish *not* to utilize the automatic handshaking will require special cabling to defeat it. This necessity to "trick" a serial interface, perhaps more than any other quality, has led to serial I/O's bad name among users.

RS-232 Status Register

Figure 6-11a shows our hypothetical *RS-232 Status Register*. Bits $0 - 3$ reflect the current status of one of the RS-232 input lines. Assuming that the UART is connected to an interface, as depicted in Figure 5-12, a TRUE bit means that the input is asserted (greater than $+3$ volts); FALSE means that the input is inhibited (less than -3 volts). Bits 4 and 5 are general-purpose inputs whose functions are not even associated with RS-232 functions.

Figure 6-11 The modem control registers. Numbers in parentheses are DTE pin numbers.

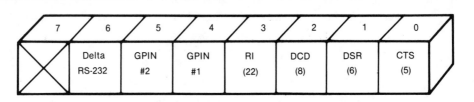

7	6	5	4	3	2	1	0
	Delta RS-232	GPIN #2	GPIN #1	RI (22)	DCD (8)	DSR (6)	CTS (5)

a. The RS-232 Input Status Register

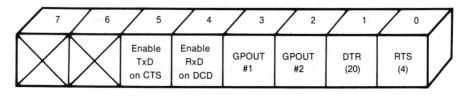

7	6	5	4	3	2	1	0
		Enable TxD on CTS	Enable RxD on DCD	GPOUT #1	GPOUT #2	DTR (20)	RTS (4)

b. RS-232 Outputs and Auto-Handshake Enables

At times, we are not interested in the actual state of an input, but whether it has changed state. Bit 6, therefore, is labeled **Delta RS-232** to suggest that this bit reports a change in any of the RS-232 inputs. This bit remains TRUE until read. The identity of the exact input that changed state can be read from another register (not shown). On UARTs that do not support general-purpose inputs, the Delta bits are usually in the same register as the status bits.

RS-232 Output Control Register

Figure 6-11b shows an idealized *RS-232 Output Control* register. In addition to the conventional RS-232 outputs, RTS and DTR, this register also contains one or two general-purpose outputs for use as the hardware designer sees fit. For example, the designer may wish to use the additional outputs to support a more complicated form of modem control, or to interact with more than one external device.

Despite the railings against the automatic hardware handshaking built into UARTs, there are certain circumstances in which it is undeniably convenient. Therefore, we devote 2 bits in the RS-232 Output Control register to enable and disable it: *Enable TD on CTS* and *Enable RxD on DCD*. This provides the flexibility to use it when we need it, and not to have to wrestle with it when we don't.

Inverted RS-232 Logic

You will recall from our discussion of logic levels in Chapter 5 that the RS-232 standard dictates positive logic (i.e., positive voltages are TRUE) for control input and output signals, but negative logic for data signals. As you read UART data sheets (or nose around with a voltmeter), you may be puzzled to discover that the polarity of the control inputs and output voltages on the UART's pins are inverted. In other words, writing a 1 to the UART's DTR bit, for example, actually causes the UART itself to generate a negative voltage. This apparent anomaly can be explained by realizing that RS-232 line driver and receiver ICs reinvert the signals to positive logic before applying them to the output connectors (see "RS-232 Level Conversion" in Chapter 5).

UART Interrupts

If your program performs only communications duties, it may have nothing to do but poll the UART waiting for an inbound byte or wait for the opportunity to transmit a byte. But in applications where the serial I/O represents only a small fraction of the total program, there are always other things to do. While the user is entering text via the word processing section, the serial I/O section can be invisibly downloading stock quotations, transmitting the week's price lists to branch offices, or printing reports. In other words, it is impractical to tie up an entire computer while the UART pokes along at a few hundred baud.

The key to this increase in functionality lies in abandoning the concept of polling in favor of *interruption*. In contrast to polling, where I/O is supervised by the CPU by periodically checking a device's "readiness," the technique of interruption transfers to the peripheral device itself the burden of notifying the CPU when an I/O operation is needed (or possible). The notification takes the form of an *interrupt request* whereby the I/O device actively solicits the CPU's attention. When the CPU finishes its current instruction, it decides if it is interested in acknowledging this request for service. If so, it issues an *interrupt acknowledgment*, then turns program control over to a section of code designed to handle the device's needs—the *interrupt service routine*, or *interrupt handler*. Once the interrupt service routine terminates, the CPU returns to the main program where execution resumes as if the interruption had never occurred.

Generating Interrupts

Because of the obvious power of interruption, our hypothetical UART must generate an interrupt under a variety of conditions:

- *Transmitter Interrupts*. An interrupt is generated when the transmitter buffer becomes empty—i.e., can accept another byte for serialization.

- *Receiver Interrupts*. An interrupt can be generated whenever an incoming byte has been assembled and placed in the receiver's FIFO. Some UARTs additionally allow interrupts on the *first* received byte only.

- *RS-232 Interrupts*. An interrupt can be generated by a change in state of any RS-232 input line—CTS, DSR, DCD, or RI.

- *Interrupt on Receiver Error or BREAK*. An interrupt can be generated by any irregular serialization condition: BREAK, parity, overrun, or framing.

The *Interrupt Enable* register shown in Figure 6-12 contains a bit to enable interrupts for each of these conditions.

It is frequently necessary to disable and re-enable UART interrupts entirely at various points in program execution. On many UARTs, this simple act requires several steps: the contents of the Interrupt Enable register must be read and stored, then all relevant bits must be reset to turn interrupts off. To turn interrupts back on, the stored bit pattern is fetched and reinstalled. To sim-

Figure 6-12 The Interrupt Enable register.

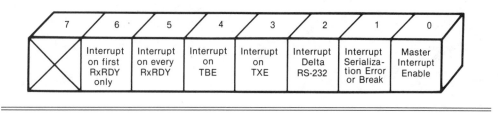

plify this cumbersome process, our Interrupt Enable register also contains a *master interrupt enable* bit, which permits UART interrupts to be turned off entirely without disturbing the bit pattern in the rest of the register.

Clearing Pending Interrupts

After the UART generates an interrupt, it will not generate another until the first one has been "cleared." On some UARTS, clearing means resetting an "interrupt pending" bit, but the most common way to clear an interrupt is to service its cause. For example, if the interrupt was generated by RxRDY, reading the available character clears the interrupt.

Interrupt Vector Determination

When an interrupt occurs, the processor must somehow ascertain which of the possible interrupts has actually occurred. From this information, the processor then calculates the *interrupt vector* (i.e., the address of the interrupt handler) that must be invoked. Although the exact method of communication between the processor and the UART differs from system to system, the result must always be the address of the function that must service the condition causing the interrupt. Because there are so many possible interrupt vectoring schemes (some processors even support multiple vectoring schemes), we will not attempt to represent vectoring in our hypothetical UART. For the sake of convenience, therefore, for now we will assume that our UART somehow magically identifies itself to the processor as the source of an interrupt. In Chapters 7 and 20, we will study in detail how interrupts on two real UARTs interact with the processor.

Conclusion

We have now created a hypothetical UART against which we can understand and measure actual devices. As we now turn to the real world to see how these abstractions translate into nuts-and-bolts integrated ICs, you will discover an amazing variety among its members. The two UARTs we will study—the Zilog Z80SIO and the National 8250—were selected for compelling reasons. Because it was designed to support the Zilog Z80 microprocessor, the Z80SIO quickly became standard in CP/M machines. The 8250's use in the entire family of IBM PCs, IBM clones, and after-market PC boards ensured its posterity. As a matter of fact, it has been estimated that one of these two UARTs is contained in at least 80 percent of all microcomputers in existence. In other words, it is almost inconceivable that you could do much asynchronous programming without at some time encountering one of these two devices.

7

Real-World Hardware: Two UARTs

In this chapter we will study two examples of UARTs: the National INS8250 and the Zilog Z80SIO. Although newer and perhaps more sophisticated devices than these certainly exist, they were chosen for two reasons. First, they are enormously popular. The 8250 example is used in the IBM PC and the Z80SIO was the heavy favorite among CP/M manufacturers. Because of the millions of these machines in existence, then, there is a high likelihood that you will encounter one of them. Aside from sheer numbers, the second reason for selecting these two devices is pedagogical. They illustrate, better than any other two devices, fundamentally different approaches to UART architecture.

Although programmers seldom need concern themselves about the physical connections between the system and the UART, an understanding of such things is sometimes (more often than we like to admit) important to puzzling out a programming problem. We will therefore take a cursory (and very superficial) look at how our UARTs fit into a typical system.

In both the UARTs we will study in this chapter, the names of the RS-232 inputs and outputs—$\overline{RTS}$, $\overline{DTR}$, $\overline{DSR}$, $\overline{DCD}$, $\overline{CTS}$, and $\overline{RI}$—are overscored to denote inverted logic. This means, for example, that a 0 in the DTR bit of a UART's RS-232 Output register produces a 1 at the $\overline{DTR}$ output. In most designs, this inversion is not apparent to the programmer because these signals are reinverted by the EIA line-driver ICs, which are interposed between the UART and the physical interface connector. (See Chapter 5 for a discussion of RS-232 level conversion.)

To avoid the notational nightmare that comes with several layers of inversion, all our discussions are based upon the assumption that this reinversion occurs. This assumption is possible because most UARTs in microcomputers are connected to an RS-232 interface. In other words, we are assuming that writing a 1 to, say, the DTR bit in the UART's RS-232 Output register ultimately produces a *positive* voltage on the DTE RS-232 interface.

To finish this line of thought, notice that the names of the *data* inputs and outputs are not overscored to indicate inversion. As we noted in Chapter 5, the RS-232 standard specifies inverted logic for data: an idling (MARKING) transmitter must generate a *negative* voltage at the interface. Since the designers of UARTs expect the transmitter to be inverted by EIA line drivers, positive logic levels must be output at the transmitter output.

The National 8250-B

Because it was designed for use with a broad range of CPUs and other support hardware, in many ways the 8250 UART[1] closely resembles the conceptual UART we studied in Chapter 6. This makes it very easy to understand and to program.

8250 Hardware Basics

Figure 7-1   A basic configuration for the National 8250.

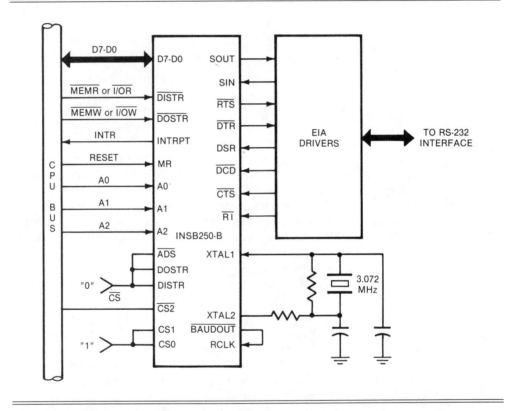

As shown in Figure 7-1, the 8250 requires three basic interfaces: the system I/O bus, the clock, and RS-232 I/O. The 8250 is connected to the low-order 8 bits of the CPU's data bus by means of data lines D0 through D7. This is the path of data in and out of the UART. Read and write operations are differentiated by the data input and output strobe lines $\overline{\text{DISTR}}$ and $\overline{\text{DOSTR}}$. The 8250 comprises several internal registers, all of which are individually addressable by means of three register selected inputs A0−A2. Transmitting a byte is therefore a three-step operation:

---

[1]National refers to the 8250 as an ACE, an Asynchronous Communications Element.

1. CPU places the outbound data byte on the 8-bit data lines D0−D7.

2. The register number of the Transmitter Buffer register is placed on register select inputs A0−A2.

3. The logic on the data strobe lines $\overline{\text{DISTR}}$ and $\overline{\text{DOSTR}}$ moves the byte from D0−D7 into the transmitter's buffer. The 8250 moves the byte from the Buffer register to the transmitter's shift register when the latter is empty.

The steps in receiving a byte are similar to those for transmission. The steps summarized below assume that an incoming byte has already been received and is waiting in the Receiver Buffer register.

1. The Receiver Buffer register's number is placed on register select inputs A0−A2.

2. A read operation is performed by the logic on the data strobe lines $\overline{\text{DISTR}}$ and $\overline{\text{DOSTR}}$.

3. The byte moves from the receive buffer to D0−D7 where it is captured by the CPU.

Although we used the transmit and receive registers in this example, reads and writes of *any* 8250 register are identical—the only difference is the register select lines A0−A2.

The final point of interface with the system I/O bus is line marked INTRPT, or interrupt. This output becomes TRUE whenever a condition exists for which the 8250 is programmed to generate an interrupt.

8250 Clock and Timing

The 8250's reference clock signal may be externally supplied or internally generated by connecting a crystal. In either case, the reference clock is injected at the XTAL1 input, whence it passes through a user-programmable divider circuit to produce a *master data clock*. This signal is 16 times higher than the desired baud rate, thus fixing the clocking factor at 16. To understand the necessity for a master data clock at a higher frequency than the baud rate, review "Receiver Timing" in Chapter 6.

The master data clock signal is internally wired to drive the transmitter logic. So that the receiver and transmitter can be operated at different baud rates, however, the master data clock's connection to the receiver logic is external. The master data clock signal is brought out of the 8250 at $\overline{\text{BAUDOUT}}$ and the receiver's clock input is made available at RCLK. When these two are connected, the receive baud rate equals the transmit baud rate. A different baud rate for the receiver can be attained by processing the signal at $\overline{\text{BAUDOUT}}$ further before reintroducing it at RCLK.

We will return to the frequency relationships among the reference clock, the master data clock, and the baud rate when we study the Baud Rate Divisor Latch registers later in this chapter.

8250 Internal Architecture

Having ever so briefly examined the 8250's contact with the outside world, let us now undertake matters of more direct interest to programmers: the internal structure of the 8250. As you can see from the block diagram in Figure 7-2, a program exerts control over the 8250 by reading and writing ten registers.[2] Except for the Interrupt Identification register, which is read-only, data written to a register can be read back.

Figure 7-2 A block diagram of the 8250.

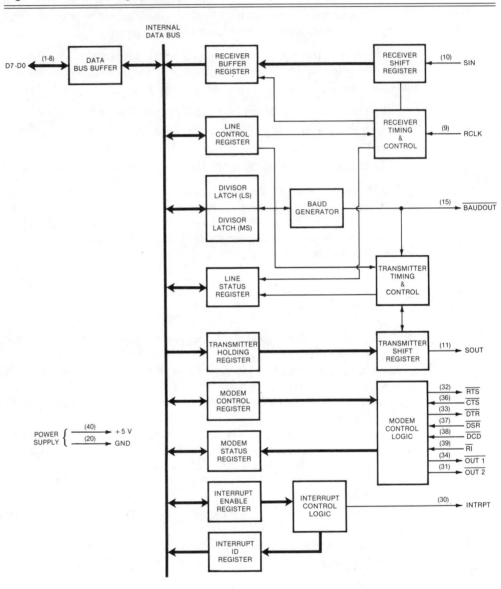

---

[2]An eleventh register—a scratch pad—also exists, although it is seldom mentioned.

Register Addressing on the 8250

If you read the section "8250 Hardware Basics" carefully, you may have already spotted an anomaly: how does the 8250 address eleven registers when there are only three physical register-select lines? Actually, only ten unique register-select addresses must be decoded because the transmitter and receiver are read/write versions of the same address. But this still leaves ten registers to address with three register-select lines. A gimmick[3] is used to extend the addressing: when bit 7 of the Data Format register is 1, registers 0 and 1 become the low- and high-order bytes of the Baud Rate Divisor Latch. (Bit 7 of the Data Format register is called the "Divisor Latch Access Bit," or DLAB.) Table 7-1 gives the register select codes for the eight "real" registers and illustrates the DLAB gimmick.

Table 7-1 Register addressing and the DLAB.

DLAB*	A0	A1	A2	Read/ Write	Register
0	0	0	0	—	Receiver (read) Transmitter (write)
0	0	0	1	R/W	Interrupt Enable
X	0	1	0	READ	Interrupt Identification
X	0	1	1	R/W	Data Format (Line Control)
X	1	0	0	R/W	RS-232 Output (Modem Control)
X	1	0	1	R/W	Serialization Status (Line Status)
X	1	1	0	R/W	RS-232 Input Status (Modem Status)
X	1	1	1	R/W	Scratch Pad
1	0	0	0	R/W	LSB Baud Rate Divisor Latch
1	0	0	1	R/W	MSB Baud Rate Divisor Latch

*"Divisor Latch Access Bit", bit 7 of the Data Format register

In most 8250 implementations, the eight "real" registers are addressed at consecutive I/O port or memory addresses, but the exact manner of address decoding is, of course, up to the hardware designer.

8250 Register Usage Summary

We will now examine the eleven functional registers in the 8250. To maintain consistency, when necessary we retain the register names invented in Chapter 6. Where these names differ substantially from those used in the 8250 data sheet, the latter follow in parentheses. The number preceding the register name is its register-select code.

---

[3]A gimmick is slightly ugly engineering. The difference between a gimmick and a kludge is that a gimmick is an intentional design, while a kludge is added later to correct for an oversight.

0: Receiver Buffer Register[4]

After a stream of bits on the 8250's SIN input has been assembled into a byte, reading this register fetches that byte. Even though the "byte" received may contain as few as 5 data bits, the CPU always fetches an 8-bit quantity. In such cases, the content of unused bits is not specified and should be masked off by software. As shown in Table 7-1, when bit 7 of the Data Format register (DLAB) is TRUE, the Receiver Buffer register becomes the read/write LSB Baud Rate Divisor Latch. The DLAB is described in detail later.

Experimentation with several vintages of 8250s shows that it contains only one buffer—the Receiver register itself.

0: Transmitter Buffer Register (Holding Register)

Writing a byte to register 0 results in its serialization and transmission at the SOUT output in the current data format and baud rate. As shown in Table 7-1, when bit 7 of the Data Format register (DLAB) is TRUE, the 0 register becomes the read/write LSB Baud Rate Divisor Latch. The DLAB is described in detail later.

1: Interrupt Enable

The bits of this read/write register, shown in Figure 7-3, enable the four types of interrupts supported by the 8250. An interrupt is enabled by a 1 in its respective bit.

Figure 7-3 The 8250's Interrupt Enable register.

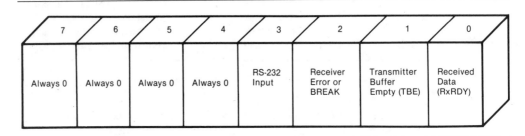

7	6	5	4	3	2	1	0
Always 0	Always 0	Always 0	Always 0	RS-232 Input	Receiver Error or BREAK	Transmitter Buffer Empty (TBE)	Received Data (RxRDY)

Bit 0 (RxRDY) If this bit is 1, an interrupt is generated when a byte is available for reading from the Receiver Buffer register.

Bit 1 (TBE) If this bit is 1, an interrupt is generated when a byte is moved from the transmitter's Holding register to the transmitter's shift register; in other words, as soon as the 8250 can accept another byte for transmission.

Bit 2 If this bit is 1, an interrupt is generated when a parity error, overrun error, framing error, or a BREAK condition is detected by the receiver during the reception of a byte.

Bit 3 (RS-232 Input) If this bit is 1, an interrupt is generated when any of the RS-232 inputs changes states.

Bits 4 − 7 Always 0.

---

[4]National Semiconductor's documentation states that the 8250 contains "full double buffering." This claim, published first in 1980 and again in 1985, has until now apparently gone untested.

As shown in Table 7-1, when bit 7 of the Data Format register (DLAB) is true, register 1 becomes the read/write MSB Baud Rate Divisor Latch whose function is described in detail below.

2: Interrupt Identification

When an interrupt occurs, the Interrupt Identification register identifies its exact source. A 0 in Bit 0 of this register means that an interrupt is pending; bits 1−3 identify the actual interrupt as shown in Table 7-2. Notice that each interrupt has a *priority*: while an interrupt is pending, interrupts with an equal or lower priority are not reported (i.e., locked out). This priority is not programmable.

Table 7-2   Interrupt Identification register.

Bit 2	Bit 1	Bit 0	Priority*	Interrupt ID
0	0	1	None	None
1	1	0	0	Serialization Error or BREAK
1	0	0	1	Received Data
0	1	0	2	Transmitter Buffer Empty
0	0	0	3	RS-232 Input

*0 is highest.

There is one interesting detail about this register. Bit 0 (the "pending" bit) is expressed in negative logic—that is, a 0 means that an interrupt is pending. Therefore, when an interrupt occurs, the number in the Interrupt Identification register is a multiple of two. In assembly language, this number is a convenient index into a table of pointers to the subroutines that handle the respective interrupts.

The Interrupt Identification register is also of great value in polled, as opposed to interrupt, operations. Suppose that the 8250's interrupts are enabled (via the Interrupt Enable register), but the *system* is programmed to ignore them. Although an 8250 interrupt under these circumstances does not invoke the system's interrupt handler, it nevertheless still sets the correct bit in the Interrupt Identification register. This makes for very efficient polled I/O: the entire UART can be checked for activity by reading a *single* register. In fact, through clever programming, the same code can be used both for interrupt and polled operations. (For a related discussion, see "The 8250 and Polled I/O" later in this chapter.)

3: Data Format (Line Control)

The byte map in Figure 7-4 shows the bit-mapping of the Data Format register.

Bit 2   If 5 data bits are used, 1½ STOP bits are automatically selected.

Bit 3−5   Most explanations of these 3 bits, including the data sheet, call bit 3 "Parity Enable," bit 4 "Parity Select," and bit 5 by the enigmatic name "Stick Parity."

Bit 6   (The BREAK bit) When 1, this bit forces the transmitter (i.e., the SOUT output) to a logical 0 state (SPACING). The transmitter remains in this state unconditionally until a 0 is written to this bit.

Bit 7   DLAB (the Divisor Latch Access Bit) As shown in Table 7-1, this bit has nothing to do with the data format, but is a gimmick that extends the number of registers that can be addressed with three register-select control lines. When this bit is 1, registers 0 and 1 (the Transmitter/Receiver and Interrupt I/O registers) become the LSB and MSB Baud Rate Divisor Latch registers.

Figure 7-4 The 8250's Data Format register.

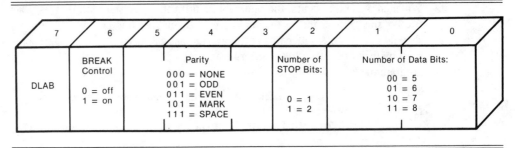

4: RS-232 Output Control (Modem Control)

This register (Figure 7-5) controls the state of the two RS-232 outputs DTR and RTS. As previously explained, these are actually inverted signals; for example, the bit labeled DTR actually controls the "NOT" output, $\overline{DTR}$. For the sake of clarity, however, we will use positive abbreviations and the term "assert" to suggest that these outputs are probably eventually re-inverted by external circuitry.

In addition to DTR and RTS, two general-purpose outputs are provided for non-RS-232 use. Although the label "General-Purpose Output" correctly implies that these are not RS-232 outputs, the distinction is artificial; these bits affect their respective outputs in all respects like RTS and DTR.

This register also contains a bit to perform a *loopback* test in which complementary inputs and outputs are temporarily connected. In this way, the continuity of the entire system can be tested by changing an output, then testing whether the change is reflected at the complementary input.

Figure 7-5 The 8250's RS-232 Output register.

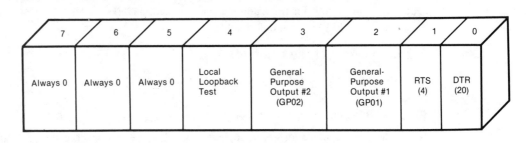

Bit 0 (DTR) Writing a 1 to this bit asserts the 8250's Data Terminal Ready output.

Bit 1 (RTS) Writing a 1 to this bit asserts the 8250's Request To Send output.

Bit 2 (GPO1) This is the first of two user-definable outputs. An example of its use can be found on the Hayes plug-in board Smartmodems, where GPO2 unconditionally resets the Smartmodem.

Bit 3 (GPO2) This is the second user-definable output. For a typical use of this bit, see "8250 Interrupts," below.

Bit 4 (Local Loopback) When this bit is 1, the following occur:

1. The transmitter's output (SOUT) is set to the logical 1 state (MARKING).

2. The receiver's input (SIN) is disconnected.

3. The output of the transmitter's shift register is directly connected to the receiver's shift register.

4. The four RS-232 control inputs are directly connected to the RS-232 outputs as follows:

$\overline{\text{CTS}}$ to $\overline{\text{RTS}}$
$\overline{\text{DSR}}$ to $\overline{\text{DTR}}$
$\overline{\text{DCD}}$ to $\overline{\text{GPO2}}$
$\overline{\text{RI}}$ to $\overline{\text{GPO1}}$

These connections provide a simple method for checking the major UART functions. Data written to the Transmitter register appears immediately at the Receiver register. Interrupts are fully operational and interrupts normally generated by RS-232 inputs can be generated simply by writing into the RS-232 Output Control register (4).

5: Serialization Status (Line Status)

This register (Figure 7-6) reports the status of the assembly and serialization process, which includes BREAK detection, receiver errors, and the readiness status of key transmitter and receiver registers.

The error conditions reported by bits 1−4 generate an interrupt when bit 2 is set in the Interrupt Enable register.

Figure 7-6 The 8250's Serialization Status register.

7	6	5	4	3	2	1	0
Always 0	Transmitter Empty (TXE)	Transmitter Buffer Empty (TBE)	BREAK Detect	Framing Error	Parity Error	Overrun Error	Data Ready (RxRDY)

Bit 0 (RxRDY) This bit is 1 when an incoming byte has been assembled and transferred into the receiver's buffer. This bit is reset when read.

Bit 1 (Receiver Overrun) A 1 in this bit indicates that a byte in the receiver buffer has been overwritten by a newly received byte. The first byte is lost. This bit is reset by reading this register.

Bit 2 (Parity Error) This bit is set to 1 when the parity bit of a received byte does not match the parity setting in the Data Format register. This bit is reset when read.

Bit 3   (Framing Error) A 1 in this bit means that after assembling an inbound byte, the STOP bit was incorrect (i.e., a SPACE instead of MARK). This bit is reset when read.

Bit 4   (BREAK Detect) A 1 appears in this bit whenever the receiver detects a SPACING condition lasting longer than one SDU. This bit is reset when read.

Bit 5   (Transmitter Buffer Empty) The TBE bit is set to 1 when a byte is moved from the transmitter's buffer (Holding register) into the transmitter's shift register. Failure to consult this bit before writing to the Transmitter Buffer register overwrites a byte already in the buffer awaiting transmission. This condition, known as *transmitter overrun*, is not reported by the 8250.

It is important to understand that although TBE signals that the 8250 is ready to accept another byte for transmission, it does *not* mean that transmission of the previous byte is complete.

Bit 6   (Transmitter Empty) The TXE bit is set to 1 when there are no bytes in the transmitter buffer *or* in the transmitter's shift register. Think of this bit as an "all bytes sent" flag. Before terminating transmission, consult this bit to avoid "leaving one in the pipe."

Bit 7   Always 0.

6: RS-232 Input Status (MODEM Status)

Bits 0−3 of this register (Figure 7-7) report a *change* in the state of their respective RS-232 pins. A 1 in any of these bits means that its input has changed since last read. Reading this register clears bits 0−3.

Bits 4−7 report the *absolute* state of their respective RS-232 inputs. Because of the logic inversion discussed earlier, a 1 in these bits ordinarily stands for a positive voltage on the RS-232 interface.

In addition to their normal duties, bits 4−7 take on special meanings during loopback testing (see Bit 4 of the RS-232 Output Control register).

Figure 7-7   The 8250's RS-232 Input Status register.

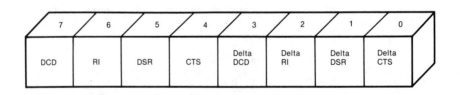

Bit 2   This bit is set on the *trailing* edge of the telephone ringer pulse from the modem.

Bit 4−7   During loopback testing (i.e., when bit 4 of RS-232 Output Control register is 1), these bits report the current state of the RS-232 *outputs*. The assignment is as follows:

    Bit 4, CTS = RTS
    Bit 5, DSR = DTR
    Bit 6, DCD = GPO2
    Bit 7, RI   = GPO1

7: Scratch Pad

This register has no function whatsoever. You may use it as you would a byte of RAM, but be advised that it does not exist on early versions of the 8250.

0/8: LSB Baud Rate Divisor Latch
0/9: MSB Baud Rate Divisor Latch

As shown in Table 7-1, when bit 7 of the Data Format register is 1, registers 0 and 1 become the LSB and MSB Divisor Latch registers, respectively. (Their register numbers, 0/8 and 0/9, reflect this gimmick.)

The 8250's reference clock is divided by the 16-bit integer contained in the LSB and MSB Divisor Latch registers. The resulting frequency is the master data clock that drives the transmitter logic and optionally (by means of an external connection on the 8250) the receiver logic as well. This master data clock is then again divided by 16 to produce the baud clock, which controls the speed at which data is received and transmitted. The divisor for any baud rate can therefore be calculated by the formula:

$$\text{Divisor} = \frac{\text{Reference clock frequency}}{16 \times \text{desired baud rate}}$$

Table 7-3 gives the divisors (in hexadecimal) for the most popular baud rates. Divisors are given for the two recommended clock frequencies.

Table 7-3 Hexadecimal baud rate divisor for two reference clock speeds.

Desired Baud Rate	Hex Divisor To Produce 16 × Clock with Clock Crystal of:	
	1.8432 MHz	3.072 MHz
50	0900	0F00
75	0600	0A00
110	0417	06D1
134.5	0359	0594
150	0300	0500
300	0180	0280
600	00C0	0140
1200	0060	00A0
1800	0040	006B
2000	003A	0060
2400	0030	0050
3600	0020	0035
4800	0018	0028
7200	0010	0016
9600	000C	0014
19200	0006	000A
38400	0003	0005
56000	0002	—

Interrupts on the 8250

The 8250's sole response to an interrupt condition is to assert its INTRPT line to inform the system (i.e., the CPU) that an interrupt occurs. The 8250 itself is not responsible for supplying the address of the associated interrupt handler. The CPU must learn the address of the 8250's interrupt handler by a combination of system hardware and software, an example of which we will study in Chapter 20.

After the CPU learns the address of the 8250's interrupt handler, it turns control over to it. When first gaining control, the handler knows only that the 8250 is the source of the interrupt; its first task, therefore, is to ascertain the precise condition that generated the interrupt. This is accomplished by reading Interrupt Identification, whose contents can easily be converted to the address of the correct subfunction to handle the pending interrupt.

Resetting a Pending Interrupt

When the 8250 generates an interrupt, all interrupts with an equal or lower priority are locked out until the current interrupt has been "cleared." The operation required to clear a pending interrupt varies according to the source of the interrupt. These relationships are given in Table 7-4.

Table 7-4   Actions required to clear pending interrupts.

Source of Interrupt	Response Required To Reset
Receiver error or BREAK	Read Serialization Status register
Received data	Read data from Receiver register
Transmit buffer empty	Write to the transmitter or read the Interrupt ID register
RS-232 input	Read the RS-232 Status register

Only one of these actions needs explanation: the response to an empty transmit buffer. This interrupt can be cleared, obviously, by writing a byte to the Transmitter Buffer register. Not so obviously, it can be cleared simply by reading the Interrupt Identification register. Suppose that 5 bytes are queued for transmission. After each byte is transmitted, a TBE interrupt is generated; writing the next byte to the Transmitter Buffer register clears the interrupt. When there are no more bytes to transmit, what will clear the interrupt generated by the fifth (and last) byte? With no more bytes to transmit, the interrupt is never cleared, locking out interrupts of lower priority. To avoid this condition, TBE interrupts can be cleared merely by reading the Interrupt Identification register.

The 8250 and Polled I/O

Several facts strongly suggest that the 8250 was designed explicitly for interrupt I/O and that support for polled operation is only halfhearted. First, the 8250 contains only a single buffer between the receiver's shift register and the data bus. This means that an unread byte is overwritten by the very next byte received. For a UART to work well in polled I/O, it must have *at least* two buffers, which are usually organized in a simple FIFO.

The second clue that the 8250 was designed primarily for interrupt mode is the lack of a simple interrupt enable/disable mechanism. As we discussed earlier in "The Interrupt Identification Register," highly efficient polled operation is possible if the 8250 reports interrupts in its Interrupt Identification register, but does not report interrupts to the CPU via the INTRPT line. Unfortunately, there is no way to accomplish this without extra hardware. (As a matter of fact, the only way to disable interrupts entirely on the 8250 is to mask and unmask bits in the Interrupt Enable register.)

The only reasonable explanation for this "oversight" is that the designers did not anticipate the 8250 running without interrupts. Serial port designers apparently do not agree with the 8250 engineers. For example, on IBM's Asynchronous Communications Adaptor, a bus-driver IC, shown in Figure 7-8, effectively blocks the 8250's INTRPT line unless the GPO2 output is asserted! With the INTRPT thus prevented from generating a processor interrupt, the 8250's internal interrupt structure can be utilized for polled operation.

Figure 7-8   The IBM PC's use of GPO1 for a Master Interrupt Enable.

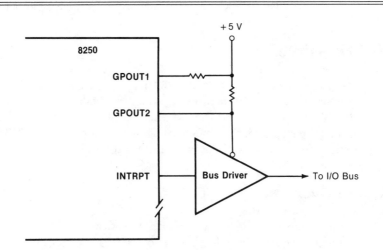

The Zilog Z80 SIO[5]
Serial Input/Output Controller

As its name suggests, the Z80SIO is primarily intended for use with the Z80 microprocessor and associated peripheral chips. Because the Z80SIO actually contains two independent UART "channels" in a single chip, it is ideal for small microcomputers where one channel is devoted to keyboard I/O and the other channel is configured as a general-purpose RS-232 serial port. The Z80SIO not only supports START/STOP asynchronous communications but also synchronous communications, including the high-level protocols SDLC and HDLC. Although we will continue to refer to it as a UART, its dual capability earns it the name USART—a Universal Synchronous/Asynchronous Receiver/Transmitter.

The Z80SIO's smaller brother, the Z80 DART (Dual Asynchronous Receiver/Transmitter) contains only the Z80SIO's asynchronous functions. Asynchronous software that runs on the

---

[5]For clarity, the remainder of this book will use the contraction *Z80SIO*.

Z80SIO runs without modification on the DART, and, with a single exception,[6] vice versa. Despite very close software compatibility (the same mask is used to manufacture both), the less complicated DART is seldom found in programmable applications such as computers, but in stand-alone products such as printer buffers, speech synthesizers, and plotters. This is not surprising, considering that the two chips have almost identical manufacturing and, consequently, selling prices. Faced with a negligible price difference, microcomputer manufacturers inevitably choose the Z80SIO's additional support for synchronous communications.

Since we are interested only in the Z80SIO as an asynchronous device, our bit-map diagrams employ a special notation for bits related to its synchronous capabilities. Bits that govern synchronous functions are marked with the phrase "SET TO 0" in write registers, "XXXX" in read registers. The "XXXX" is a reminder to mask off these bits before evaluating the register.

The Z80SIO vs the 8250

Before we look deeply into the Z80SIO, it is worth summarizing the most important differences between it and the 8250. In many areas they are similar because they are both UARTs: both predictably provide bits to monitor the readiness of the transmitter and receiver buffers to transfer data, and both provide the status and control bits for popular RS-232 lines. But beyond these generic similarities the two UARTs are about as different as can be imagined.

Register Addressing

From the programmer's point of view, the most obvious difference between the 8250 and the Z80SIO is register addressing. Instead of the "flat" addressing of the 8250 where registers are addressed at different locations, most Z80SIO registers are addressed at the *same* location by writing 2 bytes—the number of the register, followed by the desired read or write operation for that register. We will explore this form of addressing in detail shortly.

If register addressing is the most obvious difference between the two UARTs, the *nature* of the registers is the most significant. Alas, with one exception, the Z80SIO's writable registers cannot be read. On the superficial level, write-only registers are simply an aggravation, forcing us to maintain a copy of each register in RAM and to update it with each write to a UART register. On a more serious level, however, the inability to query the Z80SIO about its current state makes it impossible to write programs that, upon exit, restore the interface to its original state. As we shall see in Chapter 12, this creates insurmountable impediments to good programming.

The FIFO

One of the most obvious architectural differences is that the Z80SIO's receiver and transmitter buffers are FIFOs. This means that 4 bytes can "stack up" in the receiver and 2 in the transmitter before data is lost due to receiver overrun or transmitter underrun errors. This immunity from errors accounts for the Z80SIO's legendary robustness in polled operation. The bits that report error conditions in the receiver are also held in a FIFO, assuring that errors are not reported until the offending byte is next in line to be read.

---

[6]The DART supports an additional RS-232 input, RI. See "Read Register 0," later in this chapter.

DELTA Status Bit Latching

In the 8250 we saw how several bits in the RS-232 Input register monitor changes on the RS-232 input lines. When changes occur, the new value is remembered, or latched, until the register is read by the CPU. Latching improves the efficiency of all kinds of I/O, but especially polled I/O by allowing the programmer to defer polling until it is convenient.

The idea of latching changed inputs is carried even further on the Z80SIO, where there are two categories of latched events. The first category, referred to as an "External/Status" event, comprises the just-mentioned transition of an RS-232 input as well as the BREAK. In the second category are receiver errors—parity and receiver overrun errors, but *not* framing errors (Zilog offers no explanation for this oddity).

The scope of Z80SIO's latching action is also quite different from the 8250's. When *any* of the events in a group occurs, the status bits of *all* members are latched. If a change occurs on the DCD input, for example, the DCD, CTS and BREAK status bits are all latched.

The manner in which latched events are cleared is also different. On the 8250, the RS-232 status latches are cleared merely by reading them; on the Z80SIO, however, latches must be cleared explicitly by commands—one for each category of latched event. Lamentably, this makes reading the *current* state of a status bit a two-step operation: the latch must be cleared before it is read. (Many an hour has been squandered by programmers who didn't understand this.)

Vectoring Interrupts

The way in which interrupts are handled is perhaps the most dramatic difference between the 8250 and the Z80SIO, which uses *vectored interrupts*. These differences clearly reflect the differences in the architecture of their respective CPUs. Although we will postpone exposition of this architectural topic until later in the chapter, it should be noted that only four events on the Z80SIO are capable of generating interrupts:

1. Received Data Ready (RxRDY)
2. Transmitter Buffer Empty (TBE)
3. Receiver errors: parity, framing, or receiver overrun
4. "External/Status" events: changes in RS-232 inputs or a BREAK condition

Interrupts on these conditions can be individually enabled.

Additional Z80SIO Features

Several of the features proposed for the conceptual UART in Chapter 6 are not supported by the 8250 but are found on the Z80SIO. These include the ability to enable and disable the transmitter and the receiver, hardware handshaking between the transmitter and CTS and the receiver and DCD, and a programmable clock factor. Unfortunately, the Z80SIO has no general-purpose inputs or outputs.

Z80SIO Hardware Basics

As indicated in Figure 7-9, the Z80SIO actually consists of two UARTs in the same package, referred to as "channels" A and B.

Figure 7-9 Block and pin diagrams for the Z80SIO/2.

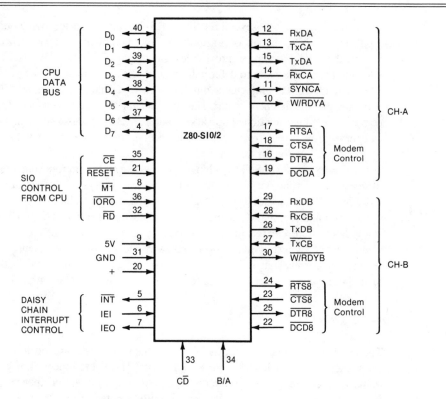

Z80SIO/2 Pin Configuration

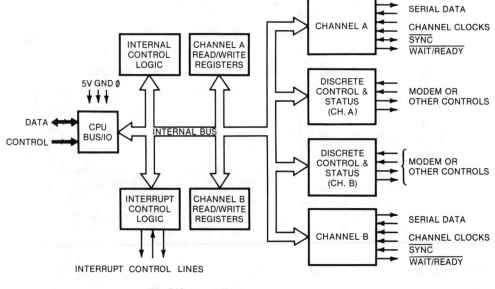

Z80SIO Block Diagram

Ordinarily, six register-select lines would be used to address the Z80SIO's twenty internal registers. The constraints of fitting two full-blown UARTs in one 40-pin package, however, demands a more economic approach.[7] The solution is evident by the fact that the Z80SIO has only two address lines: (1) $B/\overline{A}$, which selects between channels A and B, and (2) $C/\overline{D}$, which selects between a *Data register* (the receiver and the transmitter) and the *Control/Status Register* through which UART commands are issued and from which the contents of various internal registers are read. To avoid confusion between these two "master" registers and the index registers within the Control/Status register, we refer to them as the Data and Control/Status "ports." Keep in mind, though, that this in no way implies that these registers must be addressed through I/O ports instead of RAM.

The Z80SIO does not contain the circuitry to generate its own reference clock, nor the Divider registers for baud rate control. The reference clock is usually the system clock (generally $4-6$ MHz on the Z80). In each channel are separate master data clock inputs for transmitter (TxCA and TxCB) and receiver (RxCA and RxCB). After division by the *programmable* clocking factor, these signals become the baud clocks for transmitter and receiver. In most applications, the ability to transmit and receive at different baud rates is not required and the master data clock for a given channel is applied simultaneously to both transmitter and receiver inputs.

The Data Register

To the programmer, each UART in the Z80SIO package appears as two memory or port addresses, one of which provides access to the Data port. The Data port is a model of simplicity: when read, it returns the contents of the UART's receiver buffer; when written, the byte on the CPU bus is written to the UART's transmitter buffer. In other words, the Data port is both the Transmitter and Receiver register.

The TBE and RxRDY bits that software must monitor for polled operation are located in Read Register 0, access to which is gained through the Control/Status port.

Control/Status Port Addressing

As we just noted, software sees a Z80SIO channel as two address, one each for the Data port and Control/Status port. A single data register is sufficient because it has only one function: to supervise data transfers between the buses in the CPU and Z80SIO. A single Control/Status port is obviously inadequate, however, for programming the myriad communications parameters inherent in a UART. To provide access to internal registers without increasing the number of physical address lines, the Z80SIO employs *indexed* addressing. In this scheme, a byte is written to the Control/Status port; this byte, however, does not contain data for a register, but the *number* (i.e., index) of the desired register. In a sense, the first number written into the Control/Status port "exposes" that register to the I/O bus.

It is technically more accurate to view the Control/Status port simply as two arrays of registers—three read registers and eight write registers. The value of three "index" bits in Write Regis-

---

[7]The effort was not entirely successful: the Z80SIO is available in three lead-bonding options, each eliminating one signal. We are studying the Z80SIO/2, which retains full asynchronous capabilities and is the version most often used in microcomputers. A square, 44-pin package containing all leads is available as the Z80SIO/4.

ter 0 (WR[0]) determines which of the other registers in the array will be addressed by the *next* read or write of the Control/Status port.

Importantly, these indexing bits automatically reset to 0 *after each register access*; thus reads and writes of the Control/Status port are steered to RR[0] and WR[0] by default. Said another way, RR[0] and WR[0] can be addressed with a *single* read or write; addressing any other register, however, is a two-step operation: (1) the index number of the desired register is first written to the Control/Status port; (2) the next access of the Control/Status port is steered to the desired register.

To illustrate the Z80SIO's addressing procedure, let's assume that you wish to read RR[1], write WR[4], and read RR[0]:

1. Show your desire to read RR[1] by writing a 1 to the Control/Status port.

2. Read the Control/Status port to fetch the contents of RR[1].

3. Show your desire to write to WR[4] by writing a 4 to the Control/Status port.

4. Writing to the Control/Status port writes into WR[4].

5. Since the index bits are returned to 0 after each access, simply reading the Control/Status port is the same as reading RR[0].

Because RR[0] and WR[0] obviously have special importance in the Z80SIO, let's examine them first.

Write Register 0: the Basic Z80SIO Commands

We have just seen how, by default, a write to the Control/Status port is actually a write to WR[0]. Because of the efficiency in addressing WR[0], all Z80SIO *commands* are located here along with, of course, the register indexing bits described earlier.

Figure 7-10   The Z80SIO's WR[0] register.

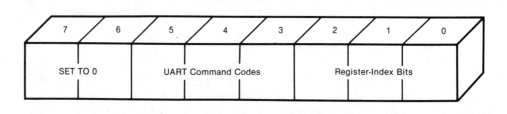

As shown in Figure 7-10, when a write to the Control/Status port is performed, the Register-Index bits (the low-order 3 bits) name the register to be addressed by the *next* access of the Control/Status port. The remaining relevant bits—3, 4 and 5—are treated as data bound for WR[0] itself. Specifically, when the Register-Index bits are 0, the byte is a *command*. Commands are listed in Table 7-5.

Command 0   When writing to WR[0] solely to select a register for the next write, all command code bits should be 0.

Command 1   Used for synchronous I/O.

Command 2   When an RS-232 input changes state or a BREAK is detected, their bits are latched in RR[0]. All bits remain latched until Command 2 is issued.

Table 7-5   Z80SIO commands in WR[0].

Command Number	Bit			Purpose of Command
	D5	D4	D3	
0	0	0	0	Null for Register-Index operations
1	0	0	1	Used for asynchronous I/O
2	0	1	0	Clear External/Status latches in RR[0]
3	0	1	1	Reset this entire channel
4	1	0	0	Enable interrupt-on-next-received-byte
5	1	0	1	Clear pending TBE (transmitter) interrupt
6	1	1	0	Reset receiver error latches in RR[0]
7	1	1	1	"Manual" return-from-interrupt instruction

Command 3   This command is equivalent to a hardware reset (i.e., a low on pin 21), but only affects a single channel. All registers must be reconfigured after a Command 3.

Command 4   When the number of bytes to receive is known in advance and can easily be polled for, an interrupt is necessary on the *first* byte, but not on subsequent ones. This form of interrupt is enabled in WR[1], and, having occurred, is reset with Command 4.

Command 5   If TBE (Transmit Buffer Empty) interrupts are enabled, some mechanism (besides transmitting another byte) must be provided for clearing the dangling interrupt that is pending after the *last* byte is transmitted. This is the function of command 5.

Command 6   Just as changes in RS-232 inputs or a BREAK condition are latched with a Command 2, so parity and receiver overrun errors are latched in RR[1] and must be cleared with Command 6. (Recall that framing errors are not latched).

Command 7   The Z80SIO is designed for interface with a Z80 processor, whose RETI (return from interrupt) instruction automatically clears the "interrupt pending" flag on the interrupting device. CPUs that do not have such an instruction can issue Command 7 instead.

It is important to understand that if Command Code bits and Register-Index bits are *both* non-0, a commmand is issued *and* a register is indexed. For example, writing 13H (0001 0010) to Write Register 0 would simultaneously issue a Command 2 and select register 3 for the next access.

Read Register 0

We have just seen that a Register Index is not required before reading RR[0]. This efficiency makes RR[0] (Figure 7-11) ideal for the bits most frequently consulted during polled operations—the RxRDY, TBE, RS-232, and BREAK status bits.

Bit 0   (Received Data) This bit is 1 when an incoming byte has been assembled and transferred into the receiver's FIFO buffer; it is 0 when the FIFO is empty.

Bit 1   This bit, which exists only in channel A, is 1 when an interrupt is pending in *either* channel. It is reset when the interrupt is serviced. This bit is mainly used in applications that do not support vectored interrupts (see "Vectored Interrupts," below). Without an "interrupt pending" bit, such applications would have to examine every bit in RR[0] and RR[1] in both channels to ascertain if an interrupt is pending anywhere on the chip. The corresponding bit of RR[0] in channel B is always 0.

Bit 2 (Transmit Buffer Empty) This bit is set to 1 when a byte is moved from the transmitter FIFO buffer into the transmitter's shift register. Failure to consult this bit before writing to the Transmitter Buffer register overwrites a byte already in the FIFO awaiting transmission. This condition, transmitter underrun, is not reported by the Z80SIO.

Bit 3 (DCD)

Bit 4 (XXX or RI on Z80DART)

Bit 5 (CTS) Bits 3 and 5 show the state of the DCD and CTS inputs, respectively. On the Z80SIO, bit 4 is devoted to synchronous functions, while on the Z80DART it is the Ring Indicator input. When *any* of these bits (or the BREAK in bit 7) changes, *all are* latched. To read the *current* state of these bits, you must therefore clear the latch by preceding your read of RR[0] with a Command 2 (to WR[0]).

If External/Status Interrupts in WR[1] have been enabled, these conditions cause an interrupt. For a discussion of how CTS and DCD can influence UART I/O, see "Automatic Handshaking" (WR[3], bit 5).

Bit 7 (BREAK detect) This bit behaves identically to the DCD and RTS RS-232 inputs in bits 3 and 5 except that it becomes 1 when a SPACING condition at the receiver input lasts longer than one SDU. Proper servicing of a BREAK condition requires issuing two Clear External/Status Latch commands—the first when the BREAK is detected, the second when it ends. Failure to issue the second command leaves the latch set.

The grouping of the BREAK bit with the RS-232 input status bits tends to make one forget that a BREAK is technically a receiver error and must be serviced as one. Specifically, when a BREAK condition is detected, the Z80SIO assembles a NULL byte and places it in the FIFO—just as with any other error. After detecting a BREAK, therefore, do not forget to read and discard the NULL from the FIFO.

Figure 7-11 The Z80SIO's RR[0] register.

7	6	5	4	3	2	1	0
BREAK Detected	XXXXXX	CTS Status	XXXXXX (RI on Z80DART)	DCD Status	Transmitter Buffer Empty (TBE)	Interrupt Pending (Ch. A only)	Received Data (RxRDY)

Z80SIO Interrupts

Interrupts play a major role in the Z80SIO, so we must examine them early in our discussion. Interrupts in channel A have priority over interrupts in channel B. Four events can cause interrupts in the following priority:

1. Received Data Ready (RxRDY)
2. Transmitter Buffer Empty (TBE)
3. Parity, framing, or receiver overrun errors
4. "External/Status" events: changes in RS-232 inputs or a BREAK

This list is slightly different from the one given earlier because receiver error interrupts are supported only if RxRDY interrupts are enabled. Before we look at the register that enables these interrupts, we must discuss the more general topic of the Z80SIO interrupt structure.

Vectored Interrupts

When an interrupt occurs, the processor must somehow ascertain which of the possible interrupts has actually occurred. From this information, the processor then calculates the *interrupt vector* (i.e., the address of the interrupt handler) that must be invoked. In the 8250 we see the simplest of relationships between the system and an interrupting peripheral. The 8250's sole responsibility is to assert its INTRPT line; it is the exclusive province of the system to identify the interrupting device, to ascertain the address of its interrupt handler, and to call that handler. The code in the handler is responsible for clearing the interrupt (i.e., inhibiting the INTRPT line).

Figure 7-12 Vectored interrupts on the Z80SIO.

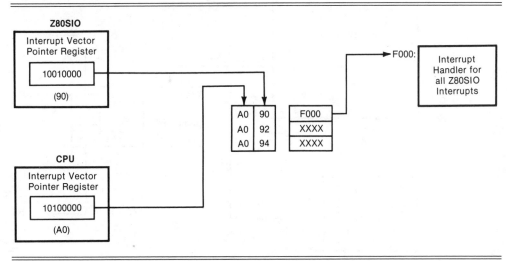

When used in conjunction with a Z80 CPU, the Z80SIO employs a more complicated, but far more efficient approach—*Peripheral Interrupt Vectoring*, in which the peripheral itself actively participates in the calculation of the interrupt vector. Figure 7-12 illustrates this process using hypothetical addresses. Before enabling interrupts on the Z80SIO, an initialization routine stores the address of (a pointer to) the interrupt handler in RAM. The handler is at location F000 and the pointer containing its address is at A090. The interrupt cycle's mission is to recover the address of the pointer, and, *indirectly through it*, the address of the handler. The initialization routine also stores the low-order byte of the pointer's address (90H) in the Z80SIO's WR[2] and its high-order byte (A0) in the CPU's Interrupt Vector Pointer[8] register.

With the stage thus set, when an interrupt occurs the Z80SIO places its half of the pointer's address on the system's data bus. The CPU fetches this byte, combines it with its own Pointer

---

[8]Once again we encounter sloppy nomenclature. Zilog's documentation refers to the Interrupt registers on the Z80 and Z80SIO as "Interrupt Vector Registers." Clearly, though, these registers do not produce the vector, but a *pointer* to the vector. (C Programmers will recognize this as a pointer to a pointer.) We use the more accurate "Vector Pointer Register."

Vector register, thus forming the full address of the pointer. With the interrupt vector pointer now in hand, the CPU turns control over to the interrupt handler by performing an *indirect* CALL to the pointer.

Automatic Vector Modification

In the approach depicted in Figure 7-12, a single interrupt handler must service the entire Z80SIO. That is, the handler must analyze registers RR[0] and RR[1] to ascertain the exact cause of the interrupt. Once the cause is known, the handler then calls the appropriate subfunction to service the interrupt. Although this is the simplest way to process interrupts for only a single source, it is inefficient when several kinds of UART interrupts are supported.

Figure 7-13   Modified vector interrupts on the Z80SIO.

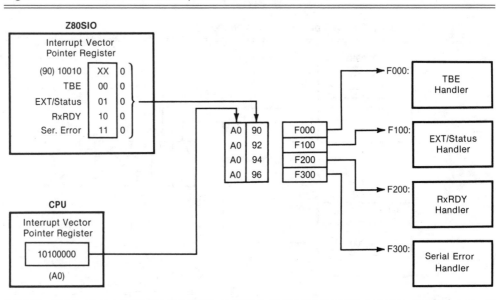

A great improvement is attained by having the Z80SIO modify its portion of the address based upon the cause of the interrupt. In this way a *unique* vector pointer is generated for each possible interrupt. Figure 7-13 illustrates modified vectoring using the hypothetical addresses from Figure 7-12. As before, the CPU's interrupt register and the Z80SIO are initialized with their respective halves of the vector pointer. This time, however, the Z80SIO outputs a different byte for each interrupt source. The portion of the address thus formed contains a pointer to the unique handler for the cause of the interrupt. If a TBE interrupt occurs, the system behaves exactly as before: the Z80SIO outputs 90H, the CPU furnishes A0, and the final address calculated is A090. In this instance, though, the address at A090 is expected to contain the address of a handler that services *only* TBE interrupts. Similarly, in response to an RxRDY interrupt, the Z80SIO outputs 94H instead of 90H. This time, the address formed is A094, which contains the address of the code to handle RxRDY interrupts.

Notice that bit 0 is not modified. In fact, the CPU forces bit 0 to 0 during address formation to guarantee that vectors are generated in intervals of 2 bytes—the storage required for 16-bit Z80 addresses. With bit 0 always 0, only *even* addresses can be formed; it is therefore up to the programmer to begin the vector table at an *even* address.

A word of warning: do not rely upon the vector modifications shown in Figure 7-13—they are incomplete. Refer to Table 7-6 for the actual modification masks, which include a third bit for channel selection.

Interrupt Control: WR[1], WR[2], and RR[2]

Interrupts are controlled entirely by means of three registers. The unmodified vector is written to WR[2] (Figure 7-14) and can be read in RR[2] (the only read-write register in the Z80SIO). RR[2] and WR[2] exist only in Channel B:

Figure 7-14   The Z80SIO's WR[2] register.

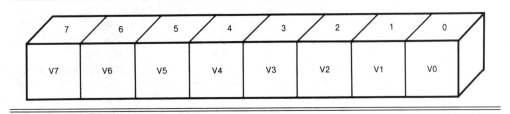

WR[1] (Figure 7-15) selects the sources of interrupts and whether the interrupt vector is modified.

Figure 7-15   The Z80SIO's WR[1] register.

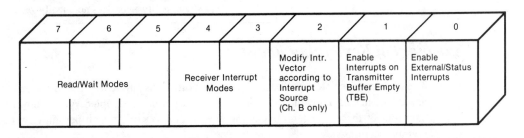

Bit 0   This is the enabling bit for External/Status interrupts—that is, interrupts originating from the RS-232 inputs or a BREAK condition. When servicing this interrupt, do not forget to clear the interrupt with Command 2, "Clear External/Status Latches."

Bit 1   This bit enables TBE interrupts. Command 5 in WR[0] provides a mechanism for clearing a pending TBE interrupt without actually writing a byte to the transmitter.

Bit 2   If set, this bit, which is active in channel B only, causes the interrupt vector pointer to be modified as shown in Table 7-6.

Bit 3
Bit 4   These two bits select one of several variations on RxRDY interrupts as indicated in Table 7-7. If vector pointer modification is enabled in bit 1, interrupts on serialization errors are also automatically enabled. To make it possible to receive data in the presence of parity errors, code 3 does not generate an interrupt on parity errors. If you wish to override this feature entirely, simply point the serialization error vector at a function containing only a Command 6, "Clear Error Latches."

Bit 5
Bit 6
Bit 7   These three bits interface the Z80SIO to other hardware devices such as DMA
controllers. The use of these bits is a topic for another time.

Table 7-6   Interrupt vector pointer modification.

V3	V2	V1	Modified by Interrupt
0	0	0	Ch.B: TBE
0	0	1	Ch.B: External/Status
0	1	0	Ch.B: RxRDY
0	1	1	Ch.B: Serialization Error
1	0	0	Ch.A: TBE
1	0	1	Ch.A: External/Status
1	1	0	Ch.A: RxRDY
1	1	1	Ch.A: Serialization Error

Table 7-7   Varieties of RxRDY interrupts.

D4	D3	RxRDY interrupt on:
0	0	No RxRDY interrupts
0	1	First byte only
1	0	Every byte, parity error modifies vector
1	1	Every byte, parity error does not modify vector

Summary of Remaining Registers

The remaining registers perform conventional functions similar to those proposed for the imaginary UART in Chapter 6 and found in the 8250 earlier in this chapter. We will now make a whistle-stop tour of these registers, bypassing WR[5] and WR[6], which pertain only to synchronous communications.

WR[3]: Receive Parameters

Most of the bits in WR[3] control some aspect of receiver operation. Of particular interest is bit 5, the "Handshaking" bit, in which control of the transmitter and receiver are tied to the CTS and DCD inputs, respectively. This feature greatly simplifies half-duplex modem control over an RS-232 interface where CTS and DCD actually control the send and receive modes. This handshaking relies upon the *current* state of these inputs, not the state of their status bits in RR[0], which might be latched.

Since half-duplex modem control has never been a popular usage for microcomputers, this feature is generally used for buffer flow control in slow peripheral devices such as printers and plotters. Flow control is achieved by connecting the printer's "Buffer Full," or BUSY output to the Z80SIO's CTS input (pin 5 on a DTE interface). When the printer has received all of the bytes it can handle, it inhibits its Buffer Full output, inhibiting the Z80SIO's CTS input and turning off the transmitter. After the character currently being assembled is sent, transmission ceases and remains in this state until CTS is asserted again.

Figure 7-16 The Z80SIO's WR[3] register.

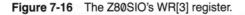

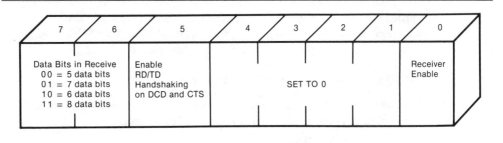

Bit 0 (Receiver Enable) When this bit is 0, the receiver does not function. On some UARTs the Receiver Enable simply holds the RxRDY FALSE while continuing to assemble characters from the communications line. The Z80SIO, on the other hand, completely disables the receiver by, one suspects, killing the clock pulses running its shift register. The complementary bit for the transmitter is WR[5], bit 3.

Bit 5 (Automatic Handshaking) When 1, this bit imparts special significance to the CTS and DCD status inputs, which effectively become secondary Receiver and Transmitter Enable bits, respectively. In other words, inhibiting the CTS and DCD inputs has the same effect as writing a 0 in WR[3], bit 0 (the Receiver Enable bit, just described) and in WR[5], bit 3 (the Transmitter Enable bit).

Bit 6
Bit 7 Bits 6 and 7 control the number of data bits assembled by the receiver. This number is independent of the transmitter's data bits number, which is set in WR[5], bits 5 and 6. Notice the lack of correlation between the bit patterns and the number of data bits they select.

WR[4]: Miscellaneous Parameters

WR[4] (Figure 7-17) controls UART functions that are common to both transmitter and receiver. Of these, only bits 6 and 7, which control the clocking factor, are interesting.

Figure 7-17 The Z80SIO's WR[4] register.

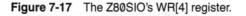

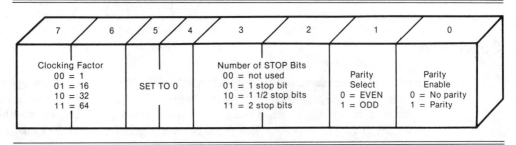

As we noted in Chapter 6, increasing the clocking factor beyond 16 produces an insignificant improvement in synchronization (see Figure 6-8). In general, a programmable clocking factor is found on UARTs that do not contain on-board baud rate generators or baud rate divisor circuitry. On such UARTs, varying the clocking factor among 16, 32, and 64 is a simple way to change the baud rate without understanding the external baud rate circuitry. This is a handy feature when the baud rate is hardwired or set by inaccessible microswitches. For example, if the switches are adjusted to produce a baud rate of, say 1200 baud, with a clocking factor of 32, changing the clocking factor to 16 and 64 then produces baud rates of 2400 and 600 baud, respectively. Selecting a clocking factor of 1 prevents START-bit synchronization.

WR[5]: Transmit and RS-232 Parameters

The bits in WR[5] (Figure 7-18) control various aspects of the transmitter, including BREAK generation. In addition, WR[5] controls the RS-232 outputs DTR and RTS.

Figure 7-18   The Z80SIO's WR[5] register.

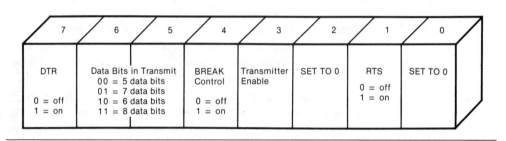

Bit 1   (Request To Send) A 1 in this bit asserts the Z80SIO's RTS output.

Bit 3   (Transmitter Enable) If this bit is 0, the transmitter does not function. The transmitter goes "offline" as soon as its shift register becomes empty. The complementary bit for disabling the receiver is WR[3], bit 0.

Bit 4   (Send BREAK) As long as there is a 1 in this bit, the output of the transmitter is forced into a SPACE condition.

Bit 5
Bit 6   These bits govern the number of data bits transmitted. This number is independent of the receiver's data bits number, which is set in WR[3], bits 6 and 7. Notice the lack of correlation between the bit patterns and the number of data bits they select.

Bit 7   (Data Terminal Ready) A 1 in this bit asserts the Z80SIO's DTR output.

Conclusion

In this chapter we examined two quite different UARTs. We shall meet them again in Chapter 9 and throughout the programming chapters. In these chapters we will use these two UARTs to demonstrate that, through careful design, communications software can achieve a high degree of generality and, yes, portability. Before we begin this quest, however, let's take a close look at another familiar face in the microcomputer crowd—the Hayes Smartmodem.

8

The Hayes Smartmodem

Before micros, the Bell 212A or 103A modems were unchallenged standards, at least in America. But in the micro world and increasingly in the rest of computerdom as well, the Hayes Smartmodem[1] product family has come to be the standard in the same fashion as the IBM line of micros has become the standard microcomputer. So dominant is the Hayes influence that market analysts estimate that upwards of 90 percent of all modems manufactured for the microcomputer market are compatible (or claim to be) with the Hayes Smartmodems. Indeed, whatever wonderful new features new modems may contain, they must still support the documented command set of the Hayes Smartmodem family. To do otherwise is to commit suicide in the market.

For our part, although we could endeavor to write a library of modem functions that encompasses the *entire* universe of modems, the generality of such functions would render them almost useless for contemporary microcomputer applications. Stated another way, designing functions broadly enough to embrace both the older ("conventional") modems *and* the "smart" modems would produce a library effective with neither. Therefore, conceding to common sense, the requirements of the everyday micro programmer, and, of course, the reality of the market place, this chapter deals exclusively with the Smartmodem.

What's So Smart About a Smartmodem, Anyway?

Before launching into the characteristics and attributes of the Hayes Smartmodem, we ought first to review (from Chapter 5) what we mean by the term "smart" modem and, by implication, a dumb one.

The rules for and extent of interaction between a modem and computer hardware are prescribed by the Electronic Industries Association Recommended Standard number 232, revision C, better known simply as RS-232C. Despite the myriad other uses, mostly illicit, to which RS-232 has been put, its sole *intended* purpose was to standardize the interaction between "Data Com-

---

[1]The trademark and copyright issues here are complicated. Hayes Microcomputer Products, Inc. claims trademark on the terms "Smartmodem 1200," "Smartmodem 1200B," "Smartmodem 2400," and "Smartmodem 2400B." Although Hayes lays no claim to the neologism "smartmodem" itself, we will use the variation "smart modem" to describe a *generic* product that supports the features and command sets of the Hayes family of modems. To avoid confusion, we will always use Smartmodem with the first letter capitalized when referring to the genuine Hayes product.

munications Equipment" (DCE, or modem) and "Data Terminal Equipment" (DTE, or computer equipment).

As defined by RS-232, all interaction between a traditional modem and the computer equipment occurs by exchanging signal voltages across wires. For example, without DTR (pin 20) asserted, modems are disabled. Similarly, the modem announces a successful carrier linkage by asserting DCD (pin 8). Without belaboring the point, then, the RS-232 interface is the sole medium through which one device may control the other. The smart modem, by contrast, interacts with peripheral equipment by exchanging ASCII character sequences. There is no *formal* difference between these character sequences and ordinary data—both are in the START/STOP asynchronous format. Rather, under certain conditions, which we will explore shortly, the modem interprets these character sequences as *command strings* instead of data. Although it has the option of relying on RS-232 signals, properly written software can effect most modem control functions on a mere pair of RS-232 data lines and signal common.

The ability to control a modem by sending it software command strings in the data stream is enormously liberating: many of the tasks with which the programmer was previously burdened are now handled by the smart modem. On an ordinary modem, for example, answering an incoming call is a major production. The program must monitor the RS-232 RI (Ring Indicator) input for a ring signal, count the RI pulses until a predetermined number is reached, at which time the program signals via RS-232 for the modem to go off-hook (i.e., answer the line) and start the carrier tone. Once the modem acknowledges these instructions (via RS-232), the program begins a timing loop looking for a transition on pin 8, DCD (Data Carrier Detect) that indicates a modem carrier link has been achieved. If the timing loop expires, the program must reverse the process—turn the carrier off, reverse the phone line, and put the modem back to sleep. The same chore on a smart modem is trivial by comparison. During initialization, the smart modem is instructed via command strings not only to answer the phone automatically, but also on which ring to answer it.

The foregoing comparison is perhaps unfair because some conventional modems are capable of automatically answering the phone. Nevertheless, the point of the comparison—that the smart modem relieves the programmer of the overwhelming minutiae of modem control—is well taken. In the remainder of this chapter we will explore the structure and behavior of smart modems. In Chapter 17 we will develop a library of functions for programming them.

The first Smartmodem was the Hayes Smartmodem 300. Although subsequent Hayes Smartmodems have greatly extended the capability of the Smartmodem 300, all are completely compatible with it. Because of its position as progenitor of the line and because of its downward compatibility, we will treat the Smartmodem 300 as *the* generic Smartmodem, referring to it simply as *the* Smartmodem. Our approach, then, will be to describe the Smartmodem 300 completely, then show how subsequent Hayes products enhance and differ from it.

An Overview of the Hayes Smartmodem 300

The generic Smartmodem (i.e., the Hayes Smartmodem 300) is a Bell 103A-type modem with data transfer rates of 110 or 300 bits per second. Under software control, it automatically answers incoming calls and, by means of an internal pulse/tone generator, automatically dials telephone numbers. The Smartmodem is designed for direct connection to the public telephone network through a single modular jack that accommodates standard RJ-11, RJ-12, RJ-13, RJ-41S, or RJ-45S plugs. The Smartmodem's intelligent features are controlled by sending commands in the form of ASCII character sequences to the Smartmodem's DCE RS-232 interface. The Smartmodem responds to commands and dialing operations with ASCII character sequences, again via its RS-232 interface.

Configuration Switch and S-Register Notation

Before proceeding in this chapter, we should pause to explain certain reference notations used. To make the information here more valuable for later use as a reference, from the outset parenthetical references will be made to topics not yet covered. In particular, certain discussions will contain references such as [S4], [SW7], or even compound references such as [S4, SW7]. The 'S' prefix refers to the Smartmodem's *S-registers*, which govern many modem functions. 'SW' prefixes refer to one of the switches of the microswitch assembly located behind the Smartmodem's front panel, from which configuration information is read at power-up and reset. Needless to say, we will study both topics in detail at the appropriate time. These forward references alert you that the topic under discussion is affected by the contents of the indicated S-register or the position of one of the indicated configuration switches.

The Smartmodem Front and Rear Panels

As illustrated in Figure 8-1, the front panel of the Hayes Smartmodem 300 is an array of seven indicator lamps. These lamps report the following conditions:

AA   (Auto Answer) The Smartmodem is ready to answer incoming calls automatically and attempt to establish a carrier link. This lamp blinks with each ring of an incoming call.

CD   (Carrier Detect) A carrier link with another modem is in progress.

OH   (Off-Hook) The Smartmodem has seized the telephone line. (This is the equivalent of manually lifting the handset from the cradle.)

SD   (Send Data) This lamp flashes when the modem outputs data on pin 2 of the RS-232 interface.

RD   (Receive Data) This lamp flashes when data arrives at the Smartmodem on pin 3 of the RS-232 interface.

TR   (Terminal Ready) This lamp illuminates whenever Data Terminal Ready (pin 20) of the RS-232 interface is asserted. [SW1]

MR   (Modem Ready) Power is applied to the Smartmodem.

The rear panel of the Smartmodem contains an on/off switch, one power pack receptacle, one DB-25P connector, one telephone connector, and a speaker volume control.

The Smartmodem's RS-232 Interface

The Hayes Smartmodems employ the minimum number of RS-232 functions necessary for full-duplex modem control. Because it is a modem, it is, by definition, a DCE device (Data Communications Equipment). RS-232 connections are made through the familiar DB-25S (female) connector. Table 8-1 shows this connector, the pins used on the Smartmodem, and a discussion of each.

Because the Smartmodem was designed for use with microcomputers, it does not pretend to implement a full-blown RS-232 interface. Nevertheless, there is nothing wildly deviant about its interface, although two of the functions should be mentioned. First, notice that DSR pin 6 follows DCD pin 8; this could cause problems for software that monitors DSR to sense when the phone has been answered. Second, CTS is permanently asserted and RTS is not implemented, so the

Smartmodem is not suited for use with software that performs traditional half-duplex handshaking protocols on these pins.

Figure 8-1   The Hayes Smartmodem 300's front and rear panels.

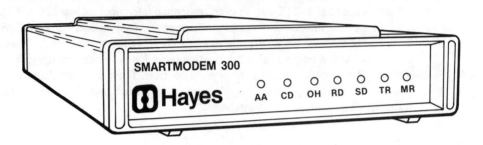

Smartmodem Front Panel

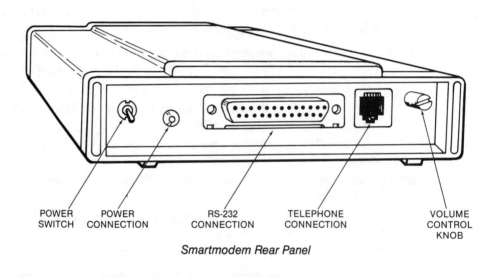

POWER SWITCH   POWER CONNECTION   RS-232 CONNECTION   TELEPHONE CONNECTION   VOLUME CONTROL KNOB

Smartmodem Rear Panel

Table 8-1.   RS-232 functions on the Smartmodem's DB-25 connector.

Pin	Function	Description
1	Frame Ground	Connected to Smartmodem chassis
2	TD	Smartmodem commands or data bound for the phone line
3	RD	Smartmodem responses or data fetched from the phone line
5	CTS	Permanently asserted
6	DSR	Hardwired to pin 8 (DCD)
7	Signal Ground	Connected to circuit common
8	DCD [SW6]	Asserted during carrier linkage
20	DTR [SW1]	Enables Smartmodem
22	RI	Asserted with each ring on the telephone line

Smartmodem States

Whenever the Smartmodem is engaged in a carrier link with another modem (called its *online state*), it behaves as a conventional modem, passing all RS-232 input directly to its transmitter. When not online, however, the Smartmodem is said to be in the *command state*, and RS-232 data is treated as potential commands. As we will see later, it is possible to switch the Smartmodem from the online to the command state and back again—without breaking the carrier link!

The "Comatose" Smartmodem

There exists a third Smartmodem state, one perhaps more properly described as a metastate: the *comatose* state. In this state, which is controlled by RS-232 DTR pin 20 [SW1], the Smartmodem does not acknowledge commands, participate in dialing activities, or exhibit modem behavior. Ring Indicator pin 22, however, remains functional. By definition, then, an asserted DTR is a prerequisite for establishing a carrier linkage; similarly, if DTR becomes inhibited *during* a carrier linkage, the Smartmodem immediately releases the line and enters the comatose state.

Smartmodem Command State

In command state, the Smartmodem monitors the bytes incoming from the RS-232 port in search of a particular sequence of bytes referred to as the *Command Sequence Introducer*, or CSI.[2] After the CSI is encountered, the Smartmodem places subsequent characters in its internal 40-character buffer, until the buffer becomes full or it encounters the *command terminator* character. Here are the few rules governing the command buffer:

- The CSI must be upper case, although subsequent characters may be either upper or lower case.
- The CSI itself is not placed in the buffer and is therefore not counted toward the 40-character maximum.
- SPace (ASCII 20H) and control characters are ignored and not counted toward the 40-character maximum.
- The backspacing character removes characters from the buffer.

When the command terminator is entered, the Smartmodem attempts to parse the buffer into individual commands. An error results if:

- More than 40 characters are entered.
- The CSI contains lower-case characters.
- An invalid command is encountered in the buffer.
- An invalid operand is encountered in the buffer.

---

[2]This lingo is from ANSI 3.64. See Chapter 1 for details.

Errors are unconditionally fatal—that is, the *entire* buffer is discarded without attempting to execute any of the commands, regardless of their individual validity. Since the Smartmodem ignores any command string containing even a single erroneous command, the programmer must exercise great care to assure the validity of the individual commands that constitute the command string.

As explained later in "Numeric Variable Commands," the Smartmodem maintains important values in programmable variables. The Smartmodem's definition of a newline is contained in two such variables. These newline variables are hereafter referred to simply as *nl1* and *nl2* [S3, S4]. By default, *nl1* and *nl2* contain CR and LF, respectively. The backspacing character is also a programmable variable [S5], by default BS (ASCII 8).

The Smartmodem's command terminator is *nl1* [S3], so by default, commands are terminated by a Carriage Return. The Smartmodem's CSI is AT, supposedly an abbreviation for "ATTENTION." This sequence is hardwired—i.e., not programmable.

Smartmodem's Response to Commands

After it has evaluated and, if possible, parsed and executed the commands in its command buffer, the Smartmodem responds with its own sequence of ASCII characters. As we will soon learn, the loquacity of this response is governed by the Smartmodem's "verbosity" mode, which is modified by the *V* (Verbose) command [SW2]. The Smartmodem waits at least 250 milliseconds between receiving the command terminator and issuing its response. This delay is important because it allows software to differentiate between characters echoed by the Smartmodem and its response to commands. In its more verbose mode, the Smartmodem reports the successful or unsuccessful execution of a command with the words OK and ERROR, respectively. In its less verbose mode, the Smartmodem responds with the single digits 0 and 4, respectively.

The newline punctuation included with Smartmodem responses also varies according to the modem's verbosity. In the more verbose mode, it surrounds its responses with both newline characters:

(nl1)(nl2)OK(nl1)(nl2)
(nl1)(nl2)ERROR(nl1)(nl2)

In its less verbose mode, however, the single digits are surrounded by *nl1*s:

(nl1)0(nl1)
(nl1)4(nl1)

To make matters slightly more complicated, when command echo is off (i.e., *ATE0*), single-digit response codes are terminated, but not preceded, by a CR (refer to Table 8-2). For special situations, the Smartmodem's default *nl1* and *nl2*, CR and LF, can be reprogrammed (See S4 and S5 in "Numeric Variable Commands," below).

Table 8-2 Newlines in Smartmodem responses. *x* is the Smartmodem's response assuming the default *nl1*, CR.

Command Echo	Disabled (E0)	Enabled (E1)
V0	*x*CR	CR*x*CR
V1	CRLF*x*CRLF	CRLF*x*CRLF

Smartmodem Responses to Dialing Commands

In addition to the OK (or 0) and ERROR (or 4) responses, the Smartmodem reports the results of dial and answer operations with a special set of responses known as *call-progress* codes. Table 8-3 shows these codes.[3] For the remainder of this book, these codes will be given in their long, or word, form.

Table 8-3   Smartmodem result codes.

Digit Code	Word Code	Description
0	OK	Non-dial command successfully executed
1	CONNECT	Carrier found at 300 baud
2	RING	Ring signal present on phone line
3	NO CARRIER	Carrier absent or never found
4	ERROR	Error in command line, unrecognized command, or command buffer exceeded 40 characters.

Now that you understand what constitutes a Smartmodem command and how the Smartmodem responds, let's survey the actual command set itself. There are two general classes of commands: first, qualitative or *mode* commands that affect general aspects of the Smartmodem's behavior; second, quantitative *numeric register* commands that supply the count, delay, or numerical parameters to important modem functions.

Smartmodem "Mode" Commands

Mode commands consist of a single printable ASCII character; an optional *mode identifier*, if present, is also a single ASCII character in the range 0−9 (30H−39H). In the string *ATE1*, the command, *E*, is followed by the mode identifier *1*. Note that this value must be an ASCII *digit*, not a binary value. In the absence of a mode identifier, 0 is assumed. Therefore *ATE* is the same as *ATE0*.

We have deliberately chosen the rather stilted term "mode identifier" to emphasize that such parameters, though represented with ASCII digits, are *not* arithmetic parameters, but mere syntactical modifiers. The Smartmodem designers could have achieved identical functionality with, say, 'Y' and 'N' as modifiers. Thus a mode command is effectively a Boolean flag variable that is toggled by its mode identifier. Actually each mode is mapped to a single bit in an internal Smartmodem register. (The single exception is the *M* command, which occupies 2 bits.)

There are four groups of Smartmodem mode commands:

1. User interface
2. Primary dial
3. Dial modifiers
4. Miscellaneous

---

[3]A summary of the response codes for the entire Smartmodem family is given in Table 8-9 at the end of this chapter.

User Interface Group

The interface group of commands alters the way in which the Smartmodem interacts with the user, but does not affect the electrical operation of the modem.

The "Echo" Mode Command

This command controls whether the Smartmodem echoes characters when in command mode (as opposed to during a carrier linkage). As soon as the Smartmodem enters a carrier link, all input is treated as data.

COMMAND: *E*

PRODUCT: Smartmodem 300

FUNCTION: Command Echo
0: Command echo off
1: Command echo on

DEFAULT: [SW4] See "Smartmodem Configuration Switches," below.

Although echo is indispensable to human users, it can cause havoc when a Smartmodem is connected to a computer that also provides echo. The first character sent becomes the object of a never-ending ping-pong match as the two devices repeatedly echo the character. Software for the Smartmodem should be carefully written so that it functions properly with or without command echo. As noted earlier, when command echo is enabled, single-digit response codes are preceded and terminated by a CR (more precisely, the *nl1* character).

The "Verbose" Mode Command

As described above, the Smartmodem can be made to respond to commands with whole words or with single-digit codes.

COMMAND: *V*

PRODUCT: Smartmodem 300

FUNCTION: Smartmodem sends single-digit or whole-word responses.
0: Digit codes
1: Word codes

DEFAULT: [SW2] See "Smartmodem Configuration Switches," below.

The single digits are easier to detect, but are much more likely to be misidentified. On the other hand, word codes are very difficult to process in some languages.

The "Quiet" Mode Command

In some environments—potential ping-pong situations, for example—it may be necessary to suppress the Smartmodem's responses entirely by using the *Q* command.

COMMAND: *Q*

PRODUCT: Smartmodem 300

FUNCTION: Suppress/enable modem command response
    0: Response
    1: No response

DEFAULT: [SW3] See "Smartmodem Configuration Switches," below.

In general, the sophistication of Smartmodem software depends on the ability to identify the Smartmodem's response codes. Since this ability is crippled if the user inadvertently enters the *Q1* command, it is not a bad idea to include 'Q0' in all commands.

Speaker Control

Once users come to rely upon the Smartmodem's loudspeaker, doing without it seems torture. (A surprising number of smart modems that claim Hayes compatibility do not even contain a speaker.) Since the Smartmodem 300 does not detect the absence of a dial tone or busy signals, the internal speaker invaluably enables you to monitor first the presence of a dial tone, then the dialing of the number string, followed by the answering of the call, a busy signal, or simply no answer.

COMMAND: *M*

PRODUCT: Smartmodem 300

FUNCTION: Loudspeaker control
    0: Always off
    1: On until carrier link established
    2: Always on

DEFAULT: 1

Once the progress of the call has been monitored, however, the noise of the carrier is annoying. The default setting of the *M* command is therefore '1'—the speaker is muted as soon as a carrier link is established.

Despite the speaker's obvious utility, some environments—a hospital ward at night or a library—require absolute quiet; or the Smartmodem user simply may not wish to announce every modem call to the rest of the world. Conversely, it may be necessary to leave the speaker on as a troubleshooting aid. ("Is that garbage on my screen caused by phone line noise or a malfunction in my Smartmodem?")

Primary Answer/Dial Group

The second group of commands affects the dialing process.

The "Answer" Command

This command is used to answer most incoming calls (i.e., calls from modems using "originate" tones. Sending any character to the Smartmodem while it is waiting for a carrier terminates the wait and returns the Smartmodem to command state.

COMMAND: *A*

PRODUCT: Smartmodem 300

FUNCTION: Takes the phone line off-hook and asserts the carrier using "answer" tones and waits [S7] for an "originate" carrier from another modem.

The length of the wait for carrier is programmable with a default of 30 seconds.

The Primary "Dial" Command

Auto-dialing is actually a controlled sequence of other Smartmodem commands. The *D* command selects "originate" tones, takes the phone line off-hook, pauses [S6] for a dial tone, dials the phone number (if present), and waits for a carrier using "answer" tones [S7].

COMMAND: *D*

PRODUCT: Smartmodem 300

FUNCTION: The primary dial command

By default, the length of the pause for a dial tone and the duration of the wait for carrier are 2 and 30 seconds, respectively. Sending any character to the Smartmodem while it is waiting for a carrier terminates the wait and returns the Smartmodem to command mode.

The punctuation ( ) - * , which may be intermixed with the digits 0−9 and spaces to improve readability, count toward the command line 40-character maximum. The characteristics of the dialing operation can be modified by including any of the dial modifiers in the command string. See "Dial Modifiers," below.

The "Hook" Command

When the modem undertakes a telephone function—auto-dial, auto-answer, hang-up—it must deal with the phone line. This command is the electronic equivalent of manually lifting and hanging up a telephone receiver.

COMMAND: *H*

PRODUCT: Smartmodem 300

FUNCTION: Seize and release phone line.
0: Hang up
1: Off-hook
2: Special off-hook

The Hayes Smartmodem contains not only a relay to operate the telephone line, but an auxiliary relay through which external equipment may be switched. These relay contacts are available on pins 5 and 2 of the phone jack on the Smartmodems. In mode 1 of the *H* command, both the phone line and the auxiliary relay are closed; in mode 2 however, only the main relay is closed. In this mode, the OH lamp on the front panel does not illuminate. In conformity with FCC regulations, there is a 2-second dead time after closing the switch hook, during which the Smartmodem neither responds to nor acknowledges commands.

Although the auxiliary relay was included primarily for the benefit of radio amateurs (to key transmitters), it can be used for any external switching operation as long as the 0.5A maximum contact current is observed.

ANSWER/DIAL Modifier Group

Dial modifiers affect the characteristics of the primary dial command, *D*. There are two types of dial modifiers—*dialing adverbs* and dialing commands.

The first kind of dial modifier, the dialing adverb, affects only the dial operation in which it appears; that is, its effect disappears as soon as the current dial operation is complete.

Calibrated Pause

It is sometimes necessary to force the Smartmodem to pause briefly during dialing. When dialing long-distance services, for example, the Smartmodem must first dial the local access number, then pause long enough for the service's dial tone. The comma is also useful when dialing from a PBX system where considerable time may elapse between requesting and getting a secondary dial tone or "outside" line.

COMMAND: , (Comma, ASCII 2C)

PRODUCT: Smartmodem 300

FUNCTION: Introduces a calibrated pause [S8] into the dial operation.

Return to Command Mode After Dial

As described above under the *D* command, the Smartmodem ordinarily dials, then immediately enters a loop awaiting an answer carrier tone from another modem. If a semicolon is present after the dial command and phone number, the Smartmodem waits for a dial tone [S6] before dialing, dials the number, but then immediately returns to the command state without waiting for a carrier or hanging up.

COMMAND: ; (Semicolon, ASCII 3B)

PRODUCT: Smartmodem 300

FUNCTION: Returns to command mode after dial.

The OH (off-hook) lamp on the front panel remains illuminated and the subsequent progress of the call can be heard through the speaker as usual. The only way to terminate a successful "semicolon" call is with the *H0* hang-up command described above or by inhibiting DTR pin 20.

This feature is not used to establish a data link with another modem, but to employ the Smartmodem as a sophisticated automatic tone dialer. Services such as electronic banking require the caller to enter information from a telephone's keypad. By programming the information in dial strings terminated with semicolons, such transactions can be performed entirely by modem and computer.

"Reverse" Dial Mode

Although *originate-only* modems are a vanishing breed, enough still exist to justify this command's existence.

COMMAND: *R*

PRODUCT: Smartmodem 300

FUNCTION: "Reverse" mode: use answer tones after dialing.

After dialing, the Smartmodem supplies answer tones instead of originate tones; this enables the Smartmodem to establish a carrier link with modems that cannot configure their tones for answering. See Chapter 5 for a full explanation of such situations.

Dial Variable Commands

The second type of dial modifiers are bona fide commands that can be issued either as part of dial commands or as stand-alone Smartmodem commands. Unlike the dialing adverbs described above and regardless of the context in which they appear, these commands are identical to other Smartmodem commands—that is, they remain in effect until they are reissued with a different parameter or until the modem is reset.

Tone/Pulse Dialing

As out of touch with technology as it may seem, the Smartmodem defaults to pulse dialing.

COMMAND: *P*

PRODUCT: Smartmodem 300

FUNCTION: Set modem to use rotary-pulse signals for dialing.

COMMAND: *T*

PRODUCT: Smartmodem 300

FUNCTION: Set modem to use tone signals for dialing.

Miscellaneous Group

Most of the remaining commands deal with the technical aspects of modem communications. Although seldom required, these commands help to solve problem situations not covered by normal Smartmodem operations.

The "Carrier" Command

During ordinary operations, the Smartmodem manages its own carrier. Normally, the Smartmodem automatically turns on its carrier signal in anticipation of and during a linkage with another modem. When the link is lost, the Smartmodem automatically turns the carrier off. The command *C0* inhibits the carrier unconditionally.

COMMAND: *C*

PRODUCT: Smartmodem 300

FUNCTION: Carrier on/off
                    0: Carrier always off
                    1: Carrier managed by Smartmodem

DEFAULT: 1

Caution should be exercised in using the *C0* command. Once it has been issued, the carrier remains inhibited—even after a dial or answer command—until an explicit *C1* or a reset command is issued.

The Full-Duplex Command

The name of this command is misleading because it does not switch the bandwidth of the communications channel, but merely provides *local echo*. In local echo, *every* received character is transmitted back, regardless of whether a carrier link exists. This is different from the echo provided by the *E* command in which input is returned only in the command mode.

COMMAND: *F*

PRODUCT: Smartmodem 300

FUNCTION: Full/half-duplex
0: Echo all characters back to sender.
1: Do not echo.

DEFAULT: 1

Last Command Repeat

The Smartmodem does not clear its buffer until the *AT* of the next command is typed. Entering *A/* (with no CR) causes the current command line to be executed again. This is useful mainly for redialing telephone numbers.

COMMAND: *A/*

PRODUCT: Smartmodem 300

FUNCTION: Repeats last command.

COMMENTS: Neither the command prefix nor command terminator is necessary.

The Reset Command

Before software configures the Smartmodem, it should issue the reset command. A reset returns the Smartmodem to its power-up condition, reinstalls all variables to their default values, reads the Smartmodem's configuration switches, then performs a self-test. See "Smartmodem Configuration Switches," below, for details.

COMMAND: *Z*

PRODUCT: Smartmodem 300

FUNCTION: Resets modem, reads configuration switches.

COMMENTS: The Smartmodem sends its response to the reset command *before* performing the reset and self-test, which take about .500 second; wait at least this long before sending another command. The reset command clears the command buffer, so any commands on the same line with the reset command are lost.

Under certain conditions the Smartmodem cannot be reset with software commands and must be switched on and off. See "Smartmodem 1200 + : Configuration Switches," below.

The "Online" Command

When the modem has "escaped" from the online to the command state (without hanging up), this command returns it to its online state. The exact procedures for this feat are described in "Escaping from and Returning to the Online State," below.

COMMAND: *O*

PRODUCT: Smartmodem 300

FUNCTION: Return to the "online" state.

Numeric Variable Commands

In our earlier discussion of the Smartmodem's commands, we emphasized that parameters for "mode" commands, though ASCII digits (i.e., 0–9), are not arithmetic in nature. The Smartmodem's numeric variables are contained in a group of thirteen 'S' (for "scalar," perhaps) registers, named S0, S1, and so on through S12. These variables are addressed in the ordinary Smartmodem command format—*AT*, followed by the register number. Unlike other Smartmodem parameters, the ASCII digits following the register name are interpreted as true arithmetic values. An S-register assignment command is created by placing an equal sign (=, ASCII 3D) between the register name and the digit-by-digit ASCII representation of the numeric value. Thus the ASCII sequence:

ATS6=125   (hex = 41 54 53 36 3D 31 32 35)

places value 125 into S-register 6. Conversely, the contents of an S-register can be fetched by placing a question mark (?, ASCII 3F) after the register name. Assuming the assignment command above is successful, the sequence:

ATS6?

causes the Smartmodem to reply:

125   (hex = 31 32 35)

surrounded by *nl1*,*nl2* (CRLF), bracketed by *nl1* (CR), or just terminated by *nl1* (CR), depending upon the settings of the *V* and *E* commands. See Table 8-2 for details. All numeric values are reported in three digits, left-padded with 0s if necessary.

Some care is required when assigning values to S-registers. Even though several of the S-registers (S3 and S5, for example) function correctly only with a limited range of characters, the Smartmodem uncomplainingly accepts any 8-bit value. To make matters worse, the Smartmodem accepts *any* number of digits as an S-register argument. For example, the Smartmodem happily accepts the following assignment:

ATS6=1234567890123456

and, when queried for the new value of S6, replies

192

From this response, we can conclude that the Smartmodem converts the ASCII digits in its argument to an internal 8-bit variable.

Based upon how they are used, S-registers can be divided into three categories: characters, counters/timers, and bit maps.

S-Register Character Variables

Four S-register variables enable the programmer to redefine the Smartmodem's concept of important ASCII characters. All four take as an argument a digit-by-digit ASCII representation of that character's rank in the ASCII character set. The command to set register S2 to the vertical bar (|, 124) are therefore

> ATS2=124

S2: Online Escape Character

This register contains the character that forces the Smartmodem from online to command state without hanging up or breaking the carrier link. Refer to "Escaping from and Returning to the Online State," below.

REGISTER:	S2
PRODUCT:	Smartmodem 300
FUNCTION:	Online escape character
VALID RANGE:	0−127
UNIT:	ASCII
DEFAULT:	43 (+, 2BH)

S3 and S4: Newline Characters *nl1* and *nl2*

By default, the Smartmodem uses a CR and LF for a newline, but each of these characters is programmable.

REGISTER:	S3
PRODUCT:	Smartmodem 300
FUNCTION:	First newline character (*nl1*) and command terminator
VALID RANGE:	0−127
UNIT:	ASCII
DEFAULT:	13 (CR, 0D)

REGISTER:	S4
PRODUCT:	Smartmodem 300
FUNCTION:	Second newline character (*nl2*)
VALID RANGE:	0−127
UNIT:	ASCII
DEFAULT:	10 (LF, 0A)

Unfortunately for C programmers, there is no way to configure the Smartmodem to achieve a single-character newline.

S3 (*nl1*) is not only the first newline character, but also the command terminator. Although an S3 value greater than 127 is correctly output as part of a newline, it is not recognized as a command terminator. This register should therefore be changed only after great thought.

S5: Programmable Backspace

This feature accommodates incomplete, eccentric, or non-ASCII keyboards. The Smartmodem accepts any character, but only ASCII control characters actually perform backspacing.

REGISTER:	S5
PRODUCT:	Smartmodem 300
FUNCTION:	Backspace character
VALID RANGE:	0−32, 127
UNIT:	ASCII
DEFAULT:	08 (BS)

S-Register Counter/Timer Variables

This category of S-register maintains count variables for fine tuning the Smartmodem's telephone interface.

S0: Ring Count for Auto-Answer

This register holds the number of rings after which the Smartmodem answers the phone.

REGISTER:	S0
PRODUCT:	Smartmodem 300
FUNCTION:	Sets ring on which to answer the phone.
VALID RANGE:	0−255
UNIT:	Rings
DEFAULT:	[SW5] in "Smartmodem Configuration Switches," below.

When set to a value greater than 0, the AA lamp on the Smartmodem's front panel illuminates and the modem answers the phone after that many ring pulses. A ring count of 0 disables auto-answer altogether and the AA lamp on the front panel is extinguished.

S1: Number of Rings So Far

This value is automatically reset to 0 between calls or if 8 seconds elapse without a ring.

REGISTER:	S1
PRODUCT:	Smartmodem 300
FUNCTION:	Counts number of rings so far.
VALID RANGE:	0−255
UNIT:	Rings
DEFAULT:	0

Oddly, this is a read/write variable. A situation in which one would wish to modify this variable is barely conceivable.

S6: Seconds To Wait for a Dial Tone

Since the Smartmodem 300 cannot detect the presence of a dial tone, a delay is introduced between taking the phone off-hook and dialing the number.

REGISTER: S6

PRODUCT: Smartmodem 300

FUNCTION: Sets number of seconds to wait for dial tone before dialing.

VALID RANGE: 2−255

UNIT: Seconds

DEFAULT: 2 (also the minimum value)

Increase this variable only to accommodate eccentric telephone systems.

S7: Seconds To Wait for Carrier

This register dictates how long after dialing the Smartmodem waits for a carrier link before returning to command mode.

REGISTER: S7

PRODUCT: Smartmodem 300

FUNCTION: Sets number of seconds to wait for carrier before giving up.

VALID RANGE: 1−255

UNIT: Seconds

DEFAULT: 30

The Smartmodem responds CONNECT if a carrier link is established during this timing interval; otherwise it sends the NO CARRIER response and returns to the command state.

Sending any byte to the Smartmodem during this interval terminates the wait, produces the NO CARRIER response, and forces a return to the command state.

S8: Length of Pause

This register holds the length of the pause produced by a comma in the dialing string.

REGISTER: S8

PRODUCT: Smartmodem 300

FUNCTION: Sets number of seconds of pause induced by comma in dial string.

VALID RANGE: 0−255

UNIT: Seconds

DEFAULT: 1

Multiple commas may be compounded for very long delays.

S9: Carrier-Present Guard Time

This register determines how long a carrier must be present before it is considered valid. This delay guards against mistaking phone line noise for a carrier.

REGISTER: S9

PRODUCT: Smartmodem 300

FUNCTION: Sets length of time the carrier must be present before announcing it.

VALID RANGE: 1−255

UNIT: Tenths of a second (Tsecs)

DEFAULT: 6 (600 milliseconds)

The default of 600 milliseconds is actually quite conservative and works fine in ordinary environments.

S10: Lost-Carrier Guard Time

This interval determines how long a carrier must be *continually* absent before the Smartmodem acknowledges it—inhibits its own carrier, turns off the front panel CD lamp, and enters the command state.

REGISTER: S10

PRODUCT: Smartmodem 300

FUNCTION: Sets length of time the carrier must be absent before announcing it.

VALID RANGE: 1−255

UNIT: Tenths of a second (Tsec)

DEFAULT: 7 (700 milliseconds)

This register, the complement to S9, guards against periodic fluctuations in carrier level (*flutter*) or momentary total loss of carrier (*dropout*).

If register S10 is set to 255, the Smartmodem behaves as if carrier were present at all times. Immediately after dialing, it asserts its carrier and issues the CONNECT response code. When the carrier linkage terminates, the Smartmodem totally ignores the loss of the receiver's carrier, continues to assert carrier, and retains control of the line. In this condition, the Smartmodem must be forced to hang up either by performing an online escape followed by a hang-up command or by inhibiting DTR. See "Smartmodem Online State," below.

S11: Touch Tone Rate

This S-register sets the speed of tone dialing.

REGISTER: S11

PRODUCT: Smartmodem 300

FUNCTION: MFTD (Touch Tone) signaling rate

VALID RANGE: 50−255

UNIT: Milliseconds

DEFAULT: 70

The dialing rate is the reciprocal of twice the value of this register (½ t). The default value of 70 milliseconds therefore produces a dialing rate of about seven digits per second. A value of 255 slows the rate to about two digits per second for applications that expect to receive tones at a human's finger-rate. Although the minimum value is listed as 50 milliseconds, the Smartmodem uncomplainingly accepts smaller values.

S12: Escape Sequence Guard Time

This is the amount of silence that must surround the command forcing the Smartmodem from online to command state.

REGISTER:	S12
PRODUCT:	Smartmodem 300
FUNCTION:	Minimum silent interval that must surround escape sequence
VALID RANGE:	20−255
UNIT:	1/50 second
DEFAULT:	50 (i.e., 1 second)

This time must be longer than one SDU (serial data unit) at the current baud rate. See "Smartmodem Online State," below for details. If S12 is 0, the escape sequence is not checked for surrounding silence.

Bit-Mapped S-Registers

In addition to the ordinary S-registers just discussed, the Smartmodem contains three bit-mapped registers: S13, S14, and S15. These enable the programmer to query the Smartmodem about the states of its internal variables, command flags, and current data format. Since the contents of these registers vary enormously across the Hayes Smartmodem product line, they are not discussed here.

Smartmodem Online State

Whenever the Smartmodem is engaged in a carrier link, it is said to be in the *online* state. Aside from the obvious presence of a carrier, the online state differs from the command state in that the modem treats input data transparently; that is, the input data stream is not placed in the Smartmodem's command buffer, but is passed along for modulation and transmission. Once in the online state, the Smartmodem automatically returns to the command state when the carrier is lost.

Escape from and Return to the Online State

There are a number of situations in which it may be necessary to return to the command mode without hanging up or dropping the carrier. Suppose, for example, that after hours of busy signals, you finally establish a carrier link, only to discover that the remote system is half-duplex. You don't want to hang up the phone line (return to command state) just for the purpose of issuing the *F0* (half-duplex) command, because it may take hours to get through again. You need a way to return to command state temporarily without disturbing the carrier linkage, issue a local command to the Smartmodem, then return to the online state.

The mechanism for moving between Smartmodem states is straightforward, if problematical. The problem is this: since the Smartmodem treats data transparently during a carrier linkage, how do we get its attention to tell it to return to the command state? When in the online state, the Smartmodem is not entirely deaf to the data stream, but listens for a string of three consecutive *escape characters* surrounded by a specified interval of silence. The value of the escape character is given in S-register 2, and the interval of silence is given in S-register 12.

Here is the procedure for performing an escape to the command state and then returning to the online state.

1. Send no data to the Smartmodem for the escape time defined in S-register 12. The default is 1 second.
2. Send three consecutive escape characters as defined in S-register 2. The default escape character is 2B (+ , ASCII 43).
3. If no data is sent during the escape time intervals, the Smartmodem responds OK, announcing that it is now in the command mode.
4. Issue local commands to the Smartmodem.
5. To return to the online state, issue the command *ATO*. The Smartmodem responds CONNECT to announce its return to the online state.

The value in S-register 12 must always be longer than the time represented by a single SDU at the current baud rate. To understand why this is so, assume that the modem is currently using a 10-bit SDU at 300 bps; here, one SDU has a duration of 33.3 milliseconds. If S-register 12 is set to 1, the guard time is only 20 milliseconds and the guard time expires while each character is being serialized. Since the Smartmodem's lowest data rate is 110 baud (an SDU of about 100 milliseconds), the default guard time of 1 second provides an order-of-magnitude safety margin under all circumstances.

Pitfalls of the Online Escape

If the value in S-register 2 is greater than 127, the escape request is ignored. If the value in S-register 12 is 0, the escape sequence is acknowledged instantaneously (i.e., without a guard band of silence).

In general, the online escape feature should be used with caution. To understand why, assume that you call a remote full-duplex system with echo-back. If the remote system happens to be using a Smartmodem, there is a danger inherent in the use of the online escape. As you send the three escape characters, the remote system also sees them and acts upon them! In other words, you not only force your modem into the command mode, you force the remote system, too. Now, you can return your modem to the online state just by typing *ATO*, but you have no control over the remote system. Your only recourse is to hang up and call again. To avoid being thus hoist with your own petard, change your Smartmodem's S-register escape character from the default or make certain that the two modems are programmed with a different escape character.

Software Hang-up

Under "normal" circumstances we can unconditionally force the Smartmodem to hang up the phone and return to the command state by inhibiting its RS-232 DTR (Data Terminal Ready, pin 20). As we will learn shortly, one of the configuration switches behind the front panel *permanently* asserts DTR, causing the Smartmodem to ignore forced hang-up. In these situations, the Smartmodem must be forced from the online mode to the command mode from where the "hang-up" command, *ATH0*, can be issued.

Smartmodem Configuration Switches

At power-up and reset, the Smartmodem acquires its default settings for several important variables from an array of eight microswitches located behind its removable front panel. The effects of changing switch 1 and 6 are immediate; the other switches are consulted only at power-up or reset. The following is a list of these switches and their functions.[4]

SWITCH #:   1

PRODUCT: Smartmodem 300

FUNCTION: DTR (Data Terminal Ready, pin 20) input override
UP: Normal DTR operation
DOWN: DTR always enabled

FACTORY: DOWN

COMMENTS: By permanently enabling DTR pin 20 (thus preventing the comatose state) this switch's DOWN position makes it possible to operate the Smartmodem without RS-232 signals or where DTR is not present. In effect, this switch is a quick alternative to making a trick cable. There is no equivalent Smartmodem command.

SWITCH #:   2

PRODUCT: Smartmodem 300

FUNCTION: Supplies default for the "verbose" command *V*.
UP: Word result codes (*V1*)
DOWN: Single-digit result codes (*V0*)

FACTORY: UP

SWITCH #:   3

PRODUCT: Smartmodem 300

FUNCTION: Supplies default for "quiet" command *Q*.
UP: Smartmodem does not send result codes (*Q1*).
DOWN: Smartmodem sends result codes (*Q0*).

FACTORY: DOWN

SWITCH #:   4

PRODUCT: Smartmodem 300

FUNCTION: Supplies default for "echo" command *E*.
UP: Smartmodem echoes its RS-232 input while in command mode (*E1*).
DOWN: Smartmodem does not echo (*E0*).

FACTORY: UP

SWITCH #:   5

PRODUCT: Smartmodem 300

---

[4]The tables at the end of this chapter cross-reference the configuration switches and their functions for the entire Smartmodem family.

FUNCTION: Disables auto-answer mode.
                      UP: Answers phone on first ring.
                      DOWN: Does not answer phone.

FACTORY: DOWN

COMMENTS: This is the default condition only and can be overridden by writing a new value into S-register 0.

SWITCH #:   6

PRODUCT: Smartmodem 300

FUNCTION: DCD pin 8 override
                      UP: DCD is asserted only during carrier link.
                      DOWN: DCD is always asserted.

FACTORY: DOWN

COMMENTS: Some software refuses to communicate with the modem unless DCD is asserted (i.e., a carrier is present). With such software, it is impossible to send Smartmodem commands. In its DOWN position, therefore, this switch permanently enables pin 8, thereby fooling the software. Like switch 1, above, this switch is a quick alternative to making a trick cable. There is no equivalent Smartmodem command.

SWITCH #:   7

PRODUCT: Smartmodem 300

FUNCTION: Telephone installation adjust
                      UP: For single-line phones
                      DOWN: For multi-line phones

FACTORY: UP

COMMENTS: With this switch in the UP position, the modem functions correctly with multi-line systems, but the status light (behind the pushbutton) does not illuminate to warn that the line is in use. This greatly vexes those who, phone already at their ears, punch onto an apparently free line only to discover the din of screeching modems. There is no equivalent Smartmodem command.

SWITCH #:   8

PRODUCT: Smartmodem 300

FUNCTION: Not used

Smartmodem Speeds and Data Format

The Smartmodem's modulator and demodulator are capable of data transfer at a maximum rate of only 300 bps. The same limitation, however, does *not* apply to the Smartmodem's serial port, which, by means of an internal baud rate and data format detector, automatically adjusts itself to operate over a wide range of baud rates. (For a discussion of the differences between baud rate and bit rate, see Chapter 5.) The Smartmodem senses the characteristics of the incoming *AT* Command Sequence Introducer and adjusts itself to match. Amazingly, the Smartmodem 300 can receive commands and send response codes anywhere in the range 50 to 2400 baud, although at 2400 it struggles to keep up with a fast typist.

The Smartmodem 300's ability to accommodate such a wide range of baud rates can lead to some interesting situations. Suppose, for example, that with the computer set for, say, 600 baud, the Smartmodem answers a 300 bps call. When the carrier linkage occurs, the Smartmodem sends its result codes at its *current* baud rate— here, 600 baud. Since the Smartmodem 300's data transfer rate is only 300 bps, the computer has to be manually switched to 300 baud. Now, when the carrier linkage is lost, the Smartmodem originally sends its result codes at 600 baud—the rate at which the call was answered. Since the computer's baud rate was adjusted to 300 baud to accommodate the modem's data rate, subsequent Smartmodem result codes are not intelligible. (The baud rate of later Smartmodems does not revert back, but remains at the data rate of the incoming call.)

In addition to its ability to adapt to many baud rates, the Smartmodem also adjusts itself to a wide variety of data formats. Table 8-4 shows the valid combinations.

Table 8-4 Data formats supported by the Smartmodem.

Data Length	Parity	Stop Bits
7	MARK	1 or more
7	SPACE	1 or more
7	Even	1 or more
7	Odd	1 or more
7	None	2 or more
8	None	1 or more
8	Even	1 or more
8	Odd	1 or more

The only exceptional item on this list is the Smartmodem acceptance of 8 data bits *with* parity.

The Anatomy of Dialing

Before moving on to other Smartmodems, you should understand the sequence of events that occur when the Smartmodem dials a call. Figure 8-2 is a flow chart of the discrete commands that constitute the dialing operation.

The Hayes Smartmodem 1200

The next product in the Hayes Smartmodem product line is the Smartmodem 1200. The Smartmodem 1200 incorporates all the features of the Smartmodem 300, but adds a new data transfer rate of 1200 bps. In its 1200 bps mode, the Smartmodem 1200 is tone-compatible with the Bell 212A modem. Like its predecessor, the Smartmodem 300, the Smartmodem 1200 eschews the Bell 212A's more "formal" RS-232 modem interface for one more suitable for microcomputer hardware.

Figure 8-2 Anatomy of a Smartmodem dial.

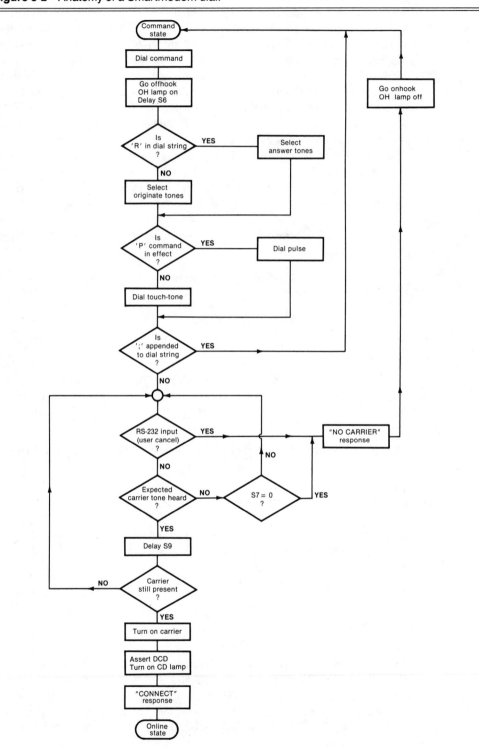

We refer to the Smartmodem 300 as the generic Smartmodem because it defines the Hayes way of doing things, and because all subsequent Smartmodem products default to the "Smartmodem 300 mode." But it is the popularity of the Smartmodem 1200 that has led to the creation of the de facto industry standard. Today there are dozens of products claiming to be "Hayes Smartmodem compatible," but it is the Smartmodem 1200 to which their compatibility alludes.

We will now examine the Smartmodem 1200, noting where it improves on or is different from its older brother. Again, the term smart modem refers to the genre, while Smartmodem 1200 refers to the genuine article from Hayes.

Although Hayes Microcomputer Products, Inc. has never changed the product's name, there are actually two Hayes Smartmodem 1200s. We are now discussing the *original* product, to which the name "Smartmodem 1200" will apply for the remainder of this chapter. Later, we will discuss a significantly revised version of the 1200, which we will examine as a separate product and for which we will even provide a nickname.

Smartmodem 1200: Front and Rear Panels

The Smartmodem 1200 sports an additional lamp at the far left of its front panel, shown in Figure 8-3. This lamp, which bears the marking HS for "High Speed," illuminates whenever the Smartmodem 1200's internal baud rate generator is set at 1200 baud.

The rear panel is unchanged from the Smartmodem 300: on/off switch, one power receptacle, one DB-25S connector, one telephone connector, and a speaker volume control.

Figure 8-3 The Smartmodem 1200's front panel. Note the addition of the lamp marked HS.

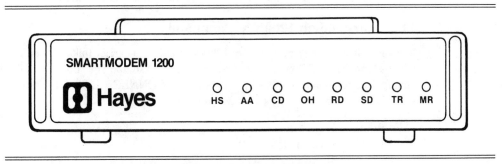

Smartmodem 1200: Configuration Switches

The Smartmodem 1200 assigns the same functions to all seven of the microswitches on the Smartmodem 300. In addition, the Smartmodem 1200 defines the previously unused eighth microswitch. To the list of Smartmodem 300 configuration switches, add the following definition for the Smartmodem 1200:

SWITCH #: 8

FUNCTION: "Dumb" switch—disables command recognition.

UP: Disables Smartmodem command recognition.

DOWN: Enables Smartmodem command recognition.

FACTORY: DOWN

COMMENTS: There is no equivalent Smartmodem command. Response codes from phone
             operations are unaffected.

If this switch strikes you as odd—that one would spend extra money for a Smartmodem then intentionally defeat its intelligence—recall the hypothetical situation described earlier in this chapter ("Pitfalls of the Online Escape"). There we pointed out how sending the escape sequence to the local Smartmodem can also force the remote system to command mode. The new eighth switch deafens the Smartmodem 1200 to all commands, thereby eliminating all possibility that echoed data will be interpreted as commands.

Smartmodem 1200: RS-232 Interface

Like the Bell 212A, pin 12 on the Smartmodem's DB-25 connector is asserted at 1200 baud. This pin was not used on the Smartmodem 300. Since most microcomputers do not support an RS-232 input on pin 12 without a hardware modification or a custom cable, software developers largely ignore the RS-232 speed indicator, relying on the Smartmodem's response codes to ascertain its data rate.

Smartmodem 1200: New Commands

The Smartmodem 1200 adds two new commands, one to enable the use of the new CONNECT 1200 or 5 response code, and one to ask the Smartmodem to identify itself.

The Smartmodem 1200's X Command

In its default state, the Smartmodem 1200 responds to a carrier linkage at either 300 or 1200 bps with the same code: CONNECT. If programmed to do so, the Smartmodem 1200, however, uses a unique code to announce 1200 bps connections: CONNECT 1200. This response code "extension" is enabled by issuing the new *X* command.

COMMAND: *X*

PRODUCT: Smartmodem 1200

FUNCTION: Enables use of the Smartmodem 1200's CONNECT 1200 response code.
             0: Issues CONNECT for all carrier linkages.
             1: Issues CONNECT 1200 after a carrier linkage at 1200 bps.

DEFAULT: 0

COMMENTS: The default maintains compatibilty with the Smartmodem 300.

The Smartmodem 1200 Product ID Command

So that software may ascertain which model of Smartmodem it is addressing, the new command *I* requests a product identification code.

COMMAND: *I*

PRODUCT: Smartmodem 1200

FUNCTION: Modem replies with Hayes product identification code or ROM checksum.
0: Returns 3-digit product id code.
1: Returns 3-digit ROM checksum.

COMMENTS: The format of the reply is the same as for S-register queries: three-digit ASCII, left-padded with 0s if necessary.

The first two digits (12) in the product id code are the product number and the last digit is the number of the ROM revision. Most return 122 or 123. Since the *I* command was introduced with the Smartmodem 1200, a Smartmodem 300 returns ERROR.

Smartmodem 1200: Speeds and Data Format

As with the Smartmodem 300, the Smartmodem 1200 senses the baud rate and data format from the *AT* portion of a command and adjusts accordingly. There are, however, two major differences between the two products' handling of baud and data rates in general. First, whereas the Smartmodem 300 accepts commands at virtually any baud rate between 50 and 2400, the Smartmodem 1200 accepts commands only at 300 and 1200 baud.

Second, after losing the carrier, the Smartmodem 300 reverts to its pre-answer baud rate for the purpose of sending reply codes. The Smartmodem 1200, however, remains at the baud rate of the last connection.

It is important to note that the Smartmodem 1200 always issues its CONNECT message *before* changing its internal baud rate in response to a carrier. Assume, for example, that both the computer and modem are set for 300 baud. When a call is detected at 1200 bps, the Smartmodem 1200 issues the CONNECT message at 300 baud, then switches immediately to 1200 baud. When the carrier is lost, the NO CARRIER response is issued at 1200 baud.

The Smartmodem 1200 supports most of the data formats of the Smartmodem 300. The Smartmodem 1200, however, does *not* support 8 data bits with parity—an insignificant loss.

The Smartmodem 1200B

The popularity of the IBM PC led to the production of a Smartmodem 1200 on a plug-in card with the volume control and phone jack mounted on the card's mounting bracket. Because the Smartmodem 1200B also includes an 8250 UART configured identically to that on IBM's *Asynchronous Communications Adaptor* (i.e., serial card), no additional hardware is required to use it. Although the 1200B is functionally equivalent to the 1200, there are some obvious differences.

Smartmodem 1200B: Product ID Code

The Smartmodem 1200B returns the same product code as a Smartmodem 1200—122 or 123. The first two digits (12) are the product number and the last number is the ROM revision of its first two digits. As we will see in Chapter 18, the inability of software to differentiate between these two modems is unfortunate indeed.

Smartmodem 1200B: Front Panel

Because the Smartmodem 1200B card resides inside the computer, Hayes decided not to include status lamps. All in all, this seems like a reasonable conclusion, although the lamps would certainly be valuable debugging aids to software developers.

Smartmodem 1200B: Configuration Switches

The Smartmodem 1200B has three configuration switches and one jumper. Note: UP=OFF and DOWN=ON.

SWITCH #:	1
PRODUCT:	Smartmodem 1200B
FUNCTION:	IBM PC Communications port UP: Assigned to COM2 DOWN: Assigned to COM1
FACTORY:	DOWN

SWITCH #:	2
PRODUCT:	Smartmodem 1200B
FUNCTION:	Telephone type installation UP: For single-line phones DOWN: For multi-line phones
FACTORY:	UP
COMMENTS:	With this switch in the UP position, the modem functions correctly with multi-line systems, but the phone's status light (behind the pushbutton) does not illuminate to warn that the line is in use.

SWITCH #:	3
PRODUCT:	Smartmodem 1200B
FUNCTION:	DCD (Data Carrier Detect) override UP: DCD is always asserted. DOWN: DCD is asserted only during carrier link.
FACTORY:	DOWN
COMMENTS:	Some software refuses to communicate with the modem unless DCD pin 8 is asserted (i.e., a carrier is present). With such software, it is impossible to send Smartmodem commands. In its DOWN position, therefore, this switch permanently enables (pulls up) pin 8, thereby fooling the software. There is no equivalent Smartmodem command.

SWITCH #:	DTR (Data Terminal Ready) Jumper
PRODUCT:	1200B
FUNCTION:	DTR override A-B: DTR inhibited puts Smartmodem in comatose state. B-C: DTR is always asserted.

FACTORY: B-C

COMMENTS: Although there is no DTR override microswitch on the 1200B, this function is accomplished by moving a jumper between two pins on the board itself.

It is puzzling why Hayes chose to omit the other configuration switches found on the Smartmodem 1200, in particular those that select the default settings for the user's interface, such as echo, verbosity, and so forth.

Smartmodem 1200B: RS-232 Interface

We have throughout cautioned against an overly close association between the names of UART inputs and outputs and RS-232 nomenclature. The Smartmodem 1200 illustrates the reason for this caution. Because the Smartmodem 1200 and the 8250 UART are on the same board, there is no need for an RS-232 interface between them. Since there is no RS-232 interface, the use of RS-232 names is, strictly speaking, absurd. The association in folks' minds between the RS-232 name and modem function is so strong, however, that RS-232 nomenclature is probably the *least* complicated way to communicate the relationship between the modem and the UART. Always keep in mind, however, that THERE IS NO RS-232 INTERFACE IN THE SMARTMODEM 1200B. Modem control is still accomplished through the 8250's "modem control" lines.

Hardware Reset

As we will see, it is not always possible to reset a Smartmodem with software commands. Since the Smartmodem 1200B has complete control of the UART and the modem, it supports a hardware reset. Making its General Purpose Output #1 TRUE causes an unconditional reset. (See Chapters 7 and 20 for explanations of the 8250 UART's general-purpose outputs.)

The Smartmodem 1200 +

We noted earlier that the Smartmodem 1200 product underwent a significant revision but not a name change. That Hayes itself considers the newer 1200's to be a new product is demonstrated by its new product number as reported by the *I* command. Objectively, however, the newer Smartmodem 1200 is, if not a distinct product, a new species in the Smartmodem genus. It is, at least for our purposes, worthy of its own name. Accordingly, then, we will continue to refer to the older as the "Smartmodem 1200." We will use the name "Smartmodem 1200 + " for the newer product.[5]

Smartmodem 1200 + : Front and Rear Panels

The front panel of the Smartmodem 1200 +, depicted in Figure 8-4, is identical to that of the Smartmodem 1200 except for the ® symbol after the corporate logo. The rear panel, however, shows important changes: there are two telephone jacks instead of one and the volume control is gone.

---

[5]The Hayes staff refers to it informally as the "1200EF" for "Extended Features."

Figure 8-4   Front and rear panels of the Smartmodem 1200 + .

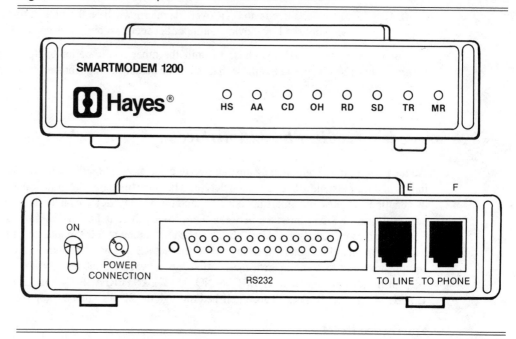

Because the Smartmodem 1200 is connected in parallel with the telephone line, lifting the telephone handset during a carrier linkage disrupts the link. By using two jacks, the Smartmodem 1200 + is placed between the line and the telephone. As long as the modem is connected to the line (i.e., while the OH indicator is illuminated), the telephone is disconnected from the line. Normal telephone operation is restored when the Smartmodem 1200 + releases the line.

Smartmodem 1200 + : Product ID Code

The 1200 + returns a product code of 13, followed by a single-digit ROM revision number. Hayes Microcomputer Products, Inc. advises that ROM revision numbers are not issued consecutively; therefore, smaller ROM revision numbers are not necessarily older.

Smartmodem 1200 + : Configuration Switches

The Smartmodem 1200 + adds two new configuration switches. Since pin 10 depends upon the setting of pin 1, the synopsis for pin 1 is repeated here for your convenience.

SWITCH #:   1

PRODUCT: Smartmodem 300, 1200, 1200 +

FUNCTION: DTR pin 20 override
UP: Normal DTR operation
DOWN: DTR always enabled

FACTORY: Down

COMMENTS: In its down position, this switch permanently enables (pulls up) pin 20 on the RS-232 interface. Since pin 20 is the Smartmodem's "master enable," this switch allows normal operation when the proper voltage is supplied externally. There is no equivalent Smartmodem command.

SWITCH #:   9

PRODUCT: Smartmodem 1200+

FUNCTION: Bell 212A/103A vs CCITT V.22 compatibility
             UP: Bell
             DOWN: CCITT

FACTORY: UP

COMMENTS: Equivalent to the *B* command described below.

SWITCH #:   10

PRODUCT: Smartmodem 1200+

FUNCTION: Hardware reset (enabled by switch 1 UP)
             UP: DTR behaves as described by switch 1.
             DOWN: DTR transition from asserted to inhibited causes an unconditional reset.

FACTORY: UP

COMMENTS: This would be a very handy feature if it were attached to any RS-232 input besides DTR (Data Terminal Ready), which is too valuable in ordinary operation to sacrifice.

Very little needs saying about switch 9: it merely allows Smartmodem users to communicate at 1200 bps with most of the rest of the world, where CCITT V.22 is the recognized standard. The hardware reset provided by switch 10, however, merits discussion.

If switch 1 is in its "DTR override" position (DOWN), the Smartmodem cannot always be reset with the *Z* command. Remember, you cannot take for granted that the Smartmodem is in command mode or, more important, that it is configured in a reasonable way. Here are three such situations.

1. The worst situation is when configuration switch 8 is set so that the Smartmodem ignores all commands.

2. The command terminator (*nl1*) has been changed to a value greater than 127 [S3]. The modem simply ignores all commands.

3. A carrier linkage exists and the escape character has been changed to a value greater than 127 [S2]. Here, there is no way to force the Smartmodem from online to command state from where the reset command can be issued.

At remote, unattended sites the lack of an RS-232 reset can require a journey to an inaccessible, out-of-the-way location merely to toggle the on/off switch. With switch 10 in the DOWN position, the software controlling a remote modem must first be programmed to interpret loss of carrier (i.e., DCD) as the need for a reset. When software senses that DCD has become inhibited, it in turn inhibits DTR, resetting the Smartmodem. The software then reinitializes the Smartmodem and attempts to reestablish communications.

Software developers were understandably pleased to learn in advance that the Smartmodem would feature an RS-232 reset. Alas, there was almost universal disappointment when it was discovered exactly how the reset was implemented. If you have ever needed an example of a Hobson's choice, this is it. By choosing the much-needed hardware reset, the programmer must sacrifice DTR's ordinary role—an unconditional return to the command mode, making the Smartmodem "dumb." It would have been interesting to have been a fly on the wall at Hayes when the decision to assign the reset function to DTR pin 20 was made. There are really only three choices:

1. Assign the reset function to a pin that is seldom used in standard RS-232 configurations—pin 11, for example.
2. Assign the reset function to one of the Smartmodem's unused inputs—RTS pin 4, for instance.
3. Assign the reset function to one of the Smartmodem's unused RS-232 inputs, but, by means of a configuration switch, allow the input to be switched back to its standard usage.

The potential success of scheme number one could easily be predicted from the success of Hayes' use of pin 12 (also a seldom used pin) for speed indication. Since microcomputers support, at most, only four or five RS-232 signals, the RS-232 reset could realistically be utilized only with a special cable.

The wisdom of option number two, not its ultimate success, probably led to its rejection. Practically speaking, manufacturers are justifiably cautious about deviating from established practices. There are, admittedly, very few established practices in microcomputer RS-232 interfaces, yet those that do exist certainly center about the pins supported by Smartmodems. To assign the reset function to one of them would invite disaster in the form of an everlasting avalanche of technical support calls.

This leaves us with the third option which, in fact, was the one finally chosen. Inexplicably, however, the RS-232 input chosen to bear this new switch-selectable function was DTR, not the unused RTS! So distasteful to programmers is the notion of giving up the normal DTR function, this wonderful feature is almost certainly to languish in disuse like the speed indicator on pin 12. We can only hope that this decision will be reversed in future products so that software developers can have both ordinary DTR control *and* a hardware reset.

Smartmodem 1200 + : Changes to the User Interface

The most striking difference between the user interface on the Smartmodem 1200 + and that on earlier Smartmodems is its acceptance of lower case *or* upper case in the *AT* portion of the command. A mixture of cases is an error. For example, *at* and *AT* are both acceptable, but *At* or *aT* are not.

Smartmodem 1200 + : New Dial Modifiers

The greatest change between the Smartmodem 1200 and 1200 + is found in the extended support for dialing and answering functions.

The Switch Hook "Flash"

In older PBX systems, momentarily hanging up the line caused a lamp to flash on the operator's panel—a request for assistance. This verb quickly became transitive ("Flash me when you're finished") and then was backformed into a new substantive noun. Following this tradition, newer automated PBX systems use a "flash" to get the assistance of the electronic "operator."

COMMAND: ! (Exclamation point, ASCII 21H)

PRODUCT: 1200 +

FUNCTION: "Flashes" the switch hook—momentarily takes the line off-hook.

One-Eighth Second Pause

A slant in the dial string generates a ⅛-second pause.

COMMAND: / (Slant, ASCII 2F)

PRODUCT: 1200 +

FUNCTION: Introduces a .125 second pause.

Wait for Silence

COMMAND: @ (Commercial "at," ASCII 40H)

PRODUCT: 1200 +

FUNCTION: Waits 30 seconds [S7] for 5 seconds of silence before proceeding.

COMMENTS: This is used to navigate through systems that require a prefix before allowing a call to proceed. Typically, these systems (often security systems) require a prefix to "break" the dial tone. If the dial tone does not break (or if a voice, busy, or other audio signal is present after the dial tone break), the call is terminated and the response code NO ANSWER or 8 is issued.

Wait for Secondary Dial Tone

The secondary wait code W is generally used to gain access to long-distance services, but can be used on any multi-tiered system that produces standard Bell dial tones. If the secondary dial tone is not forthcoming in the time allowed, the call is terminated.

COMMAND: W (ASCII 57H)

PRODUCT: 1200 +

FUNCTION: Waits 30 seconds [S7] for a secondary dial tone before proceeding.

Smartmodem 1200 + : New Commands

These commands constitute major differences between the Smartmodem 1200 + and the plain Smartmodem 1200.

CCITT V.22 Compatibility

Bell did not necessarily choose the best modulation techniques for its 1200 bps modems (212 types). In recognition of this, the world standards organization CCITT adopted a different standard, now in use in much of the world. To achieve compatibility with these modems, the Smartmodem 1200 + introduced the *B* (Bell) command.

COMMAND: *B*

PRODUCT: Smartmodem 1200 +

FUNCTION: Bell 103A/212A vs CCITT V.22 compatibility
0: CCITT
1: Bell

DEFAULT: See "SWITCH #9," just above.

COMMENTS: The Smartmodem 1200 + works in CCITT mode only at 1200 bps.

Note that no attempt was made to achieve compatibilty with CCITT V.21 300 baud modems. In fact, attempting to dial another modem at 300 baud while in CCITT mode produces an ERROR or 4 return code.

Firmware Volume Control

To make room for a second phone jack on the rear panel of the Smartmodem 1200 + , it was necessary to sacrifice the volume control. In its place is a firmware attenuator controlled by the *L* command.

COMMAND: *L*

PRODUCT: Smartmodem 1200 +

FUNCTION: Adjusts audio output of internal speaker.
0: Lowest audio output
1: Medium audio output
2: Highest audio output

DEFAULT: 1

COMMENT: Use the *M* command to turn the speaker completely off.

The attenuation between the high and medium settings is large and obvious. The difference between medium and low, however, is much less pronounced.

Call Progress Monitoring

One of the obvious weaknesses of earlier Smartmodems was their limited ability to monitor the progress of a phone call. This is because pre-1200 + Smartmodems are "blind dialers," pausing a few [S6] seconds after taking the phone line off-hook, then perfunctorily dialing the number — even if no phone line is connected to the modem. Similarly, the modem doesn't detect the busy signal from a successfully dialed number. In both cases — clearly error conditions — early Smartmodems patiently wait for their internal timers [S7] to expire before returning a NO CARRIER response.

The Smartmodem 1200 + adds the ability to detect the absence of a dial tone or the presence of a busy signal or any combination of the two.

COMMAND: *X*

PRODUCT: Smartmodem 1200 +

FUNCTION: Selects level of call progress monitoring.
                   0: Smartmodem 300 mode
                   1: Smartmodem 1200 mode
                   2: Enables dial tone detection only.
                   3: Enables busy signal detection only.
                   4: Enables both dial tone and busy signal detection.

DEFAULT: 0 (i.e., Smartmodem 300)

In one situation the direct interconnection of two Smartmodems, the X3 setting, must be employed to defeat dial tone detection (i.e. the Smartmodem must dial blindly). Although rarely done, two Smartmodems can be cabled directly together, with twisted-pair cables terminated with the appropriate RJ connectors. This interconnection is illustrated in Figure 8-5.

Figure 8-5   Two Smartmodems connected as short-haul modems.

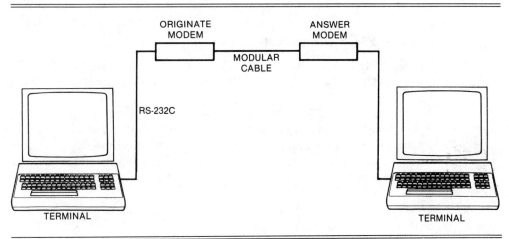

Since the Smartmodems are not connected to a phone line in this arrangement, there is no dial tone to detect and, of course, no ring signal to trigger auto-answer. After issuing the command *ATX3*, a carrier linkage is established by one end sending

    ATD

forcing one modem off-hook in the originate mode, and sending to the other modem

    ATA

to cause it to go off-hook in the answer mode.

    If dial tone detection is active, the originating Smartmodem 1200 + never goes off-hook, but returns to the command state immediately after its predetermined [S6] wait for a dial tone.

    One suspects the X2 setting—disable busy signal detection—exists simply because it was easy to implement. No situations come to mind where it is necessary to defeat busy signal detection, but it is just conceivable that the Smartmodem might mistake a grossly out-of-tolerance busy signal for a ring signal.

New Smartmodem 1200 + Responses

The new call-progress monitoring requires the new response codes shown in Table 8-5.

Table 8-5   New response codes for the 1200 + .

Digit Code	Word Code	Description
6	NO DIALTONE	No dial tone present. Note that this response can come from either a primary dial operation or a *W* dial modifier in the dial string. See "Smartmodem 1200 + : New Dial Modifiers," above.
7	BUSY	Busy signal heard.
8	NO ANSWER	Returned only after the @ dial modifier to signify that the required number of seconds of silence was not heard. In other words, dialing the preceding characters did not "break" the dial tone. See "Smartmodem 1200 + : New Dial Modifiers," above. If the @ dial modifier encounters a busy signal, it returns a BUSY response instead of NO ANSWER.

Long-SPACE Disconnect

Except for its duration, the "long SPACE" is identical to a BREAK condition. The BREAK, you will recall from Chapter 2, occurs when the communications line is held at SPACE for *at least* the duration of one SDU.

The long-SPACE disconnect, like the DTR-reset feature discussed above, is usually employed as a last resort to regain control of a Smartmodem at a remote, unattended location where a manual reset is impractical. In such installations, modems are usually permanently connected by leased lines. The software controlling the remote modem responds to the loss of carrier (caused by the long SPACE) by resetting the modem and attempting to reestablish a data linkage.

COMMAND: *Y*

PRODUCT: Smartmodem 1200 +

FUNCTION: "Long space" disconnect
0: Disabled
1: Enabled

DEFAULT: 0

COMMENTS: When enabled, the Smartmodem 1200 + immediately transmits a SPACE (BREAK) for 4 seconds. If *Y* is set to 1, the Smartmodem 1200 + drops the carrier and disconnects from the line upon receipt of 1.6 seconds of SPACE.

Smartmodem 1200 + : RS-232 Interface

The behavior of DSR pin 6 in earlier Smartmodem 1200s (i.e., DSR follows DCD) approximates standard RS-232 usage. In the 1200 + , however, DSR and CTS pin 5 are pulled up (permanently asserted) to + 10 volts through a common 470 ohm pull-up resistor. This change is apparently designed to enable software to ascertain if the modem is powered up. (See "Smartmodem 2400: RS-232 Interface" below, for more on this DSR drama.)

The Smartmodem 1200B +

The 1200B + is the circuit card version of the 1200 + designed for the IBM PC family. It behaves identically to the 1200 + . Its configuration switches are shown in Table 8-6.

Table 8-6 Configuration switches for the Smartmodem 1200B + .

SW	Function	Factory Setting (DOWN=RIGHT)
1	COM1/COM2	DOWN: COM1
2	Phone type	UP: RJ-11, -41S, -45S
3	DCD override	DOWN: DCD reflects carrier status
4	DTR override	UP: DTR forces hang-up and return to command mode.
5	BELL/CCITT	UP: BELL
6	Pulse ratio	UP: 39 percent make/61 percent break

The Smartmodem 1200 + Half-Card

The Smartmodem 1200 + Half-Card, which installs in the IBM's short expansion slot (behind the power supply), is functionally identical to the Smartmodem 1200B + . The configuration switches, located directly on the circuit board in other "B" type Smartmodems, are located on the 1200 + Half-Card's mounting bracket and are readily accessible from the rear. The number of configuration switches has been reduced from six on the 1200B + to four on the Half-Card. The function of these switches is shown in Table 8-7.

Table 8-7 Configuration switches for the Smartmodem 1200 + Half-Card.

SW	Function	Factory Setting
1	COM1/COM2	RIGHT: COM1
2	Phone type	LEFT: RJ-11, -41S, -45S
3	DCD override	RIGHT: DCD reflects carrier status
4	DTR override	LEFT: DTR forces hang-up and return to command mode.

The 1200 + Half-Card returns the same product code as a Smartmodem 1200 + (13x) where 13 is the product number and 'x' is the ROM revision.

The Smartmodem 2400

The Hayes Smartmodem 2400 is a radical enhancement from its ancestors in the Smartmodem family. Although it supports both asynchronous *and* synchronous communications, we will study only those commands that affect its behavior in asynchronous mode. The Smartmodem 2400 is externally identical to the Smartmodem 1200 (except for the model number); there are no configuration switches behind the front panel.

Smartmodem 2400: Front and Rear Panels

Aside from its model number, the Smartmodem 2400's front panel is identical to those of the Smartmodem 1200 and 1200 + . As shown in Figure 8-6a, behind the front panel, where one expects to find the Smartmodem's bank of configuration switches, is a single three-pin (two-position) jumper, referred to as the *dumb strap*. When the jumper is removed entirely or connects the center and the right-hand pins, the 2400 behaves as a Smartmodem; when the jumper connects the center and the left-hand pins, the 2400 behaves as a "dumb" modem—i.e., does not respond to commands, make or receive phone calls, and so forth.

Because the Smartmodem 2400 requires an 8.5 VAC power source instead of the 13.5 VAC of earlier Smartmodems, the power jack on the rear panel, shown in Figure 8-6b is shaped differently to prevent use of earlier power packs. The new 3-pin jack is square with the upper right corner keyed for correct orientation.

Figure 8-6   The Smartmodem 2400's "dumb" strap and rear panel.

a. The Smartmodem 2400's "Dumb" Strap Behind the Front Panel

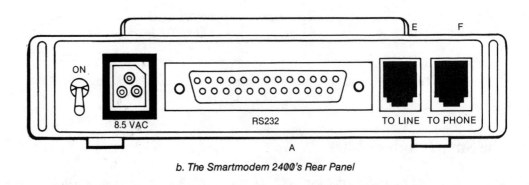

b. The Smartmodem 2400's Rear Panel

In response to the *I* command, the Smartmodem returns the standard 24x, the first two digits being the product number and 'x' its ROM revision number.

Smartmodem 2400: The "Profile" vs Configuration Switches

A combination of RAM, ROM, and non-volatile ROM replaces the Smartmodem hardware configuration switches. The default values for every programmable variable—S-registers and mode variables— are in ROM storage. Twenty-six of these variables (the *configuration group*, some of which relate to the synchronous communications mode) are referred to collectively as the *factory configuration profile*.

Like all other Smartmodems, the 2400 contains an area of "working" RAM containing variables, the command line buffer, scratch pad areas, and so forth. Hayes refers to this ordinary RAM as the "active configuration profile." At any time by means of ordinary Smartmodem commands, the *configuration group* variables from the work area can be written into an area of *non-volatile* memory referred to as the *user's configuration profile*.

As delivered from the factory, the values in the user's profile are the same as those in the factory profile. At power-up or reset, the 2400, like all Smartmodems, loads its default variables into the work area from ROM. But whereas other Smartmodems load user-configurable variables from hardware switches, the 2400 loads them from the user's configuration profile. Thus the user profile in non-volatile memory serves precisely the same function as the configuration switches— a kind of "silicon switch."

The use of memory switches instead of configuration switches has advantages, the most obvious being the ability to store values for nine of the 2400's S-registers. Since all S-registers store 8-bit numbers, the equivalent hardware storage would require 72 microswitches!

To manage this new configuration system, the Smartmodem 2400 possesses new commands to:

- Read the factory profile into working RAM
- Read the user's profile into working RAM
- Write the selected variables from working RAM into the user's profile

We will examine these commands in a later section.

Smartmodem 2400: Changes in the Command Set

The Smartmodem 2400 supports all of the commands from earlier Smartmodems except the *C* (carrier) and *F* (duplex). The Smartmodem 2400 adds several new commands. Most of the new commands consist of an ampersand (&, ASCII 38) followed by an alphabetical character, which may already be in use in the generic Smartmodem command set. For example, *ATL0* has one meaning in the generic Smartmodem command set, and *AT&L0* has an entirely different meaning in the extended command set of the Smartmodem 2400.

Dialing Modifiers

The Smartmodem 2400 introduces two new commands: one to store a phone number in the user's profile, the other to dial that number.

COMMAND: &Z
PRODUCT: 2400
FUNCTION: Stores the following dial string (phone number).

239

COMMENTS: Up to 33 characters can be stored, not including blanks. Longer numbers are truncated.

After a dial string has been stored with the *&Z* command, it can be automatically redialed by appending an *S* to the primary dial command.

MODIFIER: *S*

PRODUCT: 2400

FUNCTION: Dials stored number.

COMMENTS: This is a dial command *modifier* and must be appended to the primary dial command, for example, *ATDPS*, *ATDTS*, or simply *ATDS*.

Commands To Replace Configuration Switches

We remarked that the default configuration held in the microswitches of earlier Smartmodems is held in non-volatile memory by the Smartmodem 2400. The following commands perform the functions previously served by the hardware configuration switches.

COMMAND: *&C*

PRODUCT: 2400

FUNCTION: DCD pin 8 options
        0: Always asserted (ON)
        1: DCD asserted only during carrier linkage

DEFAULT: 0

COMMENTS: Equivalent to configuration switch SW1 on earlier Smartmodems.

COMMAND: *&D*

PRODUCT: 2400

FUNCTION: DTR pin 20 options
        0: Smartmodem 2400 is always enabled despite state of DTR.
        1: Smartmodem 2400 is comatose when DTR is inhibited.
        2: On-to-off transition of DTR resets Smartmodem.

DEFAULT: 0

COMMENTS: Equivalent to interaction of configuration switches SW1 and SW10 on Smartmodem 1200 + .

COMMAND: *&J*

PRODUCT: 2400

FUNCTION: Telephone jack selection
        0: RJ-11, -41S, -45S (single line)
        1: RJ-12, -13 (multi-line)

DEFAULT: 0

COMMENTS: Equivalent to configuration switch SW7 on other stand-alone Smartmodems.

Profile Commands

This group of commands manages the content of the RAM work area, ROM variables, and non-volatile memory.

COMMAND: &F

PRODUCT: 2400

FUNCTION: Fetches factory configuration profile.

COMMENTS: Reads selected default values from ROM into working RAM. Unlike the Z command, other commands can follow &F on the command line.

COMMAND: &Z

PRODUCT: 2400

FUNCTION: Resets a modem *and* installs user's configuration profile.

COMMENTS: Although not a new command, it is listed here to emphasize that reading the user's configuration profile is a part of resetting the modem. The 2400 requires 2 seconds for reset and self-test before accepting a subsequent command. Earlier Smartmodems require only .5 second for reset.

COMMAND: &W

PRODUCT: 2400

FUNCTION: Stores current configuration variables in non-volatile memory.

COMMENTS: For a complete list of stored variables, see Table 8-8 at the end of this chapter.

Telephone Hardware Commands

Two of these commands exist solely to expand the overseas Smartmodem market. The third enables modems to communicate over leased lines— i.e., without the dial tone protocol.

COMMAND: &G

PRODUCT: 2400

FUNCTION: Guards tone selection (not used in US)
          0: No guard tones
          1: 550 Hz guard tone
          2: 1800 Hz guard tone

DEFAULT: 0

COMMAND: &P

PRODUCT: 2400

FUNCTION: Makes/breaks ratio for mechanical pulse dialer.
          0: 39 percent/61 percent (US)
          1: 33 percent/67 percent (UK, Hong Kong)

DEFAULT: 0

COMMENTS: Controls the duty cycle of the pulse.

COMMAND: &L

PRODUCT: 2400

FUNCTION: Leased-line or dial-up operation
0: Dial-up
1: Leased-line

DEFAULT: Dial-up

COMMENTS: Point-to-point leased lines do not use dial tone protocols.

RS-232 Commands

This command addresses the complaint that the behavior of the DSR lead on earlier Smartmodems does not conform to RS-232 specifications (see "Smartmodem 2400: RS-232 Interface," below.)

COMMAND: &S

PRODUCT: 2400

FUNCTION: DSR pin 6 options
0: DSR is always asserted.
1: DSR behaves according to RS-232 standard.

DEFAULT: 0 (compatible with previous Smartmodems)

COMMAND: &M

PRODUCT: 2400

FUNCTION: Asynchronous/Synchronous mode select
0: Asynchronous operation
1-3: Synchronous operation

DEFAULT: 0

Smartmodem 2400: Changes in the S-Registers

The Smartmodem 2400 does not support S-register 11, used on earlier Smartmodems to adjust the duration of the tones in Touch Tone dialing. The default value of S-register 10 (lost-carrier guard time) is increased from its earlier value of 70 milliseconds to 1.4 seconds.

The Smartmodem 2400 adds several new S-registers, most of which are used either for synchronous operations or for self-testing the modem. The single addition for our notice is:

REGISTER: S25

PRODUCT: 2400

FUNCTION: Minimum time DTR must change state to be recognized.

VALID RANGE: 0-255

UNIT: Hundredths

DEFAULT: 7

Like S-registers 9 and 10, this register provides a delay between an RS-232 event and its recognition. This is a much-needed addition because some UARTs momentarily change the state of RS-232 outputs ("hiccup") during writes to certain registers.

Smartmodem 2400: New Response Code

The Smartmodem 2400 adds a new response code to announce a carrier linkage at 2400 bps. Notice that this response is not the next *consecutive* code number—the code 9 is skipped.

Digit Code	Word Code	'X' Level	Description
10	CONNECT 2400	2,3,4	Carrier found at 2400 bps

Smartmodem 2400: RS-232 Interface

Although the Smartmodem 2400's RS-232 interface appears to be greatly expanded, most of the change centers about the synchronous mode where rigorous standards abide.

Smartmodem 2400 RS-232 Pin 23: High Speed Indicator

As you will recall, 1200 bps Smartmodems report their higher speeds by asserting pin 12 (as on the Bell 212A). The Smartmodem 2400 also reports it on pin 23 as specified by the RS-232 standard (DSRS, Data Signal Rate Selector).

Standardized DSR

On earlier Smartmodems, DSR was asserted at all times or tied to Data Carrier Detect pin 8. Although the former is the default state of the Smartmodem 2400, the *&S1* command makes DSR behave according to the RS-232 standard. In its "RS-232" mode, DTR is asserted only when the following conditions exist *simultaneously* (Quoted phrases are from the RS-232 standard itself):

1. The Smartmodem 2400 is "connected to a communications channel," that is, off-hook and not in a self-test or "voice" mode.

2. The Smartmodem 2400 has performed "any timing functions required by the switching system to complete call establishment." In originate mode, this means dialing, monitoring call progress, and anything else required to usher the call through the phone network.

3. The Smartmodem 2400 has begun "the transmission of a discrete answer tone. . ." In answer mode, the answer tone is begun immediately after the phone goes off-hook. In originate mode, however, the originate tone is not transmitted until the answer tone is received. Hence, DSR appears to track DCD.

Variables in the Factory and User's Profile

Table 8-8 shows the asynchronous parameters that are stored in the user's profile and the command or S-register to which they correspond.

The Smartmodem 2400B

The Smartmodem 2400B is the circuit-card version of the 2400 designed for installation in the IBM PC family of microcomputers. Like other "B" Smartmodems, the 2400B contains its own

8250 UART, so it requires no serial port. There is one major difference between the 2400B and its stand-alone counterpart: the 2400B does not support synchronous communications.

Table 8-8   User profile parameters and their factory values.

Parameter	Command or S-register	Factory Profile
Data rate (300, 1200, 2400 bps)	---	2400 bps
Parity	---	Even
Bell/CCITT compatibility	B	Bell (1200 bps only)
Command echo	E	1 (echo on)
Speaker volume	L	1 (medium)
Result codes sent	Q	0 (codes sent)
Word or single-digit result codes	V	1 (word)
Tone or pulse dial	T/P	P (pulse)
Result code set selection	X	0 (Smartmodem 300)
Long SPACE disconnect option	Y	0 (disabled)
Number of rings to answer phone	S0	0 (no auto-answer)
Test timer setting	S18	0
Delay before examining DTR	S25	5 (.05 sec)
DCD option	&C	0 (ignore)
DTR option	&D	0 (ignore)
Guard tone options	&G	0 (off)
Phone jack type	&J	0 (RJ-11/-41S/45S)
Leased-line/dial-up select	&L	0 (dial-up)
Transmission mode (sync/async)*	&M	0 (asynchronous)
Pulse dial make/break ratio	&P	0 (39/61 percent)
DSR option	&S	0 (follows DCD)

*2400 stand-alone only

Smartmodem 2400B: Changes to the Command Set

Because the 2400B does not support the synchronous mode, the *&M* is absent from the command set. The *&S* command (DSR pin 6 control) is technically present, but does not support the 1 parameter—i.e., redefining DSR to conform to the RS-232 definition. In fact, the command *&S1* produces an error response from the 2400B. The Smartmodem 2400B user's manual (p. 3–9) states the reason for this omission:

> For the standalone [sic] Smartmodem 2400, some data terminals require different interpretations of DSR. Hence, the Smartmodem 2400 provides programmable options. With the Smartmodem 2400B, the modem-to-terminal interface is on the modem board and is well defined.

While this statement is certainly true, it doesn't allow for the (admittedly rare) situation where software must monitor DSR.

Summaries

Table 8-9 shows the *entire* set of Smartmodem response codes, and the *X* command setting that supports each:

Table 8-9   Complete Smartmodem response result codes and the *X* command level that produces them.

Digit Code	Word Code	X Command Level	Description
0	OK	0,1,2,3,4	Non-dial command successfully executed
1	CONNECT	0,1,2,3,4	Carrier found at 300 bps
2	RING	0,1,2,3,4	Ring signal present on phone line
3	NO CARRIER	0,1,2,3,4	Carrier absent or never found
4	ERROR	0,1,2,3,4	Error in command line, unrecognized characters
5	CONNECT 1200	1,2,3,4	Carrier found at 1200 bps
6	NO DIALTONE	2,4	No dial tone present. Note that this response can come from either a primary dial operation or a *W* dial modifier in the dial string. See "Smartmodem 1200 + : New Dial Modifiers," above.
7	BUSY	3,4	Busy signal heard
8	NO ANSWER	3,4	Returned only after the @ dial modifier to signify that the required number of seconds of silence was not heard; in other words, dialing the preceding characters did not "break" the dial tone. See "Smartmodem 1200 + : New Dial Modifiers," above. If the @ dial modifier encounters a busy signal, it returns a BUSY response instead of NO ANSWER.
9	Reserved		
10	CONNECT 2400	2,3,4	Carrier found at 2400 bps.

Table 8-10 is a cross reference between a function and its configuration switch across the entire Smartmodem family. Table 8-11 is a cross reference between a switch number and its function across the entire Smartmodem family.

Table 8-10 Configuration switches cross referenced by function.

Function	300	1200	1200B	1200+	1200B+	Half-Card	2400/2400B*
DTR mode	1	1	jumper	1	4	4	&D
Verbosity	2	2	—	2	—	—	V
Send codes	3	3	—	3	—	—	Q
Echo	4	4	—	4	—	—	E
Auto-answer	5	5	—	5	—	—	0
DCD mode	6	6	3	6	3	3	&C
Phone jack	7	7	2	7	2	2	&J
Commands ok	x	8	—	8	—	—	Q
Bell/CCITT	—	—	—	9	5	—	B
DTR resets	—	—	—	10	—	—	D2
COMM1/COMM2	—	—	1	—	1	1	(note)**
Make/Break Ratio	—	—	—	—	6	—	&P

*For the Smartmodem 2400 and 2400B, equivalent commands are given. These commands must be installed in the user profile with the &W command before they become the default settings.

**2400B: COM1/COM2 is selected by a single switch on the rear panel.

Table 8-11 Smartmodem configuration switches cross referenced by switch number.

SW	300	1200	1200B	1200+	1200B+	1200+ Half-Card	2400 2400B
1	DTR override	DTR override	COM1/COM2	DTR override	COM1/COM2	COM1/COM2	-
2	V command	V command	Phone type	V command	Phone type	Phone type	-
3	Q command	Q command	DCD override	Q command	DCD override	DCD override	-
4	E command	E command	-	E command	DTR override	DTR override	-
5	Auto-answer	Auto-answer	-	Auto-answer	Bell/CCITT	-	-
6	DCD override	DCD override	-	DCD override	Pulse ratio	-	-
7	Phone type	Phone type	-	Phone type	-	-	-
8	x	Dumb mode	-	Dumb mode	-	-	-
9	-	-	-	Bell/CCITT	-	-	-
10	-	-	-	Hardware reset	-	-	-

x = not used, hyphen = not present

II

Asynchronous Programming in C

The remainder of this book is about asynchronous serial programming. Because code execution speed is critical, serial I/O programming ought, perhaps, to be performed in the assembly language of the target machine. But in most serial communications programs, the actual I/O functions themselves are small anterooms in the program edifice, while the main portion of the program is concerned with menu selection, editing chores, and other features that support, but do not directly participate in, the serial I/O process. Clearly, then, a large part of any program containing serial communications functions can be written in a high-level language, descending occasionally into the assembler for those functions whose execution time is important.

The choice of a high-level language is important. In an effort to embrace the broadest possible audience, the few existing books on serial I/O programming have supplied programming examples in BASIC or Pascal. This choice has invariably proven disastrous: the programs themselves are clumsy, graceless, and slow. BASIC and Pascal are so fundamentally unsuited for time-critical, systems-level applications that it is difficult to justify their use solely on pedagogical grounds. Indeed, it often seems that the ugliness of the programs actually obscures the subject more than illuminates it.

The C programming language is ideally suited for our needs. C is said to be "close" to the computer on which it resides; that is, its basic operators are those of a typical microprocessor's instruction set, and its data types and data structures are general and flexible. C, it is claimed, is the language that assembly language programmers come to after burn-out. C is Spartanly elegant, compact, and terse (some even say cryptic); *fast*, well-written C on a clever compiler can rival an assembler. It is no mystery why major software houses have quietly adopted C as their in-house development language. Most important in C's list of strengths, however, is the prospect of portability not found in other languages. Simply put, portability means that, system and hardware dependencies notwithstanding, C code written for one operating environment will compile and run on others.

Our goal in writing programs, then, is to build a library of C functions that perform correctly regardless of the environment in which they are run. As a demonstration of this capability, our programs and functions are designed to run on two popular computers employing substantially different hardware, and running different operating systems—the Kaypro 4, an 8-bit, Z-80 based microcomputer running the CP/M operating system and the IBM PC AT using the 16-bit 80286 microprocessor running PC DOS 3.1. (By the way, the programs and functions also run correctly on the less powerful members of the IBM PC family.)

As you work your way through the programming section, you will build several files, the contents of which evolve as new information is added. This presents a technical problem: when figures reach a certain size, it is not practical to reiterate them in their entirety just for the sake of showing the addition of one or two lines. Therefore, elliptical versions of these figures are given, showing only the additions. For convenience of reference, the *final* contents of all header files are given in Appendixes D-G. Please note that these appendixes contain the data, but not the *functions* developed for the respective files. A function's page number is easily found by its entry in the Function Index.

9

Designing a Basic Serial I/O Library

This is the first of eleven programming chapters. Before we leap into the fray, however, we need to consider some preliminary issues. The first portion of this chapter discusses the compiler that was used for development of the programs and instructs you to make certain additions to your *STDIO.H*. A great deal of effort was expended to use only C constructions that are common to most compilers. As a matter of fact, this chapter contains a list of assumptions made about the C compiler; you will find these assumptions to be quite modest and easily satisfied by all serious C compilers. Because there is such wide variation among compilers, linkers, and librarians, there are very few instructions about how to operate these tools. Be prepared to devote much of your time in this chapter to the initial process of accommodating the idiosyncrasies in your system. If, for example, yours is a single-pass linker, the order in which object modules appear within libraries is important.

The Aztec C Compilers

Before we get down to the work of designing our library of serial I/O functions, we need first to discuss the compiler selected to develop that library. Although the goal of absolute portability is noble, it is just that — a goal — and cannot be perfectly realized. So, although C is renowned for its portability and consistency from one implementation to another, there are inevitable variations among compilers. The first consideration of a C compiler is, of course, that it produce bug-free C programs. Because the research and development for this book was conducted on an IBM PC AT, many excellent C compilers for PC DOS were evaluated. As a result, the programs and functions in this book operate correctly with only minor revision for the PC DOS compilers from Lattice, Computer Innovations, Mark Williams, C Ware (De Smet), Microsoft, and a host of others. (See Appendix C for details.)

Beyond the fundamental criterion of compiler competence, we need to produce programs that can easily be moved from one environment to another. In this regard, a compiler's most important attribute is its manufacturer's support for other operating systems and computers. Not only does this guarantee that your code will run correctly on all systems supported, but, almost as important, promises a similar set of development tools — compiler, assembler, linker, and other utilities—in all versions of the compiler. Based upon these criteria, the compilers selected for this book are the Aztec C compilers from:

Manx Software
P.O Box 55
Shrewsbury, NJ 07701

This company sells compilers for PC-DOS, MS-DOS, CP/M-80, CP/M-86, MacIntosh, Apple II, Radio Shack, Commodore, and Amiga. Manx Software even offers cross-compilers—allowing you to develop programs for one environment while working in a different environment. For example, the Kaypro versions of programs in this book were actually developed on an IBM PC AT with the Aztec IBM-to-CP/M development package. The executable files were transferred from the IBM disk format to the Kaypro format with the Xenocopy disk format-conversion program. The two Aztec C compilers used for the examples in this book were PC-DOS, Version 3.02e and CP/M-80, Version 1.06d.

Modifying the Compilers' STDIO.H Files

The code in this book assumes that certain items have been added to the *STDIO.H* files. Figures 9-1 and 9-2 show all additions for the two files. If you consider the modification of *STDIO.H* to be a sacrilegious act, feel free to create your own "*LOCAL.H*" file, but it is your responsibility to remember to include it where necessary. Many of the added items are self-explanatory, but a few need discussion.

Preprocessor Constants: NUL, NULL, and NIL

Although all three constants are defined as 0, they are used for different reasons. There are two reasons for using preprocessor constants in a program. First, they impart generality and portability to the code—enabling you to alter a constant's value without tracking down every reference to it in the code. Second, preprocessor definitions are employed to manifest the meaning of a particular constant more clearly.

The constant NULL is customarily defined as 0 in C. Construction like this is common:

```
int foo();
while (foo() != NULL)
```

Here the presence of a constant manifests the meaning—the control block will continue until the *integer* function foo returns 0. But what if foo returns a char instead of an int? Now the phrase

```
while (foo() != NULL)
```

is a bit misleading, because there is no such character as a NULL. The use of NUL, then, emphasizes that foo is some sort of ASCII function. In this role, NUL is a *manifest constant*:

```
while (foo() != NUL)
```

The constant NIL exists for both reasons. Suppose, for example, that foo returns a *pointer* to char; again

```
while (foo() != NULL)
```

would not be very informative. NIL is therefore employed to announce that the operation is a pointer operation, in which a return value of 0 has a special meaning. In this capacity, NIL is used not only as a manifest constant, but also serves a subtle, but important purpose with C compilers under PC DOS. The internal architecture of the 8086 family of processors leads to a variety of possible organizations for memory referred to as *memory models*. In the Small memory model (the one our programs use), all pointers occupy 16 bits, so for Small model programs we use the definition #define NIL 0. In some larger memory models, however, pointers are 32 bits long and attempting to assign or compare a 32-bit pointer value to the 16-bit integer NIL would be an error. In larger memory models, then, we use the definition #define NIL 0L or #define NIL (long)0. Thus the constant eases the task of writing code that runs in different environments.

Port and Memory Access Function Names

As similar as these compilers are, there are one or two system dependencies that must be cleared up before we can get underway. One of the differences is in the names of the library functions that read and write port addresses and memory locations. Luckily, these functions are identical in their calling syntax and returned value, so we can fix the problem by using the preprocessor definitions inport and outport shown in Figures 9-1 and 9-2.

An Explanation of 'unsigned chars'

A major ambiguity among C compilers is the data type char. Some compilers consider char to be an 8-bit unsigned quantity, while others consider it to be an 8-bit unsigned quantity with the high-order bit guaranteed to be 0. Others even treat it as a 7-bit signed quantity. Although the Aztec compilers explicitly support the type unsigned char, the code is easier to transport to other compilers if we use

```
typedef unsigned char BYTE
```

for the 8-bit, unsigned quantity. This guarantees that we can specify 8 bits when we need to.

Figure 9-1   Items for the *STDIO.H* file for PC-DOS.

```
#define NULL 0                   /* integer constant             */
#define NIL  (void *)0           /* portable pointer constant    */
#define NUL '\0'                 /* ASCII constant               */
#define ERR -1
#define EOF -1
#define EVER ;;                  /* used  in "for (EVER)"        */
#define FALSE 0
#define TRUE !FALSE
#define inport inportb           /* port input  for uart access  */
#define outport outportb         /* port output (see Appendix B) */
typedef unsigned char BYTE;
typedef unsigned char BOOL;
#define DOS_EOF  0x1A            /* end of file for text files   */
```

Figure 9-1 cont.   Items for the *STDIO.H* file for PC-DOS.

```
#define BLKSIZE  1024
#define MAX_NAME_LEN 80              /* name plus path                      */
```

Figure 9-2   Items for the *STDIO.H* file for CP/M.

```
#define NULL 0                       /* integer constant                   */
#define NIL  0                       /* pointer constant                   */
#define NUL  '\0'                     /* ASCII constant                     */
#define ERR -1
#define EOF -1
#define EVER ;;                      /* used  in "for (EVER)"              */
#define FALSE 0
#define TRUE !FALSE
#define inport in                    /* port input for uart access         */
#define outport out                  /* port output for uart access        */
typedef unsigned char BYTE;
typedef unsigned char BOOL;
#define DOS_EOF  0x1A                /* end of file for text files         */
#define BLKSIZE  1024
#define MAX_NAME_LEN 15              /* name plus 3 bytes of wiggle room   */
```

Incidental Functions

In this section you will occasionally find references to "incidental" C functions whose code is not given in the text. An "incidental" function is one that has nothing to do with asynchronous serial programming, but is required to compile and run the software developed in this book. Since there are only a handful of incidental functions and they are all quite short, please begin by compiling them now and adding them to a library of your choosing. This library, which we shall refer to simply as *YOUR.LIB*, is required to link most of the programs throughout the book.

Memory Models and Memory Usage

As mentioned earlier, the code is designed for the Small Memory model on the IBM PC family. This limits the size of the code and data to 64K each. The serial I/O libraries themselves occupy only about 25K in the executable file, so the Small model is adequate for the programs developed in the book and for most other applications. A major application with a sophisticated user interface, however, will probably require a larger memory model. Detailed instructions for other memory models are presented in Appendix C.

Because of the relative inefficiency of the 8088 instruction set, the code for the Kaypro computer is larger than its 8086 counterpart. This difference, coupled with the 64K memory limitation, means that even a modest increase in program size will probably require memory management with overlays.

Converting to Other Compilers

Although the code in the book was developed with the Aztec C compiler, it relies very little upon specific attributes of that compiler. Conversion to another compiler or operating system should therefore be a painless chore consisting largely of figuring out which of your compiler's header files must be included. For completeness, however, here is a list of the assumptions made about the compiler

1. **Passing Structures by Reference**—As defined by Kernighan and Ritchie (p. 121), the only valid operations upon a structure or union are to take its address and access one of its members. That is, one structure or union may not be assigned to another nor can they be passed as argument functions. But, say K&R, "These restrictions will be removed in forthcoming versions." Today, most C compilers have indeed removed these restrictions. The code in this book assumes that a structure can now be passed entirely by *value*, and that identical structures can be assigned.

Kernighan and Ritchie (p. 197) essentially mandate unique names for *all* structure members, even if they appear in different structures. In recognition of current compiler design, however, the code in this book requires that structure member names be unique only in the structure in which they appear.

2. **Integer Storage**—No assumptions are made about the size of the "natural" `int`, but a `short` or `unsigned short` is expected to occupy 16 bits.

3. **Memory Allocation**—Memory is allocated from low to high. That is, when two objects of the same type are allocated consecutively, the first one allocated has the lower address. It is difficult to imagine a compiler for which this is not true.

4. **Memory Alignment**—All structures are assumed to be *byte aligned*; that is, the compiler leaves no gaps between members. Check your compiler's documentation for the option required to produce byte alignment.

5. **Variable Names**—Names are significant to 32 characters.

The Serial I/O Libraries

Our goal in the rest of this chapter is the composition of a dumb terminal emulator—a program that alternately polls the keyboard and a serial port for activity. If a character arrives from the keyboard, it is transmitted; if one arrives from the serial port, it is displayed. Our first version of this program is named *TERM0*, with succeeding versions named consecutively *TERM1*, *TERM2*, etc. At times, however, we refer to the program concept simply as unnumbered *TERM*.

Our immediate business is to write the basic serial I/O routines necessary to effect *TERM*. As we begin to add enhancements to *TERM*, you may lament that it contains the functionality of a commercial product, but not the style or flair—keyboard input and CRT output are handled through the slow, lackluster console functions. In fact, in place of actual menus, you are likely to find comments such as "your sexy menu here." In other words, because *TERM* is an instructional tool, we waste no time on designing a flashy user interface. Besides, if you wish to develop a product from *TERM*, you will doubtless wish to apply your own notions about the user interface.

Our plan of attack in writing portable I/O functions and programs is the construction of several libraries, each containing different levels of functions. To understand the meaning of the term "level" here, let's take a look at a hypothetical level-3 function `s_puts` and its supporting lower-level functions. This function, shown in Figure 9-3 transmits a NUL-terminated string from the serial port.

Figure 9-3 A hypothetical level-3 function and its level-1 and level-2 support functions.

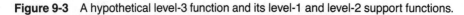

```
FUNCTION NAME: s_puts
LEVEL:          3
LIBRARY:        SIO.LIB
DESCRIPTION:    A level-3 function to transmit a NUL-terminated string from serial port.
OTHER MODULES: s_putc (level-2)
RETURNS:        void
COMMENTS:       A newline is appended.

#include "stdio.h"

BYTE s_xmitstat();                          /* return type declarations          */
void s_putc(), s_xmit();


void s_puts(str)
char *str;
{
    while (*str != '\0')
        {
        s_putc(*str);
        str++;
        }
}
```

```
FUNCTION NAME: s_putc
LEVEL:          2
LIBRARY:        BUOS.LIB
DESCRIPTION:    A level-2 function to transmit a single byte from the serial port.
OTHER MODULES: s_xmitstat (level-1)
RETURNS:        void

void s_putc(c)
unsigned char c;
{
    while (s_xmitstat == NULL)              /**** LEVEL 2 SUPPORT FUNCTION ****/
        ;
    s_xmit(c);
}
```

```
FUNCTION NAME: s_xmit
LEVEL:          1
LIBRARY:        YOURUART.LIB
DESCRIPTION:    A level-1 function to transmit a single byte via UART.
OTHER MODULES: outport
RETURNS:        void
```

Figure 9-3 cont. A hypothetical level-3 function and its level-1 and level-2 support functions.

```
void s_xmit(c)
unsigned char c;
{
      outport(0x3f8,c);                    /**** LEVEL 1 SUPPORT FUNCTION ****/

}
```

FUNCTION NAME: s_xmitstat
LEVEL: 1
LIBRARY: *YOURUART.LIB*
DESCRIPTION: A level-1 function to return the UART's transmitter status.
OTHER MODULES: inport
RETURNS: BYTE

```
BYTE s_xmitstat()
{
      return (inport(0x3fd) & 0x20 );      /**** LEVEL 1 SUPPORT FUNCTION ****/
}
```

An Explanation of 's_puts'   The s_puts function is written very much like the standard C library function puts: the byte pointed to by str becomes the argument to a function named s_putc. Clearly, however, s_puts knows nothing about the ultimate destination of the characters. Functions with this degree of abstraction are referred to as *level-3* functions.

By examining s_putc, however, we can make some generalizations about the ultimate destination of the byte—it seems to be bound for a device that is not always ready to receive data, so the program must loop until a "device ready" status is received, at which time the byte is dispatched. Notice, however, that in this *level-2* function, still nothing is known about the details of the device itself: the device's status might be derived by reading a port address, a memory address, or even a DMA (*direct memory access*) operation. The action required to dispatch the byte to its destination is equally vague.

In the pair of *level-1* functions s_xmit and s_xmitstat, however, we plainly see the hardware details of the I/O operation. In the case of s_xmitstat, the contents of port address 0x3FD is fetched, and after masking off bit 5, is returned. In s_xmit the byte is dispatched by a straightforward write to the port address 03F8.

It is assumed that you understand the distinction between source and object files. Therefore, the header for each source module contains the name of the library to which that module's *object* code belongs. It is your responsibility to keep the source code in individual files, preferably bearing the names of the functions they contain.

The Library Hierarchy

Virtually any serial I/O function can be written in the same abstract, generalized fashion as `s_puts`. By carefully applying the principles of structured programming and common sense, we can successively refine a problem by peeling away its functional levels. Specifically, we build and maintain libraries for each level of function. Thereafter, if our programs employ only functions in the high-level library, they can be easily moved to another environment just by rewriting the low-level library for the new environment.

SIO.LIB: the Level-3 Library

At the top of our library hierarchy reside the level-3 functions. These functions are generally all that are required for writing programs, although it is sometimes necessary to call level-2 functions directly as well. For the remainder of this book, the level-3 library will be referred to by the name *SIO.LIB*.

BUOS.LIB: the Level-2 Library

The next library, *BUOS.LIB*, contains functions such as `s_putc`—functions whose responsibility is to provide an interface between the hardware and the level-3 functions.

"UARTS".LIB: the Level-1 Library

Since the UART used in any application dominates the character of serial I/O, we require a level-1 library for each UART for which we intend to write code. Here reside the level-1 primitives that are called by the level-2 functions in *BUOS.LIB*. In other words, the functions in these UART libraries are responsible for resolving hardware differences for the level-2 functions. For this book, we need two such libraries: *U8250.LIB* for the IBM PC AT and *Z80SIO.LIB* for the Kaypro.

Level-0: the "COMPUTER".C Files

The examples of level-1 functions in Figure 9-3 are a bit misleading because they employ *constants* for port addresses. Such routines function correctly only with one specific computer (in this case, the IBM PC). Aside from constants that are native to the UART under consideration (such as register masks), our actual level-1 routines must contain no constant values whatsoever. The alternative to constants is, of course, variables. Our program groups all these variables together into a global data structure, `struct serial`, whose members are available to all functions that need access to them. The definition for this structure is shown in Figure 9-4.

In every program, we will declare a single instance of a `struct serial` with the name `sio`, to which all functions refer for hardware-specific data. This declaration always resides in a "level-0" file, in which all the generalities contained in the level-1 functions—port addresses, register offsets, and other machine-specific information—are finally resolved. Because the declaration of `sio` is always in this level-0 file, functions at every other level must refer to it by including the statement

```
extern struct serial sio;
```

At declaration, the `sio` declaration is also initialized with the values unique to the computer for which the program is being compiled. We refer to these computer-specific files with the file name extension 'C' *not* 'LIB', because they are ordinary object modules. The name of one and only one of these modules must appear in the linkage list when creating an executable file from the libraries. The files we build in this book are named *IBMPC.C* and *KAYPRO.C*.

We have now created a hierarchy of libraries where the unknown information for the functions at each level is supplied from the level just below, with a computer-specific module at the bottom to resolve all unknowns through the initialized values in the serial structure, sio. Those familiar with the internal structure of operating systems will recognize that the relationship of our *BUOS.LIB* and the UART libraries is essentially the same as that of the BIOS (Basic I/O System) and BDOS (Basic Disk Operating System) in DOS, CP/M, and many other systems. The parallel is intentional.

The first version of the structure is shown in Figure 9-4.

Figure 9-4   Definition of the "master" serial structure.

STRUCT DEF: serial
FILE: *SIODEF.H*
DESCRIPTION: Definition of a master structure to define a serial port.

```
struct serial
    {
    BYTE     *uart_base;      /* base address of UART                 */
    int      data_off;        /* offset of data port from base        */
    int      status_off;      /* offset of status port from base      */
    unsigned rcvmask;         /* byte received mask                   */
    unsigned xmitmask;        /* transmitter holding reg. empty       */
    };
```

An Explanation of 'struct serial'   For now, this structure, which should be placed in a file named *SIODEF.H*, contains only 5 elements—(1) the "base" address of the UART, (2) the offset of the data and (3) serialization status registers from that base, and (4) TBE and (5) RxRDY status masks required by all UARTs. Even though uart_base contains the *actual* address of the UART, it is declared to be a pointer. This may appear to be a misdeclaration, but in fact it is the only declaration possible. We need a variable large enough to hold any possible address in the system. In other words, we need a pointer. Our use of this pointer just seems strange because we are more interested in the address than the value it points to. We'll touch again on this topic in the next chapter.

Notice that the two offset structure members data_off and status_off are declared to be *signed* integers. This allows the use of negative offsets if necessary. The two masks are declared to be unsigned instead of BYTE to accommodate future UARTs that may use 16-bit registers.

Why not design the structure to contain *absolute* addresses for the Data and Status registers instead of the offsets as shown? Indeed, this approach bears no penalty as long as the computer in question supports only a single serial port. In environments where several serial ports exist, however, software usually must address UARTs at several different locations. Since the registers in every serial port have identical offsets, it greatly improves the generality of the code if all serial ports can be addressed simply by specifying a single base address. We'll return to this point later and the benefits of expressing register locations as offsets will become obvious.

For the time being, every function we write refers to an instance of the serial structure. This structure is named sio. In subsequent chapters we will develop a much more flexible way to address this ''level-0'' structure.

Constants for Masking Status Registers

Based upon the Status register descriptions discussed in Chapters 6 and 7, we can construct constant definitions of the status masks for the 8250 and Z80SIO. These constants, given in Figure 9-5, should be placed in the header files, *U8250.H* and *Z80SIO.H*, respectively.

Figure 9-5   Definitions for the constants used in level-1 transmit/receive routines.

Mask Constants for U8250.H

```
#define RCV_MASK        1               /* RxRDY mask   */
#define XMIT_MASK       0x20            /* TBE mask     */
```

Mask Constants for Z80SIO.H

```
#define RCV_MASK        1               /* RxRDY mask */
#define XMIT_MASK       4               /* TBE mask     */
```

U8250.LIB

Any level-1 library must contain functions that:

- Fetch a byte from the UART's receiver.
- Return the status of the UART's receiver.
- Dispatch a byte from the UART's transmitter.
- Return the status of the UART's transmitter.

We can now write the level-1 library routines for the 8250 and Z80SIO UARTs. Luckily, because the status bytes of most UARTs mask the transmit and receive characters in pretty much the same way, the four functions in Figure 9-6 are correct for most UART libraries. At any rate, create the two files *U8250.LIB* and *Z80SIO.LIB*. Each must contain these four functions.

Figure 9-6   Level-1 functions s_xmit, s_xmitstat, s_rcv, and s_rcvstat.

```
FUNCTION NAME:  s_rcv
LEVEL:          1
LIBRARY:        U8250.LIB and Z80SIO.LIB
DESCRIPTION:    Read a character from UART.
OTHER MODULES:  sio data structure.
RETURNS:        unsigned char (BYTE)
COMMENTS:       The base address of the UART is a member of the sio structure. The Data register is
                expressed as an offset from the base address.
```

```
#include "stdio.h"
#include "siodef.h"
extern struct serial sio;
```

Figure 9-6 cont. Level-1 functions s_xmit, s_xmitstat, s_rev, and s_revstat.

```
BYTE s_rcv()
{
     return ( inport(sio.uart_base + sio.data_off));
}
```

FUNCTION NAME: s_rcvstat
LEVEL: 1
LIBRARY: *U8250.LIB* and *Z80SIO.LIB*
DESCRIPTION: Reads the UART's Serial Status register and masks off the receiver ready bit.
OTHER MODULES: sio structure.
RETURNS: unsigned char (BYTE)
COMMENTS: The base address of the UART is a member of the sio structure. The address of the
                 UART's Serialization Status register is expressed as an offset from the base address.

```
#include "stdio.h"
#include "siodef.h"
extern struct serial sio;

BYTE s_rcvstat()
{
     return (inport(sio.uart_base + sio.status_off) & sio.rcvmask);
}
```

FUNCTION NAME: s_xmit
LEVEL: 1
LIBRARY: *U8250.LIB* and *Z80SIO.LIB*
DESCRIPTION: Writes a byte to UART.
OTHER MODULES: sio data structure.
RETURNS: void
COMMENTS: The base address of the UART is a member of the sio structure. The Data register is
                 expressed as an offset from the base address.

```
#include "stdio.h"
#include "siodef.h"
extern struct serial sio;

void s_xmit(c)
BYTE c;
{
     outport(sio.uart_base + sio.data_off, c);

}
```

FUNCTION NAME: s_xmitstat
LEVEL: 1
LIBRARY: *U8250.LIB* and *Z80SIO.LIB*
DESCRIPTION: Reads a 8250 UART's Status register and masks off the transmitter status bit.
OTHER MODULES: sio data structure.

RETURNS: `unsigned char (BYTE)`

COMMENTS: The base address of the UART is a member of the `sio` structure. The address of the UART's Serialization Status register is expressed as an offset from the base address. The value of the constant XMIT_MASK is read from SIODEF.H.

```c
#include "stdio.h"
#include "siodef.h"
extern struct serial sio;

BYTE s_xmitstat()
{
    return ( inport(sio.uart_base + sio.status_off) & sio.xmitmask);
}
```

An Explanation of the Level-1 Functions   In each case, these functions expect to find the real addresses of the respective UART ports in a `uart_base` member of the `serial` structure named `sio`. This `sio` structure, you will remember, is assumed to lie in a computer-specific file which we will declare later.

s_rcvstat   Fetches the base port address of the UART from the structure, adds `sio.stat_off` to it, then reads a byte from that port address. The status bit is masked with the value `sio.rcvmask`. Thus, the value returned is TRUE only if a character has been assembled and is available for reading.

s_rcv   Fetches the base port address of the UART from the structure, adds `sio.data_off` to it, then reads and returns the value at that port address.

s_xmitstat Fetches the base port address of the UART from the structure, adds `sio.stat_off` to it, then reads a byte from that port address. The status bit is masked with the value `sio.xmitmask`. Thus, the value returned is TRUE only if the transmitter is ready.

s_xmit   Fetches the base port address of the UART from the structure, adds `sio.data_off` to it, and outputs the BYTE argument c to that port address.

When writing level-1 functions like these for other UARTs, keep in mind that although both the 8250 and the Z80SIO report a ready status as a TRUE bit, a few UARTs employ inverted logic. Since level-2 functions are designed to interpret a non-0 to be a READY status, the level-1 routines for such UARTs must return the *1s complement* of the masked value.

Now compile these modules and create from them two (for now) identical libraries, *U8250.LIB* and *Z80SIO.LIB*.

Location of Data Objects

The `serial` structure was defined in Figure 9-4. In the four functions in Figure 9-6, the inclusion of the file *SIODEF.H* provides the compiler with a definition of the `serial` structure. The `extern struct serial sio` statement informs the compiler that the actual `sio` structure to which the functions refer is external to these files. Remember, the `serial` structure definition in *SIODEF.H* is just that, a definition. The actual *declaration*[1] and initialization of an instance of this

---

[1]A definition creates only a template; the actual instance is created by a declaration. This is reversed from Kernighan and Ritchie's *C Progamming Language*, but makes more sense to almost everyone.

structure—named `sio`—will be made later as we create level-0 modules for each computer. If your understanding of the relationships among these various modules is hazy at this point, don't worry; it will soon become clear.

Notes on C usage: pointer arithmetic

We have declared `uart_base` to be of type "pointer to `char`," but since it is actually a "dummy" pointer, it might seem that the type of object to which it points is unimportant. To understand its critical importance, assume that a `long`, `int`, and BYTE occupy 4, 2, and 1 bytes, respectively. What would the following code fragment print?

```
int    d = 5;
BYTE *a = 100;
int  *b = 100;
long *c = 100;
printf("%d\n", a + d);
printf("%d\n", b + d);
printf("%d\n", c + d);
```

The answer to this question is in the next chapter in the box on page 276.

The BUOS.LIB Level-2 Library

With the receive/transmit/status UART functions now in place in the level-1 libraries, we can begin to build the next layer of functions required to support asynchronous serial I/O functions. These routines combine the level-1 routines into new functions to read and write single bytes in various ways. For now, we need only three such routines:

s_putc   A UART write function that waits for a TRUE transmitter status, then writes a byte to the serial port.

s_getc   A UART read function that waits for a TRUE receiver status, then reads a byte from the serial port.

s_inchar   A UART read function that returns a character if the receiver status is TRUE, otherwise returns an error.

These functions are shown in Figure 9-7.

Figure 9-7 Level-2 functions for reading and writing bytes.

```
FUNCTION NAME:  s_putc
LEVEL:          2
LIBRARY:        BUOS.LIB
DESCRIPTION:    Writes a byte to the UART pointed to in the sio structure.
OTHER MODULES:  s_xmitstat and s_xmit.
RETURNS:        void
COMMENTS:       Waits for TBE to become TRUE.

#include "stdio.h"
#include "siodef.h"

BYTE s_xmitstat();                        /* return type declaration      */

void s_putc(c)
BYTE c;
{
    while (s_xmitstat() == NULL)          /* wait for uart to be ready    */
        ;
    s_xmit(c);                            /* send the character and return */
}
```

```
FUNCTION NAME:  s_getc
LEVEL:          2
LIBRARY:        BUOS.LIB
DESCRIPTION:    Reads a byte from the UART pointed to in the sio structure.
OTHER MODULES:  s_rcvstat, s_rcv
RETURNS:        BYTE
COMMENTS:       Waits forever for an available byte.

#include "stdio.h"
#include "siodef.h"

BYTE s_rcvstat(), s_rcv();

BYTE s_getc()
{
    while (s_rcvstat() == NULL)           /* wait for character to be ready */
        ;
    return (s_rcv());                     /* read the character and return it */
}
```

```
FUNCTION NAME:  s_inchar
LEVEL:          2
LIBRARY:        BUOS.LIB
DESCRIPTION:    Reads a byte from the UART pointed to in the sio structure.
OTHER MODULES:  s_rcvstat, s_rcv
RETURNS:        int
```

Figure 9-7 cont. Level-2 functions for reading and writing bytes.

COMMENTS: Does not wait for a byte to arrive. It returns the byte if ready, otherwise −1. The use of −1 permits a NUL character to be recognized as data.

```
#include "stdio.h"
#include "siodef.h"

#define NOT_READY -1

BYTE s_rcvstat(), s_rcv();

int s_inchar()
{
    return (s_rcvstat() == NULL ?  NOT_READY : s_rcv());
}
```

The most important attribute of these functions is their generality: they know nothing about the sio structure and nothing specific about the particular UART in use. Although ignorance of the sio structure is certainly not a requirement (or even a goal) for level-2 functions, it superbly illustrates the ideal of logical and physical abstraction.

The SIO.LIB Level-3 Library

Level-3 functions, *by definition*, call only level-2 functions, and, from time to time, other level-3 functions. Although this library, *SIO.LIB*, will be quite large by the end of the book, for now we will include in it only the single function shown in Figure 9-8.

Figure 9-8 s_puts: a level-3 function for transmitting a string.

FUNCTION NAME: s_puts
LEVEL: 3
LIBRARY: *SIO.LIB*
DESCRIPTION: Writes a NUL-terminated string to the UART pointed to in the sio structure.
OTHER MODULES: s_putc
RETURNS: void

```
#include "stdio.h"
#include "siodef.h"


void s_puts(str)
char *str;
{
    for (; *str != NUL; str++)
      s_putc(*str);
}
```

TERM, Version 0

We are now ready to write our first program using the SIO and UART libraries. First, though, add #define statements to the ASCII character constants shown in Figure 9-9, then create a file named *ASCII.H*. This file will be required throughout the remainder of the book.

Figure 9-9 Character constants for *ASCII.H*.

CTRL_A	0x01	TAB	0x09	CTRL_T	0x14
SOH	0x01	HT	0x09	NAK	0x15
CTRL_B	0x02	CTRL_J	0x0A	CTRL_U	0x15
STX	0x02	LF	0x0A	CTRL_V	0x16
CTRL_C	0x03	CTRL_K	0x0B	CTRL_W	0x17
ETX	0x03	CTRL_L	0x0C	CAN	0x18
CTRL_D	0x04	FF	0x0C	CTRL_X	0x18
EOT	0x04	CTRL_M	0x0D	CTRL_Y	0x19
CTRL_E	0x05	CR	0x0D	CTRL_Z	0x1A
ENQ	0x05	CTRL_N	0x0E	CTRL_LBRAK	0x1B
CTRL_F	0x06	CTRL_O	0x1F	ESC	0x1B
ACK	0x06	CTRL_P	0x10	CTRL_BAKSL	0x1C
CTRL_G	0x07	CTRL_Q	0x11	CTRL_RBRAK	0x1D
BEL	0x07	DC1	0x11	CTRL_CTRL	0x1E
CTRL_H	0x08	CTRL_R	0x12	CTRL__	0x1F
BS	0x08	CTRL_S	0x13	SP	0x20
CTRL_I	0x09	DC3	0x13	DEL	0x7f

TERM0, an extremely simple terminal program, is shown in Figure 9-10. "But wait!" you are probably thinking, "we can't write a program, because we don't yet have a computer-specific (level-0) file for resolving all the references to an SIO." To encourage you to "Think Generally!" we will write the program—a pure form of intellectual abstraction—before we attach concrete meaning to its lowest-level library. In other words, you should understand what the program does, not how the underlying hardware accomplishes it. After we have examined and discussed the program's design, we'll create a hardware file for the IBM PC and the Kaypro.

TERM0 contains two functions that are not in the standard library—inkey and getch. The function inkey returns a typed character or NOT_READY if no character is waiting. The function getch waits for a single key to be pressed, then returns it immediately. These functions are explained in detail in "Console I/O," below.

Figure 9-10 *TERM0*: a simple terminal program to illustrate the use of the serial I/O libraries.

PROGRAM TITLE: *TERM0*
DESCRIPTION: Simple dumb terminal program with function menu.
SYNTAX: TERM0
OTHER MODULES: Functions in *BUOS.LIB*, *SIO.LIB*, and the level-0 library for the target computer.
COMMENTS: The functions inkey and getch are not in the standard library, but are given in Appendix A.

Figure 9-10 cont. *TERM0:* a simple terminal program to illustrate the use of the serial I/O libraries.

```c
#include "stdio.h"
#include "siodef.h"
#include "ascii.h"

#define MENU        CTRL_A                      /* key for command summary    */
#define NOT_READY    -1                         /* return value from s_inchar */


int vers = 0;                                   /* version number (global)    */

main()
{
    void term();
    term();                              /*              TERM             */
    printf("\nEnd of TERM%d\n",vers);
    return(0);
}

void term()
{
    int c;                               /* must be int to detect -1 return   */
    printf("TERM, Version %d: Press Control-%c for a list of commands\n",\
        vers, MENU + '@');
    for (EVER)                           /*           eternal loop            */
        {
        if ( (c = s_inchar()) != NOT_READY)  /* check serial port for byte */
            putchar(c);
        if ( (c = inkey()) != NOT_READY)     /* if a key is pressed        */
            if (c == MENU)                   /* and it's the menu key      */
                {
                if (menu() != NUL)  /* if menu function returns non-zero */
                    break;                   /* return to main            */
                }
            else
                s_putc(c);
        }
}

#define EXIT    'Q'                             /* key to exit from main      */

int menu ()
{
    int c ;
    int retval = 0;
    static char *menus[] =
        {
        "\tQ.  EXIT from TERM.",
        ""                               /* null string terminates list       */
        };
```

Figure 9-10 cont. *TERM0:* a simple terminal program to illustrate the use of the serial I/O libraries.

```
char ** menup;
c = !EXIT;
while (c != EXIT)
     {
     puts("\n\n");
     for (menup = menus; **menup != NUL ; menup++)
     printf("%s\n", *menup);
     printf("\n\t\t  Enter selection  (CR to quit menu) :  ");
     if ( (c = getch()) == CR)
          break;                          /* return to term           */
     c = toupper(c);
     switch (c)
        {
        case EXIT:                        /* return to term and exit  */
             retval = 1;
             break;
        default:
             puts("Invalid choice\n\007");
             break;
        }
   }
puts("\nExiting menu");
return (retval);                         /* will be zero except if EXIT  */
}
```

An Explanation of TERM0   Upon entry to `main`, the program simply calls the function `term`, which consists of two alternating polling loops. If a byte arrives over the serial line via `s_inchar`, it is immediately displayed with `putchar`. If a character is typed on the keyboard, it is first tested to see if it is MENU, the *menu trigger key*. If not, the byte is immediately dispatched over the serial line via `s_putc` and the polling continues.

Pressing the menu trigger key (here defined as a **Ctrl-A**) calls the function `menu`, whose main duty is to present a menu of available functions. Although this list contains only one item—the request to exit the program—it will grow rapidly in future chapters. Each menu item is merely an element in an array of pointers to strings (`char * []`). To mark the end of the array, the last element in the array must always contain a pointer to a NUL string. This technique makes adding a new option to the command summary quite convenient—just insert the string in the alphabetical order of its key character.

Typing a CR at the menu causes the menu function to return a value of 0 to `main`—a signal to continue polling the keyboard/serial port. Typing the key defined as EXIT, however, returns a value of 1, the signal for `term` to return to `main`. Any other key elicits an "Invalid Choice" message and the prompt reappears.

Console I/O

The need for the functions `inkey` and `getch` stems from a severe shortcoming in most microcomputer C implementations. In virtually all CP/M and PC/MS DOS compilers, the standard library functions for console input—for example `getchar` and its derivatives—are buffered. That is, calls to `getchar` do not immediately return with the fetched character. Instead, the characters are buffered until a CR is typed. In most libraries, `putchar` by default converts CR and LF to CRLF and echoes typed characters to the console—obviously unacceptable behavior when a program such as *TERM* must fetch and process keyboard data character-by-character. Moreover, *TERM* needs each character in exactly the form which it is typed—without CR, LF, or EOF mapping.

Although C compilers usually provide console I/O functions that do not echo or otherwise process their data, these functions are not part of a standard C library. Therefore there exists no *portable* way to handle console I/O. To make matters worse, many C compilers—Aztec included—do not provide even a nonportable console *status* routine for ascertaining if a keyboard character is ready. This lack of portable level-1 console routines is inexcusable—console status and system read calls are basic to *every* operating system, large or small. Portable methods for controlling every important characteristic of console I/O exist. Lest we waste too much time bemoaning the inadequacies of our libraries, before proceeding please turn to Appendix A, where you will find the 8080 and 8086 assembly language functions for the level-1 console functions and the C source code for the two level-2 C functions `inkey` and `getch` used in *TERM0*. The linkage examples shown later in this book assume that you have added these functions, as described in Appendix A.

Linking TERM0

If we were now to link the object modules for *TERM0* and *SIO.LIB* with either *Z80SIO.LIB* or *U8250.LIB*, the linker would find one very important object to be missing—the `sio` structure itself. Without this structure, the port addresses referred to in the level-1 functions do not exist. For each computer we will now create a separate linkage module to declare and initialize the structure for that computer, thus providing the missing information: the UART's base port addresses, the offsets of its various registers, and the two status masks.

The Level-0 Modules: IBMPC.C

We will create the module for the IBM PC first. The IBM PC supports two "asynchronous communications adapters" (serial ports), which are referred to by the system device names COM1 and COM2. COM1 usually resides at port address 03F8, COM2 at 02F8. The data port and serialization status ports are located at offsets 0 and 5, respectively.

The module for *IBMPC.C* is extremely simple, as shown in Figure 9-11.

Figure 9-11   The level-0 module for the IBM PC family.

STRUCT NAME:	`sio`
COMPUTER FILE:	*IBMPC.C*
DESCRIPTION:	"Master" serial structure. Declares and initializes the `serial sio` structures used by the functions in other libraries.
COMMENTS:	Resolves all hardware references in files at higher levels.

```
#include "stdio.h"
#include "u8250.h"
#include "siodef.h"
```

Figure 9-11 cont. The level-0 module for the IBM PC family.

```
#define COMM1      (BYTE *)0x3F8     /* IBM PC's first  serial port   */
#define COMM2      (BYTE *)0x2F8     /* IBM PC's second serial port   */
#define DP_OFF             0         /* offset of UART data port      */
#define SP_OFF             5         /* offset of UART status port    */

struct serial sio =
    {
    COMM1,                           /* base address of UART          */
    DP_OFF,                          /* offset of data port from base */
    SP_OFF,                          /* offset of status port from base */
    RCV_MASK,                        /* RXRDY mask--defined in U8250.H */
    XMIT_MASK                        /* TBE mask--defined in U8250.H  */
    };
```

An Explanation of IBMPC.C Here our `sio` structure's first member, `uart_base`, is initialized to contain the port address of the first serial port in the IBM PC, 03F8H. The offsets of the Data and Serialization Status registers from the base address are 0 and 5, respectively. The values required to mask off the TBE and RxRDY bits are imported from *U8250.H*. If you are tempted to place the DP_OFF and SP_OFF constants in *U8250.H*, remember that these relationships are not *inherent* properties of the UART, but of the computer.

During linkage, `sio.uart_base`, `sio.data_off`, `sio.xmitmask`, and `sio.rcvmask` in the level-1 functions acquire the values from this structure initialization. To create an executable file *TERM0.EXE* for the IBM PC, first compile *IBMPC.C*, then issue the following command to the Aztec linker:

LN TERM0.O IBMPC.O SIO.LIB BUOS.LIB U8250.LIB YOUR.LIB C.LIB

where *C.LIB* is the Aztec compiler's standard library and YOUR.LIB is your private library containing the console functions from Appendix A. That's all there is to it. Moreover, we can easily create a version for the CP/M Kaypro computer.

The Level-0 Modules: KAYPRO.C

The various CP/M models of Kaypro computers are single-board machines without expansion slots. All models use a Z80SIO UART, with UART channel A used for the keyboard and channel B used for a general purpose serial port located at base address 4. The offset of the data registers is 0, and the offset of the serialization status register is 2. With this information, we can easily create the Kaypro module, *KAYPRO.C*, shown in Figure 9-12.

Figure 9-12 The level-0 module for the KAYPRO family of CP/M computers.

STRUCT NAME:	`sio`
COMPUTER FILE:	*KAYPRO.C*
DESCRIPTION:	Declares and initializes the `serial sio` structure used by the functions in other libraries.
COMMENTS:	Known to be accurate for models 2, 4, and 10.

Figure 9-12 cont.   The level-0 module for the KAYPRO family of CP/M computers.

```
#include "stdio.h"
#include "z80sio.h"
#include "siodef.h"

#define PORT1        (BYTE *)4
#define DP_OFF            0               /* offset of UART data port       */
#define SP_OFF            2               /* offset of UART status port     */

struct serial sio =
    {
    PORT1,                               /* base address of UART           */
    DP_OFF,                              /* offset of data port from base  */
    SP_OFF,                              /* offset of status port from base */
    RCV_MASK,                            /* RxRDY mask--defined in Z80SIO.H */
    XMIT_MASK                            /* TBE mask--defined in Z80SIO.H  */
    };
```

Because of the manner in which the level-2 and level-3 functions are written, we need only compile *KAYPRO.C* and link it as follows:

LN TERM0.O KAYPRO.O SIO.LIB BUOS.LIB DART.LIB YOUR.LIB C.LIB

Conclusion

By careful design, we have devised a reasonably general framework within which we can write the basic code for most computer systems. By designing our libraries hierarchically downward from the general to the specific, only minor revisions will be required to create workable versions for a variety of hardware configurations and operating system environments.

But lest we become content with fulsome praise, the next chapter will discard most of these functions in favor of others that are still more general and, therefore, more portable.

10

Portability Considerations

In the previous chapter we constructed a framework within which we can easily write serial I/O routines that run on almost any hardware. Although our level-2 and level-3 routines are general, they are not yet flexible enough to support every programming situation. With the concept of hierarchically structured libraries in mind, then, the purpose of this chapter is to revise these functions with an eye toward increasing their generality and therefore their portability. For the sake of consistency, whenever possible we will retain the function and library names begun in the previous chapter.

Level-1 Functions

Look closely at the level-1 function s_xmit. Do you see anything that might limit its usefulness or that ties it to a particular computer architecture? Let's answer this question with another. Suppose that you wish to write programs for a computer that does not address its UART through I/O ports, but as ordinary memory locations. Wouldn't the need for *memory-mapped* serial I/O render the inport and outport functions in the level-1 library useless? If you are like many programmers, your first inclination might be to "fix" the problem by changing inport and outport preprocessor constants in *STDIO.H* to peek and poke routines, which access RAM instead of I/O ports. This would be a solution of sorts, but you would be forced to maintain separate libraries for memory- and port-mapped UARTs. Besides, how would you handle a system that contains both kinds of addressing?

If this seems far-fetched, remember that a fair number of serial I/O boards exist for S-100 bus CP/M systems, where the user selects not only the address at which the UARTs are located, but also whether they are addressed through memory or I/O ports. Although there are innumerable circumstances where committing your library to port addressing would prove crippling, it is unnecessary to recite them. Their importance is philosophical: don't hardwire constants and other values into your code when you don't have to.

To make our level-1 functions more general, we need a UART addressing scheme that can be specified when the program is run (or linked) instead of when it is compiled. To C programmers, this means that every function in the level-1 library must employ "pointers" to as yet unknown functions that read from and write to the UART.

The almost effortless use of pointers, including the *pointers to functions* we need here, is another reason why the C language is a good choice for serial I/O programming. Before we proceed, though, let's pause for a short review of C function pointers. A trivial program, *FPTEST1*, is shown in Figure 10-1.

Figure 10-1 *FPTEST1*: a simple program to demonstrate C function pointers.

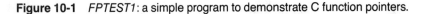

```
void function1(a)
int a;
{
    printf("This is function 1.  The value passed is %d.\n",a);
}

void function2(b)
int b;
{
    printf("This is function 2.  The value passed is %d.\n",b);
}

main()
{
    void (*functp)();        /* pointer to a void function      */
    functp = function1;      /* make it point at function1      */
    (*functp)(1);            /* call the function pointed to    */
    functp = function2;      /* make it point at function2      */
    (*functp)(-1);           /* and call it again               */
}
```

An Explanation of FPTEST1   Here are two simple functions named, imaginatively, function1 and function2. The declaration of the variable functp

```
void (*functp)();
```

is the focus of our attention. In order to understand this declaration, let's first consider it written like this:

```
void *functp();  /* pointer to a void function */
```

Here, the two operators in this expression—the pointer * and function call ()—"compete" for closest association with the variable name. Ordinarily, the function call wins because it has the highest priority (precedence); thus, functp is a *function* that returns a pointer to a void.

We can change this "natural" order of evaluation by placing *grouping parentheses* around *functp, which forces the * to bind to the function name before the function call operator[1]. The declaration then says that functp is a *pointer* to a function that returns a void.

The pointer functp is assigned to point at function1; functp is then called, passing the value 1 as an argument:

```
(*functp)(1);
```

---

[1]Do not confuse the grouping parentheses with the parentheses that denote a function call. The former are not operators at all, but punctuation directing the order of evaluation in an expression.

Notice that the parentheses *and* the pointer operator are retained in the call. Next, the function pointer is assigned to `function2` and called with the argument -1.

Function Pointers in a Structure

Since our declared strategy in composing libraries is to maintain all relevant variables in the `sio` structure, we install the pointers to the read/write functions there, too. Before we examine the changes that are required in the `sio` structure definition, declaration, and initialization, let's first see how the placing of the function pointer in a structure affects the syntax in our *FPTEST* program. Figure 10-2 shows *FPTEST2*, the revised program.

Figure 10-2 The *FPTEST2* program revised to demonstrate C function pointers as structure members.

```
void function1(a)
int a;
{
    printf("This is function 1.  The value passed is %d.\n",a);
}

void function2(b)
int b;
{
    printf("This is function 2.  The value passed is %d.\n",b);
}

struct
    {
    void (*functp)();
    } x;

main()
{
    x.functp = function1;         /* make it point to function1     */
    (*x.functp)(1);               /* call the function pointed to   */
    x.functp = function2;         /* make it point to function2     */
    (*x.functp)(-1);              /* and call it again              */
}
```

As you can see, the function pointer's residing in a structure does not substantially affect the calling syntax. Since the structure member '.' operator has higher precedence than the pointer operator, parentheses are not required around the member reference.

The 'sio' Structure with Pointers to UART Access Functions

The pointers to the UART access functions will reside in our `sio` structure. Figure 10-3 shows `sio` with these pointers installed.

Figure 10-3 The sio structure revised to contain pointers to UART access functions.

```
struct serial
    {
    unsigned *uart_base;              /* base address of UART             */
    int       data_off;              /* offset of data port from base    */
    int       status_off;            /* offset of status port from base  */
    unsigned rcvmask;                /* RxRDY mask                       */
    unsigned xmitmask;               /* TBE mask                         */
    BYTE     (*readbyte)();          /* pointer to RAM/port read routine */
    void     (*writebyte)();         /* pointer to RAM/port write routine */
    };
```

An Explanation of the Revised 'sio'   The two new structure members are readbyte, declared to be a pointer to a function returning BYTE, and writebyte, a pointer to a function returning void.

As we develop new functions throughout this book, we will modify this sio structure. When creating new versions of the structure, it is important to *append* new members to the previous version of the structure. Adding new members only to the end of the structure leaves the relationship between pre-existing members unchanged; therefore, functions previously compiled do not have to be recompiled.

The Revised UART.LIB Functions

We must now revise the level-2 functions to take advantage of the function pointers in the sio structure. These changes are shown in Figure 10-4. (Please do not add them to your library yet.) Note that only one header is shown for all four functions.

Figure 10-4 Level-2 functions s_rcv, s_rcvstat, s_xmit, and s_xmitstat.

```
FUNCTION NAME: s_rcv, s_rcvstat, s_xmit, s_xmitstat
DESCRIPTION:       Level-2 functions using function pointers.
COMMENTS:          These are not the final versions. Do not add them to your libraries.

#include "stdio.h"
#include "siodef.h"

BYTE s_rcvstat()
{
    return ((*sio.readbyte)(sio.uart_base + sio.status_off) & sio.rcvmask);

}

BYTE s_rcv()
{
    return ( (*sio.readbyte)(sio.uart_base + sio.data_off));

}
```

Figure 10-4 cont.   Level-2 functions `s_rcv`, `s_rcvstat`, `s_xmit`, and `s_xmitstat`.

```
BYTE s_xmitstat()
{
    return ( (*sio.readbyte)(sio.uart_base + sio.status_off) & sio.xmitmask);
}

void s_xmit(c)
BYTE c;
{
    (*sio.writebyte)(sio.uart_base + sio.data_off, c);

}
```

An Explanation of the Revised Level-2 Functions   In their previous versions, these level-2 routines relied on the `sio` structure only for the port addressing arguments and UART masks. The importance of the revisions in Figure 10-4 is that the reads and writes take place through pointers to functions whose exact identity need not be known at compile time. You supply the names of the *actual* read/write functions, initializing the `sio` structure in the "level-0" computer specific file. Figure 10-5 shows how the revised `sio` structure is declared and initialized. (*IBMPC.C* and *KAYPRO.C* are identical in this respect.)

Figure 10-5   Revised `sio` structure declaration and initialization for the KAYPRO and the IBM PC.

```
BYTE inport();                          /* return type declarations        */
void outport();

struct serial sio =
    {
    COMM2,                              /* base address of UART            */
    DP_OFF,                             /* offset of data port from base   */
    SP_OFF,                             /* offset of status port from base */
    RCV_MASK,                           /* RxRDY mask from U8250.H          */
    XMIT_MASK,                          /* TBE mask from U8250.H            */
    inport,                             /* pointer to RAM/port read routine */
    outport,                            /* pointer to RAM/port write routine */
    };
```

At the beginning of this module, the return types of the UART access functions are declared:

```
BYTE inport();
void outport();
```

The structure declaration initializes the `readbyte` member to point at `inport`, and the `writebyte` member to point at `outport`.

Pointers in Memory-Mapped Systems

In Chapter 9, we discussed the importance of declaring the structure variable `uart_base` to be a pointer. We can now see why this is necessary. The alternative to declaring it to be a pointer is to declare it to be an arithmetic type such as an `unsigned int`. In most systems you can expect that the size of an `int` reflects the "natural" size of the microprocessor registers on which the language is implemented. The natural size for `int`s, for example, is 16 bits on the Z80 and 8086, but 32 bits on a 68000. With this in mind, it might seem safe to store addresses as `int`s. Such assumptions about the relationship in size between data types are notoriously treacherous and eventually cause grief. One example should illustrate. Since the 68000's registers are 32 bits wide, the natural size of an `int` is 32 bits. Yet several 68000 C compilers offer a "16-bit integer option" where all integer operations are truncated to 16 bits. In this mode, attempting to store a 32-bit address in an `int` would prove fatal—half the address would be lost in truncation.

Answer to puzzle on page 261

The code on page 261 prints

    105
    110
    120

In other words, if n is an integer, and `ptr` is declared to point at an object of type x, then the expression `ptr + n` is equivalent to `ptr + (n * sizeof(x))`; the compiler automatically *scales* pointer arithmetic to account for the size of the objects pointed to. It is therefore extremely important that `uart_base` point to a `char`; otherwise, the addresses obtained from adding an offset to the UART's base address will be incorrect. In fact, this is a good general rule: when using a pointer variable expressly for address arithmetic, **make certain that it is declared as a pointer to a type that occupies a single unit of storage**.

The 'SIO' Object

Before we can proceed to write level-2 functions that rely upon these new level-1 functions, we must correct a severe limitation in our libraries—they are hardwired to a single `sio` data structure. This means that it is almost impossible to manage more than a single serial port simultaneously, because all level-1 functions refer directly to a single structure, `sio`! To appreciate how restrictive this design is, assume that you wish to write a program for the IBM PC that manages two serial ports at one time—one for a modem and one, say, to display the incoming modem data on a serial printer. The following gymnastics would be required:

```
struct serial printer, tmp;
        :
s_putc(c);          /* output to the modem              */
tmp = sio;          /* save current sio in a temporary  */
```

ORDER FORM

Name _____ Company _____

Address _____

City _____ State _____ Zip _____

Phone (____) _____ Date _____

Place of book purchase _____

Type of computer used _____

Disk format (1st choice) _____

                (2nd choice) _____

Brand of C compiler* _____ Version _____

*If your compiler is not supported, you will receive the code as it appears in the book.

Number of Copies	Title	Unit price	(US funds)
____	C Programmer's Guide to Serial Communications	@ $26.95 ea.	$ _____.___
____	Companion diskettes (2)	@ $35.00 ea. set	$ _____.___
____	Extra copies of ASCII wall chart	@ $15.00 ea.	$ _____.___

Shipping: $3.50 per book, $1.50 for other items $ _____.___

California residents add 6% sales tax $ _____.___

TOTAL $ _____.___

- -

fold

Three ways to order (no purchase orders, please):

1. Charge to: ____ Visa ____ MasterCard

                Card Number   Expiration Date

           [ ][ ][ ][ ][ ][ ][ ][ ][ ][ ][ ][ ][ ][ ][ ][ ]   [ ][ ]-[ ][ ]

                Signature _____

Fold over this card, then staple or tape it.

2. Or enclose check and mail to:

                            Campbell Productions
                            P.O. Box 7159
                            Berkeley, CA 94707

                            (Checks can be stapled inside this card)

3. Or place phone order at (415) 526-4311 (24 hrs)

Shipping charges cover First Class US Mail. Other methods are available at extra charge (credit card orders only):
____UPS   ____UPS Next Day   ____UPS Second Day   ____Federal Express

fold over, then tape or staple

Campbell Productions
P.O. Box 7159
Berkeley, CA 94707

(415) 526-4311

```
sio = printer;    /* now copy the printer over the sio */
s_putc(c);        /* now output to the printer          */
sio = tmp;        /* recover the original sio           */
        ⋮
```

Pretty cumbersome isn't it? It won't set any speed records either. Clearly this facetious example is not really a workable alternative. Ideally our code would read like this:

```
s_putc(modem, c);
s_putc(printer, c);
```

where modem and printer describe serial ports *somehow* associated with the printer and modem. To assist in this association let's now make the definition shown in Figure 10-6.

Figure 10-6 The SIO definition.

STRUCT DEF: SIO
FILE: *SIODEF.H*
DESCRIPTION: Typedef of master structure for defining a serial port.

```
typedef struct
    {
    BYTE      *uart_base;         /* base address of UART            */
    int       data_off;          /* offset of data port from base   */
    int       status_off;        /* offset of status port from base */
    unsigned  rcvmask;           /* RxRDY mask                      */
    unsigned  xmitmask;          /* TBE mask                        */
    BYTE      (*readbyte)();      /* pointer to RAM/port read routine */
    void      (*writebyte)();     /* pointer to RAM/port write routine */
    } SIO;
```

An Explanation of 'SIO'   Although this definition adds nothing to our code in the way of functionality, the typedef statement allows us to define our own data object—the SIO. As such, it possesses the attributes of all data types—scope, storage class, and so forth. This means that the compiler subjects it to the same type-checking rules as, say, an int. But perhaps the SIO's most important function is psychological—it encourages us to think of the serial port in abstract terms, as a *conceptual* instead of a physical entity. For example, instead of writing

```
struct serial sio;
```

which refers to a loose accumulation of data under the name sio, we can now write

```
SIO sio;
```

which loudly exclaims that SIO is an important *object*.

Managing Multiple 'SIO's

To manage our printer and modem simultaneously, we can now declare *two* SIOs for the two serial ports, COMM1 and COMM2:

```
SIO typeAsio =          /* declare an SIO for com1 */
    {
    COMM1,
    DP_OFF,
    SP_OFF,
    RCV_MASK,
       ⋮
    }

SIO typeBsio =          /* declare an SIO for com2 */
    {
    COMM2,
    DP_OFF,
    SP_OFF,
    RCV_MASK,
       ⋮
    }
```

Although we refer to the *ports* as COMM1 and COMM2, the SIOs, which now contain all important information about their respective serial ports, are named typeAsio and typeBsio. If every function's argument list contains a reference to an SIO, that function can address the serial port uniquely described by the SIO. With this idea in mind, a call to such a function looks like this:

```
s_putc(typeAsio, c);        /* to modem on com1   */
s_putc(typeBsio, c);        /* to printer on com2 */
```

which would pass the *entire* structure in the argument list[2]. This method, however, would be ludicrously inefficient because C would have to make a copy of the entire SIO for passing in the argument list. We can, however, easily and efficiently pass the SIO's *address* in the argument list:

```
s_putc(&typeAsio, c);       /* to modem on com1   */
s_putc(&typeBsio, c);       /* to printer on com2 */
```

Here, each call to s_putc passes the address of a different structure. The function s_putc itself can learn everything there is to learn about this SIO by examining the structure at this address. The same code can be written more eloquently using pointer variables instead of address operators:

```
SIO *modem   = &typeAsio;
SIO *printer = &typeBsio;
s_putc(modem, c);           /* pass pointer to com1 SIO */
s_putc(printer, c);         /* pass pointer to com2 SIO */
```

---

[2]The Aztec compiler used for this book permits entire structures to be passed to and returned from a function. This feature is now part of the ANSI X3J11 C standard.

This looks remarkably like our ideal a few paragraphs back, doesn't it? With this technique, we are now able to manage an unlimited number of serial ports, because we pass to our functions a description (in the form of a pointer) of the SIO describing that port. All that remains is to change our functions so that they gain access to an SIO through a pointer in the argument list instead of built-in references to sio.

Revising the Level-1 Functions

The changes required to the four level-1 functions are trivial, although to some readers the presence of the structure pointer operator makes the functions appear more daunting. The *final* version of these functions is shown Figure 10-7.

Figure 10-7 Level-1 functions now address data through SIOs.

FUNCTION NAME: s_rcvstat, s_rcv, s_xmitstat, s_xmit,
LEVEL: 1
LIBRARY: *U8250.LIB* and *Z80SIO.LIB*
DESCRIPTION: UART I/O primitives written to access their data through a pointer to an SIO (data structure).
OTHER MODULES: None
COMMENTS: Caution—calling these functions without the pointer argument produces disastrous results.

```
void s_xmit(siop, c)
register SIO *siop;
BYTE c;
{
    (*siop->writebyte)(siop->uart_base + siop->data_off, c);

}

BYTE s_xmitstat(siop)
register SIO *siop;
{

   return ( (*siop->readbyte)(siop->uart_base + siop->status_off) & siop->xmitmask);
}

BYTE s_rcv(siop)
register SIO *siop;
{
    return ( (*siop->readbyte)(siop->uart_base + siop->data_off));
}

BYTE s_rcvstat(siop)
register SIO *siop;
{
   return ((*siop->readbyte)(siop->uart_base + siop->status_off) & siop->rcvmask);
}
```

An Explanation of the UART I/O Primitives   These functions are essentially the same as those shown earlier in Figure 10-4. The sole difference is this: those in Figure 10-4 addressed their data through a fixed-named structure, `sio`, while these new functions address their data through a *pointer* to a structure, `siop`.

If you have difficulty with this notion, consider that most C programmers use an almost identical mechanism every day without really being aware of it. The *stream* I/O functions in C's standard library—`fopen`, `fclose`, `fread`, and `fwrite`—are designed in exactly this way. If you examine your compiler's *STDIO.H* file, you will find that the data type `FILE` is really a `typedef` of a structure. The function `fopen`, for example, returns a pointer to a `FILE`, which the other "stream" functions must include in their argument list. The parallel between our `SIO` and C's `FILE` is, of course, intentional. (In Chapter 14 we carry this parallel to completion by composing `s_open` and `s_close`.) There is, therefore, a very close parallel between:

```
FILE *fopen(), *fp;
fp = fopen("test.tmp","r");
    ⋮
putc(c, fp);
fclose(fp);
```

and

```
SIO *s_open, *siop;
siop = s_open(portnum);
    ⋮
s_putc(siop, c);
s_close(siop);
```

If you know how to perform stream I/O with C's library, you will almost intuitively understand the rest of the code in this book. The main difference between the `SIO` and `FILE` functions is syntactical—the `SIO` functions *always* require the `SIO` pointer to be the first argument in the list.

The 'register' Storage Class

The single disadvantage of our scheme of addressing a serial port through an `SIO` is *speed*. The `SIO` functions perform a great deal of time-consuming indexing relative to the `SIO` pointer. This, together with the use of function pointers, incurs considerable overhead. Although later in this book we will solve many of the problems caused by lack of speed, we can improve performance considerably by instructing the compiler to retain, when possible, the `SIO` pointer in one of the microprocessor's registers for more rapid access.

Revising the Level-2 Functions

Now that we have generalized the level-1 functions, we turn our attention to the level-2 functions in *BUOS.LIB*. These functions suffer from the same limitation as our early versions of the level-1 functions—inflexibility. To understand where these functions may be improved, let's review the code for `s_getc` shown in Figure 10-8.

This routine is inflexible because it assumes that bytes are received only through the level-1 functions in the UART service libraries. Yet there are circumstances where this assumption is incorrect. For example, if I/O is performed with *interrupts*, the interrupt service routine actually services the UART; that is, the very occurrence of an interrupt signals that a byte is ready. The interrupt service routine then automatically fetches the byte from the UART, placing it in a buffer

Figure 10-8 The current version of s_getc.

```
BYTE s_getc()
{
    while (s_rcvstat() == NULL)      /* wait for character to be ready  */
        ;
    return (s_rcv());                /* read the character and return it */
}
```

to be fetched later. Under these conditions, the status information must come from a function that reveals whether the interrupt buffer is empty; similarly, bytes must be read with a function that fetches characters from the interrupt buffer. The current version of s_putc suffers from the same limited vision: it assumes that bytes are dispatched only with the level-1 functions in the UART service libraries.

Without going into greater detail about interrupts right now (Chapter 20 covers interrupts), it should be obvious that a different set of routines than we currently use for polled I/O will be required for interrupt-driven I/O.

More Function Pointers

As you might have suspected, we will now (and for the *last* time) rewrite the level-2 routines to use pointers to functions, instead of hardwiring in the names of the functions themselves. In this way, our functions rely upon pointers instead of the level-1 UART service functions. With this technique, the exact identity of functions need not be decided until the program is actually run. As before, these four new function pointers are part of the SIO, the revised version of which is shown in Figure 10-9.

Figure 10-9 The SIO definition revised to contain pointers to UART service functions.

STRUCT DEF: SIO
FILE: *SIODEF.H*
DESCRIPTION: Typedef of master structure for defining a serial port.
COMMENTS: Revised to contain pointers to UART service functions.

```
typedef struct
    {
    BYTE     *uart_base;        /* base address of UART            */
    int      data_off;          /* offset of data port from base   */
    int      status_off;        /* offset of status port from base */
    unsigned rcvmask;           /* RxRDY mask                      */
    unsigned xmitmask;          /* TBE mask                        */
    BYTE     (*readbyte)();      /* pointer to RAM/port read routine */
    void     (*writebyte)();     /* pointer to RAM/port write routine */
    BYTE     (*s_rstat)();       /* pointer to serial receiver status */
    BYTE     (*s_read)();        /* pointer to serial fetch routine   */
    BYTE     (*s_xstat)();       /* pointer to serial xmiter status   */
    void     (*s_send)();        /* pointer to serial xmit routine    */
    } SIO;
```

An Explanation of the Revised 'SIO' The new additions are the two *receiver* function pointers `s_rstat` and `s_read` and the two *transmitter* function pointers `s_xstat` and `s_send`.

The Revised Level-2 Functions for BUOS.LIB

With the new function pointers in the structure we can now rewrite the level-2 functions to perform I/O through these pointers. The revised `s_getc` and `s_putc` functions for *BUOS.LIB* are given in Figure 10-10. Don't forget to include *STDIO.H*.

Figure 10-10 Revised level-2 functions for reading and writing bytes via function pointers.

```
FUNCTION NAME:  s_getc
LEVEL:          2
LIBRARY:        BUOS.LIB
DESCRIPTION:    Waits for a byte to arrive from the serial port (SIO) pointed to by siop.
OTHER MODULES:  None
RETURNS:        BYTE
COMMENTS:       Access to the port is through a pointer to an sio structure.

BYTE s_getc(siop)
register SIO *siop;
{
    while ((*siop->s_rstat)(siop) == 0 )  /* wait for char to be ready   */
        ;
    return ((*siop->s_read)(siop));            /* read and return it      */

}
```

```
FUNCTION NAME:  s_putc
LEVEL:          2
LIBRARY:        BUOS.LIB
DESCRIPTION:    Sends a byte out the serial port (SIO) pointed to by siop.
OTHER MODULES:  None
RETURNS:        void
COMMENTS:       Access to the serial port is through an sio structure.

void s_putc(siop, c)
register SIO *siop;
BYTE    c;
{
    while ((*siop->s_xstat)(siop) == 0)       /* wait for uart to be ready  */
        ;
    (*siop->s_send)(siop, c);                 /* write it and return      */
}
```

Figure 10-10 cont. Revised level-2 functions for reading and writing bytes via function pointers.

FUNCTION NAME: s_inchar
LEVEL: 2 (or MACRO)
LIBRARY: *BUOS.LIB*
DESCRIPTION: Fetches a byte from the serial port (SIO) pointed to by siop, if one is ready; otherwise returns.
OTHER MODULES: None
RETURNS: int: the byte if one is ready; otherwise −1.
COMMENTS: The function can also be written as a macro in *STDIO.H*.

```
int s_inchar(siop)
SIO *siop;
{
    if ((*siop->s_rstat)(siop))
        return ((*siop->s_read)(siop));
    return (-1);
}
```

An Explanation of 's_putc', 's_getc', 's_inchar' All three of these functions accomplish the same tasks as earlier versions. The important difference here is that the new versions have absolutely no idea *how* a byte is fetched, or written. The names of the functions pointed to by s_rstat, s_read, s_xstat, and s_send are not actually assigned until the linker sees the SIO declarations and initializations in the computer-dependent level-0 file. As we saw in Chapter 9, the pointed-to functions can even be altered during program execution to take advantage of hardware differences.

Declaring and Initializing the 'SIO'

Just as we initialized our I/O "access" pointers to inport and outport, we will now initialize our UART "service" pointers to point at their corresponding level-1 routines. Figure 10-11 shows the initialization and declaration for *IBMPC.C. KAYPRO.C* is identical in this respect.

Figure 10-11 A revised SIO declaration and initialization for the IBM PC.

'SIO' NAME: typeAsio
FILE: *IBMPC.C*
DESCRIPTION: Declaration and initialization of the SIO for the IBM PC.

```
#define COMM1 (BYTE *)0x3F8        /* IBM PC's first serial port   */
#define COMM2 (BYTE *)0x2F8        /* IBM PC's second serial port  */
#define DP_OFF 0                   /* offset of UART data port     */
#define SP_OFF 5                   /* offset of UART status port   */

BYTE inport(), s_rcv(),s_rcvstat(),s_xmitstat();
void outport(),s_xmit();

SIO typeAsio =
    {
    COMM1,                         /* base address of UART         */
```

Figure 10-11 cont. A revised SIO declaration and initialization for the IBM PC.

```
DP_OFF,                           /* offset of data port from base      */
SP_OFF,                           /* offset of status port from base    */
RCV_MASK,                         /* RxRDY mask from U8250.H             */
XMIT_MASK,                        /* TBE mask from U8250.H               */
inport,                           /* pointer to RAM/port read routine   */
outport,                          /* pointer to RAM/port write routine  */
s_rcvstat,                        /* pointer to serial receiver status  */
s_rcv,                            /* pointer to serial fetch routine    */
s_xmitstat,                       /* pointer to serial xmiter status    */
s_xmit,                           /* pointer to serial xmit routine     */
};
```

An Explanation of the Revised IBMPC.C   In this instance of the SIO, named typeAsio, all pointers are initialized to the same functions as were employed in the original libraries. After you have correctly modified the SIO definition, declaration, and initialization, and have revised the UART libraries, you should revise the *TERM* program from Chapter 9 to accommodate the new SIO functions. These revisions are shown in Figure 10-12.

Figure 10-12   *TERM* revised to use the new SIO style function calls.

PROGRAM TITLE: *TERM1*
DESCRIPTION: Simple dumb terminal program, with function menu.
SYNTAX: TERM1
OTHER MODULES: Functions in *BUOS.LIB*, *SIO.LIB*, and the level-0 library for the target computer.

```
#include "stdio.h"
#include "siodef.h"
#include "ascii.h"

#define MENU      CTRL_A                /* key for command summary          */

int vers = 1;                          /* version number (global)          */
main()
{
    extern SIO typeAsio;               /* found in computer-specific file  */
    void term();                       /* return type declaration          */
    SIO *siop = &typeAsio;             /* pointer to the level-0 SIO        */
    term(siop);                        /* pass SIO pointer to TERM          */
    printf("\nEnd of TERM%d\n", vers);
    return(0);
}
void term(siop)
SIO *siop;                             /* required by the revised functions */
{
    int c;                             /* must be int to detect -1 return   */
    printf("TERM, Version %d:  Press Control-%c for a summary of commands\n",\
        vers, MENU + '@');
```

Figure 10-12 cont. *TERM* revised to use the new SIO style function calls.

```
    for (EVER)                          /*  eternal loop            */
        {
        if ( (c = s_inchar(siop)) != NOT_READY) /* check SIO for byte     */
            putchar(c);
        if ( (c = inkey()) != NOT_READY)   /* if a key is pressed      */
            if (c == MENU)                 /* and its the menu key     */
                {
                if (menu(siop) != NUL)     /* if menu returns non-zero */
                    break;                 /* return to main           */
                }
            else
                s_putc(siop, c);           /* output to SIO            */
        }
}
#define EXIT     'Q'                        /* key to exit from main    */
int menu (siop)
SIO *siop;
{
    int c ;
    int retval = 0;
    static char *menus[] =
        {
        "\tQ.  EXIT from TERM.",
        ""                                 /* null string terminates list  */
        };
    char ** menup;
    c = !EXIT;
    while (c != EXIT)
        {
        puts("\n\n");
        for (menup = menus; **menup != NUL ; menup++)
        printf("%s\n", *menup);
        printf("\n\t\t  Enter selection  (CR to quit menu) :   ");
        if ( (c = getch()) == CR)
            break;                         /* return to term           */
        c = toupper(c);
        switch (c)
            {
            case EXIT:                     /* return to term and exit  */
                retval = 1;
                break;
            default:
                puts("Invalid choice\n\007");
                break;
            }
    }
    puts("\nExiting menu");
    return (retval);                       /* will be zero except if EXIT */
}
```

An Explanation of TERM1 A pointer to an SIO, siop, is assigned the address of the typeAsio declared in the level-0 library (e.g., *IBMPC.C*). Note that typeAsio must be declared external here. The pointer is then passed in the call to the term functions where it is needed in the arguments to s_inchar and s_putc. Although not used in this version, the SIO pointer is also passed to menu.

It is worth noting that while this revision doesn't increase the functionality of *TERM*, it lays the groundwork for enhancements that would have been impossible in the earlier version. As support functions unfold during the remainder of this book, you will gradually gain an appreciation of the power of this design.

'SIO's for Memory-Mapped UARTs

So far we have shown how to initialize an SIO for a computer that addresses its UARTs via its port structure. One naturally expects to find memory-mapped UARTs in systems built around processors that lack port I/O instructions (the 6502 and 68000, for example). However, a surprising number of systems use memory-mapped UARTs despite the presence of port I/O instructions. One such memory-mapped computer is the MAX80 by Lobo Systems, which uses a Z80 microprocessor and a Z80SIO UART. The linkage module for the MAX80, shown in Figure 10-13, is also a guide for initializing an SIO on processors without port I/O.

Figure 10-13   Level-0 module that initializes the SIO for the Lobo Systems MAX80, a CP/M computer with memory-mapped UARTs.

```
#include "stdio.h"
#include "siodef.h"
#include "z80sio.h"

void poke(memloc, byte)
unsigned *memloc;
BYTE     byte;
{
    *memloc = byte;
}


BYTE peek(memloc)
unsigned *memloc;
{
    return (*memloc);                      /* not very efficient but will do !  */
}

#define COMM1 (BYTE *)0xF7E4               /* port 'A' */
#define COMM2 (BYTE *)0xF7E6               /* port 'B' */


#define DP_OFF 0                           /* offset of UART data port          */
#define SP_OFF 1                           /* offset of UART status port        */

BYTE inport(), s_rcv(),s_rcvstat(),s_xmitstat();
void outport(), s_xmit();
```

Figure 10-13 cont.   Level-0 module that initializes the SIO for the Lobo System MAX80, a CP/M computer with memory-mapped UARTs.

```
struct serial sio =
    {
    COMM1,                              /* base address of UART              */
    DP_OFF,                             /* offset of data port from base     */
    SP_OFF,                             /* offset of status port from base   */
    RCV_MASK,                           /* RxRDY mask from U8250.H            */
    XMIT_MASK,                          /* TBE mask from U8250.H              */
    peek,                               /* pointer to RAM/port read routine  */
    poke,                               /* pointer to RAM/port write routine */
    s_rcvstat,                          /* pointer to serial receiver status */
    s_rcv,                              /* pointer to serial fetch routine    */
    s_xmitstat,                         /* pointer to serial xmiter status   */
    s_xmit,                             /* pointer to serial xmit routine    */
    };
```

An Explanation of MAX80.C   The only difference between this module and that for KAYPRO is the initialization of the function pointer with peek and poke instead of inport and outport. If your compiler provides peek and poke functions, substitute them for the ones shown here, but be certain that the order of the poke arguments is the same.

Memory-Mapped UARTs in Segmented Memory

It is improbable that a memory-mapped system exists that is based upon the Intel 8086 family, which employs segmented addressing. Indeed, even if segmented memory were not an impediment, the addressing modes of the 8086 IN and OUT assembler instructions are so flexible, it is difficult to think of a motivation for designing a memory-mapped UART. Even if such a design were desirable, it could not be implemented in the Small memory model, where pointers are representable with only 16 bits; in other words, *all* data is assumed to lie inside the C program's 64K DATA segment. Since memory dedicated to hardware locations always lies outside the program, pointers to a UART require 32 bits of storage.

Conclusion

Although this ends our formal discussion of portability, a concern for generality and its attendant hope of portability should always be present during program design. In future chapters, we'll see how this philosophy pays great dividends. In particular, we'll be able to write complicated programs that know nothing about the hardware on which they run. In Chapter 18, for example, we'll add an XMODEM supervised file transfer function to the *TERM* program we began in Chapter 9.

11

Timing Functions

The subject of software portability begun in the last chapter leads naturally to the unpleasant subject of system timing. As we develop our libraries, we will frequently be faced with decisions about timing. How long should a function wait for a byte to arrive before giving up? How long after sending a smart-modem command must a function wait for the smart modem's response? Before we can expect functions to deal with timing considerations such as these, we must first write a few lower-level timing functions.

Types of Timing Functions

Our subsequent high-level functions require two distinct types of timing functions, each with its own special requirements—delays and waits.

Time Delays

A delay routine is merely a calibrated time waster. Fixed delays of various durations are frequently required to provide a "set-up time" for another device.

Interbyte Delay

In a quest for faster communications, we hope for ever faster modems, and often write assembly language code to speed up time-hungry functions. As we saw in Chapter 4, however, sometimes we are required to slow down the communications rate by limiting the maximum rate at which bytes are transmitted. Many systems, especially multi-user dial-up systems, expect bytes to be generated by a human typist (at the rate of a few hundred bytes per *minute*). If bytes arrive much faster than this *finger rate*, the system's input buffer may be overrun and data lost. Similarly, intelligent modems often cannot process commands at their full data rate, so an *interbyte delay* must be employed whenever the modem is addressed. The most straightforward way to achieve interbyte delay is to insert a calibrated delay before each byte is transmitted.

Interline Delay

Many systems use discrete *hardware* input buffers to collect incoming characters. When a line terminator (a Carriage Return, for example) is entered, the buffer generates an interrupt to the computer, which then fetches the data from the hardware buffer. While this use of a separate hardware buffer certainly improves the overall efficiency of the system, there is one common problem. If the time required to empty the buffer exceeds the time between characters, the first few inbound characters immediately after the line terminator are lost and the system is said to "drop characters." This problem does not occur as long as data is entered at the finger rate, but during computerized transmission, there is (ideally) *no* delay between characters. When electronically uploading data at 1200 baud into a finger-rate buffer, however, five or six characters can be lost. It is the responsibility of the transmitting software to introduce a slight pause after transmitting a line terminator. An *interline* delay of one or two tenths of a second is usually sufficient to allow the host computer to service its input buffer.

Timeout Functions

The delays just described are totally passive—the wasting of time is the sole objective. In other situations, however, we are concerned not so much with the delay itself, but in making certain that other events happen (or don't happen) within an allotted amount of time. For example, as we discussed in Chapter 4, during a file transfer, we must deal with the possibility that an anticipated byte will never arrive. To protect against this possibility, we require a byte-fetching routine that waits only a *specified* time before returning. On the opposite side of this coin, we also occasionally need to know when a certain time has elapsed *without* characters arriving.

System Timers and Timekeeping

The simplest way to measure the passage of time is by causing the processor to perform a few irrelevant instructions:

```
for (i = MAGIC_NUMBER; i > 0; --i)   /* do nothing */
    ;
```

Although such a loop generates a more or less *predictable* delay, the actual time elapsed depends upon three factors: (1) the assembly code generated by your compiler, (2) the number of system interrupts that "steal" processor time during the loop, and, of course, (3) the processor speed. If any of these three factors is changed, the constant MAGIC_NUMBER has to be adjusted in order to maintain the timing interval. In other words, this sort of delay routine is inherently non-portable.

The System Metronome

This problem of portability can be solved only with an *external* temporal standard against which software can judge the passage of time. We refer to this standard as the system *timekeeper*, which comprises three parts:

1. The *metronome*'s sole function is to generate a precise timing interval. Metronomes are implemented in a variety of ways, but a common technique employs a counter/timer IC (such as the Intel 8253 or Zilog CTC) to divide the output of a crystal oscillator by a predetermined count. At the start of a timing cycle, a register in the counter/timer is loaded with a predetermined count. Each oscillator pulse then decrements the counter register, finally setting a flag in the counter/timer when the counting register reaches 0. The counter/timer then (optionally) automatically reloads the count value and recommences the counting sequence, thus producing a pulse every F/N seconds where F is the frequency of the oscillator and N is the number loaded into the down-counter.

2. The *chronometer* circuitry translates the precise timing intervals generated by the metronome into conventional time intervals of hours, minutes, seconds, and fractions of seconds. Notice that the *chronometer* does not necessarily keep the actual time of day—it begins counting at 0:00:00 (usually defined as midnight) when the system is powered up.

3. The *time of day* clock (or ''real-time clock,'' as it is sometimes naively called) is a hardware device that maintains sidereal (''real'') time. This device, which is powered by a battery when the computer is not powered on, is used to synchronize (set) the system chronometer during system power-up.

The Metronome's Software Interface

When a system metronome exists, software can measure the passage of time merely by polling the timer directly.[1] Assuming that the hypothetical function `timerstat` returns 0 if the counter has expired, a delay loop can now be written:

```
while (timerstat() )
    ;
```

A more elegant approach to timing employs system interrupts. Here, the expiration of the timer count generates an interrupt whose service routine supports the chronographic functions. For example, each metronome interrupt increments a reserved memory cell, thus supplying to the chronometer a cumulative count of timing intervals from which can be calculated hours, minutes, and seconds. In this scheme, software can monitor the activities of the metronome simply by watching the cumulative count in memory instead of polling the timer directly. The IBM PC, described below, uses this structure.

Although a system metronome makes it possible to write timing functions that are independent of both compiler and processor speed, it does little to improve portability. Even if systems contain metronomes (most do nowadays), they may use different hardware or different timing intervals. Some may be accessed through RAM, others through an I/O port. Some generate a system interrupt when the counter expires, while others are not integrated into the system interrupt structure at all. This absence of a standardized interval timing means that timing functions

---

[1]On the 8253 timer/counter, the count is monitored by actually reading the count register. But not all timer chips provide a way to examine the count in progress. On the CTC, for example, unless the *output* of the timer is reported through a memory or port address, the expiration of the timer must be reported with a system interrupt. Polling is not reliable on systems that use timer interrupts—the interrupt service routine may reset the counter before it can be detected through polling.

written for one system metronome probably will not run on another. This is not to say the cause is totally lost, however. By careful design, we can minimize the effect of system timing differences on our higher-level functions.

Designing a "Virtual" Timing System

Before we worry about resolving problems arising from inadequacies in the timing hardware, we will first make a wish list for the *ideal* timing function. A timing function has only two inherent attributes: accuracy and *resolution*. Accuracy is fairly straightforward: how well does the function measure time? The second attribute, resolution, is a bit more complicated. Here we define timing resolution (sometimes also called *granularity*) to be the "native" interval of the system metronome. For example, the best resolution that can be derived from a system metronome that ticks 1000 times per second is $\pm$ 1 msec (.001 second).

The ideal function is, of course, 100 percent accurate and resolves time intervals down to a single processor clock cycle. But, practically speaking, asynchronous I/O has much more modest requirements. Keeping in mind that the critical aspect of timing—bit timing—is handled by UARTs and other hardware devices, our requirements are really quite modest. Although we might *wish* for a timing resolution of 1 msec, the metronomes used in the popular micros are not usually that fast.

The timing interval derived from a 60 Hz metronome—17 msecs—is a logical (and historically popular) choice, but before we decide, let's see how this suits the most popular microcomputer in the market, the IBM PC.

Timing Routines for the IBM PC

The IBM PC/XT/AT all contain a metronome and a chronograph, but only the AT contains a built-in time-of-day clock as standard equipment. The metronome is an Intel 8253 counter/timer IC, which divides a 1,193,180 MHz crystal oscillator by 65536, yielding a timing interval of .0549255 seconds (a frequency of 18.206482 Hz). If this seems like a strange choice of intervals, consider that almost exactly 64K of these intervals occur in one hour. The expiration of the count in the 8253 generates an interrupt (Type 8) whose service routine (interrupt handler) increments a word in memory referred to as TIMER_LO. When TIMER_LO overflows every hour, another word, TIMER_HI is incremented. At any instant, therefore, TIMER_HI contains the hours since the system was started and TIMER_LO contains the number of 18.2-second intervals, or *timer ticks*, that have occurred. TIMER_LO is located at 0000:046CH and TIMER_HI at 0000:046EH.

Now and for the foreseeable future, it is probably safe to design software around the IBM PC's 55 msec metronome. The limitation of 55 msecs is more apparent than real; as we will soon see, there are few situations that require even this degree of resolution. Therefore, the timing arguments in our functions will be expressed in 55 msec increments which, to simplify discussion and calculation, we will treat as an even 50 msecs. We call this interval—20 to the second—a "tick-second," or *Tsec* for short.

Having decided to design our system's timing resolution around the Tsec, have we not abandoned all hope of portability? How can we accommodate other popular computers that, though not IBM compatible, none the less represent a lucrative market? The solution to these problems is not difficult if we assume that future popular computers will not employ a *longer* timing interval than one Tsec. (Since the IBM PC's use of 55 msecs has generated so much grumbling, this seems a safe assumption.) The existence of a shorter metronomic interval, therefore, makes it easy to compose functions that measure time in units of Tsecs. Despite our choice of the Tsec as a timing standard for our high-level functions, however, the details of reading the metronome are sufficiently different to deserve classification as level-0 functions, which must be rewritten for each computer. Figure 11-1 shows the delay for the *IBMPC.C*, the most basic of the three timing functions that we will compose in this chapter.

A Level-0 Timing Function ('delay')

It is important to notice that this function name does not begin with the usual "s_". This means that it does *not* require an SIO pointer in its argument list and may, in fact, be added to your general IBM PC library.

Figure 11-1   The delay function: a calibrated time-waster for the IBM PC.

FUNCTION NAME: delay
LEVEL: 0
LIBRARY: *IBMPC.C*
DESCRIPTION: Does nothing for the number of Tsecs passed in the argument.
OTHER MODULES: peekw: returns the word at offset:segment.
RETURNS: void
COMMENTS: The system interval is defined as 1 Tsec (about 50 msecs).

```
#define  TIMER_LO 0x46C

void delay(tsecs)
unsigned tsecs;
{
     unsigned tickref;
     for (; tsecs > 0; --tsecs)
          {
          tickref = peekw(TIMER_LO, 0);
          while (tickref == peekw(TIMER_LO, 0))
               ;
          }
}
```

An Explanation of 'delay' (IBM PC)   Only one argument is passed to delay: the duration of the desired delay, Tsecs. The idea here is to wait for the value in TIMER_LO to change Tsecs times. At the beginning of the for loop, a call to peek captures the value of TIMER_LO in the variable tickref. Then begins a while loop that continually compares the value of TIMER_LO to the reference value in tickref. On the next metronomic pulse, the two values no longer match, the while breaks, and count in the outer for is decremented. The new value of TIMER_LO is captured in tickref and the cycle repeats until tsecs reaches 0, terminating the function.

As written, the `delay` function doesn't produce accurate results when Tsecs is equal to 1. Can you see why? Suppose that `tickref` is captured an instant before TIMER_LO changes. Now the test,

```
while (tickref == peekw (TIMER_LO,0))
```

is TRUE on the very next iteration of the loop, resulting in an unpredicatably short delay. There is no really satisfactory fix for this problem. You may be tempted to add these two lines

```
tickref = peekw(TIMER_LO, 0);
while (tickref == peekw(TIMER_LO, 0))
    ;
```

at the beginning of the function to guarantee that the Tsec counting begins at the *start* of a metronomic interval. But this "fix" just replaces one form of inaccuracy with another—the latter produces delays too long by exactly the same amount that the former's were too short. Surprisingly, this inaccuracy causes little problem in actual use. For example, when `delay` is used to provide an interbyte delay (say, in transmitting a string), the *average* delay is, in fact, 1 Tsec because the function guarantees that at least one metronomic interval occurs between bytes. Furthermore, when called with an argument significantly larger than 1, the error on the first iteration is "swamped" by the additional iterations.

A Wait-for-Character Function

At the beginning of this section we noted that, in addition to a delay routine, we would need a routine that waits for the arrival of a byte, but returns if none is forthcoming within a specified time limit. For the remainder of this book we will rely heavily upon this *timeout input* function, without which many of the programs cannot be reliably written. In other words, the timeout function is just a safety net intended to prevent the function from waiting forever for an event that never occurs.

We require a timeout function that returns a byte from the SIO or TIMEOUT (-1), if no byte arrives in `tsecs` timing intervals. A first try at this function is likely to lead to this trap:

```
#define TIMEOUT -1

int s_waitch(siop, tsecs)
SIO *siop;
unsigned tsecs;
{
    unsigned tickref;
    int count;
    for (; count > 0; --count)
        {
        if ( (*siop->s_rstat)(siop) )
            return ( (*siop->s_read)(siop));
        tickref = peekw(TIMER_LO, 0);
```

```
        while (tickref == peekw(TIMER_LO, 0))
                ;
            }
    return (TIMEOUT);
}
```

This is much like delay, but with what amounts to a call to s_inchar thrown in between metronomic intervals. Do you see the flaw with this design? Since the function samples the SIO only once per Tsec, it loses bytes that arrive at a rate faster than the metronomic interval of 50 msec. Assuming a 10-bit SDU, this design fails at speeds above about 200 baud!

There is a second design flaw with this approach. Notwithstanding the wait interval, this function should approximate a bare call to s_inchar. But notice what happens if it is called with a tsecs argument of 0: the for loop is never entered and the SIO is never sampled. Thus this design never fetches when called with a wait argument of 0.

Both of these design flaws are rectified in the final version of s_waitch shown in Figure 11-2.

Figure 11-2 The s_waitch function: wait specified Tsecs for an inbound byte before returning.

```
FUNCTION NAME: s_waitch
LEVEL:          0
LIBRARY:        IBMPC.C
DESCRIPTION:    Waits tsecs Tsecs for a serial byte to arrive.
OTHER MODULES: peekw, s_inchar
RETURNS:        int, the byte, if one arrives; otherwise NOT_READY at timeout.
COMMENTS:       The system timing interval is defined as a "Tsec," or about 50 msec.
```

```c
#define  TIMER_LO 0x46C              /* timer located in segment 0      */

int s_waitch(siop, tsecs)
register SIO *siop;
unsigned tsecs;
{
    static unsigned tickref;
    tickref = peekw(TIMER_LO, 0);            /* initialize reference count   */
    while (tsecs > 0)
        {
        if ( (*siop->s_rstat)(siop) ) /* check UART for byte ready        */
            return ( (*siop->s_read)(siop)); /* return byte if ready        */
        if (peekw(TIMER_LO, 0) != tickref)   /* compare new count to old */
            {
            tickref = peekw(TIMER_LO, 0);    /* get new reference ....    */
            tsecs--;                         /* ...and reduce timeout     */
            }
        }
    return (s_inchar(siop));                  /* timed out--no byte received */
}
```

An Explanation of 's_waitch'   In this design, the sampling of the SIO and the testing of TIMER_LO have equal status in the main while loop. The SIO sampling is performed by first testing the receiver status (through the SIO function pointer s_rstat). If a byte is ready, it is returned immediately by a call to the function pointer s_read; otherwise TIMER_LO is checked. When TIMER_LO changes, a new reference value is immediately captured into tickref and the tsec is decremented. The entire process repeats until tsecs reaches 0. When the while loop expires, the result of a final call to s_inchar is returned, thus guaranteeing correct behavior with a wait argument of 0.

"Magic Number" Timing Functions

Since the Kaypro contains no metronome circuit, timing must be achieved by using a timing constant ("magic number") in a do-nothing timing loop.

A 'delay' for KAYPRO.C

Since we have decided to base our library on timing units of Tsecs, we must select a magic number that produces a timing interval of about 50 msecs. The version of delay for *KAYPRO.C* is shown in Figure 11-3.

Figure 11-3   The delay function: a calibrated time-waster for the Kaypro.

FUNCTION NAME: delay
LEVEL: 0
LIBRARY: *KAYPRO.C*
DESCRIPTION: Waits for a serial byte to arrive for tsecs system timing intervals.
OTHER MODULES: None
RETURNS: void
COMMENTS: In the absence of a system metronome, timing is by means of a do-nothing loop.
                MAGIC_1 is adjusted experimentally to produce a timing interval of 1 "Tsec," or
                about 50 msec.

```
#define  MAGIC_1 575

void delay(tsecs)
unsigned tsecs;
{
    unsigned i;
    for (; tsecs > 0; --tsecs)
        for (i = MAGIC_1; i > 0 ; --i)      /* do nothing */
            ;
}
```

An Explanation of 'delay'   How is the value of the magic number constant to be gleaned? By the inelegant method of trial and error—by plugging in experimental values for MAGIC_1, calling the function with an argument that produces a delay of several seconds, then timing it with a stopwatch. The value required for the Kaypro is approximately 575. More recent Kaypros run faster and this number has to be reduced. Remember, these values are different for different compilers.

An 's_waitch' for KAYPRO.C

The wait-for-character function for *KAYPRO.C* in Figure 11-4 is similar in structure to the basic timing function `delay`.

Figure 11-4 The `s_waitch` function: a calibrated character timeout function for the Kaypro.

FUNCTION NAME: s_waitch
LEVEL: 0
LIBRARY: *KAYPRO.C*
DESCRIPTION: Waits for a serial byte to arrive for `tsecs` system timing intervals.
RETURNS: `int`, the byte if one arrives; otherwise NOT_READY at timeout.
COMMENTS: In the absence of a system metronome, timing is by means of a do-nothing loop.
                `MAGIC_2` is adjusted experimentally to produce a timing interval of 1 "Tsec," or about 50 msec.

```
int s_waitch(siop, tsecs)
SIO *siop;
unsigned tsecs;
{
    unsigned i;
    for (; tsecs > 0; --tsecs)
        for (i = MAGIC_2; i > 0; --i)
            if ( (*siop->s_rstat)(siop) )       /* check UART for byte ready  */
                return ( (*siop->s_read)(siop));   /* return byte if ready */
    return (s_inchar(siop));                      /* timeout              */
}
```

An Explanation of 's_waitch' The `for` loop consists entirely of sampling the SIO for a received byte and returning immediately if one is ready. When the `while` loop expires, the SIO is sampled one final time. Note that this function uses a different constant than its sister function `delay`. This new constant, `MAGIC_2`, is substantially smaller, to account for the time spent in polling the SIO. If you have difficulty achieving accuracy by adjusting the value of `MAGIC_2`, try experimenting with various types of storage classes. Declaring `i` to be `static` produces slight changes in timing, while declaring `siop` to be `register` produces relatively large changes (if your compiler supports the `register` storage class).

Manifest Constants for Timing Arguments

Because our timing interval of 50 msecs is not expressed in even decade values (1, .1, etc.), the meaning of the arguments to delay and s_waitch is not obvious. For example, it is not readily apparent that this call produces a 1-second delay:

```
delay(18);
```

To make the code more readable, we can define constants to express the most frequently used time intervals. Place the constants shown in Figure 11-5 in the header *SIODEF.H*. The figures in the comments show the decimal values before roundoff.

Figure 11-5 Manifest decimal constants for timing arguments.

```
#define _0_SEC_05      1       /* 50  ms */
#define _0_SEC_1       2       /* 1.8     */
#define _0_SEC_15      3       /* 150 ms */
#define _0_SEC_2       4       /* 3.6     */
#define _0_SEC_25      5       /* 250 ms */
#define _0_SEC_3       6       /* 5.5     */
#define _0_SEC_4       7       /* 7.3     */
#define _0_SEC_5       9       /* 9.1     */
#define _0_SEC_6      11       /* 11.9    */
#define _0_SEC_7      13       /* 12.7    */
#define _0_SEC_8      15       /* 14.6    */
#define _0_SEC_9      16       /* 16.4    */
#define _1_SEC_0      18       /* 18.2    */
```

These constant names follow a simple convention: the string ''_SEC_'' stands for a decimal point. For example, 0_SEC_4 represents four-tenths of a second, and 1_SEC_0 is one second. Where the round-off error in the tenth-second constants is unacceptable, you can create more accurate hundreth-second constants—for example, 0_SEC_05 and 0_SEC_15 to represent 50 and 150 msecs, respectively.

These constants can be compounded to produce longer delays. For example, use

```
delay(1_SEC_0 + 0_SEC_5);
```

for a one and one-half second delay, or

```
delay(1_SEC_0 * 5);
```

to produce a delay of five seconds.

A UART Trash Collector

We mentioned at the beginning of this chapter that occasionally we desire to wait not for a character to arrive, but for one *not* to arrive. Consider the situation in which you wish to send commands to a smart modem, then wait for the modem's acknowledgment (i.e., OK). Now, if the smart modem happens to be in the command-echo mode, after each command several of the characters from the commands echoed remain in your UART's receiver buffer. When you read the SIO for the modem's reply, these characters are included. In effect, you read not only the reply, but part of the command as well, making it more difficult to interpret the modem's response. To solve the problem, we require a function that continually reads bytes from the SIO until no more are received. In addition, we must be able to limit the maximum number of bytes read. This feature protects us if the function is called during a never-ending input stream. Figure 11-6 shows such a function, s_clrsio.

Figure 11-6   A function to clear trash from the UART.

FUNCTION NAME: s_clrsio
LEVEL: 3
LIBRARY: *SIO.LIB*
DESCRIPTION: Clears numbytes bytes from UART's receive buffers.
OTHER MODULES: s_waitch
RETURNS: TIMEOUT (-1) if no bytes received, or 0 after numbytes bytes are received.
COMMENTS: To avoid inaccuracies inherent in the timing functions, a minimum delay of _0_SEC_1 must be used.

```
#define TIMEOUT -1                          /**** FOR SIODEF.H ****/


int s_clrsio(siop, numbytes)
SIO *siop;
unsigned numbytes;
{
    for (; numbytes > 0; --numbytes)
        if (s_waitch(siop, _0_SEC_1) == TIMEOUT)
            return (TIMEOUT);
    return (0);
}
```

An Explanation of 's_clrsio'   This function simply calls s_waitch the specified number of times, then returns 0 to signal that the number of bytes requested were read. If, however, no bytes arrive in _0_SEC_1 (one-tenth) seconds, the function *immediately* returns -1. These return values enable the calling function to ascertain the success of the operation.

In our discussion of delay, we noted the inherent inaccuracy of metronome-based functions when called with a timing argument equal to one timing interval. Because the duration of the first "tick" is unpredictable, an argument of *at least* two timing intervals is necessary to *guarantee* a delay one timing interval in duration.

A Test Program for the Timing Functions

Figure 11-7 shows a simple program to verify that the timing functions are functioning correctly. The constant definition TIMEOUT should now be added to *SIODEF.H*.

Figure 11-7   A simple program to test the timing functions.

PROGRAM TITLE: *TIMETEST*
SYNTAX: TIMETEST
DESCRIPTION: Tests timing functions `delay` and `s_waitch`

```
#include "stdio.h"
#include "siodef.h"


#define TIMEOUT  -1

main()
{
     extern SIO typeAsio;
     SIO *siop = &typeAsio;
     if (s_clrsio(siop, 10) == 0)
          exit(puts("Can't clear SIO for test.\007"));
     puts("Start byte wait.");
     if( s_waitch(siop, 10 * _1_SEC_0) == TIMEOUT)
          puts("No byte.");
     else
          puts("Found byte.");
     puts("Start timeout.");
     delay(10 * _1_SEC_0);
     puts("End timeout test.");
}
```

Conclusion

The two level-0 timing functions in this chapter, `delay` and `s_waitch`, though simple, form the heart of almost every other function we will compose. It is now time to plunge into the deepest, murkiest of intellectual pools—the problem of writing portable functions to deal with baud rate and data format.

12

Functions for Baud Rate and Data Format

In previous programming chapters, we have discussed asynchronous serial I/O in relatively abstract terms. That is, we have always assumed that inbound and outbound bytes are correctly formed and are at the correct baud rate. In this chapter we will develop the data structures and functions necessary to set the baud rate and to vary all elements of the SDU—data length, parity, and the number of stop bits.

There is nothing particularly glamorous about these functions. In fact, at their lowest level, such functions always consist largely of unromantic programming chores such as ORing, ANDing, and shifting. Because such chores are inherently dependent upon the system hardware, especially the UARTs, they tend to be viewed with a measure of dread by programmers, who see writing new serial "drivers" as a never-ending job. Nothing can eliminate the apprehension associated with the activity, but we can simplify it (by orders of magnitude) while simultaneously decreasing the time required and increasing the success rate.

It is only fair to warn you that this is a difficult chapter. Knowing this in advance, you should probably read it once just to gain an idea of its scope, then work, or perhaps more accurately, *hack*, your way through the code line by line. Like many of the programming chapters, this one is not designed for ingestion at a single session. As you proceed, take consolation in the knowledge that the methods and code described in this chapter have successfully tamed about thirty different UARTs on radically different systems. The great promise of this chapter, then, is that its methods will reduce from hours (or days!) to minutes the time required to "port" your software to new systems or new serial hardware. In short, by careful design and a dogged determination to "Think General!" we can bring some degree of generality and portability to an area of programming usually considered to be hopelessly hardware-dependent.

Design Goals

The primary goal of this chapter is to compose a library of functions that enable us to manipulate the UART's data format and baud rate using humane arguments and syntax such as `setbaud(300)` or `setparity(NONE)`. As always, level-3 functions such as these cannot stand alone because, by definition, they do not address the UART directly. Instead, they invoke level-2 functions, which transform the human language arguments to abstract, or logical, arguments. The level-2 functions in turn pass these logical arguments to level-1 functions where they are actually translated into reads and writes of the *physical* UART.

Level-3 functions are always simple to design—their names, arguments, and syntax are chosen for clarity and simplicity. Level-1 functions are also relatively easy to design, because the UART they address so rigidly dictates their structure. The level-2 functions present the most interesting and difficult challenge, because they must decode the "natural" syntax of the level-3 functions into abstract commands, then invoke the level-1 functions to accomplish the correct physical command.

In a real sense, level-2 functions are the interface between programmer and hardware. If this interface is correctly designed, neither side is aware of the other. To achieve generality and portability, these functions must address only the *conceptual* UART ("uartness," if you will) and make as few assumptions as possible about real UARTs.

Because of their centrality in the overall library design, and because UART functions do not lend themselves easily to abstract expression, most of our effort will go into the design of a *virtual UART*—an intellectual representation with no exact counterpart in reality. Aside from the intellectual difficulty involved in inventing a virtual device interface for the UART, there are several practical and philosophical questions to consider.

User Criteria

Users become quite annoyed when application programs disturb their primary interface with the computer. Programs that change the cursor's shape but terminate without restoring it are an obvious example. Users find the presence of an unfamiliar cursor so disturbing that they often reboot the computer to restore the "correct" one. Because the cause of and remedy for the uninvited change in cursor shape is usually obvious, such cosmetic problems are merely annoying. Unsolicited alteration of the configuration of a serial port by a program, however, is far more serious for several reasons. First, its effects are more profound—as far as the user is concerned, an important part of the system no longer functions correctly. Second, unlike the altered cursor shape, the victim may not associate the running of a specific program (perhaps hours earlier) with the mysterious change in behavior of his printer or modem. Finally, the remedy is not necessarily obvious.

If these considerations seem too philosophical let's look at a real example. In Chapter 5, we pointed out that many UARTs employ automatic transmitter handshaking with one of the RS-232 control inputs. Although the Z80SIO, one of the UARTs we are examining in detail, employs this handshaking feature, it also allows the programmer to disable it. Systems designed around the Z80SIO often anticipate that it will drive a serial printer. (The Z80SIO's automatic CTS handshaking is irresistible to software designers, because it eliminates the need to code printer handshaking into the operating system itself.) After struggling to build a proper RS-232 printer cable, the user naturally takes this handshaking for granted. Now suppose that after successfully using his printer, the user calls up a favorite modem program. As we have pointed out, modem applications do not require this form of hardware handshaking. These programs, especially those designed to work with smart modems, eschew RS-232 handshaking in favor of software codes transmitted over a three-wire cable (see Figure 5-18). In order to use this minimum cable, such programs invariably disable the Z80SIO's CTS/transmitter and DCD/receiver handshaking. (Otherwise, a custom RS-232 cable would be necessary to trick the Z80SIO's handshaking.) Unfortunately, when the modem program exits, it may fail to restore the Z80SIO's automatic handshaking. When the printer is next used, the Z80SIO's transmitter no longer responds to an inhibited CTS, the printer's input buffer is quickly overrun, and printer output is garbled.

If this scene were acted out frequently enough, we would expect the user to figure out the source of the printer malfunction. There is, in his mind at least, no manifest connection between running the modem software and the malfunctioning printer. The moral of this fiction is simple: considerable thought should go into the design of functions that manipulate important interfaces. When your software alters the interface in any way, it should, whenever possible, restore it to its original condition. In other words, always apply the maxim "Leave it as you find it." The functions in this chapter provide a mechanism to achieve this goal.

General Assumptions

Before discussing the actual design of the library functions, let's outline the characteristics of our virtual UART:

- All UART operations are byte-oriented. That is, they interface with the system data buses 8 bits at a time. No other assumptions are made about the size or architecture of the data bus.
- All writable registers may be write-only; that is, their contents may not be recoverable.
- The master clock generator is external to the UART.
- The clocking factor is at least 16, but may be programmable.
- Sixteen baud rates from 50 to 19,200 are available.
- The baud rate is under program control. The baud rates for both transmitter and receiver are *simultaneously* programmed by writing two 1-byte divisors to one or more registers.
- The following data format settings are supported:

STOP BITS	1, 1½, and 2
PARITY	NONE, ODD, EVEN, MARK, SPACE
DATA LENGTH	5 through 8

- Data format is manipulated by writing to bit-mapped, *write-only* registers. One set of parameters governs both transmitted and received data.
- Data format parameters are not necessarily represented in the same register. For example, the bits governing parity may be in a different register than those for governing the number of stop bits.
- The following RS-232 outputs are supported: RTS, DTR, and two general-purpose outputs, GPO1 and GPO2.
- The following RS-232 inputs are supported: CTS, DSR, DCD, RI, and two general-purpose inputs, GPI1 and GPI2.
- The transmitter can be forced into a SPACE state indefinitely for the purposes of creating a BREAK condition.
- Transmitter and receiver handshaking exists on the CTS and DCD RS-232 lines respectively.
- Transmitter and receiver sections may be separately enabled and disabled.

No error detection?

You may be surprised (or even shocked) by the conspicuous absence of error detection in our virtual UART. Indeed, with the exception of the BREAK, none of the errors discussed in Chapter 6 are supported by our virtual UART. This omission stems from a somewhat radical conviction (see Chapter 3) that serialization error detection is not very important in real life. If you disagree or if you have a special need to detect serialization errors, you may easily add the functions later.

This remainder of this chapter is organized into six parts:

1. "Virtual" registers
2. Data format level-2 and -3 functions
3. Data format level-0 and -1 objects for the Z80SIO (Kaypro)
4. Baud rate level-2 and -3 functions
5. Baud rate level-0 and -1 objects for the Z80SIO (Kaypro)
6. Baud rate and data format level-0 and -1 objects for the 8250 (IBM PC)
7. Configuration and restoration of the SIO
8. Enhancements to *TERM*

The Virtual Register

Some of the characteristics of the virtual UART clearly influence the library design more than others. The stipulation that all registers are write-only is perhaps the most onerous. If the UART's registers were read/write we could manipulate them as follows:

1. Fetch UART register's current bit pattern.
2. Reset selected bits with an OR.
3. Apply desired bit pattern with an AND.
4. Write new bit pattern back to the register.

Without the ability to read these registers and store their contents, however, we obviously cannot use this approach. The solution to this problem is straightforward: for each writable register in the *physical* UART, we maintain a corresponding *virtual register* in RAM. That is, each physical UART register has an identical counterpart in memory. In this scheme, a level-2 function manipulates the bit pattern of a virtual register, then passes the contents of the virtual register to a level-1 function, which is responsible for "updating" the corresponding registers in the physical UART:

1. Reset selected bits in the virtual register.
2. Apply new bit pattern to the virtual register.

3. Call a level-1 function to write the virtual register to the physical UART.

Let's see how this process works by examining Figure 12-1, a first-draft level-2 function to set the parity.

Figure 12-1   Level-2 function to set parity.

```
FUNCTION NAME:  chngparity
LEVEL:          2
LIBRARY:        (hypothetical)
DESCRIPTION:    Set parity.
OTHER MODULES:  _chngparity (also hypothetical)
RETURNS:        int
COMMENTS:       Constant values are in SIODEF.H and Z80SIO.H
```

```c
#include "siodef.h"
#include "z80sio.h"

BYTE vreg4 = 0x45;                      /* virtual register number 4    */

int chngparity(paritycode)              /* paritycode is 0 - 2          */
int paritycode;
{
    int ormask = 0;

    vreg4 &= PARITYMASK;        /* clear parity bits in virtual register */
        switch (paritycode)     /* derive correct OR mask to set bits    */
            {
            case NONE:
                ormask = NONE_MASK;
                break;
            case ODD:
                ormask = ODD_MASK;
                break;
            case EVEN:
                ormask = EVEN_MASK;
                break;
            default:
                ormask = -1;                /* parity value out of range    */
                break;
            }
    if (ormask != -1)
        {
        vreg4 |= ormask;        /* set parity bits in virtual register   */
        _chngparity(vreg4);     /* call level-1 function to write to UART */
        }
    return(ormask != -1);
}
```

305

An Explanation of 'chngparity' This function, like all the "virtual" functions in this book, expects its argument to be an *integer* code—0 for NONE, 1 for ODD, and so forth; these constants, as well as a few general constant definitions that we will need in the next few chapters, are given in Figure 12-2. These system-wide constants must reside in *SIODEF.H*.

Figure 12-2 System-wide constants and constant definitions.

General Constants for SIODEF.H

```
#define NUMMASKS      5        /* number elements in "setmask" array    */
#define NUMBAUDS     16        /* number of baud rates supported        */

#define VIRGIN       -2        /* dummy initializer (must be < -1)      */
#define SUPPLIED      0        /* dummy initializer (set during init)   */
#define NA            0        /* dummy initializer ("not  applicable") */
```

Manifest Constants for Columns in the Virtual Register Array

```
#define VIR           0
#define USR           1
```

Data Format Constants

```
/* parity constants */    /* stop bits constants */   /* data len constants */
#define NONE      0        #define STOP1       0        #define DL5      0
#define ODD       1        #define STOP1_5     1        #define DL6      1
#define EVEN      2        #define STOP2       2        #define DL7      2
#define MARK      3                                     #define DL8      3
#define SPACE     4
```

Return Code Constants

```
/* Error codes returned by SIO functions */
#define OR_ARG   1                /* Argument out of range   */
#define BAD_FCN  2                /* Function not supported */
#define BAD_ARG  3                /* Argument not supported */
#define BAD_PORT 4                /* Illegal device number   */
#define NO_PORT  5                /* Device not installed    */
#define NO_SIO   6                /* No SIO declared         */
#define OPEN_NOW 7                /* Device already open     */
#define NO_CLOSE 8                /* No such device open     */
#define KEY_CAN  9                /* aborted from keyboard   */
#define NO_FILE  10               /* file not found          */
```

The call to this hypothetical function is

```
chngparity(EVEN)
```

where EVEN is one of the data format codes from Figure 12-2. The constants PARITYMASK, NONE_MASK, ODD_MASK, and EVEN_MASK define the bit patterns required to produce the desired parity. Because these constants are unique to the UART being addressed, they must reside in the header file for the appropriate UART, in this case *Z80SIO.H*, the values for which are shown in Figure 12-3.

The bits governing parity are cleared by ANDing them with the constant PARITYMASK. The bits are then set to the desired value by ORing them with a constant (e.g., ODD_MASK), whose value is determined by switching on the paritycode argument. Since the Z80SIO's Write Register 4 governs parity, the virtual register is named v_reg4. Once the desired bit pattern has been built in the virtual register, the as yet unwritten level-1 function, _chngparity, writes the virtual register to the UART.

The important thing to notice about this function is that only the virtual register v_reg4, not the Z80SIO's Write Register 4 is manipulated; the binary value ultimately bound for the Z80SIO is first built in vreg4. In short, the level-2 function needs to know nothing about the physical UART—the act of installing the virtual register in the Z80SIO is left to the level-1 function chngparity.

You have doubtless spotted the fatal flaw in this sample function: the mask values and virtual register may be totally different for other UARTs. In other words, it is not really a level-2 function. Because it is valid for only one UART, it would have to be recompiled for every UART supported. We can overcome this problem, however, by rewriting the function to access the masks and the virtual register through structure members.

Figure 12-3 Values for the level-0 file Z80SIO.H.

Parity

PARITYMASK	0xFC	/* 1111 1100 */
NONE_MASK	0x00	
ODD_MASK	0x02	/* 0000 0010 */
EVEN_MASK	0x03	/* 0000 0011 */
MARK_MASK	----	/* Not supported */
SPACE_MASK	----	/* Not supported */

Transmitter Data Length

TxDLMASK	0x9F	/* 1001 1111 */
TxDL5_MASK	0x00	
TxDL6_MASK	0x40	/* 0100 0000 */
TxDL7_MASK	0x20	/* 0010 0000 */
TxDL8_MASK	0x60	/* 0110 0000 */

Stop Bits

STOPMASK	0xF3	/* 1111 0011 */
ONE_MASK	0x04	/* 0000 0100 */
ONE_5_MASK	0x08	/* 0000 1000 */
TWO_MASK	0x0C	/* 0000 1100 */

*Receiver Data Length**

DLMASK	0x3F	/* 0011 1111 */
DL5_MASK	0x00	
DL6_MASK	0x80	/* 1000 0000 */
DL7_MASK	0x40	/* 0100 0000 */
DL8_MASK	0xC0	/* 1100 0000 */

*Recall that the Z80SIO uses separate data length settings for transmit and receive.

Figure 12-3 cont. Values for the level-0 file *Z80SIO.H.*

Manifest Constants for Z80SIO Write Registers

```
#define WR0      0
#define WR1      1
#define WR2      2
#define WR3      3
#define WR4      4
#define WR5      5
#define VBAUDLO  6
#define VBAUDHI  7
```

The Virtual Register Array

Before we modify chngparity, however, let's first declare an array of eight virtual registers—one for each of the Z80SIO's asynchronous write registers and two for the baud rate divisor that we'll need later in the chapter. This array is shown in Figure 12-4.

Figure 12-4 A two-dimensional array of virtual registers.

ARRAY NAME: vregA
TYPE: 8×2 array of BYTE.
LEVEL: 0
LIBRARY: *KAYPRO.C*
DESCRIPTION: "Virtual" UART registers—array members used to simulate read/write UART registers.
COMMENTS: The left column (VIR) holds the values to which the UART registers are initialized; the right column is initialized to 0s for now. Two additional registers are required for the high- and low-order bytes of the baud rate divisor.

```
BYTE vregA[8][2] =                          /* "virtual" registers VIR/USR */
    {
/*  VIR ------ USR  */
    {0x18,  0},
    {0,     0},
    {0,     0},
    {0xC1,  0},
    {0x45,  0},
    {0xEA,  0},
    {0,     0},                             /* for baud rate */
    {0,     0},                             /* for baud rate */
    };
```

An Explanation of 'v_regA'   There is one small surprise in this declaration—the virtual register array is *two dimensional*. Although we will not need the second dimension of this array until later in the chapter (where it stores the "state of the UART" for later restoration), its introduction now will familiarize you with the syntax associated with its usage. The initialized values in the left column are, for tutorial convenience, assumed to be the current values of the corresponding Z80SIO write registers; just how this correspondence between the virtual array and the physical UART is achieved will be explained later. In the meantime, just assume that an as yet unnamed function was called to guarantee that the Z80SIO's physical write registers have been initialized with the values shown.

Syntax with Two-Dimension Array

You will notice that the two columns in `v_regA` are labeled VIR ("virtual") and USR ("user"). These two constants, defined in Figure 12-2 as 0 and 1 respectively, make the references to virtual registers more obvious. For example, to address cell 4,0 (the one initialized to 45H), we write

```
v_regA[4][VIR]
```

To manifest the meaning more clearly, virtual registers are also given constant names for use in initialization and in level-1 calls. For instance, for the Z80SIO, the same cell can be addressed as

```
vregA[WR4][VIR]
```

which reminds us that we are addressing the virtual register corresponding to the Z80SIO's Write Register 4.

A General Structure for Bit Manipulation ('vregbits_')

With the virtual register array now declared, we could easily define a "parity" structure. But we would eventually also have to define "stopbits" and "data length" structures. In truth, we require a *general* structure that will hold the information necessary to impose selected bit patterns on *any* virtual register. To emphasize this generality, then, we will henceforth refer to `struct regbits`, shown in Figure 12-5. Our "parity" structure will merely be an instance of this structure.

Figure 12-5   `vregbits_`: a structure for virtual register manipulation.

STRUCT DEF: `vregbits_`
HEADER FILE: *SIODEF.H*
DESCRIPTION: General structure for virtual register manipulation.

Figure 12-5 cont. `vregbits_`: a structure for virtual register manipulation.

```
struct vregbits_
    {
    BYTE        resetmask;              /* AND mask apply to virtual register */
    short       setmask[NUMMASKS];      /* array of OR masks for each setting */
    BYTE        vregnum;                /* virtual register number (row)       */
    int         offset;                 /* offset of physical uart register    */
    BYTE        now;                    /* code for current value              */
    BYTE        start;                  /* code to use at initialization       */
    struct      vregbits *next;         /* pointer to next vregbits structure  */
    };
```

The four highlighted structure members contain all the information needed by a level-2 function:

resetmask   This is the AND mask for clearing selected bits in the virtual register.

setmask[ ]   Since our virtual UART supports five parity settings—NONE, EVEN, ODD, MARK, and SPACE—we require a "five-element" array to hold the OR mask for each desired bit pattern. Since several functions need to know the size of this array, a constant is used to define NUMMASKS. In a moment, we'll explain why this is declared to be an array of short despite our assumption that UART registers are only 8 bits wide.

vregnum   This is the parity register's position (i.e., its *rank*) in the virtual register array.

offset   This is the offset (from uart_base) of the UART port controlling this function. For example, if we declare a vregbits_ to control, say, parity, offset will contain the offset of the UART register that controls parity. This value will be employed by the level-1 routine to address the correct UART register.

The remaining three members are defined now, but will be discussed later as they arise:

now   When the contents of a virtual register are changed, the code for its current rank in the setmask array is placed here for later reference. If, for example, EVEN parity is selected, 2 is stored in this member.

start   This is the setting used during initialization of the SIO (covered later in this chapter). It is expressed as a rank in the setmask array. For instance, 0 in this member tells the initialization function to set the SIO to 1 stop bit.

next   This pointer enables us to "attach" more than one vregbits_ structure to a single UART function by creating a linked list in which each structure contains a pointer to another vregbits structure. We will discuss this in detail later.

An instance of the vregbits_ structure for controlling parity can now be declared in *KAYPRO.C*. This structure, given the tag parityA, is shown in Figure 12-6.

Figure 12-6 `parityA`: a structure for describing parity functions.

STRUCT NAME: `parityA`
TYPE: `struct vregbits_`
LEVEL: *0*
FILE: *KAYPRO.C*
DESCRIPTION: Structure for describing parity functions.
COMMENTS: PARITYMASK is defined in *SIODEF.H*, other masks in *Z80SIO.H*. Unused elements of the
            `setmask` array must be initialized to −1.

```
struct vregbits_ parityA =
    {
    PARITYMASK,                              /* AND mask to apply            */
    {NONE_MASK, ODD_MASK, EVEN_MASK, -1 , -1 },  /* array of OR masks        */
    WR4,                                     /* virtual register number      */
    SP_OFF,                                  /* offset of Z80SIO's ctrl/stat port */
    SUPPLIED,                                /* don't bother to initialize this */
    NONE,                                    /* use this value for SIO config. */
    NIL                                      /* the only registers for parity */
    };
```

This declaration initializes the `resetmask` and `setmask` members from the constant values contained in *Z80SIO.H*. We can now explain why the `setmask` array is declared as `short int` instead of BYTE: each element must be able to hold a value of −1. Since the Z80SIO does not support MARK and SPACE parity, the fourth and fifth elements of the `setmask` array are initialized to the *sentinel* value of −1. This enables level-2 functions to detect requests for unsupported settings. We will use this technique for marking the ends of valid data for the remainder of this book.

Since the Z80SIO's parity bits reside in Write Register 4, the virtual register number (`vregnum`) is set to WR[4]. Because of the Z80SIO's addressing scheme, the offset of the physical register is the same as that of the Kaypro's control/status port—`SP_OFF`.

Notice that the `now` member is assigned the manifest constant SUPPLIED to remind you that no initialization is necessary. The `start` member is set for NO parity by using the NONE rank code from *SIODEF.H*.

The name of the structure is `parityA`. Although the Kaypro has only one serial port (and another cannot easily be added), we employ this nomenclature to leave the door open for using the same declarations in other Kaypro or Kaypro-compatible computers that support multiple serial ports (the Kaypro 10, for example).

Because all bits required to set parity on a Z80SIO are in a single register (WR4), the `next` member is initialized to NIL to show that there are no more relevant `vregbits` structures involved.

We are now ready to write a second (but still not final) draft of our level-2 function to change parity. Instead of the name `chngparity`, however, let's use the more general name of `vsetbits` to reflect that it can be used on *any* virtual register. This version merely uses a pointer to a `vregbits_` structure that contains the vital information:

```
vsetbits(p, rank)
struct vregbits_ *p;
int rank;
{
vregA[VIR][p->vregnum] &= p->resetmask;
vregA[VIR][p->vregnum] |= p->setmask[rank];
_vsetbits(vregA[VIR][p->vregnum]);
}
```

The call to this function looks like this:

```
vsetbits(&parityA, ODD);
```

This passes the address of (a pointer to) the `parityA` structure declared and initialized in *KAYPRO.C*. The element of `vreg` (the virtual register array) containing the parity information is described by the `vregnum` member. In this case, `vregA[VIR][p->vregnum]` refers to array element 4, 0 in the `vreg` array. Similarly, the `rank` argument is an index into the `setmask` array, providing the OR mask for the desired bit pattern. Finally, the level-1 function is called upon to perform the actual write to the UART.

Notice that we have changed the name of the still-unwritten level-1 function to `_vsetbits`. We will often employ this parallel nomenclature in the remainder of this book, deriving the name for a level-1 function by prepending an underscore to the name of a level-2 function.

Access Through an 'SIO' Pointer

The passing of a `regbits` structure pointer greatly extends the generality of this function. We now have a level-2 function that is blissfully ignorant of the system hardware: it merely manipulates a cell in the virtual register according to the contents of a `parity` structure. The development of this function now lacks only one step: to rewrite the function in terms of the `SIO`. Our new function must therefore access its virtual registers and data format structures (e.g., `parity`) through a *pointer* to an `SIO`.

Before we rewrite the function, let's first see how this affects the `SIO` definition. We must add the following elements:

- The virtual register array. Since the size of this array varies from one UART to another, the `SIO` does not contain the virtual array itself, but a *pointer* to it.
- The number of elements in the virtual register array
- A *pointer* to a `vregbits_` structure devoted to parity
- A *pointer* to a `vregbits_` structure devoted to stop bits
- A *pointer* to a `vregbits_` structure devoted to data length

If your head is beginning to reel a bit from all the pointers, consider the alternative. If we had placed the actual `regbit_` structures themselves in the `SIO` instead of pointers to them, the syntax for initializing the `SIO` would be incomprehensible.

Figure 12-7 highlights the new items as they appear in the `SIO`.

Figure 12-7   Additions to the SIO to support data format.

STRUCT DEF: SIO
FILE: *SIODEF.H*
DESCRIPTION: Typedef of master structure for defining a serial port.
COMMENTS: Support added for virtual UART and data format.

```
typedef struct
    {
    BYTE     *uart_base;              /* 0   base address of UART          */
    :
    BYTE     (*v_regp)[2];           /* 11  pointer to a 2-dim array of ints */
    int      v_regpsize;             /* 12  length of virtual array       */
    struct   vregbits_ *par;         /* 13  pointer to parity structure   */
    struct   vregbits_ *sb;          /* 14  pointer to stop bit structure */
    struct   vregbits_ *dl;          /* 15  pointer to data length structure */
    } SIO;
```

The pointer to the virtual array is worthy of discussion. Pointers to multidimensional arrays are not very common, so the definition (*v_regp)[2] may seem a bit odd. First, as with pointers to functions, parentheses are required to bind the variable name to the * operator instead of to the array brackets. In other words, without the parentheses, v_regp would be a two-dimensional array of pointers to BYTE. Less obvious, perhaps, is that the *length* of the array (number of rows) is not required in the pointer declaration. As with single-dimension arrays, the first set of brackets may be left blank, because the compiler needs to know only the *width* of the array in order to calculate the correct *scaling* for arithmetic references to its members.

Structures for Stop Bits and Data Length

Let's now look at the declaration of regbit_ structures for stop bits and data length. These are shown in Figure 12-8.

The regbit_ structures stopsA and dlenA contain the relevant information for the Z80SIO: both are addressed through the Z80SIO's "control/status port" at offset SP_OFF, and occupy virtual registers 4 (WR4) and 3 (WR3), respectively.

Figure 12-8   The vregbits_ structure for stop bits and data length.

STRUCT NAME: stopsA, txdlenA, dlenA
TYPE: regbits_
LEVEL: 0
FILE: *KAYPRO.C*
DESCRIPTION: Structures for controlling stop bits and data length.

Figure 12-8 cont. The `vregbits_` structure for stop bits and data length.

```
struct vregbits_ stopsA =
     {
        STOPMASK,                          /* AND mask to apply              */
{ ONE_MASK, ONE_5_MASK, TWO_MASK, -1, -1 }, /* array of OR masks            */
        WR4,                               /* virtual register number        */
        SP_OFF,                            /* offset of Z80SIO's ctrl/stat port */
        SUPPLIED,                          /* don't bother to initialize this */
        STOP1,                             /* use this value for SIO config.  */
        NIL                                /* no more structures for stop bits */
     };

struct vregbits_ txdlenA =               /* for tranmsit only */
     {
        TxDLMASK,
        { TxDL5_MASK, TxDL6_MASK, TxDL7_MASK, TxDL8_MASK, -1 },
        WR5,
        SP_OFF,
        SUPPLIED,
        TxDL8,
        NIL                                /* end of linked list              */
     };

struct vregbits_ dlenA =
     {
        DLMASK,                            /* AND mask to apply               */
        { DL5_MASK, DL6_MASK,DL7_MASK, DL8_MASK, -1 },/* array of OR masks    */
        WR3,                               /* virtual register number         */
        SP_OFF,                            /* offset of Z80SIO's ctrl/stat port */
        SUPPLIED,                          /* don't bother to initialize this */
        DL8,                               /* use this value for SIO config.  */
        &txdlenA                           /* Z80SIO dlen takes two registers */
     };
```

Multiple Register Operations

How do we handle a UART operation that requires more than a single operation on a single register? The last two structures in Figure 12-8 illustrate how a single operation—setting the data length—may involve more than one `v_regbits` structure.

As you recall from Chapter 7, data length for the transmitter and the receiver on the Z80SIO are independently adjustable. Because the bits governing these two settings reside in *different* registers, they cannot be described by a single `vregbits_` structure. The `next` member of the `vregbits_` structure provides the mechanism for describing functions that require *multiple* registers.

Since `next` is declared to be a pointer to another `v_regbits` structure, we can easily form a chain, or linked list of such structures. In Figure 12-8, the `next` member of the `dlen` structure (the one used to initialize the SIO) contains a pointer to the txdlen structure, thus making available the additional information needed to set the transmitter's data length. Its next member, in turn, contains NIL, indicating that it is the *final* structure in the list and that no more v_regbits structures are required to set the data length. Any function that has access to dlen will, through its next member, also have access to txdlen. If this method of list linkage is a bit fuzzy now, it will become clear when we compose our final version of vsetbits, the function that actually manipulates these virtual registers.

With these new data format structures in hand, we can now declare an instance of an SIO named, as always, typeAsio. Figure 12-9 shows this declaration.

Figure 12-9   Initialization of the new SIO members.

'SIO' NAME: typeAsio
FILE: *KAYPRO.C*
DESCRIPTION: Declaration and initialization of the SIO for the Kaypro. Highlighted items support virtual UART and data format.

```
SIO typeAsio =
    {
    PORT1,                      /* base address of UART              */
    :
    v_regA,                     /* pointer to virtual register array */
    8,                          /* number of rows in virtual array   */
    &parityA,                   /* parity structure                  */
    &stopsA,                    /* stop bit structure                */
    &dlenA,                     /* data length structure             */
    :
    };
```

Here, the pointer (v_regp) to the two-dimensional virtual register array is initialized with the address of v_regA, which was declared on page 308. Similarly, the par, sb, and dl vregbits_ pointers are initialized with the address of the parityA, stopsA, and dlenA structures.

Unsupported Virtual Functions

Naturally, not all UARTs support every feature we have designed into our virtual structure. How do we initialize the SIO member if there is no structure declaration for an unsupported function? Since all these new members are pointers, we mark them as unsupported by initializing them to NIL.

List Linkage

Keep in mind these four interrelated facts:

1. The next member of *every* vregbits structure must be initialized.
2. If there is only one structure involved, its next member must be initialized to NIL; otherwise, vsetbits acts upon this uninitialized (random) value and writes garbage at the location indicated by the non-existent next "structure."

3. For the reasons just discussed in (2), the `next` member of the *final* structure in the list MUST be initialized with NIL.

4. The `SIO` must be initialized with a pointer to the *first* structure in a linked list of structures. Using later structures in the list produces incomplete (and often puzzling) results.

'Vsetbits': the Final Version

Let's now look at Figure 12-10, the final version of `vsetbits`, the level-2 function that manipulates the bits in the virtual register. The constant definitions for return codes are from *SIODEF.H* and were given in Figure 12-2.

Figure 12-10 The `vsetbits` function: the final version.

FUNCTION NAME: vsetbits
LEVEL: 2
LIBRARY: *BUOS.LIB*
DESCRIPTION: Builds a new bit pattern in the virtual register in `v_regp` by ANDing and ORing, then calls the level-0 `_setbits` to install that bit pattern in the physical UART's register.
RETURNS: int: 0 if successful; OR_ARG if argument is out of range; BAD_FCN if the function is not supported (SIO pointer is NIL); BAD_ARG if the requested setting is not supported by hardware (mask initialized to −1).
COMMENTS: More than one virtual register may be attached to a function by the linked list of `next` pointers.

```
int vsetbits(siop, rbp, rank)
SIO *siop;
struct vregbits_ *rbp;
BYTE rank;                              /* rank of value to install        */
{
    BYTE tmp;
    if (rbp == NIL)                     /* function not supported in hardware */
        return (BAD_FCN);
    if ( rank >= NUMMASKS)              /* argument range check            */
        return (OR_ARG);
    if (rbp->setmask[rank] == -1)       /* argument not supported in hardware */
        return (BAD_ARG);
    do  {
        siop->v_regp[rbp->vregnum][VIR] &= rbp->resetmask; /* reset bits   */
        tmp = siop->v_regp[rbp->vregnum][VIR] |= rbp->setmask[rank];
        rbp->now = rank;                /* update current table rank       */
        _vsetbits(siop, rbp, tmp);      /* write vreg to the UART           */
        rbp = rbp->next;                /* another structure involved?     */
        } while (rbp != NIL);           /* no, done                        */
    return (0);
}
```

An Explanation of 'vsetbits'   This function requires three arguments:

1. Like all our functions, the first argument is the `SIO` pointer through which all other variables are accessed.

2. A pointer to a `struct vregbits_`. (This may be a pointer to a parity, stop bits, or data length structure.)

3. The code for the desired setting as defined in Figure 12-2. A request for 8 data bits, for example, would require a `rank` argument of 3 (DL8 in *SIODEF.H*).

Error testing is performed immediately upon entry to the function. An error code of BAD_FCN is returned if the structure pointer is NIL, indicating that the function described is not supported. An error code of OR_ARG is returned if the `rank` argument is greater than the size of the `vsetbits` array. Finally, an error code of BAD_ARG is returned if the `rank` element of the `vsetbits` array is unsupported (initialized to −1).

When the arguments have been validated, a `do...while` loop uses the information contained in the pointed-to `vregbits_` structure to modify the contents of the appropriate virtual register. First, the bits in the virtual register are cleared by applying the AND mask:

```
siop->v_regp[rbp->vregnum][VIR] &= rbp->resetmask;
```

This imposing-looking expression becomes rather more friendly with its variables evaluated for a call to set EVEN parity:

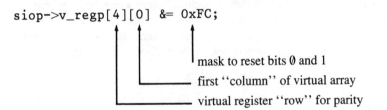

```
siop->v_regp[4][0] &= 0xFC;
```

mask to reset bits 0 and 1
first "column" of virtual array
virtual register "row" for parity

Assuming that virtual register 4 currently contains a value of 45H, the expression further evaluates to 0x45 & 0xFC, or 44H (e.g., bit 0 is cleared).

Next, the desired bit pattern is imposed upon the virtual register and, to simplify the syntax for calling _vsetbits, the results are stored in the intermediate variable `tmp`.

```
tmp = siop->v_regp[rbp->vregnum][VIR] |= rbp->setmask[rank];
```

which evaluates to

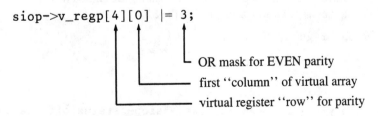

```
siop->v_regp[4][0] |= 3;
```

OR mask for EVEN parity
first "column" of virtual array
virtual register "row" for parity

and eventually becomes 0x44 | 3, or simply 47H.

Next, the rank of the current setting effect is stored in the now member of the `vregbits_` parity structure. Now that virtual register 4 contains the correct value for the Z80SIO's Write Register 4, the level-1 function _vsetbits is finally called to install the value in the virtual register in the physical UART.

Following the List Linkage

With the information passed in the vregbits structure now safely installed in the physical UART, the following innocuous-looking assignment occurs:

```
rbp = rbp->next;
```

thus loading into rbp the address of the next vregbits structure in the linked list. The body of the do...while repeats until a NIL next member signals the end of the list. This design supports the use of multiple structures for a single logical operation—the Z80SIO data-length structures in Figure 12-8, for example.

Before writing the actual _vsetbits function for the Z80SIO, let's first compose a couple of small functions that make programming life on the Z80SIO much nicer.

Level-1 Register Access Routines for the Z80SIO

As explained in Chapter 7, the Z80SIO's register-select pointer by default contains 0, so reads and writes are automatically directed to RR[0] and WR[0]. Accessing any other read or write register, however, is a two-step operation. Before a register may be read or written, the register pointer must first be *set* by writing a register number to the control status port. The next read or write operation then accesses the selected register. **Reading or writing any register automatically resets the register-select pointer to 0.** The two functions to read and write the registers are shown in Figure 12-11.

Figure 12-11   Functions regread and regwrite: low-level routines to simplify the two-step read/write operation on a Z80SIO.

FUNCTION NAME: regread, regwrite
LEVEL: 1
LIBRARY: *Z80SIO.LIB*
DESCRIPTION: Reads and writes Z80SIO registers by number.
OTHER MODULES: None
RETURNS: A register read returns BYTE; a register write returns void.
COMMENTS: Since all Z80SIO registers are accessed through the same port, these functions form I/O
                              addresses from status_off in the SIO.

```
void regwrite(siop, regnum, binval)
SIO *siop;
int regnum;
BYTE binval;
{
    (*siop->writebyte)( siop->uart_base + siop->status_off, regnum);
    (*siop->writebyte)( siop->uart_base + siop->status_off, binval);
}
```

Figure 12-11 cont. Functions `regread` and `regwrite`: low-level routines to simplify the two-step read/write operation on a Z80SIO.

```
BYTE regread(siop, regnum)
SIO *siop;
int regnum;
{
    (*siop->writebyte)( siop->uart_base + siop->status_off, regnum);
    return( (*siop->readbyte)(siop->uart_base + siop->status_off) );
}
```

An Explanation of 'regread' and 'regwrite'   These two routines simplify reading and writing Z80SIO registers by accepting a register number in their argument lists and selecting that register before performing the read or write.

Level-1 Function for the Z80SIO ('_vsetbits')

With `regwrite` to cover up the cumbersome Z80SIO addressing, `_vsetbits` in Figure 12-12 is quite simple.

Figure 12-12   The level-1 function to set bits in the Z80SIO.

FUNCTION NAME: `_vsetbits`
LEVEL: 1
LIBRARY: *Z80SIO.LIB*
DESCRIPTION: This is the primitive to write a virtual register to its corresponding UART register.
OTHER MODULES: None
RETURNS: `void`
COMMENTS: This function is called only by `vsetbits`.

```
void _vsetbits(siop, rbp, binval)
SIO *siop;
struct vregbits_ *rbp;
BYTE binval;
{
    regwrite(siop, rbp->vregnum, binval );
}
```

An Explanation of '_vsetbits'   The `offset` members of `vregbits_` structures are initialized with the offset of the Z80SIO's Control/Status register. Since we were careful to make the order of the virtual registers in the array correspond to the order of the physical registers in a Z80SIO, the structure member `vregnum` can be used to select the Z80SIO write register.

The degree to which you find this function anticlimactic is a direct measure of our success. The sole objective of our virtual UART concept is to squeeze the machine dependency out of our functions, concentrating it into innocuous droplets like `_vsetbits`.

The Level-3 Functions for Data Format

With the two lower-level functions in hand, the portable level-3 functions shown in Figure 12-13 can now be written to employ a simple, natural syntax.

Figure 12-13   Level-3 functions to set the data format.

FUNCTION NAME: `setparity, setdatalen, setstops`
LEVEL: 3
LIBRARY: *SIO.LIB*
DESCRIPTION: These functions set their respective data format elements.
OTHER MODULES: `vsetbits`
RETURNS: int: 0 if successful; OR_ARG if argument is out of range; BAD_FCN if the function is not supported (SIO pointer is NIL); BAD_ARG if the requested setting is not supported by hardware (mask initialized to −1).

```
int setparity(siop, newpar)
SIO *siop;
BYTE newpar;
{
     return (vsetbits(siop, siop->par, newpar));
}

int setdatalen(siop, newdl)
SIO *siop;
BYTE newdl;
{
     return (vsetbits(siop, siop->dl, newdl));
}


int setstops(siop, newsb)
SIO *siop;
BYTE newsb;
{
     return (vsetbits(siop, siop->sb, newsb));
}
```

An Explanation of the Level-3 Data Format Functions   Each of these functions simply calls the level-2 function `vsetbits`, passing to it the SIO pointer, the correct `struct vregbits_` pointer, and the rank code of the desired format. For example, these three calls are required to set the data format to 7EVEN2.

```
        setdatalen(siop, DL7);
        setparity(siop, EVEN);
        setstops(siop, STOP2);
```

Level-3 Error Returns

Each of these functions returns the error code passed to it from `vsetbits_`. The following snippet of code illustrates how to test this return value.

```
#include "siodef.h"
int ecode;
if ( (ecode = setparity(siop, SPACE)) != 0)
 switch (ecode)
      {
      case OR_AGR:
            puts("Invalid argument.");
            break;
      case BAD_FCN:
            puts("Invalid function.");
            break;
      case BAD_ARG:
            puts("Setting not supported.");
            break;
      }
```

Level-3 Functions To Fetch the Current Data Format

When the level-2 function has successfully written the virtual register to the physical register, it stores the rank argument in the now member of the structure for use by other functions. At any time, then, we can learn the current status of any of the data parameters by examining its structure. The level-3 functions in Figure 12-14 simply return the value of the now member.

Figure 12-14   Functions to fetch the current data format rate.

```
FUNCTION NAME: paritynow, dlnow, stopsnow
LEVEL:         3
LIBRARY:       SIO.LIB
DESCRIPTION:   Returns current setting of data format element.
RETURNS:       int: the rank of the setting as defined in SIODEF.H or −1 if the
               function is not supported.
```

```
int paritynow(siop)
SIO *siop;
{
    if (siop->par != NIL)
        return (siop->par->now);
    return (-1);

}
```

Figure 12-14 cont.   Functions to fetch the current data format rate.

```
int dlnow(siop)
SIO *siop;
{
     if (siop->dl != NIL)
          return (siop->dl->now);
     return (-1);
}
int stopsnow(siop)
SIO *siop;
{
     if (siop->sb != NIL)
          return (siop->sb->now);
     return (-1);

}
```

An Explanation of the Level-3 Fetch Functions   These simple functions merely return the current value in the now member of their respective structures. If the function is unsupported in the SIO—i.e., initialized to NIL—a −1 is returned.

Placement of the Structure Definitions

Because the declarations for v_reg, dlen, stops, and parity are all specific to the Z80SIO, they can rightly be placed in *Z80SIO.C* with the other level-1 functions. In principle, this enables you to create a new level-0 file simply by declaring an SIO with new values for PORT1, DP_OFF, SP_OFF, and BAUD. This placement is not recommended, however, because you will doubtless wish to customize the data in each of these objects for different applications or different situations. Placing all such definitions in the computer-specific file gives you the opportunity to alter this data for each new computer.

Baud Rate Functions

Support for a variable baud rate is accomplished in much the same way as data format. Specifically, there are three tiers of baud rate functions, all of which refer to a structure describing the virtual and physical characteristics affecting baud rate. But there is one important difference—we are assuming that the registers holding the Baud Rate register divisors contain no other data. That is, *all* bits in a Baud Rate register constitute the baud rate divisor. Because we do not have to concern ourselves with resetting and setting selected bits in a Baud Rate register, the Baud Rate register(s) may be *write-only*. This greatly simplifies the structure of the baud rate functions. In fact, it means that the Baud Rate registers do not necessarily have to reside in the array of virtual read/write registers. Nevertheless, placing the baud registers there bundles these functions into a neat, intellectually manageable package, providing a consistency in design by anticipating a future UART that shares its Baud Rate register with other data.

The 'vbaud_' Data Structure

You will remember from our virtual UART definition that we are assuming that the baud rate is programmed by writing a 2-byte divisor to two Baud Rate registers. Since we can assume nothing about the characteristic of the physical UART registers (are the registers contiguous? are they at different addresses?), the structure must contain the offset address and virtual register numbers for both the high and low byte of the divisor. The vbaud_ structure is shown in Figure 12-15.

Figure 12-15   A data structure to describe the baud rate.

```
STRUCT DEF:   vbaud_
FILE:         SIODEF.H
DESCRIPTION:  Control structure for baud rate.

struct vbaud_
   {
   BYTE       vregnuml;               /* high-order byte of baud rate divisor  */
   BYTE       vregnumh;               /* low-order byte of baud rate divisor   */
   int        offsetlo;               /* offset of lo-order baud rate register */
   int        offsethi;               /* offset of hi-order baud rate register */
   int        divisor[NUMBAUDS][2];   /* array of two-byte divisors            */
   BYTE       now;                    /* rank of current divisor               */
   BYTE       start;                  /* rank of value to use at start up       */
   };
```

The functions of the members in this structure are similar to those in the vregbits_ structure. Two differences, however, are worth pointing out. First, because baud rates are not bit mapped, no "resetmasks" or "setmasks" are necessary. In place of the "set" mask are the actual divisors, represented as a two-dimensional array of BYTE. For purposes of visualization, we refer to the divisor in the first array ("column" 0) as the high-order byte, and the other as the low-order byte. The now and start members store the rank of the baud rate codes, respectively, for the current baud rate and the baud rate to use at start-up.

The divisors array, like the vregbits_ structure, is declared to be int. This enables us to mark unsupported baud rates with a −1 "sentinel." The vbaud_ structure contains no next member because of our assumption that the 16-bit divisor resides in two registers.

Figure 12-16   System-wide manifest constants for baud rates. These belong in SIODEF.H.

```
#define NUMBAUDS      16            /* number of baud in divisor array   */

#define BAUD50        0             #define BAUD1800      8
#define BAUD75        1             #define BAUD2000      9
#define BAUD110       2             #define BAUD2400      10
#define BAUD134_5     3             #define BAUD3600      11
#define BAUD150       4             #define BAUD4800      12
#define BAUD300       5             #define BAUD7200      13
#define BAUD600       6             #define BAUD9600      14
#define BAUD1200      7             #define BAUD19K2      15
```

Since several functions need to know the size of the divisor array, a constant, NUMBAUDS is used to declare its dimension. This greatly simplifies changing its size in the future.

Initialization of a 'vbaud_' Structure

Figure 12-16 shows the manifest constants for the rank codes associated with the 16 baud rates assumed for our virtual UART. Because the Z80SIO itself contains no baud rate generator, the Kaypro employs an 8116 (or 5016, a 5-volt version of the same device), a dual channel clock generator, whose channel 1 output is connected to the Z80SIO's channel A clock input. The 8116 is essentially a frequency divider, down-counting a 5.0688 MHz oscillator to produce a serial data clock. It can be programmed by writing the values shown in Table 12-1 to its "divisor" port located on the Kaypro at I/O port 0.

Table 12-1 Baud Rate Divisor Constants for *KAYPRO.C.*

High Byte		Low Byte		High Byte		Low Byte	
BH__50	0x00	BL__50	0x00	BH__1800	0x00	BL__1800	0x08
BH__75	0x00	BL__75	0x01	BH__2000	0x00	BL__2000	0x09
BH__110	0x00	BL__110	0x02	BH__2400	0x00	BL__2400	0x0A
BH__134	0x00	BL__134	0x03	BH__3600	0x00	BL__3600	0x0B
BH__150	0x00	BL__150	0x04	BH__4800	0x00	BL__4800	0x0C
BH__300	0x00	BL__300	0x05	BH__7200	0x00	BL__7200	0x0D
BH__600	0x00	BL__600	0x06	BH__9600	0x00	BL__9600	0x0E
BH__1200	0x00	BL__1200	0x07	BH__19K2	0x00	BL__19K2	0x0F

A close look at this table shows that these values are not divisors in the usual sense because the smaller values correspond to lower output frequencies. Writing a value to the divisor port merely selects one of 16 hardwired internal dividers. The values shown assume a *clock factor* of 16; that is, they produce frequencies that are 16 times the actual baud rate (see Chapter 6 for an explanation). Also notice that since the baud rate device is not a part of the Z80SIO, the divisor constants shown in Table 12-1 belong in *KAYPRO.C* or, better, in a separate include file for reuse with other computers that use the 8116.

Figure 12-17 Declaration and initialization of a struct vbaud_ for the Kaypro.

```
STRUCT DEF:   vbaud_
FILE:         SIODEF.H
DESCRIPTION:  Structure for controlling baud rate through virtual registers.

struct vbaud_ baudA =
    {
    VBAUDLO,                        /* virtual register for low byte    */
    VBAUDHI,                        /* virtual register for byte        */
    BAUD,                           /* offset of 8116 baud generator    */
    NA,                             /* uses a single byte divisor       */
```

Figure 12-17 cont.   Declaration and initialization of a `struct vbaud_` for the Kaypro.

```
{
  {BH_50,   BL_50   }, {BH_75,   BL_75   }, {BH_110,  BL_110  },
  {BH_134,  BL_134  }, {BH_150,  BL_150  }, {BH_300,  BL_300  },
  {BH_600,  BL_600  }, {BH_1200, BL_1200 }, {BH_1800, BL_1800 },
  {BH_2000, BL_2000 }, {BH_2400, BL_2400 }, {BH_3600, BL_3600 },
  {BH_4800, BL_4800 }, {BH_7200, BL_7200 }, {BH_9600, BL_9600 },
  {BH_19K2, BL_19K2 }
},
SUPPLIED,                        /* rank of current baud      */
BAUD1200                         /* start at 1200 baud        */
};
```

The declaration and initialization of the `vbaud_` structure shown in Figure 12-17 reveals one or two points of interest. First, the high- and low-order bytes are initialized side-by-side in enclosing braces separated by commas. Second, although our *virtual UART* assumes a 2-byte baud rate divisor and 2 Baud Rate registers, the actual device used in the Kaypro (i.e., the SMC 8116) uses only a single byte written to a single register. This poses no problem—high byte baud rate constants (e.g., BH_50) are all 0.

The Level-2 Function To Set the Baud Rate

The level-2 function to set the baud rate looks superficially like `vsetbits`. The main difference is that `setbaud` does not manipulate individual bits in the virtual register.

Figure 12-18   `vsetbr`: the level-2 baud rate function.

FUNCTION NAME: `vsetbr`
LEVEL: 2
LIBRARY: *BUOS.LIB*
DESCRIPTION: Sets the baud rate to the `rank` element of the structure's `divisor` array. Passes high- and low-order divisors to the level-1 function, `_vsetbr`.
OTHER MODULES: `_vsetbr`
RETURNS: `int`: 0 if successful; OR_ARG if argument is out of range; BAD_FCN if the function is not supported (SIO pointer is NIL); BAD_ARG if the requested setting is not supported by hardware (divisor is −1).
COMMENTS: The `rank` argument is an index for the array of divisors, constants for which reside in *SIODEF.H*. Notice that the low byte is passed before the high byte.

```
int vsetbr(siop, brp, rank)
SIO *siop;
struct vbaud_ *brp;
BYTE   rank;                          /* rank of value to install    */
```

Figure 12-18 cont. `vsetbr`: the level-2 baud rate function.

```
{
    BYTE brlo, brhi;                    /* intermediates simplify syntax    */
    if (brp == NIL)                     /* baud rate not supported in hardware */
        return (BAD_FCN);
    if ( rank >= NUMBAUDS)              /* requested rank out of range       */
        return (OR_ARG);
    if (brp->divisor[rank][1] == -1 || brp->divisor[rank][0] == -1)
        return (BAD_ARG);              /* request baud rate not available   */
    brlo = brp->divisor[rank][1];      /* lo byte of divisor                */
    brhi = brp->divisor[rank][0];      /* lo byte of divisor                */
    brp->now = rank;                   /* update baud in effect             */
    _vsetbr(siop, brp, brlo, brhi);    /* call level-1 to do it             */
    return (0);
}
```

An Explanation of 'vsetbr'   The fundamental task of `vsetbr` is to pass the individual bytes of the baud rate divisor to the level-1 function, `_vsetbr`. Notice that the low byte of the divisor is passed *before* the high byte. The use of the intermediate variables `brlo` and `brhi` is purely stylistic, intended to clarify the expressions.

The error checking in `vsetbr` is identical to that in `vsetbits`. An error code of OR_ARG is returned if the `rank` argument is out of range; an error code of BAD_FCN is returned if the structure pointer is NIL (indicating that the baud rate is not software programmable); finally, an error code of BAD_ARG is returned if the `rank` element of the `divisor` array is unsupported (i.e., initialized to −1).

Level-1 Function To Set Baud Rate

Since the 8116 baud rate generator IC in the Kaypro is so simple, the level-1 function shown in Figure 12-19 is likewise simple.

Figure 12-19   The level-1 function to set baud rate for *KAYPRO.C*.

FUNCTION NAME: `_vsetbr`
LEVEL: 1 (well, really 0)
LIBRARY: *KAYPRO.C*
DESCRIPTION: Primitive for setting the baud rate.
OTHER MODULES: None
RETURNS: `void`
COMMENTS: The baud rate is changed by writing `brval` value to the address of the 8116 baud rate generator.

```
void _vsetbr(siop, brp, brval)
SIO *siop;
struct vbaud_ *brp;
BYTE brval;
{
    (*siop->writebyte)(siop->uart_base + brp->offsetlo, brval);
}
```

An Explanation of '_vsetbr'   This function merely writes the "divisor" to the 8116 baud rate generator. Since the level-2 function passes the low byte of the divisor first, _vsetbr doesn't declare the high-order byte. Because this function addresses non-UART hardware, it should not reside in *Z80SIO.C*. For the sake of simplicity we are assuming that this function and the constant definitions in Table 12-1 reside in *KAYPRO.C*. Placing them in a separate file named, say, *BR8116.LIB*, would modularize them for reuse with other computers.

The Level-3 Function for Baud Rate

Figure 12-20 shows setbaud, the level-3 function to set the baud rate; Figure 12-21 shows the function to fetch the current baud rate.

Figure 12-20   The level-3 baud rate function.

FUNCTION NAME: setbaud
LEVEL: 3
LIBRARY: *SIO.LIB*
DESCRIPTION: Sets the baud rate to the rank element in the divisor array.
OTHER MODULES: vsetbr (level-2)
RETURNS: int: −1 if rank is out of range or not supported by hardware; otherwise 0.
COMMENTS: The rank argument is an index into an array of divisors, constants for which reside in *SIODEF.H*.

```
int setbaud(siop, rank)
SIO *siop;
unsigned rank;
{
    return (vsetbr(siop, siop->br, rank));
}
```

Figure 12-21   Use of baudnow to fetch the current baud rate.

FUNCTION NAME: baudnow
LEVEL: 3
LIBRARY: *SIO.LIB*
DESCRIPTION: Returns rank of current baud rate as defined in *SIODEF.H*
RETURNS: int

```
int baudnow(siop)
SIO *siop;
{
    if (siop->br != NIL)                 /* if supported */
        return (siop->br->now);
    return (-1);
}
```

An Explanation of 'setbaud' and 'baudnow'   Very little needs to be said about these functions except to point out that the fetch function returns the error code from `vsetbr`. Because some hardware does not support all 16 of the baud rates of our virtual UART, the return value from `setbaud` should always be tested, especially when the call is made in response to user input. The `baudnow` function returns the rank of the current baud rate setting. If the `br` pointer in the SIO structure is not supported, a NIL is returned.

We have now completed the levels-2 and -3 functions for the data format library. We have also written level-1 functions for the Z80SIO and level-0 data for the Kaypro. Let's now turn our attention to the 8250 and IBM PC.

Data Format and Baud Rate for the IBM PC

If all UARTs were as straightforward as the 8250, there would be little need for virtual registers. All 8250 write registers—Baud, Interrupt Enable, RS-232 Output, and Line Control (Data Format)—can also be read at the same address. Although it does have idiosyncrasies and one or two shortcomings, in many ways it is the ideal UART from the point of view of the programmer. Because it is such a well thought-out device, it fits quite comfortably in our virtual UART scheme. Before installing the 8250 functions to the libraries, add the constants shown in Figure 12-22 to *U8250.LIB*.

Figure 12-22   Masks and virtual constants for the 8250.

Masks for the 8250

DLMASK	0xFC	/* 1111 1100 */	PARITYMASK	0xC7	/* 1100 0111 */
DL5_MASK	0		NONE_MASK	0	
DL6_MASK	1	/* 0000 0001 */	ODD_MASK	8	/* 0000 1000 */
DL7_MASK	2	/* 0000 0010 */	EVEN_MASK	0x18	/* 0001 1000 */
DL8_MASK	3	/* 0000 0011 */	MARK_MASK	0x28	/* 0010 1000 */
			SPACE_MASK	0x38	/* 0011 1000 */
STOPMASK	0xFB	/* 11111011 */			
ONE_MASK	0	/* 00000000 */			
ONE_5_MASK	4	/* 00000100 */			
TWO_MASK	4	/* 00000100 */			

Manifest Constants for the Virtual Register Numbers

```
#define VBAUDLO  0
#define VBAUDLO  1
#define VINTR    2
#define VFMT     3
#define V232OUT  4
```

The Virtual Register Array for the 8250

Recall from Chapter 7 that there is only one significant oddity in the 8250: the low- and high-order Baud Rate registers are addressed at the same offsets as the Transmitter and the Interrupt Enable registers. When bit 7 of the Data Format (Line Control) register is FALSE, reads and writes to these addresses are directed to the Data and the Interrupt Enable registers; conversely, when bit 7 of the Data Format register is TRUE, reads and writes to these addresses are steered to *LSB Divisor Latch* and the *MSB Divisor Latch*. The existence of these "phantom" registers precludes a one-to-one correspondence between a register's physical offset and its position in the virtual register array. Figure 12-23 shows the declaration and initialization of the array, which is substantially smaller than the Z80SIO's.

Figure 12-23   Virtual array for the IBM PC.

ARRAY NAME: v_regA
TYPE: Two-dimensional array of BYTE.
LEVEL: 0
FILE: *IBMPC.C*
DESCRIPTION: Used for virtual UART registers.

```
BYTE v_regA[5][2]=

    {
/*  VIR    USR  */
    0,    0,                          /* 0 = baud low byte        */
    0,    0,                          /* 1 = baud high byte       */
    0,    0,                          /* 2 = interrupt enable     */
    0,    0,                          /* 3 = data format          */
    0,    0                           /* 4 = RS232 output control */
    };
```

Since the IBM PC may contain more than one serial port, the name of this array contains the familiar 'A' appendage to associate it with `typeAsio`, the first serial port. If we wish to support more than one `SIO`, we need a separate virtual array for each `SIO` declared—`v_regA`, `v_regB`, and so forth.

Data Format on the IBM PC

The declaration and initialization of the `vregbits_` structures for the IBM PC is similar to that for the Kaypro, except, of course, the values are appropriate for an 8250 instead of a Z80SIO. These structures are shown in Figure 12-24. Aside from the addressing information—both virtual and physical—the most obvious difference is in the parity structure where MARK and SPACE parity are supported.

Like the virtual register array, all structure identifiers end in the letter 'A' in order to associate them mnemonically with `typeAsio`. If another port is supported, its declarations end in 'B', the next in 'C', and so on.

Figure 12-24 Data format structures for the IBM PC.

STRUCT NAME: parityA, stopsA, dlenA
TYPE: struct vregbits_
LEVEL: 0
FILE: *IBMPC.C*
DESCRIPTION: SIO control structures for parity, stop bits, and data length.

```
struct vregbits_ parityA =              /* for 8250 UART */
    {
    PARITYMASK,                     /* AND mask to apply to this register     */
    { NONE_MASK, ODD_MASK, EVEN_MASK, MARK_MASK, SPACE_MASK }, /* OR masks   */
    VFMT,                           /* virtual register--rank in v_rega       */
    3,                              /* offset of physical register from uart_base*/
    SUPPLIED,                       /* rank in mask table of current setting   */
    NONE,                           /* rank to use in initialization           */
    NIL                             /* no more structures for parity           */
    };


struct vregbits_ stopsA =               /* for 8250 UART */
    {
    STOPMASK,
    { ONE_MASK, ONE_5_MASK, TWO_MASK, -1, -1 },
    VFMT,
    3,
    SUPPLIED,
    STOP1,
    NIL                             /* no more structures for stop bits  */
    };


struct vregbits_ dlenA =                /* for 8250 UART */
    {
    DLMASK,
    { DL5 MASK, DL6_MASK, DL7_MASK, DL8_MASK, -1 },
    VFMT,
    3,
    SUPPLIED,
    DL8,
    NIL                             /* no more structures for data length */
    };
```

Because of the popularity of the IBM PC, one is tempted to place these declarations in *IBMPC.C*. If you elect to do so, keep in mind that even though the IBM method of address decoding is natural to the 8250, its physical offsets are probably not valid for boards that are not intended for use with the IBM PC.

The Level-1 Function for the 8250 ('_vsetbits')

The final chore of implementing the data format library on the IBM PC is to write the 8250 version of the level-1 function _vsetbits, shown in Figure 12-25.

Figure 12-25 Level-1 function to write to the physical UART.

FUNCTION NAME: _vsetbits
LEVEL: 1
LIBRARY: U8250.LIB
DESCRIPTION: This is the primitive to write the format in the virtual register to the corresponding UART register.
OTHER MODULES: None
RETURNS: void
COMMENTS: This function is called only by vsetbits.

```
void _vsetbits(siop, brp, binval)
register SIO *siop;
struct vregbits_ *brp;
BYTE binval;
{
    (*siop->writebyte)(siop->uart_base + brp->offset, binval);
}
```

An Explanation of '_vsetbits'   The byte passed in binval is unceremoniously written to the offset given in the regbin_ pointer, brp. On the 8250, the bits that govern parity, data length, and stop bits all reside in the same (Data Format) register at offset 3.

Baud Rate on the IBM PC

The 8250 contains the circuitry for an on-board baud generator, so setting the baud rate could hardly be simpler, at least from a logical standpoint. Two 8-bit registers, referred to as *LSB and MSB Divisor Latches*, constitute a 16-bit divisor for the clock circuitry. Because the 8250's clocking factor is *fixed* at 16 (i.e., not programmable), the frequencies actually generated by the dividing circuitry must be 16 times greater than the desired baud rate. Using the IBM PC's oscillator frequency of 1.8432 MHz, the 16-bit divisors for each baud rate can be calculated by the equation:

$$\text{divisor} = 1,843,200 \div (16 \times \text{baud rate})$$

Applying this equation to our 16 baud rates produces the divisor constant definitions for the IBM PC shown in Table 12-2.

For unexplained reasons, IBM cautions that "in no case should the data rate be greater than 9600 baud." Despite this admonition, 19,200 and even 38,400 baud cause no problems. For now, however, leave the definition of 19,200 baud at -1 in order to test the error-checking mechanism built into vsetbr (see page 325).

Table 12-2   Baud Rate Divisor Constants for *U8250.H.*

High Byte		Low Byte		High Byte		Low Byte	
BH__50	0x09	BL__50	0x00	BH__1800	0x00	BL__1800	0x40
BH__75	0x06	BL__75	0x00	BH__2000	0x00	BL__2000	0x3A
BH__110	0x04	BL__110	0x17	BH__2400	0x00	BL__2400	0x30
BH__134	0x03	BL__134	0x59	BH__3600	0x00	BL__3600	0x20
BH__150	0x03	BL__150	0x00	BH__4800	0x00	BL__4800	0x18
BH__300	0x01	BL__300	0x80	BH__7200	0x00	BL__7200	0x10
BH__600	0x00	BL__600	0xC0	BH__9600	0x00	BL__9600	0x0C
BH__1200	0x00	BL__1200	0x60	BH__19K2	−1	BL__19K2	−1 *

*Calculated values for 19,200 baud are HI = 0, LO = 06.

Declaration and Initialization of the 'vbaud_' Structure

The declaration of the vbaud_ structure, shown in Figure 12-26, looks very much like that for the Kaypro, except the 8250 uses both high-order and low-order elements of the virtual register array. Because of the peculiar fashion in which the divisor registers are addressed, their physical offsets are 0 and 1 — the same as the Data and Interrupt registers.

Figure 12-26   Declaration and initialization of a vbaud_ structure.

```
STRUCT NAME: baudA
TYPE:        struct vbaud_
LEVEL:       0
FILE:        IBMPC.C
DESCRIPTION: SIO control structure for baud rate.

struct vbaud_ baudA =
    {
    VBAUDLO,                          /* virtual register for lo byte      */
    VBAUDHI,                          /* virtual register for hi byte      */
    0,                                /* offset of UART lsb baud baud reg  */
    1,                                /* offset of UART msb baud reg       */
    {
      {BH_50,    BL_50   }, {BH_75,    BL_75   }, {BH_110,   BL_110  },
      {BH_134,   BL_134  }, {BH_150,   BL_150  }, {BH_300,   BL_300  },
      {BH_600,   BL_600  }, {BH_1200,  BL_1200 }, {BH_1800,  BL_1800 },
      {BH_2000,  BL_2000 }, {BH_2400,  BL_2400 }, {BH_3600,  BL_3600 },
      {BH_4800,  BL_4800 }, {BH_7200,  BL_7200 }, {BH_9600,  BL_9600 },
      {BH_19K2,  BL_19K2 }
    },
    SUPPLIED,                         /* rank of current baud in divisor table */
    BAUD1200                          /* start at 1200 baud                    */
    };
```

Level-1 Function Baud Rate for the 8250 ('_vsetbr')

It is the responsibility of level-1 functions to resolve the conflict arising from the 8250's use of coincident addresses. The function in Figure 12-27 resolves this conflict.

Figure 12-27 `_vsetbr`: a level-1 function for baud rate.

FUNCTION NAME:	`_vsetbr`
LEVEL:	1
LIBRARY:	*U8250.LIB*
DESCRIPTION:	Primitive for setting the baud rate.

...writing `lobaud` and `hibaud` to the 8250's LSB and MSB ...s can be addressed only if bit 7 in the Data Format register ...se two registers, the original contents of the Data Format

```
base + siop->par->offset) | 0x80;
iop->par->offset, tmpfmt);
rp->offsetlo, lobaud);
rp->offsethi, hibaud);
iop->par->offset, tmpfmt & 0x7f);
```

...en bit 7 of the Data Format register is FALSE, the registers ...register (i.e., transmit and receive) and the Interrupt Enable ...nat register is TRUE, however, these become the low- and ...isor registers. Because of this addressing anomaly, the first ...it 7 of the Data Format register. Since the low-order 7 bits of ...ttings (as well as the BREAK bit), they must be preserved. ...egister, setting its bit 7 (ORing it with 80H), then storing it ...mp is then written back to the Data Format register, "ex- ...rs for addressing. In the statement that accomplishes this,

```
iop->uart_base + siop->par->offset) | 0x80;
```

...et stands for the offset of the Data Format register. Since ...ength, and stop bits all reside in the same register, `siop->sb->offset` or `siop->bl->offset` could also have been used.

Next, the low- and high-order bytes of the divisor are written to the offsets named in the `vbaud_` pointer, `brp`. Finally, in order to restore registers 0 and 1 to their "normal" addressing modes, bit 7 of `tmp` is cleared and `tmp` is written back to the Data Format register.

Configuration and Restoration

It is nearly time to put our new libraries to work. We shall do this by enhancing *TERM* to permit changes in baud rate and data format. Before we can proceed, however, we have a bit more programming to do. It has probably occurred to you that the success of our system of virtual registers depends upon one thing: the virtual registers must start life containing the same values as the corresponding physical UART registers. Until now, we have avoided this subject merely by assuming that this initialization has already magically taken place. We must now conjure up these magical functions. To this end, we require two additional level-1 functions—s_config to save the current settings upon entry, and s_restore to restore them upon exit. Let's begin with the 8250 versions of these functions.

The 'config' and 'restore' Functions for the 8250

All registers on the 8250 are read/write. Therefore, the task on the 8250 is to fetch the contents of all registers and place them in *both* dimensions of the virtual array. Storing each physical value in the VIR dimension achieves the beginning physical-to-logical correspondence assumed by our library functions. Storing a copy of the physical registers in the USR dimension also preserves the current state of the UART so that the interface can be restored upon termination of the program. Figure 12-28 shows s_config.

Figure 12-28 Use of s_config to load virtual registers with the UART's physical registers.

FUNCTION NAME: s_config
LEVEL: 1
LIBRARY: *U8250.LIB*
DESCRIPTION: Copies the contents of the 8250's write registers into the SIO's virtual array.
OTHER MODULES: None
RETURNS: void

```
void s_config(siop)          /* copy physical UART regs into virtual regs */
register SIO *siop;
{
    BYTE tmp;
    int i;
    tmp = (*siop->readbyte)(siop->uart_base + siop->par->offset) | 0x80;
    (*siop->writebyte)(siop->uart_base + siop->par->offset, tmp);
    siop->v_regp[VBAUDLO][USR] = (*siop->readbyte)(siop->uart_base + siop->br->offsetlo);
    siop->v_regp[VBAUDHI][USR] = (*siop->readbyte)(siop->uart_base + siop->br->offsethi);
    (*siop->writebyte)(siop->uart_base + siop->par->offset,tmp & 0x7f);
    siop->v_regp[VINTR][USR]  = (*siop->readbyte)(siop->uart_base + 1);
    siop->v_regp[VFMT][USR]   = (*siop->readbyte)(siop->uart_base + siop->par->offset);
    siop->v_regp[V232OUT][USR] = (*siop->readbyte)(siop->uart_base + 4);
    for (i = 0; i < 5; i++)  /* copy USR column into VIR column */
        siop->v_regp[i][VIR] = siop->v_regp[i][USR];
}
```

An Explanation of 's_config'   The first order of business is to save the current UART values in the USR column of the virtual array. The current contents of the 8250's two Baud Rate Divisor registers are saved first. Refer to page 333 for an explanation of the idiosyncrasies of addressing the Baud Rate Divisor registers. Next, the Interrupt Enable register is saved, followed by the Data Format register, and finally the RS-232 Output (Modem Control) register. Since we have not yet developed structures for interrupts and for RS-232 control, the constants 1 and 4 are employed as addressing offsets in place of structure variables.

When every element of the USR column in the array has been initialized with its 8250 counterpart, a `for` loop copies these values into the VIR column. Thus, when the function returns, both columns contain identical, *current* copies of the 8250's write registers.

The function to restore the state of the serial port, `s_restore`, is shown in Figure 12-29.

Figure 12-29 UART restoration for the 8250.

```
FUNCTION NAME:  s_restore
LEVEL:          1
LIBRARY:        U8250.LIB
DESCRIPTION:    Restores the SIO to its original state.
OTHER MODULES:  None
RETURNS:        void

void s_restore(siop)
register SIO *siop;
{
    _vsetbr(siop,siop->br,siop->v_regp[VBAUDLO][USR], siop->v_regp[VBAUDHI][USR]);
    _vsetbits(siop,siop->par,siop->v_regp[VFMT][USR]);
    (*siop->writebyte)(siop->uart_base + 1, siop->v_regp[VINTR][USR]);
    (*siop->writebyte)(siop->uart_base + 4, siop->v_regp[V232OUT][USR]);
}
```

An Explanation of 's_restore' To restore the state of the UART, this function writes the original values stored in the USR column of the virtual register to the 8250. The level-1 primitives, `_vsetbr` and `_vsetbits` are called to restore the Baud Rate and the Data Format registers. Because we do not yet have similar primitives for dealing with interrupts or RS-232 output, the constants 1 and 4 are used in the offset calculation.

The 's_config' and 's_restore' Functions for the Z80SIO

Because only one of the Z80SIO's registers (the interrupt vector) is read/write, it is obviously impossible to restore the interface to its original condition—if we cannot read the current settings, we cannot save and therefore cannot restore them. If you re-read the paragraph on page 303 where we vowed to restore the interface, you will discover the phrase "whenever possible." Although this may sound like classic literary weaseling, it is really just the opposite. Even though the registers of many UARTs are, regrettably, write-only, the philosophical commitment to restoring the interface has compelled us to design routines that accommodate those that are read/write. In UARTs that use write-only registers, such as the Z80SIO, the restoration of the interface has to be *simulated*.

To achieve correspondence between the the 8250 and the virtual array, we simply filled the virtual register array with the contents of the UART. But since the Z80SIO's write registers cannot be read, in order to achieve this correspondence on the Z80SIO we must, paradoxically, do just the opposite—configure the UART with the contents of the virtual array. In other words, because we cannot learn the contents of the Z80SIO's registers, we peremptorily set them to acceptable values.

Restoring the interface presents a parallel problem: how can we pretend to recite what we never knew. The solution is the same: "restore" the interface to some *reasonable* value upon termination—reasonable in that you avoid leaving the port in an eccentric condition (such as 9600 5E2). The condition in which you leave the Z80SIO depends upon the manner in which the computer is typically used. The CP/M operating system on the Kaypro, for example, does not have a serial handshake driver in software for use with a serial printer, but relies upon the Z80SIO's automatic handshaking feature. On the Kaypro, therefore, we elect to restore DTR handshaking. On other computers, whose serial ports are devoted to applications that do not typically require hardware handshaking (a modem or perhaps a video display terminal), we might elect to turn off the Z80SIO's automatic handshaking before terminating.

Initialization of 'v_regA' for the Z80SIO

Once we have decided upon the configuration and restoration values for the Z80SIO, where should these values reside? Since these values must eventually find their way into the virtual registers, it makes sense to put them there in the first place. In other words, we initialize both columns of the virtual array to the desired bit patterns, then use s_config and s_restore functions to install them in the corresponding registers of the Z80SIO. Figure 12-30 shows the full declaration and initialization for the Z80SIO.

Figure 12-30   Virtual array declaration and initialization for the Kaypro.

ARRAY NAME: v_regA
TYPE: 8x2 array of BYTE
LEVEL: 0
FILE: *KAYPRO.H*
DESCRIPTION: "Virtual" UART registers—array members used to simulate read/write UART registers.
COMMENTS: The left column (VIR) holds the values to which the Z80SIO registers are initialized, the right column (USR) holds the values to restore upon exit.

```
BYTE v_regA[8][2] =     /* "virtual" registers VIR/USR */
   {
/*  VIR ------- USR  */
   {0x18,    0x18 },    /*  0 reset channel                                   */
   {0,          0 },    /*  1 no interrupts                                   */
   {0,          0 },    /*  2 interrupt vector                                */
   {0xC1,    0xE1 },    /*  3 start with no auto handshake, turn on at        */
   {0x44,    0x44 },    /*  4 async mode, x16 clk, 1 stop                     */
   {0xEA,    0x68 },    /*  5 start with RTS/DTR high, inhibit then at exit  */
   {0,          0 },    /*  6 baud rate lo */
   {0,          0 }     /*  7 baud rate hi */
   };
```

An Explanation of 'v_reg' These values, which are explained in detail in Tables 12-3 and 12-4, are fairly pedestrian. Aside from the data format, there are only two pivotal configuration decisions: (1) automatic RS-232 handshaking (on RTS/DCD) is disabled, and (2) the RS-232 inputs DTR and CTS are turned OFF. Both decisions are based upon the assumption that the Kaypro's serial port will drive a modem or perhaps a video terminal and will not need hardware handshaking and, importantly, will need to control the RS-232 output lines. Since the start-up baud rate is kept in the `vbaud_` structure itself, these elements are set to 0. The baud rate is "restored" to 1200 baud.

In truth, the initialization values require much less thought than those for restoration. Why? As part of the initialization process, soon after `s_config` is called, an as yet unwritten function calls `setparity`, `setbaud` and other level-3 "virtual" functions to install the `start` members of their structures. These functions, of course, quickly overwrite the contents of the virtual registers. This is not to say that initialization is not important; we must always rely upon it to perform the low-level configuration (magic numbers) uniquely required by the UART, but not encompassed by our definition of the virtual UART (resetting the UART, for example).

Table 12-3   "Configuration" Bytes (VIR).

Register Number	Hex	Binary	Meaning
0	18	0001 1000	Channel reset
1	0	0000 0000	No interrupts (not actually used)
2	0	0000 0000	Interrupt vector dummy (see s_config)
3	C1	1100 0001	8 bits Rx, no auto handshake, Rx enable
4	44	0100 0100	16 clock factor, 1½ stops, async mode, no parity
5	68	0101 1000	DTR/RST off, 8 bits Tx, no break, Tx enable
6	0	0000 0000	Dummy for low baud
7	0	0000 0000	Dummy for hi baud

Table 12-4   "Restoration" Bytes (USR).

Register Number	Hex	Binary	Meaning
0	18	0001 1000	Channel reset
1	0	0000 0000	No interrupts
2	0	0000 0000	Interrupt vector dummy (not actually used)
3	E1	1110 0001	8 bits Rx, enable auto handshake, Rx enable
4	44	0100 0100	16 clock factor, 1½ stops, async mode, no parity
5	EA	1110 1010	DTR/RST on, 8 bits Tx, no break, Tx enable
6	0	BL_1200	Low byte of baud rate divisor
7	0	BL_1200	High byte of baud rate divisor

The restoration bytes simply reassert the DTR and RTS outputs and enable the auto handshaking mode. These are safe choices, since the Kaypro is initialized this way at power-up. The baud rate is set to 1200 baud.

We are now ready to look at the Z80SIO version of `s_config` and `s_restore`, shown in Figure 12-31.

Figure 12-31 Configuration and restoration functions for the Z80SIO.

FUNCTION NAME:	s_config, s_restore
LEVEL:	1
LIBRARY:	*Z80SIO.LIB*
DESCRIPTION:	Output configuration and "restore" bytes to UART from the bytes contained in the virtual register array.
OTHER MODULES:	regwrite, _vsetbr
RETURNS:	void
COMMENTS:	The values in the virtual array are intended only to insure that the program execution begins and ends with the Z80SIO in a reasonable state.

```
void s_config(siop)
SIO *siop;
{

    int i;
    for (i = 0; i < 6;  i++)
       {
       if (i == 2)                           /* don't change interrupt vector */
          continue;
       regwrite(siop, i, siop->v_regp[i][VIR]);
       }
}


void s_restore(siop)
SIO *siop;
{
    int i;
    for (i = 0; i < 6;  i++)
       {
       if (i == 2)                           /* don't change interrupt vector */
          continue;
       regwrite(siop, i, siop->v_regp[i][USR]); /* write to register       */
       }
    _vsetbr(siop, siop->br, siop->v_regp[VBAUDLO][USR], siop->v_regp[VBAUDHI][USR]);
}
```

An Explanation of 's_config' and 's_restore'   These functions are almost identical—both merely output bytes to the UART from the appropriate column in the virtual register. The loop counter i becomes the register number in the call to regwrite. Because the Z80SIO does not contain its own baud generator, s_restore must call the level-1 baud rate function _vsetbr to set the baud rate. The only mysterious feature here is that neither routine writes to Write Register 2, which contains the interrupt vector. This may seem a bit odd, since this is the only register in the entire UART that is read/write. We skip this register for two reasons: first, it is accessible only from the "B" section of the Z80SIO and we have no general mechanism to address a *specific* section of a UART; second, and most important, it is *always* dangerous to cavalierly change an interrupt vector. Suppose, for example, that the other half of the Z80SIO is currently being used for *interrupt-driven* terminal I/O. Unthinkingly writing into Write Register 2 would immediately bring the system down.

String Arrays for Data Format, Baud Rate, and Errors

Figure 12-2 listed a complete set of manifest constants for data format and baud rate settings as well as constants for the errors returned by the various functions. Figure 12-32 shows the string arrays that corrrespond to each group of constants. Some of the error messages will not be needed until later chapters, but they should be installed in *SIO.LIB* now.

Figure 12-32   Strings to support data format, baud rate, and error messages.

ARRAY NAME: `sbstr, parstr, dlstr, brstr`
TYPE: Array of `char *`
LEVEL: 3
FILE: *SIO.LIB*
DESCRIPTION: ASCII strings for baud rate and data formats.
COMMENTS: Use the now member of each structure to index into these arrays.

```
char *sbstr[]   = { "1", "1 1/2", "2" };
char *parstr[]  = { "None", "Odd", "Even", "Mark", "Space" };
char *dlstr[]   = { "5", "6", "7", "8" };
char *brstr[]   = { "50", "75", "110", "134.5", "150", "300", "600", "1200",
                    "1800", "2000", "2400", "3600", "4800", "7200", "9600",
                    "19,200" };
```

ARRAY NAME: `errstr`
TYPE: Array of `char *`
LEVEL: 3
FILE: *SIO.LIB*
DESCRIPTION: Messages for error codes returned by data format and baud rate functions.

```
char *errstr[] =
    {
    "",
    "Argument out of range",               /* 1    #define OR_ARG    */
    "Function not supported",              /* 2    #define BAD_FCN   */
    "Argument not supported",              /* 3    #define BAD_ARG   */
    "Illegal device number",              /* 4    #define BAD_PORT  */
    "Device not installed",               /* 5    #define NO_PORT   */
    "Device not available",               /* 6    #define NO_SIO    */
    "Device already open",                /* 7    #define OPEN_NOW  */
    "No such device or device not open",  /* 8    #define NO_CLOSE  */
    "Transfer Cancelled from keyboard",   /* 9    #define KEY_CAN   */
    "File not found",                     /* 10   #define NO_FIL    */
    ""                                    /* NIL array terminator */
    };
```

The first four arrays are pointers to ASCII strings whose position in the array corresponds to the data format and baud rate codes they describe. For example, using the code for MARK parity (defined as 3 in *SIODEF.H*), the expression

```
              printf("%s", parstr[MARK]);
```

prints the word "Mark."

The second array, errstr, is an array of pointers to error messages that describe the errors resulting from calls to any of the level-3 "set" functions.

TERM2

We are now ready for the new version of our terminal program. The important change from *TERM1* is the support for data format and baud rate changes. Moreover, upon exit the interface is restored to its original condition on the IBM PC, and to a reasonable state on the Kaypro. *TERM2* is shown in Figure 12-33.

Figure 12-33 *TERM2*: terminal program with support for baud rate and data format.

```
#include "stdio.h"
#include "siodef.h"
#include "ascii.h"

#define MENU    CTRL_A              /* key for command summary           */

int vers = 2;                       /* version number (global)           */

main()
{
    extern SIO typeAsio;            /* found in computer-specific file   */
    void term();                    /* return type declaration           */
    SIO *siop = &typeAsio;          /* pointer to the level-0 SIO        */
    s_config(siop);                 /* save/config interface             */
    setparity(siop,siop->par->start);  /* start values for data format   */
    setdatalen(siop, siop->dl->start);
    setstops(siop, siop->sb->start);
    setbaud(siop, siop->br->start); /* install startup baud rate         */

    term(siop);                     /* pass SIO pointer to term function */

    s_restore(siop);
    printf("\nEnd of TERM%d \n", vers);
    return(0);
}

void term(siop)
SIO *siop;                          /* required by the revised functions */
{
    UNCHANGED FROM TERM2
}


#define FORMAT  'A'                 /* setup serial parameters           */
#define EXIT    'Q'                 /* key to exit from term             */
```

Figure 12-33 cont. *TERM2*: terminal program with support for baud rate and data format.

```
int menu(siop)                              /* menu now gets SIO pointer       */
SIO *siop;
{
    void setup();
    int c;
    int retval = 0;
    static char *menus[] =
        {
        "\tA.  Data Format, Baud rate",
        "\tQ.  EXIT",
        ""                                  /* null string terminates list     */
        };
    char ** menup;
    c = !EXIT;
    while (c != EXIT)
        {
        puts("\n\n");
        for (menup = menus; **menup != NUL ; menup++)
        printf("%s\n", *menup);
        printf("\n\t\t Enter selection  (CR to quit menu) :  ");
        if ( (c = getch()) == CR)
            break;              /* return to term */
        c = toupper(c);
        switch (c)
            {
            case EXIT:              /* back to DOS                    */
                retval = 1;
                break;
            case FORMAT:            /* Data format, Baud rate         */
                setup(siop);
                break;
            default:
                puts("Invalid choice\n\007");
                break;
            }
        }
    puts("\nExiting menu");
    return (retval);    /* will be zero except if EXIT */
}

void setup(siop)                                /* change data format and baud rate */
SIO *siop;
{
    extern char *errstr[], *sbstr[], *parstr[], *dlstr[], *brstr[];
    int (*fcnp)(), choice, errcode;
```

341

Figure 12-33 cont. *TERM2*: terminal program with support for baud rate and data format.

```
    for (fcnp = NIL; ;fcnp = NIL)         /* loop forever, reset pointer      */
        {
        puts("\nCURRENT SETTINGS:\n");
        printf("1. Baud Rate [ %-6.6s ]\n", brstr[baudnow(siop)]);
        printf("2. Parity    [ %-6.6s ]\n", parstr[paritynow(siop)]);
        printf("3. Stop bits [ %-6.6s ]\n", sbstr[stopsnow(siop)]);
        printf("4. Data Bits [ %-6.6s ]\n", dlstr[dlnow(siop)]);
        printf("5. Display this menu again.\n");
        printf("Enter your choice (press RETURN to exit): ");
        switch (choice = getch())                  /* assign function pointer */
            {
            case '1':
                fcnp = setbaud;
                /* sexy menu for baud rates here */
                break;
            case '2':
                fcnp = setparity;
                /* sexy menu for parity here */
                break;
            case '3':
                fcnp = setstops;
                /* sexy menu for stop bits here */
                break;
            case '4':
                fcnp = setdatalen;
                /* sexy menu for data length here */
                break;
            case '5':
                continue;
            case CR:
                puts("\nExiting format select.");
                return;
            default:
                puts("\n\007- invalid entry -");
                break;
            }
    if (fcnp != NIL)                       /* if a valid choice was made */
        do  {
            printf("\nEnter code for new value and press return: ");
            scanf("%d",&choice);
                if ( (errcode = (*fcnp)(siop, choice)) != 0)
                    printf("ERROR: %s\n\007",errstr[errcode]);
        } while (errcode != 0);
    }
}
```

An Explanation of TERM2   Considering the amount and density of information contained in this chapter, none of the new features of this program should be perplexing. After calling `s_config` to save the state of the serial port (or set it, as the case may be), the level-3 data format and baud rate functions are called to install the start-up values contained in their respective structures. Then the function `term` is called to enter the terminal section of the program. The function `term` remains unchanged from the previous versions.

As before, when **Ctrl-A** is typed, the `menu` function is called. Note that this function now makes use of the `SIO` pointer argument passed from `term`. Once in the menu, pressing ''A'' invokes `setup`, the routine to change the data format and baud rate settings. Upon entry to this function the current data format settings are displayed by calling the various ''now'' functions; the return value from these functions becomes an index into their respective string arrays. (Recall that the `now` member is kept current by the level-2 routines.)

Next, `getch` fetches the user's menu selection from the keyboard and places it in the variable `choice` to which a `switch` is applied. (The submenus for the four functions are left to your imagination.) The idea of this loop is to assign a function pointer, `fcnp`, based upon the user's selection. Beyond the switch, a non-NIL `fcnp` indicates a valid entry—the user's selection from the imaginary menu. This selection, which should be a positive integer in the range 0 to 5, is then passed as an argument to the function pointed to by `fcnp`. The level-2 functions `vsetbits` and `vsetbr` return 0 if the argument is reasonable, or an error code 1-3. An error code returned from the call to `fcnp` becomes an index into the string of error messages, `errstr`.

One final stylistic point: the function pointer is set to NIL (an illegal value for a pointer) each time through the loop, by an eternal loop with a *null conditional clause*. This produces an endless loop:

```
for (fcnp = NIL; ;fcnp = NIL)          /* no conditional */
```

The only way to exit the loop is with the CR case that executes a `return`.

For devotees of terse C coding, the following alternative is almost irresistible:

```
if (fcnp)                    /* if a valid choice was made */
    do   {
         printf("\nEnter code for new value: ");
         scanf("%d", &choice);
         puts(errstr[errcode = (*fcnp)(siop, choice)]);
         } while (errcode != 0);
```

Conclusion

Once comprehended, the functions, structures, and data in this chapter can have an enormously liberating effect upon program design. Their most striking characteristic is their portability when complemented with the necessary level-0 and -1 files. By systematically squeezing the hardware dependencies from the two highest layers of our code, we also reap an important side benefit—a suite of functions that employ a consistent, natural calling sequence and are therefore manifestly easy to understand.

In the next chapter we will complete our "virtual UART" by adding RS-232 functions and one or two miscellaneous functions.

13

RS-232 Control

Although RS-232 subjects have a history of confounding users, programmers also have difficulty with it. As we discussed in Chapter 5, there is persistent and widespread confusion between the RS-232 interface and asynchronous serial I/O. Programmers quickly discover that in the course of even the most mundane chore they are likely to run into this electrical Maginot Line. There is scarcely a serial application that is not in some way expected to control an external device through the RS-232 interface.

In previous chapters we have argued that the serial interface should *always* be restored upon exit. Yet following this advice inevitably gives rise to irresolvable conflicts. Take, for example, the case where a modem and another serial device share a single serial port (not simultaneously, of course). Good programming practice dictates that when terminating, modem software should inhibit the DTR (Data Terminal Ready) input to prevent the automatic answering of incoming calls. If a printer (or other serial device) subsequently connected to this port requires DTR to be asserted, however, it does not function properly. These two applications have fundamentally different RS-232 requirements: if DTR is asserted, the modem answers the phone; if inhibited, the printer doesn't function.

There are no pat solutions to problems of this nature because they arise from applying the RS-232 interface where it was never intended—printer handshaking, for example. Even though intelligent modems provide a partial solution to this particular problem by disabling auto-answer with software commands, other conflicts sooner or later arise that are not so easily resolved. Therefore, to enter asynchronous serial I/O applications without complete control over the RS-232 interface is to enter a duel unarmed. The purpose of this chapter is to provide the armament. Continuing with the "virtual UART" theme from Chapter 12, we will now compose the functions required to implement the following RS-232 features:

- RS-232 outputs: RTS (Request to Send), DTR (Data Terminal Ready), and two general-purpose outputs, GPO1 and GPO2

- RS-232 inputs: CTS (Clear to Send), DSR (Data Set Ready), DCD (Data Carrier Detect), RI (Ring Indicator), and two general-purpose inputs, GPI1 and GPI2

Because RS-232 output control is so similar to our previous experience with data format and baud rate, we will undertake it first. For the sake of notational convenience, abbreviations for the RS-232 functions are used for the remainder of this chapter.

RS-232 UART Outputs

The goal in this section is to develop generalized functions required to assert or inhibit RTS, DTR, and the two general-purpose outputs, GPO1 and GPO2. The general-purpose outputs are not associated with any "official" name or pin assignment in the RS-232 standard. That is, their use is completely at the discretion of the hardware designer. Sometimes circuit designers use these outputs to implement some of the more obscure RS-232 outputs. At other times they are used for internal functions (on the IBM PC, GPO1 is the 8250's "master" interrupt enable). However they are implemented, from the programmer's point of view they behave identically to "dedicated" outputs.

By the way, it is worth mentioning again that the UART names for the RS-232 outputs are invariably DTE names. When UARTs are configured as DCEs, however, DTE names are misleading and, to the inexperienced programmer anyway, perplexing. Often when UARTs are configured as DCEs, you can adjust by mentally exchanging the following name pairs:

DTE Name	becomes	DCE Name
TD		RD
RD		TD
CTS		RTS
RTS		CTS
DCD		DTR
DTR		DCD
DSR		RI
RI		DSR

You are cautioned against placing too much stock in this list because the relationship between UART outputs and their RS-232 names is inherently superficial. That is, other than the names arbitrarily given to them, there is usually no *functional* difference between, say, the DTR and RTS outputs. Since the outputs are functionally interchangeable, their names should be regarded as descriptions, not design prescriptions. Don't be surprised, for example, to discover that the output that a UART data sheet refers to as CTS is connected to pin 11 on the interface and is intended solely for hardware handshaking!

RS-232 Logic

In our virtual UART, each RS-232 output is governed by a single bit in the UART write registers. If you examine UART data sheets, you may be confused to find that the UART outputs often have names like $\overline{DCD}$ (i.e., NOT DCD), suggesting *negative* logic. As illustrated in Figure 5-12, however, UARTs do not drive the RS-232 output pins directly, but are connected to *RS-232 line driver* ICs that convert the UART's output voltages and currents to those dictated by the RS-232 standard. Since most RS-232 line drivers invert their signals, UARTs must generate a negative voltage in order to cause a positive voltage at the RS-232 output pins. From the programmer's point of view, then, most UARTs employ conventional *positive* logic—a TRUE output control bit generates a positive voltage on the corresponding interface pin. There are, of course, a few UARTs with bona fide negative logic where a TRUE bit produces a negative voltage on the interface.

RS-232 Output and the Virtual UART

It should come as no surprise that we will implement our RS-232 output functions within the framework of the virtual register scheme. Although there are no new programming techniques or constructions presented in this chapter, everything here depends upon your understanding the "virtual" concept. So be forewarned: you will find this chapter tough going without a thorough understanding of Chapter 12.

Before we begin composing the RS-232 output functions, Figure 13-1 lists the constants required for RS-232 output control. These constants should reside in *SIODEF.H*, *U8250.H*, and *Z80SIO.H* as indicated.

Figure 13-1 Constants to support RS-232 output functions.

| OFF | 0 | /* RS-232 inhibited */ |
| ON | 1 | /* RS-232 asserted */ |

Constant	U8250.H	Z80SIO.H
DTRMASK	0xFE /* 1111 1110 */	0x7F /* 0111 1111 */
RTSMASK	0xFD /* 1111 1101 */	0xFD /* 1111 1101 */
GP02MASK	0xF7 /* 1111 0111 */	/* not supported */
GP01MASK	0xFb /* 1111 1011 */	/* not supported */
BRK_MASK	0xBF /* 1011 1111 */	0xEF /* 1110 1111 */

The 'rs232out_' Structure

The structure we will use to describe an RS-232 output is shown in Figure 13-2.

Figure 13-2 A structure to describe an RS-232 output.

```
STRUCT DEF:  vout232_
LIBRARY:     SIODEF.H
DESCRIPTION: Structure of RS-232 output data.

struct vout232_
    {
    BYTE    resetmask;          /* AND mask apply to vreg      */
    BYTE    vregnum;            /* number of virtual register  */
    int     offset;             /* offset of register in uart  */
    BOOL    now;                /* rank of current setting     */
    BOOL    start;              /* rank to use at startup      */
    struct  vout232 *next;      /* pointer to next struct      */
    };
```

An Explanation of 'vout232_' This structure definition is very similar to the `vregbits_` structure in Chapter 12. There is, however, one very big difference: there is no array of "set" masks. From Boolean algebra we know that a bit is reset by ANDing it with 0 and set by ORing it with 1. Stated another way, any bit can be set by ORing with the 1s complement of the mask used to reset it. This greatly simplifies the writing of our level-2 function `vset232`, shown in Figure 13-3.

The 'vset232' Function

The `next` member of the structure serves the same function as in the `vregbits_` structure: a hedge against the virtual UART definition that each RS-232 output is governed by a single bit. In Chapter 12, we saw how the Z80SIO requires two registers to set the data length. Although it is unlikely that a UART will commit more than one bit to an RS-232 output, it certainly *is* possible. As in `vregbits_`, the `next` member allows us to form a linked list of single-bit structures.

Figure 13-3 Level-2 function to control RS-232 outputs.

FUNCTION NAME: `vset232`
LEVEL: 2
LIBRARY: *BUOS.LIB*
DESCRIPTION: Turns selected RS-232 output ON or OFF.
OTHER MODULES: None
RETURNS: `int`: OR_ARG if state argument is other than 0 or 1; BAD_FCN if the requested function is not supported in hardware; otherwise 0.
COMMENTS: The test for a NIL pointer must be the first error test. OFF and ON are defined in *SIODEF.H*

```
int vset232(siop, p232, state)
SIO *siop;
struct vout232_ *p232;
BOOL state;                  /* state in table of mask to use */
{
    if (p232 == NIL)
        return (BAD_FCN);
    if ( state != OFF && state != ON)         /* range check          */
        return (OR_ARG);
    do   {
    siop->v_regp[p232->vregnum][VIR] &= p232->resetmask;  /* reset bit      */
    if (state == ON)
        siop->v_regp[p232->vregnum][VIR] |= ~p232->resetmask;   /* set bit */
    p232->now = state;                          /* update current state variable */
    _vset232(siop, p232, siop->v_regp[p232->vregnum][VIR]);
    p232 = p232->next;
    } while (p232 != NIL);                       /* more structs in linked list?  */
    return (0);
}
```

An Explanation of 'vset232' This function first validates both arguments: OR_ARG is returned if the `state` argument is not OFF or ON; BAD_FCN is returned if the pointed-to `vout232_` structure is NIL (i.e., not supported). If the arguments are valid, the `resetmask` is applied to the virtual register, `vregnum`. As always, the test for a NIL pointer must precede all other tests.

First, the contents of the virtual register are ANDed with `resetmask` to reset the appropriate bit and turn the output OFF:

```
siop->v_regp[p232->vregnum][VIR] &= p232->resetmask;
```

If the `state` argument is ON, the bit is made TRUE by ORing the virtual register with the 1s complement of `resetmask`:

```
siop->v_regp[p232->vregnum][VIR] |= ~p232->resetmask;
```

Finally, after updating the pointed-to `vout232_` structure with the `state` argument, the level-1 function updates the physical UART and returns.

Level-1 RS-232 Output Functions for the Z80SIO and 8250

Versions of the level-1 function `_vset232` for both the Z80SIO and 8250 are shown in Figure 13-4.

Figure 13-4 Level-1 functions to control RS-232 output.

```
FUNCTION NAME:   _vset232
LEVEL:           1
LIBRARY:         U8250.LIB
DESCRIPTION:     Writes the virtual register containing the selected RS-232 output pin to the
                 corresponding UART register.
RETURNS:         void
COMMENTS:        This function is called only by vset232.
```

```
void _vset232(siop, p232, binval)
register SIO *siop;
struct vout232_ *p232;
BYTE binval;
{
    (*siop->writebyte)(siop->uart_base + p232->offset, binval);
}
```

```
FUNCTION NAME:   _vset232
LEVEL:           1
LIBRARY:         Z80SIO.LIB
DESCRIPTION:     Writes the virtual register containing the selected RS-232 output pin to the
                 corresponding UART register.
RETURNS:         void
COMMENTS:        This function is called only by vset232.
```

Figure 13-4 cont.   Level-1 functions to control RS-232 output.

```
void _vset232(siop, p232, binval)
SIO *siop;
struct vout232_ *p232;
BYTE binval;
{
    regwrite(siop, p232->vregnum, binval);
}
```

An Explanation of '_vset232'   The code for both primitives is totally uneventful. Both write a byte to the physical register indicated in the SIO's virtual array. The Z80SIO version calls regwrite, the function given in Chapter 12, to simplify the two-step process for accessing a Z80SIO register.

The BREAK Signal

As discussed in Chapter 6, the BREAK signal is the source of a great deal of confusion. It is sometimes called the BREAK ''character,'' although it is actually just the opposite of a character. Sometimes it is discussed (usually in the novice/hobbyist press) as if it were somehow part of the RS-232 standard, which it is not. To review: a BREAK is a condition in which the line is held at SPACE for longer than one SDU.

Whatever a BREAK *is*, it can certainly be well described by a vout232_ structure. If you find the use of a vout232_ structure to describe a BREAK to be intellectually disquieting, notice that a vout232_ structure is really a general mechanism for controlling one bit or an entire group of bits as one unit. In this respect, it is a complement to vregbits_, which is a general way to control individual bits. At any rate, the structure declarations and initializations necessary to implement the BREAK signal as a vout232_ structure are included here. Just remember that including the BREAK in our discussion of RS-232 outputs does not imply that it is an RS-232 condition.

RS-232 Members in the 'SIO'

The SIO definition in *SIODEF.H* requires new members to accommodate the four vout232_ functions defined by our virtual UART. The relevant additions are shown in Figure 13-5.

Figure 13-5   New SIO members to support RS-232 output.

STRUCT DEF: SIO
FILE: *SIODEF.H*
DESCRIPTION: Typedef of master structure for defining a serial port.
COMMENTS: Support for RS-232 outputs and BREAK.

Figure 13-5 cont.   New SIO members to support RS-232 output.

```
typedef struct
     {
     BYTE        *uart_base;               /* base address of UART            */
     :
     struct      vregbits_ *sb;            /* pointer to stop bit structure   */
     struct      vregbits_ *dl;            /* pointer to data length structure */
     struct      baud_     *br;            /* pointer to baud rate structure  */
     struct      vout232_  *rts;           /* pointer to RTS structure        */
     struct      vout232_  *dtr;           /* pointer to DTR structure        */
     struct      vout232_  *gpo1;          /* pointer to GPOUTPUT1 structure  */
     struct      vout232_  *gpo2;          /* pointer to GPOOUTPUT2 structure */
     struct      vout232_  *brkbit;        /* pointer to break structure      */
     } SIO;
```

An Explanation of 'SIO'   The five new members—rts, dtr, gpo1, gpo2, and brkbit—are all declared to be of type "pointer to struct vout232_"; remember, these names assume that the serial port is configured as a DTE.

Declaration of 'vout232_' Structures

Having written the level-1 and level-2 functions, we are now ready to declare and initialize instances of the vout232_ structures. The structures for *IBMPC.C* and *KAYPRO.C* are in Figure 13-6. The constants used for initialization were given in Figure 13-1.

These declarations are so straightforward they hardly merit discussion. The names of the RS-232 output structures are named after the pins defined by the RS-232 standard. Again, these pin numbers assume a DTE device (both the IBM PC and Kaypro 4 are DTEs). The 8250 supports two general-purpose outputs through its Modem Control register; the Z80SIO, however, does not.

Figure 13-6   Declaration and initialization for vout232_ structures.

STRUCT NAME: pin4A, pin20A, gp1outA, gp2outA, breakA
TYPE: vout232_
LEVEL: 0
FILE: *IBMPC.C*
DESCRIPTION: Declaration and initialization of RS-232 and BREAK output control structures.

```
struct vout232_ pin4A =             /****     RTS        ****/
     {
     RTSMASK,                       /* mask to reset RTS      */
     V232OUT,                       /* virtual reg number     */
     4,                             /* offset of UART reg     */
     SUPPLIED,                      /* state of RTS bit now   */
     OFF,                           /* state for startup      */
     NIL                            /* pointer to next        */
     };
```

Figure 13-6 cont.   Declaration and initialization for vout232_ structures.

```
struct vout232_ pin20A =              /****      DTR        ****/
        {
        DTRMASK,
        V2320UT,
        4,
        SUPPLIED,
        OFF,
        NIL
        };

struct vout232_ gploutA =             /****      GPO1       ****/
        {
        GPO1MASK,
        V2320UT,
        4,
        SUPPLIED,
        OFF,
        NIL
        };

struct vout232_ gp2outA =             /****      GPO2       ****/
        {
        GPO2MASK,
        V2320UT,
        4,
        SUPPLIED,
        OFF,
        NIL
        };

struct vout232_ breakbA =             /* BREAK signal       */
        {
        BRK_MASK,
        VFMT,
        3,
        SUPPLIED,
        OFF,
        NIL
        };
```

STRUCT NAME: pin4A, pin20A, and breakA
TYPE: vout232_
LEVEL: 0
FILE: KAYPRO.C
DESCRIPTION: Declaration and initialization of RS-232 and BREAK output control structures.
COMMENTS: Z80SIO has no general-purpose outputs.

Figure 13-6 cont. Declaration and initialization for `vout232_` structures.

```
struct vout232_ pin4A =              /****     RTS        ****/
    {
    RTSMASK,                         /* mask to reset RTS    */
    WR5,                             /* virtual reg number   */
    SP_OFF,                          /* offset of UART reg    */
    SUPPLIED,                        /* state of RTS bit now */
    OFF,                             /* state for startup    */
    NIL                              /* pointer to next      */
    };

 struct vout232_ pin20A =             /****     DTR        ****/
    {
    DTRMASK,
    WR5,
    SP_OFF,
    SUPPLIED,
    OFF,
    NIL
    };

/* NO GENERAL-PURPOSE OUTPUTS ON Z80SIO */

struct vout232_ breakbA =            /* BREAK signal */
    {
    BRK_MASK,
    WR5,
    SP_OFF,
    SUPPLIED,
    OFF,
    NIL
    };
```

'SIO' Declaration

Figure 13-7 shows the relevant fragments of the SIO declaration for both *IBMPC.C* and *KAYPRO.C*.

Figure 13-7 Declaration and initialization of the current SIO.

'SIO' NAME: `typeAsio`
FILE: *IBMPC.C*
COMMENTS: Support added for RS-232 outputs and BREAK functions.

Figure 13-7 cont. Declaration and initialization of the current `SIO`.

```
SIO typeAsio =
    {
    COMM1,                          /* base address of UART              */
    :
    &stopsA,                        /* stop bit structure               */
    &dlenA,                         /* data length structure            */
    &baudA,                         /* baud rate structure              */
    &pin4A,                         /* RS-232 RTS output                */
    &pin20A,                        /* RS-232 DTR output                */
    &gp1outA,                       /* RS-232 first user-defined output */
    &gp2outA,                       /* RS-232 2nd user-defined output   */
    &breakbA,                       /* break bit                        */
    };
```

'SIO' NAME: typeAsio
FILE: *KAYPRO.C*
COMMENTS: Support added for RS-232 outputs and BREAK functions.

```
SIO typeAsio =
    {
    PORT1                           /* base address of UART              */
    :
    &stopsA,                        /* stop bit structure               */
    &dlenA,                         /* data length structure            */
    &baudA,                         /* baud rate structure              */
    &pin4A,                         /* RS-232 RTS output                */
    &pin20A,                        /* RS-232 DTR output                */
    NIL,                            /* user-defined outputs not supported */
    NIL,                            /* user-defined outputs not supported */
    &breakbA,                       /* break bit                        */
    };
```

An Explanation of 'typeAsio'   The addresses of the structures are used to initialize the new members of the `SIO`. Since the Z80SIO does not support the two general-purpose inputs, the Kaypro's `SIO` must initialize these members to `NIL`. This value, of course, is required as a place holder in the initialization list, but it also serves another important purpose. Every level-2 function we have written so far has contained a line such as

```
if (pointer == NIL)
    return (BAD_FCN);
```

Because of this test, attempts to change the state of an unsupported bit—the general-purpose outputs on a Z80SIO, for example—return an error code.

Level-3 Functions for RS-232 Output

We have written the level-1 and level-2 functions, and declared instances of vout232_ structures for both Z80SIO and 8250; we have added the new functions to the SIO definition and added initializers to the typeAsio declarations. We are now ready to compose the level-3 functions shown in Figure 13-8.

Figure 13-8 Level-3 RS-232 output functions.

FUNCTION NAME: setrts, setdtr, setgpo1, setgpo2, setbrk
LEVEL: 3
LIBRARY: *SIO.LIB*
DESCRIPTION: These functions set or reset their respective RS-232 output pins.
OTHER MODULES: vset232
RETURNS: int: OR_ARG if state argument is other than 0 or 1; BAD_FCN if the requested function is not supported in hardware; otherwise 0.

```
int setrts(siop, state)                    /* set RST */
SIO  *siop;
BOOL state;
{
     return (vset232(siop, siop->rts, state));
}

int setdtr(siop, state)                    /* set DTR */
SIO  *siop;
BOOL state;
{
     return (vset232(siop, siop->dtr, state));
}

int setgpo1(siop, state)                   /* set 1st general-purpose output */
SIO  *siop;
BOOL state;
{
     return (vset232(siop, siop->gpo1, state));
}

int setgpo2(siop, state)                   /* set 2nd general-purpose output */
SIO  *siop;
BOOL state;
{
     return (vset232(siop, siop->gpo2, state));
}

int setbrk(siop)
SIO *siop;
{
     vset232(siop, siop->brkbit, ON);
     delay(_0_SEC_3);
     return (vset232(siop, siop->brkbit, OFF));
}
```

An Explanation of the RS-232 Output Functions   These functions strongly resemble the functions for setting the data format and the baud rate. All call the level-2 function, `vset232`, passing as arguments a pointer to the `SIO`, a pointer to the relevant `SIO` member, and the desired state (i.e., on or off) for the RS-232 output. All functions return the error codes passed back from `vset232`.

The 'setbrk' Function

This function merely turns on the UART's BREAK bit, pauses for about 300 milliseconds, then turns it off again. As we have mentioned several times, there is no such thing as a "standard" break signal; technically, UARTs interpret *any* SPACE condition that lasts longer than the current SDU as a BREAK. If the longest possible SDU is 12 (8E2 plus one start bit), and the baud rate is 50, any SPACE longer than $12 \div 50$ or roughly 250 milliseconds should be detected as a BREAK. This BREAK duration will probably suffice in most situations, but, in the absence of standardization, you must be able to adjust its duration. It is left to the reader as an exercise to write the code for a BREAK function whose duration is programmable.

RS-232 Output Status Functions

In addition to the functions in Figure 13-8, which change the state of an RS-232 output, it is sometimes useful—if not essential—to be able to read the *current* state of an output. The simple level-3 functions shown in Figure 13-9 perform that function.

Figure 13-9   Level-3 functions to return the current state of RS-232 outputs.

FUNCTION NAME: `dtrnow, rtsnow, gpo1now, gpo2now`
LEVEL: 3
LIBRARY: *SIO.LIB*
DESCRIPTION: Fetch current state of RS-232 outputs.
OTHER MODULES: None
RETURNS: `int`: BAD_FCN if the output is not supported; otherwise ON/OFF.

```
int dtrnow(siop)
SIO *siop;
{
     if (siop->dtr == NIL)
         return (BAD_FCN);
     return (siop->dtr->now);
}

int rtsnow(siop)
SIO *siop;
{
     if (siop->rts == NIL)
          return (BAD_FCN);
     return (siop->rts->now);
}
```

Figure 13-9 cont. Level-3 functions to return the current state of RS-232 outputs.

```
int gpo1now(siop)
SIO *siop;
{
    if (siop->gpo1 == NIL)
        return (BAD_FCN);
    return (siop->gpo1->now);
}

int gpo2now(siop)
SIO *siop;
{
    if (siop->gpo2 == NIL)
        return (BAD_FCN);
    return (siop->gpo2->now);
}
```

An Explanation of 'setup232' These functions return an error code if the requested RS-232 output function is not supported; otherwise, they return the now member of the relevant vout232_ structure. Since now members are updated at level-2, each function assumes that its corresponding "set" function in Figure 13-8 has been previously called, presumably during initialization.

TERM3

The new functions enable us to control RS-232 outputs in *TERM*. The ability to control the DTR output, which is almost universally supported by modems, is particularly important in terminal programs. DTR, you will recall, is the modem's "master enable," without which the modem ignores all data and, in the case of smart modems, commands.

With the wide popularity of smart modems, programmers are increasingly inclined to perform *every* modem function with software commands. This is unfortunate, and in most cases, degrades the performance of the software. The Hayes Smartmodem, for example, can be configured to assume that DTR is asserted at all times (see Chapter 8). This ability to override DTR makes it possible to use a simple three-wire cable instead of an eccentric RS-232 cable. DTR override is admittedly a convenience, but ultimately it is just that—a convenience. The truth is that intelligent modem control via DTR is immeasurably simpler than control via software commands.

Figure 13-10 gives the incidental changes and additions to *TERM3*.

Figure 13-10 *TERM3*: incidental changes from *TERM2*.

PROGRAM NAME: *TERM3*
DESCRIPTION: Terminal program

Figure 13-10 cont. *TERM3*: incidental changes from *TERM2*.

```
COMMENTS:        Features:
                 Baud rate and data format set
                 Serial interface restored upon exit
                 RS-232 output control
                 Transmitted BREAK signal

int vers = 3;                            /* version number  (global)      */
          ⋮

#define FORMAT  'A'                      /* Setup serial parmeters        */
#define RS232   'B'                      /* RS-232 output control         */
#define BRK     'C'                      /* send BREAK signal             */
#define EXIT    'Q'                      /* key to exit from term         */
          ⋮
          {
          "\tA.  Data Format, Baud rate",
          "\tB.  RS-232 control",
          "\tC.  Transmit BREAK signal",
          "\tQ.  EXIT",
          ""                             /* null string terminates list   */
          };
          ⋮
          case RS232:                    /* RS232 output control          */
              setup232(siop);
              break;
          case BRK:                      /* send BREAK                    */
              setbrk(siop);
              break;
          ⋮
```

An Explanation of TERM3   The changes to the terminal functions are slight: two new `case` statements have been added to the keyboard `switch` in `menu` in order to support BREAK transmission and RS-232 output control. The BREAK case calls the level-3 function `setbrk`, while the RS232 case calls the local function `setup232`, shown in Figure 13-11. The menu array has also been adjusted to reflect these changes.

Figure 13-11   Level-3 functions to control RS-232 and to transmit a BREAK.

```
MODULE NAME:     setup232
DESCRIPTION:     Function to transmit BREAK and control RS-232 outputs: RTS, DTR, and two general-
                 purpose outputs.
OTHER MODULES:   setdtr, dtrnow, setgo1, gpo1now, setbrk, setgpo2, gpo2now, setrts,
                 rtsnow.
```

Figure 13-11 cont.   Level-3 functions to control RS-232 and to transmit a BREAK.

RETURNS: void
COMMENTS: The two general-purpose outputs are not necessarily mapped to RS-232 pins.

```
void setup232(siop)
SIO *siop;
{
    extern char *errstr[];            /* error strings */
    extern int setrts(), setdtr(), setgpo1(), setgpo2();
    static char *statstr[] = {"OFF", "ON", "--"};
    int (*fcnp)();
    int choice, errcode, rtsstat, dtrstat, gpolstat, gpo2stat, *statp;
    rtsstat  =  rtsnow(siop); dtrstat  =  dtrnow(siop);
    gpolstat =  gpolnow(siop); gpo2stat =  gpo2now(siop);
    for (fcnp = NIL; ;fcnp = NIL)      /* loop forever, reinitialize pointer */
        {
        printf("\n1. Toggle RTS  [ %3s ]\n", statstr[rtsstat]  );
        printf( "2. Toggle DTR  [ %3s ]\n", statstr[dtrstat]  );
        printf( "3. Toggle GPO1 [ %3s ]\n", statstr[gpolstat] );
        printf( "4. Toggle GPO2 [ %3s ]\n", statstr[gpo2stat] );
        puts(   "5. Exit this function\n");
        printf("Enter your choice and press RETURN: ");
        scanf("%d", &choice);
        switch (choice)               /* assign function & status pointer  */
            {
            case 1: fcnp  = setrts;  statp = &rtsstat;  break;
            case 2: fcnp  = setdtr;  statp = &dtrstat;  break;
            case 3: fcnp  = setgpo1; statp = &gpolstat; break;
            case 4: fcnp  = setgpo2; statp = &gpo2stat; break;
            case 5:
                puts("Exiting RS232 setup.");
                return;
            default:
                puts("\007- invalid entry -");
                break;
            }
        if (fcnp != NIL)                      /* if a valid choice was made   */
            {
            if (*statp != BAD_FCN)        /* if this function is supported*/
                *statp = !(*statp);        /* toggle its status            */
            if ( (errcode = (*fcnp)(siop, *statp)) != 0)
                printf("ERROR:  %s\n\007",errstr[errcode]);
            }
        }
}
```

An Explanation of 'setup232'   The design of this function is similar to the data format function (setup) inherited from *TERM2*: an eternal for loop (with a blank conditional clause) polls the keyboard for a menu choice. The loop is broken only when the user chooses "Exit" from the menu.

Before entering the `for` loop, the status variables (e.g., `dtrstat`) are initialized by calling the level-3 "set" functions. These status variables therefore contain a positive integer in the range 0 to 2: 0 or 1 represents the state of the respective pins; a value of BAD_FCN marks a function as being unsupported. The selection menu uses these integer status variables to index into `statstr`, an array of pointers describing the three possible states: OFF, ON, or "--".

A `switch` is applied to the selection entered from the keyboard. Each valid `case` assigns a value to two pointers: the function pointer `fcnp` and the status pointer `statp`. When a valid selection is entered (i.e., if `fcnp != NIL`), the pointed-to status variable is toggled between 0 and 1 with the logical NOT operator. The "set" function, called through the pointer `fcnp`, uses the status variable as an argument. The `for` loop repeats and the new setting is reflected in the menu display.

Errors are announced by using any non-0 return code from the called function as an index into the `errstr` string array given previously in Figure 12-32.

RS-232 Input Status

If control over the RS-232 outputs enables you to signal the outside world, the ability to read the RS-232 inputs enables the outside world to signal you. In many applications, including the smartmodem library in Chapter 17, the ability to read the status of RS-232 inputs is your only contact with the hardware you are controlling. The need to monitor the status of the RS-232 inputs is not limited to modem control, but is generally required for hardware *flow control*—where the receiving device (such as a printer) can ingest data much faster than it can digest data. Despite all the efforts by printer manufacturers to promote software-controlled buffer handshaking, RS-232 control is still the most popular method. To complete our mastery over the RS-232 interface, then, we will compose a set of functions in support of the four RS-232 inputs in the virtual UART function described in Chapter 12:

CTS   (Clear to Send) In half-duplex modem connections, the modem uses CTS to signal the DTE device when the line has been successfully reversed from receive to transmit modes. Since very few microcomputer applications involve half-duplex transmission, however, CTS is employed as a general-purpose input.

DSR   (Data Set Ready) As defined by the RS-232 standard, DSR goes high when the modem's carrier has been turned on (answer mode) or when the line is off-hook waiting for a carrier (originate mode). On microcomputer equipment, DSR is often used less formally as an "I'm awake and ready" signal to the DTE. In these situations, it is essentially a power-on indicator. (On pre-2400 Hayes Smartmodems, DSR is physically tied to DCD.)

DCD   (Data Carrier Detect) When a modem achieves a data link with another modem, it asserts DCD.

RI   (Ring Indicator) The modem asserts RI during phone line ringer pulses.

In addition to the preceding four RS-232 inputs, our virtual UART supports two general-purpose inputs, GPI1 and GPI2. These inputs, if present, may or may not be connected to the RS-232 interface. Figure 13-12 shows the manifest constants required to support the RS-232 input functions that follow. Neither UART supports GPI1 or GPI2.

Figure 13-12 RS-232 input constants for *Z80SIO.H* and *U8250.H*.

Constant	U8250.H		Z80SIO.H	
CTSMASK	`0x10`	`/* 0001 0000 */`	`0x20`	`/* 0000 0010 */`
DSRMASK	`0x20`	`/* 0010 0000 */`		`/* Not Supported */`
RIMASK	`0x40`	`/* 0100 0000 */`		`/* Not Supported */`
DCDMASK	`0x80`	`/* 1000 0000 */`	`0x08`	`/* 0000 1000 */`

The 'vin232_' Structure

By now you should be accustomed to the basic plan for new virtual features: define a structure to describe the physical attributes of that feature, write three levels of functions to relate the virtual to the physical UART, then install pointers to instances of these structures in the SIO. Figure 13-13 shows the structure definition required for RS-232 inputs.

Figure 13-13 `vin232_`: a structure to describe an RS-232 input.

```
STRUCT DEF:   vin232_
FILE:         SIODEF.H
DESCRIPTION:  Structure to describe an RS-232 input.
COMMENTS:     Contains a pointer to the level-1 status function.
struct vin232_
     {
     BYTE      vregnum;          /* number of virtual register       */
     int       offset;           /* offset of physical register in UART */
     BYTE      mask;             /* mask to isolate active bit        */
     BYTE      now;              /* current value of this input       */
     BYTE      (*read232)();     /* pointer to level-1 fetch function */
     };
```

The first four members of this structure follow our familiar pattern, containing a virtual and physical description of the object, in this case an RS-232 input. The final member read232, a pointer to a function, however, is entirely new. For the time being, this pointer should be initialized to point to an ordinary level-1 function as we have learned to write them; in a few pages we will examine the reasoning behind this construction and the circumstance under which a different function would be pointed to.

Level-1 and Level-2 Functions for Fetching RS-232 Input Status

Since initialization of a `vin232_` structure requires a pointer to the level-1 function, we will break with precedent and compose the level-1 before the level-2 function. This function is shown in Figure 13-14.

Figure 13-14   Level-1 functions to fetch RS-232 input status.

```
FUNCTION NAME:  _vstat232
LEVEL:          1
LIBRARY:        U8250.LIB
DESCRIPTION:    Reads the UART register containing the status bit for the appropriate RS-232 input. A
                pointer to this function resides in each vin232_ structure.
RETURNS:        BYTE
```

```
BYTE _vstat232(siop, p232)
register SIO *siop;
struct vin232_ *p232;
{
    return ( (*siop->readbyte)(siop->uart_base + p232->offset) );
}
```

```
FUNCTION NAME:  _vstat232
LEVEL:          1
LIBRARY:        Z80SIO.LIB
DESCRIPTION:    Reads the UART register containing the status bit for the appropriate RS-232 input. A
                pointer to this function resides in each vin232_ structure.
RETURNS:        BYTE
COMMENTS:       Changes in RS-232 status are latched until "reset" by clearing the "Reset External/
                Status" bit (bit 4) in Write Register 0.
```

```
BYTE _vstat232(siop, p232)
SIO *siop;
struct vin232_ *p232;
{
    regwrite(siop, 0, 0x10);     /* reset EXT/STATUS bit in WR[0] */
    return ( (*siop->readbyte)(siop->uart_base + p232->offset) );
}
```

An Explanation of '_vstat232'   The 8250 version of this function is the model of simplicity—it passes the SIO and a pointer to a vin232_ structure, and merely returns the UART register at the offset given in the structure. The Z80SIO version, however, contains an interesting twist. When a Z80SIO's RS-232 input changes, its value is latched into a bit in the status register; subsequent changes in the input have no effect upon the status register until the latch is cleared. The latch is controlled by bit 4 in WR[0], the "External/Status Reset bit." Any read of the RS-232 status register must therefore be preceded by writing 10H to Write Register 0.

Declarations of the 'vin232_' Structures

With the level-1 function out of the way, we can now create the vin232_ structures. Figure 13-15 shows the declarations and initializations of the four vin232_ structures for *IBMPC.C* and *KAYPRO.C*.

Figure 13-15 The `vin232_` structures for RS-232 input.

STRUCT NAMES: pin5A, pin6A, pin8A, and pin22A
TYPE: vin232_
LEVEL: 0
FILE: *IBMPC.C*
DESCRIPTION: vin232_ structures for RS-232 control

```
BYTE _vstat232();    /* return type declaration */

 struct vin232_ pin5A =              /*** CTS  ***/
     {
     6,                              /* offset of UART register    */
     CTSMASK,                        /* AND mask for this bit       */
     SUPPLIED,                       /* value of bit at last test   */
     _vstat232                       /* pointer to level-1 function */
     };

struct vin232_ pin6A =               /*** DSR ***/
     {
     6,
     DSRMASK,
     SUPPLIED,
     _vstat232
     };

 struct vin232_ pin8A =              /*** DCD ***/
     {
     6,
     DCDMASK,
     SUPPLIED,
     _vstat232
     };

 struct vin232_ pin22A =             /*** RI ***/
     {
     6,
     RIMASK,
     SUPPLIED,
     _vstat232
     };
```

STRUCT NAMES: pin5A and pin6A
TYPE: vin232_
LEVEL: 0
FILE: *KAYPRO.C*
DESCRIPTION: vin232_ structures for RS-232 control

Figure 13-15 cont.   The `vin232_` structures for RS-232 input.

```
BYTE _vstat232();    /* return type declaration */


struct vin232_ pin5A =              /*** CTS   ***/
   {
   SP_OFF,                          /* offset of UART register    */
   CTSMASK,                         /* AND mask for this bit       */
   SUPPLIED,                        /* value of bit at last test   */
   _vstat232                        /* pointer to level-1 function */
   };


struct vin232_ pin8A =              /*** DCD ***/
   {
   SP_OFF,
   DCDMASK,
   SUPPLIED,
    _vstat232
   };
```

The 8250 supports all RS-232 input functions described by our virtual UART; the Z80SIO supports only CTS and DCD. Unfortunately, neither provides general-purpose inputs. As with the RS-232 outputs, the names given these structures—"pin5," for example—are their DTE names.

RI declaration for the Z80DART

Although Zilog, Inc. advertises the Z80DART as the asynchronous portion of the Z80SIO, in fact there is one difference: the Z80DART supports the RS-232 Ring Indicator (RI) input conspicuously missing from the Z80SIO. The `vin232_` structure declaration and constant definition for the Z80DART looks like this:

```
#define RIMASK    0x20
struct vin232_ pin22A =         /* RI for Z80DART */
     {
     SP_OFF,       /* offset of UART register    */
     RIMASK,       /* AND mask for this bit       */
     SUPPLIED,     /* value of bit at last test   */
     _vstat232     /* pointer to level-1 function */
     };
```

'SIO' Definitions

The new RS-232 inputs must be added to the SIO definition as shown in Figure 13-16.

Figure 13-16   Additions to the SIO definition.

```
STRUCT DEF:   SIO
FILE:         SIODEF.H
DESCRIPTION:  Typedef of master structure for defining a serial port.
COMMENTS:     Addition of members to support RS-232 input.

typedef struct
    {
    BYTE       *uart_base;                /* base address of UART          */
    :
    struct    vout232_ *brkbit;
    struct    vin232_  *cts;       /* pointer to  CTS structure     */
    struct    vin232_  *dsr;       /* pointer to  DSR structure     */
    struct    vin232_  *dcd;       /* pointer to  DCD structure     */
    struct    vin232_  *ri;        /* pointer to  RI structure      */
    struct    vin232_  *gpil;      /* pointer to  GPINPUT1 structure */
    struct    vin232_  *gpi2;      /* pointer to  GPINPUT2 structure */
    } SIO;
```

The Level-2 RS-232 Input Function ('vstat232')

Everything is now in place to compose the level-2 function required to handle the logical portion of RS-232 input. This function is shown in Figure 13-17.

Figure 13-17   Level-2 function to fetch RS-232 status.

```
FUNCTION NAME:  vstat232
LEVEL:          2
LIBRARY:        BUOS.LIB
DESCRIPTION:    Returns status of RS-232 input pointed to by p232.
RETURNS:        int: TRUE if the input is asserted; FALSE if inhibited; BAD_FCN if the input is not
                supported.
COMMENTS:       The call to the level-1 function is through a function pointer in the vin232_ structure.
int vstat232(siop, p232)
SIO *siop;
struct vin232_ *p232;                       /* pointer to a @[vin232]@ structure  */
{
    if (p232 == NIL)
        return (BAD_FCN);                    /* this input not supported     */
    p232->now = (*p232->read232)(siop, p232) & p232->mask;
    return (p232->now  ? TRUE : FALSE);     /* return status               */
}
```

An Explanation of 'vstat232'   As vsetbits and vset232 before it, this function returns an error code of BAD_FCN if the vin232_ structure in the SIO contains NIL, indicating that this particular input is not supported by the UART. The level-1 function fetches the UART register given in p232; the desired bit is masked off with an AND and stored in the now member of the structure.

The call to the level-1 function,

```
(*p232->read232)(siop, p232)
```

is performed through a function pointer in the p232 structure. Why? When we implement RS-232 interrupts in Chapter 20, the service routine will read the RS-232 input status register and place a TRUE or FALSE in the now member of the appropriate structure. When interrupts are on, it is impossible to fetch the status of an RS-232 input by polling a status register, because the interrupt service routine may have cleared the very status bit that must be tested. In other words, RS-232 input by interrupts and RS-232 input by polling require different level-1 functions. We will pick up this discusssion in more concrete terms in Chapter 20.

'SIO' Declaration and Initialization

The declaration and initialization of the new members in SIO are shown for *IBMPC.C* and *KAY-PRO.C* in Figure 13-18. So that calls to unsupported functions will return the correct error code, all unsupported members are initialized to NIL.

Figure 13-18   Declaration and initialization of the expanded SIO.

```
'SIO' NAME: typeAsio
FILE:       IBMPC.C
COMMENTS: Support added for RS-232 inputs.

SIO typeAsio =
    {
    COMM1,                  /* base of UART     */
    :
    &breakbA,
    &pin5A,                 /* RS-232 CTS input */
    &pin6A,                 /* RS-232 DSR input */
    &pin8A,                 /* RS-232 DCD input */
    &pin22A,                /* RS-232 RI  input */
    NIL,                    /* RS-232 gp1 input */
    NIL,                    /* RS-232 gp2 input */
    };
```

Figure 13-18 cont. Declaration and initialization of the expanded SIO.

```
'SIO' NAME: typeAsio
FILE:      KAYPRO.C
COMMENTS: Support added for RS-232 inputs.

SIO typeAsio =
    {
    COMM1,                          /* base of UART     */
    :
    &breakbA,
    &pin5A,                         /* RS-232 CTS input           */
    NIL,                            /* RS-232 DSR  not supported  */
    &pin8A,                         /* RS-232 DCD input           */
    NIL,                            /* RS-232 RI not supported    */
    NIL,                            /* RS-232 gp1  not supported  */
    NIL,                            /* RS-232 gp2  not supported  */
    };
```

Level-3 RS-232 Input Functions

We have now defined, declared, and initialized the vin232_ structures to support the RS-232 input function in our virtual UART. We have also written the level-1 and level-2 functions. All that remains is to compose the level-3 functions, shown in Figure 13-19.

Figure 13-19 Level-3 functions to return status of RS-232 functions.

```
FUNCTION NAME: iscts, isdsr, isdcd, isri, isgpi1, isgpi2
LEVEL:         3
LIBRARY:       SIO.LIB
DESCRIPTION:   Fetches the state of an RS-232 input.
OTHER MODULES: vstat232
RETURNS:       int: BAD_FCN if requested function is not supported; otherwise TRUE/FALSE.

int iscts(siop)
SIO *siop;                 /* pointer to the serial device structure */
{
    return (vstat232(siop, siop->cts));
}

int isdsr(siop)
SIO *siop;
{
    return (vstat232(siop, siop->dsr));
}
```

Figure 13-19 cont. Level-3 functions to return status of RS-232 functions.

```
int isdcd(siop)
SIO *siop;
{
    return (vstat232(siop, siop->dcd));
}

int isri(siop)
SIO *siop;
{
    return (vstat232(siop, siop->ri));
}

int isgpi1(siop)
SIO *siop;
{
    return (vstat232(siop, siop->gpi1));
}

int isgpi2(siop)
SIO *siop;
{
    return (vstat232(siop, siop->gpi2));
}
```

An Explanation of the Level-3 Input Functions These functions proceed in what has become a predictable manner: returning the error code from calling the level-2 function. For the sake of consistency with the other functions, these also return a value of BAD_FCN if the function requested is not supported.

TERM3A

Adding the ability to monitor the RS-232 inputs requires only minor changes to *TERM3*. When these changes are added, we shall refer to the new program as *TERM3A*. The modifications are shown in Figure 13-20.

Figure 13-20 Modifications to the `setup232` function to display status of the RS-232 inputs.

```
void setup232(siop)
SIO *siop;
{
    static char *statstr[] = {"OFF", " ON", "---"};
    int (*fcnp)();
    int choice, errcode, rtsstat, dtrstat, gpo1stat, gpo2stat, *statp;
    rtsstat = rtsnow(siop);  dtrstat  =  dtrnow(siop);
    gpo1stat = gpo1now(siop); gpo2stat =  gpo2now(siop);
```

Figure 13-20 cont. Modifications to the setup232 function to display status of the RS-232 inputs.

```
for (fcnp = NIL; ;fcnp = NIL)      /* loop forever, reinitialize pointer */
    {
    puts("\nCURRENT RS-232 INPUT STATUS:");
    puts("\tCTS   DSR   DCD   RI   GP1   GP2");
    printf("\t%s   %s   %s   %s   %s   %s\n\n",
       statstr[iscts(siop)], statstr[isdsr(siop)], statstr[isdcd(siop)],
       statstr[isri(siop)], statstr[isgpi2(siop)], statstr[isgpi2(siop)]);
    printf("\n1. Toggle RTS  [ %3s ]\n", statstr[rtsstat]  );
    printf(  "2. Toggle DTR  [ %3s ]\n", statstr[dtrstat]  );
    printf(  "3. Toggle GPO1 [ %3s ]\n", statstr[gpo1stat] );
    ⋮
```

An Explanation of 'setup232'   The RS-232 inputs are displayed by calling each status function and using its return value as an index into the array of pointers to strings, statstr. If you find deeply nested C expressions difficult to read, feel free to assign the return value from the status function to an intermediate variable, which in turn becomes the index into the string pointer array:

```
int ctsstat;
ctsstat = iscts(siop);
printf("CTS = %s\n", statstr[ctsstat]);
```

Regardless of the style you choose, the status functions return a value from 0 to 2 and one of the strings is always displayed.

Conclusion

The functions required for programming support of RS-232 input/output are now complete. To demonstrate these functions, we will use them interactively through the menu system in our terminal program. As a practical matter, however, the most powerful use of these functions is in the degree of control they impart to your programs. There will be copious examples of this control in later chapters, where we rely heavily on RS-232 functions.

14

Miscellaneous UART Functions

In the first part of this chapter we will complete our implementation of the virtual UART begun in Chapter 12 by adding four important functions to the SIO:

- A function to enable/disable the UART's transmitter
- A function to enable/disable the UART's receiver
- A function to enable/disable transmitter handshaking on RTS
- A function to enable/disable receiver handshaking on DCD
- A function to change the clocking factor

Although some common UARTs (including the 8250) do not support them, these features are conceptually important in our UART management.

In the second section of this chapter, we'll compose s_open and s_close, whose calling syntax closely parallels that of the standard C library stream functions fopen and fclose.

In the last section, we'll apply these new functions to the now-familiar program, *TERM*.

Transmitter/Receiver Functions

The first four functions listed above are important because after reset, many UARTs default to the most restrictive conditions: transmitter and receiver off and handshaking on. Without functions to correct these states, asynchronous serial I/O is impossible. Although it may be argued that low-level activity such as this rightfully belongs in the s_config file, there are many situations in which these features must be manipulated under program control. For example, turning off the UART receiver is a good way to prevent garbage from collecting in the UART's receive buffer, or, as the case may be, the interrupt buffer. Similarly, software printer drivers require absolute control over the RS-232 handshaking; it is therefore important that you be able to defeat any automatic handshaking built into the UART.

Because you are now familiar with the procedure of adding support for new items by modifying the SIO definition, these new functions will be presented with much less fanfare than in previous chapters. Figure 14-1 shows the additions that *SIODEF.H* requires to accommodate these new functions: a few general manifest constants and the modified SIO definition. Because the SIO has grown quite long, the SIO in Figure 14-1 shows the *entire* current definition and provides reference numbers in the comments for your convenience.

Figure 14-1   Additions to *SIODEF.H* for supporting transmitter/receiver enable and handshake.

Manifest Constants

```
#define X1    0        /* clock factor = 1  */
#define X16   1        /* clock factor = 16 */
#define X32   2        /* clock factor = 32 */
#define X64   3        /* clock factor = 64 */
```

STRUCT DEF: SIO
FILE: *SIODEF.H*
DESCRIPTION: Current version of the entire SIO.
COMMENTS: Highlighted items add support for transmitter/receiver enable; handshaking, clock factor, and a "device" number are highlighted. Line numbers in comments are for reference only.

```
typedef struct
    {
    BYTE      *uart_base;         /* 0  base address of UART              */
    int       data_off;          /* 1  offset of data port from base     */
    int       status_off;        /* 2  offset of status port from base   */
    unsigned  rcvmask;           /* 3  RxRDY mask                        */
    unsigned  xmitmask;          /* 4  TBE mask                          */
    BYTE      (*readbyte)();      /* 5  pointer to RAM/port read routine  */
    void      (*writebyte)();     /* 6  pointer to RAM/port write routine */
    BYTE      (*s_rstat)();       /* 7  pointer to serial receiver status */
    BYTE      (*s_read)();        /* 8  pointer to serial fetch routine   */
    BYTE      (*s_xstat)();       /* 9  pointer to serial xmiter status   */
    void      (*s_send)();        /* 10 pointer to serial xmit routine    */
    BYTE      (*v_regp)[2];       /* 11 pointer to a 2-dim array of ints  */
    int       v_regpsize;        /* 12 length of virtual array           */
    struct    vregbits_ *par;     /* 13 pointer to parity structure       */
    struct    vregbits_ *sb;      /* 14 pointer to stop bit structure     */
    struct    vregbits_ *dl;      /* 15 pointer to data length structure  */
    struct    vbaud_    *br;      /* 16 pointer to baud rate structure    */
    struct    vout232_  *rts;     /* 17 pointer to RTS structure          */
    struct    vout232_  *dtr;     /* 18 pointer to DTR structure          */
    struct    vout232_  *gpo1;    /* 19 pointer to GPOUTPUT1 structure     */
    struct    vout232_  *gpo2;    /* 20 pointer to GPOOUTPUT2 structure    */
    struct    vout232_  *brkbit;  /* 21 pointer to break structure        */
    struct    vin232_   *cts;     /* 22 pointer to  CTS structure         */
    struct    vin232_   *dsr;     /* 23 pointer to  DSR structure         */
    struct    vin232_   *dcd;     /* 24 pointer to  DCD structure         */
    struct    vin232_   *ri;      /* 25 pointer to  RI structure          */
    struct    vin232_   *gpi1;    /* 26 pointer to  GPINPUT1 structure     */
    struct    vin232_   *gpi2;    /* 27 pointer to  GPINPUT2 structure     */
    struct    vregbits_ *txenable;/* 28 "  xmitter enable structure       */
    struct    vregbits_ *rxenable;/* 39 "  receiver enable structure      */
    struct    vregbits_ *ctshs;   /* 30 "  cts handshake on xmitter       */
    struct    vregbits_ *dcdhs;   /* 31 "  dcd handshake on receiver      */
    struct    vregbits_ *clkf;    /* 32 "  clock factor structure         */
    short     devnum;            /* 33 s_opened device number            */
    } SIO;
```

Unlike the RS-232 input and output structures, we cannot assume that these new functions are governed by a single bit in a UART register. Why? On a few UARTs, the meaning of "transmitter on" or "receiver on" is subject to program control. In one mode, the receiver and transmitter are functional, but their respective status flags are permanently set to FALSE. In this mode, then, code that accesses the transmitter or receiver without checking their status performs as before, but code that polls the status bits does not. In another possible mode, the receiver and transmitter are unconditionally inhibited and serialization of data does not occur. Similar options exist for handshaking features. To accommodate these various modes, we therefore use a regbits_ structure to describe the remaining functions. Figure 14-2 shows the constant definitions for *Z80SIO.H* as well as the new vregbits_ structures required in *KAYPRO.C* only. Declarations are not shown for *IBMPC.C* because the 8250 UART in the IBM PC does not support these features.

Figure 14-2 Additions to *Z80SIO.H* and *KAYPRO.C* for supporting transmitter/receiver enable and handshake.

Constant Definitions for Z80SIO.H

TxMASK	0xF7	/* 1111 0111 */	TxHSMASK	0xDF	/* 1101 1111 */
TxON_MASK	0x08	/* 0000 1000 */	TxHSON_MASK	0x20	/* 0000 0010 */
TxOFF_MASK	0		TxHSOFF_MASK	0	
RxMASK	0xFE	/* 1111 1110 */	RxHSMASK	0xDF	/* 1101 1111 */
RxON_MASK	0x1	/* 0000 0001 */	RxHSON_MASK	0x20	/* 0000 0010 */
RxOFF_MASK	0		RxHSOFF_MASK	0	
CLKMASK	0x3F	/* 0011 1111 */			
X1_MASK	0				
X16_MASK	0x40	/* 0100 0000 */			
X32_MASK	0x80	/* 1000 0000 */			
X64_MASK	0xC0	/* 1100 0000 */			

STRUCT NAME: txonA, rxonA, txhsA, rxhsA, and clockfA
TYPE: vregbits_
FILE: *KAYPRO.C*
DESCRIPTION: Control structures for transmitter ON/OFF, transmitter and receiver handshaking, and clocking factor.

```
struct vregbits_ txonA =      /** transmitter enable **/
    {
    TxMASK,                             /* mask to reset bits              */
    { TxOFF_MASK, TxON_MASK, -1, -1 },  /* masks to set bits               */
    WR5,                                /* virtual register number         */
    SP_OFF,                             /* offset of physical register     */
    SUPPLIED,                           /* current value                   */
    ON,                                 /* value to use at start up         */
    NIL                                 /* no more structures needed       */
    };
```

Figure 14-2 cont. Additions to *Z80SIO.H* and *KAYPRO.C* for supporting transmitter/receiver enable and handshake.

```
struct vregbits_ rxonA =        /** receiver enable **/
        {
        RxMASK,
        { RxOFF_MASK, RxON_MASK, -1, -1 },
        WR3,
        SP_OFF,
        SUPPLIED,
        ON,
        NIL
        };

struct vregbits_ txhsA =        /** transmitter handshake on RTS **/
        {
        TxHSMASK,
        { TxHSOFF_MASK, TxHSON_MASK, -1, -1 },
        WR3,
        SP_OFF,
        SUPPLIED,
        OFF,
        NIL,
        };

struct vregbits_ rxhsA =        /** receiver handshake on DCD **/
        {
        TxHSMASK,
        { TxHSOFF_MASK, TxHSON_MASK, -1, -1 },
        WR3,
        SP_OFF,
        SUPPLIED,
        OFF,
        NIL
        };

struct vregbits_ clockfA =                  /** clock factor **/
        {
        CLKMASK,
        { X1_MASK, X16_MASK, X32_MASK, X64_MASK, -1 },
        WR4,
        SP_OFF,
        SUPPLIED,
        X16,                                /* start with clock factor = 16        */
        NIL
        };
```

The simple functions required to implement the new features are mirror images of earlier functions that refer to `regbits_` structures. Each calls `setbits`, passing to it the SIO, a pointer to the respective `regbits_` structure and the desired level. These functions, given in Figure 14-3, return the customary `setbits` error codes.

Figure 14-3 Level-3 functions to enable transmitter, receiver, and handshaking.

FUNCTION NAME: `xmiton, rcvon, txhson, rxhson,` and `setclk`
LEVEL: 3
LIBRARY: *SIO.LIB*
DESCRIPTION: Enable transmitter and receiver; enable transmitter handshake on CTS and receiver handshake on DCD; set clock factor.
OTHER MODULES: `vsetbits`
RETURNS: `int`: OR_ARG if argument is out of range; BAD_FCN if the function is not supported (`SIO` pointer is NIL); BAD_ARG if the requested setting is not supported by hardware; 0 if successful.

```
int xmiton(siop, state)     /** transmitter on/off **/
SIO *siop;
int state;
{
    return (vsetbits(siop, siop->txenable, state));
}

int rcvon(siop, state)      /** receiver on/off **/
SIO *siop;
int state;
{
    return(vsetbits(siop, siop->rxenable, state));
}

int txhson(siop, state)     /** transmitter handshake on/off **/
SIO *siop;
int state;
{
    return(vsetbits(siop, siop->ctshs, state));
}

int rxhson(siop, state)     /** receiver handshake on/off **/
SIO *siop;
int state;
{
    return(vsetbits(siop, siop->dcdhs, state));
}

int setclk(siop, clkfactor) /** set clock factor **/
SIO *siop;
int clkfactor;
{
    return(vsetbits(siop, siop->clkf, clkfactor));
}
```

Finally, Figure 14-4 shows the actual declaration and initialization for `typeAsio` in both *KAYPRO.C* and *IBMPC.C*. Again, the entire `SIO` is shown with line numbers in the comments.

Figure 14-4 SIO declarations and initializations for *KAYPRO.C* and *IBMPC.C*.

'SIO' NAME: `typeAsio`
FILE: *KAYPRO.C*
COMMENTS: Supports transmitter/receiver control, handshaking, clock factor, and a "device" number. Line
numbers in comments are for reference only.

```
SIO typeAsio =
     {
     PORT1,                       /*0   base address of UART                     */
     DP_OFF,                      /*1   offset of data port from base           */
     SP_OFF,                      /*2   offset of status port from base         */
     RCV_MASK,                    /*3   RxRDY mask from U8250.H                  */
     XMIT_MASK,                   /*4   TBE mask from U8250.H                    */
     inport,                      /*5   pointer to RAM/port read routine         */
     outport,                     /*6   pointer to RAM/port write routine        */
     s_rcvstat,                   /*7   pointer to serial receiver status        */
     s_rcv,                       /*8   pointer to serial fetch routine          */
     s_xmitstat,                  /*9   pointer to serial xmiter status          */
     s_xmit,                      /*10  pointer to serial xmit routine           */
     v_regA,                      /*11  pointer to virtual register array        */
     8,                           /*12  number of rows in virtual array          */
     &parityA,                    /*13  parity structure                         */
     &stopsA,                     /*14  stop bit structure                       */
     &dlenA,                      /*15  data length structure                    */
     &baudA,                      /*16  baud rate structure                      */
     &pin4A,                      /*17  RS-232 RTS output                        */
     &pin20A,                     /*18  RS-232 DTR output                        */
     NIL,                         /*19  NO RS-232 first user-defined output      */
     NIL,                         /*20  NO RS-232 2nd user-defined output        */
     &breakbA,                    /*21  break bit                                */
     &pin5A,                      /*22  RS-232 CTS input                         */
     NIL,                         /*23  NO RS-232 DSR input                      */
     &pin8A,                      /*24  RS-232 DCD input                         */
     NIL,                         /*25  NO RS-232 RIinput                        */
     NIL,                         /*26  NO 1st user-defined RS-232 input         */
     NIL,                         /*27  NO 2nd user-defined RS-232 input         */
     &txonA,                      /*28  transmitter-on structure                 */
     &rxonA,                      /*39  receiver-on structure                    */
     &txhsA,                      /*30  transmitter/RTS handshake                */
     &rxhsA,                      /*31  receiver/DCD handshake                   */
     &clockfA,                    /*32  clock factor                             */
     SUPPLIED,                    /*33  device number supplied during open       */
     };
```

'SIO' NAME: `typeAsio`
FILE: *IBMPC.C*
COMMENTS: Several of the highlighted items must be initialized to NIL because the 8250 UART lacks
support for transmitter/receiver control, handshaking, clock factor, and a "device" number.
Line numbers in comments are for reference only.

Figure 14-4 cont. SIO declarations and initializations for *KAYPRO.C* and *IBMPC.C*.

```
SIO typeAsio =
    {
    COMM1,              /*0   base address of UART                    */
    DP_OFF,             /*1   offset of data port from base           */
    SP_OFF,             /*2   offset of status port from base         */
    RCV_MASK,           /*3   RxRDY mask from U8250.H                 */
    XMIT_MASK,          /*4   TBE mask from U8250.H                   */
    inport,             /*5   pointer to RAM/port read routine        */
    outport,            /*6   pointer to RAM/port write routine       */
    s_rcvstat,          /*7   pointer to serial receiver status       */
    s_rcv,              /*8   pointer to serial fetch routine         */
    s_xmitstat,         /*9   pointer to serial xmiter status         */
    s_xmit,             /*10  pointer to serial xmit routine          */
    v_regA,             /*11  pointer to virtual register array       */
    5,                  /*12  number of rows in virtual array         */
    &parityA,           /*13  parity structure                        */
    &stopsA,            /*14  stop bit structure                      */
    &dlenA,             /*15  data length structure                   */
    &baudA,             /*16  baud rate structure                     */
    &pin4A,             /*17  RS-232 RTS output                       */
    &pin20A,            /*18  RS-232 DTR output                       */
    &gp1outA,           /*19  RS-232 first user-defined output        */
    &gp2outA,           /*20  RS-232 2nd user-defined output          */
    &breakbA,           /*21  break bit                               */
    &pin5A,             /*22  RS-232 CTS input                        */
    &pin6A,             /*23  RS-232 DSR input                        */
    &pin8A,             /*24  RS-232 DCD input                        */
    &pin22A,            /*25  RS-232 RI  input                        */
    NIL,                /*26  NO 1st user-defined RS-232 input        */
    NIL,                /*27  NO 2nd user-defined RS-232 input        */
    NIL,                /*28  NO transmitter-on structure             */
    NIL,                /*39  NO receiver-on structure                */
    NIL,                /*30  NO transmitter/RTS handshake            */
    NIL,                /*31  NO receiver/DCD handshake               */
    NIL,                /*32  NO clock factor                         */
    SUPPLIED,           /*33  device number supplied during open      */
    };
```

Opening and Closing an 'SIO'

The theme of this book is flexibility, generality, and portability of asynchronous serial I/O programs and functions. By careful design we have managed to devise a system where all references to the serial port are made through a pointer to a large structure typedef'ed as an SIO. The SIO describes a serial port completely, and contains all the data and pointers to data necessary to perform I/O with that port. Despite this maniacal insistence on generality, however, we have so far not put it into action by demonstrating how the same set of functions can be used to manage several serial devices. There is a good reason for this: we simply don't have the tools. Since our programs are written with foreknowledge of the system hardware, declaring the omnipresent variable `siop` is simple and routine:

```
SIO *siop;          /* pointer to an SIO      */
siop = &typeAsio;   /* point at "master" SIO  */
s_config(siop);     /* save/config interface  */
```

Suppose we wish to add support for a serial printer to our terminal program. We could easily manage two devices by declaring a second SIO in the level-0 file (*IBMPC.C*, for example) with the name , say, `typeBsio`, then:

```
SIO *siopA;
SIO *siopB;
siopA = &typeAsio;
siopB = &typeBsio;
s_config(siopA);
setparity(siopA,siopA->par->start);
setdatalen(siopA, siopA->dl->start);
    ⋮
s_config(siopB);
setparity(siopB,siopB->par->start);
setdatalen(siopB, siopB->dl->start);
    ⋮
```

This appears simple enough, doesn't it? Suppose, however, that the serial port described by `typeBsio` doesn't exist. With luck, reading and writing the non-existent device will not prove fatal. Or suppose, through some quirk of installation, that `siopA` and `siopB` point to the same device. Or that a single device is `s_config`'ed more than once. The list of possible pitfalls is almost endless.

In order to simplify handling multiple serial devices, we need two fundamental system-level management functions, one to "open" an SIO and the other to "close" it. Any incorrect or potentially dangerous condition—opening a non-existent port or closing a port that is not open—can then be spotted. In keeping with the other functions in this book, the syntax of these functions will be made to resemble familiar C library functions, to wit `fopen` and `fclose`. A "file" is managed as a stream like this:

```
typedef struct             /* this normally lives in stdio.h */
    {
    char *_bp;
    char *_bend;
    char *_buff;
    char _flags;
    char _unit;
    char _bytbuf;
    int _buflen;
    char *_tmpname;
    } FILE;
FILE *fopen();       /* a function returning a pointer to a FILE */
FILE *filep;         /* a pointer to a FILE                      */
if ( (filep = fopen("TEST", "r")) == NIL)
    {
    puts("Cannot close file");
    exit(1);
    }
    ⋮
```

```
if (fclose(filep) != NUL)
    {
    puts("Cannot close file");
    exit(1);
    }
```

Just as a FILE is a typedef for the structure required for buffered device I/O, so an SIO is a typedef for the structure required for asynchronous serial I/O. Just as these C library functions require a pointer to a FILE, so our functions require a pointer to an SIO. To continue this parallel, we will now prepare an SIO for serial I/O in the same way as C prepares a FILE—by "opening" it. In other words, our procedure should look like this:

```
SIO *s_open( );
SIO siop;
int portnum=0;
if ( (siop = s_open(portnum)) == NIL)
    {
    printf("Cannot open serial device # %d\n8,portnum);
    exit(1);
    }
        ⋮

if (s_close(siop) != NUL)
    {
    puts("Cannot close file");
    exit(1);
    }
```

"Opening" a Serial I/O Device

Here is a summary of the tasks that s_open must perform:

1. Return an error if:
    A. The device requested is illegal (i.e., out of range) for this computer.
    B. The device requested is legal, but the support hardware is not installed.
    C. The device requested is legal, but you do not wish to support it.
    D. The device is already open.
    E. There is not enough memory for an SIO.
2. Verify that a legally requested device is in fact present in the system.
3. Mark the SIO as open in a system-wide table.
4. Install the device number in the SIO itself.
5. Configure the UART (via s_config).
6. Initialize data format, baud rate, RS-232 outputs, transmitter/receiver, clock factor, and automatic handshaking according to the start members in their respective structures.
7. Return a pointer to the opened SIO.

Although these are not difficult programming tasks, obviously they require knowledge of the computer's hardware. For example, the maximum number of serial ports varies from computer to computer: the IBM PC supports four, but the Kaypro only one. This maximum number of ports can easily be placed in the level-0 file, but how are we to verify that a requested device is *actually* installed? If, for example, we attempt to open COMM4 on an IBM PC, how can s_open discover if COMM4 is not installed? Clearly, the level-0 file, in this case *IBMPC.C*, must contain a machine-specific routine to verify the presence or absence of the requested hardware. Aside from this pure hardware problem, we must also design a mechanism that keeps track of which devices are in use (open). This system must also map the device numbers to physical devices.

Before we begin the design of this system, here are the only two constant definitions required for SIODEF.H:

```
#define CLOSED FALSE
#define OPEN   TRUE
```

The '_siostat' Structure

To manage the devices in the system, we first must know the total number of serial ports permitted by the system. This information resides in the global integer variable _maxsios in the level-0 file. In addition to the number of possible devices in the system, we need to maintain three pieces of information about each device: the address of its SIO, a flag to indicate whether the SIO is open or closed, and a flag to indicate whether the device supports UART interrupts. (The interrupt flag is explained in Chapter 20.) These three items can be represented by the simple structure shown in Figure 14-5.

Figure 14-5   A structure for serial device management.

STRUCT DEF: _siostat
FILE: *SIODEF.H*
DESCRIPTION: Contains the address of (a pointer to) an SIO, an open/close flag, and a flag to indicate whether the SIO supports interrupts (discussed in Chapter 20).
COMMENTS: One such structure must be declared for each serial port supported.

```
struct _siostat
   {
   SIO  *typep;                    /* SIO pointer for this port   */
   BOOL openflag;                  /* currently open?             */
   BOOL intrptok;                  /* interrupts supported?       */
   };
```

With this structure in hand, let's see how to apply it to the Kaypro. We will assume that the *KAYPRO.C* file has declared an SIO structure named, as always, typeAsio. The Kaypro supports only a single serial port, resulting in the following constant definition:

```
#define MAX_PORTS   1
```

This value is then used to initialize the global variable containing the maximum number of ports and to dimension an array of _siostat structures. These are shown in Figure 14-6.

Figure 14-6   A system list of the Kaypro's supported serial ports.

```
STRUCT NAME:  _siolist
FILE:         KAYPRO.C
DESCRIPTION:  An array of struct _siostat, MAX_PORTS in length.
COMMENTS:     The global integer _maxsios contains the maximum number of serial devices possible in
              the system.

#define MAX_PORTS       1

int _maxsios = MAX_PORTS;                       /* global--max number of ports   */

struct _siostat _siolist[MAX_PORTS] =  /* an siostat structure for each port */
   {
     { &typeAsio, CLOSED, TRUE }            /* port 1 */
   };
```

An Explanation of '_siolist'   The constant MAX_PORTS is used to initialize the global variable _maxsios and to dimension _siolist, an array of _siostat structures. The typep member of element 0 (here, the only element) is initialized to contain the address of the only SIO declared in *KAYPRO.C*—typeAsio. The openflag member is initialized to mark this SIO as closed. For now, ignore the interrupt flag.

We can now write the preliminary version of s_open shown in Figure 14-7.

Notice that the portnum argument is declared to be an unsigned instead of an int—this prevents illegal indexing if a signed integer is accidentally passed.

The first part of this function verifies that the device requested is valid; if not, a NIL is returned to signal an error. An error results if the number of the requested device is larger than the maximum number of devices permitted in the system.

Next, the portnum argument is used to index into the _siolist array; an error is returned if the typep member of that element is initialized to NIL. This rejects device requests that may be legal in the system, but that you do not wish to support.

If the device number passes the foregoing tests, it is assumed to be valid. To guard against reopening an already-open device, however, the final test makes certain that the status member of the relevant _siostat array contains the value CLOSED. Finally, to simplify the syntax of subsequent function calls, the address of the SIO is copied into the now-ubiquitous pointer siop.

Figure 14-7   A preliminary version of s_open.

```
FUNCTION NAME:  s_open
LEVEL:          3
LIBRARY:        SIO.LIB
DESCRIPTION:    Prepares a serial device for I/O.
RETURNS:        SIO *, or NIL upon failure.
COMMENTS:       This is a preliminary version.
```

Figure 14-7 cont. A preliminary version of s_open.

```
SIO *s_open(portnum)
unsigned portnum;                          /* must be unsigned              */
{
    extern struct _siostat _siolist[];
    extern int _maxsios;                   /* global -- number of ports     */
    SIO *siop;                             /* @[SIO]@ pointer to return     */
    if (portnum >= _maxsios)               /* is device number legal?       */
        return (NIL);
    if (_siolist[portnum].typep == NIL)    /* does an SIO exit for it?      */
        return (NIL);
    if (_siolist[portnum].openflag != CLOSED)  /* is it already open?       */
        return (NIL);
    siop = _siolist[portnum].typep;        /* SIO to intermediate pointer   */
    s_config(siop);                        /* set up SIO's uart             */
    setclk(siop, siop->clkf->start);       /* set clock factor              */
    :
    rcvon(siop, siop->rxenable->start);    /* enable receiver               */
    _siolist[portnum].openflag = OPEN;     /* mark SIO open in list         */
    siop->devnum = portnum;                /* put device number in SIO      */
    return (siop);
}
```

Now that the device number has passed this phalanx of validity tests, it is safe to "open" the device. Opening consists of: (1) configuring the UART and/or saving its current state for subsequent restoration; and (2) calling all virtual UART functions to initialize the SIO to the values contained in the start members of its various members. Because of the design of the level-2 functions—unsupported virtual functions that are not supported in hardware return harmlessly. Finally, with the SIO fully opened, the appropriate member in the _siostat is marked OPEN, the device number is installed in the SIO, and the address of the SIO is returned.

An '_siolist' for the IBM PC

That the Kaypro has only one serial port perhaps obscures the details of s_open. To see it work in a more complicated environment, let's now construct the system data for *IBMPC.C*. The IBM PC is capable of supporting four serial cards or, as IBM calls them, "Asynchronous Communications Adaptors." Since a system rarely contains all four, we will assume the much more common configuration of two serial cards, known in IBM parlance as COM1 and COM2. (We'll see in Chapter 20 why they are not likely to be COM3 and COM4.)

As you know, we need to declare an SIO for each port. Our examples, however, have always shown only a single SIO, named typeAsio. For the remainder of this chapter we will assume that there exists *another* SIO named typeBsio and the full complement of 'B' structures (i.e., parityB, baudB, etc.) and other 'B' data (i.e., v_regB) required to initialize it. The only necessary difference between the two SIOs is their uart_base members: 3F8H for typeAsio and 2F8H for `typeBsio`. To save space, this second SIO is not shown in any figure, but it should not be difficult to imagine.

The `_siolist` for *IBMPC.C* is shown in Figure 14-8.

Figure 14-8 A system list of the IBM PC's supported serial ports.

```
STRUCT DEF:   _siolist
FILE:         IBMPC.C
DESCRIPTION:  An array of struct _siostat, MAX_PORTS in length.
COMMENTS:     The global integer _maxsios contains the maximum number of serial devices possible in
              the system.

#define MAX_PORTS = 4                          /* COMM1-4          */

int _maxsios = MAX_PORTS;                      /* global           */
struct _siostat _siolist[MAX_PORTS] =          /* IBM has 2 ports  */
    {
    { &typeAsio, CLOSED, TRUE  },              /* COMM1            */
    { &typeBsio, CLOSED, TRUE  },              /* COMM2            */
    { NIL,       CLOSED, FALSE },              /* no SIO declared  */
    { NIL,       CLOSED, FALSE }               /* no SIO declared  */
    };
```

An Explanation of IBMPC.C '_siolist'   Now s_open honors open requests for devices numbered 0 or 1. Opening device number 0 returns a pointer to `typeAsio` (mapped to COM1), while opening device number 1 returns a pointer to `typeBsio` (mapped to COM2). Attempting to open device number 2 or 3 (COM3 and COM4) fails when s_open spots that the address members contain NILs.

As written, s_open has an Achilles heel. Have you thought of it? Consider what happens when your software attempts to open device 0 or 1 on a computer with only a single serial port. Because it has no way to know what hardware is in the system, s_open succeeds and all I/O is directed to the non-existent serial port! There is, alas, no *portable* way to query a system for its hardware burden. Therefore, for each computer for which we construct a level-0 file, we must write a custom routine that returns s_open a TRUE/FALSE answer to the question, "Is this device present in the system?"

Although the details differ from machine to machine, on every expandable system there must exist some way to glean this information. When the IBM PC boots up, routines in its ROM BIOS scan configuration switches on the system board, and verify the existence of various equipment by generally nosing around in the system looking for hardware. Luckily for us, ROM BIOS builds a four-element list of serial ports pointers at memory address 0:400H. Since the port addresses on the 8086 family of processors are 16 bits wide, each element in this list is 2 bytes wide. COM1's base address (i.e., `uart_base`) can therefore be learned by reading address 0:400H, COM2's at 0:402H, and so forth.

We are concerned not so much about the values of these `uart_base` pointers as whether they are 0—the value marking non-existent devices. The port-verification functions for both *KAYPRO.C* and *IBMPC.C* are given in Figure 14-9.

Figure 14-9 The isport function for Kaypro and IBM PC.

FUNCTION NAME: isport
LEVEL: 0
LIBRARY: *KAYPRO.C*
DESCRIPTION: Verifies that the port number devnum exists.
OTHER MODULES: None
RETURNS: BOOL: TRUE if the device exists.

```
BOOL isport(devnum)
unsigned devnum;
{
     return (devnum == 0);
}
```

FUNCTION NAME: isport
LEVEL: 0
LIBRARY: *IBMPC.C*
DESCRIPTION: Verifies that the port number devnum exists.
OTHER MODULES: peekw: a 2-byte peek function.
RETURNS: BOOL: TRUE if the device exists.
COMMENTS: peekw returns an unsigned integer from offset:segment.

```
#define UART_PTR 0x400                    /* pointer to uart table in IBM PC    */

BOOL isport(devnum)
unsigned devnum;
{
     return(peekw(UART_PTR + (2 * devnum), 0));
}
```

An Explanation of 'isport'   The IBM PC version uses the device number to index into the serial port table at 400H. The value in that element, guaranteed to be non-0 if the associated card is present, is returned. In this manner, a FALSE is returned only when the corresponding serial card is not present.

The Kaypro version is shamefully simple — it simply returns the result of comparing the device number to 0.

Error Codes

At the same time we rewrite s_open to incorporate isport, we can also make its error checking more robust. At present, s_open suffers from the problem of all functions that return pointers — only a single value, NIL, is available for an error code. While the calling program can test the return value for 0 to detect when an error has occurred, it has no way to ascertain the nature of the error. The only solution to this dilemma is to have the function place an error code in a global variable for subsequent evaluation by the calling program. This is the approach we will take in s_open, where the error-return variable is s_errno. The error codes returned by s_open and s_close were presented without comment in Figure 12-2, but are repeated to make certain that you have placed them in *SIODEF.H*.

```
/* Error codes returned by SIO functions */
#define OR_ARG    1          /* Argument out of range   */
#define BAD_FCN   2          /* Function not supported  */
#define BAD_ARG   3          /* Argument not supported  */
#define BAD_PORT  4          /* Illegal device number   */
#define NO_PORT   5          /* Device not installed    */
#define NO_SIO    6          /* No SIO declared         */
#define OPEN_NOW  7          /* Device already open     */
#define NO_CLOSE  8          /* No such device open     */
#define KEY_CAN   9          /* aborted from keyboard   */
#define NO_FILE   10         /* file not found          */
```

Figure 14-10 shows the final version of s_open, incorporating isport and greatly improved error discovery.

Figure 14-10 Use of s_open to "open" an SIO.

FUNCTION NAME: s_open
LEVEL: 3
LIBRARY: *SIO.LIB*
DESCRIPTION: "Opens" an SIO.
OTHER MODULES: setdtr, setrts, setgpo1, setgpo2, setparity, setstops, setdatalen, setbaud, xmiton, rcvon, rxhson, and txhson.
RETURNS: SIO *; NIL if no storage is available, if the portnum argument is out of range, or if the portnum is not defined. Error code for the failure is placed in the global variable s_errno.
COMMENTS: The SIO (serial port) described is initialized first by calling s_config to perform any UART-specific tasks, then by calling setbaud, setparity, etc. A pointer to this SIO is returned.

```
int  s_errno;                               /***** GLOBAL VARIABLE *****/

SIO *s_open(portnum)
unsigned portnum;
{
    extern struct _siostat _siolist[];
    extern int _maxsios;                    /* global -- number of ports   */
    SIO *siop;                              /* SIO pointer to return       */
    if (portnum >= _maxsios)                /* is device number legal?     */
        {
        s_errno = BAD_PORT;
        return (NIL);
        }
    if (isport(portnum) == NUL)             /* is the hardware installed?  */
        {
        s_errno = NO_PORT;
        return (NIL);
        }
```

Figure 14-10 cont. Use of s_open to "open" an SIO.

```
        if (_siolist[portnum].typep == NIL)       /* does an SIO exist for it?   */
            {
            s_errno = NO_PORT;
            return (NIL);
            }
        if (_siolist[portnum].openflag != CLOSED)  /* is it already open?         */
            {
            s_errno = OPEN_NOW;
            return (NIL);
            }
        siop = _siolist[portnum].typep;            /* SIO pointer from table      */
        s_config(siop);                            /* set up SIO's uart           */
        setclk(siop, siop->clkf->start);           /* set clock factor            */
        setparity(siop, siop->par->start);         /* set data format             */
        setstops(siop, siop->sb->start);
        setdatalen(siop, siop->dl->start);
        setbaud(siop, siop->br->start);
        setdtr(siop, siop->dtr->start);            /* set RS-232 and GP outputs   */
        setrts(siop, siop->rts->start);
        setgpo1(siop, siop->gpo1->start);
        setgpo2(siop, siop->gpo2->start);
        rxhson(siop, siop->dcdhs->start);          /* set receiver handshaking    */
        txhson(siop, siop->ctshs->start);          /* set xmitter handshaking     */
        xmiton(siop, siop->txenable->start);       /* enable transmitter          */
        rcvon(siop, siop->rxenable->start);        /* enable receiver             */
        _siolist[portnum].openflag = OPEN;         /* mark SIO open in list       */
        siop->devnum = portnum;                    /* put device number in SIO    */
        return (siop);
}
```

An Explanation of 's_open'   Aside from the call to isport, which makes certain that the requested device is present in the system, this complete version of s_open is functionally equivalent to the one previously shown in Figure 14-7. The greatest modification is in the use of s_errno to return error codes to describe the several conditions that might cause an open failure.

"Closing" a Serial I/O Device

An SIO opened with s_open must be closed with s_close, as shown in Figure 14-11.

Figure 14-11   Use of s_close to "close" an SIO.

```
FUNCTION NAME: s_close
LEVEL:         3
```

Figure 14-11 cont.   Use of `s_close` to "close" an SIO.

LIBRARY:	*SIO.LIB*
DESCRIPTION:	Restores the SIO pointed to by `siop` to its original condition.
OTHER MODULES:	s_restore
RETURNS:	`int`: NO_CLOSE if the SIO pointer is NIL or not on the list of s_open'ed ports.
COMMENTS:	If the close fails, no attempt is made to restore the SIO.

```
int s_close(siop)
SIO *siop;
{
    extern struct _siostat _siolist[];      /* list of available @[SIO]@s    */
    extern int _maxsios;         /* global -- maximum number of serial ports */
    int i;
    if (siop == NIL)
        return (NO_CLOSE);
    for (i = 0 ;i < _maxsios; i++)
        if ( (siop == _siolist[i].typep) && (_siolist[i].openflag == OPEN))
            {
            _siolist[i].openflag = CLOSED;
            break;
            }
    if ( i == _maxsios)                      /* no match in list              */
        return (NO_CLOSE);
    s_restore(siop);                         /* restore interface             */
    siop->devnum = VIRGIN;                   /* install dummy device number   */
    return (0);
}
```

An Explanation of 's_close'   This function loops through `_siolist`, the list of available SIOs, to make certain (1) that the SIO to close is actually valid and (2) that it's already open. If both conditions obtain, the SIO is restored, the SIO is marked as CLOSED, the device number in the SIO is set to NUL, and a 0 is returned as the symbol of a successful close.

Why even bother to close an SIO? After all, it doesn't contain data in the same sense as, say, a FILE. The most important function `s_close` performs is its restoration of the interface to its original condition. Aside from that, an SIO's failure to close is a good indication that something has gone awry in your program.

Suggested Enhancements for 's_open'

At present there are two major areas in which s_open can be improved. Neither is earth-shaking nor critical to ordinary operations, but both add to the function's utility.

"Mode" Arguments

The present design of s_open opens only preexisting SIOs; that is, in order to open COM2 on the IBM PC, `typeBsio` must *already* exist. A much more flexible approach creates the SIO by allocating storage for it, then copying an existing SIO into it. This option is passed to s_open in much the same way that the "open" mode for a FILE is passed to fopen.

Dynamic 'uart_base'

Our technique of initializing an SIO requires that we install `uart_base`, a pointer to the base address of the UART. The `isport` function can be easily modified to return this information as the `uart_base` pointer or NIL if none exists. In fact, the IBM PC version of `isport` already returns the port address, but as an `int` instead of the SIO pointer required.

TERM Revisions

The ability to open and close an SIO greatly simplifies the prologue and epilog required to use a serial port. Figure 14-12 shows how the `main` portion of *TERM* is changed by these new functions.

Figure 14-12 The `main` function of *TERM* using `s_open` and `s_close`.

```
main( argc, argv)
int argc;
char *argv[];
{
    int portnum = 0;                          /* default serial card      */
    SIO *siop;                                /* pointer to an SIO        */
    if (argc > 1)
        portnum = atoi(argv[1]);
    if ( (siop = s_open(portnum)) == NIL)
        {
        printf("\007Cannot open:  %s\n", errstr[s_errno]);
        return(s_errno);
        }

    term(siop);                               /* -- TERM -- */

    if ( (s_errno = s_close(siop)) != 0 )
        {
        printf("\007Cannot close:  %s\n", errstr[s_errno]);
        return(s_errno);
        }
    puts("\nEnd of TERM\n");
    return(0);
}
```

An Explanation of the Revised 'main' Function   By default, the desired device number `portnum` is 0. To enable access to a different port (and to enable you to test the error-checking mechanism), a different device number may be specified on the command line. In practical use, programs probably should not automatically terminate when `s_open` returns an error; a more helpful approach offers the user the alternative of specifying a new device number and perhaps permanently installing it in the program.

Conclusion

We have now completed the virtual UART section of our SIO and can turn our attention to adding loftier features. In upcoming chapters, for example, we'll write a series of functions that enable you to perform ''formatted'' I/O through an SIO, to control the speed of transmission, to fix the ends of lines, to translate or remove characters, and a host of other chores vital to asynchronous serial I/O.

15

Formatted Output

All of the functions we have written so far might fairly be called "tools" —routines that, while interesting, are of little practical value by themselves. This characterization is not intended to be pejorative, but in truth, the best of tools can sustain one's interest only so long. We now turn our attention to composing a new group of functions that perform, for want of a better term, "formatted" serial output. By formatted, we mean that our functions will perform some type of processing on ordinary or *raw* output. End-of-line handling is a good example of formatted serial output. As we discussed in Chapter 1, there is little agreement among operating systems about what character should be employed to mark the end of one line and the start of a new line. Some systems use CR *and* LF and other systems use CR *or* LF. Because many utility programs, especially those that process text, rely heavily upon a particular end-of-line character(s), files produced under one operating system are problematical under another. One of the fundamental attributes of good communication software, therefore, is its ability to translate among the various end-of-line conventions.

Formatted output means that raw data is somehow adjusted to facilitate communications with a dissimilar or at least partially incompatible environment. Since there is no way to predict whether you are on the receiving or transmitting end of such an incompatibility, you require one group of functions for formatted output and another for formatted input. Each group is governed by its own control structure, a pointer to which is located (you guessed it) in the SIO structure. Because these functions are modeled after their familiar counterparts from the C standard library, you already know how to use them.

Before we begin, place the constants shown in Figure 15-1 in a new header file named *SIOCTL.H*.

Figure 15-1   Constants for a new header file, *SIOCTL.H*.

```
#define  IGNORE      -2
#define  NOECHO       1
                    /* NEW LINE TRANSLATION MODES */

#define NOXLAT        0              /* remove nothing--i.e., "raw"   */
#define LF2CR         1              /* translate LF to CR            */
#define CR2LF         2              /* translate CR to LF            */
#define EOL2SPACE     3              /* convert CR&LF to spaces       */
#define REMOVEEOL     4              /* remove all CR and LF          */
```

Figure 15-1 cont. Constants for a new header file, *SIOCTL.H.*

```
#define LF2CRLF      5            /* convert LF to CRLF                    */
#define CR2CRLF      6            /* convert CR to CRLF                    */
#define CRLF2LF      7            /* convert CRLF to LF                    */
#define CRLF2CR      8            /* convert CRLF to CR                    */

                  /* UPPER/LOWER CASE MODES */
#define UP_LOW       0            /* upper and lower--i.e., "raw"          */
#define UPPER        1            /* convert to upper                      */
#define LOWER        2            /* convert to lower                      */

                  /* XON-XOFF  CONTROL */
#define NO_XX        0            /* no XON-XOFF flow control              */
#define XON_ONLY     1            /* accept only 'xonchar' for XON         */
#define XON_ANY      2            /* accept anything for XON               */
```

Formatted Output

At the base of our formatted output functions will be the level-2 function s_putc, whose sole function is to output "raw" bytes from the SIO. Using flags and data in an output control structure, we will build the single-byte output function s_fputc to "format" the byte stream in a variety of ways. Instead of listing the various tasks we wish s_fputc to perform, we will examine the entire structure and the individual purpose of each member. Figure 15-2 shows the output control structure soctl_.

Figure 15-2 The soctl_ control structure.

STRUCT DEF: soctl_
FILE: *SIODEF.H*
DESCRIPTION: Control structure for "formatted" serial output.
COMMENTS: Numbering in comments is provided to simplify cross-reference with initializers.

```
struct soctl_
    {
    BOOL      rawflg;            /*0   perform no processing at all       */
    short     eolmode;          /*1   end-of-line formatting             */
    BOOL      consflg;          /*2   echo characters to console         */
    BOOL      wechoflg;         /*3   interbyte wait for return echo      */
    unsigned  wecho_dly;        /*4   Tsecs to wait for return echo       */
    short     casemode;         /*5   change to upper or lower case       */
    short     xxmode;           /*6   XON-XOFF control                    */
    BYTE      xoffc;            /*7   XOFF character                      */
    short     xonc;             /*8   XON character (-1 == any char)      */
    BOOL      asciiflg;         /*9   strip bit 7                         */
    BOOL      cntrlflg;         /*10  remove control characters           */
```

Figure 15-2 cont.   The soctl_ control structure.

```
short      ok_cntrls[32];          /*11 permitted control characters    */
short      numcc;                  /*12 number of controls in ok_cntrls */
BOOL       filterflg;              /*13 filter-remove characters         */
short      filtlist[128][2];       /*14 list of byte to remove or filter */
short      numfc;                  /*15 number of bytes in filter list   */
BOOL       ib_dlyflg;              /*16 interbyte delay in tsecs         */
unsigned   ib_dly;                 /*17 pause between bytes              */
BOOL       il_dlyflg;              /*18 interline pause flag             */
BYTE       il_dlyc;                /*19 char to begin interline pause    */
unsigned   il_dly;                 /*20 interline pause in tsecs         */
char       kbortc;                 /*21 key to break out of loops        */
BYTE       lastc;                  /*22 previous byte output             */
BOOL       flushflg;               /*23 an end of line decision pending  */
};
```

The members of this structure have the following functions:

rawflg   Disables all byte processing and makes a call to s_fputc equivalent to a call to s_putc.

eolmode   Determines the end-of-line translation according to the following constants (given in Figure 15-1).

NOXLAT	No end-of-line translation is performed.
LF2CR	Line Feed is replaced with Carriage Return.
CR2LF	Carriage Return is replaced with Line Feed.
EOL2SPACE	Carriage Return and Line Feed are replaced with spaces.
REMOVEEOL	Carriage Return and Line Feed are removed.
LF2CRLF	Line Feed is replaced with Carriage Return and Line Feed.
CR2CRLF	Carriage Return is replaced with Carriage Return and Line Feed.
CRLF2LF	Carriage Return and Line Feed are replaced with Line Feed.
CRLF2CR	Carriage Return and Line Feed are replaced with Carriage Return.

consflg   Outputs the byte not only to the SIO but also to standard output.

wechoflg   Outputs the byte to the SIO then waits wecho_dly Tsecs for a byte to arrive via SIO input. In effect, this feature waits until the receiver acknowledges reception of the byte just transmitted.

casemode   Translates bytes to upper or lower case according to the following constants (given in Figure 15-1):

UP_LOW	No translation
UPPER	Convert to upper case
LOWER	Convert to lower case

xxmode	XON/XOFF flow control, triggered by xoffchar, is governed by the following constants (given in Figure 15-1):

NO_XX	No XON/XOFF.
XON_ONLY	Enable XON/XOFF, accept only xonc as XON.
XON_ANY	Enable XON/XOFF, accept any byte as XON.

asciiflg	Compensates for data format errors or "normalizes" word-processed text files by clearing bit 7 of each transmitted byte.
cntrlflg	Enables control character removal. Because in practice the controls for exclusion usually outnumber those for inclusion, the list ok_cntrls[32] contains a list of control characters *not* to be removed, and the *cardinal* number numcc contains the number of characters entered in this list.
filterflg	Enables byte translation and removal. The bytes in "column" 0 of a 128-element two-dimensional array, filtlist[128][2] are translated to the corresponding bytes in column 1. If, however, the byte in column 1 is −1, the byte in column 0 is simply not transmitted. The number of entries in the array is contained in numfc, a *cardinal* number. (This must be an integer array to accommodate the −1 values.)
ib_dlyflg	Introduces an unconditional pause of ib_dly Tsecs per *byte*.
il_dlyflg	Introduces an unconditional pause of il_dly Tsecs per *line*. The il_dlyc function defines the byte that triggers this line delay, usually CR or LF.
kbortc	Key recognized to break out of wait loops.
lastc	A 1-byte scratch pad buffer required during end-of-line conversion.
flushflg	The signal that a CRLF end-of-line translation is pending. Upon receipt of a CR in the CRLF2LF mode, the decision to translate must be postponed until the next character is known to be an LF. The primary use of this flag is to broadcast to functions that call s_fputc that an untransmitted byte remains in lastc.

Declaration and Initialization of an 'soctl_' Structure

Figure 15-3 shows one possible declaration and initialization of an soctl_ structure.

Figure 15-3   Declaration and initialization of an output control structure.

STRUCT NAME: octlA
TYPE: struct soctl_
FILE: *IBMPC.C* and *KAYPRO.C*
DESCRIPTION: Declares and initializes an soctl_ output control structure.
COMMENTS: The numbering in the comments corresponds to that in the soctl_ structure definition.

```
struct soctl_ octlA =
    {
    OFF,                              /*0  "raw" output flag              */
    NOXLAT,                           /*1  end-of-line mode               */
```

Figure 15-3 cont. Declaration and initialization of an output control structure.

```
    OFF,                                  /*2   console output flag             */
    OFF,                                  /*3   echowait flag                   */
    _1_SEC_0 * 5,                         /*4   echo-wait before timeout in Tsecs */
    UP_LOW,                               /*5   upper/lower case conversion mode */
    XON_ONLY,                             /*6   flow control mode               */
    DC3,                                  /*7   XOFF character                  */
    DC1,                                  /*8   XON character if mode >= 0       */
    ON,                                   /*9   strip high bits flag            */
    ON,                                   /*10  remove unwanted controls flag   */
{NUL,BEL,BS,HT,LF,CR,FF,DC3,DC1,DOS_EOF},/*11  permitted controls             */
    10,                                   /*12  number of controls in above list */
    OFF,                                  /*13  translation/removal flag        */
    {},                                   /*14  translation/removal list        */
    0,                                    /*15  no entries in above array       */
    OFF,                                  /*16  no interbyte delay flag         */
    _0_SEC_05,                            /*17  delay in Tsecs                  */
    ON,                                   /*18  end-of-line pause flag          */
    LF,                                   /*19  character to pause after        */
    _0_SEC_4,                             /*20  pause in Tsecs                  */
    ESC,                                  /*21  keyboard abort character        */
    SUPPLIED,                             /*22  'last character' buffer         */
    SUPPLIED                              /*23  flag to flush last character    */
};
```

An Explanation of 'octlA'   Most members of the structure are initialized to common-sense values. A few, however, require discussion. First, the `rawflg` is disabled because most applications require output processing of some sort. The XON/XOFF protocol is enabled because it is supported by most networks and timesharing services, as well as many hardware devices such as printers. The XOFF "trigger" character is set to DC3 (ASCII 13H). The XON "release" character is set to DC1 (ASCII 11H) and the mode is set to XON_ONLY, meaning that only the receipt of DC1 releases the XOFF state.

Together, `asciiflg`, `cntrlflg`, and `ok_cntrls`, when enabled, can be used to translate outgoing text files to *plain ASCII text*. The high-order bit is cleared and only the ASCII control characters classified as Format Effectors (see Chapter 1) are transmitted. This, of course, precludes the transmission of binary files of all types as well as text files produced by most word processors.

The interbyte and interline delays are given typical values, but are *not* enabled.

As a level-3 object, `octlA` could claim residence in *SIO.LIB*. It is better, however, to place it in the level-0, computer-specific file where it can be easily configured for each computer.

Additions to the 'SIO' Structure

Figure 15-4 shows how the definition, declaration and initialization of the SIO is affected by the addition of the output control structure.

Figure 15-4 Changes in definition, declaration, and initialization of the SIO.

STRUCT DEF: SIO
FILE: *SIODEF.H*
DESCRIPTION: Typedef of master structure for defining a serial port.
COMMENTS: Highlighted items add support for "formatted" output.

```
typedef struct
    {
    BYTE       *uart_base;          /* 0  base address of UART         */
    :
    short    devnum;                /* 33 s_opened device number       */
    struct   soctl_   *s_octl;      /* 34 pointer to output control struct */
    } SIO;
```

'SIO' NAME: typeAsio
FILE: *IBMPC.C* and *KAYPRO.C*
COMMENTS: Highlighted items add support for "formatted" output.

```
SIO typeAsio =
    {
    COMM1,                          /*0  base address of UART          */
    :
    SUPPLIED,                       /*33 serial device number          */
    &octlA,                         /*34 output control                */
    };
```

Output Control Functions

With the soctl_ fully formed we can now write the output functions that refer to it. As is our custom, we will compose a single master function, s_fputc, then derive several "convenience" functions from it. The principle of s_fputc is simple: passed an SIO pointer and a *single* byte, it processes the byte based upon the flags and arrays in the SIO's s_octl member. While the code for this function is not complicated, it is, unfortunately, rather too large for explanation in a few sentences or paragraphs. Instead, the entire function is shown in Figure 15-5 and followed by a piece-by-piece discussion of its constituent parts.

Figure 15-5 The s_fputc function: a level-2 function for "formatted" output control.

FUNCTION NAME: s_fputc
LEVEL: 2
LIBRARY: *BUOS.LIB*
DESCRIPTION: Provides "formatted" character-by-character serial output according to the soctl_ structure.
OTHER MODULES: eputch

Figure 15-5 cont. The `s_fputc` function: a level-2 function for "formatted" output control.

RETURNS: int: NOECHO if "wait for echo" times out; KEY_CAN if a loop (e.g., XON/XOFF) is
                  aborted from keyboard; otherwise 0.

COMMENTS: Features:

Raw (no processing)	High-bit clearing
Interbyte and interline delay	Character filter
XON/XOFF flow control	Character translation
End-of-line conversion	Console output
Upper/lower-case conversion	Wait-for-echo

```c
int s_fputc(siop, c)
SIO *siop;
BYTE c;
{
    register struct soctl_ *op;              /* saves lots of indexing time */
    static int  i, txflag;
    txflag = TRUE;
    op = siop->s_octl;
    op->flushflg = FALSE;
    if (op->rawflg)                          /* -- RAW: XMIT -- */
        {
        s_putc(siop, c);
        return (0);
        }
    if (op->asciiflg)                        /* -- RESET BIT 7 -- */
        c = toascii(c);
    if (op->xxmode && s_inchar(siop) == op->xoffc)  /* -- FLOW CONTROL --  */
        for (EVER)                           /* paused awaiting release or abort  */
            {
            if (s_keybort(siop))
                return (KEY_CAN);
            if ( (i = s_inchar(siop)) == -1)
                continue;
            if (op->xxmode == XON_ANY || i == op->xonc)
                break;
            }
    if (op->filterflg)                       /* -- TRANSLATE/REMOVE BYTE -- */
        {
        for (i = op->numfc - 1; i >= 0 ; i--)
            if (c == op->filtlist[i][0])
                {
                if (op->filtlist[i][1] == -1)  /* remove             */
                    txflag = FALSE;
                else
                    c = op->filtlist[i][1];    /* translate          */
                break;
                }
        }
```

Figure 15-5 cont.   The `s_fputc` function: a level-2 function for "formatted" output control.

```
        if (iscntrl(c) && txflag)                    /*  -- REMOVE CONTROLS -- */
            {
        if (op->cntrlflg)
                {
            txflag = FALSE;
            for (i = op->numcc - 1; i >= 0 ; i--)
                    if (c == op->ok_cntrls[i])  /* loop through list       */
                        {
                        txflag = TRUE;       /* if on list              */
                        break;
                        }
            }
        if (txflag)                      /* -- END OF LINE TRANSLATION -- */
            {
        switch (op->eolmode)
                {
            case NOXLAT:                     /*     no conversion          */
                break;
            case LF2CR:                      /*       lf->cr               */
                if (c == LF)
                        {
                        s_eputc(siop, op->lastc == CR ? LF : CR);
                        txflag = FALSE;
                        }
                break;
            case CR2LF:                      /*              cr->lf        */
                if (c == CR)
                        {
                        txflag = FALSE;
                        op->flushflg = TRUE;
                        break;
                        }
                if (op->lastc == CR)
                s_eputc (siop, c == LF ? CR : LF);
                break;
            case EOL2SPACE:          /* cr and lf converted to spaces */
                if (c == CR || c == LF)   /* crlf = one space       */
                        {
                        txflag = FALSE;
                        if (c != LF && op->lastc != CR)
                            s_eputc(siop, SP);
                        }
                break;
            case REMOVEEOL:             /* cr and lf not transmitted    */
                if (c == CR || c == LF)
                        txflag = FALSE;
                break;
```

Figure 15-5 cont. The s_fputc function: a level-2 function for "formatted" output control.

```
        case LF2CRLF:                /* lf -> crlf           */
            if (c == LF && op->lastc != CR)
                    s_eputc(siop, CR);
            break;
        case CR2CRLF:                /*  cr->crlf            */
            if (c == CR)             /* wait for next byte   */
                    {
                    txflag = FALSE;
                    op->flushflg = TRUE;
                    }
            if (op->lastc == CR)
                    {
                    s_eputc(siop, CR);
                    if (c != LF)
                    s_eputc(siop, LF);
                    }
            break;
        case CRLF2LF:                /* crlf -> lf           */
            if ( c == CR)
                    {
                    txflag = FALSE;
                    op->flushflg = TRUE;
                    break;
                    }
            if (op->lastc == CR && c != LF)
                    s_eputc(siop, CR);
            break;
        case CRLF2CR:                /* crlf -> cr           */
            if (op->lastc == CR && c == LF)
                    txflag = FALSE;
            break;
        default:
            break;
        }                            /* end of end-of-line switch  */
        }
    }
    if (txflag)
        {                            /* -- FLOW CONTROL -- */
        switch (op->casemode)        /* -- CONVERT CASE -- */
            {
        case UP_LOW:
            break;
        case UPPER:
            c = toupper(c);
            break;
        case LOWER:
            c = tolower(c);
            break;
        }
```

Figure 15-5 cont. The s_fputc function: a level-2 function for "formatted" output control.

```
        if ( op->ib_dlyflg)                 /* -- INTERBYTE, -LINE DELAYS -- */
            delay(op->ib_dly);
        s_eputc(siop, c);                  /* xmit with optional console output */
        if (op->wechoflg)                        /* -- WAIT FOR REMOTE ECHO -- */
            if (s_waitch(siop, op->wecho_dly) == TIMEOUT)
                return (NOECHO);
        if (op->il_dlyflg && c == op->il_dlyc)
            delay(op->il_dly);                  /* end of line delay           */
        }
    op->lastc = c;                          /*      save this character        */
    return (0);
}
```

Speed Considerations

The matter of speed is important to serial I/O. Often the speed performance of a function can be substantially improved merely by paying close attention to how data objects are represented and by anticipating how the compiler regards certain kinds of C operations.

Pointer Efficiency

By now you should be convinced of the value of the general idea of accessing all data and functions through a pointer to an all-encompassing SIO. Although structures and pointers to structures provide great conceptual power, they also incur a heavy burden of code overhead in the form of indirect addressing and indexing. In other words, code generated from multiple layers of structures and pointers is slow and cumbersome. In s_fputc, we alleviate this problem somewhat by using a local pointer (op) to a s_octl structure instead of our usual siop->s_octl. Thus relieved of one index and one indirect (pointer) operation, the code runs faster and, an added bonus, is easier to read and understand.

Storage Class

Since op is addressed so frequently, a further (and marked) speed improvement can be achieved by declaring op to be a register variable, thus obviating a memory access at each mention. A similar, though less dramatic speed improvement may obtain by declaring often-used variables to be static instead of automatic. Why? Virtually all micro C compilers create automatic variables on the stack, then refer to them with indirect indexed addressing. This form of addressing is more burdensome on some processors than others, but it is particularly onerous on the Intel 8086 family. Consider the following fragment of 8086 code:

```
    int fnc()
    {
        int x = 5;
        ⋮
    }
```

On the 8086, the code generated by this simple use of `auto` variables is:

```
fnc:
    push bp                  ;save frame pointer
    mov  bp,sp               ;move stack to frame pointer
    add  sp, 2               ;allocate stack space for variable 'a'
    mov  word ptr -2[bp],5   ;initialize 'a' with 5
```

Compare this to the same code but using a static variable for x:

```
int fn()
{
    static int x;
    x = 5;
    ⋮
```

which produces the following assembly code:

```
mov         word ptr a_,5
```

It doesn't require a great understanding of microprocessor architecture and assembly language to guess which code runs faster. Because indexed addressing is inherently more time consuming than simple indirect addressing, this example is not intended to single out the 8086 for ridicule, rather to show how performance can often be increased dramatically simply by paying attention to details and "reading between the lines" of code. This discussion is carried even further in Chapter 16, which deals with the subject of formatted *input* where speed is relatively more critical.

An Overview of 's_fputc'

If `rawflg` == TRUE upon entry to `s_fputc`, the byte is transmitted immediately and the function returns. Beyond this, the basic structure of `s_fputc` centers around deciding whether a byte should be transmitted. The following pseudo-code illustrates how this decision is made.

```
s_fputc(siop, c)
{
        if (raw)
            transmit c;
            return(0);
        if (c is on remove/translate list)
            txflag = FALSE;
        if (c is control character)
            if (c is not on control character list)
                txflag = FALSE;
        if (c is CR or LF and eolmode is relevant)
            txflag = FALSE;
    if (txflag == TRUE)
        various processing: flow control, delays, uppercase, etc.
        transmit c;
    lastc = c;
    return(0);
}
```

As the highlighted portion shows, a character is marked for removal by setting `txflag` to FALSE. There are three conditions under which a byte is not transmitted:

- If it is marked for removal on `filtlist`
- If it is a control character and *not* on the list `ok_cntrls`
- If it is a CR or LF and end-of-line processing is in effect

These conditions assume that the respective functions are enabled—for example, `cntrlflg == TRUE`.

If the byte is not transmitted (i.e., `txflag` is TRUE), it is immediately stored in the single-character buffer, `lastc`. If, on the other hand, the byte is OK to transmit, it undergoes additional processing—flow control management, interbyte and interline delays, case conversion, and so forth. Transmitted bytes are also stored in `lastc`.

When seen in this context, `s_fputc` is actually quite straightforward, submitting quite humbly to a piece-by-piece analysis.

"Raw" Mode

The first test applied is whether to perform any processing at all:

```
if (ip->rawflg)
    {
    s_putc(siop, c);
    return (0);
    }
op->flushflg = FALSE;
```

If `rawflg` is TRUE, the byte is immediately transmitted and a 0 is returned to signify success. In order to speed up processing, both local variables are declared to be in the `register` class. If raw mode is not enabled, the buffer manager flag `flushflg` is cleared and the test for high-byte clearing is performed immediately so that subsequent byte comparisons that differ only in bit 7 produce correct results.

```
if (op->asciiflg)
    c = toascii(c);
```

For example, word processors often use the high bits of characters for special purposes. Carriage Returns in a file thus processed are 8DH (instead of 0DH) and pass unrecognized through our end-of-line processing.

Translation/Removal of Bytes

The ability to translate bytes is often a life-saving feature. It makes possible conversion of a few characters to compensate for a keyboard with a non-ASCII character set, conversion from one word processor's codes to another's, or even conversion between entire character sets (ASCII to EBCDIC, for example).

The ability to strip selected bytes during transmission can also be a boon to the receiver, removing certain characters that might disrupt the screen, printer, or operating system.

Let's assume that the `soctl_` structure is initialized like this:

```
struct soctl_octlA =
    {
    FALSE,                      /*0  perform no processing at all     */
        .
        .
    7,                          /*12 number of controls in ok_cntrls  */
    FALSE,                      /*13 filter-remove characters flag     */
    {                           /*14 list of bytes to remove or filter */
     {'#', '-'},                /* translation table in from-to format */
     {0x7F, -1}
    },
    2,                          /*15 number of bytes in filter list    */
        .
        .
    0.5                         /*23 an end-of-line decision pending    */
    };
```

Element 0, {'#', '-'} *replaces* all occurrences of nanograms with hypens. Element 1 *removes* all occurrences of DEL (7FH). Let's see how these work:

```
if (op->filterflg)                          /* TRANSLATE/REMOVE BYTE   */
    {
    for ( i = op->numfc-1; i >=0; i--)
        if (c == op->filtlist[i][0])
            {
            if (op->filtlist[i][1] == -1)  /* remove      */
                txflag = FALSE;
            else
                c = op->filtlist[i][1];   /* translate  */
            break;
            }
    }
```

If `filterflg` is TRUE, the number of elements in the two-dimensional array becomes the counter in a `for` loop that compares the byte-under-test to the byte in column 0. If a match is found, column 1 is examined. If column 1 contains a −1, the byte-under-test is marked for removal by setting `txflag` and the loop breaks. If column 1 is not −1, however, the byte in column 1 is assigned to the byte-under-test and the loop breaks.

As the pseudo code on page 311 shows, the next two tests—for control character removal and end-of-line translation—are performed only if the byte-under-test is a control character.

Control Character Removal

The list of control characters, `ok_cntrls`, is an *inclusive* list—if the byte-under-test is *not* on this list, it is removed. If this seems backwards, or if it seems to duplicate the general ability to remove/translate bytes, consider how this function is used. In the majority of situations where control characters must be removed, the list of unwanted characters is much longer than the list of wanted ones. For example, the only control characters permitted in ASCII "plain text" are the Format Effectors BEL, BS, HT, LF, VT, FF, and CR. It is obviously simpler and much faster to search an 8-byte list for acceptable characters than to search a 24-byte list for characters to exclude.

```
if (iscntrl(c) && txflag)                    /* REMOVE CONTROLS      */
    {
    if (op->cntrlflg)
        {
        txflag = FALSE;
        for ( i = op->numcc-1; i >=0; i--)
            if (c == op->ok_cntrls[i])    /* loop through list */
                {
                txflag = TRUE;            /* if on list */
                break;
                }
        }
    if (txflag)                    /* END-OF-LINE TRANSLATION  */
        :
```

Before entering the test, `txflag` is made FALSE, and is set to TRUE *only* if the control character-under-test is in the `ok_cntrls` array. The number of elements in the array becomes the counter in a `for` loop that compares the byte-under-test to each element in the array. If a match is found, `txflag` is made TRUE; otherwise, the loop expires with `txflag` FALSE and transmission is prevented.

End-of-Line Conversion

Still within the large `if ( c == iscntrl())`, the next test is for end-of-line conversion:

```
if (iscntrl(c) && txflag)                    /* REMOVE CONTROLS      */
    {
    if (op->cntrlflg)
        {
        :
    if (txflag)                    /* END-OF-LINE TRANSLATION  */
        {
        switch (op->eolmode)
            {
            case NOXLAT:                /*    no conversion    */
                break;
            case LF2CR:                 /*      lf->cr         */
                if (c == LF)
        :
```

Problems with end-of-line conventions are a source of endless grief and frustration. It is always desirable to solve these problems during I/O rather than leaving the job to the user, who may not understand the nature of the problem. In general, five types of conversion are necessary. Follow the discussion of each while referring to the corresponding `case` statements in Figure 15-5. To understand some of the code, you must keep in mind that each character is retained in `lastc` after it is transmitted. Discussion of the `flushflg` member is postponed until later.

LF2CR and CR2LF: One EOL Character to Another

At first thought, these two conversions appear as simple substitutions. But substitution is not what we are about here; we wish to perform intelligent end-of-line processing. We will create a special case for CRLF to CR or LF, but this case must work only on *solitary* CRs and LFs while letting CRLF pairs pass unmodified.

In LF2CR, CR must not be substituted for LF if the previous byte was a CR (i.e., the first byte of a CRLF pair). In CR2LF, the decision to convert CR to LF must be postponed until we find out if the next byte is an LF. Therefore `txflag` is made TRUE and the CR is not transmitted. If the next byte-under-test is an LF, no conversion is made: the buffered CR is output and `txflag` is not set, permitting the LF (byte-under-test) to be transmitted normally. If the byte-under-test is *not* an LF, an LF is transmitted, `txflag` is not set, and the byte-under-test is transmitted normally.

EOL2SPACE: Conversion of EOL Characters to Spaces

This is substitution of an SP (ASCII 20H) for either a CR or LF. This is a useful feature when transferring text to typesetting machines that add newlines dynamically. Spaces must be added to prevent concatenation of the word at the end of one line to the word at the beginning of the next. To prevent the converting of CRLF to two spaces, a one-character look-back controls the output of the SP.

REMOVEEOL: Removal of CR and LF

Although rarely needed, text totally devoid of EOL markings is sometimes needed—for example, in art departments during the paste-up phase of production. Here CR and LF are unconditionally removed by making `txflag` TRUE.

One EOL Character to a CRLF Pair: LF or CR to CRLF

These conversions use the same criteria as LF2CR and CR2LF, just explained.

Processing of Transmitted Bytes

If `txflag` has not been made FALSE by the preceding processing, the byte-under-test is output after undergoing a series of tests and manipulations, the code for most of which is obvious and requires only a little explanation.

XON/XOFF

The code to support the XON/XOFF protocol comes first. If `xxmode` is not disabled (i.e., is not NO_XX), the reception of the XOFF byte defined in `xoffchar` causes entry into a loop awaiting the reception of a ''release,'' or XON byte. The value of `xxmode` determines the value of the release byte that is recognized in the loop; if `xxmode` is XON_ANY, the loop is broken by the arrival of the next byte; otherwise, only `xonc` breaks the loop.

If an XON never arrives, there must be some means to break out of the pause loop. A timeout is impractical since the duration of an XON/XOFF cycle is often long and by definition unpredictable. This is provided by the `s_keybort` function shown in Figure 15-6. This function reads standard input and compares its value (−1 if no byte is ready) to the `soctl_` member, `kbortc`. The result of the comparison is returned.

Case Conversion

After XON/XOFF processing, bytes are converted to upper or lower case (or neither) depending upon the value of `casemode`.

Figure 15-6 Use of the s_keybort function to detect if the abort key has been typed.

```
FUNCTION NAME:   s_keybort
LEVEL:           3
LIBRARY:         SIO.LIB
DESCRIPTION:     Checks the keyboard to see if the designated abort key has been typed.
OTHER MODULES:   inkey
RETURNS:         BOOL: TRUE if the abort key has been pressed; otherwise FALSE.
COMMENTS:        The abort key is defined by the kbortc member of the soctl_ structure. This
                 function can be replaced with the following macro:
                 #define s_keybort(p) inkey() == (p)->s_octl->kbortc
```

```
BOOL s_keybort(siop)
SIO *siop;
{
     return (inkey() == siop->s_octl->kbortc);
}
```

Echoes, Waits, and Delays

At long last, the byte-under-test is ready to be transmitted. Because output is performed from several locations in the code and console output may also be required, all SIO output is made via the local function s_eputc, shown in Figure 15-7.

Figure 15-7 The s_eputc function: a subfunction providing SIO output and optional console output.

```
FUNCTION NAME:   s_eputc
LEVEL:           2
LIBRARY:         BUOS.LIB
DESCRIPTION:     Outputs the byte to the SIO and, if consflg is set, to standard output.
OTHER MODULES:   s_putc
RETURNS:         void
COMMENTS:        Declared static—i.e., local to this file.
```

```
static void s_eputc(siop, c)
SIO *siop;
int c;
{
     s_putc(siop, c);
     if (siop->s_octl->consflg)                    /* echo to standard out      */
          putchar(c);
}
```

An Explanation of 's_eputc' This function simply outputs the byte to the SIO, then, based upon the value of consflg, sends the byte to standard output.

If the echo-wait mode is enabled, a loop is entered waiting for any received character. No check is made to ascertain if the byte received matches the one transmitted. If no byte arrives in wecho_dly seconds, the function ends by returning the constant NOECHO, defined in *SIODEF.H*.

Finally come the two programmed delays, one for each byte and one for each line. With all processing steps now complete, the function returns a 0.

Level-3 Functions for Formatted I/0

The level-2 function s_fputc provides the tools to write a wealth of interesting and useful level-3 functions. Figure 15-8 shows s_fputs, our version of the standard library function puts.

Figure 15-8   Use of s_fputs for formatted string output.

FUNCTION NAME: s_fputs
LEVEL: 3
LIBRARY: *SIO.LIB*
DESCRIPTION: Outputs a string to the SIO under control of the soctl_ structure.
OTHER MODULES: s_fputc
RETURNS: void
COMMENTS: The local function s_fflush clears s_fputc's single-character buffer.

```
static void s_fflush(siop)
SIO *siop;
{
     if (siop->s_octl->flushflg &&  !siop->s_octl->rawflg)
          s_fputc(siop, siop->s_octl->lastc);
}

void s_fputs(siop, str)
SIO *siop;
char *str;
{
     while (*str != '\0')
          s_fputc(siop, *str++);
     s_fflush(siop);
     if (siop->s_octl->consflg == TRUE)
          putchar('\n');
}
```

An Explanation of 's_fputs'   The code for s_fputs is simple and predictable. Of rather more interest is the local function s_fflush. To understand why it is necessary, assume that s_fputs (with CRLF2LF processing in effect) is used to transmit a file containing CRLF's. If that file happens to end with a single CR (a not-uncommon end-of-text marker among editors), the final CR is held in the single-character buffer lastc. Return now to Figure 15-5 and notice that flushflg is always made FALSE at the beginning of s_fputc and is made TRUE *only* when a byte is placed in lastc. Therefore, flushflg serves as a kind of "dirty flag" to signal that an untransmitted byte is pending in the buffer.

Stripped-Down String Output

Despite the power and convenience of the "formatting" functions, there are some situations where speed of transmission is the sole criterion. In these cases, especially at higher baud rates, s_puts might provide a slight speed advantage over s_fputs in the rawflg mode. Figure 15-9 shows s_puts, the level-3 function we set out to write in Chapter 9. Using s_putc, our most basic means for SIO output, this simple function outputs successive bytes from the pointed-to string until a NUL byte is reached.

Figure 15-9 Use of s_puts for unformatted string output.

```
FUNCTION NAME:   s_puts
LEVEL:           3
LIBRARY:         SIO.LIB
DESCRIPTION:     Transmits a string from the SIO without control through the soctl_ structure.
OTHER MODULES:   s_putc
RETURNS:         void

s_puts(siop, str)
SIO *siop;
char *str;
{
    while (*str != '\0')
        s_putc(siop, *str++);
}
```

A 'printf' Function for the 'SIO'

Once you discover the convenience and the power of s_fputs, you quickly yearn for s_printf, the SIO version of printf. As you can surmise, printf is considerably more complicated than puts, so we won't attempt to write it from scratch. However, if you peruse your compiler's standard I/O library you may discover a wonderfully simple way to build your own s_printf from already existing tools.

In many compilers the functions printf, sprintf, and fprintf are based upon a single, more basic function. This function, which often has a name like format, requires not only the familiar string arguments, but a *pointer* to a single-character output function. Its declaration header looks like this:

```
format(outfunc, fmt, argp)
(*outfunc)();
char *fmt;
char *argp;
```

The function `printf` then becomes a simple call to `format`, using `putchar` as the single-character output function.

```
printf(fmt, argp)
char *fmt;
char *argp;
{
extern int putchar();
format(putchar, fmt, argp);
}
```

We can assume that somewhere within `format`, the pointed-to function is called with a single argument—`putchar(c)`, for instance. Because our `s_fputc` requires a pointer to an `SIO`, we must devise a mechanism for passing the additional argument to it. The solution, shown in Figure 15-10, is elementary and is how compilers pass the FILE pointer and buffer arguments to `fprintf` and `sprintf`.

Figure 15-10   The `s_printf` function: "printf" through the `SIO`.

FUNCTION NAME: `s_printf`
LEVEL: 3
LIBRARY: *SIO.LIB*
DESCRIPTION: "Printf-style" output through the SIO.
OTHER MODULES: `s_fputc` and your compiler's version of `format`.
RETURNS: `int`: the number of characters output.
COMMENTS: Depending upon the internal construction of `format`, the return value may be affected by the return value of `s_fputc`.

```
static SIO *dummyp;            /* local for passing pointer to format function */

static void dummy(c)
int c;
{
    s_fputc(dummyp, c);
}

int s_printf(siop,fmtstr,argp)
SIO     *siop;
```

Figure 15-10 cont. The `s_printf` function: "printf" through the `SIO`.

```
    char    *fmtstr;
    char    argp;          /* must be char */

{

    dummyp = siop;                      /* pass the SIO pointer in a dummy local */
    format(dummy, fmtstr, &argp);
    s_fflush(siop);
}
```

An Explanation of 's_printf'   The function begins by stashing the pointer to the `SIO` in `dummyp`. Instead of calling `format` with a pointer to `s_fputc` directly, we call it with a pointer to a dummy function whose sole purpose is to extract the `SIO` from `dummyp` before calling `s_fputc`. This same technique can be used to pass any number of arguments to `format`.

> Some compiler manufacturers do not document the `format` function, but place it in their standard libraries anyway. On the other hand, some compilers declare `format` to be local, suppressing it in the linkage symbol table and listing of library publics. In the latter case—where the compiler manufacturer has intentionally put it out of your reach—you either have to purchase source code to the library or rely upon the compiler manufacturer to tell you how to use the undocumented function. If all else fails, you can always take the hacker's approach: write your own function to snoop around in the run-time library for the address of the `format` function.

Functions To Manipulate 'soctl_' Members

To take advantage of the powerful output control system we have just developed, we need a way to manipulate the `soctl_` members conveniently. As it now stands, however, changing the contents of an `SIO`'s `soctl_` structure is cumbersome to say the least. The simplest approach is to create a separate function to read and write each of the structure members—`setraw(siop, ON)`, `setibdly(siop, O_SEC_1)`, and so forth. As you can imagine, writing a function for every member of a structure quickly becomes tedious and is certainly inefficient. A more sensible and compact approach is to create a single general function to manipulate the structure members. When composing this function, however, you need the constants shown in Figure 15-11 in your *SIOCTL.H* file. For completeness, Figure 15-11 also shows the constant definitions required in the next chapter.

For ease of design, our new function, `s_ocntrl`, will address only the *integral* data types in the structures—the `int`s and `char`s. It will be left to the reader's imagination to develop functions for manipulating the arrays.

Figure 15-11   Constant definitions for use in output and input control functions.

```
/* "FUNCTION" ARGUMENTS FOR USE WITH I/O CONTROL FUNCTIONS   */

#define  SET            0
#define  GET            1


/* CONTROL ARGUMENTS FOR USE WITH I/O CONTROL FUNCTIONS      */

                    /** FLAGS **/
#define  RAWFLAG        0          /* flag unformatted I/O                */
#define  T_OUTFLAG      1          /* used for formatted input only       */
#define  EKOBAKFLAG     2          /* used for formatted input only       */
#define  WECHOFLAG      3          /* wait-for-echo flag                  */
#define  CONSFLAG       4          /* console output flag                 */
#define  ASCIIFLAG      5          /* remove high bit flag (&0x7f)        */
#define  CNTRLFLAG      6          /* remove selected controls flag       */
#define  FILTERFLAG     7          /* filter unwanted characters flag     */
#define  IB_DLYFLAG     8          /* interbyte delay flag (output only)  */
#define  IL_DLYFLAG     9          /* interline delay flag (output only)  */
                    /** DELAYS **/
#define  WECHO_DLY      10         /* echo-wait delay (in tsecs)          */
#define  IB_DLY         11         /* interbyte delay (in tsecs)          */
#define  IL_DLY         12         /* interline delay (in tsecs)          */
#define  T_OUT          13         /* timeout on input only (in tsecs)    */
                    /** MODES **/
#define  EOLMODE        14         /* end-of-line mode argument           */
#define  CASEMODE       15         /* upper/lower mode argument           */
#define  XXMODE         16         /* xoff mode argument                  */
              /** DEFINED CHARACTERS **/
#define  XOFFC          17         /* character defined as XOFF           */
#define  XONC           18         /* character defined as XON            */
#define  IL_DLYC        19         /* character to trigger interline delay */
#define  KBORTC         20         /* keyboard abort character            */
```

We will design the function to set or fetch the structure members, depending upon a "mode" (SET or GET) passed in the argument list. The complete s_ocntrl is shown in Figure 15-12.

Figure 15-12   The s_ocntrl function: a level-3 function to change the contents of an soctl_ structure.

FUNCTION NAME:	s_ocntrl
LEVEL:	3
LIBRARY:	*SIO.LIB*
DESCRIPTION:	Sets or fetches the value of the flag, delay, and mode members of an sictl_ input control structure.
OTHER MODULES:	None
RETURNS:	int. SET: 0 if successful, otherwise −1; GET: −1 if unsuccessful.
COMMENTS:	Constants are in *SIOCTL.H*. The range of the 'code' arguments is not checked.

Figure 15-12 cont. The s_ocntrl function: a level-3 function to change the contents of an soctl_ structure.

```c
int s_ocntrl(siop, function, member, newval)
SIO      *siop;
short    function;                      /* SET or GET                    */
short    member;                        /* code for member to address    */
unsigned newval;                        /* new value for member (SET only ) */
{
    int retval  = 0;
    if ( function == SET)
        switch (member)
        {
            case RAWFLAG:    siop->s_octl->rawflg    = newval; break;
            case EOLMODE:    siop->s_octl->eolmode   = newval; break;
            case CONSFLAG:   siop->s_octl->consflg   = newval; break;
            case WECHOFLAG:  siop->s_octl->wechoflg  = newval; break;
            case WECHO_DLY:  siop->s_octl->wecho_dly = newval; break;
            case CASEMODE:   siop->s_octl->casemode  = newval; break;
            case XOFFC:      siop->s_octl->xoffc      = newval; break;
            case XONC:       siop->s_octl->xonc       = newval; break;
            case XXMODE:     siop->s_octl->xxmode     = newval; break;
            case ASCIIFLAG:  siop->s_octl->asciiflg  = newval; break;
            case CNTRLFLAG:  siop->s_octl->cntrlflg  = newval; break;
            case FILTERFLAG: siop->s_octl->filterflg = newval; break;
            case IB_DLYFLAG: siop->s_octl->ib_dlyflg = newval; break;
            case IB_DLY:     siop->s_octl->ib_dly     = newval; break;
            case IL_DLYFLAG: siop->s_octl->il_dlyflg = newval; break;
            case IL_DLY:     siop->s_octl->il_dly     = newval; break;
            case IL_DLYC:    siop->s_octl->il_dlyc    = newval; break;
            case KBORTC:     siop->s_octl->kbortc     = newval; break;
            default:
                retval = -1;
                break;
        }
    else if (function == GET)
        switch (member)
        {
            case RAWFLAG:    retval = siop->s_octl->rawflg    ; break;
            case EOLMODE:    retval = siop->s_octl->eolmode   ; break;
            case CONSFLAG:   retval = siop->s_octl->consflg   ; break;
            case WECHOFLAG:  retval = siop->s_octl->wechoflg  ; break;
            case WECHO_DLY:  retval = siop->s_octl->wecho_dly ; break;
            case CASEMODE:   retval = siop->s_octl->casemode  ; break;
            case XOFFC:      retval = siop->s_octl->xoffc      ; break;
            case XONC:       retval = siop->s_octl->xonc       ; break;
            case XXMODE:     retval = siop->s_octl->xxmode     ; break;
            case ASCIIFLAG:  retval = siop->s_octl->asciiflg  ; break;
            case CNTRLFLAG:  retval = siop->s_octl->cntrlflg  ; break;
            case FILTERFLAG: retval = siop->s_octl->filterflg ; break;
```

Figure 15-12 cont. The `s_ocntrl` function: a level-3 function to change the contents of an `soctl_` structure.

```
            case IB_DLYFLAG: retval = siop->s_octl->ib_dlyflg ; break;
            case IB_DLY:     retval = siop->s_octl->ib_dly    ; break;
            case IL_DLYFLAG: retval = siop->s_octl->il_dlyflg ; break;
            case IL_DLY:     retval = siop->s_octl->il_dly    ; break;
            case IL_DLYC:    retval = siop->s_octl->il_dlyc   ; break;
            case KBORTC:     retval = siop->s_octl->kbortc    ; break;
            default:
                retval = -1;
                break;
            }
    return (retval) ;

}
```

An Explanation of 's_ocntrl' There are no surprises here. It is important to note, however, that because of the `if...else if` expression, the function accepts only the SET or GET mode arguments. The desired member in the argument list is then applied to a `switch` that, based upon the SET/GET mode arguments, either sets the desired member to the new value passed in the argument list, or returns that member's current value. A single local variable, `retval`, serves double duty: it returns the current value of a member in the GET mode or an error code of −1 if an illegal function or member argument is accidentally passed in either mode. The constants shown in Figure 15-1 can be used in function calls to identify the `soctl_` members.

The greatest virtue of this function is its simplicity and, because of liberal use of manifest constants, its clarity. Our next topic contains copious examples of how `s_ocntrl` is used.

Temporary Storage for Output Control Structures

Frequently we wish to alter two or three members of the `SIO`'s output control structure upon entry to a function and to restore them to their original values upon exit. This can be accomplished by manually storing each structure member in a temporary variable for the duration of the call, then restoring them before terminating. An easier method is to save and restore a copy of the *entire* structure:

```
funct(siop)
SIO siop;
{
    struct soctl_ tmpctl;
    tmpctl = *siop->s_octl;
    s_ocntrl(siop, SET, IB_DLYFLAG, OFF);
    s_ocntrl(siop, SET, IL_DLYFLAG, ON);
    s_ocntrl(siop, SET, CONSFLAG, ON);
        ⋮
        much important code goes here
        ⋮
    *siop->s_octl = tmpctl;
}
```

While this is quite acceptable, it is tiresome to write the same preamble repeatedly. A better solution is to write complementary functions to save and restore copies of structures automatically. These functions, s_opush and s_opop, are shown in Figure 15-13.

Figure 15-13 The s_opush and s_opop functions: temporary storage and restoration for output control structures.

FUNCTION NAME: s_opush, s_opop
LEVEL: 3
LIBRARY: *SIO.LIB*
DESCRIPTION: Save and restore s_octl structures on local stack.
OTHER MODULES: None
RETURNS: int: 0 if stack operation is successful; otherwise 1.
COMMENTS: Both functions check for balance of the local stack, so take care that every "push" is
                 balanced with a corresponding "pop."

```
#define OSTKSIZ 10

static struct soctl_ *ostack[OSTKSIZ] = { NIL }; /* init 1st element to NIL  */
static struct soctl_ **ostackp = ostack;         /* pointer to top of stack  */


int s_opush(siop)
SIO *siop;
{
    char *malloc();
    if (ostackp >= &ostack[OSTKSIZ])            /* check for end of array      */
        {
        puts("\007Ostack overflow.");
        return (1);
        }
    *ostackp = (struct soctl_ *)malloc(sizeof(struct soctl_)); /* get mem    */
    if (*ostackp == NIL)                        /* out of memory               */
        return (1);
    **ostackp = *siop->s_octl;                  /* make copy in allocated memory*/
    ++ostackp;                                  /* point to next slot          */
    return (0);
}

int s_opop(siop)
SIO *siop;
{
    if (ostackp <= ostack)                      /* don't let stack become unbalanced */
        {
        puts("\007Istack underflow.");
        return (1);
        }
    --ostackp;                                  /* point at first active element     */
```

Figure 15-13 cont. The s_opush and s_opop functions: temporary storage and restoration for output control structures.

```
*siop->s_octl = **ostackp;      /* restore old structure from stack  */
free(*ostackp);                 /* release allocated memory          */
return (0);
}
```

An Explanation of 's_opush' and 's_opop'   These two commands work in concert like assembly language PUSH and POP instructions. Calling s_opush saves the SIO's output structure on a local stack; s_opop restores it. The design of this system is quite simple: ostack is the stack (an array of pointers to octl_ structures), and ostackp is a pointer into the stack.

Calling s_opush results in the following:

1. A pointer to storage for an ioctl structure is malloced and saved in the stack element pointed to by ostackp.

2. The SIO's output control structure is copied into the reserved storage.

3. The stack pointer is incremented to point at the next element.

An error code is returned if the stack is already full or if the requested memory is not available.

Calling s_opop results in the following:

1. The SIO's output control structure is restored from the address contained in the stack element pointed to by the stack pointer ostackp.

2. The memory allocated for temporary storage is released.

3. The stack pointer is decremented.

These functions must be used with some caution. Remember, for every s_opush, there must be a corresponding s_opop. Failure to observe this rule causes the restoration of the incorrect structures and inevitably leads to stack overflow or underflow. For example, the following code eventually leads to unexpected results when the first return is taken:

```
funct(siop, x)
SIO *siop;
int x;
{
    s_opush(siop);
    :
    if (x == 1)
        return (0);
    BODY OF CODE HERE
    :
    s_opop(siop);
    return (0);
}
```

The following coding style, however, insures that the stack is automatically balanced before return:

```
funct(siop, x)
SIO *siop;
int x;
{
    int retval = 1;
            s_opush(siop);
            :
            if (x == 1)
                retval = 1;
            else
                retval = 0;
            if (retval)
                {
                BODY OF CODE HERE
                }
            s_opop(siop);
            return (retval);
}
```

Here the balancing s_opop is always executed.

A second caution in the use of these functions centers about the issue of speed. Although innocent-looking enough, the statements

```
*siop->s_octl = **ostackp;
**ostackp = *siop->s_octl;
```

actually copy the *entire* structure from one memory location to another. While many processors have fast block move instructions to make copying more efficient, it *does* steal processor time. Since using these functions within time-sensitive loops seriously compromises performance, s_opush and s_opop are most useful when employed as prologues and epilogs to a function.

Let's now apply our newly developed standard output library functions to an important enhancement to the terminal program, *TERM*.

TERM4

Data exchange between computers has always been an important province of serial I/O, because the serial port—including the RS-232 interface—is a "portable" medium. Disk and tape formats may vary but virtually every serial device manufactured recognizes and supports the START/STOP method of serial communication.

In Chapter 3 we discussed the ugly fates that can befall a byte during transmission over a serial link. We also pointed out that, because of this unreliability, an "unsupervised" transmission (i.e., without protocol or error checking) of *binary* files is exceedingly risky. With most text files, the risk is worth taking because the errors sustained during transmission are easily spotted and, at least in the cosmic scheme of things, relatively inconsequential. In situations of high incompatibility, unsupervised character-by-character transmission of text files may indeed be the only means of communication available. We will now add the ability to upload text files to *TERM*. We will add supervised file transfers to our terminal program in a later chapter. Figure 15-14 shows the changes in the previous version of *TERM*. The main module is unchanged.

Figure 15-14 Changes in *TERM3* to produce *TERM4*. Incidental changes are highlighted.

PROGRAM NAME: *TERM4*
DESCRIPTION: Terminal program.
COMMENTS: New feature: file upload with XON/XOFF.

```
#include  "sioctl.h"

void upload();                          /* return type declaration       */

int vers = 4;                           /* version number  (global)      */

main(argv, arc)
int argc;
char *argv[];
{

    UNCHANGED FROM TERM3

}


void term(siop)
SIO *siop;
{
    int c;                              /* must be int to detect -1 return */
    s_ocntrl(siop, SET, IB_DLYFLAG, OFF);   /* interbyte delay           */
    s_ocntrl(siop, SET, IL_DLYFLAG, OFF);   /* interline  delay          */
    printf("TERM, Version %d: Press Control-%c for a list of commands\n",\
        vers, MENU + '@');
    for (EVER)                          /*          eternal loop          */
        {
        if ( (c = s_inchar(siop)) != NOT_READY) /* check SIO for byte     */
            putchar(c);
        if ( (c = inkey()) != NOT_READY)   /* if a key is pressed         */
            if (c == MENU)
                {
                if (menu(siop))
                    break;              /* if menu returns non-zero       */
                }
            else
                s_fputc(siop, c);       /* use formatted output           */
        }
}

#define UPLOAD  'D'                     /* transmit file                  */


int menu (siop)
SIO *siop;
{
    int c;
```

417

Figure 15-14 cont. Changes in *TERM3* to produce *TERM4*. Incidental changes are highlighted.

```
            ⋮
static char *menus[] =
     {
     "\tA.  Data Format, Baud rate",
     "\tB.  RS-232 control",
     "\tC.  Transmit BREAK signal",
     "\tD.  Upload Text File",
     "\tQ.  EXIT",
     ""                              /* null string terminates list  */
     };
        ⋮
     case BRK:                       /* send BREAK                   */
          setbrk(siop);
          break;
        ⋮
     case UPLOAD:                    /* transmit a disk file         */
          upload(siop);
          break;
        ⋮
     default:
        ⋮
```

MODULE NAME: upload
PROGRAM: *TERM4*
DESCRIPTION: Function to transmit (upload) a file.
COMMENTS: XON/XOFF flow control is supported.

```
void upload(siop)
SIO *siop;
{
     FILE *rfopen(), *xmitfp;                /* return type declarations    */
     char fnbuff[MAX_NAME_LEN];
     int c;
     int errflag = 0;
     putchar('\n');                          /* now open file, return *FILE */
     if ( (xmitfp = rfopen("Name of file to upload", fnbuff)) == NIL)
          return;                            /* user terminated upload      */
     s_opush(siop);                          /* save output structure_      */
     s_ocntrl(siop, SET, IB_DLY, _0_SEC_1);  /* interbyte delay of .1 secs  */
     s_ocntrl(siop, SET, IL_DLYFLAG, ON);    /* interline delay for slow ttys*/
     s_ocntrl(siop, SET, CONSFLAG, ON);      /* turn on console output       */
     while ( (c = getc(xmitfp)) != EOF)      /*   transmit the file          */
          {
          if (s_keybort(siop))               /* transfer aborted from keyboard?  */
               break;
          s_fputc(siop, c);
          }
```

Figure 15-14 cont. Changes in *TERM3* to produce *TERM4*. Incidental changes are highlighted.

```
    putchar('\n');
    errflag = ferror(xmitfp);          /* see if getc ended with an error   */
    if (errflag || fclose(xmitfp))     /* if read or close error            */
        printf("Error %s %s.\n\007", errflag ? "reading" : "closing", fnbuff);
    s_opop(siop);                      /* restore output control structure  */
    getch(puts("End of upload.\n\n-- Press any key to continue --"));
    puts("Exit upload.");
}
```

An Explanation of TERM4   Aside from the miscellaneous changes to the summary menu and the version number, *TERM4* contains one major change—in `term` itself, keyboard characters are transmitted with `s_fputc` instead of with `s_putc`. Now, the transmission of characters typed at the keyboard are governed by the `SIO`'s `soctl_` output control structure. The following lines, for example, make sure that no delays occur when keyboard characters are transmitted:

```
    s_ocntrl(siop, SET, IB_DLYFLAG, OFF);
    s_ocntrl(siop, SET, IL_DLYFLAG, OFF);
```

The most important addition to the `term` function, however, is the new UPLOAD case in the menu `switch`. In `upload` itself, a call to `rfopen` asks the user for the name of the file for transmission; `rfopen` returns when the file is successfully `fopen`ed (or when the user answers the prompt by typing a solitary CR). Note that `rfopen`, the code for which is given in Appendix B, must be passed a pointer to a prompt string and a pointer to a filename buffer. Once a file is opened for reading, the `SIO`'s output control structure is saved with

```
    s_opush(siop);
```

With the ''default'' output control structure thus saved for later restoration, its transmission parameters can be altered by calls to `s_ocntrl`: console output, no interbyte delay, and a slight interline delay. The slight interline delay is necessary for some video terminals in order to give them time to perform a CRLF, which may require scrolling the entire screen up to make a blank line at the bottom of the screen. In addition, the slight interline delay gives the receiver a hiatus in which to process the contents of its input buffer. An interbyte delay can be added merely by changing the line

```
    s_ocntrl(siop, SET, IB_DLYFLAG, OFF);
```

to

```
    s_ocntrl(siop, SET, IB_DLYFLAG, ON);
```

Once the output file has been opened, the transmission of the file begins—bytes are fetched by `getc` and transmitted via `s_fputc`, governed by the values contained in the `SIO`'s output control structure. Characters are echoed to the console during transmission. When end-of-file is encountered, the original output control structure is restored to the `SIO`, and the file is closed. If, during transmission of the file `keybort` discovers a termination request, the loop breaks and an orderly shutdown occurs. The test for errors in disk I/O is performed after the upload is complete instead of after each character. The support for XON/XOFF is totally transparent to the `upload` function because it is handled automatically in `s_fputc`.

Alternative Designs for 'upload'

Two factors limit the speed with which `upload` can transfer data. The primary limitation is console output, which can be overcome simply by turning `consflg` off. The second limitation, disk I/O, is actually not as bad as it seems. Athough the code makes it look as if the disk read is performed byte-by-byte, remember that calling `getc` is tantamount to asking `fread` for a single byte. Thus, depending upon the system, C actually buffers disk I/O by several hundred bytes; the only significant delay occurs when C must actually fill the file's I/O buffer from disk. In Chapter 16 we will see how to overcome even this limitation by performing our own buffering.

Suggested Improvements

The initialization of the `soctl_` is obviously overly conservative — only those control characters in the `ok_cntrls_` are transmitted, and every byte is transmitted with its bit 7 reset to 0. Since most applications employ control characters and, to a lesser extent, the information in bit 7, this configuration is unlikely to prove satisfactory in the real world. *TERM4*, therefore, would benefit from a configuration function to customize the `soctl_` structure's `ok_cntrls` and `filtlist` arrays. This is left for the reader as a programming project.

Conclusion

Control over serial output is only half the battle. In the next chapter we will apply much of the experience gained from writing `s_fputc` to the writing of a "formatted" input function, `s_fgetc` and its entourage of level-3 functions.

16

Formatted Input

In the previous chapter we built a library of functions to format serial output. In this chapter we will build a similar library for process serial input. The plan is essentially the same: first we will compose a level-2 single-byte serial input routine, `s_fgetc`, whose behavior is governed by a structure pointer in the `SIO`. From this function we will construct several level-3 functions to perform more complicated tasks such as string and line input. After presenting a short program to test the string input functions, we will add a remarkably simple function to our *TERM* program to permit the capture of incoming bytes into a RAM buffer and thence to a disk file.

A Formatted Input Function

In Chapter 15 we began a general discussion of how apparently inconsequential design decisions can greatly affect the performance of serial I/O functions. There we discussed how speed is but one of many performance parameters. In an output function, for instance, data is not jeopardized if it is transmitted slowly. In *input* functions, where we have no control over when bytes will arrive, speed is *the* critical performance parameter. Indeed, if an input function dawdles too long processing one inbound byte, the next byte may be missed. Due to the grave importance of speed in our input function, `s_fgetc`, we will apply all the design techniques discussed in the previous chapter plus a few new ones.

The 'sictl_' Structure

Much can be foreseen about the design of `s_fgetc` simply by examining the structure that governs it. Figure 16-1 shows the declaration of the `sictl_` structure.

Figure 16-1 Declaration of the `sictl_` structure.

STRUCT DEF: `sictl_`
FILE: *SIODEF.H*
DESCRIPTION: Control structure for "formatted" serial input.
COMMENTS: Numbering in comments is provided to simplify later cross-reference with initializers.

Figure 16-1 cont. Declaration of the `sictl_` structure.

```
struct sictl_
     {
     BOOL      t_outflg;              /*0   timeout on/off flag            */
     unsigned  t_out;                 /*1   timeout period                 */
     BOOL      rawflg;                /*2   perform no processing at all   */
     BOOL      ekobakflg;             /*3   echo all input back to sender  */
     BOOL      asciiflg;              /*4   strip bit 7                     */
     short     eolmode;               /*5   end-of-line formatting          */
     BOOL      consflg;               /*6   echo characters to console      */
     short     casemode;              /*7   change to upper or lower case   */
     BYTE      xoffc;                 /*8   XOFF character                  */
     BYTE      xonc;                  /*9   XON character                   */
     BOOL      cntrlflg;              /*10  remove control characters       */
     short     ok_cntrls[32];         /*11  permitted control characters    */
     short     numcc;                 /*12  number of controls in ok_cntrls */
     BOOL      filterflg;             /*13  filter-remove characters         */
     int       filtlist[128][2];      /*14  list of byte to remove or filter */
     short     numfc;                 /*15  number of bytes in filter list   */
     BYTE      lastc;                 /*16  previous byte output             */
     BOOL      rbakflg;               /*17  a pending eol decision resolved  */
     BYTE      rbakc;                 /*18  pending readback character       */
     };
```

Many of the structure members serve exactly the same functions as their counterparts in the `soctl_` output control structure; others have the same name but perform somewhat differently.

t_outflg   Enables `s_fgetc`'s timeout input mode. When ON, `s_fgetc` waits `t_out` Tsecs for a byte to arrive; when OFF, it returns immediately if a byte is not available.

rawflg   Disables all byte processing and makes a call to `s_fgetc` equivalent to a call to `s_inchar`.

ekobakflg   When ON, a received byte is immediately retransmitted.

asciiflg   Compensates for parity errors or "normalizes" word-processed text files by clearing bit 7 of each transmitted byte.

eolmode   Determines the end-of-line translation according to the following constants (given in Figure 15-1).

    NOXLAT   No end-of-line translation is performed.

    LF2CR   Line Feed is replaced with Carriage Return.

    CR2LF   Carriage Return is replaced with Line Feed.

    EOL2SPACE   Carriage Return and Line Feed are replaced with spaces.

    REMOVEEOL   Carriage Return and Line Feed are removed.

    LF2CRLF   Line Feed is replaced with Carriage Return and Line Feed.

    CR2CRLF   Carriage Return is replaced with Carriage Return and Line Feed.

CRLF2LF	Carriage Return and Line Feed are replaced with Line Feed.
CRLF2CR	Carriage Return and Line Feed are replaced with Carriage Return.

consflg   Outputs the byte not only to the SIO but also to standard output.

casemode   Translates bytes to upper or lower case according to the following constants (given in Figure 15-1):

UP_LOW	No translation
UPPER	Convert to upper case
LOWER	Convert to lower case

xonc

xoffc   Although s_fgetc itself does not perform XON/XOFF directly, the structure allows you to define these bytes for use by functions that do. These 2 bytes are usually, but not necessarily, DC1 (ASCII 11H, Control-Q) and DC3 (ASCII 13H, Control-S), respectively.

cntrlflg   Enables control character removal. Because in practice the controls for exclusion usually outnumber those for inclusion, the list ok_cntrls contains a list of control characters *not* to be removed and the *cardinal* number numcc contains the number of characters entered in this list.

filterflg   Enables byte translation and removal. The bytes in the first column of a 128-element two-dimensional array, filtlist[128][2], are translated to the corresponding bytes in the second column. This array is declared to be an array of int. If the byte in the second column is −1, the byte in column 1 is not transmitted. The number of bytes for translation is contained in numfc, a *cardinal* number.

lastc   A 1-byte scratch-pad buffer required during end-of-line conversion.

rbakflg   This "read-back" flag signals that the next byte is to be fetched from rbakc, below, instead of from the SIO. Used during end-of-line processing. (See "The Read-Back Mechanism," below.)

rbakc   During certain types of end-of-line processing a CR is stored here pending receipt of the next character. (See "The Read-Back Mechanism," below.)

Declaration and Initialization of an 'sictl_' Structure

Figure 16-2 shows one possible declaration and initialization of an sictl_ structure.

Figure 16-2   Declaration and initialization of an input control structure.

STRUCT NAME:	ictlA
TYPE:	struct sictl_
FILE:	*IBMPC.C* or *KAYPRO.C*
DESCRIPTION:	Declares and initializes an input control structure.
COMMENTS:	The numbering in the comments corresponds to that in the sictl_ structure definition.

Figure 16-2 cont. Declaration and initialization of an input control structure.

```
struct sictl_  ictlA =
    {
    OFF,                                  /* 0   timeout-on-input flag            */
    _0_SEC_05,                            /* 1   default timeout in Tsecs         */
    OFF,                                  /* 2   "raw" input flag                 */
    OFF,                                  /* 3   echo input back to sender flag   */
    ON,                                   /* 4   reset high bit flag              */
    NOXLAT,                               /* 5   end-of-line mode                 */
    OFF,                                  /* 6   console output flag              */
    UP_LOW,                               /* 7   upper/lower case conversion mode */
    DC3,                                  /* 8   XOFF (pause) character to send    */
    DC1,                                  /* 9   XON (release) character  to send  */
    ON,                                   /* 10  remove unwanted controls flag    */
{NUL,BEL,BS,HT,LF,CR,FF,DC3,DC1,DOS_EOF},  /* 11 permitted controls               */
    10,                                   /* 12  number of controls in above list */
    OFF,                                  /* 13  byte translation/removal mode    */
    {},                                   /* 14  translation/removal array        */
    0,                                    /* 15  no entries in above array        */
    SUPPLIED,                             /* 16  'last character' buffer          */
    SUPPLIED,                             /* 17  eol readback flag                */
    SUPPLIED                              /* 18  pending readback character       */
    };
```

An Explanation of 's_ictlA'   The structure is initialized to common-sense values. First, t_outflg is OFF; that is, the function returns immediately if no byte is ready. The rawflg is disabled because most applications require some kind of input processing. The XOFF character is set to DC3 (ASCII 13H) and the XON "release" character is set to DC1 (ASCII 11H). The asciiflg, cntrlflg, and ok_cntrls members are enabled to convert incoming bytes to *ASCII Plain Text*. Notice that in addition to the usual Format Effectors (control characters), the DC1 and DC3 control characters are permitted. Any limitation on control characters, of course, precludes the use of "unraw" mode for reception of binary data.

Like octlA in Chapter 15, ictlA is a level-3 object and can reside in SIO.LIB. Since you may wish to configure this structure for each computer, however, it is probably a better idea to place it in the level-0, computer-specific file.

Additions to the 'SIO' Structure

Figure 16-3 shows how the definition, declaration and initialization of the SIO is affected by the addition of the input control structure.

Figure 16-3 Changes in definition, declaration, and initialization of the SIO.

```
'SIO' DEF:     SIO
FILE:          SIODEF.H
```

Figure 16-3 cont.   Changes in definition, declaration, and initialization of the SIO.

DESCRIPTION: Typedef of master structure defining a serial port.
COMMENTS: Highlighted item adds support for "formatted" input.

```
typedef struct
    {
    BYTE        *uart_base;          /* 0  base address of UART         */
    :
    struct   soctl_   *s_octl;       /* 34 pointer to output control struct */
    struct   sictl_   *s_ictl;       /* 35 pointer to input  control struct */
    } SIO;
```

'SIO' NAME: typeAsio
FILE: *IBMPC.C* and *KAYPRO.C*
COMMENTS: Highlighted item adds support for "formatted" input.

```
SIO typeAsio =
    {
    COMM1,                           /*0  base address of UART          */
    :
    &octlA,                          /*34 output control                */
    &ictlA,                          /*35 input control                 */
    };
```

An Overview of 's_fgetc'

Figure 16-4 shows s_fgetc, the level-2 function that will become the heart of all level-3 functions.

Figure 16-4   The s_fgetc function: a single-byte input function.

FUNCTION NAME: s_fgetc
LEVEL: 2
LIBRARY: *BUOS.LIB*
DESCRIPTION: Provides "formatted" character-by-character serial input according to the sictl_
                structure pointed to by the SIO.
OTHER MODULES: None
RETURNS: int: TIMEOUT if t_outflg is TRUE and no byte arrives in t_out Tsecs; IGNORE
                if an EOL decision is pending; otherwise the byte received.
COMMENTS: Functions supported:
                Switchable timeout mode   Raw mode
                Control character filter   Character translation/filter
                End-of-line conversion   Console output
                XON/XOFF flow control   Upper/lower-case conversion
                Echo-back to sender   High bit clearing

Figure 16-4 cont. The s_fgetc function: a single-byte input function.

```c
int s_fgetc(siop)
SIO *siop;
{
    register struct sictl_ *ip;          /* registers and statics for speed   */
    static int retbyte, i, c;
    static BOOL rxflag;
    if (siop->s_ictl->rawflg)            /* do raw processing asap            */
        return (s_inchar(siop));
    ip = siop->s_ictl;                   /* save lots of indexing time        */

    if (ip->rbakflg)                     /* if byte pending                   */
        {
        ip->rbakflg = FALSE;
        if (ip->consflg)
            putchar(ip->rbakc);
        return (ip->rbakc);
        }
    c = (ip->t_outflg) ?  s_waitch(siop, ip->t_out)  :  s_inchar(siop);
    if (c == TIMEOUT)
        return (TIMEOUT);
    retbyte = -1;                        /* postpone initialization           */
    rxflag  = TRUE;
    if (ip->ekobakflg)                   /* -- ECHO TO SENDER -- */
        s_putc(siop, c);
    if (ip->asciiflg)                    /* -- RESET BIT 7 -- */
        c = toascii(c);
    if (ip->filterflg)                   /* -- TRANSLATE/REMOVE BYTE -- */
        {
        for ( i = ip->numfc - 1; i >= 0 ; i--)
            if (c == ip->filtlist[i][0])
                {
                if (ip->filtlist[i][1] == -1)  /*    remove          */
                    rxflag = FALSE;
                else
                    c = ip->filtlist[i][1];    /* translate          */
                break;
                }
        }
    if (iscntrl(c) && rxflag)            /* -- REMOVE CONTROLS -- */
        {
        if (ip->cntrlflg)
            {
            rxflag = FALSE;
```

Figure 16-4 cont.   The `s_fgetc` function: a single-byte input function.

```
        for (i = ip->numcc-1; i >= 0 ; i--)
            if (c == ip->ok_cntrls[i])    /* loop through list    */
                {
                rxflag = TRUE;       /* if on list               */
                break;
                }
        }
    }
if (rxflag)                               /* -- END-OF-LINE TRANSLATION -- */
    {
    switch (ip->eolmode)
        {
        case NOXLAT:                      /*    no conversion          */
            break;
        case LF2CR:                       /*              lf->cr       */
            if (c == LF)
                retbyte = CR;
            break;
        case CR2LF:                       /*              cr->lf       */
            if ( c == CR)
                retbyte = LF;
            break;
        case EOL2SPACE:                   /* cr & lf converted to spaces */
            if (c == CR || c == LF)  /*    crlf = one space       */
                if (c != LF && ip->lastc != CR)
                    rxflag = FALSE;
                else
                    retbyte = SP;
            break;
        case REMOVEEOL:                   /*    cr and lf not transmitted */
            if (c == CR || c == LF)
                rxflag = FALSE;
            break;
        case LF2CRLF:                     /*              lf -> crlf   */
            if (c == LF)
                {
                ip->rbakflg = TRUE;
                ip->rbakc   = LF;
                retbyte     = CR;
                }
            break;
        case CR2CRLF:                     /*              cr->crlf     */
            if (c == CR)
                {
                ip->rbakflg = TRUE;
                ip->rbakc   = LF;
                }
            break;
```

Figure 16-4 cont. The s_fgetc function: a single-byte input function.

```
case CRLF2LF:                    /*              crlf -> lf         */
        if ( c == CR && ip->lastc != CR)
            rxflag = FALSE;
        else
            retbyte = (ip->lastc == CR) ? LF : CR;
        break;
case CRLF2CR:                    /*              crlf -> cr         */
        if ( c == CR && ip->lastc != CR)
            rxflag = FALSE;
        else
            retbyte = CR;
        break;
default:
        break;
    }                                   /* end of end-of-line switch    */
}
    if (rxflag)
        switch (ip->casemode)           /* -- CASE CONVERSION -- */
            {
            case UP_LOW:
                break;
            case UPPER:
                c = toupper(c);
                break;
            case LOWER:
                c = tolower(c);
                break;
            }
    ip->lastc = c;                              /*      save this character     */
    if (retbyte != -1)              /* if byte to return is not byte received */
        c = retbyte;
    if ( ip->consflg && rxflag )
        putchar(c);
    return (rxflag ? c : IGNORE);
}
```

An Explanation of 's_fgetc' If you understand how s_fputc in Chapter 15 works, you should have no difficulty with s_fgetc. For this reason identical sections—"raw" mode, ASCII (high-order byte) stripping, case conversion, control character inclusion, and byte translation/removal—will not be explained. If you need an explanation of these sections, please review the parallel material in Chapter 15. Instead, we will concentrate on the differences between the two functions. The explanation consists of an overview followed by a discussion of individual parts.

Chapter 15 also explained how substituting an `soctl_` pointer for the more cumbersome `SIOP` pointer together with the judicious use of `register` and `static` variables make the code more efficient. These same techniques can be found in `s_fgetc`. The first code encountered in `s_fgetc` tests the `s_ictl` member `rbakflg`. We will resume discussion of this code in a few pages.

Why not declare all important variables to be of storage class `register`? Well, on any given processor there is clearly a limit to the number of registers available. When most compilers run out of registers for `register` variables, they convert them to `automatic`. Therefore, by greedily declaring an unreasonable number of fast variables, you may paradoxically create slow (`auto`) ones instead.

Raw Processing

So that a "raw" call to `s_fgetc` approximates the speed of an unadorned call to `s_inchar`, the test for `rawflg` is performed immediately, even before assignment of the variables. This means that `rawflg` must be addressed through the doubly indirect structure pointers, which in this case is actually faster than using the intermediate structure pointer `ip`. In other words,

```
if (siop->s_ictl->rawflg)
```

is faster than

```
ip = siop->s_ictl;
if (ip->rawflg)
```

The overhead of setting up `ip` doesn't pay unless it will be used several times later in the function. The actual read of the `SIO` is performed with a call to `s_inchar`.

Control Logic

You will recall that the organizing principle behind `s_fputc` was deciding whether to transmit a byte. The function `s_fgetc` demands a different approach: we must receive a byte before we can process it. Although `s_fgetc` cannot "read around" an incoming byte, its return value can signal that, for one reason or another, the received byte should be ignored. So, just as `txflag` in `s_fputc` serves as a transmit switch, `rxflag` in `s_fgetc` is a receive switch. If `rxflag` is TRUE at the end of the function, the received byte is returned; otherwise, IGNORE is returned (defined in Figure 15-1).

Timeout Operation

Since we are interested in maximum speed in checking the SIO for a possible byte, t_outflg determines which function is used:

```
c = (ip->t_outflg) ? s_waitch(siop, ip->t_out) : s_inchar(siop);
if (c == TIMEOUT)
      return (TIMEOUT);
```

If t_outflg is ON, the byte is fetched by calling s_waitch, which waits t_out Tsecs for the byte to arrive. If t_outflg is OFF, however, the byte is fetched with s_inchar instead. Thus, functions built upon s_fgetc can test its return value for both negative values, IGNORE and TIMEOUT.

End-of-Line Conversion

The criteria for end-of-line formatting are no different than their counterparts in s_fputc, but the fact that s_fgetc is an input routine presents special problems. In some conversions, LF2CR for instance, s_fgetc must return a different byte than the one it actually received; that is, an LF has been received but a CR must be returned. Your first impulse here is probably to assign CR to c (the received byte variable). But remember, c must invariably be assigned to lastc; furthermore, the assignment of c may occur only after all processing has concluded. The solution to this situation is the variable retbyte, which is initialized to -1 upon entry to s_fgetc:

```
case LF2CR:
      if (c == LF)
            retbyte = CR;
      break;
```

When c has been safely tucked away in ip->lastc and if the value of retbyte is no longer -1 (i.e., it has changed), retbyte is assigned to c:

```
ip->lastc = c;
if (retbyte != -1)
    c = retbyte;
```

Now, after optional console echo, rxflag determines whether to return a byte value or the constant IGNORE:

```
return (rxflag ? c : IGNORE);
```

The "Read-Back" Mechanism

In several of the end-of-line cases, 2 bytes must be substituted for 1. In the CR2CRLF case, for example, the reception of a CR must result in returning first a CR then an LF. But s_fgetc can return only a single value. A method can probably be devised where the extra byte is returned in the high-order byte of the returned value, but such schemes are *hopelessly* non-portable and eventually cause gargantuan troubles. A better solution is to store the second byte in a static variable, set a flag to note its presence, then return the first character as usual. When the function is next called, the flag is TRUE and the byte is immediately returned ("read back") without further processing:

```
if (ip->rbakflg)                /* if byte pending   */
    {
    ip->rbakflg = FALSE;
    if ( ip->consflg)
        putchar(c);
    return (ip->rbakc);
    }
```

It is, of course, essential that this code appear early in the function.

Level-3 functions that call s_fgetc need to know when a character is present in the read-back buffer. The function shown in Figure 16-5 returns the look-back character or −1 if none is present.

Figure 16-5   Use of s_iflush to flush the s_octl's "look-back" buffer.

FUNCTION NAME: s_iflush
LEVEL: 2
LIBRARY: *BUOS.LIB*
DESCRIPTION: Returns pending byte from the s_octl's "look-back" buffer.
OTHER MODULES: None
RETURNS: int: byte if available; otherwise −1.

```
int s_iflush(siop)
SIO *siop;
{
    return ((siop->s_ictl->rbakflg) ? siop->s_ictl->rbakc : -1);
}
```

More on Speed

You may have spotted that the functions of the two variables rxflag and retbyte might be combined. For example, we might initialize retbyte to −1 then change its value to −2 for IGNORE. Then, anywhere we once wrote

```
    if (rxflag)
```

we could now write

```
    if (retval != -1)
```

Why not? The answer is speed. Due to microprocessor logic, it is inherently faster to test for 0/not-0 (FALSE/TRUE) than to test one value against another. Since rxflag is tested frequently in s_fgetc, it is important to choose the faster method even at the expense of managing more variables.

XON/XOFF Bytes

In Chapter 15 we designed the management of the XON/XOFF protocol into s_fputc itself. Since XON/XOFF is used only with buffered input, it is meaningless in association with a single-byte input function such as s_fgetc. Nevertheless, the two members xonc and xoffc enable you to *define* the XON/XOFF characters you wish to employ whenever s_fgetc is used in a buffered operation. This is a great convenience, for it enables us to write the macros shown in Figure 16-6.

Figure 16-6 Macros for transmitting XON and XOFF.

MACRO NAME:	xon, xoff
FILE:	*SIODEF.H*
DESCRIPTION:	Transmit the XON/XOFF bytes defined in the SIO.
COMMENTS:	The p is a formal parameter for the SIO pointer and is replaced with the actual parameter used in the call. The parentheses around p are required by most preprocessors.

```
#define xon(p)  s_putc((p), (p)->s_ictl->xonc)
#define xoff(p) s_putc((p), (p)->s_ictl->xoffc)
```

Echo-Back

Just as s_fgetc supplies local output to standard output for communicating with equipment that does not "echo" input, s_fgetc also supplies the *echo-back* feature, which, based upon the value of the ekobakflg, simply consists of immediately retransmitting every received byte.

Level-3 Functions for Formatted Input

We now need a convenient means to change s_fgetc's behavior without worrying about its interaction with the s_ictl structure. This function, shown in Figure 16-7, allows easy configuration of the flag, mode, and delay members in the SIO's s_ictl structure. The manifest constants previously given in Figure 15-11 are used to identify the desired sictl_ member. The explanation of this function is identical to that of s_ocntrl in Figure 15-12.

Figure 16-7 Level-3 function to set/fetch integral data types from the `s_ictl`.

```
FUNCTION NAME: s_icntrl
LEVEL:         3
LIBRARY:       SIO.LIB
DESCRIPTION:   Sets or fetches the value of the flag, delay, and mode members of an sictl_ input
               control structure.
OTHER MODULES: None
RETURNS:       int: 0 if successful; otherwise, −1.
COMMENTS:      Constants are in SIOCTL.H. The range of the 'code' arguments is not checked.
```

```c
int s_icntrl(siop, function, member, newval)
SIO      *siop;
short    function;                      /* SET or GET (see SIOCTL.H)        */
short    member;                        /* code for member to address      */
unsigned newval;                        /* new value for member (SET only ) */
{
    int retval  = 0;
    if (function == SET)
        switch (member)
            {
            case T_OUT       : siop->s_ictl->t_out       = newval;  break;
            case T_OUTFLAG   : siop->s_ictl->t_outflg     = newval;  break;
            case RAWFLAG     : siop->s_ictl->rawflg       = newval;  break;
            case EKOBAKFLAG  : siop->s_ictl->ekobakflg    = newval;  break;
            case ASCIIFLAG   : siop->s_ictl->asciiflg     = newval;  break;
            case EOLMODE     : siop->s_ictl->eolmode      = newval;  break;
            case CONSFLAG    : siop->s_ictl->consflg      = newval;  break;
            case CASEMODE    : siop->s_ictl->casemode     = newval;  break;
            case XONC        : siop->s_ictl->xonc         = newval;  break;
            case XOFFC       : siop->s_ictl->xoffc        = newval;  break;
            case CNTRLFLAG   : siop->s_ictl->cntrlflg     = newval;  break;
            case FILTERFLAG  : siop->s_ictl->filterflg    = newval;  break;
            default:
                retval = -1;
            }

    else if (function == GET)
        switch (member)
            {
            case T_OUT       : retval  = siop->s_ictl->t_out      ;  break;
            case T_OUTFLAG   : retval  = siop->s_ictl->t_outflg   ;  break;
            case RAWFLAG     : retval  = siop->s_ictl->rawflg     ;  break;
            case EKOBAKFLAG  : retval  = siop->s_ictl->ekobakflg  ;  break;
            case ASCIIFLAG   : retval  = siop->s_ictl->asciiflg   ;  break;
            case EOLMODE     : retval  = siop->s_ictl->eolmode    ;  break;
            case CONSFLAG    : retval  = siop->s_ictl->consflg    ;  break;
```

Figure 16-7 cont.   Level-3 function to set/fetch integral data types from the `s_ictl`.

```
                case CASEMODE  : retval  = siop->s_ictl->casemode ;  break;
                case XONC      : retval  = siop->s_ictl->xonc    ;   break;
                case XOFFC     : retval  = siop->s_ictl->xoffc   ;   break;
                case CNTRLFLAG : retval  = siop->s_ictl->cntrlflg ;  break;
                case FILTERFLAG: retval  = siop->s_ictl->filterflg; break;
                default:
                        retval = -1;
                }
        return (retval) ;
}
```

Temporary Storage for Input Control Structures

In Chapter 15 we constructed s_opush and s_opop to save and restore an entire s_octl. This provides a simple mechanism for preserving the structure across function calls that change some of its members. Figure 16-8 shows the code for the sister functions s_ipush and s_ipop to manage an input control stucture. No explanation of these functions is necessary because they exactly parallel s_opush and s_opop, which were discussed in Figure 15-13.

Figure 16-8   The s_ipush and s_ipop functions: temporary storage for input control structures.

FUNCTION NAME: s_ipush, s_ipop
LEVEL: 3
LIBRARY: *SIO.LIB*
DESCRIPTION: Save and restore s_ictl structures on the local stack.
OTHER MODULES: None
RETURNS: int: 0 if stack operation is successful; otherwise 1.
COMMENTS: Both functions check for balance of the local stack, so take care that every "push" is
                balanced with a corresponding "pop."

```
#define ISTKSIZ 10

static struct sictl_ *istack[ISTKSIZ] = { NIL }; /* init 1st element to NIL  */
static struct sictl_ **istackp = istack;         /* pointer to top of stack  */

int s_ipush(siop)
SIO *siop;
{
    char *malloc();
    if (istackp >= &istack[ISTKSIZ])
        {
        puts("\007Istack overflow.");
        return (1);
        }
```

Figure 16-8 cont. The s_ipush and s_ipop functions: temporary storage for input control structures.

```
        *istackp = (struct sictl_ *)malloc(sizeof(struct sictl_));
        if (*istackp == NIL)
                return (1);
        **istackp = *siop->s_ictl;
        ++istackp;
        return (0);
}

int s_ipop(siop)
SIO *siop;
{

        if (istackp <= istack)
                {
                puts("\007Istack underflow.");
                return (1);
                }
        --istackp;
        *siop->s_ictl = **istackp;
        free(*istackp);
        return (0);

}
```

Level-3 Convenience Input Functions

In this section we will create s_fgets and s_fgetln, a pair of level-3 "convenience" functions built upon s_fgetc. First we'll look at s_fgets.

The 's_fgets' Function

Implicit in the idea of communications is dialog. The conversation between sender and receiver in a protocol file transfer is an example of an interdevice dialog. Most serial devices are configured by transmitting to them a train of meaningful bytes (commands), then awaiting an acknowledgment. In their simplest forms, the command and reply consist of single-byte responses—XON/XOFF, ACK/NAK, etc. But as we learned in our discussion of smart modems in Chapter 8, modern serial devices can actually be queried for highly detailed information about their internal status. Their response to such queries is often many bytes in length and may even arrive in a variety of formats. Before we can hope to approach smart-modem programming, then, we need a function that can reliably capture these multibyte replies. The functions shown in Figure 16-9 partially satisfy this need.

Figure 16-9 Use of `s_fgets` to return a series of bytes—a 0-terminated string.

FUNCTION NAME: s_fgets
LEVEL: 3
LIBRARY: *SIO.LIB*
DESCRIPTION: Inputs a NUL-terminated string of numc bytes into `buffer`.
OTHER MODULES: s_fgetc, s_iflush.
RETURNS: `int`: number of bytes in buffer (0 if timeout occurs).
COMMENTS: Buffer must be numc + 1 bytes long to accommodate the NUL terminator. Timeout mode is forced for the duration of the function.

```
int s_fgets(siop, buff, numc)
SIO *siop;
BYTE *buff;
int numc;
{
    int c, count;
    s_ipush(siop);                         /* save input structure      */
    s_icntrl(siop, SET, T_OUTFLAG, ON);    /* turn on input timeout     */
    if (s_icntrl(siop, GET, T_OUT) == 0)   /* save timeout interval     */
        s_icntrl(siop, SET, T_OUT, 1);     /* make sure there is some delay */
    count = 0;
    while (count < numc)
        {
        if ((c = s_fgetc(siop)) == TIMEOUT)
            break;
        if (c == IGNORE)                   /* exclude this character    */
            continue;
        *buff++ = c;                       /* install byte in buffer    */
        ++count;
        }
    if ( (c = s_iflush(siop)) != -1)       /* byte pending in s_fgetc?  */
        {
        *buff++ = c;
        ++count;
        }
    *buff = NUL;                           /* terminate buffer with NUL */
    s_ipop(siop);                          /* save input structure      */
    return (count);
}
```

An Explanation of 's_fgets' Almost by definition, a function to fetch bytes that arrive asynchronously must wait some reasonable period of time before giving up. In other words, a function without a timeout is not likely to fetch bytes very successfully. The first duty of s_fgets, then, is to guarantee that the soctl_'s timeout flag is TRUE and that there is a nominal amount of timeout. Before changing the structure members T_OUTFLAG and T_OUT, however, the entire structure is saved by a call to s_ipush. Upon completion, s_ipop restores the structure. The timeout interval is changed *only* if it is currently 0; this guarantees that the timeout interval is not 0, but does not disturb an existing non-0 value.

The numc argument in s_fgets is assumed to be the number of bytes you wish to fetch. To guarantee room for the NUL terminating byte, it must be one less than the actual length of the buffer.

The body of the function is a while loop inside which bytes are fetched by s_fgetc and placed in the buffer at the location pointed to by buff. The loop breaks after numc iterations or when s_fgetc's timeout interval expires. A NUL byte is then appended to the buffer and the two previously saved sictl_ members are restored. The function s_fgets returns the number of bytes in the buffer, *not* including the NUL terminator.

Keep in mind that many systems, especially those that accommodate slow TTY devices, often pad their output with NUL bytes. It is not unusual, for example, for such a system to transmit ten or more NUL bytes after a newline to give the device an opportunity to return its literal or figurative carriage. Although s_fgets itself does not exclude received NUL bytes from the buffer, this is easily accomplished by either the ok_cntrls inclusion array or the filtlist conversion/removal array.

The s_fgets function is extremely useful for retrieving a string of indefinite length. That is, s_fgets unconditionally gathers bytes until the buffer is full or until a timeout occurs. There are times, however, when we wish s_fgets to respond to a delimiter, usually a newline. Consider the simple act of writing software to fetch a user's password. Here, a timeout period of several seconds is needed to give the user plenty of time to remember and type a password. After the password is entered, s_fgets must wait an entire timeout interval before returning. A simple solution to this problem is given in the function in Figure 16-10. Since this function is usually employed to fetch *lines*, it is named s_fgetln.

Figure 16-10 The s_fgetln function: delimited input.

FUNCTION NAME: s_fgetln
LEVEL: 3
LIBRARY: *SIO.LIB*
DESCRIPTION: Inputs a NUL-terminated string of bytes into buff. Input is terminated when the specified delimiter is encountered.
OTHER MODULES: s_fgetc, s_iflush.
RETURNS: int: number of bytes in buffer (0 if timeout occurs).
COMMENTS: Buffer must be numc + 1 bytes long to accommodate the NUL terminator. Timeout mode is forced for the duration of the function.

```
int s_fgetln(siop, buff, numc, eolc)
SIO *siop;
BYTE *buff;
int numc;
BYTE eolc;
{
    int     c, count;
    s_ipush(siop);                          /* save input structure      */
    s_icntrl(siop, SET, T_OUTFLAG, ON);     /* turn on input timeout     */
```

Figure 16-10 cont. The s_fgetln function: delimited input.

```
    if (s_icntrl(siop, GET, T_OUT) == 0)    /* save timeout interval      */
        s_icntrl(siop, SET, T_OUT, 1);      /* make sure there is some delay */
    count = 0;
    while (count < numc)
        {
        if ((c = s_fgetc(siop)) == TIMEOUT)
            break;
        if (c == IGNORE)                     /* exclude this character      */
            continue;
        if (c == eolc)                       /* don't put eol byte in buffer */
            break;
        *buff++ = c;                         /* install byte in buffer      */
        ++count;
        }
    if ( (c = s_iflush(siop)) != -1)         /* byte pending in s_fgetc?    */
        {
        *buff++ = c;
        ++count;
        }
    *buff = NUL;
    s_ipop(siop);                            /* restore input structure     */
    return (count);
}
```

An Explanation of 's_fgetln' The principal differences between this function and s_fgets are the delimiter argument eolc and the line:

```
        if (c == eolc)
            break;
```

These cause the function to terminate upon receipt of the specified delimiter. The delimiter itself is not placed in the buffer. Like s_fgets, the numc argument in s_fgetln is the number of bytes to fetch. In order to guarantee room for the NUL terminating byte, numc must therefore be one less than the actual length of the buffer.

TERM5

We are now ready to add an important feature to our terminal program— the ability to capture incoming bytes into a disk file. Before we design that feature, however, Figure 16-11 shows the incidental additions to *TERM4* required to produce *TERM5*—version number, function menu, and so forth.

Figure 16-11 Changes in *TERM4* to produce *TERM5*.

PROGRAM NAME: *TERM5*
DESCRIPTION: Terminal program
COMMENTS: New feature: file download with XON/XOFF

```
int vers = 5;                                  /* version number  (global)       */

main(argv, arc)
int argc;
char *argv[];
{

    UNCHANGED FROM TERM4

}

void term(siop)
SIO *siop;
{
    int c;                              /* must be int to detect -1 return */
    s_ipush(siop);                      /* save both control structures    */
    s_opush(siop);
    s_icntrl(siop, SET, CONSFLAG, ON);  /* console echo on formatted input */
    s_ocntrl(siop, SET, IB_DLYFLAG, OFF);   /* interbyte delay             */
    s_ocntrl(siop, SET, IL_DLYFLAG, OFF);   /* interline  delay            */
    printf("TERM, Version %d: Press Control-%c for a summary of commands\n",\
        vers, MENU + '@');
    for (EVER)                          /*          eternal loop           */
        {
        s_fgetc(siop);                         /* s_fgetc will echo        */
        if ( (c = inkey()) != NOT_READY)
            if (c == MENU)
                {
                if (menu(siop))
                    break;             /* if menu returns non-zero         */
                }
            else
                s_fputc(siop, c);
        }
    s_opop(siop);                      /* restore both control structures  */
    s_ipop(siop);
}

#define DNLOAD1 'E'                             /* Download with C's buffer      */
#define DNLOAD2 'F'                             /* Download with local buffer    */
```

Figure 16-11 cont.   Changes in *TERM4* to produce *TERM5*.

```
int menu (siop)
SIO *siop;
{
    int cbuff(), locbuff();                  /* declare capture functions    */
    int  c;
    int  retval = 0;
    static char *menus[] =
        {
        "\tA.  Data Format, Baud rate",
        :
        "\tE.  Download Text File (small buffer)",
        "\tF.  Download Text File (large buffer)",
        "\tQ.  EXIT",
        ""                                   /* null string terminates list  */
        };
    char ** menup;
        :
            case UPLOAD:                     /* transmit a disk file         */
                upload(siop);
                break;
            case DNLOAD1:           /* receive a file: use C's file buffer */
                dnload(siop, cbuff);
                break;
            case DNLOAD2:           /* receive a file: use local file buffer */
                dnload(siop, locbuff);
                break;
            default:
                puts("Invalid choice\n\007");
                break;
        }
    }
        :
}
```

In earlier versions of this function, serial I/O was performed with the "raw" functions s_getc and s_putc. The use of s_fgetc and s_fputc in this version enables us to apply the entire battery of formatted control to every byte that is received or sent. As shown, we disable delays on output, and enable console echo on input. Notice that incoming bytes are no longer sent to the console by putchar, but by turning on console echo for s_fgetc. Turning on console echo for output (for half-duplex use, for example), requires only a single additional line:

```
        s_ocntrl(siop, SET, CONSFLAG, ON);
```

Design Considerations for 'dnload'

There are two distinct ways we can choose to capture data into a disk file. Since each of these methods has strengths and weaknesses, we will write both: cbuff, which captures incoming data into C's file buffer, and locbuff, which captures data into a large local buffer. In addition, we will compose a single "administrative" module named dnload to handle the common chores such as file opening, closing, error detection, and so on.

As shown in the menu function in Figure 16-11, selecting either 'E' or 'F' from the menu produces a call to dnload, passing to it the address of the chosen function. The dnload module itself must:

1. Open a file to capture inbound data.
2. Save the existing s_ictl structure and then configure it for downloading.
3. Call the selected capture function via a function pointer passed in its argument list.
4. Upon return, add the appropriate end-of-file byte to the captured file. This step is not necessary in all systems.
5. Close the file.
6. Differentiate between write errors and file-closing errors.
7. If no errors occur, display the total number of bytes in the new file.
8. Restore the s_ictl structure saved in step 2.

Figure 16-12 shows the function to accomplish this.

Figure 16-12   The dnload function: an administrative function for downloading serial data.

MODULE NAME: dnload
PROGRAM: *TERM5*
DESCRIPTION: Adminstrative function for downloading captured serial data into a disk file.
RETURNS: void
COMMENTS: This module calls the actual capture function by passing its address.

```
unsigned long bytetot;                  /* total number of bytes captured  */

void dnload(siop, captfp)
SIO *siop;
int (*captfp)();                        /* pointer to a capture function   */
{
extern FILE *wfopen();                  /* open write FILE, return pointer */
    FILE    *rcvfp;
    char    fnbuff[MAX_NAME_LEN];       /* filename buffer                 */
    int     errflag;                    /* inbound byte, counter, I/O error*/
    bytetot = 0;
    if ( (rcvfp = wfopen("File name for downloaded file", fnbuff)) == NIL)
        {
        puts("Input file not opened.");
        return;
        }
```

Figure 16-12 cont. The dnload function: an administrative function for downloading serial data.

```
s_ipush(siop);                                /* save control structure    */
s_icntrl(siop, SET, CONSFLAG, ON);      /* console echo on           */
s_icntrl(siop, SET, T_OUTFLAG, OFF); /* no timeout on input function    */
s_icntrl(siop, SET, T_OUT, _0_SEC_05);/* but set the interval for later */
printf("\n%s is now ready for capture. Press Esc key to end.\n", fnbuff);
printf("Terminal output is %s.\n",\
     s_icntrl(siop, GET, CONSFLAG) ? "on": "off");
xon(siop);                                    /* send XON to get started   */
errflag = (*captfp)(siop,rcvfp);        /* return code from disk write */
if (!errflag && bytetot)
     {
     fputc(DOS_EOF, rcvfp);              /* tack on end-of-file       */
     ++bytetot;
     errflag = fflush(rcvfp);         /* error on flush == disk prob. full */
     }
putchar('\n');
if (errflag || fclose(rcvfp))                 /* don't show stats if error */
     printf("Error %s %s.\n\007", errflag ? "writing" : "closing", fnbuff);
else
     printf("%lu bytes written to %s.\n", bytetot, fnbuff);
puts("\n-- Press any key to continue --\007");
getch();                                      /* ask user to acknowledge error */
s_ipop(siop);                                 /* restore control structure */
puts("Exiting download");
}
```

An Explanation of 'upload'   Upon entry to upload the function wfopen is called to fetch a file pointer. As given in Appendix B, wfopen prompts the user for a file name and asks permission before overwriting an existing file. It returns NIL if not successful; otherwise, it returns the file pointer of a file open for writing.

After saving the contents of the SIO's input control structure with s_ipush, the input console flag, timeout flag, and timeout delay are all set to their default values. Although to achieve maximum speed we wish s_fgetc to run with the timeout feature off during most of the file capture, it will be on from time to time; the desired timeout interval is therefore installed in advance. After displaying an announcement verifying the name of the open file and the state of the console output flag, an XON is transmitted to wake up the sender. Finally, the capture function is invoked:

```
errflag = (*captfp)(siop,rcvfp);
```

This calls the capture function selected from the menu, passing to it the ever-present siop and the FILE pointer for the disk file.

Error Handling in 'dnload'

We will design the capture functions to return a 0 if no write errors occur and non-0 otherwise. To understand the rather odd-looking error checking that follows, a quick review is in order of C's "f," or stream I/O file functions— fopen, fread, fwrite, fclose, and so forth. Recall that fwrite caches data in an internal buffer BUFSIZ bytes in length. A pointer to this buffer is contained in the FILE structure pointer returned by fopen. (The definitions for FILE and BUFSIZ are given in *STDIO.H*.) Because of the buffering, fwrites do not produce physical disk writes until the FILE buffer fills. At that time, C hands responsibility for the disk write to the operating system which, depending upon its own buffering scheme, still may not generate an immediate disk write. When the file is closed, any bytes in the buffer are written to disk before the file is closed.

That C may postpone the physical disk write creates a potential problem. To understand the problem, suppose that your C compiler employs a 512-byte FILE buffer and you fopen a file on a disk that has no free remaining space. Suppose further that you "f" write (putc or fwrite` 511 bytes to this file. This produces no physical disk write because C's buffer is only partially full; since there is no physical write, the operating system cannot inform C that there is no space remaining on the disk. In other words, you cannot trust an "f" write's "no error" return code. In the absence of a reliable positive error return from the write function, then, we can only hope that fclose will inform us of the disk-space error when it flushes the buffer to disk. But, and here's the problem, a number of popular C compilers fail to report the write error at fclose! Although the Aztec C compiler used for this book does report a write error on fclose, it seems worthwhile to write a little extra code to promote reliable, compiler-independent error operation.

Since the whole idea of the stream I/O functions is to free the programmer from such concerns as the nature or frequency of physical disk writes, we need another way to test for errors. The most reliable method is to write the contents of the buffer to disk *explicitly* with a call to fflush, which always correctly reports I/O errors. If upon return from the capture function errflag is 0, an end-of-file is written and the buffer is fflushed. The return code from the flush operation becomes the new value for errcode, which is then logically OR'ed with the return code from fclose. Thus we are able to detect whether an error occurred during any of the three phases—write, flush, or close. Notice, as an added bonus, this method enables us to uniquely identify a genuine close error, such as might result from a damaged disk directory.

Design Considerations for Data Capture Functions

When a byte is received from the SIO, we have our choice of how to capture it to disk. The first capture method, employed in our cbuff capture function, simply putcs each byte as it is received, letting C graciously and transparently buffer several hundred (i.e., BUFSIZ) bytes in its FILE buffer for us, eventually ferrying the accumulated bytes to disk. The second method, used in the locbuff function, squirrels away the incoming bytes in a large RAM buffer, performing a disk write only when the buffer is full. In this scheme, the programmer is responsible not only for ushering the bytes into the correct buffer location, but for deciding when the buffer is full and must be written to disk.

Each method clearly has its strengths and weaknesses. The automatic buffering of cbuff is convenient, but the code overhead incurred by byte-to-byte I/O (via putc) inevitably renders cbuff unsuitable as the data rate increases. Because locbuff stores incoming bytes in RAM instead of putcing them to disk immediately, it performs dramatically better at higher speeds; the penalty for locbuff's higher performance is the increased complexity of managing a large RAM buffer. There are other practical reasons for choosing one method over the other. When capturing large files onto a floppy, cbuff's frequent pauses while C writes its buffer to disk may be intolerable. The local buffer gives you the option to manipulate the data—to view and edit it, for example—before writing it to disk. On the other hand, cbuff's frequent disk writes safely tuck data away in small increments, thus limiting the amount of data that a disk or other system error can destroy.

Flow Control

As just discussed, locbuff's use of a very large buffer solves many problems by postponing time-consuming disk writes. Remember, though, that the physical disk access is just *postponed* and, as in cbuff, must sooner or later occur. Meanwhile, as the operating system is preoccupied with the physical disk access, incoming SIO bytes are lost. The classic way to prevent this sort of data loss is *flow control* (see Chapter 4). Since most of the world supports XON/XOFF, so shall we: immediately before a disk write is scheduled, we transmit an XOFF to inform the sender to pause; then, after completing the disk write, we send an XON to restart the sender. Since the details of XON/XOFF vary somewhat from cbuff to locbuff, a complete explanation will be offered along with the general discussion of each function.

Capture Function One—'cbuff'

Acknowledging the need for XON/XOFF, mindful of the relative merits of each capture method, and within the overall framework of upload, let us now look at cbuff, shown in Figure 16-13.

Figure 16-13   The cbuff function: employing C's internal FILE buffer to capture serial data into a disk file.

```
PROGRAM MODULE NAME: cbuff
PROGRAM:             TERM5
DESCRIPTION:         Subfunction for capturing serial data into a disk file using C's internal FILE
                     buffer.
RETURNS:             int: 1 if a disk write error occurs; otherwise 0.
COMMENTS:            XON/XOFF flow control supported. Size of buffer is given by the constant
                     BUFSIZ in STDIO.H.
```

```c
#define BYTESLEFT  25               /* buffer remaining after XPAUSE      */
#define XPAUSE     BUFSIZ - BYTESLEFT  /* bytes to write before sending XOFF */


int cbuff(siop, rcvfp)
SIO *siop;
FILE *rcvfp;
{
    extern unsigned long bytetot;
    int    buffcnt = 0, error = 0;           /*    bytes in C's I/O buffer   */
    int    c;
    long   i;    printf("C's %d buffer in use.\n",BUFSIZ);
    s_ipush(siop);
    for (EVER)
    {
        if ( (c = inkey()) == siop->s_octl->kbortc)  /* get keyboard byte */
            break;                              /* end download if abort     */
```

Figure 16-13 cont. The `cbuff` function: employing C's internal `FILE` buffer to capture serial data into a disk file.

```
        if (c != -1)
            s_fputc(siop, c);                /* transmit keyboard byte      */
        if ( (c = s_fgetc(siop)) < 0)        /* now check SIO for byte      */
            continue;
        putc(c, rcvfp);
        ++bytetot;
        if (++buffcnt == XPAUSE )             /* C's I/O buffer almost full? */
            {
            xoff(siop);                       /* XOFF to pause sender        */
            s_icntrl(siop, SET, T_OUTFLAG, ON); /*1 tsec for late arrivers*/
            for (i = BYTESLEFT; i > 0; i--)   /* wait for sender to stop */
                {
                if ( (c = s_fgetc(siop)) == TIMEOUT)
                    break;                     /* timeout, so sender is paused */
                else if (c == IGNORE)
                    continue;
                else
                    {
                    putc(c, rcvfp);      /* catch slow pokes, too       */
                    ++buffcnt; ++bytetot;
                    }
                }
            if (c != TIMEOUT)                  /* sender didn't respond       */
                puts("\nXOFF Ignored.\007");
            error = fflush(rcvfp) != 0;
            s_icntrl(siop, T_OUTFLAG, OFF); /* restore zero wait on input */
            if (s_icntrl(siop, GET, CONSFLAG) == OFF)
                printf("%lu total bytes written.\r", bytetot);
            buffcnt = 0;
            xon(siop);                         /* release sender stuck        */
            if (error)                         /* disk error ends capture     */
                break;
            }
        }
    puts("\nExit Menu");
    s_ipop(siop);
    return (error);                            /* return 0 if no error, 1 if error */
}
```

An Explanation of 'cbuff' The idea behind `cbuff` is to write bytes into C's `FILE` buffer, then, when the buffer is almost full, to call `fflush` to write the buffer to disk. The question is this: how do we gain insight into C's internal workings—i.e., how do we know when C's internal disk buffer is nearing capacity? Luckily (and for just such purposes as this), the size of C's buffer, `BUFSIZ`, is published in *STDIO.H*. By counting how many bytes are `putc`'ed into C's buffer, we can easily ascertain when to flush the buffer. In a sense, then, we are piggybacking XON/XOFF flow control onto C's buffered I/0 functions. Here, in pidgin C, is the simplified version of our plan of attack:

```
#define XPAUSE       BUFSIZ - (some constant)
    int buffcnt = 0;
    while (keybort() == FALSE)
        {
        read c;
        putc(c);
        if (buffcnt++ == XPAUSE)
            {
            xoff();
            flush I/O buffer
            buffcnt = 0;
            xon();
            }
        }
```

The number of bytes written is counted by the variable buffcnt. When buffcnt reaches some percentage of the buffer's capacity, XPAUSE, an XOFF is transmitted to the sender. C's I/O buffer is then flushed, buffcnt is reset, and an XON finally restarts the sender. The loop continues until terminated from the keyboard.

The use of a constant instead of a variable for XPAUSE is counter to conventional explanations of the XON/XOFF protocol, which usually conceives the XOFF point as a percentage of the total buffer size. It is difficult to understand why this concept prevails— is the celerity of the sender's response governed by the size of the receiver's buffer? Problems of scale are also produced by allocating the XOFF point based upon buffer size. Five percent of a 1K buffer is about 51 bytes, which should be plenty for almost every occasion; five percent of a megabyte, however, is a whopping 50K. If you cannot realistically expect your sender to respond in at *most* a few tens of bytes, you should seriously consider another means of transfer. The value given for use in both cbuff and locbuff has proven universally satisfactory on a wide variety of senders over several years.

This uncomplicated approach is tantalizingly close to complete. Only one interesting detail must be resolved. The transfer obviously fails if the sender totally ignores the XOFF, but what happens if the sender merely is slow to respond to the XOFF? As we have seen, the transmitter's UART probably has at least one transmit buffer. Let's assume that at the instant the XOFF is dispatched, the sending UART has just written a byte into its Transmitter Holding register and is currently outputting a byte from its transmitter. Even under perfect conditions—if the sender reacts to the XOFF *instantaneously*—the 2 bytes already in the pipeline will still be transmitted. Clearly, if the receiver proceeds with a disk write immediately after sending the XOFF, these two stragglers will be lost. This potential data loss can be avoided if, after sending the XOFF but before flushing the buffer, we first pause briefly to recover any bytes in the pipe:

```
    xoff(siop);
    s_icntrl(siop, SET, T_OUTFLAG, ON);
    for (i = BYTESLEFT; i > 0 ; i--)
        {
        if ( (c = s_fgetc(siop)) == TIMEOUT)
            break;
        else if (c == IGNORE)
            continue;
        else
            {
            putc(c, rcvfp);
            ++buffcnt; ++bytetot;
            }
        }
    if (c != TIMEOUT)         /* sender didn't respond         */
        puts("\nXOFF Ignored.\007");
```

Here, we transmit an XOFF followed immediately by a call to s_icntrl to enable time-out input operation. Then a for loop is entered to catch any late-arriving bytes and place them in the buffer. If s_fgetc times out, we know that the sender has honored the XOFF and it is now safe to fflush the buffer. If, on the other hand, the loop ends without s_fgetc's timeout ever expiring (i.e., c != TIMEOUT), a warning message "XOFF Ignored" is displayed and the flush is made anyway. The timeout flag in s_fgetc must be switched on at the beginning of the XOFF loop and back on again at the end. Since a "raw" s_fgetc can be called dozens of times before even the first straggler arrives, a nominal amount of timeout is required to prevent s_fgetc from quickly buzzing through the for loop.

With the slowpokes now safe in the buffer, the disk buffer is flushed. The error code returned by fflush is assigned to the error variable. If the flush is successful, the loop repeats. If error is TRUE, however, the loop breaks after switching off s_fgetc's timeout and transmitting the XON to the sender.

Upon return to upload an end-of-file (DOS_EOF from *STDIO.H*) is appended, the final flush is performed, and write/close errors are handled.

Something *not* present in the slowpoke for loop is worthy of mention. You may be thinking to yourself, "Each time a slowpoke arrives, let's send another XOFF in case the sender missed the first one." This is good thinking but produces perplexing results in many cases, depending on the sender's definition of the XON byte. If the sender is programmed to interpret *only* a specific byte—DC1, for example—as XON, the additional XOFF's are simply ignored. But if, as is often the case, the sender is programmed to interpret *any* byte as XON, the first redundant XOFF is paradoxically treated as an XON! It is therefore not a good idea to send multiple XOFF's unless you know the receiver's mind on the subject.

Capture Function Two—'locbuff'

Despite its need for more complicated buffer management, the design of locbuff is remarkably similar to that of cbuff. The basic ideas are the same—just before a buffer is full, write it to disk, making sure to catch the Johnny-come-latelies. The most interesting part of locbuff is not its *handling* of the buffer so much as its *declaring* the buffer. The complete locbuff is shown in Figure 16-14.

Figure 16-14   The `locbuff` function: a capture function with a large local buffer.

MODULE NAME: `locbuff`
PROGRAM: *TERM5*
DESCRIPTION: Subfunction for capturing serial data into a disk file using an externally declared RAM
                  buffer.
RETURNS: `int`: 1 if a disk error occurs; -1 if buffer allocation fails; otherwise 0.
COMMENTS: XON/XOFF flow control supported.

```
#define BYTESLEFT       25
#define HEADROOM         5                       /* blocks to save for locals    */
#define BLKSIZE        128

int locbuff(siop, rcvfp)
SIO *siop;
FILE *rcvfp;
{
extern char *bigbuff();
extern unsigned long bytetot;
    char    *buff, *p, *pausep;     /* buffer, buffer pointer, pause marker */
    int     c, i;
    int     error  = 0;
    unsigned numblks;                   /* number of BLKSIZE blocks allocated   */
    unsigned long bufflen = 1;
    p = buff = bigbuff(BLKSIZE, HEADROOM, &numblks);
    if (buff == NIL || numblks == 0)
        {
        puts("Insufficient memory for buffer.");
        return (-1);                        /* not tested upon return       */
        }
    s_ipush(siop);
    bufflen = numblks * BLKSIZE;        /* now convert from blocks to bytes  */
    pausep = (char *)(buff + (bufflen - BYTESLEFT)); /* calculate XOFF point*/
    printf("%lu byte local buffer in use.\n",bufflen);
    for (EVER)
        {
        if ( (c = inkey()) == siop->s_octl->kbortc)  /* get keyboard byte  */
            break;                          /* end download                 */
        if (c != -1)
            s_fputc(siop, c);               /* transmit keyboard byte       */
        if ( (c = s_fgetc(siop)) < 0)       /* now check SIO for byte       */
            continue;
        *p++ = c;
        if (p == pausep)
            {
            xoff(siop);                     /* XOFF to pause sender         */
            s_icntrl(siop, SET, T_OUTFLAG, ON); /* 1 sec for late arrivers*/
            for (i = BYTESLEFT; i > 0; --i)   /* wait for sender to pause */
```

Figure 16-14 cont.   The `locbuff` function: a capture function with a large local buffer.

```
                {
                if ( (c = s_fgetc(siop)) != TIMEOUT)/* catch slow pokes  */
                    *p++ = c;
                else
                        break;             /* timeout = sender acknowledged    */
                }
            if (c != TIMEOUT)              /* sender didn't respond      */
                puts("\nXOFF Ignored.\007");
            error = fwrite(buff, sizeof(BYTE), p - buff, rcvfp) != p - buff;
            bytetot += p - buff;           /* running byte total         */
            if (s_icntrl(siop, GET, CONSFLAG) == OFF  && !error)
                printf("%lu total bytes written.\r", bytetot);
            p = buff;                      /* reset buffer               */
            s_icntrl(siop, T_OUTFLAG, OFF); /* restore zero wait on input */
            xon(siop);                     /* now release sender         */
            if (error == TRUE)
                break;
            }
        }
    if(!error)
        {
        bytetot += p - buff;                   /* running byte total         */
        error = fwrite(buff, sizeof(BYTE), p - buff, rcvfp) != p - buff;
        }
    free(buff);
    s_ipop(siop);
    return (error);
}
```

An Explanation of 'locbuff'   Since we are committed to declaring a local buffer, we might as well allocate *all* memory available, reserving a few hundred bytes of heap space for subsequent function calls. This is accomplished by the function `bigbuff`, which returns a pointer to the allocated memory (the code for `bigbuff` is given in Appendix B):

```
p = buff = bigbuff(BLKSIZE, HEADROOM, &numblks);
```

The constant BLKSIZE is the block size for allocation and, though arbitrarily chosen, should be a power of 2. The constant HEADROOM is the number of these blocks to *reserve* from allocation. The values shown in Figure 16-14 result in an allocation of all memory except BLKSIZE * HEADROOM bytes—more than enough for current needs. Note that we pass a pointer to `numblks`, through which `bigbuff` informs us how many blocks were actually allocated.

Now the number of allocation blocks in `bufflen` is converted to bytes where it can be used to calculate the pointer to the XOFF pause-point in the buffer:

```
bufflen *= BLKSIZ;
pausep = (char*)(buff + (bufflen - BYTESLEFT));
```

449

Buffer Management in 'locbuff'

The buffer is managed by three pointers: `buff`, the address of the beginning of the buffer; `p`, the location in the buffer where the next byte is to be stored; and `pausep`, the address where the XON/XOFF protocol is to be engaged. In overall design, `locbuff` is no different from `cbuff`. The actual buffer writes are accomplished with

```
error = fwrite(buff, sizeof(BYTE), p - buff, rcvfp) != p - buff;
```

Since `fwrite` returns the number of bytes actually written, `error` is TRUE when the return value does not equal the number of bytes in the buffer (i.e., `buff - p`).

Conclusion

We now have a complete set of basic tools for performing asynchronous serial I/O. We can control data format, baud rate, RS-232 input, time-sensitive operations, and can meter the input and output of data in almost every conceivable fashion. From these tools we have already built an edifice of considerable utility—*TERM*. With a few more tools we can add the much-needed support for smart modems, the subject of the next chapter.

17

Smartmodem Programming

By combining the tools from preceding chapters, we are now able to compose a library of functions for controlling the Hayes Smartmodems and compatible modems. Before we begin, however, we need to discuss exactly what it means to write software for "smart" modems. As Chapter 8 clearly shows, the Smartmodem is by no means a single product, but an evolving product that has undergone substantial transformation between the original Smartmodem 300 and the current models. Thanks to careful engineering on the part of Hayes, each new modem is compatible with its predecessors. This downward compatibility gives us at least a hope of writing modem software that operates correctly with *any* Smartmodem yet exploits the unique capabilities of each. Because of the range and number of product enhancements over the years, this is a considerable challenge.

Basic Design Criteria

Since several of the Smartmodem's variables profoundly affect its behavior, our *first* and most important goal is to design library functions that are independent of these variables. Although perhaps unrealistically lofty, we can approach surprisingly near to this goal. Before we begin to compose our library, then, we will consider the design problems and formulate our approach to them.

The User Interface

No matter how carefully we plan our library, how clever our design, or how ingenious our coding techniques—none of these matter unless we restrict the user's access to the modem. In other words, if our software is to exert absolute control over a smart modem, we must have the *exclusive* right to send it commands. Our software therefore assumes an environment where the user issues smart-modem commands by making menu selections instead of by sending commands from the keyboard while in terminal mode. One way to enforce this restriction is to keep the modem's Data Terminal Ready (DTR) inhibited, keeping the modem in the comatose state where it ignores all commands. Because any security system—especially one based on the user's good behavior—is vulnerable to the canny or expert user, it is not possible to achieve the exclusivity we desire. This is not particularly worrisome—a user savvy enough to know that DTR puts the modem in command mode is also likely to understand the other consequences of his commands. At the very least, such a user is likely to infer a connection between his commands and a sudden failure of the software.

The interface variables having the greatest effect upon smart-modem behavior are (1) command echo (E command), (2) the sending (or not sending) of result codes (Q command), and (3) verbosity (V command).

Send Codes

To interact with the smart modem, we must be able to interpret its response codes. So critical are these codes to our basic design, we will actually include $Q0$ into *every* command we issue.

Use Word Codes

In our function for interpreting smart-modem responses we will compare the modem's responses to a list of valid responses. We obviously stand a greater chance of misidentifying a single-digit code than a longer word-code string. (The single-digit codes exist only for the benefit of programming languages with poor string handling.)

Command Echo: OFF

The sole purpose of command echo is to enable human users to see the commands they are typing. Since we are assuming a programming environment where the user *never* issues commands directly to the modem, command echo is of no value. In fact, it is a headache. Why? Some of our functions send commands to the modem then await a response. If command echo is enabled, these functions are unable to distinguish between an echo of command and the modem's actual response. Command echo, therefore, must be disabled.

RS-232 Control

We noted in Chapter 8 that the smart modem's "smartness" liberates programmers from the drudgery of managing the minutae of RS-232 control. We learned that most functions can be accomplished either with RS-232 signals or by sending command strings to the modem. What we didn't mention at the time is that only a masochist would choose the latter!

In fact, there is no reason to choose one method excusively—the best form of control is a combination of smart-modem command strings and RS-232 hardware signals. Our library functions, therefore, will assume that the user has set the configuration switches and, on the 1200B, the jumper to support DTR. The user need do nothing to configure the Smartmodem 2400 because the equivalent commands will be issued as part of the initialization function. Specifically, we assume DTR and DCD (Data Carrier Detect) to behave in the following manner:

- **DTR (pin 20),** when inhibited, unconditionally forces the modem into its comatose state. If already inhibited, asserting DTR puts the modem in the command state.
- **DCD (pin 8)** is asserted only during a carrier linkage.

RS-232 Cabling

One of our most rigid requirements is that the modem can be controlled with an off-the-shelf straight-through RS-232 cable. This is why our functions will not utilize the smart modem's potentially valuable speed indicator output DSRS (Data Signal Rate Selector, pin 23 on the Smartmodem 2400, pin 12 on other stand-alone modems). Because microcomputers typically do not provide RS-232 inputs on these pins, a custom cable would be required. The cable *may* contain connections for all 25 pins, but only pins 2 (TD), 3 (RD), 7 (common), 8 (DCD), and 20 (DTR) are required.

Compatibility

A great number of smart modems claim to be "Hayes compatible," but few bother to specify exactly how far that compatibility goes. There are a number of questions, some quite specific, that must be answered before the claim of compatibility can be countenanced.

- With which Hayes Smartmodem does it claim compatibility?
- How much of the Hayes Smartmodem command set does it support?
- Does it support the S-registers?
- Is the delay between receipt of and response to a command identical to a genuine Hayes Smartmodem?
- Does it return a product code?
- Does it return a ROM checksum?
- Are the bit-mapped registers supported?
- Does it support all levels of call-progress monitoring (extended result codes).

Of course, not every smart modem claiming Hayes compatibility passes these tests. As a matter of fact, very few can even answer yes to half these questions. In addition to the modems claiming Hayes compatibility, several brave manufacturers—most of whom were in the modem business before micros or Hayes even existed—have bucked the trend toward Hayes compatibility and have developed their own notions of what the "smart" in smart modem means.

Generality

Now that we have made some important decisions about the environment in which our smart-modem library will operate—no echo, word codes, RS-232, and so forth—we can set forth the number one design goal of all: independence from the environment we just specified. Complicated software built on a myriad of niggling environment specifications is like a house of cards. Sooner or later (usually sooner), an insignificant deviation from specification brings the whole construct down around the programmer's ears. For example, although it is much easier to write code for a smart modem if we make the assumption that command echo is off, we must defend against the user turning it on behind our back.

This philosophy of generality and defensive design not only immunizes us against the picayune, it fattens our wallet by embracing the multitude of modems that claim but fall slightly short of full Hayes compatibility. In a similar vein, although it appears that the market for non-Hayes style modems is slim indeed (and growing slimmer every year), we shouldn't write these products off completely, especially if accommodating them means merely broadening, as opposed to compromising, our definition of the smart modem. In other words, wherever possible, we must be careful to write functions based upon a wide definition of Hayes compatibility. Because it is impossible to support Hayes and wildly non-Hayes modems with the same code, our concern for the latter will take the form of designing code in such a general fashion that it can be easily modified for fundamentally different modem designs.

The Modem Structure

By now, you have come to expect that however we may elect to compose the modem functions, they will be implemented by means of a new structure pointer in the SIO. The name of this new member is sm (short for smartmodem) and is a pointer to an instance of the modem structure we will define in a moment. Figure 17-1 shows the new addition to the SIO.

Figure 17-1   The new modem member for the SIO.

STRUCT DEF: SIO
FILE: *SIODEF.H*
DESCRIPTION: Typedef of master structure defining a serial port.
COMMENTS: Highlighted item adds smart-modem support.

```
typedef struct
    {
    BYTE      *uart_base;          /* base address of UART           */
    int       data_off;           /* offset of data port from base  */
    int       status_off;         /* offset of status port from base */
    struct    sictl_   *s_ictl;   /* pointer to input  control struct */
    :
    struct    modem    *sm;       /* pointer to modem structure     */
    } SIO;
```

The modem structure itself contains the information, much of it ASCII, required to control a smart modem. For the sake of completeness, the entire modem structure is shown in Figure 17-2 and its initialization in Figure 17-3, but it will be explained piecemeal during development of the smart-modem functions. The definition of the modem structure and the constant definitions are assumed to be in a new file named *MODEM.H*. As with all structures, the initialization of the modem structure occurs in the level-0 files, *IBMPC.C* and *KAYPRO.C*.

Figure 17-2   The modem structure definition shown in its entirety. Both the structure and constant definitions reside in *MODEM.H*.

STRUCT DEF: modem
FILE: MODEM.H
DESCRIPTION: Support for a smart modem.

```
#define CMDBUFSIZ    41    /* capacity of Smartmodem s command buffer */
#define CMDSIZ        8    /* max storage needed for Smartmodem command */
```

Figure 17-2 cont.　The `modem` structure definition shown in its entirety. Both the structure and constant definitions reside in *MODEM.H*.

```
struct modem
    {
    unsigned ibdelay;              /*0  interbyte delay                       */
    BOOL     cmdechoflg;           /*1  modem commands to console             */
    char     csi[CMDSIZ];          /*2  command sequence introducer           */
    char     eocstr[CMDSIZ];       /*3  end-of-command character(s)           */
    char     quietcmd[CMDSIZ];     /*4  Q cmd: send result codes              */
    char     cmdbuff[CMDBUFSIZ];   /*5  build all commands here               */
    int      cmdt_out;             /*6  Tsecs to wait after a modem cmd       */
    int      cmdretry;             /*7  number of times to try a command      */
    unsigned guardtime;            /*8  escape guard time                     */
    BOOL     iscard;               /*9  is this a board modem?                */
    int      baudtry[6];           /*10 baud rates to try during init         */
    char     escape[CMDSIZ];       /*11 (S2) online escape byte = '|'         */
    unsigned baudfound;            /*12 baud rate at which modem found         */
    BOOL     rs232flg;             /*13 monitor RS-232 signals?               */
    short    smid;                 /*14 result of modem's product ID cmd      */
    short    romck;                /*15 rom checksum                          */
    short    modtype;              /*16 our code for modem                    */
    BOOL     configokflg;          /*17 modem successfully configured         */
    BOOL     baudmode;             /*18 baud rate initialization mode         */
    unsigned baudmax;              /*19 maximum baud rate of modem            */
    char     pri_config[CMDBUFSIZ];/*20 main configuration string             */
    char     dialmode[CMDSIZ];     /*21 tone or pulse dialling                */
    char     echocmd[CMDSIZ];      /*22 E cmd: echoes in command mode         */
    char     verbosecmd[CMDSIZ];   /*23 V cmd: word or digit result codes     */
    char     autoans[CMDSIZ];      /*24 (S0)# of rings before autoanswer      */
    char     dtwait[CMDSIZ];       /*25 (S6)dialtone wait  (secs)             */
    char     dcdwait[CMDSIZ];      /*26 (S7)dcd timeout wait (secs)           */
    char     speaker[CMDSIZ];      /*27 speaker mode                          */
    char     sec_config[CMDBUFSIZ];/*28 config str for evolutionary cmds      */
    char     xcmd[CMDSIZ];         /*29 result code set                       */
    char     okalpha[12];          /*30 alpha chars ok in dial string         */
    char     speakvol[CMDSIZ];     /*31 speaker volume                        */
    char     firmdcd[CMDSIZ];      /*32 2400's DCD firmware config switch      */
    char     firmdtr[CMDSIZ];      /*33 2400's DTR firmware config switch      */
    char     unconfig[CMDBUFSIZ];  /*34 string to send to smodem at exit      */
    char     dialbuff[CMDBUFSIZ];  /*35 build numeric dial string here        */
    char     dialcmd[CMDSIZ];      /*36 dial command                          */
    char     enddial[CMDSIZ];      /*37 dial suffix--e.g., ';' or 'R'         */
    char     anscmd[CMDSIZ];       /*38 answer command                        */
    BOOL     autobrflg;            /*39 switch baud rate to incoming call     */
    char     hupcmd[CMDSIZ];       /*40 hang up command                       */
    };
```

Figure 17-3 The entire modem declaration and initialization. This belongs in the computer-specific file.

STRUCT NAME: hayes
TYPE: modem
FILE: *IBMPC.C* and *KAYPRO.C*
DESCRIPTION: Initialization for a Hayes Smartmodem.

```
struct modem hayes =
    {
    _0_SEC_05,                       /*0  interbyte delay                   */
    OFF,                             /*1  no modem commands to console      */
    "AT",                            /*2  command prefix                    */
    "\015",                          /*3  command terminator = CR           */
    "Q0",                            /*4  send result codes                 */
    "",                              /*5  build all commands here           */
    _0_SEC_3,                        /*6  Tsecs to wait after a modem cmd   */
    4,                               /*7  number of times to try a command  */
    _1_SEC_0  + _0_SEC_5,            /*8  escape guard time (Tsecs)         */
    FALSE,                           /*9  not a board modem                 */
    {BAUD1200,BAUD300, BAUD2400, -1},/*10 baud rates to use during init     */
    "S2=124",                        /*11 (S2) online escape byte = ´|´     */
    SUPPLIED,                        /*12 baud rate at which modem found    */
    ON,                              /*13 monitor RS-232 signals            */
    SUPPLIED,                        /*14 result of modem´s product ID cmd  */
    SUPPLIED,                        /*15 rom checksum                      */
    VIRGIN,                          /*16 our own code for smodem type      */
    VIRGIN,                          /*17 modem successfully configured     */
    BAUD_FOUND,                      /*18 leave br where modem was found    */
    SUPPLIED,                        /*19 maximum baud rate of modem        */
    "",                              /*20 main configuration string         */
    "T",                             /*21 tones or pulse                    */
    "V1",                            /*22 word result codes                 */
    "E0",                            /*23 echo commands                     */
    "S0=0",                          /*24 (S0)# of rings before autoanswer  */
    "S6=2",                          /*25 (S6)dialtone wait  (secs)         */
    "S7=30",                         /*26 (S7) modem dcd timeout (secs)     */
    "M1",                            /*27 speaker mode                      */
    "",                              /*28 config str for evolutionary cmds  */
    "X4",                            /*39 extends result codes for clones   */
    ",*#()-R",                       /*30 alpha chars ok in dial string     */
    "L1",                            /*31 speaker volume (1, 2, or 3)       */
    "&C2",                           /*32 2400 firmware DCD switch: DCD on   */
    "&D2",                           /*33 2400 firmware DTR switch: DTR on   */
    "",                              /*34 unconfiguration                   */
    "",                              /*35 build numeric dial string here    */
    "D",                             /*36 dial command                      */
    "",                              /*37 dial suffix--e.g., ´;´ or ´R´     */
    "A",                             /*38 answer phone command              */
    "H0",                            /*30 hang up phone                     */
    ON,                              /*40 switch baud rate to incoming call */
    };
```

The constants at the top of Figure 17-3 define the size for two buffers:

CMDSIZ   Commands that set the value of an S-register require the most string storage. These commands have the form S*nn*=*NNN*, where *nn* is a two-digit register number and *NNN* is a three-digit parameter. Including the "=" and the NUL terminator, 8 bytes of storage are required.

CMDBUFSIZ   This is the size of the buffer in which our functions build commands before transmitting them to the modem. The size is defined to accommodate the smart modem's 40-character command buffer plus a terminating NUL byte.

We mentioned earlier that by careful design we can make it easier to support modems that are altogether different from the Hayes. Employing constant definitions for the size of various buffers is an example of such design.

Level-1 Modem Commands

In this section, we will compose three low-level modem functions. Because they deal with the primary actions of reading from and writing to the modem, these functions are analogous to the level-1 SIO functions in *BUOS.LIB*, although it is not necessary to segregate them into different physical libraries. In fact, the headers show and subsequent versions of *TERM* assume a single library, *MODEM.LIB*.

Structure Members Supporting Level-1 Commands

For your convenience, the structure members and their initialized values that support the level-0 functions are repeated in Figure 17-4.

Figure 17-4   The modem structure members required for level-1 modem functions. Initialization is shown in the right column. The complete structure and its initialization are given in Figures 17-2 and 17-3.

Structure Member		Initialized Value
⋮		
unsigned ibdelay;	/* 0 */	_0_SEC_05,
BOOL cmdechoflg;	/* 1 */	OFF,
char csi[CMDSIZ];	/* 2 */	"AT",
char eocstr[CMDSIZ];	/* 3 */	"\015",
char quietcmd[CMDSIZ];	/* 4 */	"Q0",
char cmdbuff[CMDBUFSIZ];	/* 5 */	"",
int cmdt_out;	/* 6 */	_0_SEC_3,
int cmdretry;	/* 7 */	4,
unsigned guardtime;	/* 8 */	_1_SEC_0 + _0_SEC_5,
⋮		

ibdelay	The interbyte delay that is used during output to the modem. A nominal interbyte delay of 1 Tsec (_O_SEC_05) is introduced.
cmdechoflg	If this flag is ON, all modem commands are sent to the console. This is useful for debugging, although you may wish to enable the user to view the modem commands.
csi[]	The Command Sequence Introducer—initialized to *AT*.
eocstr[]	This is the end-of-command string required to terminate a command—initialized to *CR* ("\r") to correspond to the modem's default *nl1* character in S-register 3.
quietcmd[]	This is the command string that forces the modem to send response codes—initialized to *Q0*.
cmdbuff[]	This is where all modem commands are built.
cmdt_out	This is the timeout interval in Tsecs while awaiting the modem's response to a command.
cmdretry	When an expected modem response is not forthcoming, this is the number of times to retry the command before giving up.
guardtime	When forcing the modem from online to command state, this is the quiet time in Tsecs that must surround the escape sequence.

A Function To Issue a Smart-Modem Command: 'm_cmd'

From the structure members discussed so far we can compose our first smart-modem function. The code for m_cmd, a function to build and send a command to the modem, is shown in Figure 17-5. Before we examine it, however, add the following error codes to *MODEM.H*.

```
#define M_SUCCEED    0
#define M_FAIL       1
#define MAXREPLY     20
#define QBUFSIZ      30
```

Figure 17-5   Use of m_cmd to send a command to the modem.

FUNCTION NAME:	m_cmd
LEVEL:	1
LIBRARY:	*MODEM.LIB*
DESCRIPTION:	Builds a smart-modem command in the modem structure's command buffer, then outputs it to the SIO.
OTHER MODULES:	s_ocntrl, s_opush, s_opop
RETURNS:	void
COMMENTS:	The following output characteristics are forced: a fixed interbyte delay and upper-case output. Commands are echoed to the console based upon the cmdechoflg structure member.

Figure 17-5 cont.   Use of m_cmd to send a command to the modem.

```
void m_cmd(siop, cmdstr)
SIO *siop;
BYTE *cmdstr;
{
     struct modem *smp = siop->sm;              /* for notational convenience*/
     BOOL dtr_stat;                             /* save state of dtr         */
     if ((dtr_stat = dtrnow(siop)) == OFF)      /* if dtr inhibited now...   */
          setdtr(siop, ON);                     /* assert it                 */
     s_opush(siop);                             /* preserve output structure */
     s_ocntrl(siop, SET, CASEMODE, UPPER);      /* convert to upper case     */
     s_ocntrl(siop, SET, ASCIIFLAG, ON);        /* strip high bits           */
     s_ocntrl(siop, SET, IB_DLYFLAG, ON);       /* interbyte delay           */
     s_ocntrl(siop, SET, IB_DLY, smp->ibdelay);
     s_ocntrl(siop, SET, CONSFLAG, smp->cmdechoflg);  /* echo commands?      */
     strcpy(smp->cmdbuff, smp->csi);            /* start with CSI prefix     */
     strcat(smp->cmdbuff, smp->quietcmd);       /* append result code mode   */
     strcat(smp->cmdbuff, cmdstr);              /* append command to buffer  */
     strcat(smp->cmdbuff, smp->eocstr);         /* append terminator to buff */
     s_fputs(siop, smp->cmdbuff);               /* output buffer to SIO      */
     if (dtr_stat == OFF)                       /* restore DTR               */
          setdtr(siop, OFF);
     s_opop(siop);                              /* restore output structure  */
}
```

An Explanation of 'm_cmd'   Our strategy here is to build a valid smart-modem command based upon the command string passed in the argument list. Commands are built in the structure member cmdbuff instead of in automatic local storage; in this way, subsequent functions can, if necessary, scrutinize the preceding command.

Since we have already vowed to use RS-232 control wherever possible, we must make certain that the Smartmodem's DTR is asserted. Remember, the Smartmodem *completely ignores* commands when DTR is inhibited. At the beginning of the function, then, we test the state of DTR and assert it if it is currently inhibited. The DTR is restored upon exit *only* if it was changed upon entry, thus avoiding unnecessary and potentially disruptive perturbations of DTR.

Before the command is built, the SIO is configured to strip the high bits from all output and to convert all output to upper case. Optionally, based upon the ibdelay and cmdechoflg members in the modem structure, an interbyte is introduced and output is echoed to the console.

With the SIO's output characteristics set, the command is assembled in the cmdbuff member of the modem structure. First, the Command Sequence Introducer is copied into the empty buffer. Because the SIO's cmdbuff may contain the previous command, the CSI must be *copied*, not *catenated*. Succeeding strings are then appended—the modem's "Quiet" command, the actual command string argument, and the command terminator.

Smart-modem software cannot hope to succeed unless the modem responds to commands in the expected fashion. The *Q* command is treated as an integral part of every command in order to make absolutely certain that the modem responds to commands.

It is worth evaluating the m_cmd function in terms of our goal of generality. The heart of the command could have easily been built mostly with constants:

```
s_ocntrl(siop, SET, IB_DLY, _0_SEC_05);
strcpy(smp->cmdbuff, "AT");
strcat(smp->cmdbuff, "Q0");
strcat(smp->cmdbuff, cmdstr);
strcat(smp->cmdbuff, "\r");
```

But consider the advantages of our method. First, it enables us to compensate for minor differences in future Hayes Smartmodems and their clones. For example, although all Hayes Smartmodems accept commands at a character rate equal to their maximum baud rate, a surprising number of clones do not. To accommodate these non-conforming clones, we must provide a slight *programmable* intercharacter delay. Although this delay causes a minor deterioration in the Hayes' performance, the loss in speed is insignificant in comparison to the benefit of widening the base of supported products.

Along broader lines, it is fairly safe to assume that the commands of even non-Hayes-compatible smart modems have the format:

command sequence introducer command *command terminator*

The use of separate string variables for each component of the command therefore greatly improves the prospect of supporting widely differing modems with the same code. Consequently, you will find that many non-Hayes modems can be supported merely by changing the initialization of the ASCII command strings in the modem structure.

Fetch a Smart-Modem Response: 'm_quiz'

It is dangerous to send a command without confirming that the modem has received it. Before we can evaluate the modem's response, however, we must write a function to fetch it. The function m_quiz, shown in Figure 17-6, fetches a string from the modem.

Figure 17-6 Use of the m_quiz function to fetch a response string from the modem.

```
FUNCTION NAME:  m_quiz
LEVEL:          1
LIBRARY:        MODEM.LIB
DESCRIPTION:    Fetches bytes from the modem. The maximum number of bytes to be fetched is
                specified in numc.
OTHER MODULES:  s_ipush, s_ipop, s_icntrl, s_fgets
RETURNS:        char *: pointer to the modem's response; NIL if no response.
COMMENTS:       The timeout interval is derived from the modem structure.
```

```
char *m_quiz(siop, numc)
SIO   *siop;
short numc;                          /* # of bytes wanted in response    */
{
    static char quizbuff[QBUFSIZ];   /* place modem's reply here         */
    char *quizp = quizbuff;          /* pointer value to return          */
    if (numc >= QBUFSIZ)             /* protect against buffer overrun   */
        numc = QBUFSIZ -1;
```

Figure 17-6 cont. Use of the m_quiz function to fetch a response string from the modem.

```
    s_ipush(siop);
    s_icntrl(siop, SET, T_OUTFLAG, ON);
    s_icntrl(siop, SET, T_OUT, siop->sm->cmdt_out);
    if (s_fgets(siop, quizbuff, numc) == 0)  /* get reply into buffer     */
        quizp = NIL;                          /* return a NIL if 0 bytes returned */
    s_ipop(siop);
    return (quizp);
}
```

An Explanation of 'm_quiz' Because the contents of its buffer are scrutinized by other functions, quizbuff is declared static. There are two other design requirements: first, the function must protect against buffer overwrite if accidentally asked to fetch bytes from a continuous stream; second, it must not hang when there are no bytes in the data stream. This protection takes three forms:

1. The maximum number of bytes to be fetched is passed in numc in the argument list.

2. numc is limited to one smaller than the size of the buffer (QBUFSIZ).

3. The "get string" function f_gets enables us to specify a timeout beyond which m_quiz will not wait.

The length of the timeout interval must reside in the modem structure because many Hayes Smartmodem clones do not observe the Hayes Smartmodem specification that guarantees 250 milliseconds between receipt of a command and issuing a response. Oddly, most of the clones that don't observe this specification err on the short side—that is, they send the response too quickly. The default value of O_SEC_3 is correct for Hayes products but may have to be adjusted for others.

Once the SIO is configured, s_fgets attempts to fetch the requested number of bytes into quizbuff. The function m_quiz returns a pointer to quizbuff or NIL if there is no response (i.e., quizbuff is empty).

Validating a Modem Response: 'm_isreply'

Once m_quiz has fetched a modem response, we must be able to ascertain if it is a valid one. After "mode" commands, we are interested only in whether the modem responds with OK or ERROR. After dialing and answering operations, however, we must differentiate between several call-progress messages—CONNECT, BUSY, and so forth. Such a validation is simple in concept: compare the modem's response to a list of all valid responses. In practice, however, several problems arise:

● There are two sets of response codes—single-digit and word.

● Single-digit response codes from the Smartmodem 300 are terminated by CR, but CRLF on all other smart modems.

● Responses from clones may contain additional spaces or newlines.

Before we discuss the function itself, let's first examine the array of smart-modem responses shown in Figure 17-7.

Figure 17-7 `m_result`: an array of smart-modem responses.

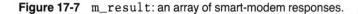

```
ARRAY NAME: m_result
TYPE:        char *
LEVEL:       3
LIBRARY:     MODEM.LIB
DESCRIPTION: A two-by-three array of string pointers containing all valid smart-modem responses.
COMMENTS:    The order of search in this array is critical (see text).
```

```c
char *m_result[][3] =
    {
        { "\r\nOK\r\n",            "\r0\r",    "0\r"  },   /* must be first */
        { "\r\nCONNECT\r\n",       "\r1\r",    "1\r"  },
        { "\r\nRING\r\n",          "\r2\r",    "2\r"  },
        { "\r\nNO CARRIER\r\n",    "\r3\r",    "3\r"  },
        { "\r\nERROR\r\n",         "\r4\r",    "4\r"  },
        { "\r\nCONNECT 1200\r\n",  "\r5\r",    "5\r"  },
        { "\r\nNO DIALTONE\r\n",   "\r6\r",    "6\r"  },   /* Hayes     */
        { "\r\nNO DIAL TONE\r\n",  "\r6\r",    "6\r"  },   /* variant   */
        { "\r\nBUSY\r\n",          "\r7\r",    "7\r"  },
        { "\r\nNO ANSWER\r\n",     "\r8\r",    "8\r"  },
        { NIL,                     NIL    ,    NIL    },
        { "\r\nCONNECT 2400\r\n",  "\r10\r",   "10\r" },
    };

int numrows = sizeof(m_result) / (3 * sizeof(m_result[0][0]));  /* cardinal */
```

An Explanation of 'm_result'   All possible result codes are stored in a *three-element* array of string pointers. Word responses are stored in column 0, and the corresponding single-digit responses in columns 1 and 2. The strings in column 1 are the single-digit responses with newline formatting produced when command echo is enabled (i.e., *E1*). Column 2 contains the single-digit responses produced when command echo is inhibited (i.e., *E0*). Refer to Table 8-2 for an explanation of how command echo effects the newline formatting of result codes. Listing every possible response code helps achieve the goal of writing functions whose behavior is independent of the current state of the *E* and *V* commands.

Notice that the entry for the tenth code contains three NIL pointers. This code is reserved by Hayes for future use. The cardinal integer `numrows` contains the number of responses in the array and is used as a row counter when searching the array.

The three-word dial tone entry NO DIAL TONE was originally installed in this array speculatively—that is, in anticipation that some manufacturer would eventually use this response. At last count, fully five products—all claiming a high degree of compatibility—use this variant.

Searching for Substrings

Many Hayes Smartmodem clones do not follow the newline formatting of the Hayes Smartmodem. A fair number, for example, use single-digit response codes with CRLFs—strictly speaking, not a Hayes format. Yet it makes no sense to exclude support for these modems simply because of this minor deviation. Besides, the problem is easily corrected: instead of attempting to match a modem's response *exactly* with one of the valid strings in the m_result array, we ascertain if any of the valid strings is a *substring* of the modem response. Using this method, a valid response can be detected even if it is surrounded on both sides by the Gettysburg address.

We now have all the tools to write a function to ascertain if a modem response is valid. The function m_isreply is shown in Figure 17-8.

Figure 17-8   Use of m_isreply to validate a modem response.

FUNCTION NAME: m_isreply
LEVEL: 1
LIBRARY: *MODEM.LIB*
DESCRIPTION: Converts result codes to an integer code.
OTHER MODULES: substr, given in Appendix B.
RETURNS: int: an integer result code or −1 if the code is not valid.
COMMENTS: This function works correctly with either long or single-digit result codes. The word
                              codes are searched first, then the digit codes. To avoid an erroneous match with any
                              message ending in '0', the array is searched backwards.

```
int m_isreply(str)
char *str;
{
    extern char *m_result[][3];
    extern int numrows;
    int row;                        /* init in for loop to start at last row */
    int col = 0;
    do  {
        for (row = numrows - 1; row >= 0; row--)  /* start with last row    */
            if (substr(str, m_result[row][col]))
                return (atoi(m_result[row][2]));
        } while (++col < 3);
    return (-1);                            /* -1 if not a substring    */
}
```

An Explanation of 'm_isreply'   This function is built around substr (see Appendix B), a general-purpose library function to search for one string within another. The function substr returns a pointer to the beginning of the smaller string within the larger string or NIL if there is no match.

The string to validate is passed to m_isreply as the formal parameter str. Since all our software assumes that word codes (i.e., *V1*) are in effect, we begin by searching all the strings in column 0 of the array, followed by those in columns 1 and 2. The control counter for the outer do...while loop is the column number, while the ordinal number of rows (numrows − 1) controls the row addressing. If a match is found, its integer equivalent is returned by applying atoi to the ASCII numerals in column 2. (The strings in the second column are unsuitable for atoi because their first characters are carriage returns.) If no match is found in the entire array, −1 is returned.

Search Order

It is almost instinctive to scan an array from low- to high-order element. This instinct, coupled with our decision to search the array for substrings, leads to a problem. Consider what happens when the modem responds with word codes to a 1200-baud connection. If the substring search begins at element 0 in m_result, the "0\r" in column 2 is matched at the end of "\r\nCONN-ECT 1200\r\n"; "0\r" is therefore correctly identified as a substring and the function returns a 0, the code for OK! The same problem, of course, occurs with the "\r\nCONNECT 2400\r\n" message or any future messages that end with "0\r"; scanning the array from high- to low-order element solves the problem by evaluating the longer responses first.

Manifest Constants for Smart-Modem Responses

Later we will be interested in associating the integer returned from m_isreply with a particular message. Using the constants in Figure 17-9 will make the code easier to read. To the eleven integers reserved by Hayes, we add a few of our own.

Figure 17-9   Manifest constants for response codes plus several codes for our own use.

```
/* manifest constants for use with modem functions */
#define M_OK        0        /* successful command              */
#define M_CONN3     1        /* carrier at 300 baud             */
#define M_RING      2        /* call incoming                   */
#define M_NODCD     3        /* no carrier detected             */
#define M_CMDERR    4        /* error in smartmodem command     */
#define M_CONN12    5        /* carrier at 1200 baud            */
#define M_NOTONE    6        /* no dial tone heard              */
#define M_BUSY      7        /* busy signal heard               */
#define M_NOANSW    8        /* silence not heard after @       */
#define M_RESERV    9        /*** don't use this!            ***/
#define M_CONN24   10        /* carrier at 2400 baud            */
#define M_NORING   11        /* no ring detected                */
#define M_BADMSG   12        /* invalid smartmodem response     */
#define M_ONLINE   13        /* can't dial into a high dcd      */
#define M_NILNUM   14        /* blank dial string               */
#define M_USRCAN   15        /* call canceled from keyboard     */
#define M_SIOERR   16        /* SIO will not clear              */
```

Level-2 Modem Functions

Now that we have the basic functions to send a command to the smart modem and fetch its reply, we will compose three more general level-2 functions. The first of these, m_query, outputs a command then fetches the modem's response.

Issue a Command and Fetch Response: 'm_query'

This function, shown in Figure 17-10, is essentially a composite of the previous two level-1 functions. The function issues a command and fetches the modem's response.

Figure 17-10 Use of `m_query` to send a command and fetch a response.

```
FUNCTION NAME:  m_query
LEVEL:          2
LIBRARY:        MODEM.LIB
DESCRIPTION:    Outputs a command, then fetches the modem's response. The maximum number of
                bytes to be fetched is specified in numc.
OTHER MODULES:  s_clrsio, m_cmd, m_quiz.
RETURNS:        char *: pointer to the modem's response; NIL if no response.
COMMENTS:       Any echoed bytes are cleared from the SIO between issuing the command and fetching
                the reply.
```

```c
char *m_query(siop, querystr, numc)
SIO   *siop;
char  *querystr;
short numc;                              /* # bytes wanted in response    */

{
    char *m_quiz();
    if (s_clrsio(siop, CMDBUFSIZ) == NUL) /* clear SIO                     */
        return (NIL);
    m_cmd(siop, querystr);               /* send desired command          */
    s_clrsio(siop, strlen(querystr));    /* clear echo                     */
    return m_quiz(siop,numc);            /* get and return pointer to reply */
}
```

An Explanation of 'm_query' Two calls to `s_clrsio` make the function interesting. In the first portion of this chapter we decided that we would base our functions on *word* result codes with *no* command echo. While establishing such parameters is an important part of software design, equally important is assuring that the code behaves reasonably if these parameters somehow do not obtain. To understand why, envision the following scene.

Your software dutifully disables command echo by including *E0* in its initialization string. However, the user of your software is a "knowledgeable" person who, upon first entering the terminal mode, is irritated with the lack of command echo. He immediately asserts DTR and types *ATE1*. After hacking around in the terminal mode, he quietly leaves the terminal mode—without, of course, restoring the echo mode to its original state. Shortly thereafter, he selects a menu choice to dial a phone number. The call is completed, carrier linkage is established, but your software (which depends upon the lack of command echo) is unable to detect the modem's CONNECT response. Instead of announcing the success of the operation, the software issues a failure message. The user, who has probably heard the progress of the entire call, is not impressed.

While this is probably an unlikely scenario and it might be argued that this person got what he deserved, you are nevertheless on the hook for the "failure" of the program. So, while we maintain our conviction to avoid command echo, we must design with the possibility that it exists. Fortunately, this is not difficult.

If the smart modem is in command-echo mode, some of the echoed bytes of the previous command will be in the SIO. Since we don't want them to be included in the modem's response, the SIO must be cleared. How many bytes to clear? To be on the safe side, we assume that

CMDBUFSIZ bytes are in the SIO buffer. If there are more, we can assume that the SIO is still receiving bytes from a source other than a smart-modem echo:

```
if (s_clrsio(siop, CMDBUFSIZ) == NUL)
        return (NIL);
```

At the present time we know that the number of echoed bytes in the SIO is equal to the number of receiver buffers in the UART—three or four at the most. Why, then, should we worry about more? In Chapter 20 we will implement UART interrupts where incoming characters are placed in a buffer of any length we choose. Again, the maxim: when possible, do not lash your software design to any one hardware concept.

Once the SIO is clear, the command is sent to the modem. Immediately, s_clrsio is called again to clear the number of bytes equal to the length of the command just transmitted. Next, m_quiz is immediately called to fetch the reply. The timing between these two calls is important. As you will recall, the timeout interval for s_clrsio is only 1 Tsec and the Hayes specifications guarantee a minimum of 250 milliseconds between the receipt of a command and the response. This leaves an ample safety margin between clearing the last character of the echo and the beginning of the modem's response.

Issue a Command and Return Its Validity: 'm_qcmd'

Since most smart-modem commands respond with either OK or ERROR, we need a function that issues a command, waits for the reply, validates the reply, then returns a code indicating success or failure. We now have all the tools to compose this extremely useful function, shown in Figure 17-11.

Figure 17-11   Use of m_qcmd to issue a command, then return SUCCEED/FAIL.

FUNCTION NAME: m_qcmd
LEVEL: 2
LIBRARY: *MODEM.LIB*
DESCRIPTION: Outputs the modem command, then waits for a response of either OK or 0.
OTHER MODULES: m_query, m_isreply
RETURNS: int: M_SUCCEED if command is successful; otherwise M_FAIL.
COMMENTS: Not intended to fetch result codes from dialing operations!

```
int m_qcmd(siop, cmdstr)
SIO *siop;
BYTE *cmdstr;
{
    int retries;
```

Figure 17-11 cont. Use of m_qcmd to issue a command, then return SUCCEED/FAIL.

```
char *reply, *m_query();
retries = siop->sm->cmdretry;              /* from structure      */
do   {                                      /* do at least once    */
       if ( ( reply = m_query(siop, cmdstr, MAXREPLY)) != NIL)
              if ( m_isreply(reply) == M_OK)
                     return (M_SUCCEED);
       } while (--retries > 0);
return (M_FAIL);
}
```

An Explanation of 'm_qcmd'   Here m_query is called to execute the smart-modem command in cmdstr. If a non-NIL pointer is returned it is immediately passed to m_isreply for validation against the strings contained in the array m_result. If the response is valid, the constant M_SUCCEED is returned. If m_query returns a NIL pointer indicating no response, or if a response is invalid, the loop repeats until the loop-controlling variable retries expires, at which time the constant M_FAIL is returned.

The constant MAXREPLY determines the maximum number of characters that m_query can fetch. Even though the longest valid reply is only 16 bytes long, MAXREPLY is set slightly larger to tolerate newlines and white space characters that some clones place before and after an otherwise valid response.

The variable retries is a copy of the modem structure member cmdretry, which is initialized to the arbitrary value of 4 in the structure. In practice, a value of 2 is usually adequate.

Fetch an Integer Response from the Smart Modem: 'm_getint'

Two types of smart-modem commands do not produce a simple OK or ERROR response. The command to ascertain the value of S-registers (see page 214) and the *I* command, which returns the product ID checksum, return three-digit ASCII integers. Figure 17-12 shows m_getint a function to query the modem and return the integer represented in its ASCII response.

Figure 17-12   Use of m_getint to query the modem for an integer.

FUNCTION NAME:	m_getint
LEVEL:	2
LIBRARY:	*MODEM.LIB*
DESCRIPTION:	Query modem for a positive integer response.
OTHER MODULES:	m_query, isdigit
RETURNS:	int: the integer or −1 if none found.
COMMENTS:	Will not convert an integer less than two digits.

Figure 17-12 cont. Use of m_getint to query the modem for an integer.

```
int m_getint(siop, cmdstr)
SIO *siop;
char *cmdstr;
{    char *buffp, *m_query();
     if ( (buffp = m_query(siop, cmdstr, 10)) != 0)
          for (; *buffp != NUL; buffp++)
               if (isdigit(*buffp) && isdigit(*(buffp+1)) )
                    return (atoi(buffp));
     return (-1);
}
```

An Explanation of 'm_getint'   This function calls m_query to issue the command and fetch the modem's response. Despite the fact that the response to such a command contains a maximum of seven characters, m_query accepts as many as ten in order to tolerate the superfluous newlines and white space emitted by some clones. If m_query returns a response, the string is scanned for two *consecutive* digits which, if found, are converted to a binary integer by atoi and returned. If the two digits are not found, −1 is returned.

Even though the Hayes specifications guarantee a return of three digits in these commands, we are content with only two. By thus widening the definition, we embrace many of the clones, some of which return a two-digit product code or even two digits of an alphabetical character (*12A*, for example). Based upon this philosophy, one might argue that searching for a single ASCII digit would be even better, accommodating clones that, say, suppress leading 0s from three-digit responses. But as an empirical, not a philosophical matter, no such clones exist at present. Moreover, it is unlikely that the clone manufacturers will stray so far from the Hayes specification.

Return Call-Progress Response: 'm_wait4dcd'

The last kind of smart-modem responses we must address are those generated by making or receiving a call. These messages, shown in Figure 17-7 above, occur during or after a telephone operation. BUSY, NO DIAL TONE, and NO ANSWER are returned as a result of a failure in the dialing operation (see Chapter 8). CONNECT, CONNECT 1200, and CONNECT 2400 occur after a successful dial or answer command. Depending upon the vintage of the Smartmodem (i.e., 1200 vs 1200+), the response NO CARRIER can occur in either of the circumstances just mentioned.

Figure 17-13 shows the function m_wait4dcd, which is designed to be called after a smart-modem dial or answer command.

Figure 17-13   Use of m_wait4dcd to wait for modem response to phone operation.

```
FUNCTION NAME:  m_wait4dcd
LEVEL:          2
LIBRARY:        MODEM.LIB
```

Figure 17-13 cont. Use of m_wait4dcd to wait for modem response to phone operation.

DESCRIPTION: Waits for modem response. The wait loop can be terminated from the keyboard. Response from the modem is converted to an integer code and returned. Codes are in *MODEM.H*.

OTHER MODULES: m_isreply, s_clrsio, s_fgets, s_icntrl, s_ipop, s_ipush, s_keybort

RETURNS: int: the modem's integer response code to dialing (M_NODCD if no response occurs within the specified time; M_USRCAN if user presses abort key; M_SIOERR if SIO will not clear; or M_BADMSG if the response is invalid.

COMMENTS: The duration of the wait for carrier is determined by the Smartmodem's S-register 7, the value of which is kept in the modem structure member dcdwait.

```
int m_wait4dcd(siop)SIO *siop;
{
    int retcode = -1;                        /** must initialize this !     **/
    char waitbuff[MAXREPLY + 1];
    if (s_clrsio(siop, CMDBUFSIZ) == NUL)    /* clear SIO                    */
        return (M_SIOERR);
    s_ipush(siop);
    s_icntrl(siop, SET, T_OUTFLAG, ON);      /* turn on timeout mode         */
    s_icntrl(siop, SET, T_OUT, _0_SEC_2);    /* timeout for s_fgets          */
    do                                       /* wait for response from modem */
        {
        if (s_fgets(siop, waitbuff, MAXREPLY) != 0)
            if ( (retcode = m_isreply(waitbuff)) == -1)
                retcode = M_BADMSG;          /* -1 if not a result code      */
        if (s_keybort(siop))
            {
            retcode = M_USRCAN;              /* canceled call from keyboard  */
            break;
            }
        } while (retcode == -1);
    s_ipop(siop);
    return (retcode);
}
```

An Explanation of 'm_wait4dcd' The substance of the function is a do...while loop that alternately polls the keyboard and calls s_fgets to test for a modem response. If the abort key is pressed, the function exits immediately, returning the M_USRCAN code. As long as there is no response, s_fgets returns a NIL and the loop continues indefinitely as long as the value in retcode remains −1. A response of any kind from the modem, however, breaks the loop immediately. If no carrier linkage occurs within the time specified in S-register 7, the modem automatically issues the NO CARRIER response. Normally, m_wait4dcd returns the integer values of the response code, but returns M_BADMSG in the event of an invalid response. The relatively short timeout delay of 200 milliseconds limits the time spent in s_fgets, thus guaranteeing that the keyboard is polled frequently.

Temporarily Force Smart Modem into Command State: 'm_gocmd'

Our final level-2 function, shown in Figure 17-14, makes it possible to issue a command while the modem is online — that is, during a carrier linkage. As you will recall from Chapter 8, the smart modem can be forced from its online state to the command state *without hanging up* by sending it three escape characters (defined in S2) surrounded by a quiet period (defined in S12). The modem acknowledges its transition to the command state by issuing the OK response. Sending *ATO0* (that's "oh zero") returns it to the online state.

Figure 17-14   Use of m_gocmd to go to the command state and issue a command.

FUNCTION NAME: m_gocmd
LEVEL: 2
LIBRARY: *MODEM.LIB*
DESCRIPTION: Forces the modem from online to command state.
OTHER MODULES: s_ipush, delay, s_icntrl, s_ipop
COMMENTS: Three "escape" characters are sent, surrounded by the quiet interval given by the modem structure member guardtime. The smart-modem escape character is kept in S-register 2 and defaults to ' + ' (ASCII 28).

```
int m_gocmd(siop, escchar)
SIO *siop;
char escchar;
{
    int i;
    int errcode = M_FAIL;
    char escbuff[MAXREPLY];
    s_ipush(siop);
    s_icntrl(siop, SET, T_OUTFLAG, ON);           /* force timeout on input  */
    s_icntrl(siop, SET, T_OUT, siop->sm->guardtime +1); /* force timeout     */
    delay(siop->sm->guardtime);
    for (i = 3; i > 0 ; --i)
        s_fputc(siop, escchar);
    if (s_fgets(siop, escbuff, 10) != 0)    /* get reply into buffer         */
        errcode = m_isreply(escbuff) == M_OK;        /* TRUE/FALSE            */
    s_ipop(siop);
    return (errcode);
}
```

An Explanation of 'm_gocmd'   For reasons that will become clear when we compose the reset function, the escape character is passed in the argument list. The timer function delay produces the quiet interval that must precede the escape sequence. The trailing quiet interval, however, is supplied by s_fgets, which also fetches the modem's response to the escape sequence. The timeout interval for s_fgets is determined by the guardtime member of the modem structure.

If the modem does not respond to the escape sequence or if its response is invalid, errcode still contains M_FAIL. Otherwise errcode contains M_SUCCEED.

There is a minor flaw with m_gocmd: s_fgets not only waits guardtime for the response, but also *after* the last byte of the response has arrived.

Level-3 Modem Functions

In this section we will write the high-level functions that must be called before the smart modem can be used. The first function, m_reset returns the modem to its default state so that it responds in a predictable fashion to commands. The second function, m_whoru, learns the exact identity of the smart modem — its product code, its ROM revision number, and its ROM checksum number.

The third function, m_config, configures the smart modem based upon the information gleaned from m_whoru.

A Function To Reset the Smart Modem: 'm_reset'

Oddly, one of the most difficult functions to design is the one to reset the smart modem. As we noted in Chapter 8, there are several circumstances under which the smart modem cannot be reset at all.

1. If the command terminator (*nl1*) [S3] has been changed to a value greater than 127, the modem simply ignores all commands.

2. A carrier linkage exists and the escape character [S2] has been changed to a value greater than 127. Here, there is no way to force the modem from online to command state whence the reset command can be issued.

3. DTR control has been overridden and cannot be used to force the modem to the command state where a reset command can be issued.

4. A configuration switch is set that forces the modem to ignore commands altogether.

Now, there are two philosophies to resetting a smart modem. In the first approach, you make *no assumptions* whatsoever about the modem's current state or configuration. Beginning with a simple reset command, and proceeding to ever more heroic measures, you try every conceivable technique to reset the modem. If, after this exhaustive testing, the modem still does not respond, you give up and sheepishly resort to asking the user to reset the modem by switching it off and back on.

The second philosophy is less energetic. Here you make only *one assumption* about the current state of the smart modem: that it was last used by your own software or, at least, is in a fathomable state. This implies that it has been correctly installed — the cable is correct, the configuration switches are in the positions required for your software, and so on.

We will take the second approach. This decision is admittedly based partially on tutorial convenience — this method is simpler to explain and understand. But there are more practical reasons for the choice. A normal reset requires only about 10 seconds. If the normal reset does not occur, it can take several more minutes to work through every possibility for resetting the modem. Is it worth it? From a statistical standpoint, once correctly installed, the modem should reset normally every time. Of the tiny fraction of cases where normal reset fails, most are hopeless — that is, no amount of effort on your part will reset it. Therefore, it seems a waste of code and user's patience to defend against a rare and almost certainly fatal malady. The effort and expense of such a futile programming effort is better spent on a good installation program, a good instruction manual, and incisive help messages.

Modem Structure Members Required for Reset

The structure members required for `m_reset` are highlighted in Figure 17-15, followed by a brief discussion of each.

Figure 17-15 The `modem` structure members required for the reset function. Initialization is shown in the right column. The complete structure and its initialization are given in Figures 17-2 and 17-3.

Structure Member			Initialized Value
	⋮		
BOOL	iscard;	/* 9 */	FALSE,
int	baudtry[6];	/* 10 */	{BAUD1200,BAUD300, BAUD2400, -1},
char	escape[CMDSIZ];	/* 11 */	"S2=124",
unsigned	baudfound;	/* 12 */	SUPPLIED,
BOOL	rs232flg;	/* 13 */	ON,
	⋮		

iscard The reset operation is greatly simplified if the modem is known in advance to be a plug-in card (i.e., 'B') type, which can be reset simply by asserting the 8250 UART's GPO1. Since there is no way for software to learn if the modem is a 'B' type, this structure member must be set to TRUE/FALSE by some sort of installation program.

baudtry[] This array contains the baud rates at which the software reset commands are sent. During installation, the user should initialize the first element of this array with the baud rate at which the modem is normally used. The list of baud rates *must* be terminated by a −1.

escape[] This is the modem's "escape" character. We initialize it to "124," the ASCII code for '|' and install it in S-register 2 during the initialization function described later. If the modem fails to respond to software reset commands, it is possible that it is in the online state and must be forced to the command state using this character in the escape sequence (see Chapter 8, "Escape from and Return to Online State," for a discusssion.)

baudfound If reset is successful, the baud rate at which the modem responds to the reset command.

rs232flg If the modem cannot be reset, this is set to FALSE to broadcast that RS-232 functions are not likely to have the desired effect.

Figure 17-16 The `m_reset` function for *MODEM.H*: a function to reset the smart modem.

```
FUNCTION NAME: m_reset
LEVEL:         3
LIBRARY:       MODEM.LIB
```

Figure 17-16 cont. The m_reset function for *MODEM.H*: a function to reset the smart modem.

DESCRIPTION: Attempts to reset the modem to default condition.
OTHER MODULES: delay, setgpol, setdtr, setbaud, m_gocmd, m_cmd, m_gocmd, m_cmd
RETURNS: int: M_SUCCESS if reset is successful; M_FAIL if user aborts.
COMMENTS: Hardware reset is used if user installs modem as a "B" (board) type. If user elects to terminate the reset, rs232flg in the modem structure is made FALSE.

```
int m_reset(siop)
SIO *siop;
{
    extern char *brstr[];
    struct modem *smp = siop->sm;
    int  i, j, errcode, user_redo;
    int tmptries, tmptime, tmpbr;          /* temporary storage             */
    if (s_clrsio(siop, CMDBUFSIZ) == NUL)       /* clear SIO of garbage     */
        return (M_SIOERR);
    tmptries = smp->cmdretry;              /* save number of retries        */
    tmptime  = smp->cmdt_out;             /* save command resposne time out */
    tmpbr    = baudnow(siop);             /* save current baud rate         */
    setdtr(siop, OFF);                    /* inhibit DTR to force comatose mode*/
    delay(_0_SEC_3);                      /* a bit of DTR delay             */
    setdtr(siop, ON);                     /* assert DTR to enable command mode */
    smp->cmdretry = 2;                    /* make m_qcmd retry only twice   */
    smp->cmdt_out = _1_SEC_0 * 2;        /* allow at least 2 secs for reset */
    user_redo = FALSE;                    /* TRUE = try online escape ('+++') */
    for(EVER)                             /* only reset or user can end loop */
        {
        for (i = 0; smp->baudtry[i] != -1; ++i)/* at every baud rate listed*/
            {
            setbaud(siop, smp->baudtry[i]);
            printf("Trying Reset at %s\n", brstr[smp->baudtry[i]]);
            for (j = tmptries; j > 0; --j)   /* issue reset command         */
                {
                smp->rs232flg = TRUE;        /* may be modified below       */
                if (user_redo && j <= 2)     /* 2nd time through; modem...*/
                    {             /* ... maybe online with DTR is disabled */
                    m_gocmd(siop, '+');       /* default escape character */
                    m_cmd(siop, "H0");        /* issue hangup command      */
                    m_gocmd(siop,atoi(&smp->escape[3])); /* ditto local */
                    m_cmd(siop, "H0");        /* hangup command again      */
                    smp->rs232flg = FALSE;   /* DTR doesn't work          */
                    }
                if ( (errcode = m_qcmd(siop, "Z")) == M_SUCCEED)
                    {
                    smp->baudfound = smp->baudtry[i];      /* save rate */
                    goto EXIT;
                    }
```

Figure 17-16 cont. The m_reset function for *MODEM.H*: a function to reset the smart modem.

```
                        if (smp->iscard == TRUE)      /* if installed as a B-type */
                            {
                            setgpol(siop, ON);        /* GP01 resets B-type modem */
                            delay(_0_SEC_05);         /* leave on a while         */
                            setgpol(siop, OFF);       /* release reset            */
                            }
                        }
                }
            puts("\007\nModem won't reset. Press any key to retry, ESC to quit");
            if (getch() == ESC)
                {
                errcode = M_USRCAN;
                smp->rs232flg = FALSE;   /* broadcast to other functions      */
                break;
                }
            if (user_redo == FALSE)     /* next time through, try online escape */
                user_redo = !user_redo;
            }

EXIT:
    setdtr(siop, OFF);
    smp->cmdt_out = tmptime;                        /* restore from temporaries */
    smp->cmdretry = tmptries;
    setbaud(siop, tmpbr);
    return (errcode);
}
```

An Explanation of 'm_reset'   Immediately after declaring variables, the following strategy is undertaken:

```
inhibit dtr;
wait;
assert dtr;
for (EVER)
    {
    for (every baud rate listed)
        {
        for (several tries)
            {
            send reset command;
            if (reset successful)
                return (M_SUCCEED);
            }
```

```
            if (user chose to retry)
                {
                send online escape;
                send hangup command;
                }
        }
    "Won't reset" message;
    user decides to redo or terminate;
    if (user redo)
        continue;
    return (M_FAIL);
    }
```

The function is essentially an eternal loop that can be broken in only two ways: through a successful reset or a user abort.[1] One by one the SIO is set to the baud rates listed in the structure's baudtry array, and the reset command is issued. If the modem responds to this command with OK, M_SUCCEED is returned. Otherwise, the modem structure member iscard is tested. If TRUE, the modem is assumed to be a pc-card modem for the IBM PC, which can unconditionally be reset by writing to the 8250 UART's general-purpose output 1. (The user should be able to change iscard during installation.) The reset command is issued twice with a 2-second timeout interval to allow for the long reset time of a Smartmodem 2400. If OK is not forthcoming, the next baud rate is selected and the reset command is sent again.

After all baud rates have been tried (about 30 seconds), the user is informed that the modem will not reset and is given the alternative to try again or terminate. If he elects to retry, the whole process repeats, beginning again with the first baud rate in the list. The next time through the loop, two new commands are issued in addition to the reset command: the online escape command followed by the "off-hook" command. If the modem is in the online state (i.e., in a carrier linkage), these commands force it back to the command mode where it then responds to the reset command. Note that the escape command is issued twice, once with the default setting of S2 and once (for good measure) with the setting contained in the modem structure. The loop continues as before until reset is successful or the user elects to quit trying.

Upon exit under any circumstances, the modem structure members that were changed upon entry are restored to their original values. Whenever it is necessary to send the online escape, the rs232flg in the modem structure is made FALSE to broadcast to other functions that the smart modem does not support RS-232 control.

This reset function is designed to be quite strict in that it does not allow the user to ignore the smart-modem failure to reset. In practice, however, there are many circumstances under which one might elect to proceed despite the failure of the modem to respond: the proper modem cable may not be available; the user may be perfectly happy with the behavior of a modem whose only shortcoming is a lack of Hayes compatibility; or, for that matter, the user may not be trying to communicate with a modem at all, but with another kind of device altogether. As we shall see, an intelligently designed communications program should provide a convenient method—perhaps in the form of a command line option or an installation variable—to allow the user to ignore the modem altogether.

---

[1]Those who feel that the goto statement should be banished from the C language should try writing a *reasonable* version of m_reset without it.

Installation

The reset process can be sped up if the user correctly installs `iscard` and the `baudtry` array. The benefit of identifying the modem as a 'B' type is obvious—reset is instantaneous and unconditional. The number and order of the baud rates in `baudtry` are also important because they prevent the reset function from addressing the modem at invalid or seldom-used baud rates. For the Smartmodem 300, for example, the user should install only baud rate BAUD300; for the Smartmodem 1200, the list can consist of both BAUD1200 and BAUD300 in the order of most frequent usage. For the Smartmodem 2400, the list can contain BAUD2400, BAUD1200, and BAUD300, also in the order of most frequent usage.

Identifying the Smart Modem: 'm_whoru'

Because various vintages and models differ so widely in their capabilities, once the smart modem has been reset, we must learn as much about it as we can. The information gained here will be used to determine the manner in which we later configure the modem.

Modem Types

We will employ the constants shown in Figure 17-17 to describe a smart modem. These values have absolutely no meaning to the modem itself, but are codes created privately by us to simplify references to the various types of modems.

Figure 17-17   Constants for defining the various types of modems.

```
/* modem identifier codes */

#define  ID_UNKNOWN      0
#define  ID_300          1
#define  ID_12           2
#define  ID_12PLUS       3
#define  ID_24           4
#define  ID_12CLONE      5
#define  ID_24CLONE      6
```

Modem Structure Members Required for Identification

Figure 17-18 highlights the `modem` structure members and their initialized values that are required by `m_whoru`.

Figure 17-18 The modem structure members required for the modem identification function. Initialization is shown in the right column. The complete structure and its initialization are given in Figures 17-2 and 17-3.

Structure Member		Initialized Value
⋮		
short smid;	/* 14 */	SUPPLIED,
short romck;	/* 15 */	SUPPLIED,
short modtype;	/* 16 */	VIRGIN,
short smdefault;	/* 17 */	VIRGIN,
⋮		

smid — This is the integer representation of the modem's product identification code received from the *I0* command.

romck — This is the integer representation of the modem's ROM checksum value received from the *I1* command.

modtype — This is our own code for the modem based upon analysis of the modem's product identification code and, potentially, its ROM checksum value. It is normally initialized to VIRGIN, but may be initialized to any of the valid modem types listed in Figure 17-17 above.

smdefault — This contains one of the valid modem types listed in Figure 17-17 above. If the identification function is unable to learn the identity of the modem, it is automatically given this type.

The actual code for m_whoru is shown in Figure 17-19.

Figure 17-19 Use of the m_whoru function to identify the type of smart modem in use.

FUNCTION NAME: m_whoru
LEVEL: 3
LIBRARY: *MODEM.LIB*
DESCRIPTION: Queries the modem for its product and ROM codes and stores them in smid and romck, respectively, in the modem structure. Also installs a modem identification code in modtype for later use.
OTHER MODULES: setdtr, m_getint, m_query, s_ipush, s_ipop, s_ictrl
RETURNS: int: M_FAIL if modem does not respond to the query or if the response is unidentifiable; otherwise M_SUCCEED
COMMENTS: REMOVEEOL is forced to guarantee the correct number of bytes. Only the first two digits in the product ID are used.

Figure 17-19 cont.   Use of the m_whoru function to identify the type of smart modem in use.

```
int m_whoru(siop)
SIO *siop;
{
    struct modem *smp = siop->sm;
    int errcode = M_SUCCEED;
    int id;
    setdtr(siop, ON);
    if ( (id = smp->smid = m_getint(siop, "I0")) == -1)    /* error              */
        errcode = M_FAIL;                            /* the only possible failure */
    if ( (smp->romck = m_getint(siop, "I1")) == -1)
        errcode = M_FAIL;
    if (id >= 100)                    /* reduce id to two digits for switch below */
        id /= 10;
    if (smp->modtype == VIRGIN)           /* modtype may already be installed */
        switch (id)
            {
            case 12:
                smp->modtype = ID_12;
                break;
            case 13:
                smp->modtype = ID_12PLUS;
                break;
            case 24:
                smp->modtype = ID_24;
                break;
            default:
                smp->modtype = ID_300;
            }
    setdtr(siop, OFF);
    return (errcode);
}
```

An Explanation of 'm_whoru'   The first effort is to fetch the modem's product identification and ROM checksum codes with the *I* command. These are stored in the modem structure members smid and romck. Once obtained, the product identification code is analyzed. The Hayes Smartmodems return a three-digit code where the first two digits are the product code and the last digit is the number of the ROM revision. Many clones do not support this command; some clones return a two-digit code while others return a two-digit code with an alphabetical character for the ROM revision number (for example, "12A"). Since our functions do not use the ROM revision number anyway, nothing is lost by analyzing only the first two digits of the identification code. The full integer returned from m_getint is stored in the structure member smid and, for local use, id. The switch analyzes the two-digit number in id and installs one of the smart-modem codes listed in Figure 17-17 in the structure member modtype.

Installation

Because it does not support the *I* command, nocase is present in the Smartmodem 300. By default, then, when the identification code does not match any of the case statements, the modem under test is assumed to be a Smartmodem 300. This obviously presents a problem: if the Smartmodem 300 can be identified only by its failure to respond to the reset command, how can we differentiate it from otherwise compatible clones—both of the Smartmodem 1200 and the Smartmodem 2400—that don't support the reset command either. The answer is to allow the user to specify the modem type instead of deriving it from the smart modem itself. This is accomplished with the structure member `modtype`, which governs the `switch` statement. If the `modtype` structure member contains the constant VIRGIN, `modtype` is calculated from the results of the *I* command. A valid modem code already in `modtype`, however, is left unchanged.

Configuring the Smartmodem

If we are to take advantage of the spiffy new features of the newer Smartmodems, we must include their commands in the configuration string. But what happens when this configuration string is sent to one of the older Smartmodems? You will recall from Chapter 8 that if a command string contains a single invalid command, *none* of the commands is executed. Clearly, we must ascertain that commands are not sent to modems that cannot understand them.

Before we compose the `m_config` command, let's discuss the structure members that will be needed. These are shown in Figure 17-20.

Figure 17-20 The `modem` structure members required for configuring the Smartmodem. Initialization is shown in the right column. The complete structure and its initialization are given in Figures 17-2 and 17-3.

	Structure Member		Initialized Value
	⋮		
BOOL	configokflg;	/* 17 */	VIRGIN,
BOOL	baudmode;	/* 18 */	BAUD_FOUND,
unsigned	baudmax;	/* 19 */	SUPPLIED,
char	pri_config[CMDBUFSIZ];	/* 20 */	"",
char	dialmode[CMDSIZ];	/* 21 */	"T",
char	echocmd[CMDSIZ];	/* 22 */	"E0",
char	verbosecmd[CMDSIZ];	/* 23 */	"V1",
char	autoans[CMDSIZ];	/* 24 */	"S0=0",
char	dtwait[CMDSIZ];	/* 25 */	"S6=2",
char	dcdwait[CMDSIZ];	/* 26 */	"S7=30",
char	speaker[CMDSIZ];	/* 27 */	"M1",
char	sec_config[CMDBUFSIZ];	/* 28 */	"",
char	xcmd[CMDSIZ];	/* 29 */	"X4",
char	okalpha[12];	/* 30 */	",*#()-R",
char	speakvol[CMDSIZ];	/* 31 */	"L1",
char	firmdcd[CMDSIZ];	/* 32 */	"&C2",
char	firmdtr[CMDSIZ];	/* 33 */	"&D2",
char	unconfig[CMDBUFSIZ];	/* 34 */	"Z"
	⋮		

The strategy for configuration is uncomplicated. We will build two separate configuration strings—`pri_config` for those commands that are supported by all Smartmodems and `sec_config` for evolutionary commands. The commands to be included in each string are shown below as subheadings of these configuration buffers.

`configokflg`	A flag to broadcast that the modem has been successfully configured.
`baudmode`	How to initialize the `SIO`'s baud rate relative to the type of modem in use.
`baudmax`	The maximum data rate for the `modtype` member of this structure.
`pri_config[ ]`	The buffer for "primary" commands—that is, commands that are valid for *all* Smartmodems. The commands are:

	`dialmode[ ]`	Selects pulse or tone dialing. Initialized for tones.
	`echocmd[ ]`	*E*, the echo command. Initialized to disable echo.
	`verbosecmd[ ]`	*V*, word or single-digit responses. Initialized for word responses.
	`autoans[ ]`	S-register 0: number of rings before auto-answer. Initialized for 0 rings, i.e., don't answer.
	`dtwait[ ]`	S-register 6: the delay between taking the phone off-hook and dialing the call. Initialized to 2 seconds.
	`dcdwait[ ]`	S-register 7: how long after dialing to wait for a carrier before giving up. Initialized to 30 seconds.
	`speaker[ ]`	*M* command that controls the speaker. Initialized to 1 (speaker on) until carrier is detected.

`sec_config[ ]`	This is the buffer for "secondary" commands—that is, commands that are valid only for *some* Smartmodems. Commands are placed in this buffer based upon the `modtype` structure member and, potentially, `smid` and/or `romck`. These commands are:

	`xcmd[ ]`	Selects the command set in use based upon the `modtype` structure member. Initialized to 4, but must be changed to 1 for the Smartmodem 1200.
	`okalpha[ ]`	This is a list of characters that are valid in a dial string.
	`speakvol[ ]`	The firmware volume control, the *L* command. Initialized to 1—medium volume.
	`firmdcd[ ]`	The Smartmodem 2400 has no configuration switches, so DCD must be configured in software. It is initialized to "&C2": pin 8 reflects the carrier.
	`firmdtr[ ]`	The Smartmodem 2400 has no configuration switches, so DTR must be configured in software. It is initialized to "&D2": pin 20 forces the modem to its comatose state.

`unconfig[ ]`	This is a string that you can optionally send to the modem upon exit. Here, it is initialized with the reset command.

A Function To Configure the Smartmodem: 'm_config'

The challenge of this function is to ascertain which commands to place in the secondary configuration buffer. Figure 17-21 shows the code for m_config.

An Explanation of 'm_config'   Once the basic strategy of this function is understood, the code becomes quite routine. The "primary" configuration string is built by concatenating only those commands that are universally palatable to all Smartmodems. The "secondary" configuration string, however, is unique for each type of Smartmodem, so its contents must be built dynamically, based upon the value of the modtype structure member supplied by m_whoru.

A switch is applied to the modtype structure variable. Each case represents a type of Smartmodem. Since "primary" commands (those shared by all Smartmodems) are initialized to the Smartmodem 300 settings, the case for the Smartmodem 300 contains only one statement—

Figure 17-21   Use of m_config to configure a Smartmodem.

FUNCTION NAME: m_config
LEVEL: 3
LIBRARY: *MODEM.LIB*
DESCRIPTION: Configures the modem as described in the modem structure.
OTHER MODULES: setbaud
RETURNS: int: M_SUCCEED or M_FAIL
COMMENTS: Builds two configuration strings: pri_config containing commands that are recognized by all Smartmodems, and sec_config containing commands that are supported by only some. Note that sec_config must be sent first.

```
int m_config(siop)
SIO *siop;
{
    struct modem *smp = siop->sm;
    int retval;
    setdtr(siop, ON);
    strcpy(smp->pri_config, "");        /* null out primary config buffer   */
    strcpy(smp->sec_config, "");        /* null out secondary config buffer */
    switch (smp->modtype)               /* build sec_config based on ID code */
        {
        case ID_300:
            smp->baudmax = BAUD300;         /* maximum baud rate            */
            break;
        case ID_12:
            smp->baudmax = BAUD1200;
            smp->xcmd[1]  = '1';            /* only X1 supported           */
            strcat(smp->sec_config, smp->xcmd);
            break;
        case ID_12PLUS:
            smp->baudmax = BAUD1200;
            strcat(smp->sec_config, smp->xcmd);
            strcat(smp->okalpha, "/!@W");               /* new dial modifiers */
            strcat(smp->sec_config, smp->speakvol);
            break;
```

Figure 17-21 cont.   Use of `m_config` to configure a Smartmodem.

```
            case ID_24:
                    smp->baudmax = BAUD2400;
                    strcat(smp->sec_config, "&F");          /* recall factory config */
                    strcat(smp->sec_config, smp->firmdtr);  /* dtr mode             */
                    strcat(smp->sec_config, smp->firmdcd);  /* dcd mode             */
                    strcat(smp->sec_config, smp->xcmd);     /* extended commands    */
                    strcat(smp->okalpha, "/!@W");           /* new dial modifiers   */
                    strcat(smp->sec_config, smp->speakvol);
                    break;
            }
    m_qcmd(siop, smp->sec_config);              /* secondary must be first!  */
    strcat(smp->pri_config, smp->dialmode);     /* pulse or tone dialing      */
    strcat(smp->pri_config, smp->echocmd);      /* modem-echo in command mode */
    strcat(smp->pri_config, smp->verbosecmd);   /* long or short result codes */
    strcat(smp->pri_config, smp->autoans);      /* # rings on auto answer     */
    strcat(smp->pri_config, smp->escape);       /* escape character           */
    strcat(smp->pri_config, smp->dcdwait);      /* secs to wait for carrier   */
    strcat(smp->pri_config, smp->dtwait);       /* secs to wait for dialtone  */
    strcat(smp->pri_config, smp->speaker);      /* speaker on/off             */
    retval = m_qcmd(siop, smp->pri_config);     /* send primary to modem      */
    switch (smp->baudmode)                      /* set baud rate              */
        {
        case BAUD_DEF:                          /* no change                  */
                break;
        case BAUD_MAX:                          /* to modem's highest         */
                setbaud(siop,smp->baudmax);
                m_qcmd(siop, "");               /* tell baud rate to modem    */
                break;
        case BAUD_FOUND:                        /* rate where modem responded */
                if (smp->modtype == ID_300 && smp->baudfound > BAUD300)
                        setbaud(siop, BAUD300);                 /* special case */
                else
                        setbaud(siop,smp->baudfound);   /* where reset found it */
                m_qcmd(siop, "");               /* tell baud rate to modem    */
                break;
        }
    if (retval == M_SUCCEED)
            smp->configokflg = TRUE;            /* broadcast init             */
    setdtr(siop, OFF);                          /* inhibit DTR                */
    return (retval);                            /* return 0 if "OK"           */
}
```

the assignment of the modem's maximum data rate into the maxbaud structure member.

With the Smartmodem 1200, the first evolutionary command is added to the secondary buffer—the *X* command for extending the call progress response codes. The *X* command is initialized to '4' in the structure but since the 1200 does not support this parameter, we alter its value to '1'.

The `case` for the Smartmodem 1200+ places not only the *X* command in the secondary buffer but also appends four characters to the list of characters permitted in dialing commands and adds the *L* command for controlling speaker volume.

The secondary configuration buffer for the Smartmodem 2400 begins with the *&F* command that recalls the factory configuration. This must be the first command in the buffer because the reset performed by `m_reset` installs the *user's* configuration profile. This means that after reset the content of many crucial Smartmodem variables is not predictable. The factory configuration, however, installs the familiar configuration used by the other Smartmodems. Next, the two commands to control the Smartmodem 2400's firmware configuration "switches" are installed in the buffer. These commands, *&C* and *&D,* enable the conventional use of the DCD and DTR RS-232 inputs respectively. Finally, the remaining relevant evolutionary commands are appended to the buffer.

As we exit from the switch, the secondary configuration contains the commands appropriate for the modem whose code is in the `modtype` structure member. Despite the "secondary" in its name, `sec_config` should be transmitted *first*. This guarantees that a Smartmodem 2400 sees the *&F* command before it sees subsequent commands. In other words, an *&F* embedded later in the string would overwrite the effects of the previous commands. (The *&F* command, unlike the *Z* command, does not cancel the effect of subseqent commands in the string.)

Next, the primary configuration buffer of primary commands is constructed by concatenating the appropriate `modem` structure members.

Installation

After sending the configuration strings, one decision remains: at what baud rate shall the `SIO` begin life? The answer to this question is embodied in the `modem` structure member `baudmode`. The three choices are represented by the constant definitions below, which should be placed in *MODEM.H.*

```
#define BAUD_DEF    0    /* use default                 */
#define BAUD_MAX    1    /* use highest possible speed  */
#define BAUD_FOUND  2    /* leave where reset occurred  */
```

The first constant, BAUD_DEF, results in no change. The second, BAUD_MAX, sets the `SIO`'s baud rate to `maxbaud`, the modem's highest data rate. The final choice, BAUD_FOUND sets the `SIO` to the baud rate at which the modem responded to the reset command in `m_reset`. If the modem is a Smartmodem 300, however, a maximum baud rate of 300 baud is set; this compensates for the odd behavior in older 300s of accepting and responding to commands at rates up to 2400 baud.

Dial and Answer Functions

We now turn to the smart-modem functions for dialing and answering the phone. We will compose functions to perform the most common operations: dialing, redialing, answering, and hanging up. The highlighted `modem` structure members in Figure 17-22 are required in these operations.

Figure 17-22 The modem structure members required for telephone functions. Initialization is shown in the right column. The complete structure and its initialization are given in Figures 17-2 and 17-3.

Structure Member			Initialized Value
⋮			
char	dialbuff[CMDBUFSIZ];	/* 35 */	"" ,
char	dialcmd[CMDSIZ];	/* 36 */	"D",
char	enddial[CMDSIZ];	/* 37 */	"" ,
char	anscmd[CMDSIZ];	/* 38 */	"A",
BOOL	autobrflg;	/* 39 */	ON,
char	hupcmd[CMDSIZ];	/* 40 */	"HO"
⋮			

dialbuff[ ] The dial string is assembled in this buffer where it will be available for subsequent redialing.

dialcmd[ ] This is the dial command itself, initialized to *D*.

enddial[ ] This buffer is for command modifiers that result in an error if they appear anywhere but at the end of a dial string. At present, only the *;* (semi-colon) command (return to command mode) currently meets this description.

anscmd[ ] The answer command, initialized to *A*.

autobrflg When the modem answers a call, this flag determines whether the baud rate of the SIO is automatically changed to match the data rate of the data link. This is initialized to "ON."

hupcmd[ ] The smart-modem command to hang up the phone and return to the command mode, initialized to *H0*.

Auto-Dial Telephone: 'm_dial'

A smart-modem dialing command is actually a series of operations (see Figure 8-2, "The Anatomy of a Smartmodem Dial"). Thanks here to the internal design of the smart modem and our low-level smart-modem library, this relatively complicated procedure is reduced to a single function, m_dial, shown in Figure 17-23.

Figure 17-23 The m_dial function: a smart-modem auto-dial function.

FUNCTION NAME: m_dial
LEVEL: 3
LIBRARY: *MODEM.LIB*
DESCRIPTION: Dials the number specified and waits for the return of a result code.
OTHER MODULES: isdcd, m_cmd, s_ipush, s_icntrl, s_putc, strcpy, strcat, strlen, setdtr, m_wait4dcd

Figure 17-23 cont.   The m_dial function: a smart-modem auto-dial function.

RETURNS: int: result code returned from dial operation.
COMMENTS: The duration of the wait for the response is given in the dcdwait structure member.
                      The filtered dial string is built into the modem structure for use by redial.

```
int m_dial(siop, phonenum)
SIO *siop;
char  phonenum[];
{
    struct modem *smp = siop->sm;
    int  resultcode;
    char dialstr[CMDBUFSIZ];            /* build dial command here       */
    char *dbp = smp->dialbuff;
    do  {                               /* filter string for illegal bytes */
        if (isdigit(*phonenum) || index(smp->okalpha, *phonenum))
            *dbp++ = *phonenum;         /* copy valid characters to dialbuff */
        } while( *++phonenum != NUL );
    strcpy(dialstr,smp->dialcmd);       /* build dial string: dial command.. */
    strcat(dialstr,smp->dialbuff);      /* ...then the number itself then .. */
    strcat(dialstr, smp->enddial);      /* ...special dial commands e.g. ';' */
    if (strlen(smp->dialbuff) == 0)     /* exit if string is NIL         */
        return (M_NILNUM);
    setdtr(siop, ON);
    m_cmd(siop, dialstr);               /* output command to SIO         */
    resultcode = m_wait4dcd(siop);      /* go wait for carrier           */
    switch (resultcode)
        {
        case M_NODCD:                   /* no carrier (or timeout)       */
        case M_NOTONE:                  /* no dial tone heard            */
        case M_BUSY:                    /* busy signal heard             */
        case M_NOANSW:                  /* silence not heard after @     */
            setdtr(siop, OFF);          /* return to command state       */
            break;
        case M_USRCAN:                  /* call cancelled from keyboard   */
            setdtr(siop, OFF);          /* return to command state       */
            s_putc(siop, SP);           /* cancel call                    */
            break;
        }
    return (resultcode);                /* exit with DTR still high      */
}
```

An Explanation of 'm_dial'   The string containing the phone number to dial is passed to
m_dial as an argument. Our plan is to copy the phone number argument into dialbuff in the
modem structure so it will be available for a subsequent redialing operation. During copying, the
phone number argument is filtered; that is, only numerals and those characters listed in the array
okalpha are placed in dialbuff. (Recall that okalpha may be modifed during smartmodem configuration.)

Once the phonenum argument has been filtered and tucked safely away in the modem structure, the actual dial string that will be sent to the modem is built in the local buffer dialstr. The dial command (i.e., *D* or *T*) is copied into the buffer first. To this buffer is then appended the filtered phonenum argument, followed by the enddial buffer of commands that may appear only at the end of the dial string.

Before sending the compound dialstr to the modem, it is tested for NIL. If no dial string is present, the function immediately returns the error code M_NILNUM. Otherwise, DTR is asserted and dialstr is passed along to m_cmd, which outputs the command to the SIO. Next, m_wait4dcd is called to await the modem's response to the dial command. The timeout interval in *seconds* for m_waitdcd is the value in S-register 9, which is set to dcdwait during configuration.

The resulting code (the variable resultcode) is then subjected to a switch. If the call is successful, DTR remains asserted; if resultcode indicates that no linkage has been established, DTR is inhibited, thus unconditionally forcing the modem into the comatose state. If DTR is not supported, however, and the user aborts from the keyboard, the modem continues to wait for a carrier until S-register 9 expires. Luckily, sending any character (here a SPACE) to the modem terminates the wait. The function ends by returning resultcode.

Special Dial Strings

Communicating with a receive-only modem requires the smart modem to go off-hook and respond to a carrier with originate tones. This is accomplished with a blank dial string, *ATD*, but m_dial's refusal to dial a blank string apparently prevents it. To overcome this problem, simply place a single comma (i.e., a 1-second delay) in the dial string.

Redial Last Number: 'm_redial'

As just described, when a call is dialed with m_dial the valid alphanumeric of the phone number is stored in the modem structure for later redialing. With no string processing required m_redial, shown in Figure 17-24, merely consists of a single call to m_dial itself.

Figure 17-24   The m_redial function: a function to redial a previously dialed number.

FUNCTION NAME: m_redial
LEVEL: 3
LIBRARY: *MODEM.LIB*
DESCRIPTION: Redials a previously dialed number.
OTHER MODULES: m_dial
RETURNS: int: response code as described in *MODEM.H*.
COMMENTS: The previously dialed number is left in the modem structure by m_dial.

```
m_redial(siop)
SIO *siop;
{
    m_dial(siop, siop->sm->dialbuff);
}
```

An Explanation of 'm_redial'   Remember that m_dial stores the alphanumeric portion of the dial string in the modem structure. The previously dialed number is therefore present in the modem structure—we need only pass the string in dialbuff to m_dial itself.

Answer the Telephone: 'm_answer'

When the answer command (*A*) is issued, the smart modem performs three operations: it (1) takes the line off-hook, (2) asserts its carrier tone using receive tones, and (3) issues a response code. Since these operations are performed automatically by the smart modem, our answer function need only send the answer command and wait for the smart modem's response. The code for m_answer is shown in Figure 17-25.

Figure 17-25   The m_answer function: a function to answer an incoming call.

FUNCTION NAME:	m_answer
LEVEL:	3
LIBRARY:	*MODEM.LIB*
DESCRIPTION:	Answers an incoming call and optionally adjusts the baud rate to the rate of the call.
OTHER MODULES:	setdtr, m_cmd, m_wait4dcd, setbaud, s_clrsio, m_quiz, m_isreply, delay.
RETURNS:	int: integer answer code from m_wait4dcd.
COMMENTS:	The duration of the wait for the carrier is given in the dcdwait structure member. Waits for a RING response from the modem before answering.

```
int m_answer(siop)
SIO *siop;
{
    char *ringmsg, *m_quiz();
    int anscode, newbaud, tmptime;
    if (s_clrsio(siop, CMDBUFSIZ) == NUL)      /* clear SIO of garbage       */
        return (M_SIOERR);
    tmptime = siop->sm->cmdt_out;           /* save command response time out */
    siop->sm->cmdt_out = _1_SEC_0 * 10;     /*   long time between rings      */
    setdtr(siop, ON);
    ringmsg = m_quiz(siop, 9);
    siop->sm->cmdt_out = tmptime;           /*   restore command time out      */
    if (ringmsg == NIL)                     /*   no response                   */
        return (M_NORING);
    if(m_isreply(ringmsg) != M_RING)        /*   wrong response                */
        return (M_NORING);
    delay (_0_SEC_3);                       /* wait for smartmodem to get ready */
    m_cmd(siop,siop->sm->anscmd);           /* ok to issue answer command      */
    anscode = m_wait4dcd(siop);
    if (siop->sm->autobrflg == ON)          /* change baud to incoming call    */
        {
        switch (anscode)
```

Figure 17-25 cont. The m_answer function: a function to answer an incoming call.

```
            {
            case M_CONN3:
                    newbaud = BAUD300;
                    break;
            case M_CONN12:
                    newbaud = BAUD1200;
                    break;
            case M_CONN24:
                    newbaud = BAUD2400;
                    break;
            }
        if (baudnow(siop) != newbaud)            /* baud may already be right */
            setbaud(siop, newbaud);
        }
    switch (anscode)
        {
        case M_USRCAN:
            s_putc(siop, SPACE);
        case M_NODCD:
        case M_SIOERR:
            setdtr(siop, OFF);
        }
    return (anscode);
}
```

An Explanation of 'm_answer'   While the smart modem is sending a response, it cannot process incoming commands. Before issuing the answer command, therefore, the SIO is cleared and the modem is queried for a RING response. If RING is not detected, the function exits with the error code M_NORING; otherwise the answer command from the modem structure is sent to the modem, then wait4dcd is called to await the modem's response, which is assigned to the variable anscode. If a carrier linkage is successfully established, anscode returns a response code that identifies the link's data rate. If autobrflg is TRUE, the baud rate of the SIO is adjusted to the data rate of the linkage by a call to setbaud (unless the rates already match).

If no linkage is established, DTR is inhibited, thus the modem is put into the comatose state. If DTR is not supported, however, and the user aborts from the keyboard, the modem continues to wait for a carrier until register S9 expires. To prevent this, a SPACE is sent to the modem to terminate the wait. The function ends by returning anscode.

The requirement that an answer command follow a RING message prevents using this function when two modems are connected directly through a cable instead of through the phone line. A "mode" argument may easily be added, however, to instruct the function to skip the check for an incoming ring signal.

Installation

After a linkage is established, autobrflg governs whether the SIO adjusts to the speed of the linkage. This is initialized to TRUE but can be installed as FALSE if the user prefers to set the rate manually or, for some reason, not to set the rate at all.

Terminate a Carrier Linkage: 'm_hup'

Since terminating a carrier linkage in progress is essentially the same as hanging up the phone, the function is called "hup." Hanging up the phone should be as simple as inhibiting DTR, but the function must also deal with the possibility that DTR is not supported. The code for m_hup is shown in Figure 17-26.

Figure 17-26 The m_hup function: a function to terminate a carrier linkage.

```
FUNCTION NAME:  m_hup
LEVEL:          3
LIBRARY:        MODEM.LIB
DESCRIPTION:    Hangs up the phone.
OTHER MODULES:  delay, setdtr, isdcd, m_gocmd, m_qcmd
RETURNS:        int: M_SUCCEED or M_FAIL
COMMENTS:       If inhibiting DTR does not force hang-up, an online escape command is issued to force
                the modem to command mode where an explicit hang-up command can be issued.
```

```c
int m_hup(siop)
SIO *siop;
{
    int err;
    setdtr(siop, OFF);
    delay(_0_SEC_3);                        /* allow for a little delay       */
    if ( (err = isdcd(siop)))               /* if DTR is still up             */
        {
        m_gocmd(siop, atoi(&siop->sm->escape[3])); /* escape to cmd state */
        err = m_qcmd(siop, siop->sm->hupcmd);      /* and hang up          */
        }
    return (err);
}
```

An Explanation of 'm_hup' Upon entry, DTR is immediately inhibited. If the modem supports DTR control, this forces it back into the comatose state, unconditionally ending the carrier linkage. After inhibiting DTR, we wait 300 milliseconds, then test DCD to make certain that the carrier is no longer present. If DCD fails to drop, we assume that the modem is still online and send it the online escape sequence followed by the explicit hang-up command, *H0*.

Consult Data Carrier Detect: 'm_warndcd'

Our final function in this section is designed to prevent accidentally calling a smart-modem function when DCD is not in the required state. It is pointless, for example, to attempt to dial a number when a carrier linkage already exists or to hang up the phone when there is no carrier linkage. This function, m_warndcd, shown in Figure 17-27, is passed the expected state of the DCD input and issues a warning if that state is not present.

Figure 17-27   The `m_warndcd` function: a function to alert the user to an incorrect carrier state.

FUNCTION NAME: `m_warndcd`
LEVEL: 3
LIBRARY: *MODEM.LIB*
DESCRIPTION: Issues a warning and overrides the prompt if the current DCD state does not match the argument.
OTHER MODULES: `isdcd`
RETURNS: `int`: M_SUCCEED if the DCD state is OK, if the user elects to ignore the DCD state, or if the `rs232flag` in the `modem` structure is TRUE; otherwise M_FAIL.
COMMENTS: The `rs232flg` may be FALSE at the user's discretion or automatically if any phase of modem reset fails.

```
int m_warndcd(siop, warnmode)
SIO *siop;
int warnmode;
{
    int  c = -1;
    char *warnp;
    if (siop->sm == NIL || siop->sm->rs232flg == FALSE)
        return (M_SUCCEED);    /* no modem structure or DCD not supported */
    warnp = (warnmode) ? "no" : "a";
    if ( isdcd(siop) != warnmode)
        {
        printf("\nTests indicate %s carrier present.\
 OK to ignore?\007 (Y/N):", warnp);
        while ( c != 'N' && c != 'Y')
            if ( ( c = toupper(getch()) ) == 'N')
                return (M_FAIL);
        }
    return (M_SUCCEED);
}
```

An Explanation of 'm_warndcd'   The argument `warnmode` is the *required* state of the carrier. If the `SIO`'s DCD input doesn't match `warnmode` a message is printed explaining the discrepancy, which the user may wish to ignore. The function returns M_SUCCEED if DCD is in the expected state or if the user elects to proceed in the face of an error. M_FAIL is returned only if the user decides not to proceed.

Before the state of DCD is even tested, we see this test:

```
if (siop->sm == NIL || siop->sm->rs232flg == FALSE)
        return (M_SUCCEED);
```

This tests (1) the presence of a `modem` structure, and (2) the flag that signals that RS-232 control is supported. Recall that this flag is set in `m_reset` if the modem fails to respond properly. If no `modem` structure is present in the `SIO`, the carrier test is pointless.

String Arrays for Smart-Modem Functions

Before we modify *TERM* to include smart-modem functions, let's first take a look at some handy string arrays. Figure 17-28 shows two string arrays. The strings in m_codes correspond to the smart-modem response constants given in Figure 17-9. The strings in m_names correspond to the constants assigned to the various types of smart modems in Figure 17-17.

Figure 17-28   Use of modnames strings for identifying smart-modem types.

ARRAY NAME: m_codes
LEVEL: 3
LIBRARY: *MODEM.LIB*
DESCRIPTION: Strings corresponding to smart-modem response codes.
COMMENTS: The smart-modem response codes—e.g., M_CONN12—are defined in *MODEM.H*.

```c
char *m_codes[] =
    {
    "Successful",
    "300 baud connection established",
    "Call incoming",
    "no connection established",
    "Command error",
    "1200 baud connection established",
    "No dialtone",
    "Dialed number is busy",
    "No answer",
    "?????",                          /* reserved */
    "2400 baud connection established",
    "No ring detected",
    "Unknown smartmodem response",
    "Call already in progress",
    "Blank dial string",
    "Operation cancelled by user",
    "Cannot clear SIO"
    };
```

ARRAY NAME: m_names
LEVEL: 3
LIBRARY: *MODEM.LIB*
DESCRIPTION: Strings corresponding to modem id codes.
COMMENTS: The modem id codes—e.g., ID_1200—are defined in *MODEM.H*.

```c
char *m_names[] =                     /* names for each id code      */
    {
    "Unknown type",
    "300",
    "1200/1200B",
    "1200+/1200B+",
    "2400/2400B",
    "Generic 1200 clone",
    "Generic 2400 clone",
    };
```

TERM6

Now that we have a full complement of modem control functions, we can add several new features to our terminal program. Figure 17-29 shows these enhancements. As usual, only the functional additions are shown.

Figure 17-29 *TERM6*: smart-modem enhancements to our terminal program.

```
PROGRAM NAME: TERM6
DESCRIPTION:    Terminal program
COMMENTS:       New features: smart-modem support—dial, answer, etc.
#include  "modem.h"

int vers = 6;                           /* version number (global      */

main(argc, argv)
int argc;
char *argv[];
{
    int err, portnum;
    SIO *siop;                                /* pointer to an SIO        */
    struct modem *smp;                /* saves typing and runs faster too */
        portnum = 0;
    if (argc > 1)
        portnum = atoi(argv[1]);
    if ( (siop = s_open(portnum)) == NIL)
        {
        printf("\007Cannot open:%s\n",errstr[s_errno]);
        return (s_errno);
        }
    smp = siop->sm;
    if ( ( err = m_reset(siop)) != M_SUCCEED)
        printf("%s.  (%d)\n",m_codes[err], err);
    else if ( (err = m_whoru(siop)) != M_SUCCEED)
        puts("Fatal modem error: no response to ID request.");
    else if ( (err = m_config(siop)) != M_SUCCEED)
            puts("Fatal error during modem configuration.");
    else if
        {
        printf("Found Smartmodem: %s at %s baud. (%d)\n",\
          m_names[smp->modtype], brstr[smp->baudfound],smp->smid);
        term(siop);                       /*              TERM          */
        }

    if ( (s_errno = s_close(siop)) != 0 )
        {
        printf("\007Cannot open:%s\n",errstr[s_errno]);
        return (s_errno);
        }
    puts("\nEnd of TERM\n");
    return (0);
}
```

Figure 17-29 cont. *TERM6*: smart-modem enhancements to our terminal program.

```
void term(siop)
SIO *siop;
{

      UNCHANGED FROM TERM5

}
#define DIAL    'G'                          /* Dial phone number        */
#define REDIAL  'H'                          /* Redial previous number   */
#define ANSWER  'I'                          /* Answer phone phone       */
#define HUP     'J'                          /* Hang up phone            */

int menu (siop)
SIO *siop;
{
            ⋮
      static char *menus[] =
            {
            "\tA.  Data Format, Baud rate",
            ⋮
            "\tG.  Dial a phone number",
            "\tH.  Redial last phone number",
            "\tI.  Answer incoming call",
            "\tJ.  Hang up phone",
            ⋮
            "\tQ.  EXIT",
            ""
            };
            ⋮

      switch (toupper(c))
            {
            case EXIT:
                  retval = 1;
                  break;
            ⋮
            case DIAL:
                  if (m_warndcd(siop, OFF) == 0)
                        dial(siop);
                  c = EXIT;                          /* leave menu after dial */
                  break;
            case REDIAL:
                  if (m_warndcd(siop, OFF) == 0)
                        printf("\n%s.  \n",m_codes[redial(siop)]);
                  c = EXIT;                          /* leave menu after redial */
                  break;
```

Figure 17-29 cont. *TERM6*: smart-modem enhancements to our terminal program.

```
            case ANSWER:
                if (m_warndcd(siop, OFF) == 0)
                    printf("\n%s. \n",m_codes[m_answer(siop)]);
                c = EXIT;                      /* leave menu after answer */
                break;
            case HUP:
                if (m_warndcd(siop, ON) == 0)
                    printf("\nHangup %s.\n",\
                        m_hup(siop) == 0 ? "OK" : "error");
                c = EXIT;                      /* leave menu after hangup */
                break;
        default:
            puts("Invalid choice\007");
            c = -1;                        /* continue looping        */
            break;
        }
        ⋮
}
```

```
MODULE NAME:    dial and redial
PROGRAM:        TERM6
DESCRIPTION:    Dials or redials telephone number on the modem.
int dial(siop)
SIO *siop;
{
    extern char *m_codes[];
    int result;
    char numbuff[CMDBUFSIZ +1];
    printf("\nEnter phone number:  ");
    gets(numbuff);
    result = m_dial(siop, numbuff);
    printf("%s. (%d)\n",m_codes[result], result);
    return (result);
}


int redial(siop)
SIO *siop;
{
    printf("\nRedialing previous number:  %s\n",siop->sm->dialbuff);
    return (m_redial(siop));
}
```

An Explanation of TERM6 The library of smart-modem functions makes these new functions seem trivially easy. After opening the SIO, m_reset, m_whoru, and m_config are called in succession. The return values from these functions are used to make certain that an identifiable smart modem is indeed connected to the SIO. If any step in this setup procedure fails, term is not called and the program simply terminates with an error message. This is an intentionally restrictive approach. You will probably wish to modify the code to accommodate non-conforming modems:

```
if (!err)
    term(siop);                        /* call term if modem OK */
else
    {
    printf("No modem found. Ok to continue? (y/n)  ");
    if (toupper(getch()) == 'Y')
        term(siop);
    else
        puts("Fatal Modem Error.");
    putchar('\n');
    }
```

Inside the `menu` function, strings are installed in the `menus` array to represent the new smart-modem functions for dialing, redialing, answering, and hanging up. Menu choices as before are applied to the `switch`, turning control over to the local functions which, in turn, call the indicated function from the smart-modem library. In all cases, the value returned from each function contains the result code of the requested operation. This code is then displayed by using it to index into the string pointer array `m_names`.

Note the use of `m_warndcd`, which makes certain that DCD is correct for the function called. If DCD does not match the `ON/OFF` argument, the user is given the opportunity to proceed or to terminate the function. His choice, in the form of `M_SUCCEED` or `M_FAIL`, determines whether the call is eventually made. Although not shown here, protective calls to `m_warndcd` should now also be retrofitted to the `upload` and `dnload` cases.

Suggested Enhancements

As designed, *TERM* provides no mechanism for exiting without closing the `SIO`. Suppose that while a call is in progress, the user wishes to exit *TERM* to the operating system temporarily, then return to *TERM*. As written, this is impossible because the `SIO` is automatically `s_opened` at entry to *TERM* and `s_closed` upon exit. The ability to exit is simple: add another case to `menu` that, upon return to `main`, causes the call to `s_close` to be skipped. The second problem—how to re-enter without disturbing the `SIO` or the modem—is a bit more difficult. First, modify `s_open` to accept a mode argument that causes it to skip all configuration and simply return the pointer to the `SIO`. Second, if DCD is present upon entry to `main`, give the user the option to call `s_open` with the "re-enter" option, and to skip modem reset and configuration altogether.

Conclusion

Some will find this chapter, with its use of structures and a hierarchy of functions, to be a classic case of overkill. "Surely," they think, "there is a simpler way to converse with a smart modem." Of course there is an alternative—hardwiring variables into the code—but it is both self-destructive and shamelessly shortsighted. Using the techniques given in this chapter, it is possible to support virtually any modem claiming even remote Hayes compatibility. In fact, a smart software developer would supply "modem profiles" for every popular brand of Hayes-compatible modem. Such a profile would merely consist of an image of the `modem` structure for that smart modem, to be overlaid during installation.

18

XMODEM File Transfers

In the first part of this chapter, we will compose the functions `x_snd` and `x_rcv` to transfer files using the popular XMODEM protocol explained in Chapter 4. Later in the chapter we will write the code to implement the checksum error-checking method used in XMODEM protocol. The functions for CRC error checking will be composed in Chapter 19.

Please note that we will develop functions only for XMODEM *single-file* transfers. The specifications for multi-file transfer, along with other technical details of the XMODEM protocol, are given in Chapter 3. The present chapter assumes you are familiar with the material in Chapter 3, so if you have not read it, please do so now.

Design Considerations in File Transfers

If our file-transfer modules had to send and receive files only at typical modem speeds—300 to 2400—we would not need to worry about speed performance. But such software is often called upon to transfer files between two directly connected computers in order to transport files between incompatible disk formats or operating systems. In such nose-to-nose configurations, the transfer speed limits the ultimate usefulness of the software. We will therefore design these functions with particular attention to speed. Unfortunately, the programming practices that lead to good speed performance often conflict with the qualities normally associated with good C programming. Let's see how.

In earlier programs, we stressed a top-down, highly structured approach to program design, relegating logical procedures to functions. We have unhesitatingly passed as many arguments to these functions as necessary to achieve our goals. We have also used temporary `auto` variables liberally to manifest meaning and make the code easier to understand.

Although the copious use of functions is considered to be a mark of good program design, we do pay a price for it. Even with the cleverest of compilers running on a microprocessor with highly efficient addressing modes, a function call *inherently* takes longer to execute than the equivalent in-line code. Furthermore, due to the architecture of popular microprocessors (8080, Z80, the 8086 family, and the 68000 family), *direct* memory addressing associated with `static` C variables is substantially faster than the *indexed-indirect* addressing associated with `auto` variables and function-call arguments. As microprocessors become more sophisticated in their memory management capabilities, this discrepancy will doubtless decrease, but for now we must take such factors into consideration. In general, we will observe the following design principles:

- Each packet should be input and output without interruption between fields.

- In time-sensitive sections, we will place as much code as possible in-line; where function calls are unavoidable, we will employ the least complicated ones available. For example, we will fetch bytes with s_waitch instead of s_fgetc.

- To take advantage of the speed advantage of direct memory addressing, we will declare critical data *global* instead of passing it in function argument lists or declaring it as local auto variables.

- When inputting and outputting packets, we will be stingy with assignments, conditionals, and other expressions.

The remainder of this chapter comprises three sections. First, we will formulate a strategy for processing *exceptions*—errors, messages, and so on. Second, we will compose the module to transmit a file using the XMODEM protocol. Third, we will compose the complementary module to receive a file. In these two modules, we will show only the code for performing error checking with the *arithmetic checksum* method. Chapter 19 is dedicated to a more comprehensive presentation of the code for the CRC error-checking method.

To make the functions easier to understand and the explanation of them easier to follow, flow charts preceding the code line numbers are used in the main modules.

Constant Definitions

Before plunging in, some general constants required by the code in this chapter are given in Figure 18-1. These constants, the significance of which will be explained as we proceed, should be placed in a new file named *XMOD.H*. All functions and modules created in this chapter are assumed to reside in a single module named *XMODEM.LIB*.

Figure 18-1 General XMODEM constant definitions for *XMOD.H*.

```
#define DBLKSIZ    128        /* size of data field in packet    */
#define HEADROOM   10         /* amount of memory to save from buffer */

#define SOH_TIMOUT _1_SEC_0   /* timeout interval for SOH        */
#define ACK_RETRY  30         /* used in loop to wait for ACK    */

#define CRCPAKSIZ  133        /* number of bytes in CRC packet   */
#define CKSPAKSIZ  132        /* number of bytes in checksum packet */
```

Exception Processing

A great many interruptions—both momentary or long-lasting—can occur during a transfer. Some of these are errors from which the transfer will recover, some are normal pauses, and still others are fatal errors which require the transfer to be terminated. We use the term *exception* to cover all the reasons why a transfer is derailed.

It may strike you as odd to begin this chapter with a discussion of exception handling, but from aesthetic as well as pedagogical points of view, strong exception processing lies at the heart of any well-made program. Moreover, the nature of the programming task at hand—file transfer under a protocol—adds new importance to the topic. Data communications being the black art it is, exceptions arise from unexpected sources and present themselves in unfamiliar guises. The most important aspect of file-transfer software—more important even than speed—is the robustness with which exceptions are handled. Other kinds of programs may respond to an exception simply by announcing that one has occurred and issuing a description of it. In communications governed by a protocol, however, every identifiable exception must result not only in sending a message to the user, but in a unique response directed at the other participant in the transfer. The inclusion of these responses (which are sometimes complicated) and the accompanying messages in the *body* of the send and receive modules would make the code impenetrably difficult to understand. This congestion would be particularly deadly in the functions where, in an effort to increase speed, we have decided to place in-line much of the code that would ordinarily be placed in functions. In the XMODEM modules we are about to compose, then, the matter of exception handling cannot be parenthetical "user-friendliness," but must be central to the structure of the code itself.

The 'errcode' Variable

The structure of both the transmit and the receive function centers about a main `while` loop within which are managed the details of the transfers. The *single* condition for sustaining this loop is the local variable `errcode`, which contains an exception code. Whereas the *detection* of exceptions occurs within the main `while` loop, the *response* to them is relegated to a central exception-processing function named `x_except`. The following snipit of code illustrates the relationship of `x_except` to the two modules `x_snd` and `x_rcv`:

```
#define CONTINUE 0
#define BREAK    1
#define X_COUNT 10
#define Y_COUNT  5

#define EXCEPT_X  0
#define EXCEPT_Y  1

char *msg[] =        /* messages corresponding to exception codes */
     {
     "Timeout waiting for X",
     "Sorry, Fatal Error Y"
     };
int x_except(siop, exceptnum, ex_cntp, maxexcepts)
SIO *siop;
int exceptnum;                      /* error code in XMOD.H            */
int *ex_cntp;                       /* pointer to an error counter     */
int maxexcepts;                     /* max number of errors permitted  */
```

```
{
    int errval = CONTINUE;
    switch (exceptnum)
        {
        case EXCEPT_X:
            puts(msg[EXCEPT_X]);
            ++*ex_cntp;
            break;
        case EXCEPT_Y:
            puts(msg[EXCEPT_Y]);
            errval = BREAK;
            break;
        }
    if (*ex_cntp > maxexcepts)
        if (ask_user_2_cancel() == TRUE)
            errval = BREAK;
    return (errval);
}


x_snd()
{
    int errcnt = 0,  errcode = 0, x;
    while(errcode == CONTINUE)
        {
        x = s_getc();
        if (x == 0)
            {
            errcode = x_except(EXCEPT_X, &errcnt, X_COUNT);
            continue;
            }
        }
}


x_rcv()
{

    int errcnt = 0,  errcode = 0, y;
    while (errcode == CONTINUE)
        {
        y = s_getc();
        if (y == 1)
            {
            errcode = x_except(EXCEPT_Y, &errcnt, Y_COUNT);
            continue;
            }
        }
}
```

When an exception occurs in the transmission module x_snd, a code, EXCEPT_X, is passed to x_except. A *pointer* to the local count variable errcnt and the maximum number of exceptions permitted are also passed. Inside x_except, the exception number in the argument list is applied to a switch. When the EXCEPT_X case is detected, the exception number also selects the corresponding message by indexing into msg an array of pointers to exception messages. Since the exception is not fatal in this case, the only action taken is the incrementation of the pointed-to exception counter (i.e., + + *ex_cntp).

Importantly, the value of errval is unchanged from its initialized value of CONTINUE. Before returning the value in errval, *ex_cntp is tested to ascertain whether the pointed-to counter has reached its maximum permitted value as passed in maxexcept. When the limit is reached, the user decides whether to proceed or terminate; if the latter, errval is assigned the value BREAK. We'll assume here that the limit has not been reached and CONTINUE is returned.

Back in x_snd, the x_except's return value is assigned to the local variable errcode and a continue statement forces execution to the top of the while loop. Since EXCEPT_X was not fatal, errcode still contains CONTINUE and the transfer proceeds.

The module x_rcv proceeds like x_snd except this time EXCEPT_Y is a fatal error. In addition to displaying the error message, the EXCEPT_Y case sets errval to BREAK. Upon return to x_rcv the continue statement is executed as before, but this time errcode contains BREAK, causing the main while loop to terminate.

Constant Definitions and String Arrays for Exceptions

Before examining the actual code for x_except, let's first look at the constants to support it in Figure 18-2. These constants should reside in *XMOD.H* along with the general constants in Figure 18-1. As always, the significance of these constants will be explained as we go along.

Figure 18-2 Exception code constant definitions for *XMOD.H*.

```
#define X_ESNDMAX   10          /* max exceptions during transmission      */
#define X_ERCVMAX   10          /* max exceptions during receiving         */
#define X_NOSOHMAX 100          /* max SOH timeout exceptions              */

#define CONTINUE     0          /* errcode value that sustains snd/rcv loop */
#define BREAK        1          /* one of the errcode value that breaks same */

         /* Exception code used in both xmit and receive */
#define E_USRCAN     0          /* user cancelled transfer        */
         /* Exception codes used only in x_snd */
#define E_FILEMTY    1          /* file to transmit is empty      */
#define E_NOACK      2          /* time out waiting on ACK        */
#define E_RCVCAN     3          /* receiver canceled              */
#define E_BADPAK     4          /* NAK instead of ACK             */
#define E_EOF        5          /* End of file read               */
#define E_LASTACK    6          /* final ack not acknowledged     */
#define E_SNDOK      7          /* successful transmission        */
#define E_DSKREAD    8          /* disk read error                */
         /* Exception codes used only in x_rcv */
#define E_NOSOH      9          /* timeout receiving SOH          */
#define E_BADCKV    10          /* invalid checkvalue received    */
#define E_SNDCAN    11          /* transmitter cancelled transfer */
#define E_BADSOH    12          /* invalid SOH received           */
#define E_NODATA    13          /* timeout receiving data in block */
#define E_PAKNUM    14          /* invalid block number received  */
#define E_SNDACK    15          /* sender missed last ack         */
```

Figure 18-2 cont.   Exception code constant definitions for *XMOD.H.*

```
#define E_PAKSEQ   16        /* FATAL: packet out of sequence  */
#define E_DSKWRITE 17        /* disk write error               */
#define E_RCVOK    18        /* successful reception           */
```

Figure 18-3 gives the array of string pointers whose elements correspond to the exception code constants in Figure 18-2. For example, the expression msgs[E_BADCKV] refers to the message "Data error detected. Requesting retransmission." This array should appear at the beginning of *XMODEM.LIB*.

Figure 18-3   Strings corresponding to the constants in Figure 18-2.

ARRAY NAME: x_msg
TYPE: char *
LIBRARY: *XMODEM.LIB*
DESCRIPTION: Array of pointers to message strings used in XMODEM file transfer modules.
COMMENTS: These rank-equivalent constants are shown in comments.

```
char *x_msg[] =
    {
    "\nTransfer cancelled from keyboard.\007",    /* E_USRCAN    0  */
    "Input file is empty\007",                    /* E_FILEMTY   1  */
    "Timeout waiting for ACK",                    /* E_NOACK     2  */
    "Receiver cancelled transfer.\007",           /* E_RCVCAN    3  */
    "Resending last packet",                      /* E_BADPAK    4  */
    "End of file read",                           /* E_EOF       5  */
    "\nWarning: receiver did not acknowledge EOT.\007",  /* E_LASTACK   6  */
    "Successful transmission",                    /* E_SNDOK     7  */
    "Fatal error reading disk.",                  /* E_DSKREAD   8  */
    "Timeout waiting for SOH",                    /* E_NOSOH     9  */
    "\nData error detected. Requesting retransmission.",  /* E_BADCKV   10 */
    "Transfer cancelled by sender.\007",          /* E_SNDCAN   11 */
    "\nByte received, but not SOH",               /* E_BADSOH   12 */
    "\nTimeout waiting for packet data",          /* E_NODATA   13 */
    "\nBad packet number",                        /* E_PAKNUM   14 */
    "\nSender missed ACK",                        /* E_SNDACK   15 */
    "Fatal packet sequence error.\007",           /* E_PAKSEQ   16 */
    "Fatal error writing disk.",                  /* E_DSKWRITE 17 */
    "Successful reception"                        /* E_RCVOK    18 */
    };
```

Global Variables

All variables shown in Figure 18-4 are declared global—some in order to increase access speed, and some to avoid cluttering up the argument lists of function calls. All are declared static to limit their scope to *XMODEM.LIB*. These variables should be placed near the top of *XMODEM.LIB*. We will discuss the use of these variables as the need arises.

Figure 18-4 Global variables for *XMODEM.LIB*.

```
/* GLOBAL variables */
int    paksize;                     /* number of bytes to xmit or rcv  */
unsigned short (*r_errckp)();       /* pointer to the error check funct */
char  *ckvname;                     /* string indicating CRC or cksum  */
BYTE  csync;                        /* "NAK" for checksum, 'C' for crc  */
unsigned short *crctblp;            /* pointer to the CRC lookup table  */
struct rcvpacket *rcvbuff;          /* pointer to receive packet buffer */
```

A Function To Process XMODEM Exceptions: 'x_except'

Figure 18-5 shows the actual code for x_except, the function to handle exceptions for both the send and receive modules.

Figure 18-5 The x_except function: an XMODEM exception handler.

FUNCTION NAME: x_except
LEVEL: 3
LIBRARY: *XMODEM.LIB*
DESCRIPTION: Handles exceptions (e.g., errors) that occur during XMODEM transfers.
RETURNS: int: one of the error codes given in *XMOD.H*.
COMMENTS: A pointer to an exception counter variable and its maximum permitted value are passed as arguments.

```
0      int x_except(siop, exceptnum, ex_cntp, maxexcept)
5      SIO *siop;
10     int exceptnum;                    /* error code in XMOD.H          */
15     int *ex_cntp;                     /* pointer to an error counter    */
20     int maxexcept;                    /* max number of errors permitted */
25     {
30          extern unsigned short x_rcvcrc(), x_rcvcksum();
35          int errval = CONTINUE;
40          switch (exceptnum)
45               {
50               case E_USRCAN:                 /* user aborts from keyboard  */
55                    puts(x_msg[E_USRCAN]) ;
60                    errval = BREAK;
65                    delay(_0_SEC_5);
70                    s_putc(siop, CAN);
75                    break;
```

Figure 18-5 cont. The x_except function: an XMODEM exception handler.

```
80      /* errors in transmission */
85              case E_FILEMTY:
90                      puts(x_msg[E_FILEMTY]);
95                      break;
100             case E_RCVCAN:                  /* transmitter aborted     */
105                     puts(x_msg[E_RCVCAN]);
110                     errval = BREAK;         /*          FATAL          */
115                     break;
120             case E_NOACK:                   /* timeout waiting for ACK  */
125                     puts(x_msg[E_NOACK]);
130                     ++*ex_cntp;
135                     break;
140             case E_BADPAK:                  /* resending previous packet */
145                     puts(x_msg[E_BADPAK]);
150                     ++*ex_cntp;
155                     s_clrsio(siop, CRCPAKSIZ); /* clear buffer          */
160                     break;
165             case E_EOF:                     /* end of disk file read    */
170                     puts(x_msg[E_EOF]);
175                     errval   = E_EOF;
180                     *ex_cntp = X_ESNDMAX;
185                     break;
190             case E_DSKREAD:                 /* disk read error          */
195                     puts(x_msg[E_DSKREAD]);
200                     errval = BREAK;         /*          FATAL          */
205                     break;
210             case E_LASTACK:                 /* no ACK response to EOT   */
215                     puts(x_msg[E_LASTACK]);
220                     s_putc(siop, CAN);
225                     break;
230             case E_SNDOK:                   /* good transfer           */
235                     errval = E_EOF;
240                     printf("%s",x_msg[E_SNDOK]);  /* use printf--no newline */
245                     break;
250     /* errors in reception */
255             case E_NOSOH:                   /* timeout waiting for SOH  */
260                     ++*ex_cntp;             /* bump caller's error count */
265                     puts(x_msg[E_NOSOH]);
270                     if (rcvbuff->pnuml == VIRGIN) /* negotiate startup mode */
275                     {
280                             r_errckp = (r_errckp == x_rcvcrc) ? x_rcvcksum : x_rcvcrc;
285                             paksize  = (r_errckp == x_rcvcrc) ? CRCPAKSIZ-1: CKSPAKSIZ-1;
290                             csync    = (r_errckp == x_rcvcrc) ? 'C'        : NAK;
295                             ckvname  = (r_errckp == x_rcvcrc) ? "CRC"      : "CHECKSUM";
300                             s_putc(siop, csync);
305                             printf("\nAttempting to synchronize in %s mode.\n", ckvname);
310                     }
```

Figure 18-5 cont. The x_except function: an XMODEM exception handler.

```
315                 else
320                     s_putc(siop, NAK);
325                 break;
330             case E_BADCKV:                  /* bad checksum or CRC         */
335                 puts(x_msg[E_BADCKV]);
340                 ++*ex_cntp;
345                 s_putc(siop, NAK);
350                 break;
355             case E_SNDCAN:                  /* transmitter aborted         */
360                 puts(x_msg[E_SNDCAN]);
365                 errval = BREAK;             /*          FATAL              */
370                 break;
375             case E_BADSOH:                  /* invalid SOH received        */
380                 puts(x_msg[E_BADSOH]);
385                 s_clrsio(siop, CRCPAKSIZ);     /* ignore rest of packet    */
390                 s_putc(siop, NAK);          /* tell sender to retry        */
395                 ++*ex_cntp;
400                 break;
405             case E_NODATA:                  /* timeout in packet           */
410                 puts(x_msg[E_NODATA]);
415                 ++*ex_cntp;
420                 s_putc(siop, NAK);
425                 break;
430             case E_PAKNUM:                  /* packet numbers don't agree  */
435                 puts(x_msg[E_PAKNUM]) ;
440                 s_clrsio(siop, CRCPAKSIZ);
445                 ++*ex_cntp;
450                 s_putc(siop, NAK);          /* ask for retransmission      */
455                 break;
460             case E_SNDACK:                  /* duplicate of previous packet */
465                 puts(x_msg[E_SNDACK]) ;
470                 ++*ex_cntp;
475                 s_putc(siop, ACK);
480                 break;
485             case E_PAKSEQ:                  /* packets out of order --FATAL */
490                 puts(x_msg[E_PAKSEQ]);
495                 errval = BREAK;             /*          FATAL              */
500                 break;
505             case E_DSKWRITE:                /* disk write error            */
510                 puts(x_msg[E_DSKWRITE]);
515                 errval = BREAK;             /*          FATAL              */
520                 s_putc(siop, CAN);
525                 break;
530             case E_RCVOK:                   /* good transfer               */
535                 errval = BREAK;
540                 printf("%s",x_msg[E_RCVOK]); /* use printf--no newline */
545                 delay(_0_SEC_5);                /* let receiver get ready */
550                 s_putc(siop, ACK);             /* send final ACK          */
555                 break;
```

Figure 18-5 cont. The x_except function: an XMODEM exception handler.

```
560                 default:
565                     break;
570                 }
575         if (errval == CONTINUE && *ex_cntp > maxexcept)
580             {
585             errval = BREAK;
590             printf("%d errors or waits have occured: Keep trying?\
592     (y/n):\007 ", maxexcept);
595             if (toupper(getch()) == 'Y')
600                 {
605                 errval   = CONTINUE;
610                 *ex_cntp = 0;            /* reset caller's error counter */
615                 }
620             putchar('\n');
625             }
630         return (errval);
635     }
```

An Explanation of 'x_except'   Several of the cases in this giant switch need no elaboration because they do nothing more than display a message and test the limits of the counter. The remaining cases will be discussed with the send and receive modules to which they apply. Notice that only one case is common to both send and receive modules:

E_USRCAN   Executed when the user presses the **Escape** key during a transfer. The message is displayed and, after a half-second wait to allow the other end to finish its current packet operation, a CAN character is sent. The value BREAK is returned, terminating the caller's main packet loop.

For now, ignore the rather complicated-looking E_NOSOH case—we will discuss this along with the receive module. Instead of a global variable to count exceptions, x_except addresses the counter through a pointer passed in its argument list. The maximum value permitted for that counter is also passed. This design enables us to manage any number of counter variables, all with different limits.

The exception-limit test is only slightly more complicated than the one shown in the sample code on page 499. If *ex_cntp has reached its limit of maxexcept at line 575, the user is asked to decide whether the transfer should proceed in the face of so many exceptions. If he chooses to abort, the pointed-to exception counter is reset and errval is set to BREAK in order to force termination of the transfer within the calling module.

XMODEM Transmission

With a basic understanding of x_except, we can now study the flow chart for the XMODEM transmission module, shown in Figure 18-6. After a general discussion of this chart, we will compose the corresponding code.

Figure 18-6 Flow chart of XMODEM transmit module.

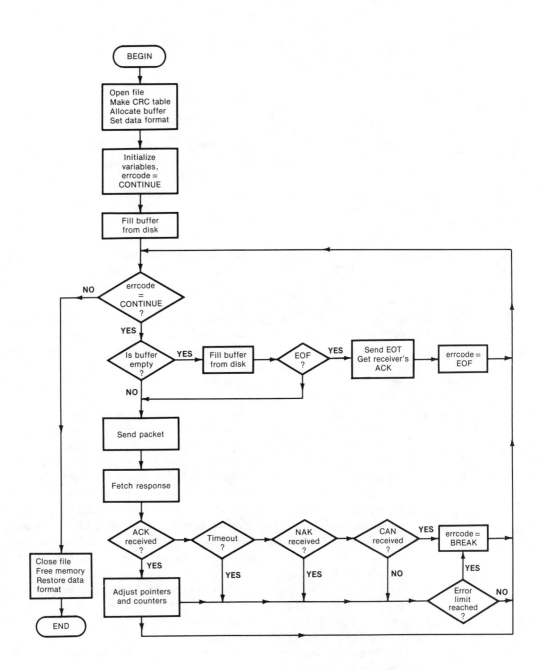

The Transmitter Flow Chart

The flow chart in Figure 18-6 can be divided into four distinct phases:

1. Variable declaration and initialization
2. Start-up
3. Packet transmission
4. Terminating transmission

Variable Declaration and Initialization

The first three blocks of the flow chart are devoted to general housekeeping chores such as setting the SIO's data format to 8-N-1, opening the file, allocating a data buffer, building the CRC table (explained in Chapter 19), and initializing variables. Please notice the emphasis on initializing the exception code variable errcode.

Start-up

In the next block, the buffer is filled from the disk *before* entering the *start-up* (synchronization) loop. Most XMODEM programs postpone this step until start-up has been established. The authors of these programs must have been thinking, "Why bother to fill the buffer until the transfer is underway?" Most of the time this is sound thinking; as a matter of fact, this is exactly how the original versions of XMODEM were designed. To understand why the buffer must be filled *before* attempting to establish communications, we need to review the start-up process.

As discussed in Chapter 3, the XMODEM protocol is *receiver driven*—that is, the receiver is responsible for initiating the transfer and for dictating the type of error checking that is used. Once the receiver is ready to begin the transfer, it commences sending a synchronization byte at 10-second intervals. When a receiver wishes to use an arithmetic checksum, it sends a NAK (15H) for the sync byte; when CRC error is desired, a 'C' (43H) is sent.

In most current programs, the receiver actually "hunts" between checksum and CRC modes. By convention, the receiver first tries to establish CRC synchronization by sending the 'C' sync. If the transmitter does not respond (by sending its first packet) within the 10-second interval, the receiver automatically switches to a NAK sync byte in an attempt to establish a transfer using checksum error checking. If there is no response to the checksum sync byte, however, the receiver switches back to the CRC sync byte at the next 10-second timeout. This alternation of sync bytes repeats until synchronization is established or a timeout limit is reached.

Early XMODEM users complained that the 10-second timeout interval was too long: when the sender missed the sync byte (even by an instant), the transfer could not commence for another 10 seconds. Ever anxious to oblige, the public-domain hackers quickly modified the start-up procedure. Instead of sending 1 sync byte every 10 seconds, the new procedure sent 1 sync byte per second for 10 seconds. A timeout—and hence the change in the value of the sync byte—is still defined as 10 seconds. This new timing causes no problems for checksum-only versions of the protocol, but can cause fatal errors in checksum/CRC versions. Let's see why.

Suppose that a receiver transmits its first 'C' sync byte at 1-second intervals. Now, and here's the fatal part, suppose the sender comes online after the eighth 'C' (out of ten) has just been sent. The sender sees this request for a CRC transfer, adjusts itself accordingly, then begins to fill its buffer from a *very* slow floppy. If 3 seconds are required to fill the buffer and send the first packet, a full 11 seconds have now elapsed since the sync byte was transmitted.

Now let's go back and see what the receiver has been up to during this 3-second hiatus. After sending two more 'C' sync bytes with no response from the transmitter, the receiver dutifully switches to checksum mode. After all, it has no way to know that the sender is being detained by the glacial floppy. "What we have here is a failure to communicate." The receiver is now looking for a 132-byte checksum packet while the slowpoke transmitter is busily sending a 133-byte CRC packet.

There is only one practical way for the sender to avoid this false sychronization: reduce the delay between receiving a sync byte and responding with the first packet. In other words, the sender must be poised, ready to send the first packet *immediately* upon receiving an acceptable sync byte. This, of course, means the sender must fill its local buffer from disk and be prepared to transmit the first packet even *before* inviting start-up.

Packet Transmission

Once synchronization has been established, program flow pivots about the answer to a single question: does the variable errcode still contain its initial value CONTINUE? As long as it does, the next packet is transmitted. The receiver's response to that packet is then evaluated: if the receiver responds with ACK, the next packet is transmitted and the process repeats; if the receiver responds with a NAK or a timeout, the same packet is transmitted and the process repeats; if the receiver responds with a CAN, x_except returns the value BREAK, terminating the main transmission loop.

Receiving a CAN is only one of the ways in which errcode can acquire a non-CONTINUE value: the user can cancel the transfer from the keyboard, a disk read error can occur, or there can be an excessive number of exceptions during transmission. The loop "normally" breaks, however, after the successful transmission of all the data in the file. When an attempt to fill the buffer from disk returns an EOF, errcode acquires the value E_EOF.

Terminating Transmission

When the main transmission loop breaks, the exact value of errcode determines how the module terminates. If errcode contains E_EOF, the transfer is assumed to have been successful and an EOT character is sent to inform the receiver that no more packets are forthcoming. The receiver acknowledges this EOT by sending a final ACK. If errcode contains *any* value other than E_EOF, no EOT is sent and, of course, no attempt is made to fetch the receiver's final ACK. Regardless of the success of the transmission, however, shutdown is orderly: the disk file is closed, memory is freed, the data format of the SIO is restored. The function returns a 0 if successful or errcode if not.

The XMODEM Transmission Module: 'x_snd'

The flow chart does not reveal the details of how packets are transmitted. In the introduction to this chapter, we set out a list of design principles one of which declares that "each packet should be input and output without interruption between fields." This may sound like a common-sense objective, but a surprising number of implementations do not follow it. Instead, it is common practice to transmit a start-of-header byte, pause to calculate the two packet-number bytes, then transmit the 128-byte data field, pause to process the checkvalue, then finally, transmit the checkvalue. These pauses, which inevitably contain time-consuming calculations, measurably reduce the effective rate of data transmission.

The solution to such jerky transmission is to build the entire packet in memory *before* transmission begins. As a matter of fact we will fill memory with as many packets as possible. To accomplish this, we must think of memory as an array of packets or, more specifically, an array of `sndpacket` *structures*, whose definition is given in Figure 18-7.

Figure 18-7   Structure definition of an XMODEM transmission packet.

STRUCT DEF: sndpacket
FILE: *XMOD.H*
DESCRIPTION: Description of an XMODEM packet for transmission.

```
struct sndpacket
      {
      BYTE soh;                         /* start of header        */
      BYTE pnum1;                       /* packet number          */
      BYTE pnum2;                       /* 1's comp packet number */
      BYTE data[DBLKSIZ];               /* data block             */
      unsigned short ckval;             /* block-check character  */
      };
```

Our transmit buffer can now be declared like this:

```
static struct sndpacket *sndbuff;
```

As you see, the buffer is really just a pointer. The actual storage is allocated by `bigbuff`, given in Appendix B. Carefully phrasing the arguments to `bigbuff`, we can allocate the buffer in units of `sndpacket`s:

```
struct sndpacket *sndbuff;
sndbuff = (struct sndpacket *)bigbuff(sizeof(struct sndpacket), HEADROOM, &numpax);
```

This instructs `bigbuff` to allocate all of memory in 133-byte blocks, leaving HEADROOM of these blocks free for local use. It also returns, via a pointer to `numpax`, the *number* of elements allocated. (The cast is necessary because `bigbuff` returns a pointer to `char`.)

Since we know the address of the first packet in the buffer array and that there are `numpax` packets in the array, we can write the function `makepacket`, shown in Figure 18-8, to fill the packets.

Figure 18-8   The `makepacket` function: a function to build transmission packets in memory.

FUNCTION NAME: makepacket
LEVEL: 3
LIBRARY: *XMODEM.LIB*
DESCRIPTION: Makes `sndpacket`s in buffer. Checkvalue character is not installed.
OTHER MODULES: None
RETURNS: `unsigned int`: the number of packets made.
COMMENTS: The checkvalues cannot be installed until after start-up.

Figure 18-8 cont.   The `makepacket` function: a function to build transmission packets in memory.

```
unsigned int makepacket(pbp, pakcnt, paknum, fp)
struct    sndpacket *pbp;                /* "packet buffer pointer"    */
unsigned  int pakcnt;                    /* number of  packets in buffer */
unsigned  long paknum;                   /* current packet count       */
FILE      *fp;
{
    unsigned paksread = 0;               /* first read in data from disk */
    while (fread(pbp->data, sizeof(BYTE), sizeof(pbp->data), fp) != 0)
        {
        pbp->soh  = SOH;                 /* install SOH                */
        pbp->pnuml = paknum++ % 256;     /* install packet number and ...*/
        pbp->pnum2 = ~(pbp->pnuml);      /* its one's complement       */
            if (++paksread == pakcnt)
                break;
        ++pbp;                           /* next packet, please        */
        }
    return (paksread);
}
```

An Explanation of 'makepacket'   Four arguments are passed:

`*pbp`   A pointer to the array of packets.

`pakcnt`   The number of packets in the buffer array (i.e., `numpax`).

`paknum`   The total number of packets already sent. The XMODEM packet sequence number is this number MOD 256.

`fp`   The file pointer from which to load the data portion of each packet.

One-by-one, using `pbp` as a buffer pointer, each packet in the buffer is loaded. First, the 128-byte data block is filled from the file indicated by `fp`, then the SOH and packet sequence numbers are added. When the entire buffer has been filled or an end-of-file is read, `makepacket` returns the number of packets actually made.

Our treatment of the buffer as an array of `sndpackets` relies on two important assumptions:

1. Your compiler builds structures from low to high memory. In a `sndpacket` structure, therefore, `soh` must have a lower address than `ckval`.

2. Structure members must be contiguous in memory. In other words, your compiler must produce byte-aligned structures with *no* gaps between members for alignment. Most compilers for microcomputers use byte alignment by default, and provide an option for other types of alignment. The `sndpacket` definition has to be adjusted to accommodate the rare compiler that does not support byte alignment, or compilers for computers that address memory only on even boundaries.

Adding Checkvalues to the Packets

You may have noticed that makepacket does not install checkvalues in the memory packets. This is because the error-checking method is not known before start-up. This presents no problem: with the time-consuming disk I/O portion of packet construction out of the way *before* start-up, we can call a separate function to add the checkvalues to the packets *afterward*. This function is shown in Figure 18-9.

Figure 18-9   Use of ckvinstall to add checkvalues to the transmission packets in RAM.

FUNCTION NAME: ckvinstall
LEVEL: 3
LIBRARY: *XMODEM.LIB*
DESCRIPTION: Installs checkvalue(s) in the array of packet structures.
OTHER MODULES: None
RETURNS: void
COMMENTS: numpaks is the cardinal size of the packet array. It is the responsibility of the error-checking function to return the checkvalue in the correct byte-order for storage in the sndpacket structure.

```
void ckvinstall(pbp, numpaks, ckvfn)
struct     sndpacket *pbp;          /* "packet buffer pointer"           */
unsigned   int  numpaks;            /* number of packets in buffer       */
unsigned   int  (*ckvfn)();         /* pointer to error-checking function */
{
     for (; numpaks > 0; --numpaks, ++pbp)
          pbp->ckval = (*ckvfn)(pbp->data);
}
```

An Explanation of 'ckvinstall'   The identity of the error-checking method is established at start-up then passed to ckvinstall as a function pointer, (*ckvfn)(). The call to the error-checking function passes the address of the data field packet and returns the checkvalue of that field, which, in turn, is assigned to the ckval member of the current sndpacket structure. Note that because ckval is an unsigned short, it is large enough to hold either a 1-byte checksum value or a 2-byte CRC.

The XMODEM Transmission Module: 'x_snd'

With preliminary design considerations out of the way and with the two important functions makepacket and ckvinstall in hand, we are now ready to tackle the code for x_snd, shown in Figure 18-10. For the sake of consistency, our explanation of x_snd follows the flow chart discussed earlier.

Figure 18-10 The XMODEM transmission module, `x_snd`.

MODULE NAME: `x_snd`
LEVEL: 3
LIBRARY: *XMODEM.LIB*
OTHER MODULES: From Appendix B: `rfopen, bigbuff`
DESCRIPTION: Transmits a file using XMODEM file-transfer protocol.
RETURNS: `int`: 0 if successful; otherwise, the terminating error code.
COMMENTS: `mk_crctbl` and `crchware` and the constant CRCCCITT will not be composed until
                 Chapter 19. In the meantime, create dummies.

```
0     int x_snd(siop)
5     SIO *siop;
10    {
15        extern FILE     *rfopen();
20        extern char     *bigbuff();
25        extern unsigned short makepacket(), crchware(), *mk_crctbl();
30    /* ----- static locals for speed of access ----- */
35        static struct sndpacket *sndbuff, *sndbuffp;  /* buff & pointer   */
40        static BYTE     *bytep;        /* for addressing structure as array */
45        static int      ack, ackcnt, i;
50        static unsigned numpax;        /* buffer size in packets          */
55        static unsigned paxmade;       /* number of packets received so far */
60        static unsigned short (*s_errckp)(); /* pointer to checkval funct */
65        static unsigned long paktot; /* running total of packets sent     */
70    /* -- */
75        FILE *sfp;
80        char fnbuff[MAX_NAME_LEN];           /* file name buffer          */
85        int  errcode;
90        int  errcnt;
95        int  paritytmp, stoptmp, dltmp;   /* to store current data format */
100       if ( (sfp = rfopen("Name for file to transmit", fnbuff)) == NIL)
105           {
110           printf("Cannot open %s.\n", fnbuff);  /* input file          */
115           return (1);
120           }
125       if ( (crctblp = mk_crctbl(CRCCCITT, crchware)) == NIL)/* CRC table*/
130           {
135           puts("Insufficient memory for CRC table.");
140           return (1);
145           }
150       sndbuff = (struct sndpacket *)bigbuff(sizeof(struct sndpacket), HEADROOM, &numpax);
155       if (sndbuff == NIL || numpax == 0)
160           {
165           puts("Insufficient memory for packet buffer.");
170           return (1);
175           }
180       printf("Buffer size = %u packets (%lu bytes).\n",numpax,(long)numpax * CRCPAKSIZ);
185       paritytmp = paritynow(siop); /* save current data format         */
190       stoptmp   = stopsnow(siop);
195       dltmp     = dlnow(siop);
200       setparity(siop, NONE);       /* now set for 8-N-1                */
205       setdatalen(siop, DL8);
210       setstops(siop, STOP1);
215   /*-------------------------------------------------------------------*/
220   /* -- the following variables MUST be explicitly initialized -- */
225   /*-------------------------------------------------------------------*/
```

Figure 18-10 cont.   The XMODEM transmission module, x_snd.

```
230         errcnt  = 0;                /* maintained by x_except         */
235         paktot  = 1;                /* running total of packets sent  */
240         paxmade = 0;                /* number of packets read from disk */
245         sndbuffp = sndbuff;         /* pointer to main buffer         */
250         errcode = CONTINUE;         /* this value sustains the main loop */
255         s_errckp = NIL;             /* use as a marker in loop below  */
260         /*-------------------------------------*/
265         if ( (paxmade = makepacket(sndbuff, numpax, paktot, sfp)) == 0)
270                 errcode = x_except(siop, E_FILEMTY, &errcnt, X_ESNDMAX);
275         if ferror(sfp)
280             errcode = x_except(siop, E_DSKREAD, &errcnt, X_ESNDMAX);
285         s_clrsio(siop, CRCPAKSIZ * numpax);     /* clear entire buffer    */
290         puts("Awaiting startup");
295         while (errcode == CONTINUE && s_errckp == NIL)
300             {
305             if (inkey() == ESC)      /* user kills from keyboard       */
310                 {
315                 errcode = x_except(siop, E_USRCAN, &errcnt, X_ESNDMAX);
320                 break;
325                 }
330             switch (s_waitch(siop, _0_SEC_1))
335                 {
340                 case 'C':                   /* receiver wants crc       */
345                     s_errckp = x_sndcrc;
350                     paksize = CRCPAKSIZ;
355                     puts("\nCRC startup received"); /* now put ckvals..*/
360                     ckvinstall(sndbuff, paxmade, s_errckp); /*in struct*/
365                     break;
370                 case NAK:               /* receiver wants checksum      */
375                     s_errckp = x_sndcksum;
380                     paksize = CKSPAKSIZ;
385                     puts("\nChecksum startup received"); /* put ckvals */
390                     ckvinstall(sndbuff, paxmade, s_errckp); /*in struct*/
395                     break;
400                 case CAN:               /* receiver quit                */
405                     errcode = x_except(siop, E_RCVCAN, &errcnt, X_ESNDMAX);
410                     break;
415                 case TIMEOUT:           /* no timeout limit             */
420                     break;
425                 default:
430                     putchar('?');       /* not meaningful               */
435                 }
440             }
445         while (errcode == CONTINUE)      /* BEGIN MAIN TRANSMIT LOOP    */
450             {
455             if (paxmade == 0)            /* all packets in buffer sent ? */
460                 {
465                 printf("\nDisk Read:  ");
470                 sndbuffp = sndbuff;
472                 paxmade = makepacket(sndbuff, numpax, paktot, sfp);
475                 if (paxmade != 0)        /* no more packets             */
480                     {
485                     ckvinstall(sndbuff, paxmade, s_errckp);
490                     printf("%d packets.\n", paxmade);
495                     }
500                 else
```

Figure 18-10 cont. The XMODEM transmission module, x_snd.

```
505                            {
510                            errcode = x_except(siop, E_EOF, &errcnt, X_ESNDMAX);
515                            --paktot;
520                            continue;
525                            }
530                    if ferror(sfp)
535                            {
540                            errcode = x_except(siop, E_DSKREAD, &errcnt, X_ESNDMAX);
545                            continue;
550                            }
555                    }
560            for (i = 0, bytep = (BYTE *)sndbuffp; i < paksize; i++)
565                    s_putc(siop, *bytep++);              /* SEND IT !          */
570            for (i = ACK_RETRY; i > 0; i--)  /* get ACK or NAK      */
575                    {
580                    if (inkey() == ESC)     /* user kills from keyboard   */
585                            {
590                            errcode = x_except(siop, E_USRCAN, &errcnt, X_ESNDMAX);
595                            break;
600                            }
605                    if ( (ack = s_waitch(siop, _1_SEC_0 )) == ACK)
610                            {
615                            printf("%lu\r", paktot);
620                            ++paktot;
625                            --paxmade;
630                            errcnt = 0;     /* this is optional           */
635                            ++sndbuffp;     /* next packet structure      */
640                            break;
645                            }
650                    if (ack == NAK)     /* receiver wants last packet again */
655                            {
660                            errcode = x_except(siop, E_BADPAK, &errcnt, X_ESNDMAX);
665                            break;
670                            }
675                    if (ack == CAN)     /* receiver wants last packet again */
680                            {
685                            errcode = x_except(siop, E_RCVCAN, &errcnt, X_ESNDMAX);
690                            break;
695                            }
700                    }
705            if (i == 0)                                  /* no ack received */
710                    {
715                    errcode = x_except(siop, E_NOACK, &errcnt, X_ESNDMAX);
720                    s_clrsio(siop, CRCPAKSIZ); /* clear buffer            */
725                    }
730            }                               /* END OF MAIN TRANSMIT LOOP   */
735    /* control comes here when receive loop breaks */
740        if (errcode == E_EOF)               /* normal transfer             */
745            {
750            errcode = 0;                    /* for final return            */
755            printf("%lu packets sent.\nAwaiting receiver's ACK: ", paktot);
760            for (i = ACK_RETRY; i > 0; i--)
765                    {
770                    s_putc(siop, EOT);
775                    if ( (ack = s_waitch(siop, _1_SEC_0 * 2)) == ACK)
780                            {
```

Figure 18-10 cont.   The XMODEM transmission module, x_snd.

```
785                             putchar('\n');
790                             x_except(siop, E_SNDOK, &errcnt, X_ESNDMAX);
795                             printf(" of %s: %lu bytes.\n", fnbuff, paktot * 128);
800                             break;
805                             }
810                 if (ack == CAN)             /* receiver cancelled         */
815                     {
820                             x_except(siop, E_RCVCAN, &errcnt, X_ESNDMAX);
825                             break;
830                     }
835                 if (inkey() == ESC)      /* user killed from keyboard   */
840                     {
845                             errcode = x_except(siop, E_USRCAN, &errcnt, X_ESNDMAX);
850                             ack = !ACK;        /* for the test below         */
855                             break;
860                     }
865                 putchar('.');            /* for each timeout           */
870                 }
875             if (ack != ACK)              /* final ACK never came       */
880                 x_except(siop, E_LASTACK, &errcnt, X_ESNDMAX);
885         }
890     if (fclose(sfp) != 0)
895         printf("\nFatal error closing %s\n", fnbuff);
900     free(sndbuff);                        /* release memory            */
905     free((char*)crctblp);
910     setparity(siop, paritytmp);          /* restore data format       */
915     setstops(siop, stoptmp);
920     setdatalen(siop, dltmp);
925     printf("\nEnd of X-Send\n");
930
935     return (errcode != E_EOF);            /* return success or fail    */
940   }      /* end of xmit */
```

Before we begin the examination of this x_snd, notice that several items dealing with CRC error checking—notably the functions mk_crctbl and crchware and the constant CRCCCITT in lines 25 and 125—do not yet exist. If you wish to test this function now using only its checksum mode, install dummies for the missing items.

Variable Declaration and Initialization

For the speed reasons discussed earlier in the chapter, several variables are declared static. This does not affect their scope; that is, they are still local to this function. Depending upon the mode defined at start-up, the function pointer s_errckp is pointed at either a checksum or CRC error-checking function.

Following variable declarations, a file and two buffers are allocated. First, rfopen opens the file to send (the code for rfopen is given in Appendix B); after rfopen, the name of the file entered by the user is in fnbuff. The as yet unwritten function mk_crctbl builds the CRC lookup table used by the as yet unwritten CRC routines. As described earlier, bigbuff returns a pointer to the largest available buffer, which is then cast into a pointer to an array of sndpacket structures. After the call to bigbuff, the variable numpax contains the number of `sndpackets` actually allocated. A failure of any of the three operations just described results in an immediate `return`. If successful, however, the current data format of the `SIO` is stored in temporary variables, then changed to 8-N-1.

Before entering the actual transmission portion of the code, several variables are initialized in lines 230-255. The comments insist that they must be explicitly initialized instead of initialized at declaration. This is not exactly true—hyperbolic comments are just a cheap way to draw your attention to the importance of initializing them at all.

`errcnt`　A *local* exception counter maintained by `x_except` through a pointer. It is initialized to 0 at line 230.

`paktot`　An `unsigned long int` containing the running total of the number of packets sent. This is initialized to 1 at line 235 so that the transmitted packet number can be derived from it. (Recall that the first packet sent in XMODEM is numbered 1, not 0.)

`paxmade`　The number of packets read into the buffer by `makepacket`. It is decremented as packets are successfully transmitted, thus indicating when another disk read is required. It begins life at 0 at line 240.

`sndbuffp`　Within the main transmission loop, this variable always points at the current `sndpacket` in the buffer. It must begin life by pointing to `sndbuff` and must be reset to this value after every disk read.

`errcode`　The presence of CONTINUE in this variable is the sole sustaining condition for the main transmission loop. Failure to initialize `errcode` therefore leads to precipitous failure.

`s_errckp`　A pointer to the error-checking function. During start-up, it is pointed at either `x_sndcrc` or `x_sndcksum`. It must be initialized to NIL (line 255) because the start-up loop tests for that value.

Start-up

For reasons explained earlier, the buffer is filled with fully constructed `sndpacket` structures before start-up synchronization is attempted. Notice that if the disk file is empty (i.e., `numpax` == 0), the transfer is *not* aborted; `x_except`'s only action is to display an informative message. In all other respects, an empty file is treated as any other.

Lines 295−440 constitute the actual synchronization polling loop. The purpose of this loop is not only to detect an incoming sync byte, but also to point `s_errckp` at the correct error-checking function and to add checkvalues to the packets already in memory. The arrival of a valid sync character also assigns a value to the global variable `paksize`, which contains the number of bytes to transmit. (Such a variable is necessary because a CRC packet is 1 byte longer than a checksum packet.)

There are two sustaining conditions for the start-up loop: `errcode` must be CONTINUE *and* `s_errckp` must contain its original, initialized value. The pointer `s_errckp` is pointed at `x_sndcrc` if a 'C' sync byte is received, or at `x_sndcksum` if a NAK is received. Any other character causes a question mark to be displayed.

The reception of a valid sync byte breaks the loop, but importantly, `errcode` still contains CONTINUE. The value of `errcode` is changed only if the user aborts the transfer by pressing the **Escape** key or if the number of invalid sync bytes exceeds the limit in `x_except`.

Although the start-up loop never times out, a dummy TIMEOUT case is provided in the event you wish to hook the module to an unattended, noninteractive application where a human is not available to press the **Escape** key.

Packet Transmission

Lines 445−735 are the body of the transmit loop, which continues as long as `errcode` still contains `CONTINUE`. If synchronization is not successful, `errcode` already contains a non-`CONTINUE` value, and control passes immediately to line 740 for orderly shutdown.

The first order of business inside the loop proper is to test for an empty buffer; if (`numpax == 0`), `makepacket` fills an empty buffer with `sndpacket` structures. If `makepacket` returns a 0, `x_except` sets `errcode` to E_EOF, and a `continue` statement forces control back to the conditional evaluation at line 445. Since `errcode` no longer contains `CONTINUE`, the main loop breaks and control passes to line 740.

"But," you are probably thinking, "didn't we fill the buffer just before beginning synchronization? Why test again so soon?" This seeming redundancy is necessary to process 0-byte files properly. Recall that if the pre-start-up disk read returns 0 blocks, the start-up *and* the transfer is allowed to continue normally. Upon entry to the main transmit loop we therefore cannot assume that the previous disk read actually placed data in the buffer. If this second disk read yields 0 blocks, the call to `x_except` now sets `errcode` to EOF and the loop breaks. For non-0 length files, however, `numpax` is not yet 0, no disk read is required, and the transmission of the buffer begins immediately. With the number of packets in memory in the variable `paxmade`, transmission of the packet begins at line 560.

If you have been less than enthusiastic about the advantages of building the packets in memory, now consider that the transmission of the entire packet is accomplished with just two lines of code:

```
560 for (i = 0, bytep = (BYTE *)sndbuffp; i < paksize; i++)
565     s_putc(siop, *bytep++);
```

Recall that the pointer `sndbuffp` points at the current packet in the buffer. The number of bytes in the packet was assigned to `paksize` during start-up. We noted earlier that we assume a `sndpacket` structure to be essentially an array of BYTE. To address the individual structure members in this manner, however, a BYTE pointer is required; this is the sole function of `bytep`. After casting the `sndpacket` structure buffer pointer to a BYTE pointer, the individual structure members are transmitted as a simple character array—all at maximum speed and without intercharacter pauses to calculate packet fields. In hacker's argot, this form of packet output really screams.

Fetching the Receiver's Reply

Once the packet has been sent, line 570 enters a `for` loop to await the receiver's response to the packet just transmitted. This "ACK" loop consists of a series of `if` statements instead of a `switch` because a `break` statement in the latter would not force an exit from the loop.

This loop checks the SIO for the receiver's response several (ACK_RETRY) times before giving up. Remember, the total wait must allow the receiver enough time to write its data to disk. As written, the wait is about 30 seconds—ample time for even the slowest of floppies. Using a single 30-second timeout interval for `s_waitch` in 570, however, would be unacceptable. Do you see why? Such a large interval would introduce an unacceptably long delay between a user's pressing the **Escape** key and the program's response. Calling a 1-second timeout 30 times guarantees that the check for keyboard input at line 570 occurs more frequently.

Upon exit from this loop, a value of 0 in the loop counter i indicates that timeout occurred. A message is issued, and control returns to the top of the main while at line 445 where the same packet is retransmitted.

Besides timing out, the reply loop can be broken by reception of any of three bytes:

CAN   If a CAN byte is received (or if the user types **Escape**), a terminating message is displayed, control returns to line 445 with a non-CONTINUE value in errcode, and the transfer ends.[1]

ACK   Reception of an ACK advances pointer and counter variables, displays the packet number, and selects the next sndpacket with the simple statement, + + sndbuffp. Now the loop breaks, and control returns to line 445, ready for the next block.

NAK   A received NAK displays a retry message and returns control to line 445 ready to retransmit.

Terminating the Transmission

At some point, makepacket finds no more data on the disk. The resulting call to x_except places EOF in errcode, breaking the main transmission loop. Control passes then to line 740, yet another timed loop. This loop "finishes off" the transmission by sending an EOT to inform the receiver that no more packets are coming. If all goes well, the receiver answers with a final ACK. The transmitter then displays a summary of packets and bytes, and performs an orderly shutdown: the input file is quietly closed, allocated memory is freed, the original data format is restored from the temporaries, and the function returns a 0. Inside the loop, the SIO is polled for 2 seconds for the final ACK. For each 2-second interval that none arrives, a period is displayed, and another EOT is sent. If the loop times out ACK_RETRY times, or if a CAN is received, or if the user presses **Escape**, x_snd terminates unsuccessfully by returning a non-0. If the main transmission loop is broken by any errcode besides E_EOF, no attempt is made to "finish off" the transmission, but the shutdown is still orderly and a non-0 result is returned.

XMODEM Reception

The design of a receiver module poses two design problems not present in the transmitter module. The first is our old nemesis, speed. Because the transmitter sets the rate of data transfer, it has no *inherent* speed requirements—a slow transmitter is just as robust as a fast one. But a slow receiver that cannot keep up with the transmitter drags *all* transfers down to its speed. In our receiver module, then, we will pay special attention to details that affect speed. As in the transmission module, one major principle will especially guide us: once the reception of a packet has begun, it should proceed *uninterrupted* until completion. That is, absolutely no testing, verification, or other operation should be performed on *any* byte until the *entire* packet is safely in memory.

Our approach will be much the same as in the transmission module where a packet for transmission is ultimately treated as a simple array. But our design of an rcvpacket structure must deal immediately with a second problem—data representation. When receiving a packet, we must be able to detect when s_waitch times out and returns a −1. But if each member is an 8-bit unsigned BYTE variable, it cannot store the 16-bit signed value −1 returned by s_waitch at timeout. The only workable solution to this problem is to create a new structure definition, the

---

[1]This use of CAN is somewhat ambiguous in XMODEM, but most implementations use it.

rcvpacket, comprising integer members instead of BYTE members. The definition for this structure is given in Figure 18-11. Note that because the SOH byte is just a precursor to a packet, a rcvpacket has no soh member.

Figure 18-11   A structure for receiving XMODEM packets.

STRUCT DEF: rcvpacket
FILE: *XMOD.H*
DESCRIPTION: Structure to describe a packet during reception.
COMMENTS: All members are declared int. There is no member for the SOH.

```
struct rcvpacket
    {
    unsigned short pnum1;              /* packet number              */
    unsigned short pnum2;              /* 1's comp packet number     */
    unsigned short data[DBLKSIZ];      /* 128-byte data block        */
    unsigned short ckvhi;             /* high byte of checkval       */
    unsigned short ckvlo;             /* low byte of checkval        */
    };
```

The Receiver Flow Chart

Continuing with our method of analysis begun in Chapter 4, we can now study the flow chart for the XMODEM reception module shown in Figure 18-12 before examining the corresponding code.

The flow chart for receiving an XMODEM file, like the one for transmission, naturally divides into four distinct phases:

1. Variable declaration and initialization
2. Start-up
3. Packet transmission
4. Terminating transmission

In addition to these phases, the manner in which the receiver module "hunts" between CRC and checksum mode will be discussed as a separate topic.

Variable Declaration and Initialization

The first few blocks in the receiver's flow chart are devoted to general housekeeping chores such as setting the SIO's data format to 8-N-1, opening a file to receive the incoming data, allocating the data buffer, and building the CRC table (discussed in Chapter 19). This phase also initializes several variables, the most important of which is errcode, which governs the main receiving loop.

Figure 18-12 Flow chart for the XMODEM receiver.

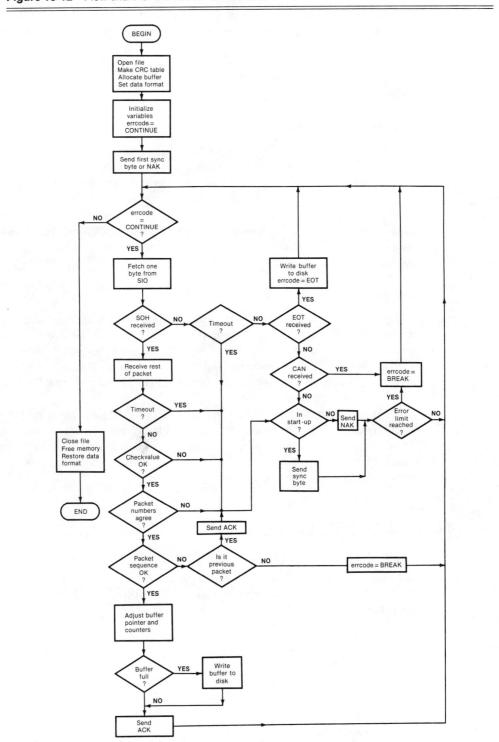

Start-up

The receiver has no start-up sequence in the same sense as the transmitter. In the XMODEM protocol, the receiver initiates the transmission by sending a synchronization byte. The identity of the synchronization byte—a 'C' or a NAK—tells the sender whether to use CRC or checksum, respectively. By convention, the receiver first attempts to establish a CRC transfer. With every timeout, the receiver alternates sync bytes until the transmitter acknowledges by sending its first packet.

Packet Transmission

A solitary sync byte is transmitted immediately before entering the familiar main receiving loop. If the transmitter is already waiting, it responds by sending its first packet. Inside the loop, the receiver polls the SIO waiting for the arrival of an SOH, the packet-signature byte. If none arrives, the receiver sends sync bytes in 10-second intervals until it reaches the timeout limit. If an SOH byte is detected, the rest of the packet is stored in RAM and evaluated later for errors. If errors are found, a NAK is sent to the receiver to request retransmission of the packet. If no errors are discovered, the receiver writes its buffer (if full) to disk, then sends an ACK to request the next packet.

Terminating Transmission

As in the transmission module, all paths lead back to the main while loop. In a successful transmission, an EOT eventually arrives instead of an SOH, indicating that no more packets are forthcoming. The receiver then writes to disk the data portions of the packets currently in the buffer, acknowledges the EOT by sending a final ACK, then breaks the main transmission loop. An orderly shutdown follows: closing the file, freeing memory, restoring the data format, and returning a 0 to the calling function.

At various points in the packet loop, the transfer may be prematurely ended by an EOT byte, a packet-sequence error, exceeding the exception limit, or by the user pressing the **Escape** key. The transmitter can end the transfer by sending a CAN byte instead of an SOH or an EOT. When a transfer is prematurely terminated, the shutdown is orderly but the buffer is not written to disk and no final ACK is sent. Notice that a prematurely terminated transfer leaves a partial file on the disk.

The XMODEM Receiver Module: 'x_rcv'

Our discussion of the receiver module shown in Figure 18-13 follows the flow chart explanation just completed. As in x_snd, the functions mk_crctbl and crchware and the constant CRCCCITT (lines 5 and 145) do not yet exist. If you wish to test this function now using only its checksum mode, install dummies for the missing items.

Figure 18-13 The x_rcv function: the XMODEM receiver module.

FUNCTION NAME: x_rcv
LEVEL: 3
LIBRARY: *XMODEM.LIB*
OTHER MODULES: From Appendix B: wfopen, bigbuff

Figure 18-13 cont. The `x_rcv` function: the XMODEM receiver module.

DESCRIPTION: Receives a file using the XMODEM protocol.
RETURNS: int: 0 if transfer is successful; otherwise, the terminating error code.
COMMENT: `mk_crctbl` and `crchware` and the constant `CRCCCITT` will not be composed until
                Chapter 19. In the meantime, create dummies.

```
0       int x_rcv(siop)
5       SIO *siop;
10      {
15      extern unsigned short crchware(), *mk_crctbl(), x_rcvcrc();
20      extern FILE *wfopen();
25      extern char *bigbuff();
30      /* ----- static locals for speed of access ----- */
35          static struct rcvpacket *rcvbuffp; /* buffer pointer is global    */
40          static int       i, j;
45          static short *intp;             /* for addressing structure as array */
50          static unsigned  long paktot;/* running packet total            */
55          static unsigned  int numpax; /* number of packets in buffer     */
60          static unsigned  int buffpax;/* number of packets received so far */
65          static int       soh;           /* received start of header byte    */
70      /* -- */
75          FILE *rfp;                      /* file pointer               */
80          char fnbuff[MAX_NAME_LEN];      /* file name buffer           */
85          int  errcode;                   /* sustains main receive loop */
90          int  errcnt;                    /* main exception counter     */
95          int  nosohtot;                  /* special counter for soh timeouts */
100         int  paritytmp, stoptmp, dltmp;    /* to store current data format */
105         if ( (rfp = wfopen("Name of file to receive", fnbuff)) == NIL)
110             {
115             if (*fnbuff)
120                 printf("Cannot open %s.\n",fnbuff);/* input file       */
130             return (1);
135             }
140         if ( (crctblp = mk_crctbl(CRCCCITT, crchware)) == NIL) /*CRC table*/
145             {
150             puts("Insufficient memory for CRC table.");
155             return (1);
160             }
170         rcvbuff = (struct rcvpacket*)bigbuff(sizeof(struct rcvpacket), HEADROOM, &numpax);
175         if (rcvbuff == NIL || numpax == 0)
180             {
185             puts("Insufficient memory for packet buffer.");
190             return (1);
195             }
200         printf("Buffer = %u packets (%lu bytes).\n", numpax, (long)numpax * DBLKSIZ);
205         paritytmp = paritynow(siop);           /* save current data format */
210         stoptmp   = stopsnow(siop);
215         dltmp     = dlnow(siop);
220         setparity(siop, NONE);                 /* now set for 8-N-1        */
225         setdatalen(siop, DL8);
230         setstops(siop, STOP1);
235     /*------------------------------------------------------------------*/
240     /* -- the following variables MUST be explicitly initialized -- */
245     /*------------------------------------------------------------------*/
250         errcnt    = 0;
255         buffpax   = 0;                          /* packets received so far  */
```

Figure 18-13 cont.   The `x_rcv` function: the XMODEM receiver module.

```
260         paktot   = 1;                          /* running packet total      */
265         errcode  = CONTINUE;
270         nosohtot = 0;                          /* SOH timeout counter       */
275         rcvbuffp = rcvbuff;                     /* pointer to main rcvbuffer */
280         rcvbuff->pnuml = VIRGIN;                /* used by for startup routine */
285         r_errckp = x_rcvcrc;                    /* starting check value routine*/
290         csync    = (r_errckp == x_rcvcrc) ? 'C': NAK; /* match r_errckp    */
295         ckvname  = (r_errckp == x_rcvcrc) ? "CRC": "CKSUM";
300         paksize  = (r_errckp == x_rcvcrc) ? CRCPAKSIZ-1 : CKSPAKSIZ-1;
305     /*-----------------------------------------*/
310         s_clrsio(siop, CRCPAKSIZ * numpax);  /* clear buffer        */
315         printf("\nAttempting to synchronize in %s mode.\n", ckvname);
320         s_putc(siop, csync);                   /* send start-up sync character */
325         while (errcode == CONTINUE)
330             {
335             if ( (soh = s_waitch(siop, SOH_TIMOUT)) != SOH)  /* bad SOH */
340                 {
345                 switch (soh)
350                     {
355                     case TIMEOUT:
360                         if (!(++nosohtot % 10))     /* every 10th time */
365                             errcode = x_except(siop, E_NOSOH, &nosohtot, X_NOSOHMAX);
370                         break;
375                     case EOT:                  /* no more packets         */
380                         for (rcvbuffp = rcvbuff, i = buffpax; i > 0; --i, ++rcvbuffp);
385                             for (j = 0; j < DBLKSIZ; j ++)
390                                 putc(rcvbuffp->data[j], rfp);
395                         if (fflush(rfp) == 0)
400                             {
405                             --paktot;
410                             errcode = x_except(siop, E_RCVOK, &errcnt, X_ERCVMAX);
415                             printf(" of %s:  %lu bytes (%lu blocks).\
420                                 \n", fnbuff, paktot * 128, paktot);
425                             }
430                         else
435                             errcode = x_except(siop, E_DSKWRITE, &errcnt, X_ERCVMAX);
440                         break;
445                     case CAN:                   /* sender canceled transfer */
450                         errcode = x_except(siop, E_SNDCAN, &errcnt, X_ERCVMAX);
455                         break;
460                     default:                    /* unmeaningful char received */
465                         errcode = x_except(siop, E_BADSOH, &errcnt, X_ERCVMAX);
470                     }
475             }
480         if (inkey() == ESC)             /* user kills from keyboard */
485             {
486             errcode = x_except(siop, E_USRCAN, &errcnt, X_ERCVMAX);
487             continue;
490             }
495         for (i = 0, intp = (short *)rcvbuffp; i < paksize; i++)
500             *intp++ = s_waitch(siop, _0_SEC_1); /* rest of packet */
505         if (rcvbuffp->ckvhi == TIMEOUT)
510             {
515             errcode = x_except(siop, E_NODATA, &errcnt, X_ERCVMAX);
520             continue;
525             }
530         if ( (*r_errckp)(rcvbuffp->data) != 0) /* bad checkvalue     */
```

Figure 18-13 cont. The x_rcv function: the XMODEM receiver module.

```
535                         {
540                         errcode = x_except(siop, E_BADCKV, &errcnt, X_ERCVMAX);
545                         continue;
550                         }
555                 if (rcvbuffp->pnum1 ^ (~rcvbuffp->pnum2 & 0x00ff))/*integrity*/
560                         {
565                         errcode = x_except(siop, E_PAKNUM, &errcnt, X_ERCVMAX);
570                         continue;
575                         }
580                 if (rcvbuffp->pnum1 != paktot % 256)    /* wrong sequence    */
585                         {
590                         if (rcvbuffp->pnum1 == (paktot % 256) -1) /* previous  */
595                                 errcode = x_except(siop, E_SNDACK, &errcnt, X_ERCVMAX);
600                         else                                    /* FATAL     */
605                                 errcode = x_except(siop, E_PAKSEQ, &errcnt, X_ERCVMAX);
610                         continue;
615                         }
620                 printf("%lu\r", paktot);            /* running total on screen*/
625                 ++rcvbuffp;                         /* next packet in array    */
630                 ++paktot;
635                 errcnt = 0;
640                 if (++buffpax == numpax)            /* buffer full             */
645                         {
650                         printf("\nDisk write\n");
655                         for (rcvbuffp = rcvbuff, i = buffpax ; i > 0 ; --i, ++rcvbuffp)
660                                 for (j = 0; j < DBLKSIZ; j ++)
665                                         putc(rcvbuffp->data[j], rfp);
670                         if (ferror(rfp))
675                                 {
680                                 errcode = x_except(siop, E_DSKWRITE, &errcnt, X_ERCVMAX);
685                                 break;
690                                 }
695                         buffpax  = 0;                /* reset counter and ...  */
700                         rcvbuffp = rcvbuff;          /* buffer pointer          */
705                         s_clrsio(siop, CRCPAKSIZ * numpax);  /* clear buffer   */
710                         }
715                 s_putc(siop, ACK);                   /* ACK is your final act   */
720                 }                                    /* end of receive loop     */
725         if (fclose(rfp) != 0)    /* come here when receive loop breaks */
730                 printf("Fatal error closing %s\n", fnbuff);
735         free((char*)rcvbuff);                        /* release buffer          */
740         free((char*)crctblp);                        /* release crc table       */
745         setparity(siop, paritytmp);                  /* restore data format     */
750         setstops(siop, stoptmp);
755         setdatalen(siop, dltmp);
760         puts("\nEnd of X-Receive");
765         return (errcode == E_RCVOK ? 0 : 1);    /* return success or fail  */
770 }
```

Variable Declaration and Initialization

For reasons discussed earlier in the chapter, several variables are declared static. All variables declared here are local.

Much of the code prior to start-up closely parallels that of x_snd. Following the declaration of variables, wfopen opens a file to capture the incoming data (the code for wfopen is given in Appendix B), and mk_crctbl builds the CRC lookup table. The receive buffer is rcvbuff, which was declared to be global in Figure 18-4. In line 170, we call bigbuff to allocate the largest buffer available and simultaneously cast its return value into an array of rcvpacket. If the three operations just described are successful, the current data format of the SIO is stored in three temporary variables, then changed to 8-N-1.

Before entering the receive loop, several variables are initialized in lines 250 through 300. Some of these have similar functions to their counterparts in x_snd:

errcnt	A *local* exception variable maintained by x_except through a pointer.
buffpax	The amount of free space remaining in the buffer, expressed as the number of rcvpackets. When this reaches 0, the buffer is written to disk.
paktot	Contains a running total of the number (unsigned long) of packets received. The current packet number is paktot MOD 256. It must be initialized to 1 so that the first packet sent in XMODEM is number 1, not 0.
errcode	The presence of CONTINUE in this variable is the sole sustaining condition for the main reception loop. Failure to initialize it leads to precipitous failure.
nosohtot	A special counter for SOH timeout errors. The reasons for its existence are explained later in "Packet Reception."
rcvbuffp	A pointer to the location in the buffer where the next incoming packet will be stored. This pointer must begin life pointing to the beginning of the buffer (i.e., rcvbuff) and must be reset after every disk write.

The remaining explicitly initialized variables—r_errckp, csync, ckvname, and paksize—all participate in the start-up process described in our discussion of the start-up procedure:

r_errckp	This is a function pointer to the error-checking method. Its initialized value dictates whether CRC or checksum error checking is tried first. According to convention, we initialize it at line 285 to x_rcvcrc.
csync	The synchronization byte used during start-up. Since its value must always correspond to the error-checking method currently being used, its initialization at line 290 depends upon the function pointer r_errckp.
ckvname	A pointer to a string used to announce the start-up mode. Its initialization at line 295 depends upon the function pointer r_errckp.
paksize	The number of bytes in the current packet. Since checksum packets and CRC packets are different sizes, paksize's initialization at line 300 depends upon the function pointer r_errckp.

Start-up

Aside from transmitting a sync byte before entering the main while loop, x_rcv itself contains no start-up procedure *per se*. That is, the first packet is treated no differently than subsequent packets.

To simplify design of x_rcv, x_except contains the start-up procedure, which "hunts" between CRC and checksum modes. Before we begin a discussion of hunting, it is important to understand that the NAK that is used as sync byte is a separate entity from the NAK that is used to negatively acknowledge a packet. A NAK byte is *always* used to negatively acknowledge a packet, even in CRC mode. Stated another way, during start-up the SOH timeout routine responds with the byte contained in a *variable*—either a NAK or a 'C'; after start-up, the *constant* NAK is used.

If, after sending a sync byte, a packet is not forthcoming from the transmitter, the receiver times out at line 355, resulting in a call x_except at line 365. In x_except, the desire is to switch "modes" from checksum to CRC (or vice versa) and begin sending the alternative sync byte. If start-up is still in progress, the sync byte must be sent; if the transfer has begun, a NAK must be sent.

Differentiating between the start-up and packet-transfer phases is not difficult to do heavy-handedly. We might, for example, simply create a global flag named, say, inxfer. Whenever a valid SOH is detected (remember, the SOH portion of an incoming packet is not saved) we set the flag:

```
inxfer = soh;
```

Inside x_except, the state of inxfer can determine whether to send a sync byte or a NAK:

```
s_putc(siop, (inxfer == 0) ? csync : NAK );
```

This concept is sound, but suffers from a familiar fatal flaw: it adds an extra assignment to the receive loop. This resulting minor degradation in receiver performance can be avoided by letting the pnum1 *packet member* inform us when start-up has occurred. We'll use a technique known as *baiting*—that is, initializing a variable to a value it can never acquire during normal operation. The assignment of this variable should reside in a unique branch of the program flow. If we later discover that this variable has acquired a different value, we know that the program flow must have taken that branch. In our case, the pnum1 member of the first buffer packet is perfectly suited to our needs. Its contents can change *only* through normal reception of a packet; that is, *after* start-up. Since the pointer rcvbuff never changes, we can use rcvbuff->pnum1 as our test variable.

Which values are illegal for pnum1? Although pnum1 is declared to be an int, XMODEM itself limits packet numbers to 8 bits. Thus the reception of a packet number can assign into pnum1 only the numbers $0-255$. It may also contain -1 if s_waitch times out. This leaves us with numbers -2 to $-32,768$ to use as bait. Once initialized to one of these values, any other value in pnum1 signals that start-up has occurred. We will use the constant VIRGIN (defined in *SIODEF.H* as -2) as our initializer.

If the main receive loop times out while waiting for an SOH, x_except looks at rcvbuff->pnum1 for guidance, at line 270:

```
270    if (rcvbuff->pnum1 == VIRGIN)   /* negotiate error-checking mode */
275        {
280        r_errckp = (r_errckp == x_rcvcrc) ? x_rcvcksum : x_rcvcrc;
285        paksize  = (r_errckp == x_rcvcrc) ? CRCPAKSIZ-1: CKSPAKSIZ-1;
290        csync    = (r_errckp == x_rcvcrc) ? 'C'         : NAK;
295        ckvname  = (r_errckp == x_rcvcrc) ? "CRC"       : "CHECKSUM";
300        s_putc(siop, csync);
305        printf("\nAttempting to synchronize in %s mode.\n", ckvname);
310        }
```

```
315    else
320        s_putc(siop, NAK);
325    break;
```

If `startp->pnum1` no longer contains `VIRGIN`, the packet transfer must be underway and a NAK is sent. However, if `startp->pnum1` still contains `VIRGIN`, start-up must still be underway, all start-up variables are switched to their alternative values, and the appropriate sync byte is transmitted.

(Notice that the variable `paksize` must be 1 byte smaller than the number of bytes in the packets because there is no SOH member in an `rcvpacket`. The definitions for the size constants are in Figure 18-1.)

Packet Reception

We have already seen how important it is to send a sync byte only every 10 seconds. Like the "ACK" loop in `x_snd` (lines 570-700), a single timeout interval of 10 seconds in `s_waitch` at line 335 is unacceptable because of the long delay before responding to the keyboard. Using a timeout of 1 second (`SOH_TIMOUT`) increases the frequency of keyboard polling, but creates another problem: when fishing for an SOH, `x_rcv` times out every second, exceeding the exception/timeout limit very rapidly. The obvious solution to the problem is also the best one—the number of SOH timeouts is maintained in the local variable `nosohtot`, and `x_except` is called only after every *tenth* SOH timeout:

```
360    if (!(++nosohtot % 10))
365        errcode = x_except(siop, E_NOSOH, &nosohtot, X_NOSOHMAX);
```

Upon reception of a valid SOH byte, the rest of the packet must be received. Because the receiver's buffer is declared as `unsigned int`, we must treat each incoming packet as a simple array of `int`. To accomplish this, the buffer pointer—a pointer to type `struct rcvpacket`—is cast to a simple integer pointer and assigned to `intp`. Incoming bytes are then stored at successive locations by incrementing `intp`:

```
495    for (i = 0, intp = (int *)rcvbuffp; i < paksize; i++)
500        *intp++ = s_waitch(siop, _O_SEC_1);
```

Once the entire packet is on board, it is scrutinized in lines 505−615 for exceptions or inconsistencies. Four exceptions are possible:

1. *Timeout receiving data* (line 505). If a timeout occurs during reception of the data portion in the packet, the loop is nevertheless completed, filling the remaining buffer elements with −1 (i.e., `TIMEOUT`). The ability to detect this negative value is why the packet elements must be an array of `int`, not BYTE. A value of −1 in the `ckvhi` structure member therefore indicates that a timeout occurred. (Question: Why can't `ckvlo` be used?).

2. *Checkvalue error* (line 530). The received checkvalue does not agree with the checkvalue calculated on the data buffer. In `x_except`, a NAK is sent to request retransmission.

3. *Packet number integrity error* (line 555). The first packet number is not the same as the 1s complement of the second. This error occurs if one of these bytes is deformed during transmission, or if a "1" byte in random `SIO` data is mistaken for the SOH of a packet. Since neither risks data corruption, retransmission is requested in `x_except`.

4. *Packet sequence error* (line 595). The packet number received is not the one expected. There are two variations on this error. A packet with the same number as the *previous* packet suggests that the transmitter somehow missed the ACK for the last packet. The condition is easily corrected (in x_except) by sending another ACK and ignoring the duplicate packet. A packet sequence in any other incorrect order (line 605) indicates a systemic problem in the transmitter and x_except aborts the transfer by returning an error code of BREAK.

Assuming that no errors are discovered in the packet, when the number of packets received (buffpax) equals the capacity of the buffer numpax (line 620) the buffer is written to disk and the buffer pointer and buffpax are reset. If there are still "unfilled" packets in the buffer, however, the relevant counters are adjusted and the buffer pointer is incremented to the next packet. Only now—with all the housekeeping out of the way—is the ACK sent at line 715. The program returns to the top of the receive loop at line 325 to await the SOH of the next packet.

Terminating Reception

The receive loop continues until an EOT (line 375) or a CAN (line 445) is received instead of an SOH. In either case, the return code from x_except terminates the receive loop. A CAN begins shutdown immediately; an EOT, however, first writes the partial buffer to disk, then acknowledges to the EOT by sending (in x_except) a final ACK. Orderly shutdown follows.

Checksum Error-Checking Functions

Both x_snd and x_rcv perform error checking through the function pointers s_errckp and r_errckp, respectively. Employing function pointers for error checking means that the send/receive loops themselves remain totally ignorant of the error-checking process. During start-up, the sender and receiver negotiate the error-checking method, pointing these two pointers at either the checksum or the CRC function. In this section, we'll compose only the two checksum functions, x_sndcksum and x_rcvcksum. In Chapter 19 we will compose the CRC functions x_sndcrc and x_rcvcrc.

Checksum Functions: 'x_sndcksum' and 'x_rcvcksum'

If the sender and receiver agree to use the checksum method during the transfer, their error-checking function pointers are aimed at x_sndcksum, shown in Figure 18-14, and x_rcvcksum, shown in Figure 18-15. Since arithmetic checksums are themselves fundamentally easy to comprehend, we need spend little time discussing this pair of functions.

Figure 18-14   Use of x_sndcksum to calculate and return an arithmetic checksum.

FUNCTION NAME: x_sndcksum
LEVEL: 3
LIBRARY: *XMOD.LIB*
DESCRIPTION: Calculates and returns an arithmetic checksum on the buffer indicated.
OTHER MODULES: None
RETURNS: unsigned short

Figure 18-14 cont. Use of `x_sndcksum` to calculate and return an arithmetic checksum.

```
unsigned short x_sndcksum(buff)          /* process checksum            */
char *buff;                              /* pointer to sndpacket->data   */
{
    static int cksum, i;
    for (cksum = i = 0; i < 128; ++i)    /* round 'em up                */
        cksum += *buff++;                /* add 'em up                  */
    return (cksum % 256);                /* take 'em back               */
}
```

An Explanation of 'x_sndcksum' This function is called only by `makepacket`, which installs its return value in the `ckval` member of an `sndpacket`. Based upon the assumption that `static` variables can be accessed faster than `auto` variables, both local variables are declared `static`. Passed a pointer to the beginning of data block, this function simply adds together the next 128 bytes, then returns their sum. Since the sum is kept in an integer, a modulo-256 operation converts it to the 8-bit format required by the XMODEM protocol.

Figure 18-15 Use of the `x_rcvcksum` function to validate the receiver's arithmetic checksum.

```
FUNCTION NAME: x_rcvcksum
LEVEL:          0
LIBRARY:        See "Portability Considerations" in text.
DESCRIPTION:    Verifies 8-bit arithmetic checksum on indicated buffer.
OTHER MODULES:  None
RETURNS:        unsigned short: 0 if checksums agree.
COMMENTS:       The checksum byte is assumed to be contiguous with the last byte of the data field.
```

```
unsigned short x_rcvcksum(data)
int *data;                               /* pointer to rcvpacket->data   */
{
    static int i;
    static unsigned short cksum;
    cksum = data[128];
    for (i = 0; i < DBLKSIZ ; ++i)
        cksum -= *data++;                /* subtract data bytes from checksum */
    return (cksum % 256);
}
```

An Explanation of 'x_rcvcksum' This function's purpose is to verify that the sum of the `data` portion of a received packet agrees with its checksum. It must return 0 if the sums agree, or non-0 if they disagree. Accordingly, this function assumes that the pointer in the argument list points to the 128-*integer* data array of `rcvpacket`. In such a structure, the 129th element is the checksum, which is captured in the local variable cksum.[2] The preceding 128 array elements are then subtracted from cksum. Since cksum is 0 only if the two checksums agree, its value (modulo-256) is returned directly.

Portability Considerations

Earlier in this chapter we admitted the assumption that a compiler builds structures from low to high memory, and that the compiler leaves no "alignment" gaps between structure members. These are safe, although not failsafe, assumptions.

The function x_sndcksum contains another assumption about the internal representation of integers that is *inherently* non-portable. To understand this, you must be aware that some microprocessors — the Intel family, for example — store words with the low-order byte lowest in memory; other processors store them in just the opposite order. The consequences of this representation are important, because in an sndpacket structure, the byte lowest in memory is transmitted first. The function x_sndcksum assumes that the 8-bit checksum occupies the low-order byte of the integer. The version of x_rcvcksum in Figure 18-15, therefore, functions correctly only if the checksum is assigned to the integer's low-order byte and that low-order byte ultimately occupies a lower memory address than the high-order byte. Because this function is inherently machine and compiler dependent, its header classifies it as a "level-0" function and as such should be placed in the computer file and not in the *XMODEM.LIB* library.

Conclusion

Although we will not compose a library of CRC functions until Chapter 19, Figure 18-16 shows the trivial changes required to add XMODEM file transfer modules to *TERM6*, producing *TERM7*. Neither the main nor the term module is affected.

Figure 18-16   XMODEM support; incidental changes required to convert *TERM6* to *TERM7*.

```
PROGRAM NAME:   TERM7
DESCRIPTION:    Terminal program
COMMENTS:       New features: XMODEM file transfers (checksum only for now).
          ⋮

#include "xmod.h"
          ⋮

int vers = 7;                           /* version number  (global)     */
          ⋮

#define XSEND    'K'                    /* send file with XMODEM protocol */
#define XRECV    'L'                    /* xmit file with XMODEM protocol */
#define EXIT     'Q'                    /* key to exit from term         */

          ⋮
```

---

[2]Even including the assignment, decrementing a static intermediate variable is faster than in directly decrementing the byte in ckvhi.

Figure 18-16 cont. XMODEM support; incidental changes required to convert *TERM6* to *TERM7*.

```
static char *menus[] =
    {
    "\tA.  Data Format, Baud rate",
    :
    "\tJ.  Hang up phone",
    "\tK.  Send a file using XMODEM protocol",
    "\tL.  Receive a file using XMODEM protocol",
    "\tQ.  EXIT",
    ""                              /* null string terminates list     */
    };
    :
        case HUP:
            if (m_warndcd(siop, ON) == 0)
                printf("\nHangup %s.\n",m_hup(siop) == 0 ? "OK" : "error");
            c = EXIT;                   /* leave menu after hangup      */
            break;
        case XSEND:
            if (m_warndcd(siop, OFF) == 0)
                x_snd(siop);
            break;
        case XRECV:
            if (m_warndcd(siop, OFF) == 0)
                x_rcv(siop);
            break;
    :
```

19

CRC Calculations

The purpose of this chapter is twofold: first, to fulfill the promise in Chapter 18 to compose the CRC functions x_sndrcrc and x_rcvcrc for use in the XMODEM protocol; second, to provide the code to implement the CRC procedures presented in Chapter 3. This chapter contains only a summary of polynomial division and its relation to the Cyclical Redundancy Check. The rather terse treatment of these subjects here therefore assumes that you have a thorough understanding of Chapter 3, where the topic is covered in depth.

Polynomials and CRC Functions

You will recall that CRC calculations are closely linked to polynomial division. In CRC parlance, a message is thought of as a long polynomial in which each 0 or 1 bit is expressed as the coefficient of a polynomial term. The exponent of each polynomial term is derived from that bit's ordinal rank in the message. For example, in a message polynomial the message 01011010 is expressed as

$$0X^7 + 1X^6 + 0X^5 + 1X^4 + 1X^3 + 0X^2 + 1X^1 + 0X^0$$
$$0 \quad\quad 1 \quad\quad 0 \quad\quad 1 \quad\quad 1 \quad\quad 0 \quad\quad 1 \quad\quad 0$$

By convention, however, terms with a 0 coefficient are omitted from the expression:

$$1X^6 + 1X^4 + 1X^3 + 1X^1$$

A second polynomial, the *generator polynomial*, is divided into the message polynomial producing a quotient and a remainder. The division is performed in modulo-2 arithmetic; that is, an XOR operation is used in place of ordinary subtraction and there are no borrows. The remainder of this division does not become a CRC until the remainder is "flushed" by appending a 0 bit to the message polynomial for every term in the remainder. For 16-bit CRC's, therefore, the dividend must be padded with sixteen 0 bits. The remainder from the modulo-2 division of the padded message polynomial is the CRC checkvalue. The quotient is discarded. All routines in this book assume a 16-bit CRC.

CRCs are employed to detect errors that occur during communication. During data transfer, the sender calculates the CRC on each block of data. After each block is transmitted, the CRC is also transmitted. The receiver divides the incoming message by the same polynomial. If the data block is received without errors, the receiver's CRC matches the CRC appended to the message. The two most commonly used 16-bit polynomials are the CCITT polynomial

$$X^{16} + X^{12} + X^5 + 1$$

and CRC-16

$$X^{16} + X^{15} + X^2 + 1$$

Polynomial Division in Hardware and Software

Polynomial division is easily simulated in hardware using flip-flops and Exclusive-OR gates. The classical hardware circuit to perform polynomial division using the CCITT polynomial is shown in Figure 19-1. Here, the high-order data bit is fed into the low-order byte of the remainder register. The remainder register shifts *left* after every step. After the division, the value in the remainder register is exactly the remainder attained by long division.

Figure 19-1 Polynomial division hardware using CRC-CCITT divisor (1021 H).

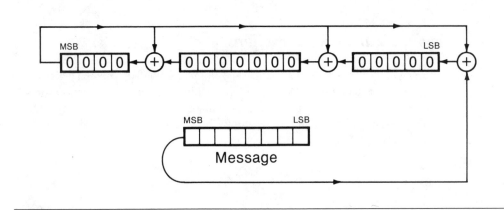

This circuit divides a byte-oriented message polynomial of any length by the specified 17-bit polynomial as follows:

1. The high-order data bit is applied to the remainder register.
2. The data bit is shifted into the remainder register's low-order bit; the remainder's high-order bit is shifted out and lost. (Actually, these high-order bits constitute the *quotient*, which is of no interest to us.)
3. If the bit shifted out of the remainder is TRUE, the entire divisor polynomial is subtracted (XORed) from the remainder.
4. The data byte is shifted left one place; the bit shifted out is of no further use.
5. Repeat steps 1–4 until all bits have been applied to the remainder register.
6. The remainder contains the remainder of polynomial division.

Simulation of Polynomial Division: 'polydiv'

Although we have no need for a function that performs this polynomial division *per se*, it is included here to enable you to verify the theoretical procedure presented in Chapter 3. The function shown in Figure 19-2 is an engine that duplicates longhand polynomial division, using the global variable remainder to hold the remainder.

Figure 19-2   A function to simulate polynomial division.

```
FUNCTION NAME: polydiv
LEVEL:         3
LIBRARY:       XMODEM.LIB
DESCRIPTION:   Simulates longhand polynomial division.
OTHER MODULES: None
RETURNS:       unsigned short
COMMENTS:      This function produces a remainder, not a CRC.
```

```
unsigned short polydiv(data, divisor, remainder)
unsigned short data;
unsigned short divisor;
unsigned short remainder;
{
    static unsigned short quotient, i;
    for (i = 8; i > 0; i--)
        {
        quotient = remainder & 0x8000;/* remember if bit 15 is set    */
        remainder <<= 1;              /* shift remainder; bit 0 = 0    */
        if ( (data <<= 1) & 0x0100)   /* shift data; if old bit 7 was 1 */
            remainder |= 1;           /* put into bit 0 of remainder   */
        if (quotient)                 /* if divisible                  */
            remainder ^= divisor;     /* subtract polynomial           */
        }
    return (remainder);
}
```

An Explanation of 'polydiv'   This function follows the preceding description almost line for line. The variable and constant names have been selected to emphasize the parallel with longhand division. As you study this function, keep four facts in mind:

1. Subtraction in modulo-2 arithmetic is the same as XORing.

2. The sole criterion for subtracting the divisor from the remainder is whether the high-order bit is TRUE *before* the shift.

3. The data is a 16-bit unsigned integer instead of an 8-bit BYTE.

4. Although the polynomial is assumed to contain 17 bits, it can be expressed in 16 bits because the division process always forces the high-order bit to 0.

Since it will be lost after every shift, the remainder's high-order bit must be stashed in the variable quotient. Inside the loop, both the remainder and the data are shifted left. With each shift, a data bit (high-order bit first), is copied into the low-order bit of the remainder register with the following couplet:

```
        if ( (data <<= 1) & 0x100)
            remainder |= 1;
```

It is not necessary to copy 0 bits because the left-shifting of the remainder automatically fills the vacated bits with 0s. After the shift, the divisor is subtracted from the remainder only if a TRUE bit is shifted out of the remainder register:

```
        if (quotient)
            remainder ^ = divisor;
```

This process is repeated for each data bit. At the end of the message, remainder contains the remainder resulting from the division of the message (i.e., the dividend polynomial) by the polynomial specified in divisor. The low-order bits shifted out constitute the quotient of that division.

To confirm that this actually simulates longhand polynomial division, Figure 19-3 shows *PDIVTEST*, a program to duplicate the example in Figure 3-1, Chapter 3.

Figure 19-3 *PDIVTEST*: a simulation of the longhand polynomial division in Figure 3-1.

PROGRAM NAME: *PDIVTEST*
DESCRIPTION: Performs longhand polynomial division on a 4-byte message.
OTHER MODULES: putbin (in Appendix B)
COMMENTS: For comparison with the longhand division, polydiv has been modified to show the intermediate remainder stages.

```
#include "stdio.h"

unsigned short p_div(data, divisor, remainder)
unsigned short data;
unsigned short divisor;
unsigned short remainder;
{
    static unsigned short quotient, i;
    for (i = 8; i > 0; i--)
        {
        quotient = remainder & 0x8000;
        remainder <<= 1;
        if ( (data <<= 1) & 0x0100)
            remainder |= 1;
        if (quotient)
            remainder ^= divisor;
        printf("         ");
        putbin(remainder);            /* display binary for each step    */
        }
return (remainder);
}
```

Figure 19-3 cont. *PDIVTEST*: a simulation of the longhand polynomial division in Figure 3-1.

```
main()                                  /* perform polynomial division on message */
{

    static char message[4] = {´C´,´f´,´y´,´U´};       /* from Chapter Three */
    int i;
    unsigned short remainder = 0;            /* must initialize to zero    */
    for (i = 0; i < 4; ++i)
        {
        remainder = p_div(message[i], 0x1021, remainder); /* CCITT poly    */
        putbin(remainder);
        }
}
```

An Explanation of 'PDIVTEST'   Since this program shows all the intermediate steps of the division, it is easy to compare its output with the intermediate ("below the line") steps of long-hand division in Chapter 3. Notice that sixteen shifts are required to arrive at the initial step of longhand division. In other words, after the first sixteen steps, the register simply contains a copy of the data. Two of the data bytes are ORed with 80H to simulate a 1 in their parity bits.

Short integer representation

Some mention should be made of the extensive use of the data type `unsigned short`. K & R (page 183) states that the data type `int` has the "natural" size suggested by the host machine architecture, and that "the other sizes (of integers) are provided to meet special needs." On microprocessor implementations of C for the 8086 family of processors, whose "natural" size is 16 bits, an `int` and a `short int` are identical and may be used interchangeably. But this picture is rapidly changing as the 32-bit microprocessors become more popular. On C compilers for 68000-based computers, where the natural size is 32 bits, a plain `int` therefore consists of 32 bits, with the `short int` reserved for 16-bit quantities. On the assumption that the `short int` will be 16 bits for the foreseeable future of micros, our functions employ it to simulate the 16-bit CRCs in this chapter.

Simulation of CRC Hardware: 'crchware'

The remainder from "pure" polynomial division is not the same as a CRC. In order to apply every term of the generator polynomial to every bit of the message, sixteen 0 bits must be put into the circuit to "flush" the remainder. The value in the remainder afterward is, *by definition*, the CRC. The necessity of flushing the remainder with 0s effectively adds 2 bytes of overhead to every message. This inefficiency is cured by modifying the basic polynomial division circuit. This new circuit, which does not require the appending of 0 bytes to the message, is shown in Figure 19-4.

Figure 19-4   The "classical" CRC hardware circuit shown with the CRC-CCITT polynomial (1021H).

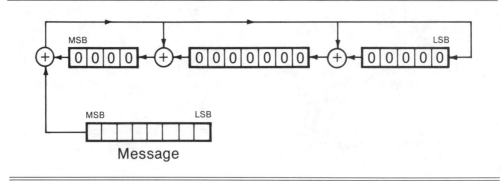

Unlike the polynomial division circuit, here the incoming data bit is XORed with the high-order bit of the accumulator, and the result is shifted into the accumulator. The important difference is the manner in which the XOR feedback is derived (i.e., how the polynomial is subtracted). Here, the result of XORing the data with the high bit of the accumulator actually becomes the feedback to the XOR gates. Using this scheme, the data bits immediately affect the feedback instead of waiting until they have propagated through the register. This circuit, then, produces the same results as the polynomial division circuit in Figure 19-1 with two 0 bytes appended to the message.

The function shown in Figure 19-5 duplicates the action of the CRC hardware. To emphasize that we are no longer simulating the longhand division technique, this function abandons the remainder/divisor terminology in favor of the accumulator/generator polynomial nomenclature. For generality, the generator polynomial and the current contents of the accumulator are passed as arguments.

Figure 19-5   The `crchware` function: simulation of CRC hardware.

FUNCTION NAME: `crchware`
LEVEL: 3
LIBRARY: *CRC.LIB*
DESCRIPTION: Simulates CRC hardware circuit.
OTHER MODULES: None
RETURNS: `unsigned short`: the new CRC.
COMMENTS: Generates a CRC directly—produces the same remainder as polynomial division with 2 NULL bytes appended to the message.

```
unsigned short crchware(data, genpoly, accum)
unsigned short data;
unsigned short genpoly;                /* the generator polynomial        */
unsigned short accum;                  /* accumulator                     */
```

Figure 19-5 cont. The `crchware` function: simulation of CRC hardware.

```
{
    static int i;
    data <<= 8;                          /* data to high byte          */
    for (i = 8; i > 0; i--)
        {
        if ((data ^ accum) & 0x8000) /* if msb of (data XOR accum) is TRUE */
            accum = (accum << 1) ^ genpoly;  /* shift and subtract poly    */
        else
            accum <<= 1;                 /* otherwise, transparent shift  */
        data <<= 1;                      /* move up next bit for XOR       */
        }
    return(accum);
}
```

An Explanation of 'crchware'   Here the sole criterion for subtracting the polynomial is the value of the bit shifted out of the accumulator XORed with the data bit. This means that the first 1 data bit immediately produces feedback to the other XOR gates, producing the characteristic CRC "bit action." Due to this immediate feedback, there is no need to flush the accumulator with 0 bits.

CRC Calculation by Table Lookup

The function `crchware` is more efficient than `polydiv` in Figure 19-2 for two reasons: first, no NULL bytes are appended to the message; second, the code is simpler—there is no need to copy each data bit into the accumulator, and no intermediate variable is required to remember the state of the "quotient" bit. Indeed, `crchware` is functionally suitable for calculating the CRC in our XMODEM modules. But although the CRC method is more efficient than the polynomial division method, it is only slightly so. In truth, both methods with their repeated shifts, ANDs, and XORs are woefully slow. Considering the care we have taken in designing the XMODEM modules for speed, using *either* of these CRC methods creates a palpable bottleneck in data transfer. The consequences of such a bottleneck can readily be seen in many commercial programs where transfers using the checksum method are four to ten times faster than their CRC counterparts. But is such a speed sacrifice necessary to gain the benefits of the more rigorous CRC error checking? Luckily, no—a better way is available.

In Chapter 3 we discovered that when an 8-bit message byte is added to the 16-bit accumulator, only the high-order *or* the low-order 8 bits of the accumulator interact with the data bits. We referred to the 8-bit result of this interaction (i.e, XORing) as the *combining value*. This leads to the observation that the new accumulator is equal to the *CRC of the combining value* plus (XOR in modulo-2) the unchanged half of the accumulator. This relationship can easily be expressed in C using an intermediate variable for clarity:[1]

[1] The high- or low-order bytes used in the steps of this procedure are reversed, depending upon the CRC model used. In this example, the high-order byte of the accumlator is XORed with the data to form the combining value and the final step uses the low-order byte. The opposite bytes would be used for models that assume bit reversals, such as the CRC-16 shown in Figure 3-6.

```
                          unsigned short tmp;
                          tmp = crchware((accum >> 8) ^ data, poly, 0);
                          accum = ((accum << 8) ^ tmp);
```

Here, crchware is called to calculate the CRC of the combining value and the result is stored in tmp. The final CRC is derived by XORing the low-order byte of the accumulator with tmp.

Building a CRC Table

Although the *combining value's* relationship to the CRC is interesting, a function derived from it obviously performs more *slowly* than crchware. Pushing our thinking just a bit further, however, we discover a startlingly simple shortcut. Since there are only 256 possible combining values, why not calculate their CRCs in advance and store them in a table. Each element of this surprisingly simple table (shown in Figure 19-7), contains the CRC of its rank in the table; for example, element 1 contains the CRC for 1, element 50 contains the CRC for 50, and so on. The function to build this table automatically is given in Figure 19-6.

Figure 19-6 Use of the mk_crctbl function to build a CRC lookup table.

FUNCTION NAME: mk_crctbl
LEVEL: 3
LIBRARY: *CRC.LIB*
DESCRIPTION: Builds a CRC lookup table based upon the specified polynomial and CRC function.
OTHER MODULES: None
RETURNS: unsigned short *: a pointer to the table.
COMMENTS: Each table element contains the CRC of its rank in the table. For example, element 50 contains the CRC of 50.

```
unsigned short *mk_crctbl(poly, crcfn)
unsigned short poly;
unsigned short (*crcfn)();                   /* pointer to CRC function    */
{
     extern char *malloc();
     unsigned short *crctp;                  /* pointer to the table       */
     int i;
     if ( (crctp = (unsigned short *)malloc(256 * sizeof(unsigned))) == NIL)
          return (NIL);
     for (i = 0; i < 256; i++ )        /* fill table with CRCs of values... */
          crctp[i] = (*crcfn)(i, poly, 0);  /* ... 0 -255                  */
     return (crctp);                         /* return a table to the pointer */
}
```

An Explanation of 'mk_crctbl' The two arguments passed to this are the generator polynomial and a pointer to a CRC function (`crchware`, for example). It not only builds the table of CRC values, it also allocates the memory for the table and returns its address. The `for` loop calculates and stores the CRC of the counter variable `i` in the `i`th element of the table. In cases where space is not critical, the table can be stored in the static array listed in Figure 19.7.

Figure 19-7 Lookup table for the CRC-CCITT for a classic hardware model.

```
ARRAY NAME: crctab
TYPE:        unsigned short
LEVEL:       3
LIBRARY:     CRC.LIB
DESCRIPTION: Lookup table for CCITT (XMODEM) polynomial.
COMMENTS:    Use this in place of mk_crctbl or just to verify that mk_crctbl generates the correct
             table.

unsigned short crctab[256] =
  {
    0x0000,  0x1021,  0x2042,  0x3063,  0x4084,  0x50A5,  0x60C6,  0x70E7,
    0x8108,  0x9129,  0xA14A,  0xB16B,  0xC18C,  0xD1AD,  0xE1CE,  0xF1EF,
    0x1231,  0x0210,  0x3273,  0x2252,  0x52B5,  0x4294,  0x72F7,  0x62D6,
    0x9339,  0x8318,  0xB37B,  0xA35A,  0xD3BD,  0xC39C,  0xF3FF,  0xE3DE,
    0x2462,  0x3443,  0x420,   0x1401,  0x64E6,  0x74C7,  0x44A4,  0x5485,
    0xA56A,  0xB54B,  0x8528,  0x9509,  0xE5EE,  0xF5CF,  0xC5AC,  0xD58D,
    0x3653,  0x2672,  0x1611,  0x0630,  0x76D7,  0x66F6,  0x5695,  0x46B4,
    0xB75B,  0xA77A,  0x9719,  0x8738,  0xF7DF,  0xE7FE,  0xD79D,  0xC7BC,
    0x48C4,  0x58E5,  0x6886,  0x78A7,  0x0840,  0x1861,  0x2802,  0x3823,
    0xC9CC,  0xD9ED,  0xE98E,  0xF9AF,  0x8948,  0x9969,  0xA90A,  0xB92B,
    0x5AF5,  0x4AD4,  0x7AB7,  0x6A96,  0x1A71,  0x0A50,  0x3A33,  0x2A12,
    0xDBFD,  0xCBDC,  0xFBBF,  0xEB9E,  0x9B79,  0x8B58,  0xBB3B,  0xAB1A,
    0x6CA6,  0x7C87,  0x4CE4,  0x5CC5,  0x2C22,  0x3C03,  0x0C60,  0x1C41,
    0xEDAE,  0xFD8F,  0xCDEC,  0xDDCD,  0xAD2A,  0xBD0B,  0x8D68,  0x9D49,
    0x7E97,  0x6EB6,  0x5ED5,  0x4EF4,  0x3E13,  0x2E32,  0x1E51,  0x0E70,
    0xFF9F,  0xEFBE,  0xDFDD,  0xCFFC,  0xBF1B,  0xAF3A,  0x9F59,  0x8F78,
    0x9188,  0x81A9,  0xB1CA,  0xA1EB,  0xD10C,  0xC12D,  0xF14E,  0xE16F,
    0x1080,  0x00A1,  0x30C2,  0x20E3,  0x5004,  0x4025,  0x7046,  0x6067,
    0x83B9,  0x9398,  0xA3FB,  0xB3DA,  0xC33D,  0xD31C,  0xE37F,  0xF35E,
    0x02B1,  0x1290,  0x22F3,  0x32D2,  0x4235,  0x5214,  0x6277,  0x7256,
    0xB5EA,  0xA5CB,  0x95A8,  0x8589,  0xF56E,  0xE54F,  0xD52C,  0xC50D,
    0x34E2,  0x24C3,  0x14A0,  0x0481,  0x7466,  0x6447,  0x5424,  0x4405,
    0xA7DB,  0xB7FA,  0x8799,  0x97B8,  0xE75F,  0xF77E,  0xC71D,  0xD73C,
    0x26D3,  0x36F2,  0x0691,  0x16B0,  0x6657,  0x7676,  0x4615,  0x5634,
    0xD94C,  0xC96D,  0xF90E,  0xE92F,  0x99C8,  0x89E9,  0xB98A,  0xA9AB,
    0x5844,  0x4865,  0x7806,  0x6827,  0x18C0,  0x08E1,  0x3882,  0x28A3,
    0xCB7D,  0xDB5C,  0xEB3F,  0xFB1E,  0x8BF9,  0x9BD8,  0xABBB,  0xBB9A,
    0x4A75,  0x5A54,  0x6A37,  0x7A16,  0x0AF1,  0x1AD0,  0x2AB3,  0x3A92,
    0xFD2E,  0xED0F,  0xDD6C,  0xCD4D,  0xBDAA,  0xAD8B,  0x9DE8,  0x8DC9,
    0x7C26,  0x6C07,  0x5C64,  0x4C45,  0x3CA2,  0x2C83,  0x1CE0,  0x0CC1,
```

Figure 19-7 cont. Lookup table for the CRC-CCITT for a classic hardware model.

```
    0xEF1F,  0xFF3E,  0xCF5D,  0xDF7C,  0xAF9B,  0xBFBA,  0x8FD9,  0x9FF8,
    0x6E17,  0x7E36,  0x4E55,  0x5E74,  0x2E93,  0x3EB2,  0x0ED1,  0x1EF0
};
```

The CRC Table Lookup Function: 'crcupdate'

Pre-calculating the CRCs of combining values and storing them in a table greatly simplifies and speeds up calculation of the CRC. Figure 19-8 shows the function to "add" a byte to the CRC accumulator.

Figure 19-8 The `crcupdate` function: CRC calculation with a lookup table.

FUNCTION NAME: `crcupdate`
LEVEL: 3
LIBRARY: *CRC.LIB*
DESCRIPTION: Calculates CRC using the table-lookup method.
OTHER MODULES: None
RETURNS: `void`
COMMENTS: Looks up the CRC of a combining value in the table pointed to by `crctab`.

```
void crcupdate(data, accum, crctab)
unsigned short data;
unsigned short *accum;                              /* pointer to a CRC accumulator */
unsigned short *crctab;          /* pointer to a table of CRC combining values */
{
    static short comb_val;
    comb_val  = (*accum >> 8) ^ data;
    *accum = (*accum << 8) ^ crctab[comb_val];
}
```

An Explanation of 'crcupdate'   The combining value is formed by XORing the data byte with the high-order byte of the accumulator (here expressed as a pointer). The CRC of the combining value—stored in the table previously built by `mk_crctbl`—is then XORed with the low-order byte of the accumulator. Freed from much of the overhead of bit shifting, this function is four to ten times faster than the `crchware` function. Importantly, because it contains no mention of a polynomial, it can be used to calculate the classical CRC using *any* generator polynomial. Actually, `crcupdate` is shown in this form only for clarity; in practice, it would be replaced with a single, more efficient statement:

```
*accum = (*accum << 8) ^ crctab[(*accum >> 8) ^ data];
```

or, better yet, by the macro shown in Figure 19-9.

CRC Functions for 'x_snd' and 'x_rcv'

The CRC calculation in XMODEM uses the classical hardware "zero-purge" model: bytes are presented MSB first and then shifted left. The CRC is identical to the remainder produced by dividing the message longhand (with two 0 bytes appended) by the CCITT generator polynomial. The high-order byte of the CRC is transmitted first.

Before we compose the CRC functions to complete the XMODEM file transfer modules begun in Chapter 18, create a new header file named *CRC.H* and install in it the constants shown in Figure 19-9. Notice that *CRC.H* contains macro expressions for two CRC lookup functions.

Figure 19-9 Constants for *CRC.H*.

```
#define CRCCCITT   0x1021        /* CCITT polynomial        */
#define CCCITT_REV 0x8408        /* reverse CCITT polynomial */
#define CRC16      0x8005        /* CRC16 polynomial        */
#define CRC16_REV  0xA001        /* reverse CRC16 polynomial */

/* remove the comment delimiters if you wish to use macros */
/*
crcupdate(d,a,t)     *(a) = (*(a) << 8) ^ (t)[(*(a) >> 8) ^ (d)];
#define crcupdate16(d,a,t) *(a)=((*(a)>>8) ^ (t)[(*(a) ^ (d)) &0x00ff])
*/
```

Reviewing the details of x_snd and x_rcv in Chapter 18, recall that the CRC functions x_sndcrc and x_rcvcrc are called via function pointers. Since their argument lists contain only a pointer to the data member of a packet structure, both functions share the variable *crctblp, a global pointer to the CRC lookup table that was built during the initialization phases of x_snd and x_rcv:

```
if ( (crctblp = mk_crctbl(CRCCCITT, crchware)) == NIL)
    {
    puts("Insufficient memory for CRC lookup table.");
    return (1);
    }
```

Transmit CRC: 'x_sndcrc'

The function x_sndcrc, shown in Figure 19-10, is called only by ckvinstall (through the function pointer r_errckp). Its purpose is to calculate and return the CRC of the data field of an sndpacket; the CRC is then installed in the ckval member of each packet.

Figure 19-10 The x_sndcrc function: the XMODEM sender's CRC function.

```
FUNCTION NAME: x_sndcrc
LEVEL:         0
```

Figure 19-10 cont.   The x_sndcrc function: the XMODEM sender's CRC function.

LIBRARY: *IBMPC.C* or *KAYPRO.C* (see text)
DESCRIPTION: Calculates CRC for indicated XMODEM data block.
OTHER MODULES: crcupdate
RETURNS: void
COMMENTS: This function is inherently non-portable because there is no way to know how the
                    processor stores words. As shown, we assume that the processor stores the LSB lower
                    in memory than the MSB.

```
unsigned short x_sndcrc(buff)
char *buff;                                  /* pointer to sndpacket->data      */
{
    extern void crcupdate();
    extern unsigned short *crctblp;       /* pointer to lookup table         */
    static unsigned short accum;          /* CRC accumulator                 */
    static int i;
    for (accum = i = 0; i < DBLKSIZ; ++buff, ++i)
    crcupdate(*buff, &accum, crctblp);           /* macro in CRC.H is better */
    return ( (accum >> 8) + (accum << 8) );      /* non-portable: see text */
}
```

An Explanation of 'x_sndcrc'   For speed of access, the CRC is calculated in a static lo-cal variable, accum. The single variable in the argument list is a pointer to the data array in an XMODEM send packet. A simple for loop calls crcupdate 128 times, on each call passing the next byte in the array. Since crcupdate requires a *pointer* to the accumulator variable, the *address* of accum is passed. The address of the CRC lookup table—the global pointer crctblp—is also passed to crcupdate.

Notice that the header for this function lists it as a "level-0" file; that is, it should reside in the computer-specific configuration file. Because the XMODEM protocol specifies that the high-order byte of the CRC is transmitted first, the high-order byte must reside at a lower memory address in the sndpacket structure. As discussed in Chapter 18 ("Portability Considerations"), the manner in which data is stored in memory varies from microprocessor to microprocessor. Therefore, x_sndcrc is inherently non-portable. Since the microprocessor in both machines for which we are developing code stores the low-order byte lower in memory, x_sndcrc byte-swaps the CRC before returning it. External variables are declared explicitly here so that this function can reside in the level-0 module.

Receive CRC: 'x_rcvcrc'

Figure 19-11 shows x_rcvcrc, the XMODEM receive CRC function. It calculates the CRC for a receive packet's data field and compares it to the CRC in the ckval field. It returns a 0 if the CRCs agree, otherwise non-0.

Figure 19-11   The x_rcvcrc function: the XMODEM receiver's CRC function.

FUNCTION NAME: x_rcvcrc
LEVEL: 3
LIBRARY: *XMODEM.C*
DESCRIPTION: Calculates CRC for an rcvpacket.
OTHER MODULES: crcupdate: pointer to a CRC lookup table.
RETURNS: unsigned short
COMMENTS: The CRC bytes in the rcvpacket are assumed to be contiguous with data bytes. The CRC (in accum) is 0 if no errors occur.

```
unsigned short x_rcvcrc(data)
short *data;                                 /* pointer to rcvpacket->data */
{
    static unsigned short i, accum;
    for (accum = i = 0; i < DBLKSIZ+2; i++)   /* include CRC bytes as data */
        crcupdate(*data++, &accum, crctblp);
    return (accum);                           /* zero if no errors         */
}
```

An Explanation of 'x_rcvcrc'   The data passed in the argument list is, of course, a pointer to the 128-byte data array of the current rcvpacket structure. Immediately following this array are the CRC members ckvhi and ckvlo. In Chapter 3, "Achieving a Zero Remainder," we discovered that when the remainder of *MessageA* is concatenated to *MessageA*, the remainder of the resulting message is 0. The function x_rcvcrc takes advantage of this happy phenomenon by treating the data as an array of 130 instead of 128 bytes, thus including in the calculation the two CRC bytes that immediately follow the data. The value in accum can be returned directly because it is 0 only if no errors occur.

CRC-16 Calculation

When most programmers think of CRCs, they think of the CRC-16 hardware circuit shown in Figure 19-12. In reality, though, the CRC-16 hardware is a specialized version of CRC-type polynomial arithmetic that compensates for peculiarities in serial I/O. Recall from our discussion of CRC-16 in Chapter 3 that the CRC-16 hardware circuit actually performs an "inverse" division to compensate for the convention of transmitting data low-order bit first. To compensate for this bit reversal, the reverse CRC-16 polynomial is applied (i.e., A001 instead of 8005 Hex), data bits are shifted into the high-order bit of the CRC accumulator, and the quotient bit is shifted out of the low-order bit.

Figure 19-12   The CRC-16 "reverse" hardware circuit. Note reversed divisor (reverse CRC-16 polynomial used).

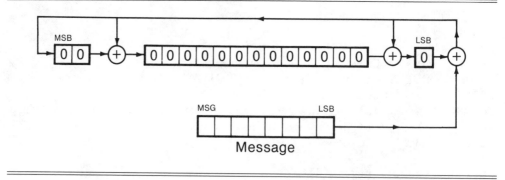

Neither of the CRC methods—classic or inverse—is superior. They are merely two versions of the same procedure, the latter designed to accommodate the peculiarities of hardware. On the rare occasion when you need to communicate with a CRC calculated in hardware, a reverse CRC algorithm comes in handy. It is certainly possible to calculate a reverse CRC using just the "classic" CRC functions we have already composed. However, the code overhead required to peform the reversals—(the order of bits in each data integer would have to be reversed and shifted right eight places)—would render CRC calculations absurdly slow. Considering the importance of speed in CRC calculations, it makes more sense to compose two special functions designed to simulate the "reverse" CRC. Figure 19-13 gives the new function crcrevhware to calculate the reverse CRC, and Figure 19-14 shows the matching table lookup function crcrevupdate. The existing mk_crctbl may be used because the CRC function is passed as a function pointer in its argument list.

Figure 19-13   Use of the crcrevhware function to simulate reverse CRC hardware.

FUNCTION NAME: crcrevhware
LEVEL: 3
LIBRARY: *CRC.LIB*
DESCRIPTION: Simulates a "reverse" CRC hardware circuit.
OTHER MODULES: None
RETURNS: unsigned short
COMMENTS: The generator polynomial in the argument list must already be reversed.

```
unsigned short crcrevhware(data, genpoly, accum)
unsigned short data;                /* NOT a char                    */
unsigned short genpoly;             /* the generator polynomial      */
unsigned short accum;               /* accumulator                   */
{
    static int i;
    data <<= 1;                     /* in preparation for loop below  */
    for (i = 8; i > 0; i--)
        {
        data >>= 1;
        if ((data ^ accum) & 0x0001) /* if msb of (data XOR accum) is TRUE */
            accum = (accum >> 1) ^ genpoly;  /* shift and subtract poly   */
```

Figure 9-13 cont. Use of the `crcrevhware` function to simulate reverse CRC hardware.

```
        else
                accum >>= 1;                /* otherwise, transparent shift    */
            }
        return(accum);
}
```

An Explanation of 'crcrevhware' This function is structurally identical to the plain `crchware` function given earlier in Figure 19-5. The difference is that the *low-order* (& 0x0001) data bit is *right* shifted into the *high-order* accumulator bit and the quotient bit is shifted out of the low-order bit of the accumulator. It is important to notice that this function does not invert the generator polynomial; that is, it is the calling function's responsibility to pass the *exact* bit pattern.

Figure 19-14 The `crcrevupdate` function: the CRC-16 table-lookup function.

FUNCTION NAME: `crcrevupdate`
LEVEL: 3
LIBRARY: *CRC.LIB*
DESCRIPTION: Calculates the "reverse" CRC-16 on data byte passed using the lookup table.
OTHER MODULES: None
RETURNS: `void`
COMMENTS: The `genpoly` is applied in the form it is passed. For CRC-16, therefore, A001 (inverse CRC-16) must be passed.

```
void crcrevupdate(data, accum, crcrevtab)
unsigned short data;
unsigned short *accum;
unsigned short *crcrevtab;
{
    static int comb_val;
    comb_val  = *accum ^ data;
    *accum = (*accum >> 8) ^ crcrevtab[comb_val & 0x00ff];
}
```

An Explanation of 'crcrevupdate' This function is identical to its sister function `crcupdate` in Figure 19-7, except the combining value is calculated by XORing the *high-order* byte of the accumulator with the data byte. This function can be simplified to

```
*accum = (*accum >> 8) ^ crcrevtab[(*accum ^ data) &0x00ff];
```

or, for even faster performance, the macro from Figure 19-8. Figure 19-15 gives the table of combining values for the reverse CRC algorithm using CRC-16. This is the table generated by the following call:

```
mk_crctbl(CRC16_REV, crcrevhware);
```

Figure 19-15   Lookup table for reverse CRC-16 hardware model.

ARRAY NAME: `crc16tab`
TYPE: `unsigned short`
LEVEL: 3
LIBRARY: *CRC.LIB*
DESCRIPTION: Combining-value lookup table for CRC-16 reverse polynomial.
COMMENTS: Use this in place of `mk_crctbl` or just to verify that the correct table is generated.

```
unsigned short crc16tab[256] =
    {
    0x0000, 0xC0C1, 0xC181, 0x0140, 0xC301, 0x03C0, 0x0280, 0xC241,
    0xC601, 0x06C0, 0x0780, 0xC741, 0x0500, 0xC5C1, 0xC481, 0x0440,
    0xCC01, 0x0CC0, 0x0D80, 0xCD41, 0x0F00, 0xCFC1, 0xCE81, 0x0E40,
    0x0A00, 0xCAC1, 0xCB81, 0x0B40, 0xC901, 0x09C0, 0x0880, 0xC841,
    0xD801, 0x18C0, 0x1980, 0xD941, 0x1B00, 0xDBC1, 0xDA81, 0x1A40,
    0x1E00, 0xDEC1, 0xDF81, 0x1F40, 0xDD01, 0x1DC0, 0x1C80, 0xDC41,
    0x1400, 0xD4C1, 0xD581, 0x1540, 0xD701, 0x17C0, 0x1680, 0xD641,
    0xD201, 0x12C0, 0x1380, 0xD341, 0x1100, 0xD1C1, 0xD081, 0x1040,
    0xF001, 0x30C0, 0x3180, 0xF141, 0x3300, 0xF3C1, 0xF281, 0x3240,
    0x3600, 0xF6C1, 0xF781, 0x3740, 0xF501, 0x35C0, 0x3480, 0xF441,
    0x3C00, 0xFCC1, 0xFD81, 0x3D40, 0xFF01, 0x3FC0, 0x3E80, 0xFE41,
    0xFA01, 0x3AC0, 0x3B80, 0xFB41, 0x3900, 0xF9C1, 0xF881, 0x3840,
    0x2800, 0xE8C1, 0xE981, 0x2940, 0xEB01, 0x2BC0, 0x2A80, 0xEA41,
    0xEE01, 0x2EC0, 0x2F80, 0xEF41, 0x2D00, 0xEDC1, 0xEC81, 0x2C40,
    0xE401, 0x24C0, 0x2580, 0xE541, 0x2700, 0xE7C1, 0xE681, 0x2640,
    0x2200, 0xE2C1, 0xE381, 0x2340, 0xE101, 0x21C0, 0x2080, 0xE041,
    0xA001, 0x60C0, 0x6180, 0xA141, 0x6300, 0xA3C1, 0xA281, 0x6240,
    0x6600, 0xA6C1, 0xA781, 0x6740, 0xA501, 0x65C0, 0x6480, 0xA441,
    0x6C00, 0xACC1, 0xAD81, 0x6D40, 0xAF01, 0x6FC0, 0x6E80, 0xAE41,
    0xAA01, 0x6AC0, 0x6B80, 0xAB41, 0x6900, 0xA9C1, 0xA881, 0x6840,
    0x7800, 0xB8C1, 0xB981, 0x7940, 0xBB01, 0x7BC0, 0x7A80, 0xBA41,
    0xBE01, 0x7EC0, 0x7F80, 0xBF41, 0x7D00, 0xBDC1, 0xBC81, 0x7C40,
    0xB401, 0x74C0, 0x7580, 0xB541, 0x7700, 0xB7C1, 0xB681, 0x7640,
    0x7200, 0xB2C1, 0xB381, 0x7340, 0xB101, 0x71C0, 0x7080, 0xB041,
    0x5000, 0x90C1, 0x9181, 0x5140, 0x9301, 0x53C0, 0x5280, 0x9241,
    0x9601, 0x56C0, 0x5780, 0x9741, 0x5500, 0x95C1, 0x9481, 0x5440,
    0x9C01, 0x5CC0, 0x5D80, 0x9D41, 0x5F00, 0x9FC1, 0x9E81, 0x5E40,
    0x5A00, 0x9AC1, 0x9B81, 0x5B40, 0x9901, 0x59C0, 0x5880, 0x9841,
    0x8801, 0x48C0, 0x4980, 0x8941, 0x4B00, 0x8BC1, 0x8A81, 0x4A40,
    0x4E00, 0x8EC1, 0x8F81, 0x4F40, 0x8D01, 0x4DC0, 0x4C80, 0x8C41,
    0x4400, 0x84C1, 0x8581, 0x4540, 0x8701, 0x47C0, 0x4680, 0x8641,
    0x8201, 0x42C0, 0x4380, 0x8341, 0x4100, 0x81C1, 0x8081, 0x4040
    };
```

So that these functions and their uses are not total abstractions to you, we will now compose a simple function to calculate both a "classical" CRC using the CCITT polynomial, and a reverse CRC using the CRC-16 polynomial on the contents of a disk file.

A CRC Test Program for the CRC Functions: 'CRCS.C'

The number of ways in which disk files can be quietly damaged is too long to list here, but the most common ways are changing floppy disks during file I/O, and (as RAM disks become more popular) unauthorized overwriting of RAM by errant software. A program for calculating the CRC for a disk file is therefore an extremely handy utility. More software publishers should follow the lead of Manx Software, which includes such a program in its Aztec C package along with a file listing the correct CRC for each file in the package. A user of Manx software is thus able to verify a file's integrity in just a few moments. Figure 19-16 uses our CRC library to create *CRCS.C*, a quick-and-dirty program to perform two kinds of CRC checks on the specified file.

Figure 19-16 *CRCS.C*: a simple program to calculate the CRCs for a file's data.

PROGRAM NAME: CRCS.C
DESCRIPTION: Calculates both CRCCCITT and CRC-16 on specified file.
OTHER MODULES: CRC functions in *CRCS.LIB*
SYNTAX: CRCS FILENAME

```
#include "stdio.h"
#include "crc.h"
main(argc, argv)                            /* CRCS.C */
int argc;
char *argv[];
{
        FILE *fopen(), *fp;
        unsigned short *mk_crctbl(), crcrevhware();
        unsigned short *tablep, accum, crchware();
        unsigned short *table16p, accum16, crcrevhware();
        int c;
        if (argc < 2)
            exit(puts("Need filename."));
        if ( (fp = fopen(argv[1], "rb")) == NIL) /* some compilers want "r" */
            exit(printf("Cannot open %s.", argv[1]));
        if ( (tablep = mk_crctbl(CRCCCITT, crchware)) == NIL)
            exit(puts("No space for CCITT table."));
        if ( (table16p = mk_crctbl(CRC16_REV, crcrevhware)) == NIL)
            exit(puts("No space for CRC-16 table."));
        accum = accum16 = 0;                 /* clear both CRC accumulators */
        while ( (c = getc(fp)) != EOF)
            {
            crcupdate(c, &accum, tablep);
            crcrevupdate(c, &accum16, table16p);
            }
        printf("CCITT for %s = %4x\n",argv[1], accum);
        accum16 = (accum16 >> 8) + (accum16 << 8);       /* byte-swap CRC-16 */
        printf("CRC-16 for %s = %4x\n ",argv[1], accum16);
        free(tablep);
        free(table16p);
        return (0);
}
```

An Explanation of CRCS.C The earlier contents of this chapter should obviate explanation. One interesting semantic point arises, however: how do we display the CRCs? This is not merely a rhetorical question, but one that exposes the ambiguity implicit in the term "CRC." For the "classical" CRC, we display the exact contents of the accumulator; that is, the high-order byte first. For the reverse CRC-16, however, we display the accumulator in the same order in which it is "naturally" transmitted—low-order byte first.

Conclusion

Do not be surprised if, having worked your way through this chapter, you feel a bit benumbed by CRCs or that your grasp of the topic is ephemeral. There is a cure for this: rereading Chapter 3, where it is suggested that you construct a physical model of a CRC register and physically move the 1s and 0s (pennies and dimes) about. Although you may have scoffed at such a blue-collar approach on the first reading, you are probably now much more receptive to the notion. Why not give it another try?

20

Interrupts

Interrupt I/O is often touted over polled I/O because it is faster. Even if this were true—and usually it is not—it misses the point horribly. It is the kind of reasoning that says jets are preferable to horses because jets use less hay; or that clocks are better than sundials because clocks can be read at night. In fact, interrupt I/O is preferable to polled I/O because it pushes the whole question of speed into the background where it belongs. In the face of the constant pressure of polling for newly arrived data, software can undertake no task longer than the time required for the UART's receive FIFO to fill. This is an intolerable constraint on any software and essentially precludes functional elegance. To the programmer, an interrupt buffer is a temporal saftey net, offering freedom to imagine, experiment, and create.

So far we have only muttered about interrupts. In fact, we haven't even bothered to define interrupt I/O, or, for that matter, its counterpart, polled I/O. Our only significant foray into the subject was our discussion of the 8250 and Z80SIO UARTs in Chapter 7. At various times throughout the book, however, we have also made certain software design decisions based upon the prospect of interrupts. There are several reasons for this obliqueness, not the least of which is the anxiety—largely unspoken—that many programmers feel about interrupts.

There is another, more philosophical reason to wait until the eleventh hour to add interrupts to the SIO. If you have plowed through the previous nineteen chapters, by now you probably have a fairly good idea about the ideology of this book: *Generality is the soul of good program design.* The major tenet of this philosophy is that hardware should not unduly influence the design of the software. To introduce interrupts—the *ultimate* hardware dependence—early in the book would have posed a temptation to optimize the design for speed and efficiency rather than generality. This commitment to generality persists to the very end where, you will notice, the accommodation of the hardware aspects of interrupt I/O is the last topic in this book.

This chapter consists of two parts: the first part is a general discussion of serial interrupts and how to integrate them into the SIO concept; the second part comprises the level-1 and level-0 functions required to interface the IBM PC's and Kaypro's interrupt hardware to the SIO.

Hardware details, once hidden in the bowels of the lower-level libraries, can quickly be forgotten. Since this is the chief benefit of employing the SIO, we can hardly bemoan it, but it probably means that the descriptions of the interrupt structures of the 8250 and Z80SIO UARTs have quietly slipped from your memory. You are therefore encouraged to review the relevant information in Chapters 7 and 12.

Interrupts

An interrupt is one example of a class of events known as *exceptions*, which are characterized by the involuntary passing of processor control from the normal path of program execution to code especially designed to "service" the event. Exceptions are not necessarily benevolent;[1] processors, for example, may generate exceptions under these unhealthy conditions:

- Addressing errors
- Bus errors
- Privilege violations
- Illegal or non-existent opcodes
- Illogical operations (division by 0, for example)

Interrupts and Asynchronous I/O

In asynchronous serial I/O, bytes arrive at unpredictable intervals — that is, asynchronously. Software must continually monitor the UART's receiver status in order to snatch each just-arrived byte before the next one arrives. Similarly, during transmission the software must monitor the transmitter's status to ascertain when the next byte may be sent. As long as the software has nothing else to do — as is the case in our *TERM* program — this perpetual *polling* imposes no hardship. But when polling is impossible or inconvenient — such as during disk I/O — incoming characters are lost or transmission ceases, or both. Interrupts offer a more efficient alternative to continual polling — the UART receives attention *only* when it needs it. That is, the occurrence of an event *automatically* and more-or-less instantaneously causes execution of code that is similar to the code executed as a result of polling. This code itself is known as an *interrupt service routine* or *interrupt handler,* but for stylistic brevity it will usually be referred to simply as "the handler." The address of the code is known as its *vector*.

Vectoring

In any given system, several interrupts may be active at any time. When an interrupt occurs, the processor must somehow ascertain which of the possible interrupts has actually occurred. From this information, the processor then calculates the vector corresponding to the interrupt. Although the exact method of communication between the processor and the UART differs from system to system, the result must always be the vector that services the condition causing the interrupt. The two processors studied in this book, the Z80SIO and the 8086, generate this interrupt vector in fundamentally different ways. We will study them in more detail as we compose their low-level interrupt functions.

Types of UART Interrupts

Generally, only four UART events generate interrupts:

1. The arrival of a byte (RxRDY)
2. The transmitter's buffer becoming empty (TBE)

---

[1]In fact, the term "exception" is often used to describe only *fault* detection, but is increasingly used in the more general sense described here.

3. A serialization error or BREAK

4. Changes on external inputs such as RS-232 status inputs

Although abstractly all such events are of equal importance, in practice the nature of the software application gives one event precedence over the others. In practice, however, the arrival of a byte (RxRDY) is granted the highest priority because of the potential for data loss if another byte arrives and overruns it. Because our space limitations make it impossible to illustrate all four kinds of interrupts, we must content ourselves with RxRDY interrupts. This is not a severe limitation because the method employed is so general that the implementation of the other interrupts is simply a matter of following the rote procedures developed for RxRDY.

Interrupts and the 'SIO'

As you have undoubtedly surmised, our implementation of interrupts requires new members to the SIO and several new functions. Before we look at these additions, however, let's briefly examine the plan of attack.

Interfacing to the RxRDY Interrupt

In Chapter 6 we noted that most UARTs' receivers are actually small FIFO buffers into which incoming bytes are moved as they are assembled from the communications line. Though typically only 2 to 5 bytes in length, a FIFO frees the programmer from writing frantic catch-it-or-lose-it routines necessary when no FIFO exists. In Chapter 6 we also noted that if the UART's FIFO could somehow be greatly enlarged, much of the pressure placed on software by polling would disappear; that is, without fear of overrunning the receiver's buffer, software could safely extend its polling interval. This, then, is the design goal for our implementation of RxRDY interrupts: to extend the size of the UART's buffer. We will approach this goal in a characteristically abstract fashion.

Interrupt Buffer Design

The type of buffer we will use for our extended RxRDY FIFO is called a *ring buffer*, so named because the action within it is circular. The movement of bytes in and out of this buffer is managed via two pointers, known by convention as the *head* and *tail* pointers. Both pointers are initialized to the beginning of the buffer. When an RxRDY interrupt occurs, its interrupt service routine reads the byte, places it at the location pointed to by the head pointer, then increments the head pointer. Bytes are fetched from the buffer by reading the byte pointed to by the tail pointer, then incrementing the tail pointer. To protect the data following the buffer, if a pointer's value after incrementation points beyond the buffer, the pointer is reset to the beginning of the buffer.

The buffer is "empty" whenever the head and tail pointers are equal. Similarly, the buffer is "full" when the *next* incrementation of the head pointer will make it equal to the tail pointer. This brings up a crucial point in ring buffer design: how should the RxRDY handler behave when it encounters a full buffer? There are only two choices: (1) to protect existing data in the buffer by discarding new bytes or (2) to allow new bytes to overwrite existing ones. Since there is no "right" way, we will choose the simpler design of ignoring the overlap of the pointers and allowing new data to overwrite old.

Figure 20-1 shows the final (!) revision of the SIOs, which supports a ring buffer and the miscellaneous variables to support RxRDY interrupts. Declaration and initialization of these new members, which is the same for both the IBM PC and the Kaypro, is also given. Only a single constant definition is required for *SIODEF.H*:

```
define IBUFSIZ 512          /* size of RxRDY interrupt buffer */
```

Figure 20-1 New SIO members required to support interrupts.

STRUCT DEF: SIO
FILE: *SIODEF.H*
DESCRIPTION: Typedef of master structure defining a serial port.
COMMENTS: Highlighted items add support for RxRDY interrupts.

```
typedef struct
    {
    BYTE      *uart_base;          /* 0  base address of UART             */
    int       data_off;            /* 1  offset of data port from base    */
    int       status_off;          /* 2  offset of status port from base  */
    unsigned  rcvmask;             /* 3  RxRDY mask                       */
    unsigned  xmitmask;            /* 4  TBE mask                         */
    BYTE      (*readbyte)();        /* 5  pointer to RAM/port read routine  */
    void      (*writebyte)();       /* 6  pointer to RAM/port write routine */
    BYTE      (*s_rstat)();         /* 7  pointer to serial receiver status */
    BYTE      (*s_read)();          /* 8  pointer to serial fetch routine    */
    BYTE      (*s_xstat)();         /* 9  pointer to serial xmiter status    */
    :
    struct    modem     *sm;       /* 36 pointer to modem structure        */
    unsigned  ibuffsiz;            /* 37 size of the  rxrdy ring buffer    */
    BYTE      *intbuff;            /* 38 pointer to     "     "      "      */
    BYTE      *eoibuff;            /* 39 pointer to end of  "        "      */
    BYTE      *iheadp;             /* 40 where in buff to put next byte    */
    BYTE      *itailp;             /* 41 where in buff to fetch next byte   */
    BYTE      (*int_rstat)();       /* 42 pointer to serial receiver status */
    BYTE      (*int_read)();        /* 43 pointer to serial fetch routine    */
    BOOL      intrptonflg;         /* 44 interrupts-are-on-flag            */
    } SIO;
```

'SIO' NAME: typeAsio
FILE: *IBMPC.C* and *KAYPRO.C*
COMMENTS: Initialization of new members that support RxRDY interrupts.

```
SIO typeAsio =
    {
    :
    &hayes,                        /*36 smartmodem                        */
    IBUFSIZ,                       /*37 size of receive interrupt buffer  */
    SUPPLIED,                      /*38 pointer to         "        "     */
    SUPPLIED,                      /*39 pointer to end of  "        "     */
    SUPPLIED,                      /*40 where in buff to put next byte    */
```

Figure 20-1 cont. New SIO members required to support interrupts.

```
SUPPLIED,            /*41 where in buff to fetch next byte    */
s_istat,             /*42 pointer to serial receiver status   */
s_iread,             /*43 pointer to serial fetch routine     */
FALSE,               /*44 interrupts-are-on-flag              */
};
```

ibuffsiz	The size of the buffer in bytes.
intbuff	A *pointer* to the ring buffer. The buffer itself is allocated when SIO is s_open'ed.
eoibuff	A pointer to the end of the buffer. Even though the end of the buffer is just the sum of ibuffsiz and intbuff members, a precalculated variable obviates repeated casting and arithmetic in pointer calculations.
headp	A pointer to the location in the buffer where the next incoming byte will be stored. The interrupt handler increments this pointer after each byte is safely tucked away.
tailp	A pointer to the location in the buffer from where the next stored byte will be read. The "byte-read" routine increments this pointer after each byte is read.
int_rstat	A pointer to a function that ascertains the buffer's "status"; i.e., whether a byte is available for reading from the buffer.
int_read	A pointer to a function that fetches a byte from the buffer.
intrptonflg	This flag broadcasts that SIO interrupts are on.

Interfacing the Ring Buffer to the Interrupt Handler

Before we concern ourselves with what sort of system-level, machine-specific tasks are required to realize interrupts, we must first integrate the buffer into the overall concept of the SIO. This is best accomplished with the top-down approach of first writing the interrupt handler itself. So, as you examine the function shown in Figure 20-2, just assume that the new SIO members have been properly initialized.

Figure 20-2 The irxrdy function—a level-3 RxRDY interrupt subhandler.

FUNCTION NAME:	irxrdy
LEVEL:	3
LIBRARY:	*SIO.LIB*
DESCRIPTION:	Byte-read interrupt subhandler for RxRDY interrupts.
OTHER MODULES:	s_rcv
RETURNS:	void
COMMENTS:	Reads a byte from the SIO, places it in the interrupt buffer at iheadp. If, after incrementation, iheadp points past the end of the buffer, it is reset to point to the beginning of the buffer.

Figure 20-2 cont.   The `irxrdy` function—a level-3 RxRDY interrupt subhandler.

```
void irxrdy(siop)
register SIO *siop;
{
    *siop->iheadp = s_rcv(siop);          /* read 8250's recevier    */
    if ( ++siop->iheadp == siop->eoibuff) /* if at end of buffer     */
        siop->iheadp = siop->intbuff;     /* reset pointer if past end */
}
```

An Explanation of 'irxrdy'   This is a classic ring buffer input manager. First, the incoming byte acquired by calling the "read" function pointer in the SIO is placed in the ring buffer at the location pointed to by `iheadp`. After incrementation, `iheadp` is boundary-checked against the end of the buffer, whose address is given in `eoibuff`. When `iheadp` points outside the allocated buffer, it is "wrapped" to the beginning.

You may be surprised to discover that the RxRDY handler is written in C instead of assembly language. Actually, the header in Figure 20-2 does not refer to it as a handler, but a subhandler. This distinction is unimportant for the time being and you should visualize `irxrdy` as if it were the entire handler. You may also be surprised that `irxrdy` is a level-3 function. As long as the interrupt handler references only the SIO data, there is no reason why it cannot be a level-3 function.

Interfacing the Interrupt Buffer to the 'SIO'

In the SIO scheme developed in this book, a function at one level "translates" its arguments for the function below it, which in turn translates its arguments, and so on. Only at the very lowest levels in this hierarchy—in our case, levels 0 and 1—is the raw hardware addressed. In this fashion, we are able to move from the abstract to the concrete in a series of gradually descending steps.

The peril of this plan is its inherent abstractness and the egghead code it tends to produce. To the accusation of overintellectualization, though, we will gladly plead guilty if it is also recognized that the process of abstraction ultimately illuminates its subject and liberates the mind of the programmer. As this discussion can quickly degenerate into a treatise on the epistemology of computer programming, let's hurry to look at a few examples that illustrate the practical benefits of an abstract way of proceeding. Consider the function `s_getc`, which simply waits for a byte to arrive, then returns the byte:

```
while ( (*siop->s_rstat)(siop) == NULL)
    ;
return ( (*siop->s_read)(siop));
```

This function knows nothing about the mechanics of fetching a byte, but it does know what is *abstractly* required—it must first wait for the receiver's "status" to become TRUE, then it "reads" and returns the just-arrived byte. The alimentary details of actually fetching the status and reading the byte are performed through the `s_rstat` and `s_read` function *pointers* in the SIO. The two pointers begin life pointing at level-1 UART functions: `s_rcvstat` returns the

UART's Serialization Status register with its RxRDY bit masked; s_rcv reads and returns a byte from the UART's receiver. In other words, the SIO is initialized to perform *polled* I/O using the UART's status bits.

To implement RxRDY interrupts—or, for that matter, any alternative method of I/O—we need only substitute two new pointers for s_rstat and s_read: pointers that return the status and data from the ring buffer instead of from UART registers. These two level-2 functions are given in Figure 20-3.

Figure 20-3   The s_istat and s_iread functions: status and read functions that interface to the RxRDY buffer.

```
FUNCTION NAME: s_istat
LEVEL:          2
LIBRARY:        BUOS.LIB
DESCRIPTION:    Character-ready function when running under interrupts.
OTHER MODULES:  None
RETURNS:        BYTE
COMMENTS:       The interrupt buffer is empty when the two pointers are equal.

BYTE s_istat(siop)
SIO *siop;
{
    return ( siop->iheadp != siop->itailp);
}
```

```
FUNCTION NAME: s_iread
LEVEL:          2
LIBRARY:        BUOS.LIB
DESCRIPTION:    Character-read function when running under interrupts.
OTHER MODULES:  None
RETURNS:        BYTE
COMMENTS:       Returns the byte in the interrupt buffer pointed to by the SIO member itailp. If,
                after incrementation, itailp points past the end of the buffer, it is reset to the
                beginning.

BYTE s_iread(siop)
register SIO *siop;                              /* for speed                 */
{
    static BYTE c;                              /* static for speed          */
    c = *siop->itailp;                          /* put in buffer at pointer  */
    if ( ++siop->itailp == siop->eoibuff)
        siop->itailp = siop->intbuff;           /* wrap back to beginning    */
    return (c);
}
```

An Explanation of 's_istat' and 's_iread'   This function is spectacularly unspectacular: it simply returns the answer to the question, "Is there a character in the buffer?" Only if the head and tail pointers are equal is the buffer empty. (Quiz: why would return (iheadp − itailp) not work?)

The byte-read function is essentially the obverse of the interrupt handler shown in Figure 20-2. Here, however, the byte at `itailp` is read before its boundary is tested and adjusted.

Switching from Polled to Interrupt I/O

We now have an RxRDY interrupt handler, a receiver-status function, and a function to read a byte. Before we write the code to switch the SIO from polled to interrupt I/O, please review Figures 14-5 to 14-8. To refresh your memory, Figure 14-5 shows the three-member structure `_siostat` that contains level-0 information about a serial port: `typep` contains a pointer to the SIO you wish to assign to that port; `openflag` is a flag to announce that the port is "open"; the last of these members, `intrptok`, is a flag to indicate whether the port is capable of interrupts. As shown in Figures 14-6 and 14-8, a global array of these structures is declared at level 0:

```
struct _siostat _siolist[MAX_PORTS]
```

The size of this array is determined by the number of serial ports supported by the system. Figure 14-6 gives the array for the Kaypro and Figure 14-8 for the IBM PC.

Modification of 's_open' and 's_close'

The logical place to perform the switchover from polled to interrupt I/O is when the SIO is s_opened. Of course, the interrupts have to be turned off again when the file is `s_close`'d. In modifying s_open and s_close we must keep in mind that they are level-3 functions and, with the exception of the `_siolist` array just mentioned, must remain ignorant of the system hardware. Figure 20-4 shows the modifications required to these two functions.

Figure 20-4   Revision to `s_open` and `s_close`.

```
FUNCTION NAME:  s_open
LEVEL:          3
LIBRARY:        SIO.LIB
DESCRIPTION:    Modifications in support of interrupt I/O.
RETURNS:        SIO*
```

```
SIO *s_open(portnum)
unsigned portnum;
{
    extern struct _siostat _siolist[];
    extern int _maxsios;                /* global -- number of serial ports */
    SIO *siop;                          /* for simplicity in syntax          */
    if (portnum >= _maxsios)            /* is device number legal?           */
        {
        s_errno = BAD_PORT;
        return (NIL);
        }
        ⋮
```

Figure 20-4 cont. Revision to s_open and s_close.

```
        _siolist[portnum].openflag = OPEN;      /* mark SIO open in list      */
        siop->devnum = portnum;                 /* put device number in SIO   */
        if ( (_siolist[portnum].intrptok == TRUE) /* set up for interrupts    */
                  && (siop->int_rstat != NIL )
                  && (siop->int_read != NIL)  )
            {
            while ( (siop->intbuff  = (BYTE*)malloc(siop->ibuffsiz)) == NIL)
                if ( (siop->ibuffsiz /= 2) < 4)
                    return (siop);              /* buffer too small           */
            siop->iheadp  = siop->itailp = siop->intbuff; /*initialize pointers*/
            siop->eoibuff = siop->intbuff + (BYTE*)siop->ibuffsiz;
            siop->s_rstat = siop->int_rstat;    /* change rxrdy pointer in SIO */
            siop->s_read  = siop->int_read;     /* change read pointer in SIO  */
            _intron(siop, portnum);             /* do the dirty work           */
            siop->intrptonflg   = TRUE;
            }
        return (siop);
}

FUNCTION NAME: s_close
LEVEL:          3
LIBRARY:        SIO.LIB
DESCRIPTION:    Modifications in support of interrupt I/O.
RETURNS:        SIO*

int s_close(siop)
SIO *siop;
{

        extern struct _siostat _siolist[];   /* list of available @[SIO]@s   */
        extern int _maxsios;          /* global -- maximum number of serial ports */
        int i;
        if (siop == NIL)
            return (NO_CLOSE);
        ⋮
        if ( i == _maxsios)                     /* no match in list           */
            return (NO_CLOSE);
        if (siop->intrptonflg == TRUE)
            {
            _introff(siop, siop->devnum);       /* turn serial interrupts off */
            free (siop->intbuff);               /* free interrupt ring buffer */
            siop->intrptonflg = FALSE;
            }
        s_restore(siop);                        /* restore interface          */
        siop->devnum = VIRGIN;                  /* install dummy device number */
        return (0);
}
```

An Explanation of 's_open'   The modification to s_open consists of the addition of a large if statement. Three conditions must be TRUE before the code inside the block is executed: the intrptok flag must indicate that interrupts for this device are supported, and the interrupt-supporting int_rstat and int_read pointers must not be NIL. If any of these conditions is FALSE, s_open exits immediately, leaving the SIO configured for polled operation. Otherwise, inside the conditional block several steps prepare for interrupt I/O.

First, the ring buffer is allocated and a pointer to it is stored in the intbuff member of the SIO. As shown in Figure 20-1, ibuffsiz is initialized to IBUFSIZE, but calling programs can modify it before s_opening the SIO.

To allocate the buffer, malloc is called to allocate a buffer of siop->ibuffsiz bytes; if this fails, malloc is called again with a request for a 50 percent smaller buffer. This progressive reducing of the buffer request continues until malloc succeeds or until the size of the request is less than 4, which causes an *immediate* return. In this way, if C is unable to supply an ample buffer, no further action is taken to activate interrupts and the SIO remains in polled mode. Your criteria of an ample buffer, of course, may be different.

Next, the ihead and itail members are initialized to point to the beginning of the buffer. The address of the end of the buffer is then calculated and stored in the eoibuff member. The "status" and "read" functions for interrupt operation are now installed:

```
siop->s_rstat = siop->int_rstat;
siop->s_read  = siop->int_read;
```

With the buffer and its pointers now correctly configured, we set intrptonflg to TRUE to announce that interrupts are on.

The stage is now set for interrupts—all that remains is to say, "Let there be interrupts." This last step is the province of the as yet unwritten level-0 function _intron, which is expected to perform the hardware and system tasks required to enable the interrupts on the current computer.

An Explanation of 's_close'   Closing the SIO is a good deal simpler than opening it. After calling the level-0 function _introff to deactivate the interrupts, the storage occupied by the buffer is returned to the free-pool and the intrptonflg is made FALSE. It is unnecessary to return the pointers to polled operation.

All the pieces are now in place for RxRDY interrupts. Our last task is to write the two level-0, hardware-specific modules _intron and _introff for both *IBMPC.C* and *KAYPRO.C*. The remainder of this chapter is devoted to this task.

Level-0 Functions for the IBM PC and Kaypro

Our goal in this section is to compose _intron and _introff for our two target computers, the IBM PC and the Kaypro 4. Because of the dissimilarity between hardware environments, these pairs of functions will resemble each other in name and purpose only. Before we begin, a few prefatory remarks may clarify what promises to be the most tedious portion of this book.

Although we have already written our handler, it is a *level-3* function irxrdy and, as such, cannot be used directly as our interrupt handler. Since an interrupt handler is always called when the processor is doing something else, its first responsibility is to preserve the state of the CPU. In other words, the handler must make certain that no CPU registers are changed during its execution. Since the code generated by compilers preserves only a *few* CPU registers, calling irxrdy directly as a handler would certainly alter one or more of the CPU registers, crashing the system.[2] Accordingly, on both our target machines, we will write the simplest possible assembly-language function whose main objective is to preserve the CPU registers during execution of the C subhandler. In both cases, these assembly-language interrupt service routines are imaginatively named __alisr or, since one is required for each SIO, __alisrA, __alisrB, and so on. The initial double underscore identifies an assembly-language function—a convention we will use throughout.

Installing RxRDY Interrupts on the IBM PC

Before we compose the level-0 functions for the IBM PC, we must understand its interrupt structure. As explained in Chapter 7, the 8250 UART's participation in the interrupt system is limited to asserting its INTRPT signal on the system's I/O bus. It is the system's responsibility to produce the proper vector for each interrupt.

Figure 20-5 The interrupt structure of the IBM PC.

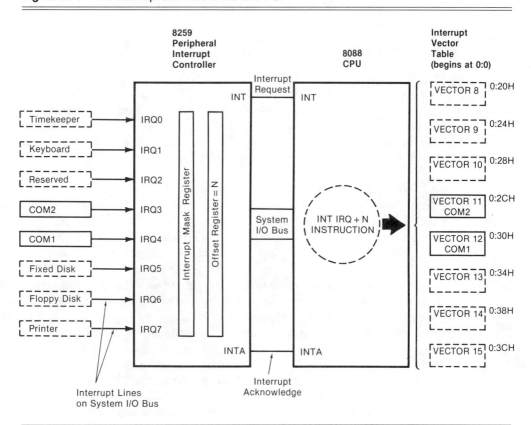

---

[2]If you are lucky. The most nightmarish bug to find is one in which an interrupt handler modifies a CPU register that the compiler uses only for numeric data.

The 8259 Peripheral Interrupt Controller

Figure 20-5 illustrates the interrupt structure of the IBM PC. The first piece in the puzzle is the 8259 Peripheral Interrupt Controller (PIC), which administrates the relationship between the CPU and as many as six peripherals plugged into the mother board. (Actually, the PIC supports eight peripherals, but two—the keyboard and the system timekeeper—are permanently wired to the I/O bus). Each peripheral's interrupt line is assigned an IRQ input on the PIC—the timekeeper gets IRQ0, the keyboard gets IRQ1, the system printer (PRN) gets IRQ7, and so forth. The two serial ports, COM1 and COM2, are assigned interrupt lines IRQ4 and IRQ3, respectively. (Notice that there are none for COM3 and COM4.)

When a peripheral generates an interrupt, the interrupt signal travels (via its IRQ) to the PIC, which relays it to the CPU. The PIC is a formidably complicated device with many responsibilities besides relaying interrupts. Only two of these features are of concern to us: the Interrupt Mask register (IMR) and the Offset register. The IMR, a read/write register located at port address 21H, is refreshingly simple. Each bit in the IMR corresponds to a peripheral interrupt input line—the timekeeper's is bit 0, COM2 is bit 3, COM1 is bit 4, and so forth. When a bit is TRUE in the IMR, the PIC does *not* relay interrupts on that IRQ; in other words, that peripheral's interrupt is masked. Before we look at the purpose of the Offset register, let's look at the other participants in the interrupt scheme.

The 8086 INT Vectoring Instruction

The most distinguishing characteristic of the 8086 instruction set is the INT instruction, which takes the form *INT nn*, where *nn* is an 8-bit argument. The CPU treats this argument as an index into a table of vectors, calling the vector at the indexed location. When an *INT nn* occurs, for example, the CPU calls the address located in element *nn* of the vector table. A call generated in this way is identical to an ordinary 8086 FAR call except that the Flag register is pushed onto the stack ahead of the FAR return address. For this reason a special RETURN instruction exists for returning from an INT instruction: IRET.

With the INT mechanism in mind, let's now see what happens when a COM1 generates an interrupt on IRQ4. If bit 4 in the IMR mask is clear, the PIC generates an interrupt request on its INT line to the CPU. When the CPU finishes its current instruction (assuming its interrupt flag is enabled), it acknowledges the PIC, which immediately blurts the IRQ number of the interrupt peripheral onto the system I/O bus. The CPU fetches this number and uses it as the argument for an INT instruction.

But wait! There is a problem: the first eight vectors in the table are usurped by the system—the divide-by-zero vector is in element 0, the print screen vector is in element 5, and so on (elements 6 and 7 are reserved). This is where the PIC's Offset register comes into play—instead of outputting the IRQ number of the peripheral directly onto the I/O bus, the PIC first adds the value in its Offset register. The PIC's Offset register is configured with a value of 8 during power-up, so as indicated in Figure 20-5, the INT arguments ultimately provided to the CPU begin at element 8 in the vector table. An interrupt from the timekeeper has the same effect as an INT 8: the 0 of IRQ0 plus the 8 in the Offset register.

There is one difference between an INT instruction generated by software and one generated by an interrupt peripheral—the PIC must be informed when it is safe to ''clear'' the current interrupt. Accordingly, at the end of every peripheral's interrupt service routine must appear a *non-specific End-of-Interrupt* command. This is accomplished by writing the value 20H to port address 20H.

The 8250 UART

The 8250 UART supports 8086 system interrupts via two registers—the Interrupt Enable register (Figure 7-3) and the Interrupt Identification register. The Interrupt Enable register contains a bit for enabling each of the four kinds of 8250 interrupts: RxRDY, TBE, RS-232 input, and serialization errors. When an interrupt occurs, the interrupt handler must read the Interrupt Identification register to ascertain which of the four possible interrupts has just occurred. The mapping of the register is given in Table 20-1.

The final piece of the interrupt puzzle involves the 8250, but it is unique to the IBM PC's use of the 8250 and *not* part of the 8250 itself. Recall from Figure 7-8 that the IBM PC uses its General-Purpose Output 2 (GPO2) to block and unblock its INTRPT output. In effect, then, GPO2 is used on the IBM PC as a Master Interrupt Enable.

Table 20-1 Interrupt Identification register.

Bit 2	Bit 1	Bit 0	Interrupt Pending
0	0	1	None
1	1	0	Serialization Error or BREAK
1	0	0	Received Data
0	1	0	Transmitter Buffer Empty
0	0	0	RS-232 Input

The '_intron' Function for the IBM PC

This completes our survey of the components in the IBM PC's interrupt system vis-a-vis the 8250 UART. To summarize, let's make a checklist of the steps necessary to activate RxRDY interrupts for IBM PC COM ports.

1. Replace the current entry in the vector table with the address of our assembly-language handler for that port. The table number for COM1 is 12, for COM2 is 11.

2. Unmask the corresponding bit in the PIC's IMR: bit 3 for COM1, bit 4 for COM2.

3. Activate UART interrupts:

   A. Enable only the RxRDY bit—bit 0—in the Interrupt Enable register.

   B. Clear any pending interrupts by reading registers 0−5.

   C. Unblock the 8250's INTRP line by asserting GPO2.

Let's now translate this checklist into `_intron` for the IBM PC. The complete function is shown in Figure 20-6

Figure 20-6 The `_intron` function for the IBM PC.

```
FUNCTION NAME:   _intron
LEVEL:           0
LIBRARY:         IBMPC.C
DESCRIPTION:     Activates interrupts for the COM port named in the argument list.
OTHER MODULES:   setgpo2, __getivec, __setivec, __getcs, __alisr
```

Figure 20-6 cont.   The _intron function for the IBM PC.

RETURNS: void
COMMENTS: Functions whose names begin with a double underscore are assembly-language
                  functions found in module INTRP.ASM. The functions __alisrA and __alisrB
                  are the interrupt handlers for COM1 and COM2, respectively. SUPPLIED is a manifest
                  constant in *SIODEF.H.*

```
typedef unsigned long INTPTR;              /* typedef for a four-byte pointer    */

#define I_RXRDY  1                         /* values of Interrupt Enable register */
#define I_TBE    2
#define I_SERERR 4
#define I_RS232  8

#define I_COM1   0x0C                      /* ranks in the system vector table */
#define I_COM2   0x0B

#define I_IMR1   0xEF                      /* mask to reset bit 4 in IMR        */
#define I_IMR2   0xF7                      /* mask to reset bit 3 in IMR        */

extern void __alisrA(), __alisrB();        /*  assembly-language handlers */

static struct
    {
    BYTE    iwanted;       /* mask for Interrupt Enable register          */
    BYTE    inum;          /* rank in interrupt vector table COM1=12,COM2=11 */
    BYTE    imask;         /* mask for Interrupt Mask Register of 8259     */
    void    (*isr)();      /* pointer to interrupt handler function        */
    INTPTR oldivec;        /* save existing vector here                    */
    BYTE    oldimr;        /* save existing Interrupt Mask Register here    */
    struct vout232_ *oldgpo2;  /* save address of gpo2 structure          */
    } _ilist[MAX_PORTS] =
        {
            { I_RXRDY, I_COM1, I_IMR1, __alisrA, SUPPLIED, SUPPLIED, SUPPLIED },
            { I_RXRDY, I_COM2, I_IMR2, __alisrB, SUPPLIED, SUPPLIED, SUPPLIED },
            { NIL  },       /* no COM3 */
            { NIL  },       /* no COM4 */
        };

void _intron(siop, portnum)
SIO *siop;
int portnum;
{
    INTPTR __getivec();
    unsigned __getcs();
    int i;
    BYTE imr;
/* STEP 1: change the interrupt vector, save current value */
    _ilist[portnum].oldivec = __getivec(_ilist[portnum].inum);
    __setivec( _ilist[portnum].inum, _ilist[portnum].isr, __getcs() );
```

Figure 20-6 cont. The _intron function for the IBM PC.

```
/* STEP 2: unmask appropriate bit in 8259's Interrupt Mask Register */
    _ilist[portnum].oldimr =  imr = inport(0x21);
    imr = (BYTE) (imr & _ilist[portnum].imask);
    outport((BYTE*)0x21,imr);                      /* outport expects a pointer */

/* STEP 3: turn on UART interrupts */
    outport(siop->uart_base + 1, _ilist[portnum].iwanted); /* enable intrpts*/
    for (i = 0; i < 6; i++)
        inport(siop->uart_base + i);        /* clear any interrupts pending */
    setgpo2(siop, ON);                      /* finally, unblock interrupts  */
    _ilist[portnum].oldgpo2 = siop->gpo2; /* save address of gpo2 structure */
    siop->gpo2 = NIL;                       /* take gpo2 control away from user */
    return;
}
```

An Explanation of '_intron'   The structure of this function is dictated by two requirements: (1) to support *every* SIO in the system and (2) to preserve the existing configuration for later restoration by _introff. Both goals are effected simultaneously by collecting the necessary variables into a structure, then declaring an array of these structures—one element for each SIO supported. Thus, the structure for the port-under-configuration is addressed as _ilist[portnum]. The members of this structure are:

iwanted	This is the value to write to the Interrupt Enable register. Although we are implementing only RxRDY interrupts here, constant definitions are provided for all four types of interrupts. The constants may be freely compounded to create any desired combination of interrupts, I_RXRDY + I_RS232, for example.
inum	This is the rank in the system vector table assigned to this peripheral card. There are no assignments for COM3 and COM4.
imask	This is the mask that must be applied to the PIC's Interrupt Mask register to activate interrupts for this peripheral.
(*isr)()	This is a pointer to the interrupt handler.
oldivec	Before installing the vector of our interrupt handler in the system table, we save the existing vector for restoration when the SIO is closed.
oldimr	Before changing the new value in the PIC's Interrupt Mask register, we store its current value for restoration when the SIO is closed.
oldgpo2	Since GPO2 enables and disables interrupts, we must remove it from user control. Before installing a NIL pointer in the SIO, however, we save its current pointer for restoration when the SIO is closed.

Small Model Pointers

An ugly problem surrounds the declaration of a pointer variable in which to store vectors. In the Small Memory model (see Appendix C) chosen for this book, data and code are expected to fit entirely in 64K bytes each—that is, within the same *physical* address segment of the CPU. Since the segment portions of all data addresses are the same in Small Model, pointers consist only of the 16-bit offset portion of the address. In other words, Small Model pointers do not supply the absolute address of an object, just its *offset* within a 64K segment.

This method of pointer representation poses a problem when dealing with system vectors (FAR pointers) that, by definition, specify the complete, 32-bit segment:offset address. The solution to the problem is to create our own data type to hold the 32-bit system pointer:

```
typedef unsigned long INTPTR;
```

With this data type to express 4-byte system vectors, we are now ready to converse with the PC DOS operating system.

Step One: Installing the Interrupt Handler in the Vector Table

Now that we have a storage type for vector address, we could easily fetch the current vector from the table, store it, and replace it with the FAR address of our assembly-language handler. Luckily, this level of fiddling is unnecessary because DOS provides services 25H and 35H to modify the vector table. To obviate assembly-language programming, every C compiler provides a function for invoking the operating system from C. If no other assembly language were required, it would be tempting to pursue this option. But since we are already committed to writing our interrupt handlers in assembler, it is no additional trouble to write two or three DOS functions. These assembly-language functions __getivec, __setivec, and __getcs are included later in Figure 20-8 along with the handler __alisr.

The assembly-language function __getivec simply returns the specified element of the system vector table. When opening COM1 (i.e, port 0), for example, the call

```
_ilist[portnum].oldivec = __getivec(_ilist[portnum].inum);
```

evaluates to

```
_ilist[0].oldivec = __getivec(12);
```

which fetchs the 4-byte contents of element 12 of the vector table and stores it in our local structure array for later recall.

With the current vector for our device safely tucked away, we are now ready to call the assembly-language function __setivec to install the address of our interrupt handler. As shown in Figure 20-6, the syntax for calling __setivec requires the FAR address of our interrupt handler; that is, the segment and offset portions of its address. As just discussed, however, addresses in Small Memory Model consist of only the offset portion. The segment portion of the __alisr is supplied by the tiny function __getcs.

When opening COM2 (i.e, port 1), the call

```
__setivec( _ilist[portnum].inum, _ilist[portnum].isr, __getcs() );
```

therefore evaluates to

```
__setivec(11, __alisrB, __getcs() );
```

Step Two: Unmasking the PIC

This section is considerably more straightforward than dealing with system vectors. The PIC's Interrupt Mask register is fetched from port 21H and stored in the structure array for later restoration. It is also assigned to a local variable `imr`, which is ANDed with the mask in the `imask` member of the structure, then written back to port 21H.

Assuming that the IMR currently contains FA, when opening COM1 (i.e, port 0), for example, the lines

```
imr = (BYTE) (imr &  _ilist[portnum].imask);
outport(0x21,imr);
```

will evaluate to

```
imr = ( 0xFA &  0xEF);        /* reset bit 4 for com1 */
outport(0x21,  0xEA );
```

Step 3: Enabling UART Interrupts

System interrupts are now enabled, so we have only to configure the 8250 UART to our needs. First, we select the desired interrupts by writing the `iwanted` structure member to the Interrupt Enable register, which is located at offset 1 from the UART's base address. Next, every UART register is read in order to clear any interrupts that might be pending.

The final step in activating RxRDY interrupts is to assert GPO2, which unblocks the 8250's INTRPT line and allows its interrupts to reach the Peripheral Interrupt Controller. After issuing the command to assert GPO2, we must "un-support" it to prevent the user or an application program from disabling it and turning off the interrupts. After saving the `SIO`'s current `gpo2` pointer, we store a NIL there. To verify that this is effective, the RS-232 control menu in *TERM* should show

4. Toggle GPO2 [---]

and selecting item four should produce the message, "Function not supported."

A Level-1 Interrupt Administrator: 's_iadmin'

So far, we have been proceeding on the assumption that our assembly-language handler will call the level-3 function `irxrdy`. This approach will, in fact, fulfill our goal of implementing RxRDY interrupts, but it is unnecessarily shortsighted, because a major modification will be required later if we wish to support the three other kinds of interrupts. A more general strategy is to write an *administrative* function that somehow learns which interrupt has occurred, then calls its handler. The level-1 function `s_iadmin` in Figure 20-7 accomplishes this.

Figure 20-7 The `s_iadmin` function: the 8250 interrupt administrator.

FUNCTION NAME: `s_iadmin`
SUBFUNCTIONS: `irxrdy` and the dummies `irs232, itbe, iserr`
LEVEL: 1

Figure 20-7 cont. The s_iadmin function: the 8250 interrupt administrator.

LIBRARY: *U8250.LIB*

DESCRIPTION: 8250 interrupt administrator. When called (from assembler ONLY!) it reads the Interrupt Identification register to identify the event that requires service, then calls the correct interrupt service routine.

OTHER MODULES: None

RETURNS: `void`

COMMENTS: Bit 0 of the Interrupt Identification register is always 0 when an event needs service. After right-shifting one place, this byte becomes an index into an array of function pointers.

```
#define INT_ENABLE  1            /* offset of Interrupt Enable register   */
#define INT_ID      2            /* offset interrupt ID register          */
#define SER_ERR     5            /* offset of Serialization Status register */
#define STAT_232    6            /* offset of Interrupt ID register        */

extern void irxrdy();            /* our level-3 function already in SIO.C */
                 /* dummies for other interrupts */
void irs232(siop)SIO *siop; {(*siop->readbyte)(siop->uart_base + STAT_232);}
void itbe(siop)  SIO *siop; {/* cleared by reading INT_ID */}
void iserr(siop) SIO *siop; {(*siop->readbyte)(siop->uart_base + SER_ERR);}

void s_iadmin(siop)
SIO *siop;
{
    static unsigned index;
    static void (*isr[4])() =          /* an array of pointers to handlers */
        {
        irs232,                        /* adjusted code in IIR = 0   */
        itbe,                          /*                       = 1   */
        irxrdy,                        /*                       = 2   */
        iserr,                         /*                       = 3   */
        };

    for (;;)                           /* loop until there are no more */
        {                              /* interrupts to service        */
        index = (unsigned)inport(siop->uart_base + INT_ID);
        if (index & 01)                /* LSB = no more interrupts     */
            break;
        index >>= 1;                   /* adjust index                 */
        (*isr[index])(siop);           /* call the correct handler     */
        }
}
```

An Explanation of 's_iadmin'   The design of this function is based upon the 8250's Interrupt Identification register shown in Table 20-1. A 0 in bit 0 signifies a pending interrupt whose identity is encoded in bits 1—2. If right-shifted one place, this register becomes a handy index into an array containing pointers to our four interrupt functions. Since irxrdy already exists, it is declared extern. As long as only RxRDY interrupts are selected in _intson, the index is always 2 and only irxrdy is called. The other functions irs232, itbe, and iserr contain the minimum code required to clear the respective interrupt. At your convenience, these dummies can be augmented into full-fledged level-3 functions.

Now that we have s_iadmin to sort out interrupts, we are ready to look at the assembly-language handler that calls it.

The Assembly-Language Interrupt Handler: '__alisr'

One of the most noticeable things about the code shown in Figure 20-8 is a strong stylistic use of upper and lower case. The rule is simple: actual assembly-language instructions are in lower case and *assembler directives* are in upper case.

Figure 20-8   Assembly-language functions for the IBM PC.

FUNCTION NAME: __alisrA
LIBRARY: *PCDOS.LIB*
DESCRIPTION: An assembly-language interrupt handler for device 0 (typeAsio).
RETURNS: void
SYNTAX FROM C: Not called from C
COMMENTS: For Aztec Small Memory Model. See Appendix C for instructions on Large models and other compilers. Line numbers are for reference only.

```
ARG1        EQU 4               ; offset first stack argument
ARG2        EQU 6               ;       2nd
ARG3        EQU 8               ;       3rd
NUMARGS     EQU 2


PUBLIC __alisrA_, __getivec_, __setivec_, __getcs_


DATASEG SEGMENT WORD PUBLIC 'DATA'
    EXTRN typeAsio_:WORD
DATASEG ENDS

CODESEG SEGMENT WORD PUBLIC 'CODE'
ASSUME CS:CODESEG, DS:NOTHING
EXTRN   s_iadmin_:NEAR

STACKSIZ    EQU 128
            ;; new stack and storage for SS/SP during interrupt
            DB   STACKSIZ-2 dup (?)       ; define STACKSIZE bytes for local stack
newstack    DW 0
oldss       DW 0
oldsp       DW 0

__alisrA_ PROC NEAR
0           push  ax                ; this on system's stack
5           mov   oldss, ss         ; save SS
10          mov   oldsp, sp         ; save SP
15          push  cs                ; set SS:SP ...
20          pop   ss                ; ...to address ...
25          mov   sp, OFFSET newstack ; ... our local stack
30                ;; -- remaining stack operations use local stack --
35          push  bp
40          push  bx
45          push  cx
```

Figure 20-8 cont.   Assembly-language functions for the IBM PC.

```
50              push    dx
55              push    si
60              push    di
65              push    es
70              push    ds
75              mov     ax, OFFSET typeAsio_  ; pass the address of typeAsio on stack
80              push    ax
85              mov     ax, SEG typeAsio_     ; address C's data
90              mov     ds, ax
95              call    s_iadmin_             ; call C interrupt administrator
100             add     sp, NUMARGS           ; remove siop argument from stack
105             pop     ds                    ; restore registers from local stack
110             pop     es
115             pop     di
120             pop     si
125             pop     dx
130             pop     cx
135             pop     bx
140             pop     bp
145             mov     ss, oldss             ; restore the caller's stack (SS:SP)
150             mov     sp, oldsp
155             mov     al, 20H               ; bid adieu to the 8259 PIC
160             out     20H, al
165             pop     ax
170             iret                          ; allons!
__alisrA_ ENDP
```

FUNCTION NAME: `__getcs`
LIBRARY: *PCDOS.LIB*
DESCRIPTION: An assembly-language function to fetch the program's current CS register.
RETURNS: `unsigned short int`
SYNTAX FROM C: `csreg = __getcs();`
                  `unsigned short int cs;`
COMMENTS: Many compilers furnish this function.

```
__getcs_    PROC NEAR            ; return current code segment
    mov     ax, cs
    ret
__getcs_    ENDP
```

FUNCTION NAME: `__getivec`
LIBRARY: *PCDOS.LIB*
DESCRIPTION: An assembly-language function to fetch the vector of a specified interrupt.
RETURNS: INTPTR (typedef as `long` in Small Model)
SYNTAX FROM C: `vector = _getivec(intnum);`
                  `INTPTR vector;`
                  `int intnum;`

Figure 20-8 cont. Assembly-language functions for the IBM PC.

COMMENTS: DOS returns segment in ES, offset in BX, but it may be necessary to modify this
         function to accommodate your compiler's conventions for returning 4-byte data types.

```
GET_IVEC    EQU      35H              ; fetch interrupt vector
SET_IVEC    EQU      25H              ; change interrupt vector
;;
;;
__getivec_ PROC NEAR
     push   bp
     mov    bp,sp                     ; copy stack pointer int base pointer
     mov    al, [bp + ARG1]           ; interrupt number off stack
     mov    ah, GET_IVEC
     int    21H
     mov    dx, es                    ; Aztec returns segment in DX and ...
     mov    ax, bx                    ; ... OFFSET in AX
     pop    bp                        ; restore base pointer
     ret
__getivec_ ENDP
```

FUNCTION NAME: __setivec

LIBRARY: *PCDOS.LIB*

DESCRIPTION: An assembly-language function to install the specified vector in the interrupt vector table
         at the rank specified by intnum.

RETURNS: void

SYNTAX FROM C: _setivec(intnum, offset, segment);
         int intnum;
         unsigned short int offset;
         unsigned short int vector;

COMMENTS: DOS requires the segment in DS, the offset in DX, but it may be necessary to modify
         this function to accommodate your compiler's method of passing 4-byte data types.

```
__setivec_ PROC NEAR
     push   bp
     mov    bp, sp
     mov    al, [bp + ARG1]                 ; get interrupt number off stack
     mov    ah, SET_IVEC
     push   ds
     lds    dx, DWORD PTR [bp + ARG2] ; now get 4-byte interrupt vector
     int    21H
     pop    ds
     pop    bp
     ret
__setivec_   ENDP
CODESEG      ENDS
END
```

An Explanation of the Assembler Functions The mission of `__alisrA` is simple — to protect the CPU registers during execution of the level-1, C interrupt handler `s_iadmin`. The caller's stack must also be protected because when an interrupt occurs there may not be enough room on the caller's stack to save the CPU's registers. PC DOS's internal stack, for example, is guaranteed to be just large enough to hold the PUSH of all the registers. Since C makes heavy use of the stack for passing arguments and for automatic storage, we must create our own local stack. In lines 5 and 10 the caller's SS and SP registers are saved in local variables, and the address of the local 128-byte stack is loaded into them in lines 15 to 25. With the new stack in effect, the remaining CPU registers can be safely PUSHed. Line 85 guarantees that the DS register points to C's data. Since `s_iadmin` expects an `siop` argument, line 75 pushes the address of `typeAsio` onto the stack prior to calling it. After return from `s_iadmin`, the protection process is reversed: the saved registers are POPed off the local stack and the caller's stack is restored. Just before the IRET instruction, line 155 sends an End-of-Interrupt command to the Peripheral Interrupt Controller. Upon exit at line 170, the caller's environment is restored except for the 4 bytes of stack space used in lines 0 — 15.

Compiler Dependencies

The code in Figure 20-8 is written for the Aztec assembler and for interface to the Small Model library. Only miniscule changes are required for other assembler and for other memory models. Please consult Appendix C for instructions and comments. The underscore *appended* to each assembler variable is to accommodate the Aztec compiler, but most compilers have similar requirements, also listed in Appendix C.

The '_introff' for the IBM PC

The code for turning off interrupts, shown in Figure 20-9, consists of deactivating system and UART interrupts for the port named in the argument list. No further explanation is required, except to point out that the values used are fetched from the `_ilist` structure array.

Figure 20-9 The `_introff` function for the IBM PC.

```
FUNCTION NAME:  _introff
LEVEL:          0
LIBRARY:        IBMPC.C
DESCRIPTION:    Deactivates system and UART interrupts for the port specified.
OTHER MODULES:  __setivec
RETURNS:        void
COMMENTS:       Values are restored from the _ilist structure array.

void  _introff(siop, portnum)
SIO *siop;
{
    outport((BYTE *)0x21, _ilist[portnum].oldimr);/* restore Int. Mask Reg   */
    __setivec(_ilist[portnum].inum, _ilist[portnum].oldivec); /* restore vect*/
    siop->gpo2 = _ilist[portnum].oldgpo2 ;          /* restore gpo2 operation */
    setgpo2(siop, OFF);             /* clear bit 3 in UART's RS-232 Output reg */
}
```

Installing RxRDY Interrupts on the Kaypro 4

The Kaypro is a microcosm of the problems one can encounter when installing interrupts. Despite the apparent simplicity of its architecture and hardware components, the lowly Kaypro lies quietly in ambush of the complacent programmer. For this reason it is an excellent object lesson in humility, poignantly illustrating the programming maxim, "Assume Nothing!"

The Kaypro's Interrupt Structure

The Kaypro contains a Z80 microprocessor and a Z80SIO UART. In Chapter 7 we learned how both CPU and an interrupting peripheral cooperate to form a pointer to the interrupt handler. This address formation is illustrated in Figure 7-12. Here the CPU and Z80SIO supplied the MSB and LSB, respectively, of the address of a vector table. When an interrupt occurs, the Z80 performs an indirect (function pointer) call of the address pointed to by the vector. In its most basic mode, the Z80SIO's portion of the address is always the same. In this mode, it is the interrupt handler's duty to discover the source of the interrupt and provide the appropriate service. In the other mode, the Z80SIO automatically modifies its portion of the address based upon the source of the interrupt. In this scheme, the base address supplied to the Z80SIO must be the beginning of a table of vectors corresponding to each interrupt.

Figure 20-10   Interrupt vector formation on a Z80 system.

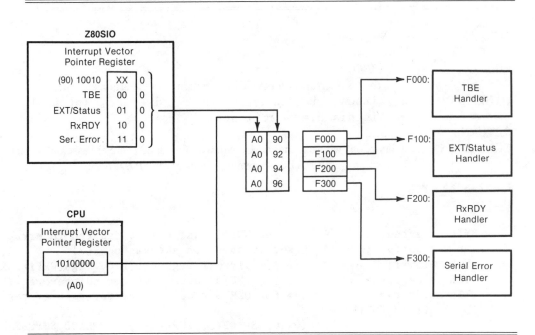

Unlike the IBM PC, where the vector table is part of and supported by the system, the vector table must be supplied by the program.

The '_intron' Function for the Kaypro

As with the IBM PC, our strategy will be to construct an assembly-language interrupt service routine whose primary task is to call `irxrdy`, the level-3 RxRDY handler given earlier in Figure 20-7.

Before we begin writing `_intron` and `_introff`, let us compose a checklist of what is required to activate RxRDY on the Kaypro.

1. Create a vector table containing the addresses of the interrupt handler.
2. Program the Z80SIO with the LSB of the address of the vector table.
3. Clear any interrupts pending on the Z80SIO.
4. Enable the desired UART interrupts and select automatic vector modification.
5. Program the CPU with the MSB of the address of the vector table.

As was our strategy for the IBM PC, we must also create an assembly language ''shell'' to protect the call to the level-3 function `irxrdy`. Because we cannot allow interrupts to occur during the time we are preparing for them, we also require the two simple assembly-language functions `__intenable` and `__intdisable`. In addition, we will create dummy assembly-language functions for the other kinds of interrupts: TBE, RS-232, and serialization errors. We will save these chores until the end of this section. Figure 20-11 shows the code for the Kaypro version of `_intron`.

Figure 20-11   The Kaypro version of `_intron`.

```
FUNCTION NAME:   _intron
LEVEL:           0
LIBRARY:         KAYPRO.C
DESCRIPTION:     Activates interrupts for the COM port named in the argument list.
OTHER MODULES:   __itbeA,__irs232A, __irxrdyA, __iserrA, __intenable,
                 __intdisable, __activate
RETURNS:         void
COMMENTS:        Functions whose names begin with a double underscore are assembly-language
                 functions. SUPPLIED is a mainfest constant in SIODEF.H.
```

```c
#define SP_OFFB 3
static struct
    {
    BYTE    iwanted;      /* byte for WR[1] that select desired interrupts    */
    int     chboffset;    /* offset of ch.B for access to WR[2]               */
    BYTE    oldwrl;       /* save for virtual register 1 (v_regA[WR1][USR[)   */
    BYTE    oldcpuvec;    /* save for CPU's current vector pointer register    */
    BYTE    oldsiovec;    /* save for UARTS's current vector pointer register */
    } _ilist[MAX_PORTS] = {
                      {0x1C, SP_OFFB, SUPPLIED, SUPPLIED,SUPPLIED },
                  };

void _intron(siop, portnum)
SIO *siop;
int portnum;
```

Figure 20-11 cont.   The Kaypro version of _intron.

```
{
        extern void __itbeA(),__irs232A(), __irxrdyA(), __iserrA();
        BYTE uartvec, cpuvec;          /* respective halves of the vector pointer */
        static BYTE ivtable[17];       /* vector table expressed as bytes          */
        void (**ivtp)();               /* pointer to start of vector table         */
/* STEP 1:  make vector table that begins at an even address  */
        if( (unsigned)ivtable % 2)                 /* if table is odd        */
            ivtp = (void (**)()) &ivtable[1];      /* move one byte down     */
            else
            ivtp = (void (**)()) &ivtable[0];
        /* initialize the vector table with the assembly-language functions */
        ivtp[0] = NIL;                             /* 4 nil vectors for ch b        */
        ivtp[1] = NIL;
        ivtp[2] = NIL;
        ivtp[3] = NIL;
        ivtp[4] = __itbeA;                         /* dummy */
        ivtp[5] = __irs232A;                       /* dummy */
        ivtp[6] = __irxrdyA;       /* real: eventually calls C function _irxrdyA */
        ivtp[7] = __iserrA;        /* dummy */
        ivtp = &ivtp[6]; /* no modified vectors, so use rxrdy handler as vector */
/* STEP 2: program LSB of vector table pointer into Z80SIO */
        uartvec = (int)ivtp & 0x00ff;
        siop->status_off = _ilist[portnum].chboffset;      /* WR2 is in ch B only */
        _ilist[portnum].oldsiovec = regread(siop, WR2);  /* save current vector */
        __intdisable();                            /* -- turn interrupts off -- */
        regwrite(siop, WR2, uartvec);              /* install new uart vector   */
        siop->status_off = SP_OFF;                 /* now address ch A again    */
/* Step 3: Clear any pending interrupts */
        regwrite(siop, 0, 0x10);                   /* clear "Ext./Status interrupts */
        regwrite(siop, 0, 0x28);                       /* clear TxRdy interrupts    */
        regwrite(siop, 0, 0x30);                   /* clear Serial error interrupts */
        s_rcv(siop); s_rcv(siop); s_rcv(siop);         /* clear rcv buffers         */
/* Step 4: Enable UART interrupts */
        _ilist[portnum].oldwrl = v_regA[WR1][VIR]; /* save virtual regl         */
        v_regA[WR1][VIR] &= ~( _ilist[portnum].iwanted);   /* reset virtual regl */
        v_regA[WR1][VIR] |= _ilist[portnum].iwanted;   /* apply intrupt mask    */
        regwrite(siop, WR1, v_regA[WR1][VIR]);     /* update Z80SIO's WR1       */
/* Step 5: program CPU with MSB of vector pointer, set interrupt mode          */
        cpuvec  = ((int)ivtp & 0xff00) >> 8;       /* CPU gets msg              */
        _ilist[portnum].oldcpuvec = __activate(cpuvec);
        __intenable();                             /* -- turn interrupts back on -- */
}
```

An Explanation of the Kaypro '_intron'   Like _intron for the IBM PC, the Kaypro version gathers all variables required for configuration into an *ad hoc* structure, then declares an array of these structures, MAX_PORTS in length. This may seem to be an absurd way to proceed considering that there is only one single port on the Kaypro 4. Other computers in the Kaypro family support as many as three ports, so taking a slightly broader approach may pay dividends later. We will explain the contents as we go along.

Two important facts greatly influence the design of _intron. First, the CPU forces bit 0 of the vector pointer to 0. This means that the vector table must begin on an even address. Second, the Kaypro uses channel A of the Z80SIO for the serial port, while the Vector register (WR[2]) is addressable only in channel B.

Step 1: Creating the Vector Table

The declaration of the vector table in C is theoretically simple:

```
void (*ivtable[])();     /* an array of pointer to void functions */
```

In practice, however, this is not possible because of the requirement that the vector table begin on an *even* address. If we declare the vector table as an array of function pointers, however, we cannot guarantee this alignment. Instead we declare two objects: the vector table ivtable, an array of BYTE with two elements for each vector, plus one; and ivtp, a *pointer* to an array of void function pointers. If the array happens to begin on an even boundary, ivtp is assigned (with the appropriate cast) to the address of its initial element; otherwise, it is assigned to its second element. Since the addresses of consecutive elements in a BYTE array differ by only one, the pointer variable ivtp contains an even address.

The vectors for the Z80SIO's channel B occupy elements 0−3 of the table and the channel A vectors elements 4−7. Indexing from ivtp, then, the first four elements of the vector table get NIL pointers while the next four get the addresses of the four (as yet unwritten) interrupt handlers.

Step 2: Installing the Vector in the Z80SIO

Since the Kaypro's serial port is channel A, we can get at the Interrupt Vector register (WR[2]) only if we know the address of the Control/Status port of channel B (located at uart_base + 3). By temporarily substituting the offset of channel B for the SIO member status_off, calls to regread and regwrite are directed to channel B instead of channel A:

```
siop->status_off = _ilist[portnum].chboffset;
```

where chboffset is an _ilist structure member initialized with the constant 3 (SP_OFFB).

Now addressing channel B in the Z80SIO, we first store the current vector in the _ilist structure array; the variable uartvec, which holds the low-order portion of the vector table address, is written into the UART. After this configuration is complete, the status_off member of the SIO is restored to channel A.

Step 3: Clear Any Pending Interrupts

Before we enable the desired interrupts, we "clear" any pending interrupts by perfunctorily performing the prescribed action. TBE, RS-232, and error interrupts are cleared with WR[0] commands, while RxRDY interrupts are cleared by reading the UART's data port.

Step 4: Enable UART Interrupts

It is now time to enable Z80SIO interrupts in WR[1]. As always, before changing a register we save it for later restoration. Because Z80SIO registers—except for register 2—are write-only, this must be accomplished though *virtual* register 1. (The virtual UART was developed in Chapters 12 and 13.) After saving the virtual register, the appropriate mask is applied and the new value is written to both the physical UART WR[1] and its virtual counterpart. The mask chosen, 1C, enables RxRDY interrupts *and* selects automatic vector modification through the vector table just constructed.

Step 5: Configure the CPU

The final step is to configure the CPU for interrupts. This is accomplished by the assembly-language function `__activate`, which supplies the CPU with the MSB of the address of the vector table. The `__activate` function also performs several other low-level tasks, one of which is to return the CPU's current Vector Pointer register for saving in `_ilist` for later restoration. With all elements in place to support interrupts, the tiny assembly-language function `__intenable` is called to enable Z80 CPU interrupts.

Assembly-Language Functions for the Kaypro

The assembly functions for the Kaypro are assembled with Aztec's assembler, which does not accept Z80 mnemonics. Since several of the instructions are unique to the Z80, they are represented with in-line defined bytes in Figure 20-12. The corresponding Z80 mnemonics are given in the commentary.

Figure 20-12 Assembly-language functions for the Kaypro.

```
FUNCTION NAME:   __alisrA
LIBRARY:         CPM80.LIB
DESCRIPTION:     Assembly-language interrupt handler for device 0 (typeAsio).
RETURNS:         void
SYNTAX FROM C:   Not called from C
COMMENTS:        Code shown is in 8080 assembler. Z80 codes are expressed with in-line defined bytes,
                 with Z80 mnemonics in comments. Line numbers are for reference only.
```

```
STACKSIZ   EQU 128
           PUBLIC    __irxrdyA_, __itbeA_,__irs232A_,__iserrA_, __irxrdyA_
           EXTRN     _irxrdy_, typeAsio_

           DS  STACKSIZ                  ; DS = "define space"
newstack:  DW  0
oldstack:  DW  0


BITPORT    EQU  1CH

5     __irxrdyA_:                        ; real handler for RxRDY interrupts
10        di                             ; lock out further interrupts
15        push psw                       ; save accum
20        in   BITPORT                   ; read bank-switch port
25        push psw                       ; save it on stack
30        ani  7fH                       ; bit7  0 = ram; 1 = ram + rom
35        out  BITPORT                   ;
```

Figure 20-12 cont. Assembly-language functions for the Kaypro.

```
40              push h              ; this goes on current stack
45              lxi   h,0           ; now switch to local stack
50              dad   sp            ;        -- add stack to hl
55              shld oldstack       ;        -- store
60              lxi   sp,newstack   ;        -- local stack now in effect
65              push psw
70              push b
75              push d
80        ;     DW 0E5DDH           ; PUSH IX
85        ;     DW 0E5FDH           ; PUSH IY
90              lxi   h, typeAsio_  ; place sio's address on stack
95              push h
100             call _irxrdy_       ; call handler written in C
105             pop   h             ; clear sio's address from stack
110       ;     DW 0E1FDH           ; POP IY
115       ;     DW 0E1DDH           ; POP IX
120             pop   d
125             pop   b
130             lhld oldstack       ; get previous stack in hl
135             sphl                ; exchange it with stack pointer
140             pop   h
145             pop   psw           ; get bank switcher off stack
150             out   BITPORT
155             pop   psw           ; now pop accumulator
160             ei                  ; enable interrupts
165             DW    04DEDH        ; (RETI) return from interrupt
        ;;dummy functions for  TBE, RS-232, and Serialization Error interrutps
PORT1       EQU   4

__itbeA_:
    push psw
    mvi   a,28H                     ; command: clear TxRdy interrupts
    out   PORT1
    pop   psw
    DW    04dedH                    ; (RETI) return from interrupt
_irs232A_:
    push psw
    mvi   a,10H                     ; command: clear Ext./Status interrupts
    out   PORT1
    pop   psw
    DW    04dedH                    ; (RETI) return from interrupt
__iserrA_ :
    push psw
    mvi   a,30H                     ; command: clear Serial error interrupts
    out   PORT1
    pop   psw
    DW    04dedH                    ; (RETI) return from interrupt
```

An Explanation of the Assembler Functions   Aside from using the more confining 8080 instruction set, `__alisrA` is functionally identical to its IBM PC counterpart—the state of the CPU is preserved across the call to `_irxrdy`. In addition, "clearing" functions are given for the three other interrupt types.

The Kaypro's interrupt handler must address one very important aspect in the system's design—bank switching. In case you have never encountered bank switching, it is a scheme whereby a memory-poor system such as CP/M, which is limited to 64K, keeps most of its operating system and other system-level code in ROM. The catch here is that the ROM addresses duplicate *ordinary RAM addresses*. At any instant, the bank—RAM or ROM—that occupies the address space is determined by a "hot bit" in RAM or, in this case, an I/O port.

During system calls, the system switches in the ROM bank for the duration, then switches back to ordinary RAM upon exit. If an interrupt occurs while the ROM bank is engaged (that is, when the interrupt vector points to a ROM routine instead of `__alisrA`), the results are predictably fatal. Since only the Kaypro's lower 32K (8000H) of memory is bank switched, we can escape this dilemma by making certain that all interrupt handlers reside above 8000H in the executable file. Typically, this is accomplished in one of five ways, listed in increasing order of difficulty:

1. In programs of average size, mentioning the handler module *last* on the linker's command line places it highest in the executable file's code segment, perhaps above 8000H. This is perfectly satisfactory; when linking *TERM* in this manner, for example, the handlers reside at a safe 9500H.

2. On smaller programs, use the linker's option that forces the entire code segment higher in the executable file. The Aztec linker's "− c" option does this.

3. Use a relocating assembler and linker to place the handlers safely.

4. Use an overlay manager such as Aztec's.

5. During initialization, move the handlers into high memory (just under the resident CP/M code), then patch in new addresses.

Just organizing memory so that the interrupt handler resides above 8000H is not the full story. Remember, when the lower bank is engaged, much of C's data may be replaced with ROM's. Memory reads return garbage and writes fall quietly on read-only ears. It is the interrupt handler's responsibility, therefore, to make certain that the RAM bank is engaged during calls (lines 15−35), and upon exit to restore the bank that was in effect upon entry (lines 145−155). As you can see, programming in a phone-booth requires considerable ingenuity.

The '_introff' Function for the Kaypro

After wrestling with bank switching, multi-channel UARTs, and the like, `_introff` in Figure 20-13 is a self-explanatory, serene little function requiring no commentary.

Figure 20-13   The `_introff` function for the Kaypro.

FUNCTION NAME:	`_introff`
LEVEL:	0
LIBRARY:	*KAYPRO.C*
DESCRIPTION:	Deactivates system and UART interrupts for the port specified.

Figure 20-13 cont. The `_introff` function for the Kaypro.

OTHER MODULES: `__regwrite` (level-1), `__activate`
RETURNS: `void`
COMMENTS: Values are restored from the `_ilist` structure array.

```
void _introff(siop, portnum)
SIO *siop;
int portnum;
{
    v_regA[WR1][VIR] =_ilist[portnum].oldwrl;      /* restore virtual regl */
    regwrite (siop, WR1, v_regA[WR1][VIR]);        /*    "      Z80SIO     */
    siop->status_off = _ilist[portnum].chboffset;  /* WR2 only in ch B     */
    regwrite(siop, WR2, _ilist[portnum].oldsiovec); /*   Z80SIO's vector   */
    siop->status_off = SP_OFF;                     /* restore current offset */
    __activate(_ilist[portnum].oldcpuvec);         /*    "      CPU's vector */
}
```

Finally, Figure 12-14 gives the auxiliary assembler functions required by `_intron` and `_introff`.

Figure 20-14 Auxiliary functions to support interrupts on the Kaypro.

FUNCTION NAME: `__activate`, `__intenable`, `__intdisable`
LIBRARY: *CPM80.LIB*
DESCRIPTION: Auxiliary functions to support interrupts; `__activate` sets the Z80's Vector Pointer register and returns its previous value.
RETURNS: `__activate: unsigned short int:` Z80's vector pointer before registering the call.
SYNTAX FROM C: `oldvec = __activate(newvec);`
                `unsigned short int: oldvec;`
                `unsigned short int: newvec;`
COMMENTS: Code shown is in 8080 assembler. Z80 codes are expressed with in-line defined bytes, with Z80 mnemonics in comments.

```
PUBLIC    __intenable_, __intdisable_, __activate_

__intenable_:                       ; for calling from C
    ei
    ret

__intdisable_:
    di
    ret

__activate_:
    lxi  h, 2                       ; set up argument frame pointer
    dad  sp
    mov  c,m                        ; get MSB of interrupt vector from stack
```

Figure 20-14 cont. Auxiliary functions to support interrupts on the Kaypro.

```
push  b                      ; save it
DW    57EDh                  ; (LD A, I) get current interrupt vector
mov   b,a                    ; save in b for return
mov   a,c                    ; restore MSB of new vector
DW    47EDh                  ; (LD I,A) store MSB of vector
DW    5EEDh                  ; (IM 2) set interrupt mode 2
lxi   h,0                    ; clear h for return
mov   l,b                    ; return current interrupt vector in hl
pop   b
ret
```

An Explanation of the Auxiliary Assembler Functions   The first two functions simply issue the CPU command to turn interrupts on and off. The __activate function fetches the Z80's portion of the vector pointer from the stack, then writes it to the Z80's Interrupt Vector Pointer register (the I register). The Z80 interrupt mode (as opposed to the 8080 mode) is selected and the function returns the original contents of the I register.

Implementing other Interrupts

Because of space limitations, interrupt functions are not given to support transmitter, RS-232, and serialization errors. Nevertheless, a few tips and guidelines are in order, particularly concerning transmitter interrupts, which are seldom discussed.

Kick-Starting Transmitter Interrupts

In Chapter 7 we noted that a transmitter interrupt is generated by the transmitter buffer *becoming empty*—that is, the interrupt is *edge-triggered* by the change in the buffer's condition. We noted in passing that the transmitter interrupt handler must be smart enough to disable further interrupts after the last character has been transmitted. We have not yet discussed the companion problem of starting transmitter interrupts in the first place. The problem is simple: since interrupts are triggered after a byte has been transmitted, how do we generate the *initial* interrupt to get the process started.

The most obvious way to start transmitter interrupts is to write a fill byte such as NUL or DEL to the SIO. The flaw with this method is that the receiver must recognize and discard the unwanted byte in the data stream. A better solution lies in the clever design of the transmitter interrupt handler itself. Communication between the main program and the interrupt handler usually takes place through a *transmit queue*,[3] an array of pointers to buffers and, of course, the

---

[3]The queue is usually an array of structures:

```
struct {
    BYTE *xbuffp;             /* pointer to a buffer to send */
    int  xbuffcnt;            /* number of bytes in buffer   */
    } xqueue[MAX_XMITS];      /* the "transmit queue"        */
```

number of bytes in them. To transmit a buffer, the main program inserts the buffer's address and byte count in the queue. When the handler has sent all bytes from a given buffer, it checks to see if there are any more buffers in the queue. If so, it proceeds as before; if not, the handler disables transmitter interrupts and sets a "queue empty" flag for the calling program (the flag must be a new SIO member). When another buffer is added to the queue, the disabled transmitter interrupts must be reenabled, then "kick-started" to generate the first TBE condition.

Transmitter queue management can easily be performed in a level-3 function. If, when adding a buffer to the queue, this function discovers that the queue is currently empty, it places a pointer to the *second* byte in the queue and outputs the first byte itself. Manually transmitting the first byte in the buffer thus generates the initial TBE condition required.

RS-232 Interrupts

Implementation of RS-232 interrupts is quite simple. First, for each input supported, add a new variable to the SIO. When an interrupt occurs, the handler stores the current state of the interrupting RS-232 input in the SIO. For each input supported, also write a simple routine to return the state of that SIO. The function for DCD, for example, is

```
int i_isdcd(siop)
SIO *siop;
{
        return (siop->dcdstate);

}
```

where dcdstate is the name of the SIO variable.

If you recall, the vin232_ structure in Chapter 12 contains a *pointer* to a function that fetches the status of that RS-232 input. By default, each of the structures is initialized to point to a routine that polls the RS-232 status register.

```
struct vin232_pin8A =
        {
        6,
        DCDMASK,
        SUPPLIED,
        _vstat232
        };
```

To support RS-232 interrupts, simply swap this pointer when opening the SIO:

```
siop->dcd->read232 = i_isdcd;
```

Calls to isdcd now return the contents of the SIO's dcdstate member, which is serviced by interrupts.

Serialization Error Interrupts

Some readers may have been puzzled by the conspicuous absence of functions to report serialization errors. These were omitted because, in real life, they are not particularly useful. If you find a need for such a library, however, the procedure *exactly* duplicates the manner in which RS-232 input status is supported. First, create new vin232_ structure pointers in the SIO for framing, parity, overrun, underrun, and BREAK conditions. Then write the complementary functions (both polled and interrupt) to return the state of the appropriate bits.

Conclusion

In the introduction to this chapter, our argument against speed as a consideration in choosing between interrupt and polled I/O was not meant to disparage the cosmic benefits of speed. Indeed, if computers were fast enough, interrupt I/O wouldn't be necessary. Still, granted the premise that interrupt I/O sometimes is slower than polling, there is no reason not to write the fastest interrupt I/O possible. Let's examine some of the steps for speeding up the functions in this chapter.

Stylistic Modifications

The code throughout this book has been written more with an eye to clarity than to execution speed or size. A modicum of speed improvement can therefore be achieved simply by compressing some of the expanded statements. In Figure 20-7, for example, the lines

```
index = (unsigned)inport(siop->uart_base + INT_ID);
index >>= 1;
(*isr[index])(siop);
```

can be replaced with

```
(*isr[inport(siop->uart_base + INT_ID) >> 1])(siop);
```

However, for the sake of others who follow, leave the more expansive version in the commentary.

Design Modifications

Speed performance can be improved somewhat by giving up the notion of level-3 handlers—a very great sacrifice. For example, changing the following line in ixrdy,

```
*siop->iheadp++ = s_rcv(siop);
```

to

```
*siop->iheadp++ = inport(siop->uart_base);
```

eliminates several levels of indirection for each received byte.

Rewriting in Assembler

The technique for optimizing the code of early micro compilers was always the same—rewrite it in assembler. The code was, well, not very tight, to be polite. Today's compilers, however, are good assembly-language programmers. The code for the *entire* suite of interrupt handler functions for the IBM PC was originally coded in assembler, but something startling happened: the compiler's assembly-language output was very similar to the hand-coded version. Athough a touch-up here and there would have improved the compiler code's efficiency, the improvement would have been slight and would not have justified sacrificing the portability of C.

Do not mistake this anecdote for a recommendation to blindly accept the assembler output from your compiler. In fact, this approach works only if you are thinking along the correct lines in C in the first place. To understand what "correct" means, compare your compiler's assembler output for the level-1 function i_admin for the IBM PC (in Figure 20-7) and its output for this version:

```
void s_iadmin(siop)
SIO *siop;
{
    unsigned index;
    index = (unsigned)inport(siop->uart_base + INT_ID);
    switch (index >>= 1)
        {
        case 0:
            irs232(siop);
            break;
        case 1:
            itbe(siop);
            break;
        case 2:
            irxrdy(siop);
            break;
        case 3:
            iserr(siop);
            break;
        }
}
```

Unless your compiler is very clever indeed, the code to call the handlers through a case table will be more ponderous than the code to implement an array of function pointers.

III

Appendixes

A

Console I/O

The programming section of this book centers about the composition and step-by-step enhancement of a dumb terminal program *TERM*. This appendix contains the console functions required for this program. Instructions for adding these functions to your libraries are given at the end of this appendix.

Authors of C libraries often slavishly follow the examples in the UNIX system. It is all the more surprising, then, that more haven't imitated UNIX's I/O system call, `ioctl`, which allows the programmer almost complete control of the console device driver. This is one of the best ideas in UNIX and merits some discussion, if for no other reason than to illuminate the shortcomings of console handling in microcomputer C libraries.

The operation of the `ioctl` call is straightforward, at least in principle: the system maintains for every console device a structure describing the parameters of the device. The device driver then formats I/O according to the flags (members) in this structure. In UNIX, this structure is quite large—fifty-odd flags govern every imaginable aspect of device I/O: baud rate, data format, newline conversion, flow control, and echo, as well as the characters used for erase, backspace, and line kill.[1]

In UNIX's "stream" I/O concept, which is adopted by every microcomputer C compiler, keyboard characters fetched by functions such as `getchar` are not returned to the calling program one-by-one as they are typed, but are stored in a buffer and returned all at once when a newline is typed. Despite the flexibility and power of this concept, it is important that any console driver also provide a mode that is unbuffered and in which no processing is performed on the characters. In UNIX this is called "raw" mode: the console input is passed along unscathed. If *"cbreak"* mode is also selected, internal I/O buffering is defeated so that each character is returned as soon as it is typed. In other words, choosing raw mode plus cbreak mode overrides all other options and features.

To their everlasting credit, the Aztec compilers actually offer an excellent `ioctl` function fashioned after UNIX. Their implementation is, of course, much more modest than the UNIX version. While the intention to provide a portable console I/O handler is admirable, the Aztec implementation, like that of every microcomputer compiler, is inadequate for our purposes for two reasons. First, because of its integration into the UNIX I/O concept, console I/O is painfully slow.

---

[1] For an excellent discussion of this topic, see Rochkind, Mark J. *Advanced UNIX Programming*, 82-89, Prentice-Hall, 1985.

Second, and most deadly, there is no console "status" function to ascertain if a character has been typed.[2]

These two deficiencies make it impossible to write the program undertaken in this book, *TERM*, whose basic structure depends upon the ability to discover if data is available either from the keyboard or from the serial port. *TERM* requires only two level-3 console functions: one that waits for a keypress, then returns the key (without echo); and one that does not wait for a key to be pressed, but checks the keyboard status and returns *either* the key or a "not ready" status byte. These two functions are given in Figure A-1.

Figure A-1   "Raw" C console input functions. The Lattice and Microsoft compilers are directly supported by an #ifdef preprocessor directive.

FUNCTION NAME: getch
LEVEL: 3
LIBRARY: *YOUR.LIB*
DESCRIPTION: Waits until a key is pressed, then returns it without echo.
OTHER MODULES: __keystat and __getkey low-levels.
RETURNS: int, which allows for modification to detect "special" keys.
COMMENTS: This should be a "raw" function with no character processing. Lattice and Microsoft compilers are supported via an #ifdef preprocessor directive.

```
#define NOT_READY -1
#define NO_KEY     0

#ifdef MS_LATT                          /* for Microsoft or Lattice      */
#define __keystat() kbhit()
#define __getkey() getch()
#endif


int getch()                             /* fetch keyboard char, no echo  */
{
    while (__keystat() == NO_KEY)       /* while no character is ready.... */
        ;                               /* ... wait ...                  */
    return (__getkey());                /* then return it when ready     */
}
```

FUNCTION NAME: inkey
LEVEL: 3
LIBRARY: *YOUR.LIB*
DESCRIPTION: Returns a keyboard character if available; otherwise −1.
OTHER MODULES: __keystat, __getkey
RETURNS: int: −1 if no character ready.
COMMENTS: This should be a "raw" function with no character processing. Lattice and Microsoft compilers are supported via an ifdef preprocessor directive.

---

[2]The absence of a portable keyboard status call under PC DOS is not a flaw in the design of the libraries, but in the system itself, where a read of the console device *always* waits for a character to be typed. This is not true in all micro operating systems.

Figure A-1 cont. "Raw" C console input functions. The Lattice and Microsoft compilers are directly supported by an #ifdef preprocessor directive.

```
int inkey()
{
      return ( (__keystat() == NO_KEY) ? NOT_READY : __getkey() );
}
```

An Explanation of the "Raw" Functions   These functions assume the existence of two keyboard "primitives": __keystat, which returns a non-0 only when a key has been pressed, and __getkey, which fetches the key. Notice that these names begin with *initial* double underscores—a convention used throughout this book to identify assembly-language or other low-level functions.

"Raw" Console Functions for Lattice/Microsoft Compilers

Fortunately, many compilers supply level-0 console functions in their standard libraries. The Lattice and Microsoft compilers, for example, provide similar functions named kbhit and getch. The functions in Figure A-1 support these compilers with an #ifdef preprocessor conditional compilation. If you are using one of these compilers, simply add the statement

```
#define MS_LATT
```

directly in the code, or pass the definition via the compiler's equivalent command-line switch. Be advised, however, when the level-0 functions are taken from these compilers' libraries, the resulting inkey and getch are only "semi-raw"; that is, they honor **Ctrl-Break** and **Ctrl-C,** and may process Control-Z as EOF.

Assembly-Language Console Primitives

If your compiler does not supply the two level-0 console I/O routines, or if you require *absolutely* unadorned I/O, you have to compose them using operating system calls. In CP/M and PC DOS, the system call that produces "raw" console I/O is DOS Function 6, which is outlined in Figure A-2.

Using this information, you may be able to write console primitives using your compiler's C functions that interface to the operating system. A better, and in some ways more portable, method is to write the primitives in assembly language. Figures A-3 and A-4 show the level-0 assembly-language functions for PC DOS and CP/M, respectively. Both use Function 6 of their respective systems. The *trailing* single underscores are necessary to satisfy the Aztec compiler and linker for which these functions are written; please refer to Appendix C for directions for other systems.

Figure A-2   A single DOS function for unadorned console input *and* output.

DOS FUNCTION: 6
DESCRIPTION: ''Direct'' or ''raw'' console I/O.
REGS ON ENTRY:

           AH   6
           DL   FF if call is for input or character for output

REGS ON EXIT:

           AL   *PC DOS*: On input calls, if zero flag is reset, AL contains a valid character.
                 CP/M: On input calls, AL contains a valid character or a 0 byte if no character is
                 ready.

COMMENTS: In PC DOS only, a 0 byte returned as a valid character indicates that the key was a non-ASCII or ''special'' key; a second call to Function 6 returns the code for the special key.

Figure A-3   The 8088 functions to fetch keyboard status.

FUNCTION: __keystat and __getkey
DESCRIPTION: PC DOS (8088 assembly-language) keyboard fetch and status functions.
LEVEL: 0
LIBRARY: Your compiler's standard library.
SYNTAX FROM C: status = __keystat();
                 int status;

                 c = __getkey();
                 BYTE c
COMMENTS: Under PC DOS, Function 6 returns a NUL as a special key with keycode 3. This is properly translated to 0 here so that ASCII NULs can be processed from the keyboard.

```
DIRECTIO_DOS       EQU  6              ; unadorned DOS keyboard input
DOS_NUL            EQU  3              ; DOS special code for NUL
NO_KEY             EQU  0

CODESEG SEGMENT WORD PUBLIC 'CODE'
ASSUME CS:CODESEG, DS:NOTHING

PUBLIC    __keystat_
PUBLIC    __getkey_

buff DW 0                             ; little buffer for key character

__keystat_ PROC    NEAR
        ;
        call    stdin_              ; check if char ready
        jz      noexit             ; exit if no char ready
        cmp     al,0               ; is character a special
        jne     readyexit          ; no, ordinary ascii character,put in buffer
        call    stdin_             ; yes, it's a special--read again
        cmp     al,DOS_NUL         ; is special NUL?
        jnz     noexit             ; no, return not ready
        mov     al,0               ; yes, return the NUL
```

Figure A-3 cont.   The 8088 functions to fetch keyboard status.

```
readyexit:
        mov     buff,ax                 ; put new char into buffer
        ret
noexit:
        mov     ax,NO_KEY
        ret
__keystat_   ENDP
        ;;
stdin_   PROC   NEAR
        mov     ah,DIRECTIO_DOS
        mov     dl,0FFh                 ; input request
        int     21h
        mov     ah,0                    ; null high byte
        ret
        ;
stdin_   ENDP

__getkey_   PROC    NEAR
        mov     ax,buff                 ; get character out of buffer
        ret
        ;
__getkey_   ENDP

CODESEG ENDS
END
```

Figure A-4   The 8080 (CP/M) functions to fetch keyboard status.

FUNCTION:	__keystat and __getkey
DESCRIPTION:	CP/M (8080 assembly-language) keyboard fetch and status functions.
LEVEL:	0
LIBRARY:	Your compiler's standard library.
SYNTAX FROM C:	status = __keystat();
	int status;
	c = __getkey();
	BYTE c
RETURNS:	int
COMMENTS:	Under CP/M, Function 6 returns a NUL as a special key with keycode 3. This is properly translated to 0 here so that ASCII NULs can be processed from the keyboard.

```
NO_KEY              EQU  -1

DIRECTIO_DOS        EQU  6              ; unadorned DOS keyboard input
BDOS                EQU  5
```

Figure A-4 cont.   The 8080 (CP/M) functions to fetch keyboard status.

```
DSEG
keybuff DW 0
CSEG

        PUBLIC __keystat_, __getkey_
__keystat_:
        mvi  c,DIRECTIO_DOS
        mvi  e,0ffh                   ; request for console input
        call BDOS
        ora  a                        ; set zero flag if AL = 0
        jnz  ready                    ; zero means not ready
        lxi  h,NO_KEY
        ret
   ready:
        lxi  h,0                      ; null in high-order register
        mov  l,a                      ; character into low-order register
        shld keybuff                  ; store key value in buffer
        ret

__getkey_:
        lhld  keybuff                 ; get key from buffer
        ret
END
```

An Explanation of '__keystat' and '__getkey'   Function 6 in both DOS and CP/M provides raw console input without echo, character processing, and so forth. There is a small but important difference in the way it returns a "ready" status. In CP/M, alas, Function 6 returns a 0 in AL if no character is ready. This means that an ASCII NUL cannot be returned by this function. In DOS, however, a character is ready in AL if the zero flag is reset after the function call. A 0 byte returned in AL means that a "special" (Home, F1, etc.) key has been pressed. The code for the *exact* special key can be learned by calling Function 6 again. Under this scheme, the code for an ASCII NUL character is 3. The code in Figure A-3 translates this special code for a NUL into a 0 byte. Other specials are returned as "not ready."

The assembly-language functions given in Figures A-3 and A-4 can be assembled and linked without modification in the Aztec system. Appendix C provides the guidelines for adapting these assembly-language routines to other compilers. If you are not immediately successful, if you do not feel up to the task, or if you are just uninterested in this aspect of computer programming, the companion disks offered in this book contain ready-to-link assembly-language libraries for popular PC DOS compilers.

Building Console Libraries

The C console functions in Figure A-1 should be placed in your private library, which we refer to under the hypothetical name, *YOUR.LIB*. If you are using either PC DOS or CP/M, supply the level-0 functions from your compiler's library or select the appropriate assembly-language primitives from Figures A-3 or A-4.

If you are using a different operating system, you will have to compose your own level-0 console functions. Luckily, console I/O is supported in much the same way on all micro operating systems, so the structures of the functions for other systems are likely to mirror those in Figures A-3 and A-4. The functions for CP/M-86, for example, are identical to those for CP/M-80 except, of course, they must be written in 8086 assembler.

If you create your own functions for __keystat and __getkey (either assembly-language or in C), add them to your compiler's standard C library. In the unlikely event that its library cannot be modified, you will have to build a separate console library and remember to include it in every linkage of the *TERM* program.

If you are using UNIX or ZENIX, use `ioctl` to place the console driver in raw and cbreak modes, then write __keystat and __getkey in C using `read` calls.

B

Incidental Functions

This appendix contains C functions that, though necessary to compile and run the software developed in this book, have nothing to do with asynchronous serial programming. If your C compiler supplies similar functions, and many do, you will be able to utilize them by modifying the calling syntax for the functions presented here. In any case, these functions are all useful in their own right and you will doubtless find use for them in many areas. The functions are:

bigbuff.c — Allocates very large buffer.

putbin.c — Prints integer in binary.

rfopen.c — Opens a stream for reading—gets name from user.

substr.c — Discovers if one string is a substring of another.

wfopen.c — Opens a stream for writing—gets name from user.

The headers for these functions show them as residing in your private library, here given the hypothetical name of *YOUR.LIB*. Don't forget to include the name of this library in every linkage.

Figure B-1 The bigbuff function.

FUNCTION NAME:	bigbuff
LEVEL:	3
LIBRARY:	*YOUR.LIB*
DESCRIPTION:	Allocates large buffer.
OTHER MODULES:	None
RETURNS:	char *: the address of the allocated buffer or NIL if no memory is available.
COMMENTS:	Allocates nblks of memory, in blksize chunks. The headroom argument is the number of blksize chunks to return to the system for local use. The actual number of blocks allocated is returned to the caller via the pointer numblkp.

```
#include  "stdio.h"
#include  "errno.h"

char *bigbuff(blksize, headroom, numblkp)
unsigned blksize;                          /* block size for allocation      */
unsigned headroom;                         /* number of blocks NOT to allocate */
unsigned *numblkp;                         /* pointer caller's count variable */
```

595

Figure B-1 cont.   The `bigbuff` function.

```
{
    extern char *malloc();
    char *p;
    unsigned nblks = 1;
    while ( (p = malloc(nblks * blksize)) != NIL)      /* call until failure */
        {
        free(p);                                 /* release it            */
        ++nblks;                                 /* ask for more next time */
        }
    if (headroom >= --nblks)                      /* not enough memory     */
        {
        nblks = 0;
        return (NIL);
        }
    nblks -= headroom;                            /* adjust for headroom   */
    *numblkp = nblks;                             /* pass back to caller   */
    return (malloc(nblks * blksize));             /* allocate & return the pointer */
}
```

An Explanation of 'bigbuff'   Situations frequently arise when you need all the heap available. Some systems have functions with names like `heapleft` or `corenow` to let you know how much to allocate:

```
char  *buff,  *malloc();
buff = malloc(heapleft());
```

Other systems maintain global pointers that can be subtracted to ascertain the amount of heap space remaining.

The `bigbuff` function is for systems where none of these methods is available. It returns a pointer to the allocated heap space requested or NIL if the request cannot be fulfilled. Its arguments provide great flexibility in the way in which the storage is allocated:

`blksize`   This enables allocation of storage in multiples of aggregate data objects.

`headroom`   Exhausting the heap is often dangerous because there is no storage left for subsequent function calls. Usually, then, we need to leave some storage for the system. This is the number of `blksize` units to leave on the heap; that is, the number of units *not* to allocate.

`numblkp`   Since the function must return a pointer to the storage actually allocated, it returns the *number of blocks* successfully allocated in the variables whose address is supplied in the argument list.

Here is an example of how to allocate a buffer for an array of "xyz" structures:

```
struct xyz
    {
    long a;
    char b;
    int  c[25];
    };

unsigned numstructs;
struct xyz *buffp;
buffp = bigbuff(sizeof(struct xyz),  10,  &numstructs);
if (buffp == NIL)
        exit();
```

This call asks for storage to hold the maximum number of xyz structures, minus 10. After the call, buffp contains a pointer to the storage (or NIL) and numstructs contains how many xyz structures the storage will hold.

Figure B-2 The putbin function.

FUNCTION NAME: putbin
LEVEL: 3
LIBRARY: *YOUR.LIB*
DESCRIPTION: Displays a 16-bit integer in binary.
RETURNS: void
COMMENTS: Newline at the end is to accommodate the program in Figure 19-3.

```
void putbin(data)
unsigned short data;                            /* 16 bit int */
{
    unsigned short shifter = 0x8000;
    for (; shifter > 0; shifter >>= 1)
        putchar((data &shifter) ? '1' : '0');
    putchar('\n');
}
```

Figure B-3 The rfopen function.

FUNCTION NAME: rfopen
LEVEL: 3
LIBRARY: *YOUR.LIB*
DESCRIPTION: Continually prompts for filename until a file is opened for reading or the user aborts.
OTHER MODULES: None
RETURNS: FILE *: the FILE pointer or NIL if the open is unsuccessful.
COMMENTS: The filename buffer passed must be long enough to hold the largest valid system name
                (79 bytes in PC DOS , 14 in CP/M).

Figure B-3 cont. The rfopen function.

```
#include  "stdio.h"
#include  "errno.h"

FILE *rfopen(promptstr, fnbuff)
char *promptstr;                            /* user prompt string      */
char *fnbuff;                               /* file name buffer        */
{
extern int errno;
extern FILE *fopen();
    FILE *rfp;
    int c;
    int errflag = 0;
    do    {
        printf("\n%s: ",promptstr);
        gets(fnbuff);
        if (strcmp(fnbuff,"") == 0)          /* user typed CR to exit  */
            return (NIL);
        if ( (rfp = fopen(fnbuff, "r")) == NIL)       /* open failure  */
            if (errno == ENOENT)
                printf("%s not found.", fnbuff);
            else
                printf("\nOpen error on %s.", fnbuff);  /* error message */
    } while (rfp == NIL);                    /* repeat until open succeeds */
    return (rfp);
}
```

An Explanation of 'rfopen'   This function simplifies the common process of querying the user for a filename, opening it, and returning a pointer to it. The prompt to issue to the user is passed in the argument list. Also passed is the location of a filename buffer into which the filename should be placed. It is the caller's responsibility to make certain that this buffer is large enough to accommodate the maximum filename possible on the system. For more protection, the length of the buffer should be passed in the argument list and enforced in rfopen.

The design of rfopen is fairly straightforward. The prompt is issued and the user's response is captured by gets into the filename buffer. An "empty" filename buffer is taken as a signal to terminate the function; otherwise fopen is called repeatedly until the file is successfully opened.

Figure B-4   The substr function.

FUNCTION NAME: substr
LEVEL: 3
LIBRARY: *YOUR.LIB*
DESCRIPTION: Ascertains if one string is a substring of the other.
OTHER MODULES: index (strchr on some compilers)

Figure B-4 cont.   The `substr` function.

RETURNS: char *: pointer to the first character of `minstr` within `majstr`; otherwise, NIL.
COMMENTS: An ''ignore case'' mode would be useful.

```
#include "stdio.h"

char *substr(majstr, minstr)
char *majstr;                          /* big string    */
char *minstr;                          /* little string */
{
    extern char *index();
    char *gp = majstr;
    int  sublen;
    if ( (sublen = strlen(minstr)) > strlen(majstr) )
        return (NIL);                      /* substring shorter than main string */
    while ( (gp = index(gp, *minstr)) != NIL )  /* find match of first char */
        {
        if (strncmp(gp, minstr, sublen) == NUL)
            return (gp);
        ++gp;
        }
    return (NIL);
}
```

An Explanation of 'substr'   The strategy here is to find a match of the strings' first characters, then see if the entire strings match. Note that the function protects against the absurd situation where the minor string is longer than the major. If the end of the major string is reached before finding a complete match, `substr` returns NIL; otherwise it returns a pointer to the first character of the substring within the main string.

Figure B-5   The `wfopen` function.

FUNCTION NAME: wfopen
LEVEL: 3
LIBRARY: *YOUR.LIB*
DESCRIPTION: Continually prompts for the name of an output file until the file is successfully opened
               or the user aborts.
OTHER MODULES: None
RETURNS: FILE *: the FILE pointer or NIL if the open is unsuccessful.
COMMENTS: Asks permission before overwriting a pre-existing file. The filename buffer passed
               must be long enough to hold the largest valid system name (79 bytes in PC DOS,
               14 in CP/M).

Figure B-5 cont.   The wfopen function.

```
#include  "stdio.h"
#include  "errno.h"        /* maybe just "error.h" */

FILE *wfopen(promptstr, fnbuff)
char *promptstr;
char *fnbuff;
{
    FILE *wfp;
    char locbuff[10];
    for (EVER)
        {
        printf("\n%s: ",promptstr);
        gets(fnbuff);
        if (strcmp(fnbuff,"") == 0)                   /* newline typed  */
            return (NIL);
        fclose(wfp = fopen(fnbuff, "r"));/* open ( and close) it for reading*/
        if (wfp == NIL)                               /* doesn't already exist   */
            return (fopen(fnbuff, "w"));
        printf("\n%s already exists. Overwrite\007?  ", fnbuff);
        gets(locbuff);
        if (toupper(locbuff[0]) == 'Y')
            break;                                    /* ok to overwrite        */
        }
    return (fopen(fnbuff, "w"));
}
```

An Explanation of 'wfopen'   This function serves the same function as rfopen, except that it opens a file for writing, and asks permission before overwriting an existing file.

C

The PC DOS Assembly-Language Interface

Without successfully assembling the console I/O functions in Appendix A, none of the versions of *TERM* performs as intended. Likewise, the code in Chapter 20 for interrupt-driven serial I/O depends upon your assembling several simple assembly-language routines. The purpose of this appendix is to explain what steps are required to interface these assembly-language routines to your compiler. If you do not feel up to the task or if you are simply uninterested in this aspect of computer programming, the companion disks offered in this book contain ready-to-link assembly-language function libraries for most popular compilers.

There is little to discuss about the 8080 assembly language because it can be assembled on virtually any 8080 assembler. Variations occur, however, such as Digital Research's RMAC assembler forbidding the use of the underscore. Generally speaking, though, these variations are minor.

There is a wide variation among the assembly-language requirements of PC DOS compilers. This appendix deals systematically with adapting the assembly-language functions in this book to other compilers. We will approach the subject in four sections:

1. The conventions for passing data between C and assembly language

2. Adapting the assembly-language functions in Chapter 20 and in Appendix A for compilers that use the Microsoft object file format

3. Modifying the assembly-language functions from Chapter 20 and Appendix A for PC DOS compilers that support Large Memory models

4. A Large Memory Model version of the C function `outport`

Data Passing Conventions

A discussion of the conventions for passing data is really two subjects—how data is passed from the calling C function and how the called function *returns* a data value back to the caller.

Passing Data from C to Assembler

All PC DOS C compilers pass arguments by pushing them on the stack. In order to support functions with a variable number of arguments (e.g., `printf`), function call arguments are pushed onto the stack from *right to left*.

1-Byte and 2-Byte Values

Since single bytes cannot be pushed onto the stack in the Intel architecture, 8-bit objects such as `chars` are pushed onto the stack as *words* with the `char` in the least significant byte. (Intel processors store the low-order byte in lower memory than the high-order byte.) Since `chars` are promoted to `int` before passing, compilers are supposed to null the high-order byte before pushing a `char` onto the stack, but do not take this for granted. Sixteen-bit values such as `short ints` are pushed onto the stack in the same manner as `chars`; that is, with high-order byte above low-order byte.

Multi-Word Values

There is no formal rule for passing multi-word values such as `longs`. In order to take advantage of the 8086's double-register load instructions LDS and LES and to facilitate forming FAR addresses, however, compilers push the low-order word onto the stack followed by the high-order word. Although it is difficult to conceive of a credible compiler that doesn't use this passing order, be cautious.

Returning Data from Assembler to C

By definition, only a single data object may be returned from assembler to C. This simplicity makes it feasible to return 1- and 2-byte objects such as `chars` and `short ints` in *registers*, not on the stack. Since the code in this book uses no `floats` or `doubles`, they are not discussed here.

Returning 1-Byte and 2-Byte Values

Because some 8086 instructions execute faster in the AX register, all compilers I have seen return `chars` and `ints` there.

Returning Multi-Word Values

While there is essential unanimity among compilers on how to return single words of data, there is no such agreement on how to return longer data types such as `longs`. Since the `__getivec` function in Figure 20-8 returns a segment:offset address as an `unsigned` long, you must ascertain the order your compiler uses to return `longs`. Most popular compilers—including Aztec, Microsoft, Desmet, Computer Innovations, and Mark Williams—return `longs` in DX:AX (high:low). Lattice, however, returns them in AX:BX.

Adapting Assembly-Language Functions to Other Compilers

The versions of `__alisr`, `__getcs`, `__getivec`, and `__setivec` in Chapter 20 as well as `__keystat` and `__getkey` in Appendix A are written for the Aztec compiler. The conversion to compilers that use the Microsoft (Intel) Object File format is a trivial chore, however, because the Aztec assembler is a fully compatible subset of the Microsoft Assembler.

Most of the necessary modifications center about the *linkage headers*, shown here in this fragment from Figure 20-8.

```
PUBLIC __alisrA_, __getivec_, __setivec_, __getcs_
DATASEG SEGMENT WORD PUBLIC 'DATA'
     EXTRN typeAsio_:WORD
DATASEG ENDS
CODESEG SEGMENT WORD PUBLIC 'CODE'
ASSUME CS:CODESEG, DS:NOTHING
EXTRN   s_iadmin_:NEAR
        ⋮
CODESEG ENDS
```

The necessary changes can be summarized as follows:

1. EXTRN and PUBLIC naming conventions
2. Linkage headers
3. The GROUP directive
4. The ASSUME directive

EXTRN and PUBLIC Naming Conventions

So that the linker is able to match up the names in your hand-written assembly-language modules with those produced by the compiler, you must follow the internal naming conventions of your compiler. Many compilers "tag" public and external names with an underscore. The Aztec compiler, for example, *appends* the underscore, while the Microsoft compiler *prepends* it; the Lattice compiler does neither, but uses names in their natural form. *Every* instance of public and external names must be modified, including those that appear in the body of the code. Local names need not be modified.

Linkage Headers

The Aztec compiler gives its code and data segments the names CODESEG and DATASEG. The names of these segments vary from one compiler to another. Most compilers document these carefully, but they are sometimes incorrect. The most reliable method for discovering the correct linkage headers is to compile this simple C program and examine its assembly-language output:

```
main()
{
     printf("Hello, world");
}
```

Examining the ASM file produced by the Microsoft C compiler (version 4.0), for example, reveals the information:

```
_TEXT    SEGMENT  BYTE PUBLIC 'CODE'
_DATA    SEGMENT  WORD PUBLIC 'DATA'
```

That is, the Microsoft compiler names its code and data segments _TEXT and _DATA, respectively. When you have discovered your compiler's segment names, exchange them for the CODESEG and DATASEG shown for the Aztec compiler. Don't forget to change the segment names preceding the ENDS statements.

The GROUP Directive

Many compilers partition their data into several separate segments, then bind them together with a GROUP directive. If your compiler supports GROUPs (the Aztec compiler does not), two additions are required to Figure 20-8. First, declare the GROUP's name as in this example from the the Microsoft compiler's assembly-language output:

```
DGROUP   GROUP     CONST,    _BSS,     _DATA
```

which groups the three segments CONST, _BSS, and _DATA into a single unit that can be addressed as "DGROUP." Place your GROUP directive immediately above the SEGMENT directive.

If your compiler uses groups, two changes to the actual code are required: the operands to OFFSET and SEG operators must be preceded by a *GROUP override operator*. Only three lines are affected:

```
25          mov    sp, OFFSET newstack
75          mov    ax, OFFSET typeAsio_
85          mov    ax, SEG    typeAsio_
```

For example, if your complier uses a group named "DGROUP", these lines would be rewritten:

```
25          mov    sp, OFFSET DGROUP:newstack
75          mov    ax, OFFSET DGROUP:typeAsio_
85          mov    ax, SEG    DGROUP:typeAsio_
```

The ASSUME Directive

Examining the Microsoft compiler's assembly-language output again, we find the following directives:

```
ASSUME CS: _TEXT, DS: DGROUP, SS: DGROUP, ES: DGROUP
```

Because none of the PC DOS assembler routines in this book declares data in the data segment, only the

```
ASSUME    CS: _TEXT
```

portion of this directive is needed. Regardless of your compiler, retain the line

```
ASSUME DS:NOTHING
```

as shown in Figure 20-8. Do **not** use your compiler's DS:ASSUME for the modules in this book.[1] In summary, let's look at the entire linkage header for the Microsoft assembler.

```
PUBLIC ___alisrA, ___getivec, ___setivec, ___getcs
DGROUP  GROUP  CONST, _BSS, _DATA
_DATA   SEGMENT WORD PUBLIC 'DATA'
        EXTRN _typeAsio:WORD
_DATA   ENDS
_TEXT   SEGMENT WORD PUBLIC 'CODE'
ASSUME  CS:_TEXT, DS:NOTHING
EXTRN   _s_iadmin:NEAR

    ⋮

_TEXT ENDS
```

Notice that the trailing underscores used by the Aztec assembler are now leading underscores, producing several odd-looking names that begin with three underscores.

Adapting to Large Memory Model

Because of the difference between pointer sizes in Large and Small Models, both C and assembler modules require modifications. Luckily, the changes in the C code are trivial and, if you wish, can be handled with a #define and conditional compilation. While there are more modifications to the assembly-language functions, the changes are largely word-processing chores that can also be handled with conditional assembly.

Adapting C Functions to Large Memory Model

Adapting the C functions to the Large Memory model requires only that you recompile them with the appropriate compiler switch (" +L" for the Aztec, "/AL" for Microsoft) and use the Large Model version of the standard libraries during linkage.

---

[1]This is not generally true, but since some of the data in the interrupt handler *must* go in the code segment, I arbitrarily chose to place it *all* there, even in the console routines in Appendix A. One ASSUME therefore works for the entire book.

The single exception is the Small Model version of _intron on page 564 which covers up the discrepancy between Large and Small Model pointer sizes by using a typedef for a type "pointer to void function":

```
typedef unsigned long INTPTR;
```

To use in Large Model, simply change this line to

```
typedef void(*INTPTR)();
```

The 32-bit pointers under Large Model make the function __getcs superfluous, so delete both it and its return-type declaration. The line

```
__setivec( _ilist[portnum].inum, _ilist[portnum].isr,__getcs() );
```

becomes the far simpler

```
__setivec( _ilist[portnum].inum, _ilist[portnum].isr);
```

Adapting Assembly-Language Functions to Large Model

Converting the assembly-language functions is more complicated, but still quite straightforward. As with the Small Model, the first step is to ascertain the correct linkage headers (GROUP, SEGMENT, and ASSUME) for your compiler's Large Model. Compile a small function under Large Model and examine the compiler's assembly-language output.

The remaining changes center about the two fundamental differences between Large and Small Models: the CALL instruction and pointer size.

Modifications for the CALL Instruction

In the Small Model, all code lies within a single 64K segment, so function calls are performed with a NEAR CALL instruction and return via a NEAR RETURN. Code in the Large Model, however, may be larger than 64K, so function calls require a FAR CALL instruction to specify the *complete* 8086 address; that is, the full 32-bit segment:offset address. Large Model functions must return with a FAR RETURN. Luckily, the compiler supplies the correct form (i.e., NEAR or FAR) of these instructions based upon the information we supply in function ("PROCedure") and data declarations. Therefore, the next step in conversion is simply to change all PROC NEAR directives to PROC FAR directives. All function declarations must be modified to reflect the need for 32-bit addresses as shown in Table C-1 below.

Table C-1 Conversion of PROC NEAR directives to PROC FAR directives.

Small Model		Large Model*	
__alisrA__	PROC NEAR	__alisrA__	PROC FAR
__getivec__	PROC NEAR	__getivec__	PROC FAR
__setivec__	PROC NEAR	__setivec__	PROC FAR
__keystat__	PROC NEAR	__keystat__	PROC FAR
__getkey__	PROC NEAR	__getkey__	PROC FAR
EXTRN s_iadmin__:NEAR		EXTRN s_iadmin__: FAR	
EXTRN typeAsio__:WORD		EXTRN typeAsio__ : DWORD	

*__getcs is not needed in Large Model.

Pointer-Size Adjustments

When s_admin is called inside the interrupt handler, under the Small Model the SIO's address is passed onto the stack as a 16-bit offset. After the call, these 2 bytes are removed from the stack with the instruction

```
add sp, NUMARGS
```

where NUMARGS is 2, the number of bytes in the SIO's address. For Large Model, change the NUMARGS definition to

```
NUMARGS EQU 4
```

then add the additional code to push the entire offset:segment address onto the stack before the CALL:

```
mov  ax, SEG  DGROUP:typeAsio_   ; put segment on stack first
push ax
mov  ax, OFFSET DGROUP:typeAsio_ ; push *siop offset on stack
push ax
```

Make certain that the two new lines appear just as shown above (i.e., before the existing code to push the offset portion of the address onto the stack).

Stack Indexing

When a function is called, the return address pushed onto the stack occupies 2 bytes in Small Model (i.e., offset) but 4 bytes in Large Model (segment:offset). Since arguments are placed on the stack *before* the function call, the argument list resides 2 bytes deeper in the stack in Large than in Small Model. We can adjust for this change in addressing by changing the EQUATE given at the beginning of the __alisr module, as shown in Table C-2 below.

Table C-2 Stack indexing constants.

Small Model		Large Model	
ARG1	EQU 4	ARG1	EQU 6
ARG2	EQU 6	ARG2	EQU 8
ARG3	EQU 8	ARG3	EQU 10

The Outport Function in Large Model

The I/O port access function that writes to the IBM PC's UART is declared as follows by most compilers:

```
unsigned outport(portnum, data);
unsigned portnum;
BYTE      data;
```

From these declarations it is clear that these functions are designed with the knowledge that 8086 port addresses are limited to 16 bits. When we call these functions, however, the port address is passed like this:

```
outport(siop->uart_base, data);
```

If we think carefully about `uart_base`'s declaration in the SIO we can see a problem in data typing: `uart_base` is defined as a *pointer* to type BYTE. This discrepancy causes no problems in Small Model because pointers and `unsigned ints` both occupy 2 bytes when passed onto the stack. In Large Model, however, the call to `outport` pushes a *4-byte* pointer onto the stack. The net effect is that `outport` takes the segment portion of the pointer as the data.

The best solution is to rewrite the function in assembly language. Figure C-1 shows `outport` for the Aztec compiler; the Large Model stack-index constants are repeated from Table C-2.

Figure C-1 Large-model port output routine for the IBM PC.

FUNCTION NAME: outport
LIBRARY: *YOUR.LIB*
DESCRIPTION: Large-model port output routine for the IBM PC.
RETURNS: outport: void
SYNTAX FROM C: outport(portp, data);
                      BYTE *portp, data;
COMMENTS: Linkage header is for Aztec, Large Model.

```
       ;; Large Model Equates
ARG1   EQU 6                    ; offset of first stack argument
ARG2   EQU 8                    ;         2nd
ARG3   EQU 10                   ;         3rd
```

Figure C-1 cont. Large-model port output routine for the IBM PC.

```
;;----------------
LARGECODE                          ;; this statement needed only for Aztec
;;----------------

        PUBLIC outport_
CODESEG SEGMENT WORD PUBLIC 'CODE'

outport_ PROC FAR
        push bp
        mov  bp,sp
        mov  dx, [bp + ARG1]    ; low order byte of pointer (port address)
        mov  ax, [bp + ARG3]    ; data argument
        out  dx,al
        pop  bp
        ret
outport_ ENDP
CODESEG ENDS
END
```

An Explanation of 'outport'   The 8086 instruction set does not permit indexing directly from SP, the stack pointer register. The register BP is provided especially for this purpose. After pushing BP itself onto the stack, a frame for indexing is created by pushing BP then copying SP into BP. Figure C-2 shows how the indexing is configured upon entry to a call to outport.

Figure C-2   Stack indexing for Large and Small Models.

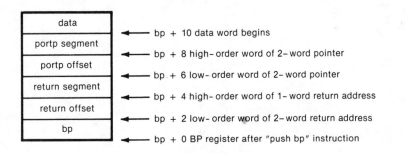

Large Model Stack Indexing Using the BP Register

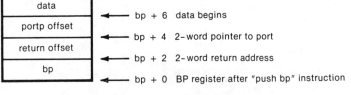

Small Model Stack Indexing Using the BP Register

D

#Include Files

ASCII.H

#define CTRL_A	0x01	#define TAB	0x09	#define CTRL_T	0x14
#define SOH	0x01	#define HT	0x09	#define NAK	0x15
#define CTRL_B	0x02	#define CTRL_J	0x0A	#define CTRL_U	0x15
#define STX	0x02	#define LF	0x0A	#define CTRL_V	0x16
#define CTRL_C	0x03	#define CTRL_K	0x0B	#define CTRL_W	0x17
#define ETX	0x03	#define CTRL_L	0x0C	#define CAN	0x18
#define CTRL_D	0x04	#define FF	0x0C	#define CTRL_X	0x18
#define EOT	0x04	#define CTRL_M	0x0D	#define CTRL_Y	0x19
#define CTRL_E	0x05	#define CR	0x0D	#define CTRL_Z	0x1A
#define ENQ	0x05	#define CTRL_N	0x0E	#define CTRL_LBRAK	0x1B
#define CTRL_F	0x06	#define CTRL_O	0x1F	#define ESC	0x1B
#define ACK	0x06	#define CTRL_P	0x10	#define CTRL_BAKSL	0x1C
#define CTRL_G	0x07	#define CTRL_Q	0x11	#define CTRL_RBRAK	0x1D
#define BEL	0x07	#define DC1	0x11	#define CTRL_CTRL	0x1E
#define CTRL_H	0x08	#define CTRL_R	0x12	#define CTRL__	0x1F
#define BS	0x08	#define CTRL_S	0x13	#define SP	0x20
#define CTRL_I	0x09	#define DC3	0x13	#define DEL	0x7f

U8250.H

#define VBAUDLO	0	#define VINTR	2	#define V232OUT	4
#define VBAUDHI	1	#define VFMT	3		

#define XMIT_MASK	0x20	#define PARITYMASK	0xC7	#define DTRMASK	0xFE
#define RCV_MASK	1	#define NONE_MASK	0	#define RTSMASK	0xFD
#define DL5_MASK	0	#define ODD_MASK	8	#define GPO1MASK	0xFb
#define DL6_MASK	1	#define EVEN_MASK	0x18	#define GPO2MASK	0xF7
#define DL7_MASK	2	#define MARK_MASK	0x28	#define BRK_MASK	0xBF
#define DL8_MASK	3	#define SPACE_MASK	0x38		

U8250.H cont.

#define STOPMASK	0xFB	#define CTSMASK	0x10	#define BRKOFF_MASK	0x00			
#define ONE_MASK	0	#define DSRMASK	0x20	#define BRKON_MASK	0x40			
#define ONE_5_MASK	4	#define RIMASK	0x40	#define TWO_MASK	4			
		#define DCDMASK	0x80					

#define BH_50	0x09	#define BH_600	0x00	#define BH_3600	0x00
#define BL_50	0x00	#define BL_600	0xC0	#define BL_3600	0x20
#define BH_75	0x06	#define BH_1200	0x00	#define BH_4800	0x00
#define BL_75	0x00	#define BL_1200	0x60	#define BL_4800	0x18
#define BH_110	0x04	#define BH_1800	0x00	#define BH_7200	0x00
#define BL_110	0x17	#define BL_1800	0x40	#define BL_7200	0x10
#define BH_134	0x03	#define BH_2000	0x00	#define BH_9600	0x00
#define BL_134	0x59	#define BL_2000	0x3A	#define BL_9600	0x0C
#define BH_150	0x03	#define BH_2400	0x00	#define BH_19K2	0x00
#define BL_150	0x00	#define BL_2400	0x30	#define BL_19K2	0x06
#define BH_300	0x01				
#define BL_300	0x80				

Z80SIO.H

#define RCV_MASK	1	#define WR0	0	#define WR4	4
#define XMIT_MASK	4	#define WR1	1	#define WR5	5
#define RR0	0	#define WR2	2	#define VBAUDLO	6
#define RR1	1	#define WR3	3	#define VBAUDHI	7
#define RR2	2				

#define DLMASK	0x3F	#define TxDLMASK	0x9F	#define CLKMASK	0x3F
#define DL5_MASK	0	#define TxDL5_MASK	0	#define X1_MASK	0
#define DL6_MASK	0x80	#define TxDL6_MASK	0x4F	#define X16_MASK	0x40
#define DL7_MASK	0x40	#define TxDL7_MASK	0x2F	#define X32_MASK	0x80
#define DL8_MASK	0xC0	#define TxDL8_MASK	0x6F	#define X64_MASK	0xC0

#define TxMASK	0xF7	#define RxMASK	0xFE	#define RxHSMASK	0xDF
#define TxON_MASK	0x08	#define RxON_MASK	0x01	#define RxHSON_MASK	0x20
#define TxOFF_MASK	0	#define RxOFF_MASK	0	#define RxHSOFF_MASK	0

#define DTRMASK	0x7F	#define STOPMASK	0xF3	#define PARITYMASK	0xFC
#define RTSMASK	0xFD	#define ONE_MASK	0x04	#define NONE_MASK	0
#define CTSMASK	0x20	#define ONE_5_MASK	0x08	#define ODD_MASK	2
#define DCDMASK	0x08	#define TWO_MASK	0x0C	#define EVEN_MASK	3

#define TxHSMASK	0xDF	#define BRK_MASK	0xEF
#define TxHSON_MASK	0x20	#define BRKOFF_MASK	0x00
#define TxHSOFF_MASK	0	#define BRKON_MASK	0x10

Z80SIO.H cont.

```
#define BH_50        0x00    #define BL_300      0x05    #define BH_3600     0x00
#define BL_50        0x00    #define BH_600      0x00    #define BL_3600     0x0B
#define BH_75        0x00    #define BL_600      0x06    #define BH_4800     0x00
#define BL_75        0x01    #define BH_1200     0x00    #define BL_4800     0x0C
#define BH_110       0x00    #define BL_1200     0x07    #define BH_7200     0x00
#define BL_110       0x02    #define BH_1800     0x00    #define BL_7200     0x0D
#define BH_134       0x00    #define BL_1800     0x08    #define BH_9600     0x00
#define BL_134       0x03    #define BH_2000     0x00    #define BL_9600     0x0E
#define BH_150       0x00    #define BL_2000     0x09    #define BH_19K2     0x00
#define BL_150       0x04    #define BH_2400     0x00    #define BL_19K2     0x0F
#define BH_300       0x00    #define BL_2400     0x0A
```

SIOCTL.H

```
struct soctl_
    {
    BOOL     rawflg;             /*0    perform no processing at all     */
    short    eolmode;            /*1    end-of-line formatting            */
    BOOL     consflg;            /*2    echo characters to console        */
    BOOL     wechoflg;           /*3    interbyte wait for return echo    */
    unsigned wecho_dly;          /*4    Tsecs to wait for return echo     */
    short    casemode;           /*5    change to upper or lower case     */
    short    xxmode;             /*6    XON-XOFF control                  */
    BYTE     xoffc;              /*7    XOFF character                    */
    short    xonc;               /*8    XON character (-1 == any char)    */
    BOOL     asciiflg;           /*9    strip bit 7                       */
    BOOL     cntrlflg;           /*10   remove control characters         */
    short    ok_cntrls[32];      /*11   permitted control characters      */
    short    numcc;              /*12   number of controls in ok_cntrls   */
    BOOL     filterflg;          /*13   filter-remove characters          */
    short    filtlist[128][2];   /*14   list of bytesto remove or filter  */
    short    numfc;              /*15   number of bytes in filter list    */
    BOOL     ib_dlyflg;          /*16   interbyte delay in tsecs          */
    unsigned ib_dly;             /*17   pause between bytes               */
    BOOL     il_dlyflg;          /*18   interline pause flag              */
    BYTE     il_dlyc;            /*19   char to begin interline pause     */
    unsigned il_dly;             /*20   interline pause in tsecs          */
    char     kbortc;             /*21   key to break out of loops         */
    BYTE     lastc;              /*22   previous byte output              */
    BOOL     flushflg;           /*23   an end of line decision pending   */
    };
```

SIOCTL.H cont.

```
struct sictl_
    {
    BOOL        t_outflg;               /*0  timeout on/off flag               */
    unsigned    t_out;                  /*1  timeout period                    */
    BOOL        rawflg;                 /*2  perform no processing at all      */
    BOOL        ekobakflg;              /*3  echo all input back to sender     */
    BOOL        asciiflg;               /*4  strip bit 7                       */
    short       eolmode;                /*5  end-of-line formatting            */
    BOOL        consflg;                /*6  echo characters to console        */
    short       casemode;               /*7  change to upper or lower case     */
    BYTE        xoffc;                  /*8  XOFF character                    */
    BYTE        xonc;                   /*9  XON character                     */
    BOOL        cntrlflg;               /*10 remove control characters         */
    short       ok_cntrls[32];          /*11 permitted control characters      */
    short       numcc;                  /*12 number of controls in ok_cntrls   */
    BOOL        filterflg;              /*13 filter-remove characters          */
    int         filtlist[128][2];       /*14 list of byte to remove or filter  */
    short       numfc;                  /*15 number of bytes in filter list    */
    BYTE        lastc;                  /*16 previous byte output              */
    BOOL        rbakflg;                /*17 a pending eol decision resolved   */
    BYTE        rbakc;                  /*18 pending readback character        */
    };
```

```
#define  SET       0      #define LF2CRLF    5      #define UP_LOW     0
#define  GET       1      #define CR2CRLF    6      #define UPPER      1
#define  NOXLAT    0      #define CRLF2LF    7      #define LOWER      2
#define  LF2CR     1      #define CRLF2CR    8      #define NO_XX      0
#define  CR2LF     2      #define NOECHO     1      #define XON_ONLY   1
#define  EOL2SPACE 3      #define IGNORE    -2      #define XON_ANY    2
#define  REMOVEEOL 4
```

```
#define  RAWFLAG      0      #define FILTERFLAG  7      #define  EOLMODE    14
#define  T_OUTFLAG    1      #define IB_DLYFLAG  8      #define  CASEMODE   15
#define  EKOBAKFLAG   2      #define IL_DLYFLAG  9      #define  XXMODE     16
#define  WECHOFLAG    3      #define WECHO_DLY  10      #define  XOFFC      17
#define  CONSFLAG     4      #define IB_DLY     11      #define  XONC       18
#define  ASCIIFLAG    5      #define IL_DLY     12      #define  IL_DLYC    19
#define  CNTRLFLAG    6      #define T_OUT      13      #define  KBORTC     20
```

XMOD.H

```
#define SOH_TIMOUT _1_SEC_0

#define DBLKSIZ      128      #define X_ESNDMAX    10      #define CONTINUE     0
#define HEADROOM      10      #define X_ERCVMAX    10      #define BREAK        1
#define CRCPAKSIZ    133      #define X_NOSOHMAX  100      #define ACK_RETRY   30
#define CKSPAKSIZ    132


#define E_USRCAN       0      #define E_LASTACK     6      #define E_BADSOH    12
#define E_FILEMTY      1      #define E_SNDOK       7      #define E_NODATA    13
#define E_NOACK        2      #define E_DSKREAD     8      #define E_PAKNUM    14
#define E_RCVCAN       3      #define E_NOSOH       9      #define E_SNDACK    15
#define E_BADPAK       4      #define E_BADCKV     10      #define E_PAKSEQ    16
#define E_EOF          5      #define E_SNDCAN     11      #define E_DSKWRITE  17
                                                          #define E_RCVOK     18


struct sndpacket
     {
     BYTE soh;                                 /* start of header            */
     BYTE pnum1;                               /* packet number              */
     BYTE pnum2;                               /* 1's comp packet number     */
     BYTE data[DBLKSIZ];                       /* data block                 */
     unsigned short ckval;                     /* block-check character      */
     };

struct rcvpacket
     {
     unsigned short pnum1;                     /* packet number              */
     unsigned short pnum2;                     /* 1's comp packet number     */
     unsigned short data[DBLKSIZ];             /* 128-byte data block        */
     unsigned short ckvhi;                     /* high byte of checkval      */
     unsigned short ckvlo;                     /* low byte of checkval       */
     };
```

CRC.H

```
#define CRCCCITT      0x1021
#define CCCITT_REV    0x8408
#define CRC16         0x8005
#define CRC16_REV     0xA001
```

MODEM.H

```
#define CMDBUFSIZ    40      #define M_SUCCEED    0      #define MAXREPLY    20
#define CMDSIZ        7      #define M_FAIL       1      #define QBUFSIZ     30

#define M_OK         0       #define M_NOTONE     6      #define M_BADMSG    12
#define M_CONN3      1       #define M_BUSY       7      #define M_ONLINE    13
#define M_RING       2       #define M_NOANSW     8      #define M_NILNUM    14
#define M_NODCD      3       #define M_RESERV     9      #define M_USRCAN    15
#define M_CMDERR     4       #define M_CONN24    10      #define M_SIOERR    16
#define M_CONN12     5       #define M_NORING    11
```

```
    struct modem
       {
       unsigned ibdelay;              /*0  interbyte delay                     */
       BOOL     cmdechoflg;           /*1  modem commands to console           */
       char     csi[CMDSIZ];          /*2  command sequence introducer         */
       char     eocstr[CMDSIZ];       /*3  end-of-command character(s)         */
       char     quietcmd[CMDSIZ];     /*4  Q cmd: send result codes            */
       char     cmdbuff[CMDBUFSIZ];   /*5  build all commands here             */
       int      cmdt_out;             /*6  tsecs to wait after a modem cmd     */
       int      cmdretry;             /*7  number of times to try a command    */
       unsigned guardtime;            /*8  escape guard time                   */
       BOOL     iscard;               /*9  is this a board modem?              */
       int      baudtry[6];           /*10 baud rates to use during init       */
       char     escape[CMDSIZ];       /*11 (S2)on-line to cmd mode escape      */
       unsigned baudfound;            /*12 maximum baud rate of modem          */
       BOOL     rs232flg;             /*13 monitor RS-232 signals?             */
       short    smid;                 /*14 result of modem's product ID cmd    */
       short    romck;                /*15 rom checksum                        */
       short    modtype;              /*16 our code for modem                  */
       BOOL     configokflg;          /*17 modem successfully configured       */
       BOOL     baudmode;             /*18 baud rate initialization mode       */
       unsigned baudmax;              /*19 maximum baud rate of modem          */
       char     pri_config[CMDBUFSIZ];/*20 main configuration string           */
       char     dialmode[CMDSIZ];     /*21 tone or pulse dialling              */
       char     echocmd[CMDSIZ];      /*22 E cmd: echoes in command mode       */
       char     verbosecmd[CMDSIZ];   /*23 V cmd: word or digit result codes   */
       char     autoans[CMDSIZ];      /*24 (S0)# of rings before autoanswer    */
       char     dtwait[CMDSIZ];       /*25 (S6)dialtone wait  (secs)           */
       char     dcdwait[CMDSIZ];      /*26 (S7)dcd timeout wait (secs)         */
       char     speaker[CMDSIZ];      /*27 speaker mode                        */
       char     sec_config[CMDBUFSIZ];/*28 config str for evolutionary cmds    */
       char     xcmd[CMDSIZ];         /*29 result code set                     */
       char     okalpha[12];          /*30 alpha chars ok in dial string       */
       char     speakvol[CMDSIZ];     /*31 speaker volume (0, 1, or 2          */
       char     firmdcd[CMDSIZ];      /*32 2400's DCD firmware config switch   */
       char     firmdtr[CMDSIZ];      /*33 2400's DCD firmware config switch   */
       char     unconfig[CMDBUFSIZ];  /*34 string to send to smodem at exit    */
       char     dialbuff[CMDBUFSIZ];  /*35 build numeric dial string here      */
       char     dialcmd[CMDSIZ];      /*36 dial command                        */
       char     enddial[CMDSIZ];      /*37 dial suffix--e.g., ';' or 'R'       */
       char     anscmd[CMDSIZ];       /*38 answer command                      */
       BOOL     autobrflg;            /*39 switch baud rate to incoming call   */
       char     hupcmd[CMDSIZ];       /*40 hang up command                     */
       };
```

MODEM.H cont.

```
#define BAUD_DEF      0    #define BAUD_MAX      1    #define BAUD_FOUND    2

#define ID_UNKNOWN    0    #define ID_12PLUS     3    #define ID_12CLONE    5
#define ID_300        1    #define ID_24         4    #define ID_24CLONE    6
#define ID_12         2
```

```
struct modem hayes =
        {
        _0_SEC_05,                        /*0   interbyte delay                   */
        OFF,                              /*1   no modem commands to console      */
        "AT",                             /*2   command prefix                    */
        "\015",                           /*3   command terminator = CR           */
        "Q0",                             /*4   send result codes                 */
        "",                               /*5   build all commands here           */
        _0_SEC_3,                         /*6   Tsecs to wait after a modem cmd    */
        4,                                /*7   number of times to try a command  */
        _1_SEC_0  + _0_SEC_5,             /*8   escape guard time (Tsecs)         */
        FALSE ,                           /*9   not a board modem                 */
        { BAUD1200, BAUD300, BAUD2400, -1},/*10 baud rates to use during init     */
        "S2=124",                         /*11  (S2) online escape bye = ´|´      */
        SUPPLIED,                         /*12  baud rate at which modem found     */
        ON,                               /*13  monitor RS-232 signals            */
        SUPPLIED,                         /*14  result of modem´s product ID cmd   */
        SUPPLIED,                         /*15  rom checksum                      */
        VIRGIN,                           /*16  our own code for smodem type       */
        VIRGIN,                           /*17  modem sucessfully configured       */
        BAUD_FOUND,                       /*18  leave br where modem was found      */
        SUPPLIED,                         /*19  maximum baud rate of modem         */
        "",                               /*20  main configuration string         */
        "T",                              /*21  tones or pulse                    */
        "E0",                             /*22  echo commands                     */
        "V1",                             /*23  word result codes                 */
        "S0=0",                           /*24  (S0)# of rings before autoanswer   */
        "S6=2",                           /*25  (S6)dialtone wait  (secs)         */
        "S7=30",                          /*26  (S7) modem dcd timeout (secs)     */
        "M1",                             /*27  speaker mode                      */
        "",                               /*28  config str for evolutionary cmds   */
        "X4",                             /*29  extends result codes for compat.   */
        ",*#()-R",                        /*30  alpha chars ok in dial string      */
        "L1",                             /*31  speaker volume (1, 2, or 3)        */
        "&C2",                            /*32  2400 firmware DCD switch: DCD on    */
        "&D2",                            /*33  2400 firmware DTR switch: DTR on    */
        "",                               /*34  unconfiguration                   */
        "",                               /*35  build numeric dial string here     */
        "D",                              /*36  dial command                      */
        "",                               /*37  dial suffix--e.g., ´;´ or ´R´      */
        "A",                              /*38  answer phone command              */
        ON,                               /*39  switch baud rate to incoming call  */
        "H0",                             /*40  hang up phone                     */
        };
```

SIODEF.H

```
#define xon(p)  s_putc((p), (p)->s_ict1->xonc)
#define xoff(p) s_putc((p), (p)->s_ict1->xoffc)
/*
#define s_inchar(p)  ((*(p)->s_rstat)((p)) == NULL ? -1 : (*(p)->s_read)((p)))
#define s_keybort(p) inkey() == (p)->s_oct1->kbortc
*/
#define NOT_READY    -1      #define OFF         0      #define IBUFSIZ   256
#define SUPPLIED      0      #define OPEN        1      #define TIMEOUT    -1
#define NA            0      #define CLOSED      0      #define VIRGIN     -2
#define ON            1

#define _0_SEC_05     1      #define _0_SEC_4    7      #define _0_SEC_8   15
#define _0_SEC_1      2      #define _0_SEC_5    9      #define _0_SEC_9   16
#define _0_SEC_2      4      #define _0_SEC_6   11      #define _1_SEC_0   18
#define _0_SEC_3      6      #define _0_SEC_7   13

#define OR_ARG        1      #define NO_PORT     5      #define KEY_CAN     9
#define BAD_FCN       2      #define NO_SIO      6      #define NO_FILE    10
#define BAD_ARG       3      #define OPEN_NOW    7      #define NO_IMEM    11
#define BAD_PORT      4      #define NO_CLOSE    8

#define X1            0      #define NUMMASKS    5      #define VIR         0
#define X16           1      #define NUMBAUDS   16      #define USR         1
#define X32           2
#define X64           3

#define NONE          0      #define DL5         0      #define TxDL5       0
#define ODD           1      #define DL6         1      #define TxDL6       1
#define EVEN          2      #define DL7         2      #define TxDL7       2
#define MARK          3      #define DL8         3      #define TxDL8       3
#define SPACE         4

#define STOP1         0
#define STOP1_5       1
#define STOP2         2

#define BAUD50        0      #define BAUD600     6      #define BAUD3600   11
#define BAUD75        1      #define BAUD1200    7      #define BAUD4800   12
#define BAUD110       2      #define BAUD1800    8      #define BAUD7200   13
#define BAUD134_5     3      #define BAUD2000    9      #define BAUD9600   14
#define BAUD150       4      #define BAUD2400   10      #define BAUD19K2   15
#define BAUD300       5
```

SIODEF.H cont.

```
struct vregbits_
    {
    BYTE        resetmask;              /* AND mask apply to virtual register */
    int         setmask[NUMMASKS];      /* array of OR masks for each setting */
    BYTE        vregnum;                /* virtual register number (row)      */
    int         offset;                 /* offset of physical uart register   */
    BYTE        now;                    /* code for current value             */
    BYTE        start;                  /* code to use at initialization      */
    struct vregbits_ *next;             /* next struct for this function      */
    };

struct vbaud_
    {
    BYTE        vregnuml;               /* virtual array of baud rate lo      */
    BYTE        vregnumh;               /* virtual array of baud rate hi      */
    int         offsetlo;               /* offset of lo-order baud rate register */
    int         offsethi;               /* offset of hi-order baud rate register */
    int         divisor[NUMBAUDS][2];   /* array of two-byte divisors         */
    BYTE        now;                    /* rank of current divisor            */
    BYTE        start;                  /* rank of value to use at start up    */
    };

struct vout232_
    {
    BYTE        resetmask;              /* AND mask apply to virtual register */
    BYTE        vregnum;                /* virtual register number (row)      */
    int         offset;                 /* offset of physical uart register   */
    BOOL        now;                    /* code for current value             */
    BOOL        start;                  /* code to use at initialization      */
    struct      vout232_ *next;         /* next struct for this function      */
    };

struct vin232_
    {
    BYTE        vregnum;                /* number of virtual register         */
    int         offset;                 /* offset of physical register in UART */
    BYTE        mask;                   /* mask to isolate active bit         */
    BYTE        now;                    /* current value of this input        */
    BYTE        (*read232)();           /* pointer to level-1 fetch function  */
    };

struct _siostat
    {
    SIO *typep;                         /* SIO pointer for this port          */
    BOOL openflag;                      /* currently open?                    */
    BOOL intrptok;                      /* interrupts supported?              */
    };
```

SIODEF.H cont.

```
typedef struct
     {
     BYTE      *uart_base;          /* 0  base address of UART            */
     int       data_off;           /* 1  offset of data port from base   */
     int       status_off;         /* 2  offset of status port from base */
     unsigned rcvmask;             /* 3  RxRDY mask                      */
     unsigned xmitmask;            /* 4  TBE mask                        */
     BYTE      (*readbyte)();       /* 5  pointer to RAM/port read routine */
     void      (*writebyte)();      /* 6  pointer to RAM/port read routine */
     BYTE      (*s_rstat)();        /* 7  pointer to serial receiver status */
     BYTE      (*s_read)();         /* 8  pointer to serial fetch routine  */
     BYTE      (*s_xstat)();        /* 9  pointer to serial xmiter status  */
     void      (*s_send)();         /* 10 pointer to serial xmit routine   */
     BYTE      (*v_regp)[2];        /* 11 pointer to a 2-dim array of ints */
     int       v_regpsize;          /* 12 length of virtual array          */
     struct    vregbits_ *par;      /* 13 pointer to parity structure      */
     struct    vregbits_ *sb;       /* 14 pointer to stop bit structure    */
     struct    vregbits_ *dl;       /* 15 pointer to data length structure */
     struct    vbaud_    *br;       /* 16 pointer to baud rate structure   */
     struct    vout232_  *rts;      /* 17 pointer to RTS structure         */
     struct    vout232_  *dtr;      /* 18 pointer to DTR structure         */
     struct    vout232_  *gpo1;     /* 19 pointer to GPOUTPUT1 structure   */
     struct    vout232_  *gpo2;     /* 20 pointer to GPOOUTPUT2 structure  */
     struct    vout232_  *brkbit;   /* 21 pointer to break structure       */
     struct    vin232_   *cts;      /* 22 pointer to  CTS structure        */
     struct    vin232_   *dsr;      /* 23 pointer to  DSR structure        */
     struct    vin232_   *dcd;      /* 24 pointer to  DCD structure        */
     struct    vin232_   *ri;       /* 25 pointer to  RI structure         */
     struct    vin232_   *gpi1;     /* 26 pointer to  GPINPUT1 structure   */
     struct    vin232_   *gpi2;     /* 27 pointer to  GPINPUT2 structure   */
     struct    vregbits_  *txenable; /* 28 "  xmitter enable structure     */
     struct    vregbits_  *rxenable; /* 39 "  receiver enable structure    */
     struct    vregbits_  *ctshs;   /* 30 "  cts handshake on xmitter      */
     struct    vregbits_  *dcdhs;   /* 31 "  dcd handshake on receiver     */
     struct    vregbits_  *clkf;    /* 32 "  clock factor structure        */
     short     devnum;              /* 33 s_opened device number           */
     struct    soctl_   *s_octl;    /* 34 pointer to output control struct */
     struct    sictl_   *s_ictl;    /* 35 pointer to input  control struct */
     struct    modem    *sm;        /* 36 pointer to modem structure       */
     unsigned ibuffsiz;            /* 37 size of the  rxrdy ring buffer   */
     BYTE      *intbuff;            /* 38 pointer to      "     "     "    */
     BYTE      *eoibuff;            /* 39 pointer to end of  "        "    */
     BYTE      *iheadp;             /* 40 where in buff to put next byte   */
     BYTE      *itailp;             /* 41 where in buff to fetch next byte */
     BYTE      (*int_rstat)();      /* 42 pointer to serial receiver status */
     BYTE      (*int_read)();       /* 43 pointer to serial fetch routine  */
     BOOL      intrptonflg;         /* 44 interrupts-are-on-flag           */
     } SIO;
```

E

Listing of IBMPC.C

```c
/* This listing contains no functions */
/* WARNING: this listing contains no SIO declaration for COM2 */

#include "stdio.h"
#include "modem.h"
#include "siodef.h"
#include "u8250.h"
#include "ascii.h"
#include "sioctl.h"

#define COMM1 0x3F8
#define COMM2 0x2F8
#define DP_OFF 0
#define SP_OFF 5
#define BAUDLO 0
#define BAUDHI 1

#define MAX_PORTS    4

extern BYTE inport(), s_rcv(), s_rcvstat(), s_xmitstat(), _vstat232();
extern BYTE s_istat(), s_iread();
extern void outport(), s_xmit();
extern unsigned peek();

BYTE v_regA[5][2]=                      /* register array for virtual UART    */
    {
/*  VIR    USR  */
    0,    0,                            /* 0 = baud low byte          */
    0,    0,                            /* 1 = baud high byte         */
    0,    0,                            /* 2 = interrupt enable       */
    0,    0,                            /* 3 = data format            */
    0,    0                             /* 4 = RS232 output control   */
    };
```

```
struct vregbits_ parityA =          /* for 8250 UART                               */
    {
    PARITYMASK,                     /* AND mask to apply to this register          */
    { NONE_MASK, ODD_MASK, EVEN_MASK, MARK_MASK, SPACE_MASK }, /* OR masks    */
    VFMT,                           /* virtual register--rank in v_rega            */
    3,                              /* offset of physical register from uart_base*/
    SUPPLIED,                       /* rank in mask table of current setting       */
    NONE,                           /* rank to use in initialization               */
    NIL                             /* no more structures for parity               */
    };

struct vregbits_ stopsA =           /* for 8250 UART */
      {
      STOPMASK,
      { ONE_MASK, ONE_5_MASK, TWO_MASK, -1, -1 },
      VFMT,
      3,
      SUPPLIED,
      STOP1,
      NIL                           /* no more structures for stop bits  */
      };

struct vregbits_ dlenA =            /* for 8250 UART */
    {
    DLMASK,
    { DL5_MASK, DL6_MASK, DL7_MASK, DL8_MASK, -1 },
    VFMT,
    3,
    SUPPLIED,
    DL8,
    NIL                             /* no more structures for data length */
    };

struct vbaud_ baudA =
      {
      VBAUDLO,                                  /* virtual register for lo byte      */
      VBAUDHI,                                  /* virtual register for hi byte      */
      0,                                        /* offset of UART lsb baud baud reg  */
      1,                                        /* offset of UART msb baud reg       */
      {
        {BH_50,    BL_50   }, {BH_75,   BL_75   }, {BH_110,  BL_110  },
        {BH_134,   BL_134  }, {BH_150,  BL_150  }, {BH_300,  BL_300  },
        {BH_600,   BL_600  }, {BH_1200, BL_1200 }, {BH_1800, BL_1800 },
        {BH_2000,  BL_2000 }, {BH_2400, BL_2400 }, {BH_3600, BL_3600 },
        {BH_4800,  BL_4800 }, {BH_7200, BL_7200 }, {BH_9600, BL_9600 },
        {BH_19K2,  BL_19K2 }
      },
      SUPPLIED,                           /* rank of current baud in divisor table */
      BAUD1200                            /* start at 1200 baud                    */
      };
```

622

```
struct vout232_ pin4A =              /****      RTS         ****/
    {
    RTSMASK,                         /* mask to reset RTS      */
    V232OUT,                         /* virtual reg number     */
    4,                               /* offset of UART reg      */
    SUPPLIED,                        /* state of RTS bit now */
    OFF,                             /* state for startup      */
    NIL                              /* pointer to next         */
    };

struct vout232_ pin20A =             /****      DTR         ****/
    {
    DTRMASK,
    V232OUT,
    4,
    SUPPLIED,
    OFF,
    NIL
    };


struct vout232_ breakbA =            /* BREAK signal         */
    {
    BRK_MASK,
    VFMT,
    3,
    SUPPLIED,
    OFF,
    NIL
    };

struct vout232_ gp1outA =            /****      GPO1        ****/
    {
    GPO1MASK,
    V232OUT,
    4,
    SUPPLIED,
    OFF,
    NIL
    };

struct vout232_ gp2outA =            /****      GPO2        ****/
    {
    GPO2MASK,
    V232OUT,
    4,
    SUPPLIED,
    OFF,
    NIL
    };
```

623

```
struct vin232_ pin5A =                  /*** CTS  ***/
    {
    6,                                  /* offset of UART register    */
    CTSMASK,                            /* AND mask for this bit       */
    SUPPLIED,                           /* value of bit at last test   */
    _vstat232                           /* pointer to level-1 function */
    };


struct vin232_ pin8A =                  /*** DCD ***/
    {
    6,
    DCDMASK,
    SUPPLIED,
    _vstat232
    };


struct vin232_ pin6A =                  /*** DSR ***/
    {
    6,
    DSRMASK,
    SUPPLIED,
    _vstat232
    };

struct vin232_ pin22A =                 /*** RI ***/
    {
    6,
    RIMASK,
    SUPPLIED,
    _vstat232
    };
```

```
struct soctl_ oct1A =
    {
    OFF,                                /*0   "raw" output flag              */
    NOXLAT,                             /*1   end-of-line mode                */
    OFF,                                /*2   console output flag             */
    OFF,                                /*3   echowait flag                   */
    _1_SEC_0 * 5,                       /*4   echo-wait before timeout in Tsecs */
    UP_LOW,                             /*5   upper/lower case conversion mode */
    XON_ONLY,                           /*6   flow control mode               */
    DC3,                                /*7   XOFF character                  */
    DC1,                                /*8   XON character if mode >= 0       */
    ON,                                 /*9   strip high bits flag            */
    ON,                                 /*10  remove unwanted controls flag   */
{NUL,BEL,BS,HT,LF,CR,FF,DC3,DC1,DOS_EOF},/*11 permitted controls             */
    10,                                 /*12  number of controls in above list */
    OFF,                                /*13  translation/removal flag        */
    {},                                 /*14  translation/removal list        */
    0,                                  /*15  no entries in above array       */
    OFF,                                /*16  no interbyte delay flag         */
    _0_SEC_05,                          /*17  delay in Tsecs                  */
    ON,                                 /*18  end-of-line pause flag          */
    LF,                                 /*19  character to pause after        */
    _0_SEC_4,                           /*20  pause in Tsecs                  */
    ESC,                                /*21  keyboard abort character        */
    SUPPLIED,                           /*22  'last character' buffer         */
    SUPPLIED                            /*23  flag to flush last character    */
    };

struct sictl_ ict1A =
    {
    OFF,                                /* 0   timeout-on-input flag          */
    _0_SEC_05,                          /* 1   default timeout in Tsecs       */
    OFF,                                /* 2   "raw" input flag               */
    OFF,                                /* 3   echo input back to sender flag */
    ON,                                 /* 4   reset high bit flag            */
    NOXLAT,                             /* 5   end-of-line mode               */
    OFF,                                /* 6   console output flag            */
    UP_LOW,                             /* 7   upper/lower case conversion mode */
    DC3,                                /* 8   XOFF (pause) character to send */
    DC1,                                /* 9   XON (release) character  to send */
    ON,                                 /* 10  remove unwanted controls flag  */
{NUL,BEL,BS,HT,LF,CR,FF,DC3,DC1,DOS_EOF}, /* 11  permitted controls          */
    10,                                 /* 12  number of controls in above list */
    OFF,                                /* 13  byte translation/removal mode  */
    {},                                 /* 14  translation/removal array      */
    0,                                  /* 15  no entries in above array      */
    SUPPLIED,                           /* 16  'last character' buffer        */
    SUPPLIED,                           /* 17  eol readback flag              */
    SUPPLIED                            /* 18  pending readback character     */
    };
```

625

```
SIO typeAsio =
    {
    COMM1,              /*0   base address of UART            */
    DP_OFF,             /*1   offset of data port from base   */
    SP_OFF,             /*2   offset of status port from base */
    RCV_MASK,           /*3   RxRDY mask from U8250.H          */
    XMIT_MASK,          /*4   TBE mask from U8250.H            */
    inport,             /*5   pointer to RAM/port read routine */
    outport,            /*6   pointer to RAM/port read routine */
    s_rcvstat,          /*7   pointer to serial receiver status */
    s_rcv,              /*8   pointer to serial fetch routine  */
    s_xmitstat,         /*9   pointer to serial xmiter status  */
    s_xmit,             /*10  pointer to serial xmit routine   */
    v_regA,             /*11  pointer to virtual register array */
    5,                  /*12  number of rows in virtual array  */
    &parityA,           /*13  parity structure                 */
    &stopsA,            /*14  stop bit structure               */
    &dlenA,             /*15  data length structure            */
    &baudA,             /*16  baud rate structure              */
    &pin4A,             /*17  RS-232 RTS output                */
    &pin20A,            /*18  RS-232 DTR output                */
    &gp1outA,           /*19  RS-232 first user-defined output */
    &gp2outA,           /*20  RS-232 first user-defined output */
    &breakbA,           /*21  break bit                        */
    &pin5A,             /*22  RS-232 CTS input                 */
    &pin6A,             /*23  RS-232 DSR input                 */
    &pin8A,             /*24  RS-232 DCD input                 */
    &pin22A,            /*25  RS-232 RI  input                 */
    NIL,                /*26  NO 1st user-defined RS-232 input */
    NIL,                /*27  NO 2nd user-defined RS-232 input */
    NIL,                /*28  NO transmitter-on structure      */
    NIL,                /*39  NO receiver-on structure         */
    NIL,                /*30  NO transmitter/RTS handshake     */
    NIL,                /*31  NO receiver/DCD handshake        */
    NIL,                /*32  NO clock factor                  */
    SUPPLIED,           /*33  device number supplied during open */
    &octlA,             /*34  output control                   */
    &ictlA,             /*35  input control                    */
    &hayes,             /*36  smartmodem                       */
    IBUFSIZ,            /*37  size of receive interrupt buffer */
    SUPPLIED,           /*38  pointer to        "         "    */
    SUPPLIED,           /*39  pointer to end of "         "    */
    SUPPLIED,           /*40  where in buff to put next byte   */
    SUPPLIED,           /*41  where in buff to fetch next byte */
    s_istat,            /*42  pointer to serial receiver status */
    s_iread,            /*43  pointer to serial fetch routine  */
    FALSE,              /*44  interrupts-are-on-flag           */
    };
```

```
int _maxsios = MAX_PORTS;               /* global                      */
struct _siostat _siolist[MAX_PORTS] =   /* IBM has two serial ports    */
    {
    { &typeAsio, CLOSED, TRUE },        /* COM1                        */
    { NIL,       CLOSED,      },        /* COM2 not shown here         */
    { NIL,       CLOSED,      },        /* no SIO declared             */
    { NIL,       CLOSED,      }         /* no SIO declared             */
    };
```

F

Listing of KAYPRO.C

```c
/* This listing contains no functions */

#include "stdio.h"
#include "siodef.h"
#include "z80sio.h"
#include "ascii.h"
#include "sioctl.h"
#include "modem.h"


#define PORT1      4
#define DP_OFF     0
#define SP_OFF     2
#define BAUD      -4
#define MAX_PORTS 1

BYTE inport(), s_rcv(), s_rcvstat(), s_xmitstat(), _vstat232();
BYTE  s_istat(), s_iread();
void outport(), s_xmit();
unsigned peek();

BYTE v_regA[8][2] =                     /* register array for virtual UART   */
    {
/*  VIR ------ USR  */
    {0x18,     0x18 },    /*  0 reset channel                                 */
    {0,           0 },    /*  1 no interrupts                                 */
    {0,           0 },    /*  2 interrupt vector                              */
    {0xC1,     0xE1 },    /*  3 start with no auto handshake, turn on at      */
    {0x44,     0x44 },    /*  4 async mode, x16 clk, 1 stop                   */
    {0xEA,     0x68 },    /*  5 start with RTS/DTR high, inhibit then at exit */
    {0,           0 },    /*  6 baud rate lo */
    {0,           0 }     /*  7 baud rate hi */
    };
```

```
struct vregbits_ parityA =                      /** FOR Z80SIO UART **/
    {
    PARITYMASK,                         /* AND mask to apply             */
    {NONE_MASK, ODD_MASK, EVEN_MASK, -1 , -1 },   /* array of OR masks   */
    WR4,                                /* virtual register number       */
    SP_OFF,                             /* offset of Z80SIO's ctrl/stat port */
    SUPPLIED,                           /* don't bother to initialize this */
    NONE,                               /* use this value for SIO config. */
    NIL                                 /* the only registers for parity  */
    };

struct regbits_ stopsA =
      {
      STOPMASK,                         /* AND mask to apply             */
{ ONE_MASK, ONE_5_MASK, TWO_MASK, -1, -1 }, /* array of OR masks         */
      WR4,                              /* virtual register number       */
      SP_OFF,                           /* offset of Z80SIO's ctrl/stat port */
      SUPPLIED,                         /* don't bother to initialize this */
      STOP1,                            /* use this value for SIO config. */
      NIL                               /* no more structures for stop bits */
      };

struct regbits_ txdlenA =             /* for tranmsit only */
      {
      TxDLMASK,
      { TxDL5_MASK, TxDL6_MASK, TxDL7_MASK, TxDL8_MASK, -1 },
      WR5,
      SP_OFF,
      SUPPLIED,
      TxDL8,
      NIL                               /* end of linked list            */
      };

struct regbits_ dlenA =
    {
    DLMASK,                             /* AND mask to apply             */
    { DL5_MASK, DL6_MASK,DL7_MASK, DL8_MASK, -1 },/* array of OR masks   */
    WR3,                                /* virtual register number       */
    SP_OFF,                             /* offset of Z80SIO's ctrl/stat port */
    SUPPLIED,                           /* don't bother to initialize this */
    DL8,                                /* use this value for SIO config. */
    &txdlenA                            /* Z80SIO dlen takes two registers */
    };
```

```
struct vbaud_ baudA =
    {
    VBAUDLO,                        /* virtual register for lo byte */
    VBAUDHI,                        /* virtual register for hi byte */
    BAUD,                           /* offset of UART lsb baud baud reg */
    NA,                             /* single byte divisor */
    {
        {BH_50,    BL_50   }, {BH_75,    BL_75   }, {BH_110,  BL_110  },
        {BH_134,   BL_134  }, {BH_150,   BL_150  }, {BH_300,  BL_300  },
        {BH_600,   BL_600  }, {BH_1200,  BL_1200 }, {BH_1800, BL_1800 },
        {BH_2000,  BL_2000 }, {BH_2400,  BL_2400 }, {BH_3600, BL_3600 },
        {BH_4800,  BL_4800 }, {BH_7200,  BL_7200 }, {BH_9600, BL_9600 },
        {BH_19K2,  BL_19K2 }
    },
    SUPPLIED,                       /* rank of current baud in divisor table */
    BAUD1200                        /* start at 1200 baud */
    };

struct vout232_ pin4A =                 /**** RTS ****/
    {
    RTSMASK,                        /* mask to reset RTS     */
    WR5,                            /* virtual reg number    */
    SP_OFF,                         /* offset of UART reg    */
    SUPPLIED,                       /* state of RTS bit now  */
    OFF,                            /* state for startup     */
    NIL                             /* pointer to next       */
    };

struct vout232_ pin20A =                /**** DTR ****/
    {
    DTRMASK,
    WR5,
    SP_OFF,
    SUPPLIED,
    OFF,
    NIL
    };

struct vout232_ breakbA =               /* BREAK signal */
    {
    BRK_MASK,
    WR5,
    SP_OFF,
    SUPPLIED,
    OFF,
    NIL
    };
```

631

```
struct vin232_ pin5A =                /*** CTS   ***/
   {
   SP_OFF,                            /* offset of UART register     */
   CTSMASK,                           /* AND mask for this bit       */
   SUPPLIED,                          /* value of bit at last test   */
   _vstat232                          /* pointer to level-1 function */
   };


   struct vin232_ pin8A =             /*** DCD ***/
      {
      SP_OFF,
      DCDMASK,
      SUPPLIED,
      _vstat232
      };


struct vregbits_ txonA =    /** transmitter enable **/
      {
      TxMASK,                         /* mask to reset bits             */
      { TxOFF_MASK, TxON_MASK, -1, -1 },  /* masks to set bits          */
      WR5,                            /* virtual register number        */
      SP_OFF,                         /* offset of physical register    */
      SUPPLIED,                       /* current value                  */
      ON,                             /* value to use at start up       */
      NIL                             /* no more structures needed      */
      };


struct vregbits_ rxonA =    /** receiver enable **/
      {
      RxMASK,
      { RxOFF_MASK, RxON_MASK, -1, -1 },
      WR3,
      SP_OFF,
      SUPPLIED,
      ON,
      NIL
      };


struct vregbits_ txhsA =    /** transmitter handshake on RTS **/
      {
      TxHSMASK,
      { TxHSOFF_MASK, TxHSON_MASK, -1, -1 },
      WR3,
      SP_OFF,
      SUPPLIED,
      OFF,
      NIL,
      };
```

```
struct vregbits_ rxhsA =      /** receiver handshake on DCD **/
    {
    TxHSMASK,
    { TxHSOFF_MASK, TxHSON_MASK, -1, -1 },
    WR3,
    SP_OFF,
    SUPPLIED,
    OFF,
    NIL
    };

struct vregbits_ clockfA =              /** clock factor **/
    {
    CLKMASK,
    { X1_MASK, X16_MASK, X32_MASK, X64_MASK, -1 },
    WR4,
    SP_OFF,
    SUPPLIED,
    X16,                                /* start with clock factor = 16      */
    NIL
    };

struct soctl_ octlA =
    {
    OFF,                            /*0  "raw" output flag                   */
    NOXLAT,                         /*1  end-of-line mode                    */
    OFF,                            /*2  console output flag                 */
    OFF,                            /*3  echowait flag                       */
    _1_SEC_0 * 5,                   /*4  echo-wait before timeout in Tsecs   */
    UP_LOW,                         /*5  upper/lower case conversion mode    */
    XON_ONLY,                       /*6  flow control mode                   */
    DC3,                            /*7  XOFF character                      */
    DC1,                            /*8  XON character if mode >= 0          */
    ON,                             /*9  strip high bits flag                */
    ON,                             /*10 remove unwanted controls flag       */
{NUL,BEL,BS,HT,LF,CR,FF,DC3,DC1,DOS_EOF},/*11 permitted controls            */
    10,                             /*12 number of controls in above list    */
    OFF,                            /*13 translation/removal flag            */
    {},                             /*14 translation/removal list            */
    0,                              /*15 no entries in above array           */
    OFF,                            /*16 no interbyte delay flag             */
    _0_SEC_05,                      /*17 delay in Tsecs                      */
    ON,                             /*18 end-of-line pause flag              */
    LF,                             /*19 character to pause after            */
    _0_SEC_4,                       /*20 pause in Tsecs                      */
    ESC,                            /*21 keyboard abort character            */
    SUPPLIED,                       /*22 'last character' buffer             */
    SUPPLIED                        /*23 flag to flush last character        */
    };
```

```
struct sictl_  ictlA =
     {
     OFF,                                /* 0   timeout-on-input flag             */
     _0_SEC_05,                          /* 1   default timeout in Tsecs          */
     OFF,                                /* 2   "raw" input flag                  */
     OFF,                                /* 3   echo input back to sender flag    */
     ON,                                 /* 4   reset high bit flag               */
     NOXLAT,                             /* 5   end-of-line mode                  */
     OFF,                                /* 6   console output flag               */
     UP_LOW,                             /* 7   upper/lower case conversion mode  */
     DC3,                                /* 8   XOFF (pause) character to send     */
     DC1,                                /* 9   XON (release) character  to send   */
     ON,                                 /* 10  remove unwanted controls flag     */
{NUL,BEL,BS,HT,LF,CR,FF,DC3,DC1,DOS_EOF}, /* 11 permitted controls              */
     10,                                 /* 12  number of controls in above list */
     OFF,                                /* 13  byte translation/removal mode     */
     {},                                 /* 14  translation/removal array         */
     0,                                  /* 15  no entries in above array         */
     SUPPLIED,                           /* 16  'last character' buffer           */
     SUPPLIED,                           /* 17  eol readback flag                 */
     SUPPLIED                            /* 18  pending readback character        */
     };

SIO typeAsio =
     {
     PORT1,                              /*0   base address of UART               */
     DP_OFF,                             /*1   offset of data port from base      */
     SP_OFF,                             /*2   offset of status port from base    */
     RCV_MASK,                           /*3   RxRDY mask from U8250.H             */
     XMIT_MASK,                          /*4   TBE mask from U8250.H               */
     inport,                             /*5   pointer to RAM/port read routine    */
     outport,                            /*6   pointer to RAM/port read routine    */
     s_rcvstat,                          /*7   pointer to serial receiver status   */
     s_rcv,                              /*8   pointer to serial fetch routine     */
     s_xmitstat,                         /*9   pointer to serial xmiter status     */
     s_xmit,                             /*10  pointer to serial xmit routine      */
     v_regA,                             /*11  pointer to virtual register array   */
     8,                                  /*12  number of rows in virtual array     */
     &parityA,                           /*13  parity structure                   */
     &stopsA,                            /*14  stop bit structure                 */
     &dlenA,                             /*15  data length structure              */
     &baudA,                             /*16  baud rate structure                */
     &pin4A,                             /*17  RS-232 RTS output                   */
     &pin20A,                            /*18  RS-232 DTR output                   */
     NIL,                                /*19  NO RS-232 first user-defined output */
     NIL,                                /*20  NO RS-232 first user-defined output */
     &breakbA,                           /*21  break bit                          */
     &pin5A,                             /*22  RS-232 CTS input                    */
     NIL,                                /*23  NO RS-232 DSR input                 */
     &pin8A,                             /*24  RS-232 DCD input                    */
```

```
        NIL,                          /*25 NO RS-232 RI   input              */
        NIL,                          /*26 NO 1st user-defined RS-232 input  */
        NIL,                          /*27 NO 2nd user-defined RS-232 input  */
        &txonA,                       /*28 transmitter-on structure          */
        &rxonA,                       /*39 receiver-on structure             */
        &txhsA,                       /*30 transmitter/RTS handshake         */
        &rxhsA,                       /*31 receiver/DCD handshake            */
        &clockfA,                     /*32 clock factor                      */
        SUPPLIED,                     /*33 device number supplied during open */
        &oct1A,                       /*34 output control                    */
        &ict1A,                       /*35 input control                     */
        &hayes,                       /*36 smartmodem                        */
        IBUFSIZ,                      /*37 size of receive interrupt buffer  */
        SUPPLIED,                     /*38 pointer to           "        "   */
        SUPPLIED,                     /*39 pointer to end of    "        "   */
        SUPPLIED,                     /*40 where in buff to put next byte    */
        SUPPLIED,                     /*41 where in buff to fetch next byte  */
        s_istat,                      /*42 pointer to serial receiver status */
        s_iread,                      /*43 pointer to serial fetch routine   */
        FALSE,                        /*44 interrupts-are-on-flag            */
        };

int _maxsios = MAX_PORTS;             /* global--max number of serial ports */
struct _siostat _siolist[MAX_PORTS] = /* an siostat structure for each port */
    {
    { &typeAsio, CLOSED, TRUE, }             /* port 1 */
    };
```

G

Listing of TERM6

```c
#include   "stdio.h"
#include   "modem.h"
#include   "siodef.h"
#include   "ctype.h"
#include   "ascii.h"
#include   "sioctl.h"
#include   "errno.h"

#define MENU        CTRL_A                       /* key for command summary   */

void term(), setup(), setup232(), upload(), dnload();  /* return types      */
int setparity(); setdatalen(), setstops(), setbaud();
int  setdtr(), setrts(), setgpol(),setgpo2();
SIO *s_open();

extern int s_errno;
extern char *errstr[], *m_codes[], *m_names[], *brstr[];

int vers = 6;                                    /* version number (global)   */

main(argc, argv)
int argc;
char *argv[];
{
    int err, portnum;
    SIO *siop;                               /* pointer to an SIO            */
    struct modem *smp;                       /* saves typing and runs faster too */
    portnum = 0;
    if (argc > 1)
        portnum = atoi(argv[1]);
    if ( (siop = s_open(portnum)) == NIL)
        {
        printf("\007Cannot open:%s\n",errstr[s_errno]);
        return (s_errno);
        }
```

```
    smp = siop->sm;
    if ( ( err = m_reset(siop)) != M_SUCCEED)
        printf("%s.  (%d)\n",m_codes[err], err);
    else if ( (err = m_whoru(siop)) != M_SUCCEED)
        puts("Fatal modem error: no response to ID request.");
    else if ( (err = m_config(siop)) != M_SUCCEED)
            puts("Fatal error during modem configuration.");
    else
        {
        printf("Found Smartmodem: %s at %s baud. (%d)\n",\
          m_names[smp->modtype], brstr[smp->baudfound],smp->smid);
        term(siop);                         /*              TERM                */
        }
    if ( (s_errno = s_close(siop)) != 0 )
        {
        printf("\007Cannot open:%s\n",errstr[s_errno]);
        return (s_errno);
        }
    puts("\nEnd of TERM\n");
    return (0);
}

void term(siop)
SIO *siop;
{
    int c;                                  /* must be int to detect -1 return  */
    s_ipush(siop);                          /* save both control structures     */
    s_opush(siop);
    s_icntrl(siop, SET, CONSFLAG, ON);  /* console echo on formatted input  */
    s_ocntrl(siop, SET, IB_DLYFLAG, OFF);   /* interbyte delay              */
    s_ocntrl(siop, SET, IL_DLYFLAG, OFF);   /* interline  delay             */
    printf("TERM, Version %d:  Press Control-%c for a summary of commands\n",\
        vers, MENU + '@');
    for (EVER)                              /*              eternal loop        */
        {
        s_fgetc(siop);                      /* s_fgetc will echo                */
        if ( (c = inkey()) != NOT_READY)
            if (c == MENU)
                {
                if (menu(siop))
                    break;                  /* if menu returns non-zero         */
                }
            else
                s_fputc(siop, c);
        }
    s_opop(siop);                           /* restore both control structures  */
    s_ipop(siop);
}
```

```
#define FORMAT  'A'                        /* Setup serial parmeters          */
#define RS232   'B'                        /* RS-232 output control           */
#define BRK     'C'                        /* send BREAK signal               */
#define UPLOAD  'D'                        /* transmit file                   */
#define DNLOAD1 'E'                        /* Download with C's buffer        */
#define DNLOAD2 'F'                        /* Download with local buffer      */
#define DIAL    'G'                        /* Setup serial parmeters          */
#define REDIAL  'H'                        /* Setup serial parmeters          */
#define ANSWER  'I'                        /* Setup serial parmeters          */
#define HUP     'J'                        /* Hang up phone                   */
#define XSEND   'K'                        /* send file with XMODEM protocol  */
#define XRECV   'L'                        /* xmit file with XMODEM protocol  */
#define EXIT    'Q'                        /* key to exit from term           */

int menu (siop)
SIO *siop;
{
    int cbuff(), locbuff();                    /* download functions          */
    char c;
    int  retval = 0;
    static char *menus[] =
        {
        "\tA.  Data Format, Baud rate",
        "\tB.  RS-232 control",
        "\tC.  Transmit BREAK signal",
        "\tD.  Upload Text File",
        "\tE.  Download Text File (small buffer)",
        "\tF.  Download Text File (large buffer)",
        "\tG.  Dial a phone number",
        "\tH.  Redial last phone number",
        "\tI.  Answer incoming call",
        "\tJ.  Hang up phone",
        "\tK.  Send a file using XMODEM protocol",
        "\tL.  Receive a file using XMODEM protocol",
        "\tQ.  EXIT",
        ""                              /* null string terminates list    */
        };
    char ** menup;
    c = !EXIT;
    while (c != EXIT)
        {
        puts("\n");
        for (menup = menus; **menup != NUL ; menup++)
        printf("%s\n", *menup);
        printf("\n\t\t  Enter selection  (CR to quit menu) : ");
        if ( ( c = getch()) == CR)
            break;                          /* return to term             */
        c = toupper(c);
```

```
switch (c)
    {
    case EXIT:                          /* back to DOS               */
        retval = 1;
        break;
    case FORMAT:                        /* Data format, Baud rate    */
        setup(siop);
        break;
    case RS232:                         /* RS232 output control      */
        setup232(siop);
        break;
    case BRK:                           /* send BREAK                */
        setbrk(siop);
        break;
    case UPLOAD:                        /* transmit a disk file      */
        upload(siop);
        break;
    case DNLOAD1:           /* receive a file: use C's file buffer */
        dnload(siop, cbuff);
        break;
    case DNLOAD2:           /* receive a file: use local file buffer */
        dnload(siop, locbuff);
        break;
    case DIAL:
        if (m_warndcd(siop, OFF) == 0)
            dial(siop);
        c = EXIT;                           /* leave menu after dial */
        break;
    case REDIAL:
        if (m_warndcd(siop, OFF) == 0)
            printf("\n%s. \n",m_codes[redial(siop)]);
        c = EXIT;                         /* leave menu after redial */
        break;
    case ANSWER:
        if (m_warndcd(siop, OFF) == 0)
            printf("\n%s. \n",m_codes[m_answer(siop)]);
        c = EXIT;                         /* leave menu after answer */
        break;
    case HUP:
        if (m_warndcd(siop, ON) == 0)
            printf("\nHangup %s.\n",\
                m_hup(siop) == 0 ? "OK" : "error");
        c = EXIT;                         /* leave menu after hangup  */
        break;
    case XSEND:                             /* Send a file with XMODEM */
        if (m_warndcd(siop, ON) == 0)
            x_snd(siop);
         break;
```

```
            case XRECV:                              /* Receive a file with XMODEM */
                if (m_warndcd(siop, ON) == 0)
                    x_rcv(siop);
                break;
            default:
                puts("Invalid choice\n\007");
                break;                               /* continue looping          */
        }
    }
    puts("\nExiting menu");
    return (retval);                                 /* will be zero except if EXIT  */
}
```

Bibliography

Periodicals

Bremer, R.W. "All about ASCII." *The Best of Interface Age*. Forest Grove Oregon: dilithium Press, 1978. This series of articles, by one of the authors of ASCII, contains a wealth of information unavailable elsewhere. Unfortunately, neither the magazine nor the publisher is still in business.

da Cruz, Frank, and Catchings, Bill. "Kermit: A File-Transfer Protocol for Universities. Part 1: Design Considerations and Specifications." *BYTE*. (June, 1984): 255. "Part 2: States and Transitions, Heuristic Rules, and Examples." *BYTE*. (July, 1984): 143. A highly condensed explanation of the Kermit protocol by its authors.

Hansen, Augie. "Kermit." *PC Tech Journal*. (January 1986): 110. This is a short but informative article about the Kermit File-Transfer Protocol.

Morse, Greg. "Calculating CRCs by Bits and Bytes." *Byte*. (September, 1986): 115-124.

Perez, A. "Byte-wise CRC Calculations." *IEEE Micro*. (June 1983): 40-50. This article explains how byte-sized CRCs combine with the existing 16-bit accumulator. It contains a chart giving all 16 intermediate combining values for CRC-16. The author builds the combining lookup table through a tortuous mathematical procedure unique for each CRC divisor. The programming examples are in Fortran and 8080 assembler.

Ritter, Terry. "The Great CRC Mystery." *Dr. Dobb's Journal of Software Tools*. (February, 1986): 26. This is the best of the CRC articles and the only one to perceive the simple way of building the combining value lookup table explained in Chapter 19. Programming examples are in Pascal.

Segal, Mark L. "Toward Standardized Video Terminals." *BYTE*. (April 1984): 365. An overview of how ANSI 3.64 relates to video terminals.

Schwaderer, W. David. "CRC Calculations." *PC Tech Journal*. (April 1985): 118-32. Similar in scope to the Perez article, including the method of building the lookup table. The programming examples are in C.

Books

Brooks, John. *Telephone: The First Hundred Years*. New York: Harper and Row, 1976. Although a puff piece on the history of AT&T, it is nonetheless worthwhile because, unlike most accounts, it stresses the business aspects of the company.

Campbell, Joe. *Crafting C Tools for the IBM PCs*. Englewood Cliffs, N.J.: Prentice-Hall, Inc., 1986. A book on systems programming in C, stressing the interface between C and the PC DOS operating system. It contains important background information about the IBM PC's interrupt system as well as an alternative serial interrupt handler.

Campbell, Joe. *The RS-232 Solution*. Berkeley: SYBEX, Inc., 1984. A book on the distressing realities of interfacing non-standard RS-232 hardware. Case studies are given for major deviations.

da Cruz, Frank. *Kermit Protocol Manual*. 5th ed. New York: Columbia University Center for Computing Activities. The original Kermit documentation, but there is probably a new one now. Supplement this book with the second da Cruz book.

da Cruz, Frank. *Kermit: A File Transfer Protocol*. Bedford, Mass.: Digital Press, 1987. This book was available too late for me to read thoroughly, but it looks delightful. It appears to be one of those rare books that speaks with equal clarity to novice and expert alike. It is also a treasure chest of practical information about the problems involved in adapting Kermit to a variety of hardware environments.

Grofton, Peter W. *Mastering Serial Communications*. Berkeley: SYBEX, Inc., 1986. If you are relatively new to communications, this is a useful, if slightly breathless, introductory treatment of the technical issues. Older SYBEX catalogs may list the author of this book as Joe Campbell.

Harrison, H. H. *Printing Telegraph Systems and Mechanisms*. London: Longmans, Green, and Co., 1923. Like the Pendry book, a look at the design and functioning of the teleprinter.

Kruglinski, David. *Guide to IBM PC Communications*. Berkeley: Osborne/McGraw-Hill, 1984. Intended mostly for the knowledgeable user, this book contains some technical material, as well as an informative discussion of telecommunications history.

Marland, E.A. *Early Electrical Communication*. New York: Abelard-Schuman, 1964. Early history of telecommunications with emphasis on Wheatstone and Cooke.

McNamara, John E. *Technical Aspects of Data Communication*. Bedford, Mass.: Digital Press, 1977. An indispensable volume of practical information plainly written.

Martin, James. *Telecommunications and the Computer*. Englewood Cliffs, N.J.: Prentice-Hall, Inc., 1976. A good text for a college-survey course.

Nichols, Elizabeth A.; Nichols, Joseph C.; and Musson, Keith R. *Data Communications for Microcomputers*. New York: McGraw-Hill, 1982. A stiff-necked look at communications by engineers. Not much fun here.

Pendry, H. W. *The Baudot Printing Telegraph*. London: Whittaker & Co., 1913. A wonderful book of explanations and incredible drawings of the Baudot teleprinter.

Peterson, W. W., and Weldon, Jr., E.J. *Error-Correcting Codes*. Cambridge: MIT Press, 1972. Considering the subject matter, this book is amazingly readable to non-mathematicians.

Pierce, John R. *Signals*. San Francisco: W.H. Freeman and Company, 1981. An interesting, if somewhat dilettantish, survey of the history of electronic communications in general, with emphasis on and much praise for the accomplishments of Bell Labs.

Pless, Vera. *Introduction to the Theory of Error-Correcting Codes*. New York: John Wiley & Sons, 1982. Its title says it all. If you want to know why one CRC divisor polynomial is better than another, this is your book.

Schwaderer, W. David. *Digital Communications Programming on the IBM PC*. New York: John Wiley & Sons, Inc., 1984. This book is full of good, useful information written in an entertaining style. Unfortunately, its programming examples are in BASIC. This book was re-released in 1987 under the title *Modems and Communications on the IBM PC*.

Seyer, Martin D. *RS-232 Made Easy*. Englewood Cliffs, N.J.: Prentice-Hall, Inc., 1984. I never read books with "Made Easy" or "Made Simple" in the titles.

Shiers, George. *The Electric Telegraph: An Historical Analogy*. Salem, N.H.: The Arno Press, 1977. This is a collection of articles by and about those involved in the early years of telegraphy. The book is worth looking at if only for the drawings of early equipment.

Stallings, William. *Data and Computer Communications*. New York: Macmillan Publishing Co., 1985. This is a good college-level text with more of an engineering flavor than the Martin book.

Stevens, David. *A Programmer's Guide to Video Display Terminals*. Dallas: Atlantis Publishing Corp., 1985. This book contains control codes for dozens of video terminals.

Thompson, R.L. *Wiring A Continent*. Princeton, N.J.: Princeton Univ. Press, 1947. This book documents the spread of the telegraph.

Standards and Documentation

American National Standards Institute
1430 Broadway
New York, NY 10018

ANSI X3.15	For Bit Sequencing of American Standard Code for Information Interchange.
ANSI X3.25	Character Structure and Character Parity Sense for Parallel-by-bit Data Communications in American Standard Code for Information Interchange.
ANSI X3.28	Procedures for the Use of the Communication Control Characters of American Standard Code for Information Interchange in Specified Data Communications Links.
ANSI X3.2	Graphic Representation of the Control Characters of American Standard Code for Information Interchange.
ANSI X3.4	Code for Information Exchange.
ANSI X3.41	Code Extension Techniques for use with the 7-bit Character Set of American Standard Code for Information Interchange.
ANSI X3.45	Character Set for Handprinting.
ANSI X3.64	Additional Controls for use with American Standard Code for Information Interchange.

CCITT (The International Consultative Committee for Telephone and Telegraph)
Documents available from
Global Engineering Documents
2625 Hickory St.
Santa Ana, CA 92707

The Red Book, Volume Eight

Electronic Industries Association
2001 Eye St.
Washington, D.C. 20006

RS-232-C   Interface between Data Terminal Equipment and Data Communications
Equipment Employing Serial Binary Data Interchange.

Data Sheets and Technical Manuals:

Z80DART/Z80SIO
Ziolog, Inc.
1315 Dell Ave.
Campbell, CA 9508

INS8250
National Semiconductor
2900 Semiconductor Dr.
Santa Clara, CA 95052

Function Index

Index

Programming in C, Revised Edition

Stephen G. Kochan

This timely revision provides complete coverage of the C language, including language features and over 90 program examples. The comprehensive tutorial approach teaches the beginner how to write, compile, and execute programs and teaches the experienced programmer how to write applications using features unique to C.

Program examples include a step-by-step explanation of all the procedures involved. The book covers all the essentials of C, including program looping, decision-making, arrays, functions, structures, character strings, bit operations, enumerated data types, and ANSI C.

Topics covered include:

■ Introduction and Fundamentals
■ Writing a Program in C
■ Variables, Constants, Data Types, and Arithmetic Expressions
■ Program Looping
■ Making Decisions
■ Arrays
■ Functions
■ Structures
■ Character Strings
■ Pointers
■ Operations on Bits
■ The Preprocessor
■ Working with Larger Programs
■ Input and Output
■ Miscellaneous and Advanced Features

476 Pages, 7½ x 9¾, Softbound
ISBN: 0-672-48420-X
No. 48420, $24.95

Programming in ANSI C

Stephen G. Kochan

This comprehensive programming guide is the newest title in the Hayden Books C Library, written by the series editor Stephen G. Kochan. A tutorial in nature, the book teaches the beginner how to write, compile and execute programs even with no previous experience with C.

The book details such C essentials as program looping, decision making, arrays, functions, structures, character strings, bit operations, and enumerated data types. Examples are complete with step-by-step explanations of each procedure and routine involved as well as end-of-chapter exercises, making it ideally suited for classroom use.

Topics covered include:

■ Introduction and Fundamentals
■ Writing a Program in ANSI C
■ Variables, Data Types, and Arithmetic Expressions
■ Program Looping
■ Making Decisions
■ Arrays, Functions, Structures
■ Character Strings, Pointers
■ Operations on Bits
■ The Preprocessor
■ More on Data Types
■ Working with Larger Programs
■ Input and Output
■ Miscellaneous Features and Topics
■ Appendices: ANSI C Language Summary, The UNIX C Library, Compiling Programs Under UNIX, The Program LINT, The ASCII Character Set

450 Pages, 7½ x 9¾, Softbound
ISBN: 0-672-48408-0
No. 48408, $24.95

Advanced C: Tips and Techniques

Paul L. Anderson and Gail Anderson

If you have a working knowledge of the C language and want to enhance your programming skills, the examples and techniques found in this new book are just what you need. It is an in-depth look at the C programming language with special emphasis on portability, execution efficiency, and application techniques.

With entire chapters devoted to special areas of C such as debugging techniques, C's run-time environment, and the memory object allocator, the book contains detailed explanations and examples that will show you how to speed up your C programs. Techniques for creating and deciphering expressions, moving data, and coding expressions that execute predictably are included as well as end-of-chapter exercises that help you learn what has been explained.

Topics covered include:

■ C Refresher
■ The Run-Time Environment
■ Bits of C
■ There's No Such Thing as an Array
■ A Closer Look at C
■ C Debugging Techniques
■ A Memory Object Allocator
■ Appendices: Portable C Under UNIX System V, Microsoft C Under XENIX, Microsoft C Under DOS, Turbo C Under DOS

325 Pages, 7½ x 9¾, Softbound
ISBN: 0-672-48417-X
No. 48417, $24.95

Topics in C Programming

Stephen G. Kochan and Patrick H. Wood

Here is the most advanced and comprehensive coverage of the maturing C market. This sequel to *Programming in C* describes in detail some of the most difficult concepts in the C language—structures and pointers. It also explores the standard C library and standard I/O library, dynamic memory allocation, linked lists, tree structures, and dispatch tables.

Experienced C programmers can examine the UNIX System Interface through discussions on controlling processes, pipes, and terminal I/O. *Topics in C Programming* also explains how to write terminal-independent programs, how to debug C programs and analyze their performance, and how to use "make" for automatic generation of a programming system.

Topics covered include:

■ Structures and Pointers
■ The Standard C Library
■ The Standard I/O Library
■ UNIX System Interface
■ Writing Terminal-Independent Programs with "curses" Library
■ Debug and Performance Analysis of C Programs
■ Generating Programs with "make"

528 Pages, 7½ x 9¾, Softbound
ISBN: 0-672-46290-7
No. 46290, $24.95

Visit your local book retailer, use the order form provided, or call 800-428-SAMS.